Lecture Notes in Computer Science 5799

Commenced Publication in 1973
Founding and Former Series Editors:
Gerhard Goos, Juris Hartmanis, and Jan van Leeuwen

Zhiming Liu   Anders P. Ravn (Eds.)

Automated Technology for Verification and Analysis

7th International Symposium, ATVA 2009
Macao, China, October 14-16, 2009
Proceedings

 Springer

Volume Editors

Zhiming Liu
United Nations University
International Institute of Software Technology (UNU-IIST)
Macao, China
E-mail: z.liu@iist.unu.edu

Anders P. Ravn
Aalborg University
Department of Computer Science
9220 Aalborg, Denmark
E-mail: apr@cs.aau.dk

Library of Congress Control Number: 2009935680

CR Subject Classification (1998): D.2, D.3, F.3, G.4, I.2.2, F.4, B.6, B.7, C.5.4

LNCS Sublibrary: SL 2 – Programming and Software Engineering

ISSN   0302-9743
ISBN-10   3-642-04760-2 Springer Berlin Heidelberg New York
ISBN-13   978-3-642-04760-2 Springer Berlin Heidelberg New York

springer.com

© Springer-Verlag Berlin Heidelberg 2009
Printed in Germany

Typesetting: Camera-ready by author, data conversion by Scientific Publishing Services, Chennai, India
Printed on acid-free paper   SPIN: 12768271   06/3180   5 4 3 2 1 0

Preface

This volume contains the papers presented at the 7th International Symposium on Automated Technology for Verification and Analysis held during October 13-16 in Macao SAR, China. The primary objective of the ATVA conferences remains the same: to exchange and promote the latest advances of state-of-the-art research on theoretical and practical aspects of automated analysis, verification, and synthesis.

Among 74 research papers and 10 tool papers submitted to ATVA 2009, the Program Committee accepted 23 as regular papers and 3 as tool papers. In all, 33 experts from 17 countries worked hard to make sure that every submission received a rigorous and fair evaluation. In addition, the program included three excellent tutorials and keynote talks by Mark Greenstreet (U. British Columbia), Orna Grumberg (Technion), and Bill Roscoe (Oxford University). The conference organizers were truly grateful to have such distinguished researchers as keynote speakers.

Many worked hard and offered their valuable time so generously to make ATVA 2009 successful. First of all, the conference organizers thank all 229 researchers who worked hard to complete and submit papers to the conference. The PC members, reviewers, and Steering Committee members also deserve special recognition. Without them, a competitive and peer-reviewed international symposium simply cannot take place.

Many organizations sponsored the symposium. They include: The United Nations University, International Institute of Software Technology (UNU-IIST); Macao Polytechnic Institute (MPI); Macao POST; and Formal Methods Europe (FME). The conference organizers thank them for their generous support and assistance.

Many individuals offered their enthusiastic help to the conference. We are grateful to Lei Heong Iok, President of MPI, Cheang Mio Han, Head of the Academic Affairs Department of MPI, and Hau Veng San, Head of the Division for Pedagogical Affairs of MPI, for their support. We would like to thank Chris George, the Conference Chair, Antonio Cerone, the Local Organization Chair, and Jun Pang, the Publicity Chair, for their hard work; Wang Zhen for writing the online registration program; Charles Morisset for his help in managing the proceedings and the program; and last, but not least, the general staff of UNU-IIST, Wendy Hoi, Kitty Chan, Michelle Ho, Sandy Lee, and Kyle Au, for their help with the local organization.

We sincerely hope that the readers find the proceedings of ATVA 2009 informative and rewarding.

August 2009

Zhiming Liu
Anders P. Ravn

Organization

ATVA 2009 was organized by the United Nations University, International Institute for Software Technology (UNU-IIST) in cooperation with the Macao Polytechnic Institute.

Conference Chairs

General Chair	Chris George (UNU-IIST, Macao)
Program Chairs	Zhiming Liu (UNU-IIST, Macao)
	Anders P. Ravn (Aalborg University, Denmark)
Organization Chair	Antonio Cerone (UNU-IIST, Macao)
Publicity Chair	Jun Pang (University of Luxembourg)

Program Committee

Rajeev Alur	Marta Kwiatkowska	Irek Ulidowski
Christel Baier	Insup Lee	Mahesh Viswanathan
Jonathan Billington	Xuandong Li	Farn Wang
Laurent Fribourg	Shaoying Liu	Xu Wang
Masahiro Fujita	Kedar Namjoshi	Ji Wang
Susanne Graf	Hanne Nielson	Hsu-Chun Yen
Mark Greenstreet	Ernst-Ruediger Olderog	Wang Yi
Wolfgang Grieskamp	Jun Pang	Tomohiro Yoneda
Teruo Higashino	Doron A. Peled	Wenhui Zhang
Moonzoo Kim	Abhik Roychoudhury	
Orna Kupferman	Natarajan Shankar	

Steering Committee

E. Allen Emerson	U. Texas at Austin
Teruo Higashino	Osaka University
Oscar H. Ibarra	U. California, Santa Barbara
Insup Lee	U. Pennsylvania
Doron A. Peled	Univ. Warwick, Univ. Bar Ilan
Farn Wang	National Taiwan Univ.
Hsu-Chun Yen	National Taiwan Univ.

External Referees

Eugene Asarin
Souheib Baarir
Rena Bakhshi
Bruno Barras
Denes Bisztray
Laura Bocchi
Benedikt Bollig
Olivier Bournez
Lei Bu
Doina Bucur
Lin-Zan Cai
Radu Calinescu
Rohit Chadha
Taolue Chen
Vivien Chinnapongse
Thao Dang
Arnab De
Ton van Deursen
Alin Deutsch
Catalin Dima
Bruno Dutertre
Jochen Eisinger
Dana Fisman
Guy Gallasch
Pierre Ganty
Han Gao

Vijay Gehlot
Ankit Goel
Stefan Haar
Stefan Hallerstede
Alejandro Hernandez
Hsi-Ming Ho
Shin Hong
Guo-Chou Huang
Chung-Hao Huang
Lei Ju
Barbara Kordy
Mark Kattenbelt
Joachim Klein
Vijay Korthikanti
Jaewoo Lee
Wanwei Liu
Christof Loeding
Gavin Lowe
Yoad Lustig
Xiaodong Ma
Stephane Messika
Gethin Norman
Chun Ouyang
Jorge A. Perez
Henrik Pilegaard
Pavithra Prabhakar

Jan-David Quesel
Nataliya Skrypnyuk
Martin Stigge
Tim Strazny
Mani Swaminathan
Ashish Tiwari
Paolo Torrini
Ashutosh Trivedi
Somsak Vanit-Anunchai
Jeffrey Vaughan
Ramesh Viswanathan
Xi Wang
Zhaofei Wang
Shaohui Wang
Andrew West
Anton Wijs
Hong-Hsin Wu
Rong-Hsuan Wu
Shaofa Yang
Hsuen-Chin Yang
Lu Yang
Ender Yuksel
Jianhua Zhao
Gethin Norman
Christian W. Probst

Sponsoring Institutions

United Nations University – International Institute for Software Technology
Macao Post
Macao Polytechnic Institute
Formal Methods Europe

Table of Contents

Invited Talks

State Space Reduction

Tools

Probabilistic Systems

Medley

Temporal Logic I

Abstraction and Refinement

Fault Tolerant Systems

Temporal Logic II

Verifying VLSI Circuits

Mark R. Greenstreet

Department of Computer Science
University of British Columbia
Vancouver, BC, Canada
mrg@cs.ubc.ca

1 Introduction

Circuit-level verification is a promising area for formal methods research. Simulation using tools such as SPICE remains the main method for circuit validation. Increasing integration densities have increased the prevalence of analog/mixed-signal designs. It is now common for analog components such as DLLs and phase correction circuits to be embedded deep in digital designs, making the circuits critical for chip functional yet hard to test. While digital design flows have benefited from systematic methodologies including the use of formal methods, circuit design remains an art. As a consequence, analog design errors account for a growing percentage of design re-spins. All of these have created a pressing need for better circuit-level CAD and motivated a strong interest in formal verification.

There are many properties of circuit-level design that make it attractive for formal approaches: key circuits tend to be small. Thus, unlike digital designs, the problems are not primarily ones of scale. Instead, the challenge is to correctly specify, model and verify circuit behavior. Furthermore, circuit-level design for both analog and digital cells is the domain of design experts who expect to spend a substantial amount of time on each cell designed. Thus, they can consider working with a verification expert if that interaction leads to a reduction in design time or risk.

In this paper, we identify three types of verification problems: introductory, intermediate, and open challenges, give examples of each, and present verification results. Section 2 presents "introductory problems" using a simple tunnel diode oscillator that has been extensively studied by formal methods researchers. These introductory problems have low-dimensional dynamics described by models chosen for mathematical convenience rather than physical realism. Such problems can provide a useful introduction to circuit behavior for verification researchers with expertise developed in other application domains.

Intermediate problems are introduced in Section 3. These are circuits that are used on real integrated circuits and modeled with a reasonable level of physical fidelity. Examples include the ring-oscillator challenge put forward by Rambus last year. Verification results for these problems may be of immediate use to design experts. Equally important, the process of formalizing the specification and circuit model provides a common language for designers, verifiers, and CAD tool developers.

Finally, Section 4 presents challenge problems whose solutions would have significant impact on the circuit design community but at present have not been addressed by

Z. Liu and A.P. Ravn (Eds.): ATVA 2009, LNCS 5799, pp. 1–20, 2009.
© Springer-Verlag Berlin Heidelberg 2009

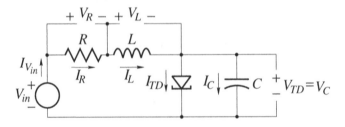

Fig. 1. A Tunnel-Diode Oscillator

formal methods. Chief among these are design problems that arise from uncertainty in device parameters. On chip analog circuits such as oscillators, voltage regulators and sense amplifiers often include a large number of digital control inputs that compensate for uncontrollable variations in the fabrication process and operating conditions.. These circuits are genuine hybrid systems with a digital control loop regulating analog components. CAD tools that could verify such designs over a the full range of operating modes and fabrication parameters would be of great interest to designers and present a great challenge and opportunity for formal methods research.

2   Introductory Examples

Research in applying formal methods to circuit-level verification dates back Kurshan and MacMillan's verification of an nMOS arbiter using COSPAN in 1991 [1]. Interest in the topic has rapidly grown in the past five years as advances in reachability tools have made increased the range of problems that can be addressed formally, and as advances in fabrication technology have led to a prevalence of mixed-signal designs and to a wide range of circuit-level behaviors that must be considered to obtain a working design but for which existing CAD flows provide no automated means of verification or validation. Not surprisingly, much of the early research in this area has focused on simple circuits and/or used simple models. These simplifications serve two purposes: first, they provide problems that are tractable with current verification tools; second, they serve a pedagogical role for formal methods researchers by providing examples that can be easily understood without a deep knowledge of circuit design and analysis techniques.

In this section, I will use the tunnel diode oscillator circuit first considered in a formal verification context by Hartong *et al.* [2] as an example of an "introductory problem" and as a way to illustrate dynamical systems concepts that can be applied to circuit verification. This section closes with a brief description of other problems of a similarly introductory nature.

2.1   The Tunnel-Diode Oscillator

The tunnel-diode oscillator consists of four components:

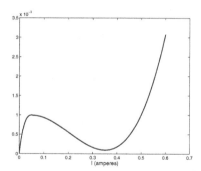

$$I_{TD}(V_{TD}) = \begin{cases} 6.0105V_{TD}^3 - 0.9917V_{TD}^2 + 0.0545V_{TD} & 0.000 \le V_{TD} \le 0.055 \\ 0.0692V_{TD}^3 - 0.0421V_{TD}^2 + 0.0040V_{TD} + 8.85794 \times 10^{-4}, & 0.055 \le V_{TD} \le 0.350 \\ 0.2634V_{TD}^3 - 0.2765V_{TD}^2 + 0.0968V_{TD} - 0.0112, & 0.350 \le V_{TD} \end{cases}$$

Fig. 2. Current vs. Voltage for a Tunnel Diode

a voltage source provides the voltage (corresponds to mechanical force) that drives the oscillator.

a resistor, the unavoidable friction or drag in circuit components. By Ohm's law, $I = V/R$ where I is the current flowing through the resistor, V is the voltage applied across the resistor, and R is the "resistance" of the resistor. In the mechanical analogy, current is the velocity of an object, and charge is the distance that it has moved.

an inductor, the electrical equivalent of "mass" in mechanical systems. The current flowing through an inductor grows at a rate proportional to the voltage applied across the inductor, just as the velocity of a mass grows at a rate proportional to the force applied to it. The circuit equation for the inductor is: $\frac{d}{dt}I_L = \frac{V}{L}$.

a capacitor, the electrical equivalent of a spring. The charge held in a (linear) capacitor is proportional to the voltage applied just as the displacement of a (linear) spring is proportional to the force applied. The circuit equation for a capacitor is: $\frac{d}{dt}V = \frac{I}{C}$.

a tunnel diode, a non-linear device that compensates for the energy dissipated by the resistor. The distinctive feature of the tunnel diode is the region where the current *decreases* with increasing applied voltage. This creates a "negative incremental resistance" that can be used to cancel the resistive losses in the inductor (and other components). Figure 2 shows the piecewise cubic relationship between current and voltage from [3] that we use for this example.

We can obtain an ordinary differential equation that models the oscillator circuit using Kirchoff's current and voltage laws. Kirchoff's current law (KCL) states that the sum of currents entering any node must be zero. This yields:

$$I_{V_{in}} = I_R = I_L = I_{TD} + I_C \qquad (1)$$

Kirchoff's voltage law (KVL) states that the sum of the voltages around any loop must be zero. This yields:

$$\begin{aligned} V_{TD} &= V_C \\ V_{in} &= V_R + V_L + V_C \end{aligned} \qquad (2)$$

Combining these with the component models described above yields:

$$\begin{aligned} \dot{I}_L &= \tfrac{1}{L}(V_{in} - I_L R - V_C) \\ \dot{V}_C &= \tfrac{1}{C}(I_L - I_{TD}(V_C)) \end{aligned} \qquad (3)$$

where $\dot{I}_L$ denotes the time derivative of I_L and likewise for $\dot{V}_C$.

Numerically integrating Equation 3 yields waveforms for the tunnel-diode oscillator. Here, we use the circuit parameters from [4]: $V_{in} = 0.3V$, $L = 1\mu H$, $C = 1pF$, and the tunnel-diode model from Figure 2, and we illustrate the behavior for three values of R, 100Ω, 200Ω and 300Ω with the initial condition that $I_L = 0$ and $V_C = 0$ for all three cases. Figure 3(a) shows that the circuit oscillates for $R = 100\Omega$ and $R = 200\Omega$ but locks-up at a fixpoint when $R = 300\Omega$. Natural questions that a designer could have about this circuit include: "For what values of R will the circuit oscillate?" "Does oscillation occur from all initial states, or does proper operation depend on the initial conditions?" "How much variation amplitude and period variation will appear at the output of the oscillator?" "How is power supply noise converted into amplitude and phase noise by the oscillator?" I examine the first two of these questions using methods from dynamical systems theory in the next section and then conclude this treatment of this simple oscillator by comparing this dynamical systems approach with time-domain analysis methods published earlier.

A Dynamical Systems Analysis of the Tunnel-Diode Oscillator. The ODE model for the tunnel-diode oscillator has two state variables: I_L and V_C. Thus, the ODE has a two-dimensional phase-space. Solutions to Equation 3 can be visualized as trajectories in this $I_L \times V_C$ space. Figure 3(b) shows two such trajectories for the oscillator circuit with $R = 200\Omega$. The first starts at the point $(I_L, V_C) = (1.2\text{mA}, 0.0591\text{V})$ which is very close to the (unstable) equilibrium point of the the oscillator. The other trajectory starts

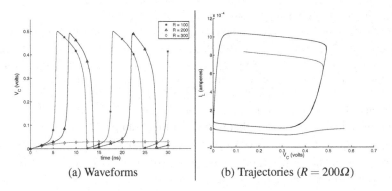

(a) Waveforms   (b) Trajectories ($R = 200\Omega$)

Fig. 3. Waveforms and Trajectories for the Tunnel Diode Oscillator

at $(I_L, V_C) = (0\text{mA}, 0.75\text{V})$ which is well "outside" of the stable orbit of the oscillator. As can be seen, both trajectories converge rapidly to a clockwise, periodic orbit – the convergence is fast enough, that they two trajectories are visually indistinguishable for most of the orbit.

Because the phase-space for the tunnel-diode oscillator's ODE is two-dimensional, the trajectory originating at any given initial condition must either converge to a fixed equilibrium point, diverge to infinity, or enter a periodic orbit [5]. Thus, we first consider the equilibrium points of the oscillator; these are the points at which $\dot{I}_L = 0$ and $\dot{V}_C = 0$. We can find all such points by solving for the roots of three cubic polynomials, one for each of the regions of the tunnel-diode model. When $R = 200\Omega$ the oscillator has one equilibrium point with $I_L = 0.84\text{mA}$ and $V_C = 0.132\text{V}$. Let f be the function such that $(\dot{I}_L, \dot{V}_C) = f(I_L, V_C)$. We check the stability of the equilibrium point to computing the eigenvalues of the Jacobian matrix for f at the equilibrium point:

$$
\text{Jac}(f, (0.84\text{mA}, 0.132\text{V})) = \left[\begin{array}{cc} \frac{\partial}{\partial I_L} \dot{I}_L & \frac{\partial}{\partial I_L} \dot{V}_C \\ \frac{\partial}{\partial V_C} \dot{I}_L & \frac{\partial}{\partial V_C} \dot{V}_C \end{array} \right]_{I_L = 0.84\text{mA}, V_C = 0.132\text{V}}
$$
$$
= \left[\begin{array}{cc} -2 & \times 10^8 \text{s}^{-1} & -1 & \times 10^6 \Omega^{-1}\text{s}^{-1} \\ 1 & \times 10^{12}\Omega\text{s}^{-1} & 3.51 \times 10^9 \text{s}^{-1} \end{array} \right] \tag{4}
$$

The eigenvalues of this Jacobian matrix are $9.3 \times 10^7 \text{s}^{-1}$ and $3.2 \times 10^9 \text{s}^{-1}$. Both have positive real parts, which shows that this equilibrium point is a repeller: trajectories starting near this point diverge exponentially away from it.

Having characterized the one equilibrium point of the oscillator, we now know that every trajectory except for the one that starts *exactly* at the equilibrium point must converge to a periodic attractor. Furthermore, every periodic attractor in a two-dimensional system must have an equilibrium point in its interior. Because the the tunnel diode oscillator has only one equilibrium point, it has only one periodic attractor. We conclude that from all initial conditions (except for the equilibrium point itself), trajectories converge to the desired oscillation. In other words, the oscillator is guaranteed to start-up, and to enter the desired oscillation mode.

For concreteness, the preceding discussion analyzed the tunnel-diode oscillator circuit assume that $R = 200\Omega$. The conclusions only require that the circuit have a unique equilibrium point that is a repeller. It is straightforward to show that this condition holds for any $R < 243.59\Omega$. For larger values of R, the equilibrium point becomes an attractor, and all trajectories converge to this point. This is an example of a *Hopf bifurcation*, where the qualitative behavior of the system changes at a critical value of a parameter. Furthermore, the analysis can be extended to consider other values of V_{in}. We note that for values of V_{in} greater than the local minimum in the tunnel-diode's current-vs.-voltage function (see Figure 2), it is possible to have multiple equilibrium points. For example, with $V_{in} = 0.5\text{V}$ and $R = 600\Omega$, there are equilibria for $(I_L, V_C) \in \{(0.955\text{mA}, 0.023\text{V}), (0.561\text{mA}, 0.219\text{V}), (0.407\text{mA}, 0.186\text{V})\}$. The first and last of these are stable equilibria while the middle one is unstable. In this case, the circuit has two stable states, and the middle equilibrium is the saddle point (a.k.a. "metastable" point) between them.

In this section, I've shown that the behavior of the tunnel-diode oscillator can be understood using standard methods from dynamical systems theory. The two-dimensional phase space makes a detailed analysis tractable. I've shown that for appropriate values of the series resistor, the oscillator is guaranteed to oscillate from all initial conditions except for a single point in the phase space. I've presented constraints on the value of R that are necessary and sufficient for correct oscillation. Without external disturbances, the oscillator settles to a unique, periodic attractor which means that the amplitude and phase noise go to zero as the oscillator operates. Similar techniques can be used to determine the sensitivity of the output amplitude and period to power supply noise and answer other questions that a designer might have about the circuit.

Time Domain Analysis of the Tunnel Diode Oscillator. Many formal methods researchers have used the tunnel-diode oscillator circuit from Figure 1 starting with Hartong *et al.* who introduced the problem in [2]. Hartong used a recursive subdivision algorithm to partition the continuous state space into smaller boxes, constructed a next-state relation on these boxes, and then used CTL model checking on this relation. They showed that nearly all boxes lead to the desired oscillating behavior and identified a fairly tight approximation of the stable orbit. They could not verify that start-up occurs everywhere except for a single point as in our analysis because of their discretization. This results in many small boxes near the equilibrium point for which they could not prove that oscillation is guaranteed. There are also boxes near along the border of their discretization for which the verification fails because they can't show that trajectories remain in with in the discretization.

Other researchers have verified the tunnel-diode oscillator example, generally following the same basic approach as Hartong *et al.* of discretizing the state space and model checking the discretization. The variations are mainly in how the discretization is performed and how the next state relation is determined. Gupta *et al.* [6] present a verification of the oscillator CheckMate which represents the reachable space with *flowpipes*. They show how they can verify proper oscillation for a 200Ω resistor, but show that the circuit fails to oscillate with a 242.13Ω resistor. They don't give the polynomial coefficient for their tunnel-diode model, and given that there seem to be slight variations in these coefficients from different papers, this could account for their slight discrepancy with our conclusion that the circuit oscillates for any $R < 243.59\Omega$. For example [7] verify the oscillator using PHAVer which uses high-dimensional polyhedra to represent reachable sets or over-approximations thereof. Little *et al.* [3] present a verification of the tunnel-diode oscillator where the circuit is modeled with a labeled hybrid Petri net (LHPN) and the reachable state space is represented using difference bound matrices.

Other Introductory Examples. There are numerous other examples that have appeared in the research literature that I will include in the category of introductory example. These are characterized by using simplified, often idealized, circuit models and having models with a low number of dimensions, typically four or less. Much of the early work was done at UBC including the verification of an asynchronous arbiter [8], a toggle flip-flop [9], and a van der Pol oscillator [10]. Like the tunnel-diode oscillator, these examples have simple, cubic polynomials for their derivative functions, and the verification approaches were built on results from dynamical systems theory. These simple examples show how it is possible to specify a wide range of circuit behaviors, both analog and digital, as topological properties of invariant sets of trajectories. The simple models make the analysis tractable, and intuitive.

In addition to the tunnel-diode oscillator, Hartong's paper [2] also also presented a Schmitt trigger and a low pass filter. Gupta *et al.* [6] added a Delta-Sigma modulator (analog-to-digital converter) circuit to the set of "standard" examples. This design differs from the oscillators and other circuits described above as it is modeled with discrete time. Thus, the verification problem is one of computing the reachable space for an iterated sequence of linear mappings, where each mapping is selected according to the sequence of threshold decisions made by the comparator. Little *et al.* [3] presented a switched capacitor integrator which has continuous, linear dynamics with discrete event transitions between different dynamics. In a different direction, Seger citeSeger08 described the use of the Forte verification tool to find state assignments that minimize the leakage current of logic blocks in standby, power-saving modes.

3   Intermediate Examples

This section presents design and verification examples that use accurate circuit models for deep-submicron fabrication processes, are larger circuits that hence have higher-dimensional state spaces and are problems of interest to practicing VLSI designers. Section 3.1 examines a differential ring oscillator that was put forward by Jones *et al.* [11] as challenge problem: "For what transistor sizings in the oscillator guaranteed to start-up properly." I will then describe some recent work on computing synchronizer failure probabilities. Synchronizers are used to implement reliable communication in systems that have multiple, independent clocks. It is well-known that it is impossible to implement a perfect synchronizer. Instead, our goal is to show that the failure probability for the synchronizer is sufficiently low. While this is not "formal" verification, the techniques that we present build on the same dynamical systems framework that we are using throughout this paper, and the problem is critical for today's chip designs. Section 3.3 concludes this section with brief descriptions of other intermediate examples and their verification.

3.1   The Rambus Ring Oscillator

Figure 4 shows the four-stage instantiation of the differential ring-oscillator circuit put forward by researchers at Rambus [11] as a verification challenge. Although the circuit has been used by VLSI designers since long before it was proposed as a challenge

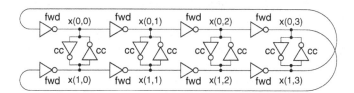

Fig. 4. A Four-Stage Differential Ring Oscillator

problem, it's introduction to the verification community has given it the moniker, the "Rambus Oscillator" problem, and I will refer to it as the "Rambus Oscillator" in the following. Designers have at times had versions of this circuit that worked in simulation, but once fabricated on a chip would occasionally fail to start. It was understood that these lock-up issues were related to the relative sizes of the transistors in the "forward" and "cross-coupling" inverters in the design. If the "forward" inverters (labeled fwd in the figure), are much larger than the "cross-coupling" inverters (labeled cc), then the circuit acts like a ring of $2n$ inverters and will settle to one of two states:

State 1: $x(0,0)$, $x(1,0)$, $x(0,2)$, $x(0,2)$ are high, and
$\qquad x(0,1)$, $x(1,1)$, $x(0,3)$, $x(0,3)$ are low.
State 2: $x(0,1)$, $x(1,1)$, $x(0,3)$, $x(0,3)$ are high, and
$\qquad x(0,0)$, $x(1,0)$, $x(0,2)$, $x(0,2)$ are low.

$$(5)$$

Conversely, if the cross-coupling inverters are much larger than the forward ones, then the circuit acts like n separate static latches and has 2^n stable states. If the forward and cross-coupling inverters have comparable strength, then the circuit should oscillate in a stable fashion. The Rambus challenge problem is to determine conditions on the sizes of the inverters that guarantee that the circuit will enter a stable oscillating condition from any initial condition. We note that it is easy to show that if a Rambus oscillator has an odd-number of stages, then it is has two stable DC equilibria. Thus, we only consider oscillators where n is even in the following.

A Dynamical Systems Analysis of the Rambus Oscillator. Our analysis proceeds in two phases (see [12] for details). First we describe a method for locating all DC-equilibria of a ring-oscillator circuit as depicted in Figure 4. We then analyze the stability of each equilibrium point. If all equilibria are unstable, then it is impossible for the circuit to settle at some stationary state. However, our analysis does not rule out the possibility that the circuit has some chaotic or higher-harmonic behavior. For an oscillator with a small number of stages, chaotic solutions seem unlikely, and our demonstration that it does not "lock up" addresses the main initialization concern of practicing designers.

An n-stage Rambus oscillator has $2n$ nodes. We model MOSFETs as voltage controlled current sources with associated capacitances, and we model the interconnect in the oscillator as additional capacitances. We use HSPICE generate tables of current data for the transistors in our circuit and use bilinear interpolation within this table. By using a fine grid for the table (0.01V steps with a 1.8V power supply), our models are very close to the HSPICE model. For simplicity, we ignore wire resistance and inductance noting that they should be negligible for any reasonably compact layout of the circuit. The state of the circuit is given by a vector of $2n$ elements, corresponding to the voltages on the $2n$ nodes of the circuit. A state is a DC equilibrium if the total current flowing into each node through the transistors is zero.

A brute-force analysis of the ring-oscillator would require searching a $2n$-dimensional space for DC equilibria. In addition to being time consuming, it would be difficult to show that such a search was exhaustive. Instead, we first show how we can simplify the problem to the search of a 2-dimensional space, and then further reduce it to a

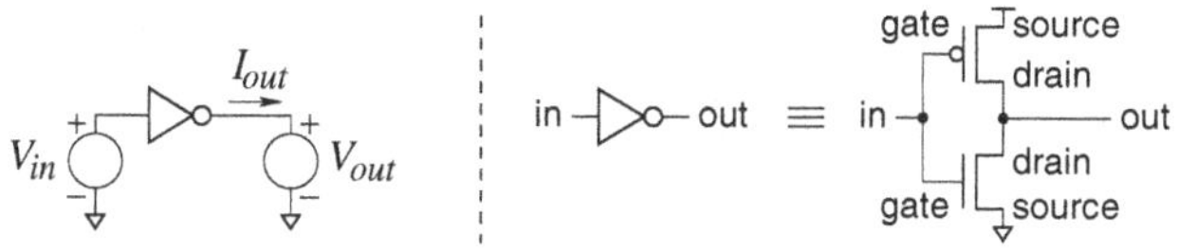

Fig. 5. An Inverter

1-dimensional search problem. This formulation makes the identification of DC equilibria straightforward.

Our analysis is based on simple observations of the monotonicity of the drain source current of a MOSFET. In particular, the drain-to-source current for a transistor (n-channel or p-channel) is positive monotonic in both the gate-to-source and drain-to-source voltages. As a consequence, the output current of an inverter (see Figure 5) is negative monotonic in both the input and output voltages of the inverter.

Because the I_{inv} function is monotonic, its inverses are also functions. In particular, we define $in_{inv}(V_{out}, I_{out})$ to be the input voltage to the inverter such that if the output voltage is V_{out}, then the output current will be I_{out}. In other words:

$$I_{inv}(in_{inv}(V_{out}, I_{out}), V_{out}) = I_{out} \tag{6}$$

We assume that all forward inverters have the same transfer function and that all cross-coupling inverters have the same transfer function – this assumption is not essential to the remaining analysis, but it simplifies the presentation. Let $I_{inv,fwd}$ and $I_{inv,cc}$ denote these two transfer functions, and let $in_{inv,fwd}$ denote the in_{inv} function for a forward inverter. For $i \in \{0, 1\}$ and $0 \le j < n$, let $V_{i,j}$ denote the voltage on node x(i,j) as indicated in Figure 4. We note that V is a DC equilibrium iff

$$
\begin{aligned}
&I_{inv,fwd}(x(1, n-1), x(0,0)) + I_{inv,cc}(x(1,0), x(0,0)) = 0\\
\wedge\ &I_{inv,fwd}(x(0, n-1), x(1,0)) + I_{inv,cc}(x(0,0), x(1,0)) = 0\\
\wedge\ &I_{inv,fwd}(x(0,i), x(0,i+1)) + I_{inv,cc}(x(1,i+1), x(0,i+1)) = 0,\\
&\quad 0 \le i < n-1\\
\wedge\ &I_{inv,fwd}(x(1,i), x(1,i+1)) + I_{inv,cc}(x(0,i+1), x(1,i+1)) = 0,\\
&\quad 0 \le i < n-1
\end{aligned}
\tag{7}
$$

Let

$$
\begin{aligned}
back(V_{0,i}, V_{1,i}) = (&in_{inv,fwd}(V_{0,i}, -I_{inv,cc}(V_{1,i}, V_{0,i})),\\
&in_{inv,fwd}(V_{1,i}, -I_{inv,cc}(V_{1,i}, V_{0,i})))
\end{aligned}
\tag{8}
$$

In English, given the voltages on the outputs of an oscillator stage, *back* calculates the voltages that must be present on the inputs of the stage if the outputs are to be in DC equilibrium.

We can use *back* repeatedly to work backwards all the way around the oscillator ring. In particular, if $back^n(x,y) = (y,x)$, then we've found a DC equilibrium. Otherwise, we note that $back^n(x,y)$ is positive monotonic in both x and y. Thus for any choice of x, there exists exactly one choice of y such that there is some z with $back^n(x,y) = (z,x)$, and this value of y can be found using standard root-finding techniques. Our verification procedure now is:

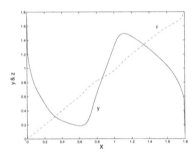

Fig. 6. Searching for DC Equilibria

1. Sweep x from ground to the power supply voltage in small steps.
2. For each choice of x, find the y such that there exists a z with $back^n(x,y) = (z,x)$.
3. Find consecutive choices of x such that the sign of $y - z$ changes. perform binary search on these intervals to find a pair, (x,y). such that $back^n(x,y) = (y,x)$. The pairs found this way are the DC-equilibrium points of the circuit.

The soundness of this method depends on having a small enough step in the sweep of the x values. In practice, we observe that the value of z changes smoothly with x, for example, Figure 6 shows the values of y and z that we obtain while sweeping x – the smoothness of these curves suggests that we are not missing any equilibrium points. Thus, we have reduced the problems of finding all DC equilibria to a single, one-dimensional sweep.

To determine whether or not a DC equilibrium is stable, we construct the small-signal, transient model at each equilibrium point. This gives us a linear model for circuit behavior in a small neighborhood of the equilibrium:

$$\dot{V} \approx J_{eq}(V - V_{eq}) \tag{9}$$

where $\dot{V}$ is the time derivative of V, V_{eq} is the voltage vector for the equilibrium point, and J_{eq} is the matrix representation of the linear approximation for $\dot{V}$ when V is near V_{eq}. The solution to Equation 9 is

$$V(t_0 + t) = V_{eq} + e^{tJ_{eq}}(V - V_{eq}) \tag{10}$$

If all of the eigenvalues of J_{eq} have negative real parts, then $e^{tJ_{eq}}$ goes to zero as t increases, and $V(t_0 + t)$ converges to V_{eq}. Thus, such a DC equilibrium is stable (See [5] for an introduction to the dynamical systems theory). Conversely, if J_{eq} has any eigenvalues with positive real parts, then its DC equilibrium is unstable.

To compute the Jacobian of $-C^{-1}I_m(V)$, we note that J is a matrix with

$$J(i,j) = \frac{\partial \dot{V}_i}{\partial V_j} \tag{11}$$

For simplicity, we assume that C is constant, and it suffices to compute the partial derivatives of $I_m(V)$ with respect to the components of V.

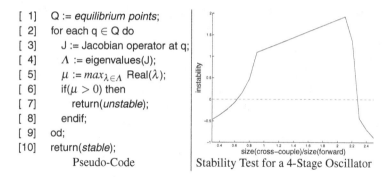

Pseudo-Code

Stability Test for a 4-Stage Oscillator

Fig. 7. Classifying DC Equilibria

Figure 7(a) shows how we combine these pieces to obtain an algorithm to verify that a Rambus ring-oscillator has no stable DC-equilibria.

We tested the methods described in the previous section by applying them to a family of Rambus ring oscillator circuits designed in the TSMC 180nm CMOS process. We implemented our analysis algorithms as Matlab scripts and compared our results with HSPICE simulations. The p-channel device in each inverter has twice the width of the n-channel transistor. We varied the transistor width to determine the inverter sizings required to guarantee oscillation. Figure 7(b) displays the results. Let

$$r = \frac{size(cross-coupling\ inverter)}{size(forward\ inverter)}$$
$$instability(r) = \min_{q \in Q(r)} \max_{e \in \Lambda(q)} real(e) \tag{12}$$

where $Q(r)$ is the set of all DC equilibria for an oscillator with an inverter size ratio of r, and $\Lambda(q)$ is the set of eigenvalues of the Jacobian matrix for $\dot{V}$ at q. Thus, if $instability(r) > 0$, all DC equilibria are unstable and the oscillator will not lock up. Conversely if $instability(r) < 0$, the circuit can lock-up for some initial conditions. We determined that lock-up is excluded for $0.638 < r < 2.243$.

We then simulated the oscillator circuit using both HSPICE and Matlab's numerical integrator function (ode113) to explore the behavior near the critical values. As expected, we found lock-up behaviors for values of $r < 0.638$ and $r > 2.243$. To our surprise, we found that the four-stage oscillator can support stable oscillations for values of r very close to zero.

For $\varepsilon < r < 0.638$ (with a very small, positive ε), the four-stage ring has three stable behaviors: it can lock-up at either of the two stable DC equilibria described in Equation 5, or it can oscillate. The actual behavior depends on the initial conditions. This is a potentially treacherous situation for an analog circuit designer. It shows that there are designs for which many initial conditions (including the default in HSPICE) lead to the desired behavior, but some conditions can lead to lock-up. Thus, this is a failure mode that could easily go undetected using standard simulation methods and only be discovered in the test lab, or after the chip has been shipped in products. We believe that examples such as this demonstrate the value of a formal approach to analyzing analog circuits.

The method presented here (and in more detail in [12]) establishes conditions that ensure that the oscillator circuit is free from lock-up. While we used a four-stage oscillator as an example, the method works for any (even) number of stages because it only searches a one-dimensional space regardless of the number of stages in the oscillator. In particular, it works for the two-stage version originally presented in [11] or for oscillators with more stages However, this analysis here does not guarantee that there is only one, stable oscillatory mode, nor does it ensure that unstable, higher-order modes die out quickly. Showing the uniqueness of the desired oscillatory mode could be attempted by reachability techniques such as those developed of hybrid systems or through finding appropriate Lyapunov functions. These remain areas for future research.

Other Approaches to Verifying the Oscillator. Little and Myers [13] analyzed a two-stage oscillator where they obtained a LHPN model derived from simulation traces and user-defined thresholds for node voltages. There goal was to establish the stability of the oscillation and they did not attempt to show that the oscillator starts correctly from any initial condition. To find lock-up traces with their method requires starting from an appropriate set of simulation traces and choosing the right set of node voltage thresholds for partitioning the state space. Tiwary *et al.* [14] used the Rambus oscillator as an example of their SAT-solver based approach to circuit verification. In particular, they used a SAT solver to identify regions of the state space that *might* contain DC equilibrium points. They did not classify the stability of these equilibrium points, and the regions that they identified covered a large fraction of the total space. They noted that more exact analysis may be possible by using abstraction refinement. More recently, Zaki *et al.* [15] presented a similar approach using HySat [16] that identifies a very small region for each equilibrium point and characterizes the stability of the point. Comparing the relative strengths and weaknesses of satisfiability based methods such as [15] and the dynamical systems approach of [12] is a topic for future research.

3.2   Synchronizer Failure Probabilities

Today's VLSI designs are often "System-on-a-Chip" [17] that combine a large number of independently designed "intellectual property" blocks. These blocks can operate at different clock frequencies because of different I/O requirements, different design targets, power optimization, etc. Consider two, communicating blocks that operate from different clocks. A signal from the sending block may change at an arbitrary time relative to the receiver's clock. This can create a synchronization failure as depicted in Figure 8.

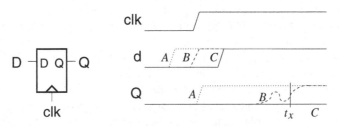

Fig. 8. A D Flip-Flop and Metastability

If the D input to the flip-flop changes well before the triggering transition of the clock, then the value of the Q output well after this rising edge (e.g. at time t_x) will reflect the new value of D. This scenario is depicted by the traces labeled A in Figure 8. On the other hand, if D changes well after the triggering transition of the clock, the Q output will retain its old value as depicted by the traces labeled C in the figure. The flip-flop is implemented by circuits that can be accurately modeled by ODEs with smooth derivative functions. Thus, the value of Q at any time is a *continuous* function of the parameters of the system. In particular, the value of Q at time t_x is a continuous function of the time of the transition of the D input. Thus, there is some time (depicted in the figure with the traces labeled B) that the D input can change such that the Q output will be at an intermediate value at time t_x **no matter how long t_x is after the clock event.** Such a scenario is called a *metastability failure*.

Metastability has been known since the early work of Chaney and Molnar [18], and many proofs have been published showing that metastability is unavoidable given any reasonable model of the physical implementation of the synchronizer (e.g. [19,20,21]). Thus, we cannot hope to prove that a synchronizer circuit will never fail. Fortunately, the probability of failure decreases exponentially with the time allotted for the synchronizer output to settle. Thus, with a sufficient settling time, the probability of a synchronization failure can be made extremely small. On the other hand, designers do not want to make the settling time too large as the extra latency of the synchronizer can adversely impact system performance. Kinniment *et al.* [22] have presented experimental measurements that show that simple linear models fail to give accurate estimates of synchronizer failure probabilities because they neglect non-linear circuit behaviors that occur as metastability "moves" from one latch to the next in a synchronizer chain. Thus, there is a need to be able to analyze synchronizer failure probabilities.

Consider a synchronizer that must handle an input transition every 10ns. To achieve a mean time between failure (MTBF) of one year, then the synchronizer must have a failure probability of less than 10^{-15}. This is close to the resolution of double precision arithmetic and is impossible to verify with traditional circuit simulators. In fact, from our experience, simulators such as HSPICE have sufficient numerical accuracy to establish MTBFs of a few milliseconds, but they cannot establish any MTBF that would be acceptable for a practical design.

Figure 9 shows a simple latch that could be used in the implementation of a flip-flop – a typical flip-flop consists of two latches, a master and a slave, that are enable on opposite polarities of the clock signal. Metastability occurs when a transition on the d input occurs just before the falling edge of clk bringing nodes x and x̄ to nearly the

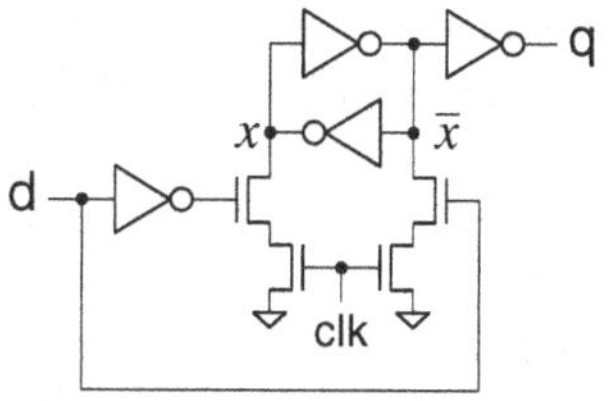

Fig. 9. A Jamb Latch

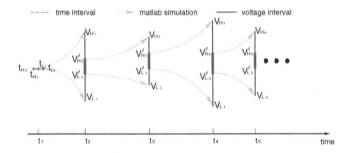

Fig. 10. Simulation with Interpolation and Restart

same voltage. In particular, the latch has an equilibrium point where both x and x̄ are at point where the input and output voltages of the inverters are equal. For any reasonable inverter designs, this equilibrium point is unstable. In fact, the Jacobian matrix for the derivative operator must have one positive eigenvalue (the instability) and the other eigenvalues must be negative. This is what makes the circuit challenging for the numerical integrators used in circuit simulators: the positive eigenvalue means that errors are amplified in the forward-time direction, and the negative eigenvalues mean that trying to integrate backwards in time is also numerically unstable.

This instability has an important physical interpretation. Consider two trajectories that both spend a long time near the metastable point before one settles with q high and the other settles with q low. For most of this time, both trajectories are very close to the unstable equilibrium point, and therefore they are very close to each other. This means that a small-signal, linear model can be used to model the *difference* between the two trajectories. The full, non-linear circuit model must be used to determine the *common* component of the two trajectories.

Figure 10 shows how we used these observations to obtain an accurate way to compute synchronizer failure probabilities. As with traditional methods, we start with two simulations with two different input transition time times: one that leads to the synchronizer settling high and the other that leads to it settling low. We bisect on this time interval until we get two trajectories that are close enough together to safely use linear interpolation to derive intermediate trajectories, but still sufficiently separated to allow a clear numerical distinction between these two path. Our algorithm finds a time, t_2 in the diagram, such that linear interpolation is valid in the interval $[t_1, t_2]$, and the points in phase space, V_{L_1} and V_{H_1} are sufficiently separated as to allow a new round of bisection to be performed. Our algorithm repeats this process, finding a sequence of time points and trajectory endpoint that move closer and closer to "perfectly metastable" trajectory. Crucial to our analysis is that at each step, the algorithm has a linear mapping from states at t_{i+1} back to states at t_i. Because the circuit model is highly non-linear, this mapping is only valid for trajectories that are close to the ones that we have found, but that is sufficient in out case. Composing these linear mappings, we can determine the width of the equivalent time interval at t_1 that leads to synchronization failures at any given settling time. We do not attempt to compute the location of this interval any more accurately than traditional simulation methods as the precise location is unimportant for determining failure probabilities. We only need to know the width of the interval, and our algorithm computes very small widths without any numerical difficulties. More details on this approach are given in [23], and [24] shows how this approach can be used to generate waveforms, the "counterexamples" that show how metastability failures occur for particular circuits.

Recently, our software has been used by research collaborators at SUN [25]. The analysis revealed failure modes that had not been previously considered and showed ways to improve the reliability of the synchronizer circuits being used in commercial designs.

This is a paper for a formal verification conference; so the reader might ask: "Is this really formal verification?" In many ways, the answer to this question is "Of course not." As noted above, no synchronizer can be perfect; so, we cannot hope to prove that a synchronizer never fails. We might hope to prove that its failure probability is acceptably small. While this is possible, our current techniques are very pragmatically numerical, and they don't offer that kind of proof. Nevertheless, I believe that this kind of research is relevant to the formal methods community. First, it came out of the same dynamical systems perspective that is behind many of the techniques used for formal verification of circuits. By learning how to specify and verify circuits, we developed many of the conceptual tools (as well as much of the software) for computing synchronizer failure probabilities. Second, when an analysis tool indicates that changes should be made to a design, we need a high level of confidence that these changes really will improve the quality of the product. Design changes are expensive and risky, and when they come out of newly developed analysis tools, project managers have a good reason to scrutinize the claims and results very carefully. Although we have not formally verified the correctness of our approach, we have carefully checked the results by many different methods. A formal correctness proof would contribute even more confidence to using new methods like these, and we see this as a valuable area for future work.

3.3   Other Intermediate Examples

To the best of my knowledge, the first published research on circuit-level verification was by Kurshan and MacMillan [1]. They verified an arbiter, the asynchronous cousin of the synchronizers described above. I classify this as an "intermediate" example as they used fairly realistic transistors models with a real circuit. Their verification assumed that inputs to the arbiter change instantaneously.

Dastidar and Chakrabarti [26] implemented a model checker for analog circuits. As in [13], they discretized the state space and used SPICE simulations to achieve a next-state relation. They extended their discretized state space model to discretizing the possible input waveforms; in other words, inputs are fine-grained "stair-step" functions. I'm including this as an "intermediate" example because they presented a systematic procedure for enumerating all possible state transitions relative to these discretizations. They used their model checker to verify properties of several circuits including a comparator, an operational amplifier, a VCO and a successive-approximation analog-to-digital converter.

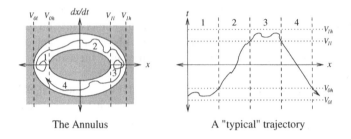

The Annulus   A "typical" trajectory

Fig. 11. Brockett's Annulus

Recently, we have verified the CMOS counterpart of Kurshan and MacMillan's arbiter [27]. Our verification uses a Brockett's annulus construction [28] shown in Figure 11 to specify the allowed input transitions. The annulus defines a relation between signal voltage and its time derivative. This bounds signals into appropriate intervals for logical low and logical high values; it also specifies monotonic transitions, and bounds the slopes, and thus transition times, for these transitions. Our verification applies for *any* input functions that satisfy these constraints. More details of the construction are in [27]. We have used similar techniques to verify a toggle flip-flop [29].

4   Open Problems

The previous two sections presented examples that show how traditional formal methods techniques such as reachability analysis and model checking can be combined with concepts from dynamical systems theory to verify circuits of simple or moderate complexity. Where to we go from here?

Presently, one of the biggest concerns of circuit designers is device parameter variability [30]. Traditionally, circuit designers have had to cope with the fact that there could be large parameter variation between different wafers or different die, but that devices on the same die tend to be very well matched. More recently, this matching has been limited to devices that are physically proximate, but designers have been extremely adept at exploiting this matching. As fabrication technology enables the manufacture of chip with extremely small transistors and wires, statistical fluctuations between devices have become relatively large, and the traditional design methods no longer work. Instead, designers use digital control inputs to analog circuits to adaptively correct for variations in process parameters and operating conditions. For example, many microprocessors adaptively adjust the power supply voltage and the body bias (the voltage on the "fourth" terminal of the transistor that we often don't bother to include in schematics) to balance speed and leakage power trade-offs [31,32]. Many chips include on-chip, dedicated processors simply to manage power supply voltage, clock skew, body bias, and other variations (e.g. [33]). Thus, chips really are hybrid systems: analog circuits with non-linear dynamics with discrete control inputs whose values are determined by a software program.

This mix of analog circuitry with digital, adaptive control creates numerous verification challenges. First, detailed simulation with circuit simulators such as SPICE is too slow to be used while simulating the adaptive algorithm. Thus, designers use mixed-mode simulation languages such as Verilog-AMS [34] or VHDL-AMS to describe their designs. Individual circuits are simulated extensively with SPICE, and then the designer writes a Verilog-AMS model to match the observed behavior. Presently, there is little or no automatic support to verify that the Verilog-AMS model matches the actual circuit. Furthermore, the detailed simulations may omit some assignments of the control inputs, but the Verilog-AMS code does something "sensible" with that input, even though it may not be what the actual circuit does. This creates many opportunities for errors to be hidden in a design.

Based on these observations, I expect that the many of the critical issues for circuit-level verification will be related to handling design with parameter variations in a systematic way. This leads to three critical areas for further research:

1. Developing tools to verify that simplified circuit models such as those used in Verilog-AMS are valid abstractions of the actual circuit. Formal methods researchers have developed many ways of describing and verifying abstractions. I expect that there are good opportunities for formal methods research to contribute to this area.
2. Verifying the correct operation of the circuit over the range of possible parameter values. While a designer can often obtain a high level of confidence in digital designs by simulating the "corner cases," analog circuits can exhibit more subtle failures that require consideration of parameters in the interior of the parameter space as well. While symbolic tools such as PHAVer [4] can analyze a circuit with parameters left as symbolic quantities and then derive relations that must hold amongst the parameters for correct operation, these tools are presently limited to designs that have a small number of dimensions to their phase space and/or have very simple dynamics.
3. Verifying the composition of analog circuits with adaptive, digital control. As noted above, this is a true hybrid systems problem, and there appears to be a good opportunity to build on the experience and and techniques of the hybrid systems community to make contributions here. Again, the complexity of the circuits and control algorithms along with the non-linearity of the circuit models present challenges that go beyond current hybrid systems research.

5 Conclusions

I have presented an introduction and survey into results and opportunities for formal verification of circuits using continuous models. My emphasis has been on using basic results from dynamical systems theory to specify and analyze circuits. In Section 2, I described the tunnel-diode oscillator problem that has often been used as an example for reachability tools, and showed how it can be verified and characterized using straightforward dynamical systems methods. This does not invalidate the reachability approach. Indeed, the challenge of circuit-level verification is largely one of the "curse of dimensionality:" with continuous variables, a state spac of only five to ten variables can be challenging for existing tools. Thus, progress will almost certainly rely on combining reachability methods from the formal methods community with key results from dynamical systems theory to create tractable methods.

In Section 3, I described "intermediate problems" that are of interest to practicing circuit designers and can be addressed with existing techniques. Again, I used an oscillator as the primary example, in this case the differential ring oscillator challenge problem posed by researchers at Rambus. I again used a dynamical systems approach, first finding the equilibrium points of the circuit and then characterizing their stability. Unlike the tunnel-diode oscillator, refuting the possibility of fixed-point attractors does not prove that the circuit oscillates as intended. This is because the higher dimensionality of the Rambus oscillator's phase space opens the possibility of more complicated behaviors than are possible with the tunnel-diode circuit. I also sketched how a dynamical systems approach can be applied to synchronizer analysis and has been used by industrial designers.

Finally, I posed challenge problems for where we could go next with this work. Chief among these are finding ways of verifying analog circuits that have digital control inputs to compensate for variations in device parameters and operating conditions. These are genuine hybrid systems that pose challenges for modeling, abstraction, and verification. In the past ten years, circuit-level verification has progressed from being academic curiosity to a topic that addresses concerns of designers working with cutting-edge fabrication processes. The high-cost of design and fabrication, the prevalence of mixed-signal designs, and the challenges of designing deep-submicron processes all motivate developing new approaches to circuit design. Formal methods has the potential to make significant contributions to emerging design techniques.

Acknowledgements

I am grateful for interaction with many students and colleagues including Robert Drost, Kevin Jones, Ian Mitchell, Frank O'Mahony, Chao Yan and Suwen Yang. This work has been supported in part by grants from Intel, SUN Microsystems, and NSERC CRD–356905-07.

References

1. Kurshan, R., McMillan, K.: Analysis of digital circuits through symbolic reduction. IEEE Transactions on Computer-Aided Design 10(11), 1356–1371 (1991)
2. Hartong, W., Hedrich, L., Barke, E.: Model checking algorithms for analog verification. In: Proceedings of the 39th ACM/IEEE Design Automation Conference, June 2002, pp. 542–547 (2002)
3. Little, S., Seegmiller, N., Walter, D., Myers, C., Yoneda, T.: Verification of analog/mixed-signal circuits using labeled hybrid petri nets. In: Proceedings of the International Conference on Computer Aided Design, November 2006, pp. 275–282 (2006)
4. Frehse, G.: PHAVer: Algorithmic verification of hybrid systems past HyTech. In: Morari, M., Thiele, L. (eds.) HSCC 2005. LNCS, vol. 3414, pp. 258–273. Springer, Heidelberg (2005)
5. Hirsch, M.W., Smale, S.: Differential Equations, Dynamical Systems, and Linear Algebra. Academic Press, San Diego (1974)

6. Gupta, S., Krogh, B.H., Rutenbar, R.A.: Towards formal verification of analog designs. In: Proceedings of 2004 IEEE/ACM International Conference on Computer Aided Design, November 2004, pp. 210–217 (2004)
7. Frehse, G., Krogh, B.H., Rutenbar, R.A.: Verifying analog oscillator circuits using forward/backward abstraction refinement. In: Proceedings of Design Automation and Test Europe, March 2006, pp. 257–262 (2006)
8. Mitchell, I., Greenstreet, M.: Proving Newtonian arbiters correct, almost surely. In: Proceedings of the Third Workshop on Designing Correct Circuits, Båstad, Sweden (September 1996)
9. Greenstreet, M.R., Huang, X.: A smooth dynamical system that counts in binary. In: Proceedings of the 1997 International Symposium on Circuits and Systems, Hong Kong, vol. II, pp. 977–980. IEEE, Los Alamitos (1997)
10. Greenstreet, M.R., Mitchell, I.: Integrating projections. In: Henzinger, T.A., Sastry, S. (eds.) HSCC 1998. LNCS, vol. 1386, pp. 159–174. Springer, Heidelberg (1998)
11. Jones, K.D., Kim, J., Konrad, V.: Some "real world" problems in the analog and mixed-signal domains. In: Proc. Workshop on Designing Correct Circuits (April 2008)
12. Greenstreet, M.R., Yang, S.: Verifying start-up conditions for a ring oscillator. In: Proceedings of the 18th Great Lakes Symposium on VLSI (GLSVLSI 2008), May 2008, pp. 201–206 (2008)
13. Little, S., Myers, C.: Abstract modeling and simulation aided verification of analog/mixed-signal circuits. Presented at the 2008 Workshop on Formal Verification for Analog Circuits (FAC 2008) (July 2008)
14. Tiwari, S.K., Gupta, A., et al.: fSpice: a boolean satisfiability based approach for formally verifying analog circuits. Presented at the 2008 Workshop on Formal Verification for Analog Circuits (FAC 2008) (July 2008)
15. Zaki, M.H., Mitchell, I., Greenstreet, M.R.: Towards a formal analysis of DC equilibria of analog designs. Presented at the 2009 Workshop on Formal Verification for Analog Circuits (FAC 2009) (June 2009)
16. Fränzle, M., Herde, C., Ratschan, S., Schubert, T., Teige, T.: Efficient solving of large nonlinear arithmetic constraint systems with complex boolean structure. JSAT Special Issue on Constraint Programming and SAT 1, 209–236 (2007)
17. Saleh, R., Wilton, S., Hu, A.J., Greenstreet, S.M., Ivanov, A., Lemieux, G., Pande, P., Grecu, C.: System-on-chip: Reuse and integration. Proceedings of the IEEE 94(6), 1050–1069 (2006)
18. Chaney, T., Molnar, C.: Anomalous behavior of synchronizer and arbiter circuits. IEEE Transactions on Computers C-22(4), 421–422 (1973)
19. Hurtado, M.: Structure and Performance of Asymptotically Bistable Dynamical Systems. PhD thesis, Sever Institute, Washington University, Saint Louis, MO (1975)
20. Marino, L.: General theory of metastable operation. IEEE Transactions on Computers C-30(2), 107–115 (1981)
21. Mendler, M., Stroup, T.: Newtonian arbiters cannot be proven correct. In: Proceedings of the 1992 Workshop on Designing Correct Circuits (January 1992)
22. Kinniment, D., Heron, K., Russell, G.: Measuring deep metastability. In: Proceedings of the Twelfth International Symposium on Asynchronous Circuits and Systems, March 2006, pp. 2–11 (2006)
23. Yang, S., Greenstreet, M.R.: Computing synchronizer failure probabilities. In: Proceedings of the 13th Design, Automation and Test, Europe Conference, April 2007, pp. 1361–1366 (2007)
24. Yang, S., Greenstreet, M.R.: Simulating improbable events. In: Proceedings of the 44th ACM/IEEE Design Automation Conference, June 2007, pp. 154–157 (2007)

25. Jones, I.W., Yang, S., Greenstreet, M.: Synchronizer behavior and analysis. In: Proceedings of the Fifthteenth International Symposium on Asynchronous Circuits and Systems, May 2009, pp. 119–126 (2009)
26. Dastidar, T., Chakrabarti, P.: A verification system for transient response of analog circuits using model checking. In: Proceedings of the 18th International Conference on VLSI Design (VLSID 2005), January 2005, pp. 195–200 (2005)
27. Yan, C., Greenstreet, M.R.: Verifying an arbiter circuit. In: Proceedings of the 8th Conference on Formal Methods in Computer Aided Design (FMCAD 2008) (November 2008)
28. Brockett, R.: Smooth dynamical systems which realize arithmetical and logical operations. In: Nijmeijer, H., Schumacher, J.M. (eds.) Three Decades of Mathematical Systems Theory: A Collection of Surveys at the Occasion of the 50th Birthday of J. C. Willems. LNCIS, vol. 135, pp. 19–30. Springer, Heidelberg (1989)
29. Yan, C., Greenstreet, M.R.: Circuit level verification of a high-speed toggle. In: Proceedings of the 7th Conference on Formal Methods in Computer Aided Design (FMCAD 2007) (November 2007)
30. Bowman, K.A., Duvall, S.G., Meindl, J.D.: Impact of die-to-die and within-die parameter fluctuations on the maximum clock frequency distribution for gigascale integration. IEEE Journal of Solid-State Circuits 37(2), 183–190 (2002)
31. Tschanz, J., Kao, J., et al.: Adaptive body bias for reducing impacts of die-to-die and within-die parameter variations on microprocessor frequency and leakage. IEEE Journal of Solid-State Circuits 37(11), 1396–1402 (2002)
32. Chen, T., Naffziger, S.: Comparison of adaptive body bias (ABB) and adaptive supply voltage (ASV) for improving delay and leakage under the presence of process variation. IEEE Transactions on VLSI Systems 11(5), 888–899 (2003)
33. Naffziger, S., Stackhouse, B., et al.: The implementation of a 2-core, multi-threaded Itanium family processor. IEEE Journal of Solid-State Circuits 41(1), 197–209 (2006)
34. Kundert, K.S.: The Designer's Guide to Verilog-AMS. Kluwer, Dordrecht (2004)

3-Valued Abstraction for (Bounded) Model Checking

Orna Grumberg

Computer Science Department, Technion, Haifa, Israel

Abstract. Model Checking is the problem of verifying that a given model satisfies a specification, given in a formal specification language. Abstraction is one of the most successful approaches to avoiding the state explosion problem in model checking. It simplifies the model being checked, in order to save memory and time.

3-valued abstraction is a strong type of abstraction that can be used for both verification and refutation. For hardware verification, 3-valued abstraction can be obtained by letting state variables and inputs range over the ternary domain 0,1,X, where X stands for "unknown". X is used to abstract away parts of the circuit that are irrelevant for the property being checked. For 3-valued abstractions, checking an abstract model may result in 1 or 0, indicating that the checked property holds or fails, respectively, on the original model. Alternatively, model checking may result in X, indicating that it is impossible to determine whether the property holds or fails due to a too coarse abstraction. In the latter case, the abstract model is refined by replacing some of the X's with the relevant parts of the circuit. The 3-valued abstraction and refinement can be applied either automatically or manually.

In this talk we present an automata theoretic approach to 3-valued abstraction in hardware model checking. We show how our 3-valued framework can be incorporated into SAT based bounded model checking and induction based unbounded model checking.

Our method enables applying formal verification of LTL formulae on very large industrial designs. We developed our method within Intel's bounded and unbounded model checking framework, implemented on top of a state-of-the-art CNF SAT solver. We used it for checking real life assertions on a large CPU design, and obtained outstanding results.

This is a joint work with Avi Yadgar, Alon Flaisher, and Michael Lifshits.

Z. Liu and A.P. Ravn (Eds.): ATVA 2009, LNCS 5799, p. 21, 2009.

Local Search in Model Checking

A.W. Roscoe, P.J. Armstrong, and Pragyesh

Oxford University Computing Laboratory
Bill.Roscoe@comlab.ox.ac.uk

Abstract. We introduce a new strategy for structuring large searches in model checking, called *local search*, as an alternative to depth-first and breadth-first search. It is designed to optimise the amount of checking that is done relative to communication, where communication can mean either between parallel processors or between fast main memory and backing store, whether virtual memory or disc files. We report on it in the context of the CSP refinement checker FDR.

1 Introduction

Recent years have seen an enormous increase in the power of model checking technology, thanks in part to the more powerful computers that we now have to run them on and in part to improved algorithms such as techniques for SAT checking [2,8], partial order reduction [14] and state-space compression [13]. It is clear, however, that there is still a need for the basic function of searching through the states of a large but finite automaton to test whether each reachable state is satisfactory.

The first author has yet to find a problem where FDR, the refinement checker for CSP (using explicit searching combined with the compression of subprocesses) could not prove a property (i.e. the absence of a counter-example) faster than the SAT checking models of [10,16]. Even when finding counter-examples, the option of using FDR in DFS mode is very competitive with these, as shown in [10].

It is well known that the state spaces of parallel systems tend to grow exponentially with the number of parallel components, and also grow rapidly with the sizes of the types used in defining systems. This means that many of the examples one might wish to run on a tool such as FDR either take only a trivial time or are well beyond the bounds of possibility. What we are going to investigate in this paper is the region between these two extremes where, for example, either it becomes desirable to split the effort of a particular run across several CPUs, the number of states needing to be stored exceeds the limits of fast memory on the computer, or both.

In any case it is clear that for the foreseeable future there will be demand for tools that can handle as large as possible a system as quickly as possible. In what follows we will examine how model-checking technology for explicitly searching through a state space has evolved with time, and has been affected by the developments in computing technology over the last two decades. In this

Z. Liu and A.P. Ravn (Eds.): ATVA 2009, LNCS 5799, pp. 22–38, 2009.
© Springer-Verlag Berlin Heidelberg 2009

last respect technology has been hugely positive and is alone responsible for the complete transformation of the capabilities of FDR and other methods. However it is also true to say that, relative to the huge increase in processing power these years have brought, the rate at which large amounts of data can be moved around, in particular on and off backing store such as disc, has not developed so rapidly on typical workstations. There has therefore been a gradually increasing need for search algorithms that minimise and optimise the needs for such data shifting. One particular statistic that is immediately visible to the user of a tool like FDR is the change in speed that occurs when it comes to occupy more space than is available to it in fast memory. We will refer to this as the *slow down* factor: 1 implying none, 2 meaning that it goes to half speed, and so on.

A crude measure of the slow-down factor is the reciprocal of the proportion of CPU time that the search tool gets when operating on backing store. (In the authors' experience they always use 100% when not fettered in this way.)

This paper presents techniques that we believe will greatly improve this factor. It represents work in progress in the sense that only relatively primitive and experimental versions of our methods have been implemented at the time of writing. The relative importance and effectiveness of the heuristics we introduce will only become clear after a good deal more work.

The main concepts of local search were proposed by the first author, and developed by all three during a period when the third author was an intern in Oxford during the summer of 2009. We expect that an implementation of it will be released in version 2.91 of FDR towards the end of 2009.

In the next section we review the background to the problem, and see how model checking algorithms have evolved in relation to this slow-down, and how both have been affected by the developments in computing technology. We then introduce the main ideas of local searching, before concentrating on the problem of how to partition state spaces effectively. We then review the results we have obtained to date before reviewing how local searching will transfer to parallel architectures.

This paper focuses on FDR. While we describe those parts of its behaviour directly relevant to this paper, inevitably we leave out a large amount of related detail. The interested reader can discover much more in, for example, [4,9], [11] (especially Appendices B and C) and [12] (forthcoming 2010).

2   Background

Early model checkers, including the first version of FDR, stored state information in hash tables. To discover if one of the successor states S' of the current state S you are examining has been seen before, just see if it is in the table. This works well provided the hash table will fit in the main memory of the computer, but extremely badly otherwise because of the way in which hash tables tend to create truly random access into the memory they consume: a section of backing store that is fetched into main memory (and this happens in large blocks) is unlikely to be much used before being written back.

This problem generated a number of ingenious techniques such as *one bit hashing* [5,6,15] in which one did not worry about hash collisions (so the search one performed was not complete). In this, only one bit is allocated per hash value, which simply records whether a state with that value has been seen before.

Such techniques were never implemented in FDR1, which saw slow-down factors approaching 100, making it entirely unusable for checks exceeding the bounds of RAM. The release of FDR2 in 1994 saw the first introduction of a searching technique in which, instead of performing each membership test individually, they are grouped together into large batches in such a way that the stored state space can be accessed effectively, with all checks against a particular block of stored state space being performed together.

The specific technique used by early versions of FDR, and described in [9], was to store the entire explored state space in a sorted list. The search was then performed in breadth-first search order, so that all the membership tests of each level of the check can be done together as follows:

- Initially, the explored state list $E(0)$ is empty and we need to explore the root state r. The initial *ply* of the search $Ply(0)$ is therefore $\{r\}$.
- Each ply $Ply(n)$ is sorted and combined with the explored states $E(n)$ by merging to create $E(n+1)$, by adding only those members of $Ply(n)$ not in $E(n)$. $Ply(n+1)$ is created as the set of all successors of these added states.
- The search is over when $Ply(n)$ is empty.

At the same time FDR started to apply compression techniques to these sorted lists, storing them in blocks that were either delta-compressed (i.e. only the bytes that were different between consecutive states were stored, together with a table showing where to put them), or compressed using the `gzip` utility, which was more expensive in terms of computing, but created compressed files that were perhaps 30% smaller than delta-compression.

When this was implemented the typical slow-down was reduced to somewhere between 2 and 4, so this represented a considerable success. In many cases the more aggressive compression regime gave lower execution times for complete checks.

The fact that disc access speed did not keep up with processor speed had the effect, however, of gradually increasing the slow-down factor between 1994 and the early 2000's, so that by this time the typical slow-down associated with this method had increased to perhaps 8-12. This was particularly noticeable towards the end of a refinement check, when relatively small numbers of new states are introduced per ply of the BFS, but the above algorithm was still ploughing through the entire state space each time.

To counter that, from FDR 2.64 onwards, the simple sorted list structure was replaced by a B-tree, still a sorted structure, but where it is possible to gain rapid access to a particular state and to omit whole blocks of states that are not required in a particular pass. Thus the merge of the algorithm reported above was replaced by repeated insertion into the B-tree represented by the already-explored states. This was particularly effective towards the end of searches, and perhaps halved the slow-down factor overall.

Of course this was not as good as we would have liked, and we are naturally now once again seeing an increase in this factor. It is this issue that the present paper addresses: we are looking for ways to reduce the amount of data that has to be moved to and from memory for each state explored.

Although the memory size of modern workstations is huge compared to those of a few years ago (2-4Gb being typical at the time of writing) it nevertheless seems to be the case that this limit is reached more quickly by FDR than in previous years. This means that, if anything, the problems of a high slow-down factor has become greater.

Believing that the new technology of disc drives built from flash memory would help greatly with the problems identified here, we obtained such a machine in 2008. We were disappointed that, at least with that particular version, the performance was actually marginally worse than with the same machine's conventional disc. This led us to believe that, though this type of technology may well improve in the future, it is very unlikely to solve the slow down problem sufficiently.

As we will discuss later, may of the same issues also apply to the parallel execution of model checking, where a significant barrier may be amount of data that has to be communicated between processors.

3   Local Search

As we have seen, BFS permits all of the membership tests in each ply of the search to be combined, which greatly reduces the amount of memory churn that is required. Nevertheless, even when improved by B-tree structures, it still more-or-less requires the entire accumulated state space to pass through the CPU on each ply. This would not matter if the memory bandwidth were sufficiently high that this happened without diminishing performance, but this is not true.

It gradually became apparent to the first author that the present BFS strategy required improvement, and so he proposed the following alternative method:

- Begin the search using the same BFS strategy as at present, with a parameter set for how much physical memory FDR is supposed to use. Maintain statistics on the states that are reached, the details of which will be discussed later.
- Monitor the position at the end of each play of the BFS, and when the memory used by the combination of the accumulated state space $X(n)$ and the unexplored successors $S(n+1)$ exceeds the defined limit, these two sets are split into a small number (at least two) *blocks* by applying some *partitioning function*.
- This partitioning might either be done as a separate exercise, or be combined with the next ply of the search.
- From here on the search always consists of a number of these blocks, and a partitioning function Π that allocates states between them. Each such block $B(i)$ will have an explored state space $EB(i)$ and a set of unexplored states $UB(i)$, which may intersect $EB(i)$.

– At any time FDR pursues the search on a single block B only, as a BFS, but the successors generated are partitioned using Π. The successors belonging to $B(i)$ are pursued in this BFS. Those belonging to other blocks are added to $UB(j)$ in a way that does not require operations on the existing body of $UB(j)$ that require this to be brought into memory.
– The search on $B(i)$ might terminate because after some ply $UB(i)$ becomes empty. In this case begin or resume the search on some other block with a nonempty $UB(j)$: if there is none, the search is complete and in FDR the refinement check gives a positive result. If there is another block to resume we must realise that $B(i)$ may not be finished for all time since other $B(j)$ might create a new $UB(i)$ for the block that has just terminated.
– On the other hand the size of the search of $B(i)$ might grow beyond our limit. In this case Π is refined so that $B(i)$ is split as above. After that a block which may or may not be one of the results of this last split is resumed.
– On resuming a block $B(i)$ the set $UB(i)$ might have grown very large thanks to input from other blocks, and furthermore it is possible that there might be much repetition. There is therefore a strong argument for (repetition removing) sorting of $UB(j)$ before assessing whether to split $B(i)$ at this stage.

It is clear that this search will find exactly as many states and successor states as either BFS or DFS: we explore the successors of every state exactly once. The objective of this approach is to minimise the amount of transfer in and out of main memory during the search. The basic rationale is that it makes sense to explore the successors of some states without always backgrounding them before doing so. In other words,

– Like DFS, tend to explore states that are already in the foreground.
– Seek to reduce the amount of memory churning performed by BFS.

There are three major parameters to this search method:

– How many pieces to divide blocks into? There are clear arguments for making this depend on the evolution of the search. If it is growing quickly we would expect a larger number of pieces to be better.
– Where there is a choice of blocks to resume, which one one should one pick? One could, for example, pick the largest one, follow a depth-first strategy (where blocks are arranged into a stack, with new blocks being pushed onto the stack, and the top of the stack being chosen for resumption), a breadth first search (where they are organised into a queue), or a hybrid in which, when a split occurs, we pursue one of the resulting blocks but push the rest to the back of a queue. Suppose, for example, an initial split generates blocks A and B, pursuing A generates AA and AB, and that pursuing AA at that point means that it terminates before splitting. Then the three strategies would initially follow $\langle A, AA, AB \rangle$, $\langle A, B \rangle$ and $\langle A, AA, B \rangle$.
– Perhaps most importantly, what algorithm should we use for partitioning the state space? There are two desiderata here: firstly that the parts we divide

the state space into are the sizes we want. While we might well want them to be equal in size, this is not inevitable. The second objective is that as large a proportion of the transitions from a state in each block should be to the same block: that way there will be relatively little state space to transfer to other blocks, and the search of a generated block is unlikely to peter out quickly. We will term this property that transitions tend to be to "nearby" states as *locality* and measure it as a percentage: the percentage of computed transitions that lie inside a single block. It follows that we should hope to do better than we would with a randomised partition.

How successful we are with this second objective might well influence the other choices that have to be made.

Whilst we hope that this approach will give us advantages thanks to better memory management, we also need to be aware of the extra work it introduces.

- Based on the above, we would expect each state to have partitioning functions applied to it as often as the blocks it happens to be in are split.
- Similarly we would expect there to be a cost in re-organising the data structures used to store states each time a block is split.
- There will also be costs in devising partitioning functions and collecting and analysing statistics to help in this.

4   Partitioning the State Space

We will assume in what follows that the overall state space is stored in a sorted structure in the general style of FDR as described earlier. We do not, however, discount the possibility that the same ideas might work in conjunction with hash tables.

Given this choice, there is an obvious way of partitioning a state space quickly: to break it into k pieces choose $k - 1$ states as pivots, with the pieces being the $k - 2$ sections between consecutive pairs of pivots, and the other two being the those less than, and greater than, all pivots. We might conventionally include the pivots themselves in the section immediately above them.

The most obvious way of picking these pivots is to spread them evenly either in the relevant $UB(i)$ or $EB(i)$ or both. The most obvious advantage of this approach is that the partitioning and restructuring work essentially disappears.

A clear disadvantage is that there is no good reason to suspect that this partitioning approach will give good locality properties: for this to happen we would need to design an order where most transitions are to states that are close (in the order) to their origins. We will show later how this can be achieved.

If we are to look for ways of improving the locality of a partition we must understand how one's tool, in our case FDR, represents states and generates transitions.

Since FDR is checking the refinement of a "specification" process *Spec* by an 'implementation" process *Impl*, the things it searches through are not single states but actually "state-pairs": the pairs (ss, is) where ss is a state of the specification and *is* is a state of the implementation that are reachable on some trace t.

ss is an integer index into an *explicit* representation of the *normal form* of *Spec*. An explicit state machine is an array of states, each of which carries a list of transitions, with each transition being the label of the action and the index of the target state. In some cases the states might have additional labelling. A normal form state machine is one in which (i) there are no τ (invisible) actions and (ii) no state has more than one action with any given label. Thus given the root state of a normal form machine, and a trace, then if it can perform the trace t then after t its state is completely determined.

If the refinement check is over any model other than $\mathcal{T}$, the traces model, then the normal form state will be labelled with information representing, for example, divergence and refusal-set information.

In most cases FDR computes the normal form in advance, but there is also the option to use the function `lazynorm(Spec)`, which means that only those normal form states relevant to traces of *Impl* are explored. The motivation for `lazynorm` is that sometimes the normalisation of *Spec* is a time-consuming activity, and `lazynorm` means that only the necessary parts of the normalisation are done. This is potentially an important distinction for our partitioning activities, since preliminary analysis can be carried out on a complete *Spec*, but less on one that has yet to be evaluated.

In a large proportion of FDR checks, the specification is extremely simple, frequently having just one or two states. For example, the specifications for "deadlock-free" and "the event a never occurs" each have just one state. There is clearly very little potential for partitioning the space of state pairs based on the specification state in cases like this[1].

The situation with the implementation state *is* is analogous to that with lazy normalisation: at the start of the check we have no idea which states will be reached or what their transitions will be. They are both examples of *implicit* state machines: a representation of the root state together with a set of recipes for computing the actions and resulting target states from any given state.

To understand the structure of an implementation state we need to understand the two-level treatment of CSP's operational semantics in FDR. The CSP$_M$ input language of FDR allows the user to lay out a network using functional programming. Broadly speaking FDR will reduce (in functional programming terms) the description of a network until it either hits a true recursion or gets below the level of all "high-level" operators, the most important of which are parallel, hiding and renaming. The syntax it encounters below that dividing line is compiled into explicit state machines using a symbolic representation of the operational semantics: these must be finite state and will be called *components*. Above that level it devises one or more recipes for combining together the states and actions

---

[1] It is possible in these cases artificially to increase the number of states in the specification, and indeed in our trial implementations we have sometimes done this. There are various good reasons such as loss of compression and the difficulty of automating this process that make this option very unattractive as a long-term solution.

of the components into states and actions of the whole implementation. We call these recipes *supercombinators*: see below.

Components do not only arise from compiling low-level syntax. They can also be generated by one of the various operators in CSP that compresses the state space of a process, typically because it has been applied to the parallel/hiding combination of a proper subset of what would otherwise have been the components of the complete system. Components can vary in size from a single state to hundreds of thousands or even millions.

Each of the recipes for combining components is called a *format*. In the majority of practical checks, there is just a single format that is effectively a parallel composition of the N (say) components, with perhaps some hiding and renaming mixed in.

Where there is more than one format, it is because one or more CSP operators that are usually low level get pushed up to high level by having some parallel operator beneath them in the reduced syntax tree, as in

$$(P \parallel Q); R \quad \text{and} \quad (a \to (P \parallel Q)) \square (b \to R)$$

In both of these there will be format that consists of a state of P and one of Q, and a format that consists of a state of R. In the right-hand process there is also a format representing the initial state that has no components.

FDR already stores the different formats separately, but where there are more than one they will frequently have very different numbers of states. So while it may well make sense to incorporate formats into a partitioning strategy, they are unlikely ever to be an important part of it. For the rest of this section, therefore, we will concentrate on partitioning an implementation process that has only a single format.

FDR calculates the actions of such a state in one of two ways. Firstly, any τ action of one of the components is promoted to be an action of the complete system, in which only the component that performs the τ changes state. Secondly, FDR produces a number of *supercombinator rules*. Each of these can be described by a partial function ϕ from the component indices to Σ, the visible event labels, together with a result action, which may either be in Σ or τ. This rule can fire just when, for each $i \in dom(\phi)$, component i can perform the event $\phi(i)$. Just the components that are in $dom(\phi)$ change state.

Thus each component processes simply moves around its own state space as the complete implementation progresses. One of the best prospects for partitioning the complete state space is to partition one of the components, and simply assign each state or state pair to a group determined by what state that component is in. This can clearly be generalised to look at the states of a small collection of the components, particularly in the case where the individual components each have very few states.

The mapping that sends each overall state to the state of the jth component may be far from uniform: some states may be represented many more times than others. It follows that what seems like a well-balanced partition of this component may not yield a well-balanced partition of the complete space. It is not at all unusual, for example, for a component process to have one or more error states that we hope will never be reached in the entire system. It therefore seems unlikely that there will be good *automatic* ways of deciding what component-based partition will be used in advance of running the search. We will, however, later show how to create a range of *options* for this in advance.

In our single format case, where the format has N components, we can think of each state pair as an $N + 1$-tuple of states, the extra one being the specification. There is no reason why partitions cannot be based on the specification state just as for a component of the implementations, but nor is there any reason to expect specification state distributions to be any more uniform.

We offer two different strategies for partitioning the state space, which we term *pre-computed* and *dynamic*.

4.1   Pre-computed Partitioning

In pre-computed partitioning, we decide on some partitioning options in advance, based on the state spaces of one or more of the $N + 1$ processes that represent a state pair.

We need an algorithm which will take a state machine and divide it into two or more state machines that are relatively self-contained, in the sense that as few transitions as possible pass between these parts.

This algorithm will come in two parts. The first part will assign weights to the various nodes and transitions of the component state machine. These will assess how likely it is that the machine will be in a given state or take a given transition. The second part will be to choose partition(s) of the state machine that attempt to deliver roughly equal node weight in each part and minimal edge weight between them so as to improve the locality of the search.

Each of these two algorithms will inevitably only give approximations to optimal results. In the first case this is because we cannot predict the weights that apply to a given search without running the search, and in the second case because even if we could formulate the correct balance between the two criteria, it would almost certainly be NP-hard to optimise them. Since the size of components we will want to partition will vary from 2 to millions, we will have to choose extremely efficient algorithms, place an upper bound on the size of component we will apply our algorithms to, or have different algorithms for different sizes of component.

This is not the place to go into great detail about these algorithms, but we give a few ideas below.

Weighting algorithms. In the absence of evidence about how a system behaves in practice, we can make intelligent guesses about how often particular transitions and nodes are used.

The state explosion problem arises because potentially, and frequently, the state spaces of the component processes multiply to give the state space of the entire system. Though in many cases this is not literally true, it is hard to think of a general way other than running the search to identify statistical information about which of these potential states are reachable and which are not. What we will therefore do is to build up a stochastic model built on the assumption that all combinations of component states are reachable. We exclude the specification from the computation of this model since it participates in *every* visible action.

What we will estimate is the probability, for each state γ of each component i of the system, that if the ith component of a global state Γ is γ, and Γ's other components are random, a randomly chosen action of Γ leads component i being in each of γ and the states immediately reachable from it. The sum of the probabilities of those states that are in the same partition as γ provides a measure of the locality of the actions starting from a randomly chosen Γ, conditional on this ith component.

We will call γ an *i-state*. We note that it might stay in γ either because it took an action that did not change the state, or because the global action did not involve component i.

For each labelled action x that each component j can make, we can compute $E_j(x)$ the expected number of times j can perform x from a random state: this is simply the number of x actions from its states divided by the number of states i has. Note that some of the states might have more than one x, so this expectation can be greater than 1.

We can therefore calculate, for each supercombinator $\rho = (\phi, x)$ the expected number of times $E(\rho)$ it can fire in an random state, namely the product of $E_j(\phi(j))$ as j ranges over $dom(\phi)$. We can similarly calculate $E_j(\rho \mid \gamma)$ the expected number of times that ρ can fire given that the i-state is γ.

- If $i \notin dom(\phi)$, it is $E(\rho)$.
- If $i \in \text{dom}(\phi)$, then it is the product of the number of $\phi(i)$ actions γ has and all the $E_j(\phi(j))$ as j ranges over $\text{dom}(\phi) - \{i\}$.

The total number of actions $EA_i(\gamma)$ we can expect a random state Γ whose i-state is some fixed γ to perform is

$$ct(\tau, \gamma) + \Sigma\{E_j(\tau) \mid j \in \{1..N\} - \{i\}\} + \Sigma\{E_i(\rho) \mid \rho \in SC\}$$

where $ct(x, \gamma')$ is the number of different x actions that the state γ' can perform from its initial state.

The expected number of times $E1_i(x \mid \gamma)$ that component i has a single one of its x actions enabled is then

- 1 if $x = \tau$.
- If $x \neq \tau$, it is the sum, over all supercombinators (ϕ, y) with $\phi(i) = x$, of the product of $E_j(\phi(j))$ as j ranges over $\text{dom}(\phi) - \{i\}$.

We can now say that the probability of a specific action (x, γ') of γ firing from Γ whose other components are randomly chosen is $E1_i(x \mid \gamma)/EA_i(\gamma)$, namely the number of times we expect it to fire as an action of such a Γ divided by the total number of actions of Γ. If $EA_i(\gamma) = 0$ then it is also 0.

The probability $PT_i(\gamma, \gamma')$ of γ making a transition to $\gamma' \neq \gamma$ is therefore the sum of this value over all labels x such that $\gamma \xrightarrow{x} \gamma'$. The probability the state is unchanged is

$$PT_i(\gamma, \gamma) = 1 - \Sigma_{\gamma' \neq \gamma} PT(\gamma, \gamma')$$

which takes into account the possibility of some x with $\gamma \xrightarrow{x} \gamma$ firing, and component i not being involved in the transition.

The above model depends crucially on our simplifying assumption that all states of the Cartesian product of the component state spaces are reachable. Under that assumption we know that every state of a given component i is reached equally often, so there is no point in trying to assign weights to these states representing how often each is represented in the complete system. There may, however, be reason to assign weights to them which include the number of times we expect that state to appear as a successor in the search, since that will affect the memory consumption of each block. This is because some component states may be represented more often than others in successors, even though they all appear equally often in the final state space. We do not propose a specific method at this time.

4.2 Example

In Chapter 15 of [11], the first case study given is peg solitaire, see Figure 1. We have added the letters A–G to show typical examples of the seven symmetry classes of slot under rotation and reflection. Games like this are useful benchmarks for FDR because they demonstrate the complexity of the problems

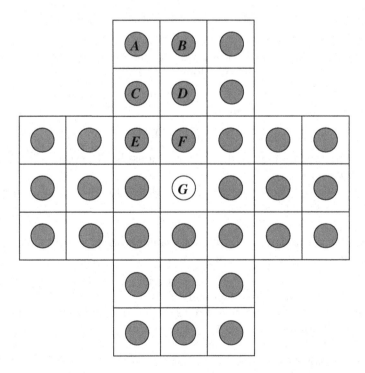

Fig. 1. Solitaire board with representatives of symmetry classes

being solved, because they usually give a counter-example (which is much more appealing than demonstrating an example where refinement holds) and because in FDR's standard breadth-first search the counter-example is found (as in solitaire) at the very end of the search, meaning that the search profile is almost identical to a check that succeeds. The model consists of 33 two-state processes, one representing each peg. A solitaire move is the in one of the directions *up, down, left* and *right*, and hops a peg over another peg into an empty slot. The complete alphabet has 19 moves in each of the four directions, plus a special event *done* that all the processes synchronise on when they reach their target state. The diagram shows the initial configuration, and the target is the opposite one – a single peg in the middle.

None of the processes can perform a τ. The nine central slots (in classes E, F and G) can each perform 12 different moves: they can be hopped out of, over, or into in any of the four directions. The twelve slots adjacent to them (classes C and D) can each perform 6 different move events, and the twelve slots around the edges (A and B) can each perform only 4. Since there is one supercombinator for each event – the one that demands that each of the 3 or 33 processes that can perform the event do so – and since only one of the two states of each event can perform it, our probability model calculates the probability of each move event being enabled as 2^{-3} and the probability that *done* is enabled as 2^{-33}. In other words $E_i(x) = 0.5$ for every event x and slot i.

The model predicts that the probability of any component process being involved in an arbitrary transition is close to the number of moves it is involved in, divided by the total number of move (76). This model, of course, is based on the assumption that all the 2^{33} states are reachable[2] whereas in fact $187,636,299$ are (about 2.2%).

By symmetry of the puzzle, it follows immediately from the fact that not all reachable configurations can be carried forward to a solution that more of the states will be encountered beyond the half-way point (i.e the 16th move of 31) than before it. This means, that $E_i(x)$ is, on average, less than 0.5 since each move requires two pegs present and one absent. Thus it is not surprising that the actual number of successor states found (1,487M) is less than the 1,781M that the model of $(76/8) \times 187M$ suggests. While the model suggests that all 76 moves will be enabled roughly equally often, in fact they vary from 12.4M times to 24.1M.

Both the model and the statistics from the check itself suggest that the outer pegs (classes A and B) are the best ones to partition on, since they change state in the smallest proportion of the transitions.

Partitioning a weighted graph. Now suppose that we have computed, for each component i, a *node weight* for each state γ, representing the proportion by which we expect to encounter Γs with this γ during the search, and an *edge*

---

[2] As discussed in [1], the 2^{33} states break down naturally into 16 equal-size equivalence classes such that every reachable state is in the same class as the starting one. Thus the 2.2% reachability actually represents about 35% of the equivalence class of the starting state.

weight on each pair (γ, γ') such that $\gamma \neq \gamma'$ and γ' is reachable in one step from γ. The edge weight represents the probability that, given that the ith component of Γ is γ, a successor Γ will have γ'.

The previous section we assumed that all node weights are equal, and that the edge weights are $PT_i(\gamma, \gamma')$. We will suggest some more possibilities later. In a case where node weights are not equal, then the edge weights from a state γ should be an estimate of the product $w(\gamma)$ and the probabilities of the various actions *given* we are in γ.

In partitioning component i into roughly equal weight but localised parts (localised meaning that most of its transitions lie within the part), there is a tension between these two objectives. In general, of course, we will want to divide a component machine into more than two pieces, or two be able to subdivide a machine that has already been partitioned. Some possibilities are as follows.

– We could deploy algorithms for finding a *minimum cut* between two regions of the state machine that have been identified an have non-trivial node weight. An example of this (and the one we have deployed in our preliminary implementation) is the Kerninghan-Lin algorithm [7].
– We could successively remove inter-node edges in reverse order of weight until the machine becomes disconnected, again with restrictions to ensure the pieces do not become too large.
– Starting from a number of well-spaced points in the graph of nodes, build up components C_i. Successively add a node to the lightest C_i: the node for which the sum of edge weights between C_i and it (both ways) is maximised.

Where we have partitioned a component into more than two parts $C_1, \ldots, C_n$, whatever algorithm we use for the above task should also generate a linear order on the C_i with a view to each of the $\bigcup_{i=r}^{s} C_i$ also making sense in terms of locality. One way of achieving this is to join together the two C_i with the largest (sum of edge weights) connection between them, and then successively add on another whose connection at either end makes most sense.

To follow the pre-computed partitioning algorithm, we then arrange the components into order by the quality of the partitioning, judged in some way. Suppose the jth part (in its linear order) of the ith component process (ordered in decreasing order of quality) is $C_{i,j}$. We then define the *partitioning function Π*, when applied to a state Γ to be a tuple whose ith component is j, where the ith component $\gamma(i)$ of Γ lies in $C_{i,j}$.

The range of Π is naturally linearly ordered by lexicographic order (i.e., the first component takes precedence, then the second, and so on).

Recalling that FDR stores the accumulated state space in a sorted structure, we can make $\Pi(\Gamma)$ the primary sorting key for the states Γ. Then to partition the state space all we have to do is find the point(s) in the range of $\Pi(\Gamma)$ which is closest to giving the desired sizes of the sections, or (probably) better, find points determined by as few components $\gamma(i)$ as possible that are within some tolerance of the desired division points.

The effect of this technique is to pre-compute many potential ways to partition the state space, and then structure the search so that it is trivial to split either B-trees or sorted lists of states.

Only experience can tell us how effective the probability-based weight calculations set out above are. It is reasonable to expect that we will find methods that are effective for searches that are in some sense "typical". It is also very likely that it will be possible to construct possibly pathological examples for which it works badly.

There are two alternatives to this: one is to use Monte Carlo methods to conduct a partial exploration of the state space in advance, simply to be able to give estimates for the node and edge weights of the components. Using this is will still be possible to use the partitioning function Π that stays constant during a search. The other alternative is to use a dynamic partitioning method.

4.3   Dynamic Partitioning

We have seen that there is a significant data structuring advantage in using a pre-computed, linearly ordered, partitioning function. There are also the disadvantages that we have to work to give predictions about the structure of the check, and that we are committed to using the $N + 1$ component processes in a fixed order regarding partitioning.

The alternative is to gather information about the node and edge weights of the various components as the check progresses: we can actually count how many times each of the states of these processes is represented in the accumulated state space, and how often each of their transitions is possible in these states.

This is very easy and relatively cheap to collect during a search, and we can then use whatever part of it we wish when a particular block of states has to be partitioned. A possible approach to this is, for each block that is searched, to collect information about those states in it that arose since that block either began as the initial one with the root state, or was last split.

We should, however, notice that the statistics from the part of the check already done may not be a good predictor of the future. For example, in the solitaire example, we would expect that the probability that any given slot is empty will increase during a run.

It is likely that in many cases it will be possible to choose a better-performing partition of such a block, probably based on only one component, that using the fixed function.

The algorithms for choosing the best ways to partition a given component process will, however, follow the same lines as those above.

Whether using dynamic or pre-computed partitioning, we always have the option of deciding how many pieces to break a block into at the point when the split is made. We note that it may be wise to estimate the eventual size of the block to be partitioned in order to guide this decision.

5   Preliminary Practical Results

There are two main options as to how to use FDR in respect of memory management. The default mode is to have it run as a simple UNIX process, storing everything as part of process state. Typical Linux implementations limit the size of a process to 2Gb or 4Gb. A modern processor typically fills this up in less than an hour when running FDR, in many cases without needing backing store at all.

The other option is via FDRPAGEDIRS and FDRPAGESIZE, environment variables which direct the tool to store blocks of states, whose size are determined by the latter, in directories specified by the former. The latter, naturally, represent backing store, but of course in many cases these are buffered in main memory.

Our main experiments have been based on two classes of example: variants of the peg solitaire puzzle discussed earlier, and the distributed database example set out in Chapter 15 of [11].

Our implementations to date use a partitioning algorithm based on the specification process only, without edge or node weighting calculations of the sort set out earlier. Nevertheless they have shown reasonable locality on the above examples: 93% (of states leading to same partition) in the database example, and 84% for solitaire.

They have shown considerable promise in speeding up large checks, in particular in the database example where we found better locality, but are still considerably sub-optimum in the way they handle the sets of states that are passed around between blocks.

For this reason we have decided not to publish a performance table in this version of this paper, but will instead include one in a later version to appear on the web.

6   Parallel Implementation

A parallel version of FDR was reported in [3], the *modus operandi* of which is to allocate states between processors using a randomising hash function whose range is the same size as the number of processors, and which implements the usual BFS by having the processors "trade" successors at the end of each ply.

Though its performance was excellent in terms of speed up (linear in most cases), this parallel version has never been included in the general FDR release because its usability would be restricted to just one of the many parallel architectures in existence. It is clear, however, that a parallel version for at least multi-core architectures is now required.

The concepts of local search clearly transfer extremely well to parallel execution, and offer the prospects of reducing the amount of communication between processors and reducing the amount of time that one process will spend waiting for another. One possible implementation would be to use the idea of *processor farming*: keep a set of search blocks in a queue and, each time a processor becomes free, give it the next member of this queue.

The effectiveness of local search versus BFS, and the most efficient way to use it, is likely to differ between parallel architectures. Let us examine the difference between a cluster of processors with independent memory and discs, and multi-core architectures that share these things. It is, of course, likely that we will have two-level architectures consisting of clusters of multi-core processors.

- In a shared-resource multi-core architecture we should have very fast inter-core communication. On the other hand the imbalance (from the point of view of model checking) between processor power and fast memory (i.e. the problem that local search is designed to alleviate) will simply be multiplied when running a check on more than one core, and disc bandwidth-per-core will be divided. It may therefore prove a good idea to concentrate on high locality between the *set* of blocks currently being explored on all the cores, and the set of blocks presently stored on disc. There might also be an argument for performing different aspects of the search on different cores, though that might be harder to balance and scale.
- The behaviour of a cluster of processors is likely to be governed by the relative rates at which data (transfers of states) is passed between processors, and the speeds at which the processors can (a) transfer data in and out of their own disc store and (b) process the results.

Our initial aim will be to release a multi-core parallel implementation, hopefully by the end of 2009.

7   Conclusions

In this paper we have analysed the issue of keeping the usage of slow forms of memory down to the level where this does not force processing to be delayed, and seen that this challenge has gradually increased as processing capability has grown faster, and will increase further with the number of processor cores.

We have developed the *local search* strategy in an attempt to solve this problem, which is crucially dependent on our ability to partition the state space into pieces whose transitions are primarily *local*, namely to other members of this partition.

We have shown that by analysing the transition patterns of the component processes that are combined by FDR generate the transitions of a particular refinement check, there is a good prospect that we can choose good partitioning algorithms.

Since local search is not BFS it removes the guarantee that the first counterexample it finds will be a shortest one. There is, however, still a choice akin to the distinction between DFS and BFS that we have to make, namely in which order do we process the outstanding blocks of our search. We discussed three possibilities for this earlier.

The next state of our work will be to implement these possibilities and a variety of partitioning algorithms in FDR and experiment with their effectiveness. Our objective is to provide a limited range of options so that the user does not have to understand all of this technology to use it.

Acknowledgements

We are grateful for discussions with Michael Goldsmith. The computing support staff at Oxford University Computing Laboratory were very helpful by providing the machines with a *small* amount of memory that we requested. This work has benefited from funding from the US Office of Naval Research and EPSRC.

References

1. Beasley, J.D.: The ins and outs of peg solitaire. Oxford University Press, Oxford (1985)
2. Een, N., Sorenson, N.: An extensible SAT solver. In: Giunchiglia, E., Tacchella, A. (eds.) SAT 2003. LNCS, vol. 2919, pp. 502–518. Springer, Heidelberg (2004)
3. Goldsmith, M.H., Martin, J.M.R.: The parallelisation of FDR. In: Proc. Workshop on Parallel and Distributed model Checking (2002)
4. Goldsmith, M.H., et al.: Failures-Divergences Refinement (FDR) manual (1991-2009)
5. Holzmann, G.: An improved reachability analysis technique. Software P&E 18(2), 137–161 (1988)
6. Holzmann, G.: Design and validation of computer protocols. Prentice Hall, Englewood Cliffs (1991)
7. Kernighan, B.W., Lin, S.: An efficient heuristic procedure for partitioning graphs. Bell System Tech. Journal 49, 291–307 (1970)
8. McMillan, K.L.: Interpolation and SAT-based model checking. In: Hunt Jr., W.A., Somenzi, F. (eds.) CAV 2003. LNCS, vol. 2725, pp. 1–13. Springer, Heidelberg (2003)
9. Roscoe, A.W.: Model checking CSP. In: A classical mind: essays in honour of C.A.R. Hoare. Prentice Hall, Englewood Cliffs (1994)
10. Palikareva, H., Ouaknine, J., Roscoe, A.W.: Faster FDR counter-example generation using SAT solving. To appear in proceedings of AVoCS 2009 (2009)
11. Roscoe, A.W.: The theory and practice of concurrency. Prentice-Hall, Englewood Cliffs (1997)
12. Roscoe, A.W.: Understanding concurrent systems. Springer, Heidelberg (forthcoming, 2010)
13. Roscoe, A.W., Gardiner, P.H.B., Goldsmith, M.H., Hulance, J.R., Jackson, D.M., Scattergood, J.B.: Hierarchical compression for model-checking CSP *or* how to check 10^{20} dining philosophers for deadlock. In: Brinksma, E., Steffen, B., Cleaveland, W.R., Larsen, K.G., Margaria, T. (eds.) TACAS 1995. LNCS, vol. 1019. Springer, Heidelberg (1995)
14. Valmari, A.: Stubborn sets for reduced state space generation. In: Proceedings of 10th International conference on theory and applications of Petri nets (1989)
15. Wolper, P.L., Leroy, D.: Reliable hashing without collision detection. In: Courcoubetis, C. (ed.) CAV 1993. LNCS, vol. 697. Springer, Heidelberg (1993)
16. Sun, J., Liu, Y., Dong, J.S.: Bounded model checking of compositional processes. In: Proc. 2nd IEEE International Symposium on Theoretical Aspects of Software Engineering, pp. 23–30. IEEE, Los Alamitos (2008)

Exploring the Scope for Partial Order Reduction

Jaco Geldenhuys[1], Henri Hansen[2], and Antti Valmari[2]

[1] Computer Science Division, Department of Mathematical Sciences
Stellenbosch University, Private Bag X1, 7602 Matieland, South Africa
jaco@cs.sun.ac.za
[2] Department of Software Systems, Tampere University of Technology
PO Box 553, FI-33101 Tampere, Finland
{henri.hansen,antti.valmari}@tut.fi

Abstract. Partial order reduction methods combat state explosion by exploring only a part of the full state space. In each state a subset of enabled transitions is selected using well-established criteria. Typically such criteria are based on an upper approximation of dependencies between transitions. An additional heuristic is needed to ensure that currently disabled transitions stay disabled in the discarded execution paths. Usually rather coarse approximations and heuristics have been used, together with fast, simple algorithms that do not fully exploit the information available. More powerful approximations, heuristics, and algorithms had been suggested early on, but little is known whether their use pays off. We approach this question, not by trying alternative methods, but by investigating how much room the popular methods leave for better reduction. We do this via a series of experiments that mimic the ultimate reduction obtainable under certain conditions.

1 Introduction

Partial order reduction is a widely-used and particularly effective approach to combat the state explosion problem. Broadly speaking, partial order reduction rules out a part of the state space as unnecessary for verifying a given property. This is achieved by exploiting the commutativity of transitions that arises from their concurrent execution or other reasons. The term "partial order reduction" is somewhat inaccurate, but it is used for historical reasons.

There are several approaches to partial order reduction. For the purpose of this paper, we consider methods that for each state expand some subset of enabled transitions. Such methods are highly similar; the sets of transitions that are expanded are called either stubborn sets [12], ample sets [11], or persistent sets [4]. The methods differ slightly in the way they are defined, and each method has a number of different formulations. Nonetheless, the key ideas in all of them are more or less equivalent [13].

In this paper we use the ample set method as presented in [1] as the starting point of our investigation. It is easy to implement, and its primitive operations are fast but, in return, it wastes some reduction power. We investigate experimentally how much potential there is for better reduction. We are interested in

Z. Liu and A.P. Ravn (Eds.): ATVA 2009, LNCS 5799, pp. 39–53, 2009.

the ultimate results that would be obtainable by an ideal method that is based on partial order principles.

We restrict our attention to reductions that preserve deadlocks. More sophisticated verification questions use additional rules such as visibility of transitions and various cycle closing conditions. We postpone them for future work, because they introduce more complications than can be discussed in this paper.

The concept of *dependency* between transitions refers to situations where two transitions may interfere with each other. Dependency is central in the calculation of ample sets, and some approximation that overapproximates dependency is used. We explore how much additional reduction in the resulting state space is to be gained from using a more accurate dependency relation. Analysis of dependency could be taken further by engaging in *dynamic analysis* as in [3,10], where the notion of dependency is refined during the generation of state spaces.

There is even more variability in the treatment of disabled transitions that are dependent on transitions in the ample set. The correctness of the methods requires that they remain disabled until a transition in the ample set occurs. This can be ensured using different heuristics, some more complicated and presumably also more powerful than others. In this paper we use a rather straightforward *precedence* heuristic and leave the allegedly stronger ones for future work.

In addition to the issues above, there is the question of calculating ample sets. The basic algorithm considers only subsets that are local to a single process. If no suitable process is found, it gives up and returns the set of all enabled transitions. However, a more sophisticated algorithm can often do better in this situation. How much further reduction is gained from using the more sophisticated algorithm, is also a matter of investigation here.

Section 2 defines the formal model of concurrent systems that is used throughout the paper. Section 3 describes exactly how ample sets and the transition dependency and precedence we employ are calculated. In Section 4 we compare experimental results from using the different algorithms for ample sets and different versions of dependencies and precedences, and conclusions are presented in Section 5.

2   Mathematical Background

In the first part of this section we present a formal description of our model of computation. This is not mere formality for its own sake. Although the formalization is detailed, its purpose is to make it possible to describe the computation of ample sets in a precise manner.

2.1   Model of Computation

Our model of computation has three components: a set of variables, a set of transitions, and a set of processes.

Definition 1. *Let $V = (v_1, v_2, \ldots, v_n)$ be an ordered set of variables. The values of variable v_i are taken from some finite domain X_i. Let $X = X_1 \times X_2 \times \cdots \times X_n$.*

- *An* evaluation $e \in X$ *associates a value with each variable.*
- *A guard* $g: X \to B$ *is a total function that maps each evaluation to a Boolean value.* $B = \{\mathsf{true}, \mathsf{false}\}$.
- *An* assignment $a: X \to X$ *is a total function that maps one evaluation to another.* □

Each process is described fully by its transitions and a designated variable called a *program counter*. A transition is a pair of the form (g, a) where g is a guard and a is an assignment. A transition is enabled in states where its guard evaluates as true. If the transition fires (i.e., is executed), it changes the values of variables as described by its assignment component. In almost all cases, the guard checks that the program counter has an appropriate value, and the assignment changes the value of the program counter.

Definition 2. *A* process *over variables* V *is a pair* (Σ, pc), *where* Σ *is a set of transitions, and* $pc \in V$ *is a variable called the* program counter. *For each transition* (g, a) *in* Σ *there is a value* x *such that the guard* g *is of the form* $(pc = x) \wedge \varphi$. □

For $e \in X$, we write $pc(e)$ to denote the value of the program counter at e.

Definition 3. *Let* V *be an ordered set of variables over the finite domain* X *and let* $\mathcal{P} = \{P_1, P_2, \ldots, P_k\}$ *be a set of processes over* V, *such that* $P_i = (\Sigma_i, pc_i)$. *We assume all the* pc_i *are different. Let* $\hat{e}$ *be an evaluation. The* state space *of* $\mathcal{P}$ *from* $\hat{e}$ *is* $M = (S, \hat{e}, \Sigma, \Delta)$, *where* $\hat{e} \in X$ *is the initial state,* $\Sigma = \Sigma_1 \cup \ldots \cup \Sigma_k$, *and* S *and* Δ *are the smallest sets such that* $S \subseteq X$, $\Delta \subseteq S \times \Sigma \times S$, $\hat{e} \in S$, *and if* $t = (g, a) \in \Sigma$ *and* $s \in S$ *and* $g(s) = \mathsf{true}$, *then* $a(s) \in S$ *and* $(s, t, a(s)) \in \Delta$. □

We say that S is the set of *states* and $\hat{e}$ is the *initial state*. The elements of Σ above are referred to as *structural transitions*, while the elements of Δ are called *semantic transitions*. From now on, when we write just "transition", we are referring to the structural ones. This convention agrees with Petri net terminology and disagrees with process algebra and Kripke structure terminology.

The following notation is used throughout the paper:

Definition 4. *Let* $M = (S, \hat{e}, \Sigma, \Delta)$ *be the state space of* $\mathcal{P}$ *from* $\hat{e}$, *and let* s *be some state of* M.

- *The* enabled transitions *of* s *are* $en(s) = \{t \in \Sigma \mid \exists s' \in S: (s, t, s') \in \Delta\}$.
- *We write* $s \xrightarrow{t}$ *when* $t \in en(s)$.
- *We write* $s \xrightarrow{t} s'$ *when* $(s, t, s') \in \Delta$.
- *We write* $s \xrightarrow{t_1 t_2 t_3 \cdots}$, *when* $\exists s_1, s_2, \ldots \in S : s \xrightarrow{t_1} s_1 \xrightarrow{t_2} s_2 \xrightarrow{t_3} \ldots$
- *The* local transitions *of process* P_i *in state* s *are* $current_i(s) = \{(g, a) \in \Sigma_i \mid \exists e \in X : pc_i(s) = pc_i(e) \wedge g(e) = \mathsf{true}\}$.
- *The* enabled local transitions *of* P_i *are* $en_i(s) = current_i(s) \cap en(s)$.
- *The* disabled local transitions *of* P_i *are* $dis_i(s) = current_i(s) \setminus en(s)$. □

Lastly, we need to know which other variables are involved in which transitions. These relationships are only defined in the context of a state space.

Definition 5. *Let $V = (v_1, v_2, \ldots, v_n)$ be an ordered set of variables, let $\mathcal{P}$ be a set of processes over V, and let $M = (S, \hat{e}, \Sigma, \Delta)$ be the state space of $\mathcal{P}$ from $\hat{e}$. Given evaluations $e, e' \in X$, for $1 \le i \le n$:*

- *e_i denotes the value of v_i in e, and*
- *$\delta(e, e') = \{i \mid e_i \ne e'_i\}$ is the set of indices on which e and e' disagree.*

If $t = (g, a) \in \Sigma$, then

- *the test set of t is $Ts(t) = \{v_i \mid \exists e, e' \in X : \delta(e, e') = \{i\} \wedge g(e) \ne g(e')\}$,*
- *the write set of t is $Wr(t) = \{v_i \mid \exists e \in X : e_i \ne a(e)_i\}$,*
- *the read set of t is $Rd(t) = \{v_i \mid \exists e, e' \in X : \delta(e, e') = \{i\} \wedge \exists j : v_j \in Wr(t) \wedge a(e)_j \ne a(e')_j\}$, and*
- *the variable set of t is $Vr(t) = Ts(t) \cup Rd(t) \cup Wr(t)$.*   □

The test, write, and read sets are conservative syntactic estimates of those variables that may be involved in the different aspects of a transition's execution. Variables with disjoint variable sets are clearly independent, but an even finer condition will be given in Section 3.1..

2.2 Ample Sets, Dependency and Precedence

It is important to distinguish which transitions may interfere with one another and to this end we define the following:

Definition 6. *Let $M = (S, \hat{e}, \Sigma, \Delta)$ be the state space of $\mathcal{P}$ from $\hat{e}$, and $S' \subseteq S$. A dependency relation $D \subseteq \Sigma \times \Sigma$ for S' is a symmetric, reflexive relation such that $(t_1, t_2) \notin D$ implies that for all states $s \in S'$, the following are true:*

1. *If $s \xrightarrow{t_1} s'$ and $s \xrightarrow{t_2}$, then $s' \xrightarrow{t_2}$ (independent transitions do not disable one another).*
2. *If $s \xrightarrow{t_1 t_2} s'$ and $s \xrightarrow{t_2 t_1} s''$ then $s' = s''$ (the final state is independent of the transition order).*

Given D and $T \subseteq \Sigma$, we write $dep(T) = \{t \mid \exists t' \in T : (t, t') \in D\}$.   □

The definition implies that if D is a dependency relation, D' is symmetric, and $D \subseteq D'$, then D' is also a dependency relation. If $S' = S$ in this definition, we get the usual notion of dependency. We shall, however, also use other S'.

Here we use the definition of ample sets from [1], modified to accommodate S' instead of S.

Definition 7. *Let $M = (S, \hat{e}, \Sigma, \Delta)$ be the state space of $\mathcal{P}$ from $\hat{e}$, let $S' \subseteq S$ and let D be a dependency relation for S'. A set $ample(s) \subseteq \Sigma$ of transitions is an ample set for state $s \in S'$ if and only if the following hold:*

A0 $ample(s) = \emptyset$ if and only if $en(s) = \emptyset$.
A1 For every path of the state space that begins at s, no transition that is not in $ample(s)$ and is dependent on a transition in $ample(s)$, can occur without some transition in $ample(s)$ occurring first.

Because condition A1 talks about future transitions, some of which may not be enabled in the current state, we need information about not only those transitions that are currently enabled, but also those that may become enabled in the future.

Definition 8. *Let $M = (S, \hat{e}, \Sigma, \Delta)$ be the state space of $\mathcal{P}$ from $\hat{e}$, and $S' \subseteq S$. A precedence relation $R \subseteq \Sigma \times \Sigma$ for S' is such that if there is some state $s \in S'$ such that $\neg s \xrightarrow{t_2}$ and $s \xrightarrow{t_1 t_2}$, then $(t_1, t_2) \in R$.*

Given R and $T \subseteq \Sigma$, we write $pre(T) = \{t \mid \exists t' \in T : (t, t') \in R\}$. ☐

The definition implies that if R is a precedence relation and $R \subseteq R'$, then R' is also a precedence relation. The precedence relation makes it possible to detect all the transitions that can enable a given transition. It is a coarse heuristic. A finer heuristic, commonly used in the stubborn set method, takes advantage of the fact that if the guard of t is of the form $\varphi \wedge \psi$ where φ evaluates to true and ψ evaluates to false in the current state, then it would suffice to only consider those transitions which may affect ψ.

3 The Calculation of D, R, and Ample Sets

3.1 Calculating D and R

In Section 2.1 we carefully make a distinction between structural and semantic transitions, and between the description of a model (its variables and processes) and the state space it generates. This difference plays an important role when it comes to the calculation of the D and R relations.

Specifically, the static (structural) description of a model is almost always available and can be used to calculate an overapproximation of the smallest possible D and R. The full state space, on the other hand, is seldom available for realistic models; the purpose of partial order methods is to avoid its construction!

In this paper we consider three versions of D/R. The first, which we refer to as D_s/R_s, is based on the static model description and is calculated as follows: Let $M = (S, \hat{e}, \Sigma, \Delta)$ be a state space, and $t_1, t_2 \in \Sigma$.

- $(t_1, t_2) \in D_s$ if and only if $Wr(t_1) \cap Vr(t_2) \neq \emptyset$ or $Wr(t_2) \cap Vr(t_1) \neq \emptyset$.
- $(t_1, t_2) \in R_s$ if and only if $Wr(t_1) \cap Ts(t_2) \neq \emptyset$.

It is easy to see that these dependency and precedence relations are not the smallest possible. For example, consider the two transitions

$$t_a : \quad \text{true} \longrightarrow x := (x + 1) \bmod 5$$
$$t_b : \quad \text{true} \longrightarrow x := (x + 2) \bmod 5$$

(Here we use Dijkstra's guarded command notation to describe the guards and assignments of the transitions.) If t_a and t_b belong to two different processes, they are clearly independent: they cannot disable each other and the order in which they execute has no effect on the final state. Nevertheless, according to the rules above $(t_a, t_b) \in D_s$ because each transition reads a variable (x) that is written to by the other.

The second version of the relations is called D_f/R_f, and is based on the full state space:

- $(t_1, t_2) \in D_f$ if and only if for some state $s \in S$ where $s \xrightarrow{t_1} s_1$ and $s \xrightarrow{t_2} s_2$, either $\neg s_1 \xrightarrow{t_2}$ or $s_1 \xrightarrow{t_2} s' \wedge \neg s_2 \xrightarrow{t_1} s'$.
- $(t_1, t_2) \in R_f$ if and only if for some state $s \in S$, both $\neg s \xrightarrow{t_2}$ and $s \xrightarrow{t_1 t_2}$.

The third and final version of the relations, D_d/R_d, is based on the full state space and the current state:

- $(t_1, t_2) \in D_d(s)$ if and only if for some state $s' \in S$ reachable from s and where $s' \xrightarrow{t_1} s_1$ and $s' \xrightarrow{t_2} s_2$, either $\neg s_1 \xrightarrow{t_2}$ or $s_1 \xrightarrow{t_2} s'' \wedge \neg s_2 \xrightarrow{t_1} s''$.
- $(t_1, t_2) \in R_d(s)$ if and only if for some state $s' \in S$ reachable from s, both $\neg s' \xrightarrow{t_2}$ and $s' \xrightarrow{t_1 t_2}$.

Note that the definition of ample sets in Definition 7 is only sensitive to what happens in the current state and its subsequent states. It is therefore correct to restrict D_d and R_d to the part of the state space that is reachable from the current state. Here we make use of the S' in Definitions 6 and 8: for $D_d(s)$ and $R_d(s)$, we let S' be the set of all those states that are reachable from s.

D_s/R_s are based on structural transitions, whereas both D_d/R_d and D_f/R_f are defined with respect to semantic transitions. While in practice the latter two versions may be expensive to calculate in full, they provide some idea of the limits of partial order reduction.

3.2   Calculating Ample Sets

It is reasonable to always consider all the current transitions in a given process as dependent, and therefore the smallest possible sets that are eligible as ample sets are the sets $en_i(s)$ of enabled local transitions in each process. A conservative estimate of when such a set can be selected is based on the following sufficient condition [1]:

Proposition 1. $en_i(s)$ is an ample set if for each process $P_j \neq P_i$ we have

1. $pre(dis_i(s)) \cap \Sigma_j = \emptyset$, and
2. $dep(en_i(s)) \cap \Sigma_j = \emptyset$.   □

A straightforward method for using this information tests the en_i sets one by one. If either of the conditions fails to hold, the set is discarded and we consider the next candidate. If no suitable candidate is found, the set $en(s)$ is used as an ample set. This approach is shown in Figure 1, and it is also roughly how partial order reduction is implemented in SPIN [7].

As it stands, the algorithm returns the first valid ample set it encounters. This is somewhat arbitrary, since it depends on the order in which the processes are examined, which, in turn, often depends on their order of declaration. This may

```
AMPLE1(S)
1  for i ∈ {1, . . . , k} such that enᵢ(s) ≠ ∅ do
2      A ← true
3      for j ≠ i do
4          if pre(disᵢ(s)) ∩ Σⱼ ≠ ∅ or dep(enᵢ(s)) ∩ Σⱼ ≠ ∅ then
5              A ← false
6              break
7      if A then return enᵢ(s)
8  return en(s)
```

Fig. 1. Ample set selection from [2]

give the user some control over the selection of ample sets, but it is doubtful whether such control is ever exercised and whether it is effective. Instead, we refer to this default version in Figure 1 as *first choice*, and we consider two alternative approaches:

– *Minimum choice:* The algorithm is modified to compute all the valid ample sets of the form $en_i(s)$ (it merely records the set index in line 7), and returns the smallest set (or one of the smallest sets) in line 8, reverting to $en(s)$ if no $en_i(s)$ qualifies.
– *Random choice:* As for minimum choice, the algorithm computes all valid ample sets of the form $en_i(s)$ and then randomly picks one of these to return in line 8, reverting to $en(s)$ if necessary.

On the surface, random choice seems just as arbitrary as first choice. However, in Section 4 the same partial order reduction run is repeated many times with the random choice approach. This allows us to measure experimentally how sensitive the reduction is to the choice of ample set.

3.3   Using SCCs for Ample Sets

One drawback of the approach in the previous section is that the ample set contains the enabled transitions of either all or exactly one of the processes. It is easy to imagine a scenario of four processes $P_1 \ldots P_4$ where en_1 and en_2 are mutually dependent, and en_3 and en_4 are mutually dependent, and all other pairings are independent. In this scenario it is possible to choose $ample = en_1 \cup en_2$ or $ample = en_3 \cup en_4$, but this is never done.

In [12] an algorithm that constructs a graph whose maximal strongly connected components (SCCs) are used as candidates for *ample* is presented.

Definition 9. *Let* $M = (S, \hat{e}, \Sigma, \Delta)$ *be the state space of* $\mathcal{P}$ *from* $\hat{e}$, D *be a dependency relation,* R *be a precedence relation, and* $s \in S$ *a state of* M.

– *For two processes* P_i *and* P_j, *if one or both of the conditions in Proposition 1 are violated, then* P_j *is a* conflicting process *for* P_i *in state* s.

AMPLE2(s)
1   $E \leftarrow \emptyset$
2   **for** $i \in \{1, \ldots, k\}$ **do**
3       $A \leftarrow true$
4   **for** $j \neq i$ **do**
5   **if** $pre(dis_i(s)) \cap \Sigma_j \neq \emptyset$ **or** $dep(en_i(s)) \cap \Sigma_j \neq \emptyset$ **then**
6               $A \leftarrow false$
7               $E \leftarrow E \cup \{(i, j)\}$
8   **if** $A \wedge en_i(s) \neq \emptyset$ **then return** $en_i(s)$
9   **return** $en_H(s)$ where H is some SCC of $G_s = (\{1, \ldots, k\}, E)$
    that satisfies the conditions of Proposition 2

Fig. 2. Ample set selection using a conflict graph

- $G_s = (W, E)$ *is a* conflict graph *for state s such that the vertices are process indices:* $W = \{1, \ldots, k\}$ *and* $(i, j) \in E$ *if and only if P_j is a conflicting process for P_i in state s.*
- *If H is an SCC of the conflict graph G_s, then $en_H(s) = \cup_{i \in H} en_i(s)$.*   □

Then we have the following:

Proposition 2. *Let $M = (S, \hat{e}, \Sigma, \Delta)$ be the state space of $\mathcal{P}$ from $\hat{e}$, $s \in S$ be some state of M, and G_s be the conflict graph for state s. If H is an SCC of G_s such that*

1. *$en_H(s) \neq \emptyset$, and*
2. *for all SCCs $H' \neq H$ that are reachable from H, $en_{H'}(s) = \emptyset$,*

then $en_H(s)$ is an ample set for state s.   □

This gives us the correctness of the algorithm in Figure 2.

To see how this approach can improve upon AMPLE1, consider the model of the philosophers' banquet, shown in Figure 3. The whole system consists of two completely independent copies of the classic four dining philosophers system, as illustrated in Figure 3(b). (The details of a single philosopher are shown in Figure 3(a).)

No reduction is possible with AMPLE1, because each $en_i(s)$ set of each philosopher contains transitions that are dependent on the transitions of the philosopher to the left or right, and is therefore invalid according to Proposition 1. On the other hand, AMPLE2 is able to select an ample set $\cup_{i \in \text{Table1}} en_i(s)$. The full system has 6400 states and 33920 transitions, which AMPLE2 reduces to 95 states and 152 transitions; as mentioned, AMPLE1 does not reduce the state space at all.

As in the case of AMPLE1, we shall consider three versions of AMPLE2:

- *First choice:* The algorithm as it stands.
- *Minimum choice:* The algorithm modified to compute all valid en_H, and to return the smallest such candidate.
- *Random choice:* The algorithm modified to compute all valid en_H, and to return a random candidate.

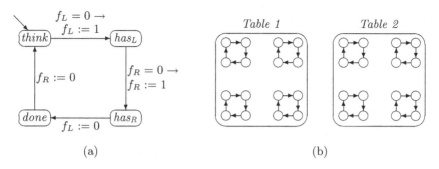

Fig. 3. Model of the philosophers' banquet. (a) Details of a single philosopher; f_L and f_R refer to a philosopher's left and right forks. (b) A banquet consisting of two independent copies of the classic dining philosophers model.

4   Experimental Results

The previous section presented three different versions of the D and R relations, two different algorithms (AMPLE1 and AMPLE2) that use the relations to compute potential ample sets, and three different ways (*first*, *minimum*, and *random*) of choosing an actual ample set.

Each of the 18 combinations of techniques are evaluated by applying them to models taken from the BEEM repository [8]. The full repository contains 300 variants of 57 basic models, and covers a range of genres: protocols, mutual exclusion and leader election algorithms, hardware control, scheduling and planning, and others. Since the experiments are long-running, only the 114 smallest models were chosen, but with at least one variant for each basic model. The sizes of the models range from 80 to 124 704 states, and 212 to 399 138 transitions.

For each model, the original model source code is converted to a C program that generates the full state space and writes the resulting graph (without detailed state contents) to a file. The D_s/R_s and D_f/R_f relations are also computed and stored along with the graphs. In all cases the full state space is identical to those described on the BEEM website.

All the numbers in the tables that follow refer to the percentage of states in the full state space explored by a method. This provides some measure of savings with respect to memory consumption, independent of specific data structures and architecture. The overhead costs involved in calculating ample sets make it hard to give a similarly independent measure for computation time.

4.1   Conflict Graph in the Static Case

The first question we address is whether the use of the conflict graph makes any difference. Algorithm AMPLE2 never fares worse than algorithm AMPLE1; Table 1(a) shows those cases where it fares better. For all but a small number of models its impact is negligible.

Table 1. Comparison of AMPLE1 and AMPLE2 algorithms in the static case. (a) Instances where AMPLE1 and AMPLE2 differ. (b) Further instances where AMPLE1 or AMPLE2 or both achieve reduction.

	(a)				(b)		
	AMPLE1	AMPLE2			AMPLE1	AMPLE2
Model	D_s/R_s	D_s/R_s		Model	D_s/R_s	D_s/R_s
phils3	100.00	32.37		mcs4	5.88	5.88
trgate2	100.00	54.77		anders4	46.47	46.47
trgate3	100.00	55.61		anders2	61.55	61.55
trgate1	100.00	59.12		peters1	62.25	62.25
phils1	100.00	60.00		mcs2	65.06	65.06
bopdp1	100.00	95.74		szyman1	69.46	69.46
elev21	100.00	96.30		ldrfil2	76.57	76.57
				peters2	82.42	82.42
				ldrfil4	82.71	82.71
				mcs1	89.30	89.30
				ldrfil3	96.39	96.39
				krebs2	97.60	97.60

This is partly due to the fact that the D_s/R_s relations are crude overapproximations of the true dependency between transitions, that do not provide much information for either AMPLE1 or AMPLE2 to exploit. Table 1(b) shows all further models for which any reduction at all was achieved. For the remaining 92 models both AMPLE1 and AMPLE2 explored the entire state space.

In all tables the rows are ordered according to the reduction reported in the rightmost column. In some tables we omit results for the same model with a different parameterization, due to lack of space.

4.2   The Static v. Full Calculation of D/R

With the exception of the msc4 model, the results in Tables 1(a) and (b) could be seen as disappointing. On the other hand, they demonstrate what can be achieved with very basic static analysis.

The question that arises is how much can be gained by refining the D/R relations. There are essentially two ways of achieving this.

Firstly, a more sophisticated analysis of the structural transition guards and assignments can eliminate unnecessary dependencies between some transitions. Such an analysis may include, for example, the kind of reasoning employed to conclude that transitions t_a and t_b in Section 3.1 are independent of one another. This is what Godefroid and Pirottin call *refined dependency* [5].

Secondly, some dependencies can be computed on-the-fly. For example, in models of concurrency with asynchronous communication, the emptiness or fullness of a bounded-length communication channel affects the dependency of some operations on the channel. Godefroid and Pirottin refer to this approach as *conditional*

Table 2. Comparison of static and full D/R relations

Model	AMPLE2 D_s/R_s	AMPLE1 D_f/R_f	AMPLE2 D_f/R_f	Model	AMPLE2 D_s/R_s	AMPLE1 D_f/R_f	AMPLE2 D_f/R_f
cycsch1	100.00	1.19	1.19	prots3	100.00	72.45	70.75
mcs4	5.88	4.13	4.13	peters2	82.42	71.54	71.54
fwtree1	100.00	6.25	6.25	drphls2	100.00	72.25	72.25
phils3	32.37	29.63	10.84	collsn2	100.00	73.94	73.94
mcs1	89.30	18.35	18.35	prodcl1	100.00	74.08	74.08
anders4	46.47	22.78	22.78	teleph1	100.00	75.16	75.16
iprot2	100.00	26.16	25.97	lamp3	100.00	75.18	75.18
mcs2	65.06	34.45	34.45	fwlink1	100.00	81.61	78.83
phils1	60.00	60.00	47.50	pgmprt4	100.00	80.82	80.82
fwlink2	100.00	51.37	50.66	ldrfil3	96.39	83.20	83.20
krebs1	100.00	90.06	51.09	bopdp2	95.35	85.81	84.78
ldrelc3	100.00	54.26	54.26	fischr1	100.00	87.38	87.38
teleph2	100.00	59.55	59.55	bakery3	100.00	87.51	87.51
ldrelc1	100.00	60.52	60.52	exit2	100.00	100.00	87.78
szyman1	69.46	62.98	62.98	brp21	100.00	87.96	87.96
prodcl2	100.00	63.12	63.12	pubsub1	100.00	94.48	88.97
at1	100.00	65.71	65.35	fwtree2	100.00	98.93	89.43
szyman2	72.22	65.76	65.76	pgmprt2	100.00	89.49	89.49
ldrfil2	76.57	65.94	65.94	brp2	100.00	99.51	96.46
lamp1	100.00	66.24	66.24	extinc2	100.00	98.95	96.87
prots2	100.00	72.51	67.69	cycsch2	100.00	100.00	98.55
collsn1	100.00	68.46	68.46	synaps2	100.00	100.00	99.75
drphls1	100.00	68.54	68.54	plc1	100.00	99.95	99.95

dependency [5], and a related technique is briefly described by Peled [9] and more fully by Holzmann [6].

Both these approaches are subsumed by D_f/R_f as defined in Section 3.1. In other words, the full versions of the D and R relations supply an upper bound to the reduction that can be achieved with refined and conditional dependency. Table 2 compares the AMPLE2 algorithm for the static D/R, and the AMPLE1 and AMPLE2 algorithms for the full D/R.

As the table shows, a significant reduction can be achieved for some models, even when using AMPLE1. Nevertheless, the SCC approach is able to exploit the improved dependency relations even further.

These results lead to a further question: given the choice of improving D or improving R, which of the two relations should be refined, if possible? To answer this question, we combined the *static* version of D with the *full* version of R, and vice versa. The results of these experiments are shown in Table 3.

Only for the four topmost models in the table does the D_s/R_f combination make a greater impact than the D_f/R_s combination. In all other cases, a more accurate version of D leads to greater reduction.

Table 3. Combinations of static/full D/R

Model	AMPLE2 D_s/R_s	AMPLE2 D_s/R_f	AMPLE2 D_f/R_s	AMPLE2 D_f/R_f
fwtree1	100.00	9.19	100.00	6.25
bopdp2	95.35	93.24	95.11	84.78
bopdp1	95.74	93.42	95.33	86.88
exit2	100.00	87.78	100.00	87.78
phils3	32.37	32.37	10.84	10.84
mcs1	89.30	89.30	20.11	18.35
anders4	46.47	46.47	22.78	22.78
iprot2	100.00	100.00	27.40	25.97
iprot1	100.00	100.00	30.82	28.94
mcs2	65.06	65.06	38.28	34.45
brp1	100.00	100.00	99.15	96.98
brp2	100.00	100.00	99.51	96.46
plc1	100.00	100.00	99.97	99.95

Table 4. Comparison of the full and dynamic D/R relations

Model	AMPLE2 D_f/R_f	AMPLE2 D_d/R_d
mcs2	34.45	22.73
fwtree2	89.43	28.51
ldrflt1	88.70	50.62
cycsch2	98.55	53.73
prots3	70.75	70.18
pubsub1	88.97	88.10
needhm1	100.00	89.54
bakery1	94.42	93.63
bakery2	100.00	98.87
gear1	100.00	99.40

4.3　Dynamic Version of D/R

The effect of using the dynamic version of D/R is compared to the full version in Table 4. For the majority of the 114 models, little further reduction is achieved, and only a couple of models (mcs2, fwtree2, ldrflt1, cycsch2, and needhm1) exhibit significant reduction (more than 10%). Of course, the use of D_f/R_f already reduces the state space for many models, and there is less "room" for additional reduction. Furthermore, if the state space of a system is strongly connected, the D_f and D_d relations are identical, as are R_f and R_d.

Table 5. Comparison of the first, minimum, and random choice

| | AMPLE2, D_f/R_f | | | | AMPLE2, D_f/R_f | | |
Model	1st	min	random	Model	1st	min	random
fwtree1	6.25	6.25	6.25....6.99	ldrflt2	65.94	65.94	65.86...65.99
mcs1	18.35	18.35	18.05...18.37	szyman2	65.76	65.76	66.05...66.22
iprot2	25.97	25.98	27.48...29.61	drphls1	68.54	68.54	68.54...68.55
iprot1	28.94	28.96	29.78...34.00	prots2	67.69	68.25	68.99...69.52
mcs2	34.45	34.45	34.38...34.87	drphls2	72.25	72.25	72.30...72.36
fwlink2	50.66	50.68	50.66...50.68	at2	72.73	72.73	72.73...72.75
ldrelc3	54.26	54.28	54.12...54.21	prots3	70.75	72.31	71.28...73.09
ldrelc1	60.52	60.55	60.27...60.57	prodcl1	74.08	74.08	74.40...75.45
szyman1	62.98	62.98	63.12...63.33	*prots1*	78.77	78.11	78.27...79.51
prodcl2	63.12	63.12	63.30...64.06	pgmprt4	80.82	80.82	80.87...80.92
ldrelc2	64.38	64.05	64.07...64.20	fwlink4	82.06	82.06	82.45...82.73
krebs2	65.17	65.17	65.18...65.22	collsn2	73.94	73.94	83.09...85.50
at1	65.35	65.35	65.35...65.38	*exit2*	87.78	87.10	87.84...88.01
krebs1	51.09	47.95	57.92...65.51	fischr1	87.38	87.38	86.75...88.17

| | AMPLE2, D_d/R_d | | | | AMPLE2, D_d/R_d | | |
Model	1st	min	random	Model	1st	min	random
mcs2	22.73	22.87	23.08...24.43	*teleph1*	75.78	70.00	77.42...82.97
fwtree2	28.51	28.76	31.54...35.35	pubsub1	88.10	88.10	87.41...88.10
ldrflt1	50.62	50.28	50.24...52.17	needhm1	89.54	89.54	89.34...91.15
cycsch2	53.73	57.42	54.09...55.15	bakery1	93.63	93.63	93.63...94.02
prots3	70.18	72.31	71.67...72.91	bakery2	98.87	98.87	98.95...99.48
prots1	78.77	78.11	78.44...79.42	gear1	99.40	99.55	99.44...99.70

4.4   First, Minimum, and Random Choice

Lastly, Table 5 shows the results of experiments in which a different choice of valid ample sets is exercised. In the case of D_f/R_f, the choice of first, minimum, and random ample sets produces no effect for either the AMPLE1 or AMPLE2 approaches. This may be explained by the fact that the choices are so limited that it does not matter which ample set is selected.

In the case of the full and dynamic versions of D/R, however, some variation can be observed. For six models, selecting the SCC with the smallest number of enabled transitions produces an improvement in the reduction; their names are shown in italics. Note, however, that this strategy does not consistently improve the reduction and that the same model behaved differently in the full and dynamic versions. The improvement is largest for teleph1 (-5.78%) and for krebs1 (-3.14%); for the other models it is less than 1%. For 12 models the minimum choice leads to losses of reduction, although these are generally smaller than the improvements.

The situation is somewhat similar when a valid SCC is chosen at random. Each experiment was repeated 50 times for D_f/R_f and 20 times for D_d/R_d to produce the results in Table 5. In the case of D_f/R_f, this strategy produces a range of 7.59% for the krebs1 model, and for D_d/R_d a range of 5.55% for the teleph1 model. All other ranges are smaller than 5% for the remaining models shown, and zero for the rest.

The relatively small ranges seem to indicate that in the majority of cases, reduction is not overtly sensitive to the choice of ample set. However, this does not rule out the possibility that more advanced, systematic heuristics for choosing an ample set could produce significant savings.

5   Discussion

The use of partial order reduction is widespread, and many improvements to the basic techniques have been proposed. Before such proposals are pursued, it is worthwhile to try to determine whether any significant improvement is possible at all. This paper has attempted to partially address this question. We have

- presented empirical lower bounds for partial order reduction based on a rough approximation of the dependency relation between transitions;
- presented empirical upper bounds based on information derived from the full state space;
- demonstrated that it is possible to improve reduction using a relatively simple technique such as a conflict graph that exploits information about transition dependency more fully than the standard technique; and
- shown that, given a choice of ample sets, choosing the smallest set, or a random set does not lead to significantly greater reduction in any of our experiments.

It is important to point out that it is unlikely that the upper bounds we present here are achievable. We have left the effect of the cycle-closing conditions and visibility for future work. Both tend to reduce the effect of partial order reduction. Generally speaking, the reduction does not appear to be as significant as reported elsewhere.

References

1. Clarke, E.M., Grumberg, O., Minea, M., Peled, D.: State space reduction using partial order techniques. Software Tools for Technology Transfer 2(3), 279–287 (1999)
2. Clarke, E.M., Grumberg, O., Peled, D.A.: Model Checking. MIT Press, Cambridge (1999)
3. Flanagan, C., Godefroid, P.: Dynamic partial-order reduction for model checking software. In: Palsberg, J., Abadi, M. (eds.) Proceedings of the 32nd Annual ACM Symposium on Principles of Programming Languages, January 2005, pp. 110–121 (2005)
4. Godefroid, P.: Partial-order Methods for the Verification of Concurrent Systems: an Approach to the State-explosion Problem. LNCS, vol. 1032. Springer, Heidelberg (1996)

5. Godefroid, P., Pirottin, D.: Refining dependencies improves partial-order verification methods (extended abstract). In: Courcoubetis, C. (ed.) CAV 1993. LNCS, vol. 697, pp. 438–449. Springer, Heidelberg (1993)
6. Holzmann, G.J.: The SPIN Model Checker: Primer and Reference Manual. Addison-Wesley, Reading (2004)
7. Holzmann, G.J., Peled, D.: An improvement in formal verification. In: Hogrefe, D., Leue, S. (eds.) Proceedings of the 7th IFIP TC6/WG6.1 International Conference on Formal Description Techniques (FORTE 1994), June 1994, pp. 197–211 (1994)
8. Pelánek, R.: BEEM: Benchmarks for explicit model checkers. In: Bošnački, D., Edelkamp, S. (eds.) SPIN 2007. LNCS, vol. 4595, pp. 263–267. Springer, Heidelberg (2007), http://anna.fi.muni.cz/models/
9. Peled, D.: Combining partial order reductions with on-the-fly model-checking. In: Dill, D.L. (ed.) CAV 1994. LNCS, vol. 818, pp. 377–390. Springer, Heidelberg (1994)
10. Peled, D., Valmari, A., Kokkarinen, I.: Relaxed visibility enhances partial order reduction. Formal Methods in System Design 19(3), 275–289 (2001)
11. Peled, D.A.: All from one, one for all: on model checking using representatives. In: Courcoubetis, C. (ed.) CAV 1993. LNCS, vol. 697, pp. 409–423. Springer, Heidelberg (1993)
12. Valmari, A.: A stubborn attack on state explosion. Formal Methods in System Design 1(1), 297–322 (1992)
13. Varpaaniemi, K.: On the Stubborn Set Method in Reduced State Space Generation. PhD thesis, Digital Systems Laboratory, Helsinki University of Technology (May 1998)

State Space Reduction of Linear Processes Using Control Flow Reconstruction

Jaco van de Pol and Mark Timmer*

University of Twente, Department of Computer Science, The Netherlands
Formal Methods & Tools
{pol,timmer}@cs.utwente.nl

Abstract. We present a new method for fighting the state space explosion of process algebraic specifications, by performing static analysis on an intermediate format: linear process equations (LPEs). Our method consists of two steps: (1) we reconstruct the LPE's control flow, detecting control flow parameters that were introduced by linearisation as well as those already encoded in the original specification; (2) we reset parameters found to be irrelevant based on data flow analysis techniques similar to traditional liveness analysis, modified to take into account the parallel nature of the specifications. Our transformation is correct with respect to strong bisimilarity, and never increases the state space. Case studies show that impressive reductions occur in practice, which could not be obtained automatically without reconstructing the control flow.

1 Introduction

Our society depends heavily on computer systems, asking increasingly for methods to verify their correctness. One successful approach is *model checking*; performing an exhaustive state space exploration. However, for concurrent systems this approach suffers from the infamous *state space explosion*, an exponential growth of the number of reachable states. Even a small system specification can give rise to a gigantic, or even infinite, state space. Therefore, much attention has been given to methods for reducing the state space.

It is often inefficient to first generate a state space and then reduce it, since most of the complexity is in the generation process. As a result, intermediate symbolic representations such as Petri nets and linear process equations (LPEs) have been developed, upon which reductions can be applied. We concentrate on LPEs, the intermediate format of the process algebraic language μCRL [12]. Although LPEs are a restricted part of μCRL, every specification can be transformed to an LPE by a procedure called *linearisation* [13, 19]. Our results could also easily be applied to other formalisms employing concurrency.

An LPE is a flat process description, consisting of a collection of summands that describe transitions symbolically. Each summand can perform an action and advance the system to some next state, given that a certain condition based

* This research has been partially funded by NWO under grant 612.063.817 (SYRUP).

Z. Liu and A.P. Ravn (Eds.): ATVA 2009, LNCS 5799, pp. 54–68, 2009.

on the current state is true. It has already been shown useful to reduce LPEs directly (e.g. [5, 14]), instead of first generating their entire (or partial) state spaces and reducing those, or performing reductions on-the-fly. The state space obtained from a reduced LPE is often much smaller than the equivalent state space obtained from an unreduced LPE; hence, both memory and time are saved.

The reductions we will introduce rely on the order in which summands can be executed. The problem when using LPEs, however, is that the explicit control flow of the original parallel processes has been lost, since they have been merged into one linear form. Moreover, some control flow could already have been encoded in the state parameters of the original specification. To solve this, we first present a technique to reconstruct the *control flow graphs* of an LPE. This technique is based on detecting which state parameters act as program counters for the underlying parallel processes; we call these *control flow parameters* (CFPs). We then reconstruct the control flow graph of each CFP based on the values it can take before and after each summand.

Using the reconstructed control flow, we define a parameter to be *relevant* if, before overwritten, it might be used by an enabling or action function, or by a next-state function to determine the value of another parameter that is relevant in the next state. Parameters that are not relevant are *irrelevant*, also called *dead*. Our syntactic reduction technique resets such irrelevant variables to their initial value. This is justified, because these variables will be overwritten before ever being read.

Contributions. (1) We present a novel method to reconstruct the control flow of linear processes. Especially when specifications are translated between languages, their control flow may be hidden in the state parameters (as will also hold for our main case study). No such reconstruction method appeared in literature before.

(2) We use the reconstructed control flow to perform data flow analysis, resetting irrelevant state parameters. We prove that the transformed system is strongly bisimilar to the original, and that the state space never increases.

(3) We implemented our method in a tool called `stategraph` and provide several examples, showing that significant reductions can be obtained. The main case study clearly explains the use of control flow reconstruction. By finding useful variable resets automatically, the user can focus on modelling systems in an intuitive way, instead of formulating models such that the toolset can handle them best. This idea of automatic syntactic transformations for improving the efficiency of formal verification (not relying on users to make their models as efficient as possible) already proved to be a fruitful concept in earlier work [21].

Related work. Liveness analysis techniques are well-known in compiler theory [1]. However, their focus is often not on handling the multiple control flows arising from parallelism. Moreover, these techniques generally only work locally for each block of program code, and aim at reducing execution time instead of state space.

The concept of resetting dead variables for state space reduction was first formalised by Bozga et al. [7], but their analysis was based on a set of sequential processes with queues rather than parallel processes. Moreover, relevance of variables was only dealt with locally, such that a variable that is passed to a queue or written to another variable was considered relevant, even if it is never used afterwards. A similar technique was presented in [22], using analysis of control flow graphs. It suffers from the same locality restriction as [7]. Most recent is [10], which applies data flow analysis to value-passing process algebras. It uses Petri nets as its intermediate format, featuring concurrency and taking into account global liveness information. We improve on this work by providing a thorough formal foundation including bisimulation preservation proofs, and by showing that our transformation never increases the state space. Most importantly, none of the existing approaches attempts to reconstruct control flow information that is hidden in state variables, missing opportunities for reduction.

The μCRL toolkit already contained a tool `parelm`, implementing a basic variant of our methods. Instead of resetting state parameters that are dead given some context, it simply removes parameters that are dead in all contexts [11]. As it does not take into account the control flow, parameters that are sometimes relevant and sometimes not will never be reset. We show by examples from the μCRL toolset that `stategraph` indeed improves on `parelm`.

Organisation of the paper. After the preliminaries in Section 2, we discuss the reconstruction of control flow graphs in Section 3, the data flow analysis in Section 4, and the transformation in Section 5. The results of the case studies are given in Section 6, and conclusions and directions for future work in Section 7.

Due to space limitations, we refer the reader to [20] for the full version of the current paper, containing all the complete proofs, and further insights about additional reductions, potential limitations, and potential adaptions to our theory.

2   Preliminaries

Notation. Variables for single values are written in lowercase, variables for sets or types in uppercase. We write variables for vectors and sets or types of vectors in boldface.

Labelled transition systems (LTSs). The semantics of an LPE is given in terms of an *LTS*: a tuple $\langle S, s_0, A, \Delta \rangle$, with S a set of states, $s_0 \in S$ the initial state, A a set of actions, and $\Delta \subseteq S \times A \times S$ a transition relation.

Linear process equations (LPEs). The LPE [4] is a common format for defining LTSs in a symbolic manner. It is a restricted process algebraic equation, similar to the Greibach normal form for formal grammars, specifications in the language UNITY [8], and the precondition-effect style used for describing automata [16]. Usenko showed how to transform a general μCRL specification into an LPE [13, 19].

Each LPE is of the form

$$X(\boldsymbol{d} \colon \boldsymbol{D}) = \sum_{i \in I} \sum_{\boldsymbol{e_i} \colon \boldsymbol{E_i}} c_i(\boldsymbol{d}, \boldsymbol{e_i}) \Rightarrow a_i(\boldsymbol{d}, \boldsymbol{e_i}) \cdot X(g_i(\boldsymbol{d}, \boldsymbol{e_i})),$$

where $\boldsymbol{D}$ is a type for *state vectors* (containing the global variables), I a set of *summand indices*, and $\boldsymbol{E_i}$ a type for *local variables vectors* for summand i.

The summations represent nondeterministic choices; the outer between different summands, the inner between different possibilities for the local variables. Furthermore, each summand i has an *enabling function* c_i, an *action function* a_i (yielding an atomic action, potentially with parameters), and a *next-state function* g_i, which may all depend on the state and the local variables. In this paper we assume the existence of an LPE with the above function and variable names, as well as an initial state vector *init*.

Given a vector of formal state parameters d, we use d_j to refer to its jth parameter. An actual state is a vector of values, denoted by v; we use v_j to refer to its jth value. We use D_j to denote the type of d_j, and J for the set of all parameters d_j. Furthermore, $g_{i,j}(d, e_i)$ denotes the jth element of $g_i(d, e_i)$, and pars(t) the set of all parameters d_j that syntactically occur in the expression t.

The state space of the LTS underlying an LPE consists of all state vectors. It has a transition from v to v' by an atomic action $a(p)$ (parameterised by the possibly empty vector p) if and only if there is a summand i for which a vector of local variables e_i exists such that the enabling function is true, the action is $a(p)$ and the next-state function yields v'. Formally, for all $v, v' \in D$, there is a transition $v \xrightarrow{a(p)} v'$ if and only if there is a summand i such that

$$\exists e_i \in E_i \cdot c_i(v, e_i) \wedge a_i(v, e_i) = a(p) \wedge g_i(v, e_i) = v'.$$

Example 1. Consider a process consisting of two buffers, B_1 and B_2. Buffer B_1 reads a datum of type D from the environment, and sends it synchronously to B_2. Then, B_2 writes it back to the environment. The processes are given by

$$B_1 = \sum_{d:\, D} read(d) \cdot w(d) \cdot B_1, \qquad B_2 = \sum_{d:\, D} r(d) \cdot write(d) \cdot B_2,$$

put in parallel and communicating on w and r. Linearised [19], they become

$$X(a\colon \{1, 2\}, b\colon \{1, 2\}, x\colon D, y\colon D) =$$

$$
\begin{array}{llll}
& \sum_{d:\, D} & a = 1 & \Rightarrow read(d) \cdot X(2, b, d, y) \quad (1) \\
+ & & b = 2 & \Rightarrow write(y) \cdot X(a, 1, x, y) \quad (2) \\
+ & & a = 2 \wedge b = 1 & \Rightarrow c(x) \cdot X(1, 2, x, x) \quad (3)
\end{array}
$$

where the first summand models behaviour of B_1, the second models behaviour of B_2, and the third models their communication. The global variables a and b are used as program counters for B_1 and B_2, and x and y for their local memory.

Strong bisimulation. When transforming a specification S into S', it is obviously important to verify that S and S' describe equivalent systems. For this we will use *strong bisimulation* [17], one of the most prominent notions of equivalence, which relates processes that have the same branching structure. It is well-known that strongly bisimilar processes satisfy the same properties, as for instance expressed in CTL* or μ-calculus. Formally, two processes with initial states p and q are strongly bisimilar if there exists a relation R such that $(p, q) \in R$, and

- if $(s, t) \in R$ and $s \xrightarrow{a} s'$, then there is a t' such that $t \xrightarrow{a} t'$ and $(s', t') \in R$;
- if $(s, t) \in R$ and $t \xrightarrow{a} t'$, then there is a s' such that $s \xrightarrow{a} s'$ and $(s', t') \in R$.

3   Reconstructing the Control Flow Graphs

First, we define a parameter to be *changed* in a summand i if its value after taking i might be different from its current value. A parameter is *directly used* in i if it occurs in its enabling function or action function, and *used* if it is either directly used or needed to calculate the next state.

Definition 1 (Changed, used). *Let i be a summand, then a parameter d_j is changed in i if $g_{i,j}(\boldsymbol{d}, \boldsymbol{e_i}) \neq d_j$, otherwise it is unchanged in i. It is directly used in i if $d_j \in \mathrm{pars}(a_i(\boldsymbol{d}, \boldsymbol{e_i})) \cup \mathrm{pars}(c_i(\boldsymbol{d}, \boldsymbol{e_i}))$, and used in i if it is directly used in i or $d_j \in \mathrm{pars}(g_{i,k}(\boldsymbol{d}, \boldsymbol{e_i}))$ for some k such that d_k is changed in i.*

We will often need to deduce the value s that a parameter d_j must have for a summand i to be taken; the *source* of d_j for i. More precisely, this value is defined such that the enabling function of i can only evaluate to true if $d_j = s$.

Definition 2 (Source). *A function $f\colon I \times (d_j{:}J) \to D_j \cup \{\bot\}$ is a source function if, for every $i \in I$, $d_j \in J$, and $s \in D_j$, $f(i, d_j) = s$ implies that*

$$\forall \boldsymbol{v} \in \boldsymbol{D}, \boldsymbol{e_i} \in \boldsymbol{E_i} \cdot c_i(\boldsymbol{v}, \boldsymbol{e_i}) \implies v_j = s.$$

Furthermore, $f(i, d_j) = \bot$ is always allowed; it indicates that no unique value s complying to the above could be found.

In the following we assume the existence of a source function source.

Note that $\mathrm{source}(i, d_j)$ is allowed to be $\bot$ even though there might be some source s. The reason for this is that computing the source is in general undecidable, so in practice heuristics are used that sometimes yield $\bot$ when in fact a source is present. However, we will see that this does not result in any errors. The same holds for the destination functions defined below.

Basically, the heuristics we apply to find a source can handle equations, disjunctions and conjunctions. For an equational condition $x = c$ the source is obviously c, for a disjunction of such terms we apply set union, and for conjunction intersection. If for some summand i a *set* of sources is obtained, it can be split into multiple summands, such that each again has a unique source.

Example 2. Let $c_i(\boldsymbol{d}, \boldsymbol{e_i})$ be given by $(d_j = 3 \lor d_j = 5) \land d_j = 3 \land d_k = 10$, then obviously $\mathrm{source}(i, d_j) = 3$ is valid (because $(\{3\} \cup \{5\}) \cap \{3\} = \{3\}$), but also (as always) $\mathrm{source}(i, d_j) = \bot$.

We define the destination of a parameter d_j for a summand i to be the unique value d_j has after taking summand i. Again, we only specify a minimal requirement.

Definition 3 (Destination). *A function $f\colon I \times (d_j{:}J) \to D_j \cup \{\bot\}$ is a destination function if, for every $i \in I$, $d_j \in J$, and $s \in D_j$, $f(i, d_j) = s$ implies*

$$\forall \boldsymbol{v} \in \boldsymbol{D}, \boldsymbol{e_i} \in \boldsymbol{E_i} \cdot c_i(\boldsymbol{v}, \boldsymbol{e_i}) \implies g_{i,j}(\boldsymbol{v}, \boldsymbol{e_i}) = s.$$

Furthermore, $f(i, d_j) = \bot$ is always allowed, indicating that no unique destination value could be derived.

In the following we assume the existence of a destination function dest.

Our heuristics for computing $\text{dest}(i, d_j)$ just substitute $\text{source}(i, d_j)$ for d_j in the next-state function of summand i, and try to rewrite it to a closed term.

Example 3. Let $c_i(\boldsymbol{d}, \boldsymbol{e_i})$ be given by $d_j = 8$ and $g_{i,j}(\boldsymbol{d}, \boldsymbol{e_i})$ by $d_j + 5$, then $\text{dest}(i, d_j) = 13$ is valid, but also (as always) $\text{dest}(i, d_j) = \bot$. If for instance $c_i(\boldsymbol{d}, \boldsymbol{e_i}) = d_j = 5$ and $g_{i,j}(\boldsymbol{d}, \boldsymbol{e_i}) = e_3$, then $\text{dest}(i, d_j)$ can only yield $\bot$, since the value of d_j after taking i is not fixed.

We say that a parameter *rules* a summand if both its source and its destination for that summand can be computed.

Definition 4 (Rules). *A parameter d_j rules a summand i if $\text{source}(i, d_j) \neq \bot$ and $\text{dest}(i, d_j) \neq \bot$.*
The set of all summands that d_j rules is denoted by $R_{d_j} = \{ i \in I \mid d_j \text{ rules } i \}$. Furthermore, V_{d_j} denotes the set of all possible values that d_j can take before and after taking one of the summands which it rules, plus its initial value. Formally,

$$V_{d_j} = \{ \text{source}(i, d_j) \mid i \in R_{d_j} \} \cup \{ \text{dest}(i, d_j) \mid i \in R_{d_j} \} \cup \{ init_j \}.$$

Examples will show that summands can be ruled by several parameters.

We now define a parameter to be a *control flow parameter* if it rules all summands in which it is changed. Stated differently, in every summand a *control flow parameter* is either left alone or we know what happens to it. Such a parameter can be seen as a *program counter* for the summands it rules, and therefore its values can be seen as *locations*. All other parameters are called *data parameters*.

Definition 5 (Control flow parameters). *A parameter d_j is a control flow parameter (CFP) if for all $i \in I$, either d_j rules i, or d_j is unchanged in i. A parameter that is not a CFP is called a data parameter (DP).*
The set of all summands $i \in I$ such that d_j rules i is called the cluster of d_j. The set of all CFPs is denoted by $\mathcal{C}$, the set of all DPs by $\mathcal{D}$.

Example 4. Consider the LPE of Example 1 again. For the first summand we may define $\text{source}(1, a) = 1$ and $\text{dest}(1, a) = 2$. Therefore, parameter a rules the first summand. Similarly, it rules the third summand. As a is unchanged in the second summand, it is a CFP (with summands 1 and 3 in its cluster). In the same way, we can show that parameter b is a CFP ruling summands 2 and 3. Parameter x is a DP, as it is changed in summand 1 while both its source and its destination are not unique. From summand 3 it follows that y is a DP.

Based on CFPs, we can define *control flow graphs*. The nodes of the control flow graph of a CFP d_j are the values d_j can take, and the edges denote possible transitions. Specifically, an edge labelled i from value s to t denotes that summand i might be taken if $d_j = s$, resulting in $d_j = t$.

Definition 6 (Control flow graphs). *Let d_j be a CFP, then the control flow graph for d_j is the tuple (V_{d_j}, E_{d_j}), where V_{d_j} was given in Definition 4, and*

$$E_{d_j} = \{ (s, i, t) \mid i \in R_{d_j} \wedge s = \text{source}(i, d_j) \wedge t = \text{dest}(i, d_j) \}.$$

(a) Control flow graph for a.   (b) Control flow graph for b.

Fig. 1. Control flow graphs for the LPE of Example 1

Figure 1 shows the control flow graphs for the LPE of Example 1.

The next proposition states that if a CFP d_j rules a summand i, and i is enabled for some state vector $\boldsymbol{v} = (v_1, \ldots, v_j, \ldots, v_n)$ and local variable vector $\boldsymbol{e_i}$, then the control flow graph of d_j contains an edge from v_j to $g_{i,j}(\boldsymbol{v}, \boldsymbol{e_i})$.

Proposition 1. *Let d_j be a CFP, $\boldsymbol{v}$ a state vector, and $\boldsymbol{e_i}$ a local variable vector. Then, if d_j rules i and $c_i(\boldsymbol{v}, \boldsymbol{e_i})$ holds, it follows that $(v_j, i, g_{i,j}(\boldsymbol{v}, \boldsymbol{e_i})) \in E_{d_j}$.*

Note that we reconstruct a local control flow graph per CFP, rather than a global control flow graph. Although global control flow might be useful, its graph can grow larger than the complete state space, completely defeating its purpose.

4   Simultaneous Data Flow Analysis

Using the notion of CFPs, we analyse to which clusters DPs belong.

Definition 7 (The belongs-to relation). *Let d_k be a DP and d_j a CFP, then d_k belongs to d_j if all summands $i \in I$ that use or change d_k are ruled by d_j. We assume that each DP belongs to at least one CFP, and define CFPs to not belong to anything.*

Note that the assumption above can always be satisfied by adding a dummy parameter b of type Bool to every summand, initialising it to `true`, adding $b = $ `true` to every c_i, and leaving b unchanged in all g_i.

Also note that the fact that a DP d_k belongs to a CFP d_j implies that the complete data flow of d_k is contained in the summands of the cluster of d_j. Therefore, all decisions on resetting d_k can be made based on the summands within this cluster.

Example 5. For the LPE of the previous example, x belongs to a, and y to b.

If a DP d_k belongs to a CFP d_j, it follows that all analyses on d_k can be made by the cluster of d_j. We begin these analyses by defining for which values of d_j (so during which part of the cluster's control flow) the value of d_k is relevant.

Basically, d_k is *relevant* if it might be directly used before it will be changed, otherwise it is *irrelevant*. More precisely, the relevance of d_k is divided into three conditions. They state that d_k is relevant given that $d_j = s$, if there is a summand i that can be taken when $d_j = s$, such that either (1) d_k is directly used in i; or (2,3) d_k is indirectly used in i to determine the value of a DP that is relevant after taking i. Basically, clause (2) deals with temporal dependencies within one cluster, whereas (3) deals with dependencies through concurrency between different clusters. The next definition formalises this.

Definition 8 (Relevance). *Let $d_k \in \mathcal{D}$ and $d_j \in \mathcal{C}$, such that d_k belongs to d_j. Given some $s \in D_j$, we use $(d_k, d_j, s) \in R$ (or $R(d_k, d_j, s)$) to denote that the value of d_k is relevant when $d_j = s$. Formally, R is the smallest relation such that*

1. *If d_k is directly used in some $i \in I$, d_k belongs to some $d_j \in \mathcal{C}$, and $s = \text{source}(i, d_j)$, then $R(d_k, d_j, s)$;*
2. *If $R(d_l, d_j, t)$, and there exists an $i \in I$ such that $(s, i, t) \in E_{d_j}$, and d_k belongs to d_j, and $d_k \in \text{pars}(g_{i,l}(\boldsymbol{d}, \boldsymbol{e_i}))$, then $R(d_k, d_j, s)$;*
3. *If $R(d_l, d_p, t)$, and there exists an $i \in I$ and an r such that $(r, i, t) \in E_{d_p}$, and $d_k \in \text{pars}(g_{i,l}(\boldsymbol{d}, \boldsymbol{e_i}))$, and d_k belongs to some cluster d_j to which d_l does not belong, and $s = \text{source}(i, d_j)$, then $R(d_k, d_j, s)$.*

If $(d_k, d_j, s) \notin R$, we write $\neg R(d_k, d_j, s)$ and say that d_k is irrelevant when $d_j = s$.

Although it might seem that the second and third clause could be merged, we provide an example in [20] where this would decrease the number of reductions.

Example 6. Applying the first clause of the definition of relevance to the LPE of Example 1, we see that $R(x, a, 2)$ and $R(y, b, 2)$. Then, no clauses apply anymore, so $\neg R(x, a, 1)$ and $\neg R(y, b, 1)$. Now, we hide the action c, obtaining

$$X(a\colon \{1,2\}, b\colon \{1,2\}, x\colon D, y\colon D) =$$

$$
\begin{array}{llll}
\sum_{d\colon D} & a = 1 & \Rightarrow \text{read}(d) \cdot X(2, b, d, y) & (1) \\
+ & b = 2 & \Rightarrow \text{write}(y) \cdot X(a, 1, x, y) & (2) \\
+ & a = 2 \wedge b = 1 & \Rightarrow \tau \cdot X(1, 2, x, x) & (3)
\end{array}
$$

In this case, the first clause of relevance only yields $R(y, b, 2)$. Moreover, since x is used in summand 3 to determine the value that y will have when b becomes 2, also $R(x, a, 2)$. Formally, this can be found using the third clause, substituting $l = y$, $p = b$, $t = 2$, $i = 3$, $r = 1$, $k = x$, $j = a$, and $s = 2$.

Since clusters have only limited information, they do not always detect a DP's irrelevance. However, they always have sufficient information to never erroneously find a DP irrelevant. Therefore, we define a DP d_k to be relevant given a state vector $\boldsymbol{v}$, if it is relevant for the valuations of *all* CFPs d_j it belongs to.

Definition 9 (Relevance in state vectors). *The relevance of a parameter d_k given a state vector $\boldsymbol{v}$, denoted $\text{Relevant}(d_k, \boldsymbol{v})$, is defined by*

$$\text{Relevant}(d_k, \boldsymbol{v}) = \bigwedge_{\substack{d_j \in \mathcal{C} \\ d_k \text{ belongs to } d_j}} R(d_k, d_j, v_j).$$

Note that, since a CFP belongs to no other parameters, it is always relevant.

Example 7. For the LPE of the previous example we derived that x belongs to a, and that it is irrelevant when $a = 1$. Therefore, the valuation $x = d_5$ is not relevant in the state vector $\boldsymbol{v} = (1, 2, d_5, d_2)$, so we write $\neg \, Relevant(x, \boldsymbol{v})$.

Obviously, the value of a DP that is irrelevant in a state vector does not matter. For instance, $\boldsymbol{v} = (w, x, y)$ and $\boldsymbol{v}' = (w, x', y)$ are equivalent if $\neg \, Relevant(d_2, \boldsymbol{v})$. To formalise this, we introduce a relation $\stackrel{\sim}{=}$ on state vectors, given by

$$\boldsymbol{v} \stackrel{\sim}{=} \boldsymbol{v}' \iff \forall d_k \in J \colon \left(Relevant(d_k, \boldsymbol{v}) \implies v_k = v_k' \right),$$

and prove that it is a strong bisimulation; one of the main results of this paper.

Theorem 1. *The relation $\stackrel{\sim}{=}$ is a strong bisimulation.*

Proof (sketch). It is easy to see that $\stackrel{\sim}{=}$ is an equivalence relation (1). Then, it can be proven that if a summand i is enabled given a state vector $\boldsymbol{v}$, it is also enabled given a state vector $\boldsymbol{v}'$ such that $\boldsymbol{v} \stackrel{\sim}{=} \boldsymbol{v}'$ (2). Finally, it can be shown that if a summand i is taken given $\boldsymbol{v}$, its action is identical to when i is taken given $\boldsymbol{v}'$ (3), and their next-state vectors are equivalent according to $\stackrel{\sim}{=}$ (4).

Now, let $\boldsymbol{v_0}$ and $\boldsymbol{v_0'}$ be state vectors such that $\boldsymbol{v_0} \stackrel{\sim}{=} \boldsymbol{v_0'}$. Also, assume that $\boldsymbol{v_0} \stackrel{a}{\to} \boldsymbol{v_1}$. By (1) $\stackrel{\sim}{=}$ is symmetric, so we only need to prove that a transition $\boldsymbol{v_0'} \stackrel{a}{\to} \boldsymbol{v_1'}$ exists such that $\boldsymbol{v_1} \stackrel{\sim}{=} \boldsymbol{v_1'}$.

By the operational semantics there is a summand i and a local variable vector $\boldsymbol{e_i}$ such that $c_i(\boldsymbol{v_0}, \boldsymbol{e_i})$ holds, $a = a_i(\boldsymbol{v_0}, \boldsymbol{e_i})$, and $\boldsymbol{v_1} = g_i(\boldsymbol{v_0}, \boldsymbol{e_i})$. Now, by (2) we know that $c_i(\boldsymbol{v_0'}, \boldsymbol{e_i})$ holds, and by (3) that $a = a_i(\boldsymbol{v_0'}, \boldsymbol{e_i})$. Therefore, $\boldsymbol{v_0'} \stackrel{a}{\to} g_i(\boldsymbol{v_0'}, \boldsymbol{e_i})$. Using (4) we get $g_i(\boldsymbol{v_0}, \boldsymbol{e_i}) \stackrel{\sim}{=} g_i(\boldsymbol{v_0'}, \boldsymbol{e})$, proving the theorem. □

5   Transformations on LPEs

The most important application of the data flow analysis described in the previous section is to reduce the number of reachable states of the LTS underlying an LPE. Note that by modifying irrelevant parameters in an arbitrary way, this number could even increase. We present a syntactic transformation of LPEs, and prove that it yields a strongly bisimilar system and can never increase the number of reachable states. In several practical examples, it yields a decrease.

Our transformation uses the idea that a data parameter d_k that is irrelevant in all possible states after taking a summand i, can just as well be reset by i to its initial value.

Definition 10 (Transforms). *Given an LPE X of the familiar form, we define its transform to be the LPE X' given by*

$$X'(\boldsymbol{d} \colon \boldsymbol{D}) = \sum_{i \in I} \sum_{\boldsymbol{e_i} \colon \boldsymbol{E_i}} c_i(\boldsymbol{d}, \boldsymbol{e_i}) \Rightarrow a_i(\boldsymbol{d}, \boldsymbol{e_i}) \cdot X'(g_i'(\boldsymbol{d}, \boldsymbol{e_i})),$$

with

$$g_{i,k}'(\boldsymbol{d}, \boldsymbol{e_i}) = \begin{cases} g_{i,k}(\boldsymbol{d}, \boldsymbol{e_i}) & \text{if} \bigwedge_{\substack{d_j \in \mathcal{C} \\ d_j \ rules \ i \\ d_k \ belongs \ to \ d_j}} R(d_k, d_j, \text{dest}(i, d_j)), \\ init_k & \text{otherwise.} \end{cases}$$

We will use the notation $X(v)$ to denote state v in the underlying LTS of X, and $X'(v)$ to denote state v in the underlying LTS of X'.

Note that $g'_i(d, e_i)$ only deviates from $g_i(d, e_i)$ for parameters d_k that are irrelevant after taking i, as stated by the following lemma.

Lemma 1. *For every $i \in I$, state vector v, and local variable vector e_i, given that $c_i(v, e_i) = \mathtt{true}$ it holds that $g_i(v, e_i) \overset{\sim}{=} g'_i(v, e_i)$.*

Using this lemma we show that $X(v)$ and $X'(v)$ are bisimilar, by first proving an even stronger statement.

Theorem 2. *Let $\overset{\approx}{=}$ be defined by*

$$X(v) \overset{\approx}{=} X'(v') \Longleftrightarrow v \overset{\sim}{=} v',$$

then $\overset{\approx}{=}$ is a strong bisimulation. The relation $\overset{\sim}{=}$ is used as it was defined for X.

Proof. Let v_0 and v'_0 be state vectors such that $X(v_0) \overset{\approx}{=} X'(v'_0)$, so $v_0 \overset{\sim}{=} v'_0$.

Assume that $X(v_0) \overset{a}{\to} X(v_1)$. We need to prove that there exists a transition $X'(v'_0) \overset{a}{\to} X'(v'_1)$ such that $X(v_1) \overset{\approx}{=} X'(v'_1)$. By Theorem 1 there exists a state vector v''_1 such that $X(v'_0) \overset{a}{\to} X(v''_1)$ and $v_1 \overset{\sim}{=} v''_1$. By the operational semantics, for some i and e_i we thus have $c_i(v'_0, e_i)$, $a_i(v'_0, e_i) = a$, and $g_i(v'_0, e_i) = v''_1$. By Definition 10, we have $X'(v'_0) \overset{a}{\to} X'(g'_i(v'_0, e_i))$, and by Lemma 1 $g_i(v'_0, e_i) \overset{\sim}{=} g'_i(v'_0, e_i)$. Now, by transitivity and reflexivity of $\overset{\sim}{=}$ (Statement (1) of the proof of Theorem 1), $v_1 \overset{\sim}{=} v''_1 = g_i(v'_0, e_i) \overset{\sim}{=} g'_i(v'_0, e_i)$, hence $X(v_1) \overset{\approx}{=} X'(g'_i(v'_0, e_i))$. By symmetry of $\overset{\sim}{=}$, this completes the proof.   □

The following corollary, stating the desired bisimilarity, immediately follows.

Corollary 1. *Let X be an LPE, X' its transform, and v a state vector. Then, $X(v)$ is strongly bisimilar to $X'(v)$.*

We now show that our choice of $g'(d, e_i)$ ensures that the state space of X' is at most as large as the state space of X. We first give the invariant that if a parameter is irrelevant for a state vector, it is equal to its initial value.

Proposition 2. *For $X'(\mathbf{init})$ invariably $\neg Relevant(d_k, v)$ implies $v_k = init_k$.*

Using this invariant it is possible to prove the following lemma, providing a functional strong bisimulation relating the states of $X(\mathbf{init})$ and $X'(\mathbf{init})$.

Lemma 2. *Let h be a function over state vectors, such that for any $v \in D$ it is given by $h_k(v) = v_k$ if $Relevant(d_k, v)$, and by $h_k(v) = init_k$ otherwise. Then, h is a strong bisimulation relating the states of $X(\mathbf{init})$ and $X'(\mathbf{init})$.*

Since the bisimulation relation is a function, and the domain of every function is at least as large as its image, the following corollary is immediate.

Corollary 2. *The number of reachable states in X' is at most as large as the number of reachable states in X.*

Example 8. Using the above transformation, the LPE of Example 6 becomes

$$X'(a\colon \{1,2\}, b\colon \{1,2\}, x\colon D, y\colon D) =$$
$$\sum_{d\colon D}\quad a = 1 \qquad\qquad \Rightarrow \mathrm{read}(d) \cdot X'(2, b, d, y) \qquad (1)$$
$$+ \qquad\quad b = 2 \qquad\qquad \Rightarrow \mathrm{write}(y) \cdot X'(a, 1, x, d_1) \quad (2)$$
$$+ \qquad a = 2 \wedge b = 1 \quad \Rightarrow \tau \cdot X'(1, 2, d_1, x) \qquad\qquad (3)$$

assuming that the initial state vector is $(1, 1, d_1, d_1)$. Note that for X' the state $(1, 1, d_i, d_j)$ is only reachable for $d_i = d_j = d_1$, whereas in the original specification X it is reachable for all $d_i, d_j \in D$ such that $d_i = d_j$.

6 Case Studies

The proposed method has been implemented in the context of the μCRL toolkit by a tool called `stategraph`. For evaluation purposes we applied it first on a model of a *handshake register*, modelled and verified by Hesselink [15]. We used a MacBook with a 2.4 GHz Intel Core 2 Duo processor and 2 GB memory.

A handshake register is a data structure that is used for communication between a single reader and a single writer. It guarantees *recentness* and *sequentiality*; any value that is read was at some point during the read action the last value written, and the values of sequential reads occur in the same order as they were written). Also, it is *waitfree*; both the reader and the writer can complete their actions in a bounded number of steps, independent of the other process. Hesselink provides a method to construct a handshake register of a certain data type based on four so-called safe registers and four atomic boolean registers.

We used a μCRL model of the handshake register, and one of the implementation using four safe registers. We generated their state spaces, minimised, and indeed obtained identical LTSs, showing that the implementation is correct. However, using a data type D of three values the state space before minimisation is already very large, such that its generation is quite time-consuming. So, we applied `stategraph` (in combination with the existing μCRL tool `constelm` [11]) to reduce the LPE for different sizes of D. For comparison we also reduced the specifications in the same way using the existing, less powerful tool `parelm`.

For each specification we measured the time for reducing its LPE and generating the state space. We also used a recently implemented tool[1] for symbolic reachability analysis [6] to obtain the state spaces when not using `stategraph`, since in that case not all specifications could be generated explicitly. Every experiment was performed ten times, and the average run times are shown in Table 1 (where $x{:}y.z$ means x minutes and $y.z$ seconds).

---

[1] Available from `http://fmt.cs.utwente.nl/tools/ltsmin`

Table 1. Modelling a handshake register; `parelm` versus `stategraph`

	constelm states	parelm time (expl.)	constelm time (symb.)	constelm states	stategraph time (expl.)	constelm time (symb.)
$\lvert D\rvert = 2$	540,736	0:23.0	0:04.5	45,504	0:02.4	0:01.3
$\lvert D\rvert = 3$	13,834,800	10:10.3	0:06.7	290,736	0:12.7	0:01.4
$\lvert D\rvert = 4$	142,081,536	–	0:09.0	1,107,456	0:48.9	0:01.6
$\lvert D\rvert = 5$	883,738,000	–	0:11.9	3,162,000	2:20.3	0:01.8
$\lvert D\rvert = 6$	3,991,840,704	–	0:15.4	7,504,704	5:26.1	0:01.9

Observations. The results show that `stategraph` provides a substantial reduction of the state space. Using `parelm` explicit generation was infeasible with just four data elements (after sixteen hours about half of the states had been generated), whereas using `stategraph` we could easily continue until six elements. Note that the state space reduction for $\lvert D\rvert = 6$ was more than a factor 500. Also observe that `stategraph` is impressively useful for speeding up symbolic analysis, as the time for symbolic generation improves an order of magnitude.

To gain an understanding of why our method works for this example, observe the μCRL specification of the four safe registers below.

$$Y(i\colon \text{Bool}, j\colon \text{Bool}, r\colon \{1,2,3\}, w\colon \{1,2,3\}, v\colon D, vw\colon D, vr\colon D) =$$

$$
\begin{array}{lll}
& r = 1 & \Rightarrow \text{beginRead}(i,j) \cdot Y(i,j,2,w,v,vw,vr) & (1) \\
+ & r = 2 \wedge w = 1 \Rightarrow \tau \cdot Y(i,j,3,w,v,vw,v) & (2) \\
+ \sum_{x\colon D} & r = 2 \wedge w \neq 1 \Rightarrow \tau \cdot Y(i,j,3,w,v,vw,x) & (3) \\
+ & r = 3 & \Rightarrow \text{endRead}(i,j,vr) \cdot Y(i,j,1,w,v,vw,vr) & (4) \\
+ \sum_{x\colon D} & w = 1 & \Rightarrow \text{beginWrite}(i,j,x) \cdot Y(i,j,r,2,v,x,vr) & (5) \\
+ & w = 2 & \Rightarrow \tau \cdot Y(i,j,r,3,vw,vw,vr) & (6) \\
+ & w = 3 & \Rightarrow \text{endWrite}(i,j) \cdot Y(i,j,r,1,vw,vw,vr) & (7)
\end{array}
$$

The boolean parameters i and j are just meant to distinguish the four components. The parameter r denotes the read status, and w the write status.

Reading consists of a beginRead action, a τ step, and an endRead action. During the τ step either the contents of v is copied into vr, or, when writing is taking place at the same time, a random value is copied to vr. Writing works by first storing the value to be written in vw, and then copying vw to v.

The tool discovered that after summand 4 the value of vr is irrelevant, since it will not be used before summand 4 is reached again. This is always preceded by summand 2 or 3, both overwriting vr. Thus, vr can be reset to its initial value in the next-state function of summand 4. This turned out to drastically decrease the size of the state space. Other tools were not able to make this reduction, since it requires control flow reconstruction. Note that using parallel processes for the reader and the writer instead of our solution of encoding control flow in the data parameters would be difficult, because of the shared variable v.

Table 2. Modelling several specifications; `parelm` versus `stategraph`

specification	constelm time	parelm states	constelm summands	pars	constelm time	stategraph states	constelm summands	pars
bke	0:47.9	79,949	50	31	0:48.3	79,949	50	**21**
ccp33	–	–	1082	97	–	–	**807**	**94**
onebit	0:25.1	319,732	30	26	**0:21.4**	**269,428**	30	26
AIDA-B	7:50.1	3,500,040	89	35	**7:11.9**	**3,271,580**	89	**32**
AIDA	0:40.1	318,682	85	35	**0:30.8**	**253,622**	85	**32**
ccp221	0:28.3	76,227	562	63	**0:25.6**	76,227	**464**	**62**
locker	1:43.3	803,830	88	72	**1:32.9**	803,830	88	**19**
swp32	0:11.7	156,900	13	12	0:11.8	156,900	13	12

Although the example may seem artificial, it is an almost one-to-one formalisation of its description in [15]. Without our method for control flow reconstruction, finding the useful variable reset could not be done automatically.

Other specifications. We also applied `stategraph` to all the example specifications of μCRL, and five from industry: two versions of an Automatic In-flight Data Acquisition unit for a helicopter of the Dutch Royal Navy [9]; a cache coherence protocol for a distributed JVM [18]; an automatic translation from Erlang to μCRL of a distributed resource locker in Ericsson's AXD 301 switch [2]; and the sliding window protocol (with three data elements and window size two) [3]. The same analysis as before was performed, but now also counting the number of summands and parameters of the reduced LPEs. Decreases of these quantities are due to `stategraph` resetting variables to their initial value, which may turn them into constants and have them removed. As a side effect, some summands might be removed as their enabling condition is shown to never be satisfied. These effects provide a syntactical cleanup and fasten state space generation, as seen for instance from the `ccp221` and `locker` specifications.

The reductions obtained are shown in Table 2; values that differ significantly are listed in boldface. Not all example specifications benefited from `stategraph` (these are omitted from the table). This is partly because `parelm` already performs a rudimentary variant of our method, and also because the lineariser removes parameters that are syntactically out of scope. However, although optimising LPEs has been the focus for years, `stategraph` could still reduce some of the standard examples. Especially for the larger, industrial specifications reductions in state space, but also in the number of summands and parameters of the linearised form were obtained. Both results are shown to speed up state space generation, proving `stategraph` to be a valuable addition to the μCRL toolkit.

7   Conclusions and Future Work

We presented a novel method for reconstructing the control flow of linear processes. This information is used for data flow analysis, aiming at state space reduction by resetting variables that are irrelevant given a certain state. We introduced a transformation and proved both its preservation of strong bisimilarity, and its property to never increase the state space. The reconstruction process enables us to interpret some variables as program counters; something other tools are not able to. Case studies using our implementation `stategraph` showed that although for some small academic examples the existing tools already suffice, impressive state space reductions can be obtained for larger, industrial systems. Since we work on linear processes, these reductions are obtained before the entire state space is generated, saving valuable time. Surprisingly, a recently implemented symbolic tool for μCRL also profits much from `stategraph`.

As future work it would be interesting to find additional applications for the reconstructed control flow. One possibility is to use it for invariant generation, another (already implemented) is to visualise it such that process structure can be understood better. Also, it might be used to optimise confluence checking [5], since it could assist in determining which pairs of summands may be confluent.

Another direction for future work is based on the insight that the control flow graph is an abstraction of the state space. It could be investigated whether other abstractions, such as a control flow graph containing also the values of important data parameters, might result in more accurate data flow analysis.

Acknowledgements. We thank Jan Friso Groote for his specification of the handshake register, upon which our model has been based. Furthermore, we thank Michael Weber for fruitful discussions about Hesselink's protocol.

References

[1] Aho, A.V., Sethi, R., Ullman, J.D.: Compilers: Principles, Techniques, and Tools. Addison-Wesley, Reading (1986)

[2] Arts, T., Earle, C.B., Derrick, J.: Verifying Erlang code: A resource locker case-study. In: Eriksson, L.-H., Lindsay, P.A. (eds.) FME 2002. LNCS, vol. 2391, pp. 184–203. Springer, Heidelberg (2002)

[3] Badban, B., Fokkink, W., Groote, J.F., Pang, J., van de Pol, J.: Verification of a sliding window protocol in μCRL and PVS. Formal Aspects of Computing 17(3), 342–388 (2005)

[4] Bezem, M., Groote, J.F.: Invariants in process algebra with data. In: Jonsson, B., Parrow, J. (eds.) CONCUR 1994. LNCS, vol. 836, pp. 401–416. Springer, Heidelberg (1994)

[5] Blom, S., van de Pol, J.: State space reduction by proving confluence. In: Brinksma, E., Larsen, K.G. (eds.) CAV 2002. LNCS, vol. 2404, pp. 596–609. Springer, Heidelberg (2002)

[6] Blom, S., van de Pol, J.: Symbolic reachability for process algebras with recursive data types. In: Fitzgerald, J.S., Haxthausen, A.E., Yenigun, H. (eds.) ICTAC 2008. LNCS, vol. 5160, pp. 81–95. Springer, Heidelberg (2008)

[7] Bozga, M., Fernandez, J.-C., Ghirvu, L.: State space reduction based on live variables analysis. In: Cortesi, A., Filé, G. (eds.) SAS 1999. LNCS, vol. 1694, pp. 164–178. Springer, Heidelberg (1999)

[8] Chandy, K.M., Misra, J.: Parallel program design: a foundation. Addison-Wesley, Reading (1988)

[9] Fokkink, W., Ioustinova, N., Kesseler, E., van de Pol, J., Usenko, Y.S., Yushtein, Y.A.: Refinement and verification applied to an in-flight data acquisition unit. In: Brim, L., Jančar, P., Křetínský, M., Kucera, A. (eds.) CONCUR 2002. LNCS, vol. 2421, pp. 1–23. Springer, Heidelberg (2002)

[10] Garavel, H., Serwe, W.: State space reduction for process algebra specifications. Theoretical Computer Science 351(2), 131–145 (2006)

[11] Groote, J.F., Lisser, B.: Computer assisted manipulation of algebraic process specifications. Technical report, SEN-R0117, CWI (2001)

[12] Groote, J.F., Ponse, A.: The syntax and semantics of μCRL. In: Proc. of the 1st Workshop on the Algebra of Communicating Processes (ACP 1994), pp. 26–62. Springer, Heidelberg (1994)

[13] Groote, J.F., Ponse, A., Usenko, Y.S.: Linearization in parallel pCRL. Journal of Logic and Algebraic Programming 48(1-2), 39–72 (2001)

[14] Groote, J.F., van de Pol, J.: State space reduction using partial τ-confluence. In: Nielsen, M., Rovan, B. (eds.) MFCS 2000. LNCS, vol. 1893, pp. 383–393. Springer, Heidelberg (2000)

[15] Hesselink, W.H.: Invariants for the construction of a handshake register. Information Processing Letters 68(4), 173–177 (1998)

[16] Lynch, N., Tuttle, M.: An introduction to input/output automata. CWI-Quarterly 2(3), 219–246 (1989)

[17] Milner, R.: Communication and Concurrency. Prentice-Hall, Englewood Cliffs (1989)

[18] Pang, J., Fokkink, W., Hofman, R.F.H., Veldema, R.: Model checking a cache coherence protocol of a Java DSM implementation. Journal of Logic and Algebraic Programming 71(1), 1–43 (2007)

[19] Usenko, Y.S.: Linearization in μCRL. PhD thesis, Eindhoven University (2002)

[20] van de Pol, J., Timmer, M.: State space reduction of linear processes using control flow reconstruction (extended version). Technical report, TR-CTIT-09-24, CTIT, University of Twente (2009)

[21] Winters, B.D., Hu, A.J.: Source-level transformations for improved formal verification. In: Proc. of the 18th IEEE Int. Conference on Computer Design (ICCD 2000), pp. 599–602 (2000)

[22] Yorav, K., Grumberg, O.: Static analysis for state-space reductions preserving temporal logics. Formal Methods in System Design 25(1), 67–96 (2004)

A Data Symmetry Reduction Technique for Temporal-epistemic Logic

Mika Cohen[1], Mads Dam[2], Alessio Lomuscio[1], and Hongyang Qu[3]

[1] Department of Computing, Imperial College London, UK
[2] Access Linnaeus Center, Royal Institute of Technology, Sweden
[3] Oxford University Computing Laboratory, UK

Abstract. We present a data symmetry reduction approach for model checking temporal-epistemic logic. The technique abstracts the epistemic indistinguishably relation for the knowledge operators, and is shown to preserve temporal-epistemic formulae. We show a method for statically detecting data symmetry in an ISPL program, the input to the temporal-epistemic model checker MCMAS. The experiments we report show an exponential saving in verification time and space while verifying security properties of the NSPK protocol.

1 Introduction

Abstraction by data symmetry reduction [1] is one of the techniques put forward to tackle the state-explosion problem in model checking reactive systems. While the effectiveness of the methodology is well understood in the context of temporal logics, this is not the case for richer logics. Specifically, no analysis has been conducted so far in the context of temporal-epistemic logic [2]. This seems unsatisfactory as efficient symbolic checkers for epistemic languages have been put forward recently [3,4,5] and the usefulness of temporal-epistemic specifications demonstrated in a number of application-critical scenarios including web-services [6], automatic fault-detection [7], and security [8].

The models for the applications above display large numbers of initial states, often resulting from randomisation of data parameters (such as nonces and messages), exacerbating further the problem of checking large models. In such models, as it is known, a group of computation paths may well be the same up to renaming the data parameters in question. While in pure temporal logic we can safely collect representatives on these traces and conduct our checks only on these, this is not immediately possible in the presence of temporal-epistemic specifications. In fact, as we recall below, in these frameworks the epistemic operators are defined analysing all possible global states in which the local component for the agent in question is the same even if these belong to different computation paths. Because of this, simply collapsing traces would make some epistemic specifications satisfied in the abstract model even if they were not in the concrete one.

In this paper we show that an alternative methodology solving this problem may be defined. Specifically, we show how we can still reduce the number of

Z. Liu and A.P. Ravn (Eds.): ATVA 2009, LNCS 5799, pp. 69–83, 2009.

initial states to be considered by using an "abstracted" version of the epistemic relations for agents in the system. We show this reduction is sound and complete for temporal-epistemic specifications, in the sense that no false positives or false negatives are found in the reduced model. We also show how to compute the abstract epistemic relations efficiently, and how to statically detect data symmetry in the input to the temporal-epistemic model checker MCMAS [5] by means of scalarset annotations [1]. The experiments we report on a prototype extension to MCMAS show an exponential reduction in time and space for the verification of the security protocol NSPK.

Related work. *Data symmetry reduction* is a known abstraction technique aiming to collapse states that are equivalent up to a renaming of data, thereby yielding a bisimilar quotient model [1]. There has been no attempt in the literature to extend data symmetry reduction from temporal logic to epistemic logic. Indeed, while abstraction for temporal properties is a well-established research area, abstraction for epistemic properties has only recently begun to receive some attention. In [9,10], Kripke models for epistemic logic are abstracted by approximating the epistemic relations. However, the models are not computationally grounded, which hampers concrete applications [11]. In [12], computationally grounded systems are abstracted by collapsing local states and actions of agents.

Closer to our contribution, [13] gives a technique for *component symmetry reduction* [14,15] not too dissimilar from the *data* symmetry reduction technique in this paper. Indeed, Theorem 1 in this paper has a close analogue in [13], although the semantics for the epistemic modality is abstracted there into a counterpart semantics [16]. Beyond this, the main contribution in this paper is to address abstraction and symmetry detection in terms of concrete models represented in the MCMAS model checker. Specifically, we introduce a symbolic extension of MCMAS on which a syntactic criteria can be given that guarantees data symmetry, and we compute the abstract semantics without quantifying over permutations. This allows significantly improved savings in relation to [13].

Overview of paper. The rest of the paper is organised as follows. In section 2 we review the interpreted systems framework, the temporal-epistemic logic CTLK, and the model checker MCMAS. In Section 3 we present the data symmetry reduction technique for CTLK properties of interpreted systems. In Section 4 we show how to detect data symmetry in an interpreted system description in the input language to MCMAS. In Section 5 we report on experimental results for a prototype extension to MCMAS. Finally, Section 6 concludes.

2 Interpreted Systems, CTLK, and MCMAS

We model multi-agent systems in the mainstream *interpreted systems* framework [2] and express system requirements in the temporal-epistemic logic CTLK [17]; this section summarises the basic definitions. More details can be found in [2]. We also describe MCMAS [5], a model checker for the verification of CTLK properties of interpreted systems.

Interpreted systems. Consider a set $Ag = \{1...n\}$ of agents. For each agent i, assume a non-empty set L_i of local states that agent i can be in, and a non-empty set ACT_i of actions that agent i can perform. Assume also a non-empty set L_{Env} of states for the environment and a non-empty set ACT_{Env} of actions for the environment. Let $S = L_1 \times \cdots \times L_n \times L_{Env}$ be the set of all possible global states and $ACT = ACT_1 \times \cdots \times ACT_n \times ACT_{Env}$ the set of all possible joint actions. For each agent i assume a local protocol $P_i : L_i \longrightarrow 2^{ACT_i}$ selecting actions depending on the local state of i, and a local evolution function $t_i : L_i \times ACT \longrightarrow L_i$ specifying how agent i evolves from one local state to another depending on its action, the actions of the other agents, and the action of the environment. Analogously, assume an environment protocol $P_{Env} : L_{Env} \longrightarrow 2^{ACT_{Env}}$, and an environment evolution function $t_{Env} : L_{Env} \times ACT \longrightarrow L_{Env}$. Let $P = \langle P_1, \cdots, P_n, P_{Env} \rangle$ be the joint protocol and $t = \langle t_1, \cdots, t_n, t_{Env} \rangle$ be the joint evolution function. Finally, consider a non-empty set $I_0 \subseteq S$ of initial states, and an evaluation function $V : A \longrightarrow 2^S$ for some non-empty set A of propositional atoms.

Definition 1 (Interpreted system). *An interpreted system is a tuple* $\mathcal{I} = \langle S, ACT, P, t, I_0, V \rangle$ *with a set S of possible global states, a set ACT of possible joint actions, a joint protocol P, a joint evolution function t, a set I_0 of initial states, and an evaluation function V.*

For any global state $g = \langle l_1, \ldots, l_n, l_{Env} \rangle \in S$, we write g_i for the local state l_i of agent i in g, and g_{Env} for the environment state l_{Env} in g.

The local protocols and the local evolution functions together determine how the system of agents proceeds from one global state to the next. The global transition relation $R \subseteq S \times S$ is such that $\langle g, g' \rangle \in R$ if and only if there exists $\bar{a} = \langle a_1, \ldots, a_n, a_{Env} \rangle \in ACT$ such that for all $i \in Ag \cup \{Env\}$, $t_i(\bar{a}, g_i) = g'_i$ and $a_i \in P_i(g_i)$. We assume throughout the paper that the global transition relation R is serial, i.e., for every $g \in S$, there is $g' \in S$ such that gRg'.

A path in $\mathcal{I}$ is an infinite sequence $g^0, g^1, \ldots$ of global states in S such that each pair of adjacent states forms a transition, i.e., $g^j R g^{j+1}$ for all j. The set G of reachable states in $\mathcal{I}$ contains all global states $g \in S$ for which there is a path $g^0, g^1, \ldots, g, \ldots$ starting from some $g^0 \in I_0$.

Intuitively, the local state g_i contains all the information available to agent i: if $g_i = g'_i$ then global state g could, for all agent i can tell, be global state g'. This observation can be used to employ a knowledge modality defined on the relation given by the equality on the local components [2]:

Definition 2 (Epistemic relation). *The epistemic indistinguishability relation* $\sim_i \subseteq G \times G$ *for agent i is such that $g \sim_i g'$ iff $g_i = g'_i$.*

Computation Tree Logic of Knowledge. We consider specifications in the temporal-epistemic logic CTLK which extends CTL with epistemic modalities.

Definition 3 (CTLK). *Assume a set $Ag = \{1..n\}$ of agents i and a non-empty set A of propositional atoms p. CTLK formulae are defined by the expression:*

$$\phi ::= p \mid \neg\phi \mid \phi \wedge \phi \mid K_i\phi \mid EX\phi \mid EG\phi \mid E(\phi U \phi)$$

The knowledge modality K_i is read "Agent i knows that", the quantifier E is read "For some computation path" and the temporal operators X, G and U are read "In the next state", "Always" and "Until" respectively. We assume customary abbreviations: $\overline{K}_i$ encodes the diamond epistemic modality $\neg K_i \neg$; $AG\,\phi$ represents $\neg E(true\,U\,\neg\phi)$ ("For all paths, always ϕ"); $AF\,\phi$ abbreviates $\neg EG\,\neg\phi$ ("For all paths, eventually ϕ").

Satisfaction of the language above with respect to interpreted systems is defined as standard. Specifically, the knowledge modality K_i is evaluated on an interpreted system $\mathcal{I}$ on a point g by means of Definition 2 as follows:

- $(\mathcal{I}, g) \models K_i\phi$ iff for all g' such that $g \sim_i g'$ we have that $(\mathcal{I}, g') \models \phi$.

The CTL modalities are interpreted on the serial paths generated by the global transition relation R: $(\mathcal{I}, g) \models EX\phi$ iff for some path $g^0, g^1, \ldots$ in $\mathcal{I}$ such that $g = g^0$, we have $(\mathcal{I}, g^1) \models \phi$; $(\mathcal{I}, g) \models EG\phi$ iff for some path $g^0, g^1, \ldots$ in $\mathcal{I}$ such that $g = g^0$, we have $(\mathcal{I}, g^i) \models \phi$ for all $i \geq 0$; $(\mathcal{I}, g) \models E(\phi U\phi')$ iff for some path $g^0, g^1, \ldots$ in $\mathcal{I}$ such that $g = g^0$, there is a natural number i such that $(\mathcal{I}, g^i) \models \phi'$ and $(\mathcal{I}, g^j) \models \phi$ for all $0 \leq j < i$.

We write $[[\phi]]$ for the extension of formula ϕ in $\mathcal{I}$, i.e., the set of reachable states $g \in G$ such that $(\mathcal{I}, g) \models \phi$. We say that formula ϕ is true in system $\mathcal{I}$, written $\mathcal{I} \models \phi$, iff $I_0 \subseteq [[\phi]]$.

MCMAS. The tool MCMAS is a symbolic model checker for the verification of CTLK properties of interpreted systems [5]. We illustrate its input language, the *Interpreted Systems Programming Language* (ISPL), with the bit-transmission protocol, a standard example in temporal-epistemic logic [2].

Example 1 (Bit-transmission protocol [2]). A sender and a receiver communicate over a lossy channel. Their goal is to transmit a bit value $b \in \{0, 1\}$ from the sender to the receiver in such a way that the sender will know that the receiver knows the value of b. The sender sends the bit value and continues to do so until it receives an acknowledgement of receipt. The receiver waits until it receives a bit value and then sends an acknowledgement and re-sends it indefinitely.

The protocol can be modelled as an interpreted system $\mathcal{I}$ with a sender agent S, a receiver agent R and the environment Env as the unreliable channel. We would like to verify that once the sender receives the acknowledgement, the bit held by the receiver is the same as the bit held by the sender, that the receiver knows this, and that the sender knows that the receiver knows this:

$$AG\,(\texttt{recack} \longrightarrow K_S\,K_R\texttt{agree}) \tag{1}$$

where K_S and K_R are the epistemic modalities for the sender and receiver agents respectively, and the propositional atom **agree** holds at a global state g if the variable **bit** in the receiver agrees with the variable **bit** in the sender, i.e., $g_R(\texttt{bit}) = g_S(\texttt{bit})$, and the propositional atom **reckack** holds when the sender has received an acknowledgement. The code in Fig.1 describes the system $\mathcal{I}$ and the CTLK specification (1) in ISPL. The code should be straightforward to understand in view of the above. We refer to [5] for more details.

```
Agent S                             Agent R
Vars                                Vars
 bit: {0,1};                          bit: {0, 1};
 rec_ack: {true,false};               rec_bit: {true, false};
 Actions = {send__0,send__1,null};    -- Actions, Protocol omitted
Protocol                            Evolution
 rec_ack=false and bit=0: {send__0};   bit=0 and rec_bit=true if
 rec_ack=false and bit=1: {send__1};      S.Action=send__0 and
 rec_ack=true: {null};                    Env.Action=transmit;
end Protocol                           bit=1 and rec_bit=true if
Evolution                                 S.Action=send__1 and
 rec_ack=true if                          Env.Action=transmit;
   R.Action=sendack and             end Evolution
   Env.Action=transmit;             end Agent
end Evolution
end Agent                           InitStates
                                     S.rec_ack=false and
Agent Env                            R.rec_bit=false;
Vars:                               end InitStates
 state: {ok, error};
end Vars                            Evaluation
Actions = {transmit,drop};           agree if S.bit=R.bit;
Protocol:                            recack if S.rec_ack=true;
 state=ok: {transmit};              end Evaluation
 state=error: {drop}
end Protocol                        Formulae
-- Evolution omitted                 AG recack -> K(S,K(R,agree))
end Agent                           end Formulae
```

Fig. 1. Bit-transmission protocol in ISPL

We briefly describe the features of basic ISPL needed to follow the discussion below; Fig.1 can be consulted for an example. An ISPL programs σ reflects the structure of the defined interpreted system $\mathcal{I}(\sigma)$, with one program section for each agent, and for each agent section four subsections containing, respectively:

- Local variable and domain definitions of the form $X: \{d_0, \ldots, d_n\}$.
- Action declarations listing the actions such as **send_0** available to the agent.
- Local protocol specifications of the form $lcond : \{a_0, \ldots, a_n\}$ where the a_i are actions and $lcond$ is a boolean combination of (domain correct) *local equalities* of the form $X = X'$ or $X = d$.
- Local evolution function specifications of the form *assign* **if** *acond* where *assign* is a conjunction of local equalities and *acond* is a boolean combination of atoms $i.\texttt{Action} = a$, where a is an action declared in the agent named i.

In addition, an ISPL program provides an initial state condition and truth conditions for atomic propositions, all in the form of *global state conditions* built from (domain correct) equalities of the form $i.X = j.Y$ or $i.X = d$, where X and Y are local variables of agents i and j respectively.

3   A Data Symmetry Reduction Technique

In this section we present a data symmetry reduction technique for CTLK properties of interpreted systems. Subsection 3.1 extends the notion of data symmetry [1] to interpreted systems; Subsection 3.2 establishes the reduction result; Subsection 3.3 shows how to compute the reduced epistemic relations.

3.1   Data Symmetry

We assume that local states are built from variables (as they are in ISPL programs). In detail, an interpreted system $\mathcal{I}$ is given together with a set Var_i of local variables for every agent $i \in Ag \cup \{Env\}$, where each $X \in Var_i$ is associated with a non-empty set D_X, the data domain of X. A local state $l \in L_i$ of agent i is a type respecting assignment to the variables in Var_i, i.e., $l(X) \in D_X$ for every $X \in Var_i$. We write $\mathcal{D}$ for the collection of all domains.

Following [1] we mark domains as either *ordered* or *unordered*.[1] Informally, a system is expected to treat all data from the same unordered domain in a symmetric fashion: Every permutation of data from such a domain should preserve the behaviours of the system.

Definition 4 (Domain permutation). *A domain permutation is a family* $\pi = \{\pi^D\}_{D \in \mathcal{D}}$ *of bijections* $\pi^D : D \longrightarrow D$ *that only change values in unordered domains, i.e., if D is ordered, then $\pi^D(d) = d$, for $d \in D$.*

The domain permutation π naturally defines a bijection on the local states L_i of agent i and a bijection on the global states S by point-wise application on data elements inside the states. In detail, for each $l \in L_i$, $\pi(l) \in L_i$ is defined by $\pi(l)(X) = \pi^{D_X}(l(X))$ for local variable $X \in Var_i$; For each global state $g \in S$, $\pi(g) = \langle \pi(g_1), ..., \pi(g_n), \pi(g_{Env}) \rangle$.

Definition 5 (Data symmetry). *A set $\Delta \subseteq S$ of states is data symmetric iff $g \in \Delta$ iff $\pi(g) \in \Delta$ for all domain permutations π. A relation $\Delta \subseteq S \times S$ between states is data symmetric iff $\langle g, g' \rangle \in \Delta$ iff $\langle \pi(g), \pi(g') \rangle \in \Delta$ for all domain permutations π. The system $\mathcal{I}$ is data symmetric iff the induced global transition relation R, the set I_0 of initial states, and each extension $V(p)$ of a propositional atom p are data symmetric.*

Example 2. Consider the protocol model $\mathcal{I}$ in Example 1 and mark the bit domain $\{0,1\}$ as an unordered domain. Two domain permutations are possible: the identity ι leaving all values unchanged, and the transposition $flip$ such that $flip^{\{0,1\}}(0) = 1$ and $flip^{\{0,1\}}(1) = 0$. It can be checked that both ι and $flip$ preserve the global transition relation, the set of initial states, and the extension of the propositional atom agree. Therefore the system $\mathcal{I}$ is data symmetric.

Lemma 1. *If system $\mathcal{I}$ is data symmetric, then so is the set G of reachable states, each epistemic relation $\sim_i$, and any formula extension $[[\phi]]$.*

Proof. (Sketch) G is data symmetric: Since I_0 and R are data symmetric, $\sim_i$ is data symmetric: Assume $g \sim_i g'$; then $g_i = g_i'$ and $g, g' \in G$. From the former, $\pi(g_i) = \pi(g_i')$, i.e., $\pi(g)_i = \pi(g')_i$. But, since G is data symmetric, $\pi(g), \pi(g') \in G$. Thus, $\pi(g) \sim_i \pi(g')$. $[[\phi]]$ is data symmetric: By induction on ϕ we can show that $(\mathcal{I}, g) \models \phi$ iff $(\mathcal{I}, \pi(g)) \models \phi$. For the base step note that the extension $V(p)$ of an atomic proposition is data symmetric. Induction step, epistemic modalities: Since $\sim_i$ is data symmetric. Induction step, temporal modalities: Since the global transition relation R is data symmetric.

---

[1] Unordered domains are called *scalarsets* in [1].

Given a data symmetric system $\mathcal{I}$, the global states $g, g' \in S$ are said to be data symmetric, written $g \equiv g'$, if and only if, $\pi(g) = g'$ for some domain permutation π. The equivalence class $[g]$ of global state g with respect to $\equiv$ is called the *orbit of g*. Analogously, the local states $l, l' \in L_i$ are said to be data symmetric, $l \equiv l'$, if and only if, $\pi(l) = l'$ for some domain permutation π.

3.2 Data Symmetry Reduction

In this section we present a technique that exploits data symmetries to reduce the number of initial states in interpreted systems.

Let $\mathcal{I}$ be a data symmetric interpreted system. An *abstraction of $\mathcal{I}$* is an interpreted system $\mathcal{I}^A = \langle S, ACT, P, t, I_0', V \rangle$ where $I_0' \subseteq I_0$ is minimal such that $I_0 = \{[g] : g \in I_0'\}$. Thus, the abstract system has a single representative initial state g for each orbit $[g]$ of symmetric initial states in I_0.

Example 3. Consider the system $\mathcal{I}$ from Example 2. There are eight initial states in I_0 reflecting the eight possible joint assignments to the variable `bit` in the sender/receiver and the variable `state` in the environment. We can form an abstraction $\mathcal{I}^A = \langle S, ACT, P, t, I_0', V \rangle$ of $\mathcal{I}$ such that I_0' contains only four initial states and in each of these `S.bit=1`. Observe that $\mathcal{I}^A \models K_R \, \mathtt{agree} \vee K_R \, \neg\mathtt{agree}$, i.e., in the abstract system initially the receiver knows whether its variable agrees with the senders variable. This follows from the fact that $\mathtt{agree} \leftrightarrow \mathtt{R.bit = 1}$ holds at all reachable states in $\mathcal{I}^A$. By contrast, $\mathcal{I} \not\models K_R \, \mathtt{agree} \vee K_R \, \neg\mathtt{agree}$.

As the example illustrates temporal-epistemic formulae are not preserved from the abstraction $\mathcal{I}^A$ to the original system $\mathcal{I}$ (or vice versa). However, we show that we can make formulae invariant between the original system and the abstract system by abstracting the satisfaction relation.

Definition 6 (Abstract epistemic relation). *The abstract epistemic indistinguishability relation $\sim_i^A \subseteq G \times G$ for agent i is such that $g \sim_i^A g'$ iff $g_i \equiv g_i'$.*

In other words, data symmetric local states are indistinguishable under the abstract epistemic relation $\sim_i^A$. In the abstract semantics the knowledge modality K_i for agent i is defined by the abstract epistemic relation $\sim_i^A$ for agent i.

Definition 7 (Abstract satisfaction). *Abstract satisfaction of ϕ at g in $\mathcal{I}$, written $(\mathcal{I}, g) \models_A \phi$, is defined inductively by:*

- *Non-epistemic cases are the same as for standard satisfaction (Section 2)*
- *$(\mathcal{I}, g) \models_A K_i \phi$ iff $(\mathcal{I}, g') \models_A \phi$ for all $g' \in G$ such that $g \sim_i^A g'$*

Example 4. Continuing Example 3, the abstract semantics avoids the unintended validity, i.e., $\mathcal{I}^A \not\models_A K_R \, \mathtt{agree} \vee K_R \, \neg\mathtt{agree}$. Pick an initial state $g \in I_0'$ in which $g_S(\mathtt{bit}) = g_R(\mathtt{bit}) = 1$. Then, $g' = \langle g_S, flip(g_R), g_{Env} \rangle \in I_0'$ and $g \sim_R^A g'$, since $g_R \equiv flip(g_R)$. However, the atom `agree` has different truth values in g and g'.

Standard satisfaction on a data symmetric interpreted system $\mathcal{I}$ is equivalent to abstract satisfaction on the abstract system $\mathcal{I}^A$.

Theorem 1 (Reduction). $\mathcal{I} \models \phi$ *iff* $\mathcal{I}^A \models_A \phi$, *assuming* $\mathcal{I}$ *is data symmetric.*

Proof. (Sketch) By Lemma 1, G is data symmetric, and so $G = \{\pi(g) \mid \text{any } \pi, g \in G^A\}$, where G and G^A are the sets of reachable states in $\mathcal{I}$ and $\mathcal{I}^A$ respectively. Therefore, we can evaluate the epistemic modality in $\mathcal{I}$ by scanning the reduced space G' and apply agent permutations "on the fly", expanding each state g' into its equivalence class $[g']$. So, $(\mathcal{I}, g) \models K_i\phi$ iff $\forall g' \in G^A : \forall \pi : g \sim_i \pi(g') \Rightarrow (\mathcal{I}, \pi(g')) \models \phi$. By Lemma 1, $[[\phi]]$ is data symmetric, and so we can replace the test of the property ϕ at $\pi(g')$ with the test of ϕ at g', and so obtain: $(\mathcal{I}, g) \models K_i\phi$ iff $\forall g' \in G^A : \forall \pi : g \sim_i \pi(g') \Rightarrow (\mathcal{I}, g') \models \phi$. In other words, $(\mathcal{I}, g) \models K_i\phi$ iff $\forall g' \in G^A : g_i = g'_i \Rightarrow (\mathcal{I}, g') \models \phi$. By induction over ϕ, therefore, we obtain: $(\mathcal{I}, g) \models \phi$ iff $(\mathcal{I}^A, g) \models_A \phi$, for all $g \in G^A$. The theorem follows from this, since $[[\phi]]$ is data symmetric by Lemma 1.

3.3   Computing the Abstract Epistemic Relations

Computing the abstract epistemic relations may seem expensive when there is a large number of domain permutations. However, as we show below, we can compute the abstract epistemic relations without applying any domain permutation at all; two local states l and l' are data symmetric if l and l' satisfy the same equalities between variables with the same unordered domain, and in addition each variable with an ordered domain has the same value in l and l'.

Proposition 1 (Equivalence check). *For any* $l, l' \in L_i$, $l \equiv l'$, *if and only if, for all variables* $X, Y \in Var_i$ *with the same unordered domain* $D_X = D_Y$,

1. $l(X) = l(Y)$ *iff* $l'(X) = l'(Y)$

and for all variables $X \in Var_i$ *with an ordered domain* D_X,

2. $l(X) = l'(X)$

Proof. Pick two local states $l, l' \in L_i$. For each domain $D \in \mathcal{D}$, define the relation $\pi^D = \{\langle l(X), l'(X) \rangle | X \in Var_i, D_X = D\}$. Condition (1) holds iff for each unordered domain D, π^D is functional and injective, i.e., can be extended to a bijection on D. Condition (2) holds iff for each ordered domain D, π^D preserves values, i.e., can be extended to the identity on D.

For symbolic model checkers, Proposition 1 provides a constructive way of computing a boolean formula encoding of the abstract epistemic relations.

4   Data Symmetry Detection

In this section we establish a static test on ISPL programs that establishes whether a given interpreted system is data symmetric, and so amenable to reduction. A natural check [1] is to verify whether or not the program explicitly distinguishes between different values from an unordered domain.

```
Agent S                               Agent R
-- Vars, Evolution as in Fig.1        -- Vars, Actions, Protocol
Actions = {send(?bit),null};          -- as in Fig.1
Protocol                              Evolution
 rec_ack=false: {send(bit)};           bit=?bit and rec_bit=true if
 rec_ack=true: {null};                  S.Action=send(?bit) and
end Protocol                            Env.Action=transmit;
end Agent                             end Evolution
-- Agent Env, InitStates,             end Agent
-- Evaluation as in Fig.1
```

Fig. 2. Bit-transmission protocol in extended ISPL

Definition 8 (Symbolic program). *Assume an ISPL program σ and a partition of the variables' domains in σ into ordered and unordered. The program σ, or a program section of σ, is symbolic iff ground values from an unordered domain appear only in domain definitions.*

For the concept of symbolic ISPL program to be useful, the actions in it need to carry parameters from unordered domains.

Example 5. Consider the program in Fig.1 with the bit-domain marked as unordered; the program is not symbolic. Intuitively, the atomic actions send_0 and send_1 could be replaced by one action and a parameter.

4.1 Extended ISPL

We extend ISPL with structured actions that explicitly carry parameters from a specified domain; the parameter can be indicated symbolically by a variable.

The syntax of the extended version of ISPL is as follows; Fig.2 can be consulted for an example. Local variables X of agents are declared as in basic ISPL. Each entry in the list of actions has the form $a(?X)$, where X is a local variable.[2] Intuitively, the *macro-variable* $?X$ represents an arbitrary value of the domain of X. A *term* t is either a local variable X, a macro variable $?X$, or a ground element d (drawn from some domain). A *parametric action* is an expression of the form $a(t)$ where the operation a and the argument term t have identical domains. The syntax for protocol sections and evolution sections are given in the same way as for basic ISPL but using the above definitions of *term* and *parametric action*. The initial states condition and the evaluation section are the same as in basic ISPL (i.e., no macro variables are allowed in equalities).

Intuitively, local variables such as bit are evaluated and bound at time of execution in the expected fashion. For instance, in the protocol of S, Fig.2, the parametric action send(bit) represents both send_0 and send_1 depending on how the term bit is instantiated. By contrast, the macro-variable ?bit in the protocol of R represents an arbitrary bit value.

Translation into basic ISPL. Extended ISPL programs are expanded into basic ones by means of the rewrite rules given in Fig. 3. As an illustration, the

---

[2] For ease of presentation we restrict attention to the unary case.

$$\{a_1(?X_1), \ldots, a_n(?X_n)\} \rightarrow \{a_1(d_{1,1}), \ldots, a_1(d_{1,m_1}), \ldots, a_n(d_{n,1}), \ldots, a_n(d_{n,m_n})\} \quad (2)$$

$$lcond : actions(\overline{x}, \overline{y}) \rightarrow \bigwedge_{\overline{d_1}, \overline{d_2}} \overline{x} = \overline{d_1} \text{ and } lcond : actions(\overline{d_1}, \overline{d_2}) \quad (3)$$

$$assign(\overline{y}) \text{ if } acond(\overline{x}, \overline{y}) \rightarrow \bigwedge_{\overline{d_1}, \overline{d_2}} assign(\overline{d_2}) \text{ if } acond(\overline{d_1}, \overline{d_2}) \quad (4)$$

Fig. 3. Extended ISPL Translation Rules

(symbolic) program in Fig.2 translates to the (non-symbolic) program in Fig.1. Action lists are expanded according to (2) where $\{d_{i,1}, \ldots, d_{i,m_i}\}$ is the domain of $?X_i$. Protocol and evolution rules are expanded to sets of rules (denoted as conjunctions) where $\overline{x}$ is the list of local variables and $\overline{y}$ is the list of macro variables occurring in the rule under consideration, and where we assume that substitutions respect domain assignments. Thus, each macro-variable is replaced during the translation by the elements from its domain.

4.2   Detection Theorem

We show that symbolic programs in extended ISPL define data symmetric systems. We assume throughout an extended ISPL program Σ which translates into a basic ISPL program σ, and we write $\mathcal{I}(\Sigma)$ for the interpreted system $\mathcal{I}(\sigma)$ defined by σ. We assume domains are divided into ordered and unordered.

Observe that a domain permutation π defines a substitution of code fragments of σ. In particular, $\pi(a\_\_d) = a\_\_\pi(d)$ for atomic actions $a\_\_d$, and $\pi(x = d) = (x = \pi(d))$ for local equalities $(x = d)$. Continuing, π lifts to a bijection on the set ACT of joint actions by component-wise application: $\pi(\overline{a}) = \langle \pi(a_1), \ldots, \pi(a_n), \pi(a_E)\rangle$.

According to the following lemma, if program Σ is symbolic then agent i is "syntactically data symmetric" in the sense that the set of protocol rules and the set of evolution rules in the translation σ are closed under domain permutations.

Lemma 2 (Syntactic agent closure). *Assume agent i is symbolic in Σ.*

1. *If Δ is a rule i's protocol in σ, then so is $\pi(\Delta)$.*
2. *If Δ is a rule in i's evolution in σ, then so is $\pi(\Delta)$.*

Proof. (Sketch) (1): By rewrite rule (3) of Fig. 3, there is a "source" protocol entry $lcond : actions(\overline{x}, \overline{y})$ in agent i in Σ such that Δ is the rule $(\overline{x} = \overline{d_1}$ and $lcond : actions(\overline{d_1}, \overline{d_2}))$, for some $\overline{d_1}, \overline{d_2}$. By rewrite rule (3) again, $(\overline{x} = \pi(\overline{d_1})$ and $lcond : actions(\pi(\overline{d_1}), \pi(\overline{d_2}))$ is a protocol rule in agent i in σ. But, this rule is precisely $\pi(\Delta)$, since both $lcond$ and $actions(\overline{x}, \overline{y})$ are symbolic. (2): By rewrite rule (4) of Fig. 3, there is an evolution entry $assign(\overline{y})$ if $acond(\overline{x}, \overline{y})$ in agent i in Σ such that Δ is the rule $(assign(\overline{d_2})$ if $acond(\overline{d_1}, \overline{d_2}))$, for some

$\overline{d_1}, \overline{d_2}$. By rewrite rule (4) again, $(assign(\pi(\overline{d_2}))$ if $acond(\pi(\overline{d_1}), \pi(\overline{d_2})))$ is also an evolution rule in agent i in σ. But, this rule is $\pi(\Delta)$, since both $assign(\overline{y})$ and $acond(\overline{x}, \overline{y})$ are symbolic.

It follows that agents are "semantically data symmetric" as defined below.

Definition 9 (Symmetric agent). *Agent i is data symmetric in $\mathcal{I}(\Sigma)$ iff*

1. $a \in P_i(l)$ *iff* $\pi(a) \in P_i(\pi(l))$
2. $t_i(\overline{a}, l) = l'$ *iff* $t_i(\pi(\overline{a}), \pi(l)) = \pi(l')$.

Lemma 3. *If agent i is symbolic in Σ, agent i is data symmetric in $\mathcal{I}(\Sigma)$.*

Proof. (Sketch) The local protocol P_i is data symmetric: Assume $a \in P_i(l)$. By the semantics of basic ISPL, there is a protocol rule $lcond : actions$ in agent i in the translation σ such that $a \in actions$ and l satisfies $lcond$, and so $\pi(a) \in \pi(actions)$ and $\pi(l) \models \pi(lcond)$. But, by Lemma 2.1, $\pi(lcond : actions)$ is also a protocol rule in agent i in σ, and so $\pi(a) \in P_i(\pi(l))$. We conclude that $a \in P_i(l)$ implies $\pi(a) \in P_i(\pi(l))$. The converse implication follows by applying π^{-1}. The local evolution function t_i is data symmetric: Assume $t_i(\overline{a}, l) = l'$. By the semantics of basic ISPL, there is an evolution entry $assign$ if $acond$ in agent i in σ such that $\overline{a}$ satisfies $acond$ and $l\,[assign]\,l'$, using Floyd–Hoare logic style notation for local state updates. It follows that $\pi(\overline{a})$ satisfies $\pi(acond)$ and $\pi(l)\,[\pi(assign)]\,\pi(l')$. But, by Lemma 2.2, $\pi(assign$ if $acond)$ is an evolution rule in agent i in σ, and so $t_i(\pi(\overline{a}), \pi(l)) = \pi(l')$. We conclude that $t_i(\overline{a}, l) = l'$ implies $t_i(\pi(\overline{a}), \pi(l)) = \pi(l')$. The converse implication follows by applying π^{-1}.

If agents are data symmetric then so is the induced global transition relation.

Lemma 4. *If each agent is data symmetric in $\mathcal{I}(\Sigma)$, then so R.*

Proof. By definition of R, $\langle g, g' \rangle \in R$ iff there is $\overline{a}$ such that $\langle g_i, g'_i \rangle \in t_i(\overline{a})$ and $a_i \in P_i(g_i)$ for $i \in Ag \cup \{E\}$. Since i is data symmetric, this is equivalent to $\langle \pi(g_i), \pi(g'_i) \rangle \in t_i(\pi(\overline{a}))$ and $\pi(a_i) \in P_i(\pi(g_i))$ for $i \in Ag \cup \{E\}$. In turn this is equivalent to $\langle \pi(g)_i, \pi(g')_i \rangle \in t_i(\pi(\overline{a}))$ and $\pi(a_i) \in P_i(\pi(g)_i)$ for $i \in Ag \cup \{E\}$. By definition of R, this is equivalent to $\langle \pi(g), \pi(g') \rangle \in R$.

We reach the symmetry detection result stating that every symbolic program in the extended ISPL defines a data symmetric interpreted system.

Theorem 2 (Detection). *If extended ISPL program Σ is symbolic then interpreted system $\mathcal{I}(\Sigma)$ is data symmetric.*

Proof. (i) R is data symmetric: By Lemmas 3 and 4. (ii) I_0 is data symmetric: The initial states condition cond in the translation σ of Σ is symbolic, and so g satisfies cond iff $\pi(g)$ satisfies cond. (iii) $V(p)$ is data symmetric: Shown as (ii).

5   Implementation and Experiments

In this section we describe a prototype extension to MCMAS implementing the data symmetry reduction presented above and report on its performance for a well-known security protocol.

Implementation. The prototype extension takes as input an extended ISPL program in which some domains are marked as unordered, checks that the supplied program is data symmetric (using Detection Theorem 2), compiles it to basic ISPL (using the translation in Section 4), reduces the initial states (as described below) and, finally, checks the supplied CTLK specifications against the abstract semantics (using Proposition 1).

To reduce the initial states, the prototype constructs the symbolic representation of a set S' which contains exactly one representative state for each orbit class, i.e., $S' \subseteq S$ is minimal such that $S = \{[s] : s \in S'\}$, where S is the set of possible global states for the supplied program. Roughly, the symbolic representation of S' is a disjunction of assignments, one assignment for each possible pattern of identities between variables with unordered domains. In detail, let $\mathcal{V}$ be the set of variables with unordered domains, and let $\Delta \subseteq 2^{\mathcal{V}}$ be a partition of $\mathcal{V}$ such that each block $\delta \in \Delta$ contains only variables that share the same domain. Intuitively, the partition Δ represents a pattern of identities between variables in $\mathcal{V}$: $X = Y$ if and only if X and Y belong to the same block $\delta \in \Delta$. For every such partition Δ, the prototype selects an assignment to variables in $\mathcal{V}$ that "agrees" with Δ; The symbolic representation of S' is the disjunction of all such assignments:

$$sym_{S'} = \bigvee_{\Delta} \bigwedge_{\delta \in \Delta, X \in \delta} X = d(\delta) \qquad (5)$$

where $d(\delta)$ is a value from the domain shared by variables in block δ; the value $d(\delta)$ is different for different blocks $\delta \in \Delta$ from the same partition.

A symbolic representation of the reduced set I'_0 of initial states can then be obtained by conjuncting $sym_{S'}$ with the initial states condition sym_{I_0} in the supplied program. To optimise the construction, the prototype distributes sym_{I_0} over the disjunction in $sym_{S'}$:

$$sym_{I'_0} = \bigvee_{\Delta} (sym_{I_0} \wedge \bigwedge_{\delta \in \Delta, X \in \delta} X = d(\delta)) \qquad (6)$$

i.e., it conjuncts with sym_{I_0} "on the fly" as $sym_{S'}$ is being constructed. As a further optimisation, the prototype generates only some of the possible variable partitions Δ. In particular, if $(X = Y) \wedge sym_{I_0}$ is empty for two variables $X, Y \in \mathcal{V}$, the prototype excludes variable partitions Δ that have a subset δ containing both X and Y.

The prototype computes the symbolic representation of the extension $[[K_i\phi]]$ with respect to the abstract satisfaction relation as follows:

$$sym_{[[K_i\phi]]} = sym_G \wedge \neg\bigvee_{\Delta}(sym_{\Delta} \wedge PreImage(sym_{[[\neg\phi]]} \wedge sym_{\Delta}, \approx))$$

where sym_G is the symbolic representation of the set of reachable states; Δ ranges over partitions of the set of agent i's local variables with unordered domains; sym_{Δ} expresses that variables in agent i agree with Δ, i.e., the conjunction of equalities $X = Y$ and inequalities $X \neq Z$ for X, Y belonging to the same block in Δ and X, Z belonging to different blocks in Δ; $sym_{[[\neg\phi]]}$ is the symbolic representation of the extension $[[\neg\phi]]$; $\approx$ relates global states with identical values for the variables in agent i with ordered domains, i.e., $\approx$ is the condition $\bigwedge_X X = prim(X)$ where X ranges over agent i's variables with ordered domains.

NSPK. To evaluate the performance of the technique we tested the prototype on the Needham-Schroeder Public Key protocol (NSPK), a standard example in the security literature [18]. The NSPK protocol involves a number of A–agents and B–agents; each A–agent starts with a nonce (*unique, unpredictable number*) Na, and each B–agent starts with a nonce Nb. We considered the following CAPSL [19] authentication goal for the protocol:

$$Knows\,B : Knows\,A : agree\,A : B : Na, Nb \qquad (7)$$

stating that when a protocol session between an A–agent and a B–agent ends, the agents share the nonces Na and Nb, the A–agent knows this and the B–agent knows that the A–agent knows this.[3]

To verify the CAPSL goal (7) we modelled the NSPK protocol as an extended ISPL program with N agents, some of them A–agents and others B–agents. In addition, we modelled a Dolev-Yao attacker [21] in the environment agent. The intruder and all agents start with a unique, non-deterministic nonce value – a value for Na in the case of A–agents and value for Nb in the case of B–agents. Thus we assumed a domain of $N + 1$ nonces; one nonce for the intruder and one for each agent.[4] We marked the domain of nonces as unordered. Finally, we translated the CAPSL goal (7) into the following CTLK formula:

$$\bigwedge_{i:B} AG\,(i.\texttt{Step} = 3 \rightarrow K_i \bigvee_{j:A}(agree(i,j) \land K_j \bigvee_{i:B} agree(i,j))) \qquad (8)$$

where $i : B$ ranges over B–agents, and $j : A$ ranges over A–agents, and $agree(i,j)$ states that agents i and j agree on the protocol variables Na, Nb, A and B, i.e., $i.Na = j.Na$, $i.Nb = j.Nb$, etc. The specification (8) states that whenever a B–agent i has completed all three protocol steps, the agent i knows that *some* A–agent j agrees with i, and agent i knows that this agent j knows that *some* B–agent i agrees with j.

Experiments. Table 1 shows the total verification time (including the time it takes to reduce the initial states) in seconds and the number of reachable states for CTLK specification (8) and different number of participating agents. The experiments ran on a 2 GHz Intel machine with 2GB of memory running Linux. Each run was given a time limit of 24 hours. For this experiment we observed an exponential reduction in both time and space in the number N of agents. Specifically, the state space is reduced by the factor $(N + 1)!$, while the reduction in verification time is more irregular given that MCMAS is a symbolic

---

[3] The goal was derived manually in [20].

[4] It would be reasonable to provide the intruder with more than just one initial nonce; the reduction would then yield even bigger savings.

Table 1. Verification results for NSPK

Agents	Without reduction		With reduction	
	States	Time	States	Time
3	1 536	3	64	1
4	11 400	28	95	4
5	651 600	7 716	905	9
6	–	> 86 400	12 256	24
7	–	> 86 400	21 989	91

model checker. We can expect even greater savings for security protocols that involve more than just one unique, unpredictable data value (nonce, session key, password, etc.) per agent.

6   Conclusions

We presented a data symmetry reduction technique for temporal-epistemic logic in the mainstream interpreted systems framework. The technique uses an abstract satisfaction relation in the reduced system; this was shown to make the reduction sound and complete, i.e., there are no false positives or false negatives in the reduced system. To facilitate the detection of data symmetric systems, i.e., systems amenable to reduction, we extended the interpreted systems programming language (ISPL) with parametric actions. We showed that symbolic programs in the extended ISPL define data symmetric systems. Experiments on the NSPK security protocol show an exponential reduction in verification time and state space for temporal-epistemic security goals.

The reduction technique in this paper reduces initial states only. However, we emphasize that for some applications, such as the security protocol model considered in this paper, collapsing data symmetric initial states alone yields the same reduced state space as collapsing all data symmetric states, i.e., it yields the quotient model with respect to the orbit relation.

Acknowledgments. The research described in this paper is partly supported by EPSRC funded project EP/E035655, by the European Commission Framework 6 funded project CONTRACT (IST Project Number 034418), and by grant 2003-6108 from the Swedish Research Council.

References

1. Ip, C.N., Dill, D.L.: Better verification through symmetry. Form. Methods Syst. Des. 9(1-2), 41–75 (1996)
2. Fagin, R., Halpern, J.Y., Vardi, M.Y., Moses, Y.: Reasoning about knowledge. MIT Press, Cambridge (1995)
3. Gammie, P., van der Meyden, R.: MCK: Model checking the logic of knowledge. In: Alur, R., Peled, D.A. (eds.) CAV 2004. LNCS, vol. 3114, pp. 479–483. Springer, Heidelberg (2004)

4. Nabialek, W., Niewiadomski, A., Penczek, W., Pólrola, A., Szreter, M.: VerICS 2004: A model checker for real time and multi-agent systems. In: Proc. CS&P 2004, pp. 88–99. Humboldt University (2004)
5. Lomuscio, A., Qu, H., Raimondi, F.: MCMAS: A model checker for multi-agent systems. In: Bouajjani, A., Maler, O. (eds.) CAV 2009. LNCS, vol. 5643, pp. 682–688. Springer, Heidelberg (2009)
6. Lomuscio, A., Qu, H., Solanki, M.: Towards verifying contract regulated service composition. In: Proc. ICWS 2008, pp. 254–261. IEEE Computer Society, Los Alamitos (2008)
7. Ezekiel, J., Lomuscio, A.: Combining fault injection and model checking to verify fault tolerance in multi-agent systems. In: Proc. AAMAS 2009 (to appear, 2009)
8. van der Meyden, R., Su, K.: Symbolic model checking the knowledge of the dining cryptographers. In: Proc. CSFW 2004, Washington, DC, USA, p. 280. IEEE Computer Society, Los Alamitos (2004)
9. Dechesne, F., Orzan, S., Wang, Y.: Refinement of kripke models for dynamics. In: Fitzgerald, J.S., Haxthausen, A.E., Yenigun, H. (eds.) ICTAC 2008. LNCS, vol. 5160, pp. 111–125. Springer, Heidelberg (2008)
10. Enea, C., Dima, C.: Abstractions of multi-agent systems. In: Burkhard, H.-D., Lindemann, G., Verbrugge, R., Varga, L.Z. (eds.) CEEMAS 2007. LNCS (LNAI), vol. 4696, pp. 11–21. Springer, Heidelberg (2007)
11. Wooldridge, M.: Computationally grounded theories of agency. In: Proc. ICMAS 2000, pp. 13–22. IEEE Press, Los Alamitos (2000)
12. Cohen, M., Dam, M., Lomuscio, A., Russo, F.: Abstraction in model checking multi-agent systems. In: Proc. AAMAS 2009 (to appear, 2009)
13. Cohen, M., Dam, M., Lomuscio, A., Qu, H.: A symmetry reduction technique for model checking temporal epistemic logic. In: Proc. IJCAI 2009 (to appear, 2009)
14. Clarke, E.M., Enders, R., Filkorn, T., Jha, S.: Exploiting symmetry in temporal logic model checking. Form. Methods Syst. Des. 9(1-2), 77–104 (1996)
15. Emerson, E.A., Sistla, A.P.: Symmetry and model checking. Form. Methods Syst. Des. 9(1-2), 105–131 (1996)
16. Lewis, D.: Counterpart theory and quantified modal logic. Journal of Philosophy 65, 113–126 (1968)
17. van der Meyden, R., Wong, K.S.: Complete axiomatizations for reasoning about knowledge and branching time. Studia Logica 75(1), 93–123 (2003)
18. Needham, R.M., Schroeder, M.D.: Using encryption for authentication in large networks of computers. Commun. ACM 21(12), 993–999 (1978)
19. Denker, G., Millen, J.: Capsl integrated protocol environment. In: Proc. DISCEX 2000, pp. 207–221. IEEE Computer Society, Los Alamitos (2000)
20. Burrows, M., Abadi, M., Needham, R.: A logic of authentication. ACM Trans. Comput. Syst. 8(1), 18–36 (1990)
21. Dolev, D., Yao, A.: On the security of public key protocols. IEEE Transactions on Information Theory 29(2), 198–208 (1983)

TAPAAL: Editor, Simulator and Verifier of Timed-Arc Petri Nets

Joakim Byg, Kenneth Yrke Jørgensen, and Jiří Srba*

Department of Computer Science, Aalborg University,
Selma Lagerlöfs Vej 300, 9220 Aalborg Øst, Denmark

Abstract. TAPAAL is a new platform independent tool for modelling, simulation and verification of timed-arc Petri nets. TAPAAL provides a stand-alone editor and simulator, while the verification module translates timed-arc Petri net models into networks of timed automata and uses the UPPAAL engine for the automatic analysis.

We report on the status of the first release of TAPAAL (available at www.tapaal.net), on its new modelling features and we demonstrate the efficiency and modelling capabilities of the tool on a few examples.

1 Introduction

Petri net is a popular mathematical model of discrete distributed systems introduced in 1962 by Carl Adam Petri in his PhD thesis. Since then numerous extensions of the basic place/transition model were studied and supported by a number of academic as well as industrial tools [8]. Many recent works consider various extensions of the Petri net model with time features that can be associated to places, transitions, arcs or tokens. A recent overview aiming at a comparison of the different time dependent models (including timed automata) is given in [15].

In the TAPAAL tool we consider *Timed-Arc Petri Nets* (TAPN) [4, 7] where an age (a real number) is associated with each token in a net and time intervals are placed on arcs in order to restrict the ages of tokens that can be used for firing a transition. The advantages of this model are an intuitive semantics and the decidability of a number of problems like coverability and boundedness (for references see [15]). On the other hand, the impossibility to describe urgent behaviour limited its modelling power and wider applicability. TAPAAL extends the TAPN model with new features of *invariants* and *transport arcs* in order to model urgent behaviour and transportation of tokens without resetting their age.

TAPAAL has an intuitive modelling environment for editing and simulation of TAPN. It also provides a verification module with automatic checking of bounded TAPN models against safety and liveness requirements via a translation to networks of timed automata and then using the UPPAAL [16] engine as a back-end for verification.

---

* Author was partially supported by Ministry of Education of the Czech Republic, project No. MSM 0021622419.

Z. Liu and A.P. Ravn (Eds.): ATVA 2009, LNCS 5799, pp. 84–89, 2009.

The connection between bounded TAPN and timed automata was studied in [13, 14, 5] and while theoretically satisfactory, the translations described in these papers are not suitable for a tool implementation as they either cause an exponential blow-up in the size or create a new parallel component with a fresh local clock for *each place* in the net. As UPPAAL performance becomes significantly slower with the growing number of parallel processes and clocks, the verification of larger nets with little or no concurrent behaviour (few tokens in the net) becomes intractable.

In TAPAAL we suggest a novel translation technique where a fresh parallel component (with a local clock) is created only for *each token* in the net. The proposed translation also transforms safety and liveness properties (EF, AG, EG, AF) into equivalent UPPAAL queries. One of the main advantages of this translation approach is the possibility to use *active clock reduction* and *symmetry reduction* techniques recently implemented in UPPAAL. As a result the verifiable size of models increases by orders of magnitude.

To the best of our knowledge, TAPAAL is the first publicly available tool which offers modelling, simulation and verification of timed-arc Petri nets with continuous time. There is only one related tool prototype mentioned in [1] where the authors discuss a coverability algorithm for general (unbounded) nets, though without any urgent behaviour. Time features (time stamps) connected to tokens can be modelled also in Coloured Petri Nets using CPN Tools [10], however, time passing is represented here using a global clock rather than the local ones as in TAPN, only discrete time semantics is implemented in CPN Tools and the analysis can be nondeterministic as the time stamps are in some situations ignored during the state-space construction.

2   TAPAAL Framework

TAPAAL offers an editor, a simulator and a verifier for TAPN. It is written in Java 6.0 using Java Swing for the GUI components and it is so available for the majority of existing platforms.

TAPAAL's graphical *editor* features all necessary elements for a creation of TAPN models, including invariants on places and transport arcs. The user interface supports, among others, a select/move feature for moving a selected subnet of the model as well as an undo/redo buttons allowing the user to move backward and forward in the history during a creation of larger models. Constructed nets and queries are saved in an interchangeable XML format using the Petri Net Markup Language (PNML) [12] further extended with TAPAAL specific timing features. An important aspect of the graphical editor is that it disallows to enter syntactically incorrect nets and hence no syntax checks are necessary before calling further TAPAAL modules.

The *simulator* part of TAPAAL allows one to inspect the behaviour of a TAPN by graphically simulating the effects of time delays and transition firings. When firing a transition the user can either manually select the concrete tokens that will be used for the firing or simply allow the simulator to automatically select the tokens based on some predefined strategy: youngest, oldest or random. The simulator also allows the user to step back and forth in the simulated trace, which makes it easier to investigate alternative net behaviours.

TAPAAL's *verification* module enables us to check safety and liveness queries in the constructed net. Queries are created using a graphical query dialog, completely eliminating the possibility of introducing syntactical errors and offering an intuitive and easy to use query formulation mechanism. The TAPAAL query language is a subset of the CTL logic comprising EF, AG, EG and AF temporal operators[1], however, several TCTL properties can be verified by encoding them into the net. The actual verification is done via translating TAPN models into networks of timed automata and by using the model checker UPPAAL. The verification calls to UPPAAL are seamlessly integrated inside the TAPAAL environment and the returned error traces (if any) are displayed in TAPAAL's simulator. For safety questions concrete traces are displayed whenever the command-line UPPAAL engine can output them, otherwise the user is offered an untimed trace and can in the simulation mode experiment with suitable time delays in order to realize the displayed trace in the net. A number of verification/trace options found in UPPAAL are also available in TAPAAL, including a symmetry reduction option which often provides orders of magnitude improvement with respect to verification time, though at the expense of disallowing trace options (a current limitation of UPPAAL). Finally, it is possible to check whether the constructed net is k-bounded or not, for any given k. The tool provides a suitable under-approximation of the net behaviour in case the net is unbounded.

The TAPAAL code consists of two parts: the editor and simulator, extending the Platform Independent Petri net Editor project PIPE version 2.5 [9], which is licensed under the Open Software License 3.0, and a framework for translating TAPN models into UPPAAL, licensed under the BSD License.

3 Experiments

We shall now report on a few experiments investigating the modelling capabilities and verification efficiency of TAPAAL. All examples are included in the TAPAAL distribution and can be directly downloaded also from www.tapaal.net.

3.1 Workflow Processes with Deadlines

Workflow processes provide a classical case study suitable for modelling in different variants of Petri nets. A recent focus is, among others, on the addition of timing aspects into the automated analysis process. Gonzalez del Foyo and Silva consider in [6] workflow diagrams extended with task durations and the latest execution deadline of each task. They provide a translation into Time Petri Nets (TPN), where clocks are associated with each transition in the net, and use the tool TINA [3] to analyze schedulability questions. An example of a workflow process (taken from [6]) is illustrated in Fig. 1.

---

[1] At the moment the EG and AF queries are supported only for nets with transitions that do not contain more than two input and two output places.

Task	Duration	Deadline
A_0	5	5
A_1	4	9
A_2	4	15
A_3	2	9
A_4	2	8
A_5	3	13
A_6	3	18
A_7	2	25

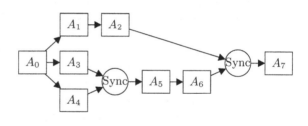

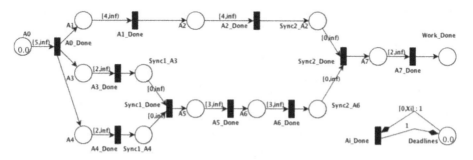

Fig. 1. A simple workflow diagram and its timed-arc Petri net model

The translation described in [6] relies on preprocessing of the workflow so that the individual (relative) deadlines for each task must be computed before a TPN model can be constructed.

In our model of extended timed-arc Petri nets a more direct translation without any preprocessing can be given. See Fig. 1 for a TAPAAL Petri net model resulting from the translation of the workflow example. Every transition with the naming schema **Ai_done** corresponds to the finalisation of the execution of the task A_i. The duration constraints are encoded directly into the net and the global deadlines are handled by adding a fresh place called **Deadlines**, containing one token (initially of age 0). The latest execution deadline X_i of a task A_i (where $0 \leq i \leq 7$) is then ensured by adding (for each i) a pair of transport arcs constrained with the time interval $[0, X_i]$ between the place **Deadlines** and the corresponding transition **Ai_done**. A schematic illustration is given in Fig. 1. Notice that transport arcs have different arrow tips than the standard arcs and are annotated with the label **1** to denote which arcs are paired into a route for the age-preserving token transportation (the annotations are relevant only in the presence of multiple transport arcs connected to a single transition). As the age of the token in the place **Deadlines** is never reset, it is guaranteed that the latest execution deadlines of all tasks are met.

The workflow example was verified in TAPAAL against the query EF (**Work_Done** = 1) and by selecting the fastest trace option the tool returned in

0.1s the following scheduling of task executions together with the necessary time delays: 5, A0_Done, 2, A3_Done, A4_Done, Sync1_Done, 2, A1_Done, 1, A5_Done, 3, A2_Done, A6_Done, Sync2_Done, 2, A7_Done.

3.2　Fischer's Protocol and Alternating Bit Protocol

Fischer's protocol [11] for mutual exclusion and alternating bit protocol [2] for network communication via lossy communication medium are well-known and scalable examples used for a tool performance testing. In our experiments we managed to verify Fischer's protocol (with a TAPN model taken from [1]) for 200 processes (each with its own clock) within 29 minutes, while an equivalent timed automaton model of the protocol provided in the UPPAAL distribution verified 200 processes in 2 hours and 22 minutes. The experiment showed a speed-up of 205% for 100 processes, 293% for 150 processes and 393% for 200 processes. The explanation to this seemingly surprising phenomenon is that the translated timed automata model of the protocol contains on one hand more discrete states than the native UPPAAL model (about twice as many), but on the other hand the zones that are tested for inclusion are smaller. As a result, the verification times for the TAPAAL produced automata are significantly faster.

Correctness of the alternating bit protocol was verified for up to 50 messages (each message has its own time-stamp) currently present in the protocol in less than two hours, while a native UPPAAL model verification took more than a day without any result. The speed-up was even more significant than in the case of Fischer's protocol: for 15 messages UPPAAL used 136 seconds and TAPAAL 7.3 seconds, for 17 messages UPPAAL needed 32 minutes and TAPAAL 13.7 seconds. There was also a difference in the tool performance depending on what kind of verification options were used, demonstrating a similar pattern of behaviour as in the case of Fischer's protocol (models with more discrete states and smaller zones verify faster).

4　Conclusion

TAPAAL offers a graphical environment for editing, simulation and verification of timed-arc Petri nets and the introduction of novel elements like invariants on places and transport arcs provides useful features particularly suitable for modelling of workflow processes, time sensitive communication protocols and other systems. The tool shows a promising performance in verification of safety and liveness properties.

The future development will focus on incorporating C-like functions and data structures into tokens in the net, on extending the firing policies with urgency and priorities, and on generalizing the query language. The aim is also to provide concrete error traces for liveness properties, rather than only the abstract or untimed ones (a current limitation of UPPAAL). We also plan to extend the model with cost, probability and game semantics and then use the corresponding UPPAAL branches (CORA, PROB and TIGA) for verification.

Acknowledgments. We would like to thank the UPPAAL team at Aalborg University and in particular Alexandre David for numerous discussions on the topic.

References

[1] Abdulla, P.A., Nylén, A.: Timed petri nets and BQOs. In: ICATPN 2001. LNCS, vol. 2075, pp. 53–70. Springer, Heidelberg (2001)

[2] Bartlett, K.A., Scantlebury, R.A., Wilkinson, P.T.: A note on reliable full-duplex transmission over half-duplex links. Commun. ACM 12(5), 260–261 (1969)

[3] Berthomieu, B., Ribet, P.-O., Vernadat, F.: The tool TINA — construction of abstract state spaces for Petri nets and time Petri nets. International Journal of Production Research 42(14), 2741–2756 (2004)

[4] Bolognesi, T., Lucidi, F., Trigila, S.: From timed Petri nets to timed LOTOS. In: Proceedings of the IFIP WG 6.1 Tenth International Symposium on Protocol Specification, Testing and Verification, Ottawa, pp. 1–14 (1990)

[5] Bouyer, P., Haddad, S., Reynier, P.-A.: Timed Petri nets and timed automata: On the discriminating power of Zeno sequences. Information and Computation 206(1), 73–107 (2008)

[6] Gonzalez del Foyo, P.M., Silva, J.R.: Using time Petri nets for modelling and verification of timed constrained workflow systems. In: ABCM Symposium Series in Mechatronics. ABCM, vol. 3, pp. 471–478. ABCM - Brazilian Society of Mechanical Sciences and Engineering (2008)

[7] Hanisch, H.M.: Analysis of place/transition nets with timed-arcs and its application to batch process control. In: Ajmone Marsan, M. (ed.) ICATPN 1993. LNCS, vol. 691, pp. 282–299. Springer, Heidelberg (1993)

[8] Heitmann, F., Moldt, D., Mortensen, K.H., Rölke, H.: Petri nets tools database quick overview,
http://www.informatik.uni-hamburg.de/TGI/PetriNets/tools/quick.html

[9] Platform Independent Petri net Editor 2.5, http://pipe2.sourceforge.net

[10] Jensen, K., Kristensen, L., Wells, L.: Coloured Petri nets and CPN tools for modelling and validation of concurrent systems. International Journal on Software Tools for Technology Transfer (STTT) 9(3), 213–254 (2007)

[11] Lamport, L.: A fast mutual exclusion algorithm. ACM Transactions on Computer Systems 5(1), 1–11 (1987)

[12] Petri Net Markup Language, http://www2.informatik.hu-berlin.de/top/pnml

[13] Sifakis, J., Yovine, S.: Compositional specification of timed systems. In: Puech, C., Reischuk, R. (eds.) STACS 1996. LNCS, vol. 1046, pp. 347–359. Springer, Heidelberg (1996)

[14] Srba, J.: Timed-arc Petri nets vs. networks of timed automata. In: Ciardo, G., Darondeau, P. (eds.) ICATPN 2005. LNCS, vol. 3536, pp. 385–402. Springer, Heidelberg (2005)

[15] Srba, J.: Comparing the expressiveness of timed automata and timed extensions of Petri nets. In: Cassez, F., Jard, C. (eds.) FORMATS 2008. LNCS, vol. 5215, pp. 15–32. Springer, Heidelberg (2008)

[16] UPPAAL, http://www.uppaal.com

CLAN: A Tool for Contract Analysis and Conflict Discovery*

Stephen Fenech[1], Gordon J. Pace[1], and Gerardo Schneider[2]

[1] Dept. of Computer Science, University of Malta, Malta
[2] Dept. of Informatics, University of Oslo, Norway
{sfen002,gordon.pace}@um.edu.mt, gerardo@ifi.uio.no

Abstract. As Service-Oriented Architectures are more widely adopted, it becomes more important to adopt measures for ensuring that the services satisfy functional and non-functional requirements. One approach is the use of contracts based on deontic logics, expressing obligations, permissions and prohibitions of the different actors. A challenging aspect is that of service composition, in which the contracts composed together may result in conflicting situations, so there is a need to analyse contracts and ensure their soundness. In this paper, we present CLAN, a tool for automatic analysis of conflicting clauses of contracts written in the contract language $\mathcal{CL}$. We present a small case study of an airline check-in desk illustrating the use of the tool.

1 Introduction and Background

In Service-Oriented Architectures services are frequently composed of different sub-services, each with its own contract. Not only does the service user require a a guarantee that each single contract is conflict-free, but also that the combination of the contracts is also conflict-free — meaning that the contracts will never lead to conflicting or contradictory normative directives. This is even more challenging in a dynamic setting, in which contracts may only be acquired at runtime.

A common view of contracts is that of properties which the system must (or is guaranteed) to satisfy. However, when analysing contracts for conflicts, the need to analyse and reason about contracts is extremely important, and looking at contracts simply as logical properties may hide conflicts altogether. The use of deontic logic to enable reasoning explicitly about normative information in a contract and about exceptional behaviour is one alternative approach to contract analysis. $\mathcal{CL}$ [3] is a formal language to specify deontic electronic contracts. The language has a trace semantics [2], which although useful for runtime monitoring of contracts, lacks the deontic information concerning the obligations, permissions and prohibitions of the involved parties in the contract, and thus it is not suitable for conflict analysis. We have recently developed conflict analysis techniques for $\mathcal{CL}$ [1], and in this paper, we present a tool implementing these techniques for the automatic analysis of contracts written in $\mathcal{CL}$.

---

* Partially supported by the Nordunet3 project COSoDIS: "Contract-Oriented Software Development for Internet Services".

Z. Liu and A.P. Ravn (Eds.): ATVA 2009, LNCS 5799, pp. 90–96, 2009.

The Contract Language $\mathcal{CL}$. Deontic logics enable explicit reasoning about, not only the actual state of affairs in a system e.g. 'the client has paid,' but also about the *ideal* state of affairs e.g. 'the client is *obliged* to pay' or 'the client is *permitted* to request a service.' $\mathcal{CL}$ is based on a combination of deontic, dynamic and temporal logics, allowing the representation of the deontic notions of obligations, permissions and prohibitions, as well as temporal aspects. Moreover, it also gives a mean to specify *exceptional* behaviours arising from the violation of obligations (what is to be demanded in case an obligation is not fulfilled) and of prohibitions (what is the penalty in case a prohibition is violated). These are usually known as *Contrary-to-Duties* (CTDs) and *Contrary-to-Prohibitions* (CTPs) respectively. $\mathcal{CL}$ contracts are written using the following syntax:

$$C := C_O | C_P | C_F | C \wedge C | [\beta] C | \top | \bot$$
$$C_O := O_C(\alpha) | C_O \oplus C_O$$
$$C_P := P(\alpha) | C_P \oplus C_P$$
$$C_F := F_C(\delta) | C_F \vee [\alpha] C_F$$
$$\alpha := 0 | 1 | a | \alpha \& \alpha | \alpha \cdot \alpha | \alpha + \alpha \qquad \beta := 0 | 1 | a | \beta \& \beta | \beta \cdot \beta | \beta + \beta | \beta^*$$

A contract clause C can be either an obligation (C_O), a permission (C_P) or a prohibition (C_F) clause, a conjunction of two clauses or a clause preceded by the dynamic logic square brackets. $O_C(\alpha)$ is interpreted as the obligation to perform α in which case, if violated, then the reparation contract C must be executed (a CTD). $F_C(\alpha)$ is interpreted as forbidden to perform α and if α is performed then the reparation C must be executed (a CTP). Permission is represented as $P(\alpha)$, identifying that the action expression α is permitted. Note that repetition in actions (using the $*$ operator) is not allowed inside the deontic modalities. They are, however allowed in dynamic logic-style conditions. $[\beta]C$ is interpreted as if action β is performed then the contract C must be executed — if β is not performed, the contract is trivially satisfied. $\wedge$ allows the conjunction of clauses, $\oplus$ is used as an exclusive choice between certain clauses, $\top$ and $\bot$ are the trivially satisfied (violated) contract. Compound actions can be constructed from basic ones using the operators $\&$, $\cdot$, $+$ and $*$ where $\&$ stands for the actions occurring concurrently, $\cdot$ stands for the actions to occur in sequence, $+$ stands for choice, and $*$ for repetition. 1 is an action expression matching any action, while 0 is the impossible action. In order to avoid paradoxes the operators combining obligations, permissions and prohibitions are restricted syntactically. See [3,2] for more details on $\mathcal{CL}$.

As a simple example, let us consider the following clause from an airline company contract: 'When checking in, the traveller is obliged to have a luggage within the weight limit — if exceeded, the traveller is obliged to pay extra.' This would be represented in $\mathcal{CL}$ as $[checkIn]O_{O(pay)}(withinWeightLimit)$.

Trace Semantics. The trace semantics presented in [2] enables checking whether or not a trace satisfies a contract. However, deontic information is not preserved in the trace and thus it is not suitable to be used for conflict detection. By a conflict we mean for instance that the contract permits and forbids performing the same action at the same time (see below for a more formal definition).

We will use lower case letters $(a, b \ldots)$ to represent atomic actions, Greek letters $(\alpha, \beta \ldots)$ for compound actions, and Greek letters with a subscript $\&$ $(\alpha_\&, \beta_\&, \ldots)$ for compound concurrent actions built from atomic actions and the concurrency operator $\&$. The set of all such concurrent actions will be written $A_\&$. We use $\#$ to denote mutually exclusive actions (for example, if a stands for 'opening the check-in desk' and b for 'closing the check-in desk', we write $a\#b$). A trace is a sequence of sets of actions, giving the set of actions present at each point in time. The Greek letter σ will be used to represent traces, using functional notation for indexing starting at zero i.e. $\sigma(n)$ is the $(n-1)$th element of trace σ.

For a trace σ to satisfy an obligation, $O_C(\alpha_\&)$, $\alpha_\&$ must be a subset of $\sigma(0)$ or the rest of the trace must satisfy the reparation C, thus for the obligation to be satisfied all the atomic actions in $\alpha_\&$ must be present in the first set of the sequence. For prohibitions the converse is required, e.g. not all the actions of $\alpha_\&$ are executed in the first step.

In order to enable conflict analysis, we start by adding deontic information in an additional trace, giving two parallel traces — a trace of actions (σ) and a trace of deontic notions (σ_d). Similar to σ, σ_d is defined as a sequence of sets whose elements are from the set D_a which is defined as $\{O_a \mid a \in A\} \cup \{F_a \mid a \in A\} \cup \{P_a \mid a \in A\}$ where O_a stands for the obligation to do a, F_a stands for the prohibition to do a and P_a for permission to do a. Also, since conflicts may result in sequences of finite behaviour which cannot be extended (due to the conflict), we reinterpret the semantics over finite traces. A conflict may result in reaching a state where we have only the option of violating the contract, thus any infinite trace which leads to this conflicting state will result not being accepted by the semantics. We need to be able to check that a finite trace has not yet violated the contract and then check if the following state is conflicting. Furthermore, if α is a set of concurrent atomic actions then we will use O_α to denote the set $\{O_a \mid a \in \alpha\}$. Note that the semantics is given in the form of $\sigma, \sigma_d \vDash C$, which says that an action trace σ and a trace with deontic information σ_d satisfies a contract C. We show the trace semantics for the obligation as an example:

$$\langle\rangle, \langle\rangle \vDash O_C(\alpha_\&)$$
$$(\beta : \sigma), (\beta_d : \sigma_d) \vDash O_C(\alpha_\&) \text{ if } (\alpha_\& \subseteq \beta \text{ and } O(\alpha_\&) \in \beta_d) \text{ or } \sigma, \sigma_d \vDash C$$

Note that in the above, pattern matching is used to split the traces into the head (β and β_d) and the tails (σ and σ_d). The above says that empty traces satisfy an obligation, while non-empty traces satisfy the contract if either (i) the obligation is satisfied, and the obligation is registered in the deontic trace; or (ii) the reparation (CTD) is satisfied by the remainder of the trace. See [1] for more details.

Conflict Analysis. Conflicts in contracts arise for four different reasons:[1] (i) obligation and prohibition on the same action; (ii) permission and prohibition on the same action; (iii) obligation to perform mutually exclusive actions; and (iv) permission and obligation to perform mutually exclusive actions.

With conflicts of the first type one would end up in a state where performing any action leads to a violation of the contract. The second conflict type results in traces

---

[1] By tabulating all combinations of the deontic operators, one finds that there are two basic underlying cases of conflict — concurrent obligation and prohibition, and concurrent permission and prohibition. Adding constraints on the concurrency of actions, one can identify the additional two cases. More complex temporal constraints on actions may give rise to others, but which can also be reduced to these basic four cases.

which also violate the contract even though permissions cannot be broken, since the deontic information is kept in the semantics. The remaining two cases correspond to mutually exclusive actions. Freedom from conflict can be defined formally as follows: Given a trace σ_d of a contract C, let $D, D' \subseteq \sigma_d(i)$ (with $i \geq 0$). We say that D is *in conflict with* D' iff there exists at least one element $e \in D$ such that:

$$e = O_a \wedge (F_a \in D' \vee (P_b \in D' \wedge a\#b) \vee (O_b \in D' \wedge a\#b))$$
$$\text{or } e = P_a \wedge (F_a \in D' \vee (P_b \in D' \wedge a\#b) \vee (O_b \in D' \wedge a\#b))$$
$$\text{or } e = F_a \wedge (P_a \in D' \vee O_a \in D')$$

A contract C is said to be *conflict-free* if for all traces σ and σ_d such that $\sigma, \sigma_d \vDash C$, then for any $D, D' \subseteq \sigma_d(i)$ ($0 \leq i \leq len(\sigma_d)$), D and D' are not in conflict.

As an example, let us consider the contract $C = [a]\mathbb{O}(b + c) \wedge [b]\mathbb{F}(b)$, stipulating the obligation of the choice of doing b or c after an a, and the prohibition of doing b if previously a b has been done. We have that C is not conflict-free since $\langle \{a, b\}, \{b\} \rangle, \langle \{\emptyset\}, \{\{O_b, O_c\}, \{F_b\}\} \rangle \vDash C$, and there are $D, D' \subseteq \sigma_d(1)$ such that D and D' are in conflict. To see this, let us take $D = \{O_b, O_c\}$ and $e = O_b$. We have then that for $D' = \{F_b\}$, $F_b \in D'$ (satisfying the first line of the above definition).

By unwinding a $\mathcal{CL}$ formula according to the finite trace semantics, we create an automaton which accepts all non-violating traces, and such that any trace resulting in a violation ends up in a violating state. Furthermore, we label the states of the automaton with deontic information provided in σ_d, so we can ensure that a contract is conflict-free simply through the analysis of the resulting reachable states (non-violating states). States of the automaton contain a set of formulae still to be satisfied, following the standard sub-formula construction (e.g., as for CTL). Each transition is labelled with the set of actions that are to be performed in order to move along the transition.

Once the automaton is generated we can check for the four types of conflicts on all the states. If there is a conflict of type (i) or (iii), then all transitions out of the state go to a special violation state. In general we might need to generate all possible transitions before processing each sub-formula, resulting on a big automaton. In practice, we improve the algorithm in such a way that we create all and only those required transitions reducing the size considerably. Conflict analysis can also be done on-the-fly without the need to create the complete automaton. One can process the states without storing the transitions and store only satisfied subformulae (for termination), in this manner, memory issues are reduced since only a part of the automaton is stored in memory.

2   A Tool for Contract Analysis

CLAN[2] is a tool for detection of normative conflicts in $\mathcal{CL}$ contracts, enabling: (i) The automatic analysis of the contract for normative conflicts; (ii) The automatic generation of a monitor for the contract. The analyses are particularly useful when the contract is being written (enabling the discovery of undesired conflicts), before adhering to a given contract (to ensure unambiguous enforcement of the contract), and during contract enforcement (monitoring).

---

[2] CLAN can be downloaded from
http://www.cs.um.edu.mt/~svrg/Tools/CLTool

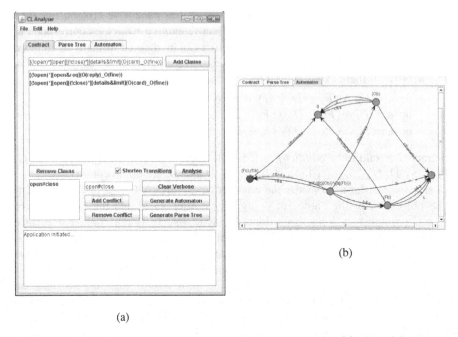

(a)

(b)

Fig. 1. (a) Screen shot of the tool; (b) Automaton generated for $[c]\mathbb{O}(b) \wedge [a]\mathbb{F}(b)$

The core of CLAN is implemented in Java, consisting of 700 lines of code. This does not include the additional code, over and above the conflict discovery algorithm, for the graphical user interface (a screen shot can be seen in Fig. 1-(a)). $\mathcal{CL}$ contracts and additional information (such as which actions are mutually exclusive) are given to the tool which then performs the conflict analysis. Upon discovery of a conflict, it gives a counter-example trace. The tool also offers an aid to analyse traces, and the possibility of visualising the generated automaton, as the one shown in Fig. 1-(b).

CLAN has been used to analyse a large contract resulting in a graph with 64,000 states, consuming approximately 700MB of memory; the analysis took around 94 minutes. The analysis seems to scale linearly in memory and polynomially in the number of states. The complexity of the automaton increases exponentially on the number of actions, since all the possible combinations to generate concurrent actions must be considered. We are currently working on how to optimise the analysis to avoid such exponential state-explosion.

3   Case Study

We briefly present here a portion of a small case study, starting from a draft contract written in English, which is formalised in $\mathcal{CL}$ and analysed using CLAN. The full example can be found in [1]. The case study concerns a contract between an airline company and a company taking care of the ground crew (mainly the check-in process) Some clauses of the contract expressed in English and $\mathcal{CL}$, are given below:

1. *The ground crew is obliged to open the check-in desk and request the passenger manifest two hours before the flight leaves.*

   $[1^*][twoHBefore]O_{O(issueFine)}(openCheckIn \ \& \ requestInfo)$

2. *After the check-in desk is opened the check-in crew is obliged to initiate the check-in process with any customer present by checking that the passport details match what is written on the ticket and that the luggage is within the weight limits. Then they are obliged to issue the boarding pass.*

   $[1^*][openCheckIn][1^*](\mathbb{O}(correctDetails \ \& \ luggageInLimit) \ \wedge$
   $[correctDetails \ \& \ luggageInLimit]O_{O(issueFine)}(issueBoardingCard))$

3. *The ground crew is obliged to close the check-in desk 20 minutes before the flight is due to leave and not before.*

   $([1^*][20mBefore]O_{O(issueFine)}(closeCheckIn)) \ \wedge$
   $([\overline{20mBefore}^*]\mathbb{F}_{O(issueFine)}(closeCheckIn))$

4. *If any of the above obligations and prohibitions are violated a fine is to be paid.*

   $[1^*][closeCheckIn][1^*](F_{O(issueFine)}(openCheckIn) \wedge F_{O(issueFine)}(issueBoardingCard))$

On this size of example, the tool gives practically instantaneous results, identifying conflicts such as the concurrent obligation and prohibition to perform action *issueBoardingCard*, together with a counter-example trace. Looking at clause 2, once the crew opens the check-in desk, they are always obliged to issue a boarding pass if the client has the correct details. However, according to clause 4 it is prohibited to issue of boarding pass once the check-in desk is closed. These two clauses are in conflict once the check-in desk is closed and a client arrives to the desk with the correct details.

To fix this problem one has to change clause 2 so that after the check-in desk is opened, the ground crew is obliged to issue the boarding pass as long as the desk has not been closed. In the full case study, other conflicts due to mutual exclusion are also found and fixed in the English contract.

4   Conclusions

The analysis of contracts for the discovery of potential conflicts can be crucial to enable safe and dependable contract adoption and composition at runtime. In this paper we have presented CLAN, a tool for automatic detection of conflicting clauses in contracts written in the deontic language $\mathcal{CL}$. Currently the tool only provides the functionality of detecting conflicts. However, many other analysis may be done by slightly modifying the underlying algorithm, as for instance the generation of a model from the contract which can be processed by a model checker. Furthermore, other contract analysis techniques are planned to be added to the tool to enable analysis for overlapping, superfluous and unreachable sub-clauses of a contract. See [1] for related works.

References

1. Fenech, S., Pace, G.J., Schneider, G.: Automatic Conflict Detection on Contracts. In: Leucker, M., Morgan, C. (eds.) ICTAC 2009. LNCS, vol. 5684, pp. 200–214. Springer, Heidelberg (2009)
2. Kyas, M., Prisacariu, C., Schneider, G.: Run-time monitoring of electronic contracts. In: Cha, S., Choi, J.-Y., Kim, M., Lee, I., Viswanathan, M. (eds.) ATVA 2008. LNCS, vol. 5311, pp. 397–407. Springer, Heidelberg (2008)
3. Prisacariu, C., Schneider, G.: A Formal Language for Electronic Contracts. In: Bonsangue, M.M., Johnsen, E.B. (eds.) FMOODS 2007. LNCS, vol. 4468, pp. 174–189. Springer, Heidelberg (2007)

UnitCheck: Unit Testing and Model Checking Combined*

Michal Kebrt and Ondřej Šerý

Charles University in Prague
Malostranské náměstí 25
118 00 Prague 1
Czech Republic
`michal.kebrt@gmail.com, ondrej.sery@dsrg.mff.cuni.cz`
`http://dsrg.mff.cuni.cz`

Abstract. Code model checking is a rapidly advancing research topic. However, apart from very constrained scenarios (e.g., verification of device drivers by SLAM), the code model checking tools are not widely used in general software development process. We believe that this could be changed if the developers could use the tools in the same way they already use testing tools. In this paper, we present the UNITCHECK tool, which enhances standard unit testing of Java code with model checking. A developer familiar with unit testing can apply the tool on standard unit test scenarios and benefit from the exhaustive traversal performed by a code model checker, which is employed inside UNITCHECK. The UNITCHECK plugin for ECLIPSE presents the checking results in a convenient way known from unit testing, while providing also a verbose output for the expert users.

1 Introduction

In recent years, the field of code model checking has advanced significantly. There exist a number of code model checkers targeting mainstream programming languages such as C, Java, and C# (e.g., SLAM [2], CBMC [6], BLAST [11], JAVA PATHFINDER [15], and MOONWALKER [7]). In spite of this fact, the adoption of the code model checking technologies in the industrial software development process is still very slow. This is caused by two main reasons (i) limited scalability to large software, and (ii) missing tool-supported integration into the development process.

The current model checking tools can handle programs up to tens of KLOC and often require manual simplifications of the code under analysis [13]. Unfortunately, such program size is still several orders of magnitude smaller than the size of many industrial projects.

---

* This work was partially supported by the Czech Academy of Sciences project 1ET400300504, and the Q-ImPrESS research project (FP7-215013) by the European Union under the Information and Communication Technologies priority of the Seventh Research Framework Programme.

Z. Liu and A.P. Ravn (Eds.): ATVA 2009, LNCS 5799, pp. 97–103, 2009.

Apart from the scalability issues, there is virtually no support for integration of the code model checkers into the development process. Although some tools feature a user interface in the form of a plugin for a mainstream IDE (e.g., SATABS [5]), creation of a particular checking scenario is not often discussed or supported in any way. A notable exception is SLAM and its successful application in the very specific domain of kernel device drivers.

These two obstacles might be overcome by employing code model checking in a way similar to unit testing – we use the term *unit checking* first proposed in [10]. Unit testing is widely used in industry and developers are familiar with writing test suites. Providing model checking tools with a similar interface would allow developers to directly benefit from model checking technology (e.g., of exploration of all thread interleavings) without changing their habits. Moreover, applying model checking to smaller code units also helps avoiding the state explosion problem, the main issue of the model checking tools.

Goals and structure of the paper. We present the UNITCHECK tool, which allows for creation, execution and evaluation of checking scenarios using the JAVA PATHFINDER model checker (JPF). UNITCHECK accepts standard JUNIT tests [1] and exhaustively explores the reachable state space including all admissible thread interleavings. Moreover, the checking scenarios might feature nondeterministic choices, in which case all possible outcomes are examined. The tool is integrated into the ECLIPSE IDE in a similar way as the JUNIT framework and also an ANT task is provided. As a result, users familiar with unit testing using JUNIT might immediately start using UNITCHECK.

```java
public class Account {
    private double balance = 0;

    public void deposit(double a) {
        balance = balance + a; //(1)
    }
    public void withdraw(double a) {
        balance = balance - a;
    }
    public double getBalance() {
        return balance;
    }
}

public class Banker
        implements Runnable {
    private Account account;
    private double amount;
    private int cnt;

    @Override
    public void run() {
        for (int i=0; i < cnt; ++i) {
            account.deposit(amount);
        }
    }
}
```

```java
@Test
public void testDepositInThreads() {
    Account account = new Account();
    Thread t1 = new Thread(
        new Banker(account, 5, 5));
    Thread t2 = new Thread(
        new Banker(account, 10, 5));

    t1.start(); t2.start();
    t1.join(); t2.join();
    assertEquals(account.getBalance(),
        25 + 50, 0);
}

@Test
public void testDepositWithdraw() {
    Account account = new Account();
    int income = Verify.getInt(0, 10);
    int outcome = Verify.getInt(0, 10);

    account.deposit(income);
    assertEquals(account.getBalance(),
        income, 0);
    account.withdraw(outcome);
    assertEquals(account.getBalance(),
        Math.max(income - outcome, 0), 0);
}
```

Fig. 1. Tests that benefit from UNITCHECK's features

Test example. Examples of two JUNIT tests that would benefit from the analysis performed by UNITCHECK (in contrast to standard unit testing) are listed in Figure 1. The code under test, on the left, comprises of bank accounts and bankers that sequentially deposit money to an account. The first test creates two bankers for the same account, executes them in parallel, and checks the total balance when they are finished. UNITCHECK reports a test failure because the line marked with (1) is not synchronized. Therefore, with a certain thread interleaving of the two bankers the total balance will not be correct due to the race condition. In most cases, JUNIT misses this bug because it uses only one thread interleaving. The second test demonstrates the use of a random generator (the `Verify` class) to conveniently specify the range of values to be used in the test. UNITCHECK exhaustively examines all values in the range and discovers an error, i.e., the negative account balance. When using standard unit testing, the test designer could either use a pseudorandom number generator (the `Random` class) and take a risk of missing an error, or explicitly loop through all possible values, thus obfuscating the testing code.

2   Tool

In this section, the internal architecture of UNITCHECK is described. Additionally, we discuss three user interfaces to UNITCHECK which can be used to employ the tool in the development process.

2.1   Architecture

An overview of the UNITCHECK's architecture is depicted in Figure 2. The core module of UNITCHECK, the actual integration of JPF and JUNIT, is enclosed in the central box. It is compiled into a Java library so that it can be easily embedded into other Java applications (e.g., into an IDE). As an input, the core module takes an application under analysis, the JUNIT-compliant test cases, and optionally additional properties to fine-tune JPF. The analysis is then driven and monitored via the `UnitCheckListener` interface.

It is important to note that neither JPF nor JUNIT functionality and structures are directly exposed outside the core. The `UnitCheckListener` interface hides all JPF and JUNIT specific details. This solution brings a couple of advantages. (i) Extensions (e.g., ECLIPSE plugin) implement only the single (and simple) listener interface. (ii) In future, both JPF and JUNIT can be replaced with similar tools without modifying existing extensions.

Inside the core, `UnitCheckListener` is built upon two interfaces – JPF's `SearchListener` and JUNIT's `RunListener`. `SearchListener` notifies about property violations (e.g., deadlocks) and provides complete execution history leading to a violation. `RunListener` informs about assertion violations and other uncaught exceptions. UNITCHECK processes reports from both listeners and provides them in a unified form to higher levels through `UnitCheckListener`.

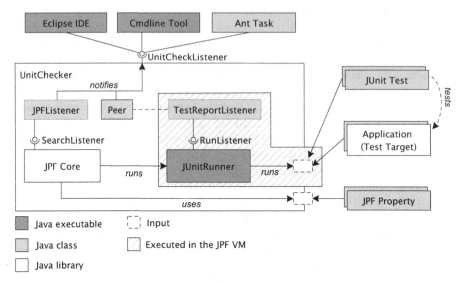

Fig. 2. JPF and JUnit integration

When analyzing the test cases, two Java virtual machines are employed. The first one is the host virtual machine in which UnitCheck itself and the underlying JPF are executed. The second one is JPF, a special kind of virtual machine, which executes JUnit. Subsequently, JUnit runs the input test cases (in Figure 2, the code executed inside the JPF virtual machine is explicitly marked). The information about test case progress provided by the JUnit's `RunListener` interface is available only in the JPF virtual machine. To make this information accessible in the host virtual machine, the JPF's Model Java Interface (MJI) API is used. It allows to execute parts of the application under analysis in the host virtual machine instead of the JPF virtual machine. Each class that is to be executed in the host VM has a corresponding peer counterpart. This mechanism is used for the `TestReportListener` class.

2.2 User Interface

Currently, there are three different extensions that provide user interface for checking JUnit tests using UnitCheck – simple command-line application, Ant task, and Eclipse plugin. The interfaces are designed to make their usage as close to the usage of the corresponding JUnit tools as possible. As an example, the Eclipse plugin provides a user interface very similar to the JUnit plugin for Eclipse, including test summaries, progress reports, and run configurations. On the other hand, the tools provide also a verbose output for the expert users which are familiar with model checking tools. In addition to the easy-to-understand

JUNIT-like result summaries, the ECLIPSE plugin provides also a navigable panel with a detailed error trace obtained from JPF with different levels of verbosity.[1]

3   Related work

The notion of unit checking was first used in [10]. The authors study the problem of symbolic model checking of code fragments (e.g., individual functions) in separation. In a similar vein, we use the term unit checking in parallel to unit testing. However, the focus of UNITCHECK is in providing users with tool support for integration of model checking into the software development process.

To our knowledge, the SLAM project [2] is by far the most successful application of code model checking in real-life software development process. Nevertheless, its success stems from the very constrained domain of device drivers, where the environment is fixed and known in advance by the tool's developers. In contrast, UNITCHECK offers benefits of code model checking in a convenient (and familiar) interface to developers of general purpose Java software.

Another related project is CHESS, which is a testing tool that can execute the target .NET or Win32 program in all relevant thread interleavings. CHESS comes in a form of a plugin into Microsoft Visual Studio and can be used to execute existing unit tests. As well as with UNITCHECK, the user of CHESS is not forced to change his/her habits with unit testing and gets the benefit of test execution under all relevant thread interleaving for free. In contrast to UNITCHECK, CHESS cannot cope with random values in tests, because it uses a layer over the scheduler-relevant API calls. The presence of a random event in a test would result in the loss of error reproducibility.

Orthogonal to our work is the progress on generating test inputs for unit tests for achieving high code coverage [9,16,17]. To name one, the PEX tool [14] uses symbolic execution and an automated theorem prover Z3 [12] to automatically produce a small test suite with high code coverage for a .NET program. We believe that similar techniques can be used in synergy with unit checking.

There are other approaches for assuring program correctness than code model checking. Static analysis tools (e.g., SPLINT [8]) are easy to use and scale well. However, there is typically a trade off between amount of false positives and completeness of such analysis. The design-by-contract paradigm (e.g., JML [4], SPEC# [3]) relies on user provided code annotations. Specifying these annotations is a demanding task that requires an expertise in formal methods.

4   Conclusion

We presented the UNITCHECK tool that brings the benefits of code model checking to the unit testing area the developers are familiar with. Of course, not all tests are amenable for unit checking. Only tests for which the standard testing

---

[1] The UNITCHECK tool and all three user interfaces are available for download at http://aiya.ms.mff.cuni.cz/unitchecking

is not complete (i.e., tests that feature random values or concurrency) would benefit from exhaustive traversal using UNITCHECK[2]. As UNITCHECK accepts standard JUNIT tests, developers can seamlessly switch among the testing engines as necessary.

References

1. JUnit testing framework, http://www.junit.org
2. Ball, T., Bounimova, E., Cook, B., Levin, V., Lichtenberg, J., McGarvey, C., Ondrusek, B., Rajamani, S.K., Ustuner, A.: Thorough static analysis of device drivers. SIGOPS Oper. Syst. Rev. 40(4), 73–85 (2006)
3. Barnett, M., DeLine, R., Fähndrich, M., Jacobs, B., Leino, K.R.M., Schulte, W., Venter, H.: The spec# programming system: Challenges and directions. In: Meyer, B., Woodcock, J. (eds.) VSTTE 2005. LNCS, vol. 4171, pp. 144–152. Springer, Heidelberg (2008)
4. Chalin, P., Kiniry, J.R., Leavens, G.T., Poll, E.: Beyond assertions: Advanced specification and verification with JML and eSC/Java2. In: de Boer, F.S., Bonsangue, M.M., Graf, S., de Roever, W.-P. (eds.) FMCO 2005. LNCS, vol. 4111, pp. 342–363. Springer, Heidelberg (2006)
5. Clarke, E., Kröning, D., Sharygina, N., Yorav, K.: SATABS: SAT-Based Predicate Abstraction for ANSI-C. In: Halbwachs, N., Zuck, L.D. (eds.) TACAS 2005. LNCS, vol. 3440, pp. 570–574. Springer, Heidelberg (2005)
6. Clarke, E., Kröning, D., Lerda, F.: A tool for checking ANSI-C programs. In: Jensen, K., Podelski, A. (eds.) TACAS 2004. LNCS, vol. 2988, pp. 168–176. Springer, Heidelberg (2004)
7. de Brugh, N.H.M.A., Nguyen, V.Y., Ruys, T.C.: Moonwalker: Verification of.net programs. In: Kowalewski, S., Philippou, A. (eds.) TACAS 2009. LNCS, vol. 5505, pp. 170–173. Springer, Heidelberg (2009)
8. Evans, D., Larochelle, D.: Improving security using extensible lightweight static analysis. IEEE Software 19(1), 42–51 (2002)
9. Godefroid, P., Klarlund, N., Sen, K.: Dart: directed automated random testing. In: PLDI 2005: Proceedings of the 2005 ACM SIGPLAN conference on Programming language design and implementation, pp. 213–223. ACM, New York (2005)
10. Gunter, E.L., Peled, D.: Unit checking: Symbolic model checking for a unit of code. In: Dershowitz, N. (ed.) Verification: Theory and Practice. LNCS, vol. 2772, pp. 548–567. Springer, Heidelberg (2004)
11. Henzinger, T.A., Jhala, R., Majumdar, R., Sutre, G.: Lazy abstraction. SIGPLAN Not. 37(1), 58–70 (2002)
12. de Moura, L., Bjørner, N.S.: Z3: An efficient SMT solver. In: Ramakrishnan, C.R., Rehof, J. (eds.) TACAS 2008. LNCS, vol. 4963, pp. 337–340. Springer, Heidelberg (2008)
13. Mühlberg, J.T., Lüttgen, G.: Blasting linux code. In: Brim, L., Haverkort, B.R., Leucker, M., van de Pol, J. (eds.) FMICS 2006 and PDMC 2006. LNCS, vol. 4346, pp. 211–226. Springer, Heidelberg (2007)
14. Tillmann, N., de Halleux, J.: Pex white box test generation for.net. In: 2nd International Conference on Tests and Proofs, April 2008, pp. 134–153 (2008)

---

[2] Of course, only the (increasing) portion of the standard Java libraries supported by JPFcan be used in the tests.

15. Visser, W., Havelund, K., Brat, G., Park, S., Lerda, F.: Model Checking Programs. Automated Software Engineering 10(2), 203–232 (2003)
16. Visser, W., Păsăreanu, C.S., Khurshid, S.: Test input generation with java pathfinder. In: Proceedings of the International Symposium on Software Testing and Analysis (ISSTA 2004), pp. 97–107. ACM, New York (2004)
17. Xie, T., Marinov, D., Schulte, W., Notkin, D.: Symstra: A framework for generating object-oriented unit tests using symbolic execution. In: Halbwachs, N., Zuck, L.D. (eds.) TACAS 2005. LNCS, vol. 3440, pp. 365–381. Springer, Heidelberg (2005)

LTL Model Checking of
Time-Inhomogeneous Markov Chains*

Taolue Chen[1], Tingting Han[2,3],
Joost-Pieter Katoen[2,3], and Alexandru Mereacre[2]

[1] Design and Analysis of Communication Systems, University of Twente, The Netherlands
[2] Software Modelling and Verification, RWTH Aachen University, Germany
[3] Formal Methods and Tools, University of Twente, The Netherlands

Abstract. We investigate the problem of verifying linear-time properties against inhomogeneous continuous-time Markov chains (ICTMCs). A fundamental question we address is how to compute reachability probabilities. We consider two variants: time-bounded and unbounded reachability. It turns out that both can be characterized as the least solution of a system of integral equations. We show that for the time-bounded case, the obtained integral equations can be transformed into a system of ordinary differential equations; for the time-unbounded case, we identify two sufficient conditions, namely the *eventually periodic assumption* and the *eventually uniform assumption*, under which the problem can be reduced to solving a time-bounded reachability problem for the ICTMCs and a reachability problem for a DTMC. These results provide the basis for a model checking algorithm for LTL. Under the *eventually stable assumption*, we show how to compute the probability of a set of ICTMC paths which satisfy a given LTL formula. By an automata-based approach, we reduce this problem to the previous established results for reachability problems.

1 Introduction

Continuous-time Markov chains (CTMCs) are one of the most important models in performance and dependability analysis. They are exploited in a broad range of applications, and constitute the underlying semantical model of a plethora of modeling formalisms for real-time probabilistic systems such as Markovian queueing networks, stochastic Petri nets, stochastic variants of process algebras, and, more recently, calculi for system biology. These Markov chains are typically *homogeneous*, i.e., the rates that determine the speed of changing state as well as the probabilistic nature of mode transitions are constant. However, in some situations constant rates do not adequately model real behaviors. This applies, e.g., to failure rates of hardware components [10] (that usually depend on the component's age), battery depletion [7] (where the power extraction rate non-linearly depends on the remaining amount of energy), and random phenomena that are subject to environmental influences. In these circumstances, Markov models

---

* Financially supported by the DFG research training group 1295 AlgoSyn, the Dutch Bsik project BRICKS, the NWO project QUPES, the EU project QUASIMODO, and the SRO DSN project of CTIT, University of Twente.

Z. Liu and A.P. Ravn (Eds.): ATVA 2009, LNCS 5799, pp. 104–119, 2009.

with *inhomogeneous* rates, i.e., rates that are time-varying functions, are much more appropriate [17].

Temporal logics and accompanying model-checking algorithms have been developed for discrete-time Markov chains (DTMCs for short), against linear-time properties [8,9] and branching-time properties [11]; for CTMCs against branching-time properties [2,3] and linear real-time properties [6]. And some of them have resulted in a number of successful model checkers such as PRISM [12] and MRMC [14]. However, the verification of *time-inhomogeneous* CTMCs (ICTMCs) has – to the best of our knowledge – not yet been investigated in depth, with the notable exception [15], which considered model checking a simple stochastic variant of Hennessy-Milner Logic (without fixed points) for *piecewise-constant* ICTMCs. The main aim of the current paper is to fill this gap by considering model checking ICTMCs w.r.t. *linear-time* properties.

One of the most fundamental linear-time properties are reachability problems. Here we address two variants: time-bounded and unbounded reachability. The former asks, given a set of goal states and a time bound, what is the probability of paths of a given ICTMC that reach the goal states within the time bound. Time-unbounded reachability is similar except that the time bound is infinity. To solve both of them, we first provide a characterization in terms of the least solution of a system of *integral equations*. This can be regarded as a generalization of similar results for CTMCs [2,3] to ICTMCs. Furthermore, we show that for the time-bounded case, the obtained integral equations can be transformed into a system of (homogeneous) ordinary differential equations, which often enjoys an efficient numerical solution; for the time-unbounded case, generally this is not possible and one has to solve the system of integral equations directly, which is not so efficient and numerically unstable. To remedy this deficiency, we identify two sufficient conditions, i.e., the *eventually periodicity* and *eventually uniformity*, under which the problem can be reduced to the time-bounded reachability problem for ICTMCs and a (time-unbounded) reachability problem for DTMCs and thus can be solved efficiently. These classes subsume some interesting and important subclasses of ICTMCs, such as, the piecewise-constant case studied in [15] and ICTMCs with rates function representing *Weibull failure rates*. The latter distributions are important to model hazards and failures, and are popular in, e.g., reliability engineering. We then turn to model checking ICTMCs against LTL. Strictly speaking, we focus on computing the probability of the set of paths of a given ICTMC which satisfy the LTL formula. One of the main difficulties here compared to CTMCs is that in ICTMC, rates between states are functions over time instead of constants, and thus the topological structure of ICTMCs, when considered as a digraph, is not stable. To circumvent this problem, we identify a condition, i.e., the *eventually stable assumption* which intuitively means that after a (finite) time, the topological structure of the ICTMC does *not* change any more. Under this assumption, we can adapt the standard automata-based approach. A crucial ingredient is that we can construct a corresponding *separated* Büchi automaton from an LTL formula[1], based on which, one can build the product of the given ICTMC and the separated Büchi automaton while obtaining a well-defined stochastic process. We then reduce the LTL model checking problem to the previous established results for reachability problems.

---

[1] Note that one can also use deterministic automata, but that would incur an extra (unnecessary) exponential blowup.

2   Preliminaries

Given a set S, let $Distr(S)$ denote the set of probability distributions over S.

Definition 1 (ICTMC). *A (labeled) inhomogeneous continuous-time Markov chain (ICTMC) is a tuple* $\mathcal{C} = (S, \mathrm{AP}, L, \alpha, \mathbf{R}(t))$, *where* S *is a* finite *set of* states; AP *is a* finite *set of* atomic propositions; $L : S \rightarrow 2^{\mathrm{AP}}$ *is a* labeling function; $\alpha \in Distr(S)$ *is an* initial distribution; $\mathbf{R}(t) : S \times S \times \mathbb{R}_{\geqslant 0} \rightarrow \mathbb{R}_{\geqslant 0}$ *is a rate matrix.*

Let diagonal matrix $\mathbf{E}(t) = \mathrm{diag}\,[E_s(t)] \in \mathbb{R}_{\geqslant 0}^{n \times n}$, where $n = |S|$ and $E_s(t) : S \times \mathbb{R}_{\geqslant 0} \dashrightarrow \mathbb{R}_{\geqslant 0}$ be defined as $E_s(t) = \sum_{s' \in S} \mathbf{R}_{s,s'}(t)$ for all $s \in S$, i.e., $E_s(t)$ is the *exit rate* of state s at time t. We require that all rates and exit rates, as functions of time t, are integrable. If all rates (and thus exit rates) are constant, we obtain a CTMC. A state s is *absorbing* if $\mathbf{R}_{s,s'}(t) = 0$, for $s' \neq s$.

Semantics. An ICTMC induces a stochastic process. The probability to take a transition from s to s' at time t within Δt time units is given by:

$$Prob\{s \rightarrow s', t, \Delta t\} = \int_0^{\Delta t} \mathbf{R}_{s,s'}(t + \tau) e^{-\int_0^{\tau} E_s(t+v)dv} d\tau = \int_t^{t+\Delta t} \mathbf{R}_{s,s'}(\tau) e^{-\int_t^{\tau} E_s(v)dv} d\tau.$$

Definition 2 (Timed paths). *Let* $\mathcal{C}$ *be an* ICTMC. *An infinite path starting at time* x *is a sequence* $\rho_x = s_0 \xrightarrow{t_0} s_1 \xrightarrow{t_1} s_2 \cdots$ *such that for each* $i \in \mathbb{N}$, $s_i \in S$, $t_i \in \mathbb{R}_{>0}$ *and* $\mathbf{R}_{s_i, s_{i+1}}(t) > 0$ *where* $t = x + \sum_{j=0}^{i} t_j$. *A finite path is a prefix of an infinite path ending in a state.*

We will sometimes omit the subscript of ρ_x if the starting time x is irrelevant. Let $Paths^{\mathcal{C}}$ and $Paths^{\mathcal{C}}(s, x)$ denote the set of (finite and infinite) paths in $\mathcal{C}$ and those starting from state s at time x, respectively. The superscript $\mathcal{C}$ is omitted whenever convenient. Let $\rho[n] := s_n$ be the n-th state of ρ (if it exists) and $\rho\langle n \rangle := t_n$ the time spent in state s_n. Let $\rho_x@t$ be the state occupied in ρ at time $t \in \mathbb{R}_{\geqslant 0}$, i.e. $\rho_x@t := \rho_x[n]$ where n is the smallest index such that $x + \sum_{i=0}^{n} \rho_x\langle i \rangle > t$. We assume w.l.o.g. that the time to stay in any state is strictly greater than 0.

Let $\mathcal{I}$ denote the set of all nonempty intervals $I \subseteq \mathbb{R}_{\geqslant 0}$ and let $I \oplus t$ (resp. $I \ominus t$) denote $\{x + t \mid x \in I\}$ (resp. $\{x - t \mid x \in I \wedge x \geqslant t\}$). The definition of a *Borel space* over paths through ICTMCs follows [3]. An ICTMC $\mathcal{C}$ with initial state s_0 and initial time x yields a probability measure $\mathrm{Pr}^{\mathcal{C}}_{s_0, x}$ on paths as follows: Let $C_x(s_0, I_0, \ldots, I_{k-1}, s_k)$ denote the *cylinder set* consisting of all paths $\rho \in Paths(s_0, x)$ such that $\rho[i] = s_i$ ($i \leqslant k$) and $\rho\langle i \rangle \in I_i$ ($i < k$). $\mathcal{F}(Paths(s_0, x))$ is the smallest σ-algebra on $Paths(s_0, x)$ which contains all cylinder sets $C_x(s_0, I_0, \ldots, I_{k-1}, s_k)$ for all state sequences $(s_0, \ldots, s_k) \in S^{k+1}$ and $I_0, \ldots, I_{k-1} \in \mathcal{I}$. The probability measure $\mathrm{Pr}^{\mathcal{C}}_{s_0, x}$ on $\mathcal{F}(Paths(s_0, x))$ is the unique measure recursively defined by:

$$\mathrm{Pr}^{\mathcal{C}}_{s_0, x}\big(C_x(s_0, I_0, \ldots, I_{k-1}, s_k)\big)$$
$$= \int_{I_0 \oplus x} \mathbf{R}_{s_0, s_1}(\tau_0) \cdot e^{-\int_x^{\tau_0} E_{s_0}(v)dv} \cdot \mathrm{Pr}^{\mathcal{C}}_{s_1, \tau_0}\big(C_{\tau_0}(s_1, I_1, \ldots, I_{k-1}, s_k)\big) d\tau_0$$

Example 1. An example ICTMC is illustrated in Fig. 2(a) (page 113), where $AP = \{a, b, c\}$ and the rate functions are $r_i(t)$ $(1 \leqslant i \leqslant 6)$. In particular, the exit rate function of s_1 is $r_2(t) + r_3(t)$. The initial distribution is $\alpha(s_0) = 1$ and $\alpha(s) = 0$ for $s \neq s_0$. A possible rate function can be the ones depicted in Fig. 1 (page 110).

Linear temporal logic. The set of linear temporal logic (LTL) formulae over a set of atomic propositions AP is defined as follows:

Definition 3 (LTL syntax). *Given a set of atomic propositions* AP *which is ranged over by a,b,..., the syntax of* LTL *formulae is defined by:*

$$\varphi ::= \mathsf{tt} \mid a \mid \neg\varphi \mid \varphi \wedge \varphi \mid \boldsymbol{X}\varphi \mid \varphi \, \mathsf{U} \, \varphi.$$

The semantics of LTL for ICTMC $\mathcal{C}$ is defined in a standard way by a satisfaction relation, denoted $\models$, which is the least relation $\models \subseteq Paths^{\mathcal{C}} \times \mathbb{R}_{\geqslant 0} \times \mathbf{LTL}$ (here we use **LTL** to denote the set of LTL formulae) satisfying:

$$
\begin{array}{llll}
(\rho, t) \models \mathsf{tt} & & (\rho, t) \models \varphi_1 \wedge \varphi_2 & \text{iff} \quad (\rho, t) \models \varphi_1 \text{ and } (\rho, t) \models \varphi_2 \\
(\rho, t) \models a & \text{iff} \quad a \in L(\rho@t) & & (\rho, t) \models \neg\varphi \quad \text{iff} \quad (\rho, t) \not\models \varphi \\
(\rho, t) \models \boldsymbol{X}\varphi & \text{iff} \quad \exists \Delta t \geqslant 0. \ (\rho, t{+}\Delta t) \models \varphi \text{ and } \rho[1] = \rho@(t{+}\Delta t) \\
(\rho, t) \models \varphi_1 \, \mathsf{U} \, \varphi_2 & \text{iff} \quad \exists \Delta t \geqslant 0. \ (\rho, t{+}\Delta t) \models \varphi_2 \text{ and } \forall t' < t{+}\Delta t. \ (\rho, t') \models \varphi_1
\end{array}
$$

We use $at_s \in AP$ as an atomic proposition which holds solely at state s. For $F \subseteq S$, we write at_F for $\bigvee_{s \in F} at_s$. Let $Paths(s, x, \varphi) = \{\rho \in Paths(s, x) \mid (\rho, x) \models \varphi\}$. Note that a timed path $\rho = s_0 \xrightarrow{t_0} s_1 \xrightarrow{t_1} \cdots$ satisfies a formula φ iff the "discrete part" of ρ, namely, $s_0 s_1 s_2 \cdots (= \rho[0]\rho[1]\rho[2]\cdots)$ satisfies φ. It thus can be easily shown that the set $Paths(s, x, \varphi)$ is *measurable*. We denote the probability measure of $Paths(s, x, \varphi)$ as $Prob(s, x, \varphi) = \mathrm{Pr}_{s,x}(Paths(s, x, \varphi))$ and let $Prob^{\mathcal{C}}(\varphi) = \sum_{\alpha(s_0) > 0} \alpha(s_0) \cdot Prob(s_0, 0, \varphi)$ be the probability that ICTMC $\mathcal{C}$ satisfies φ.

3 Reachability Analysis

In this section, we tackle reachability problems for ICTMCs. We distinguish two variants: *time-bounded* reachability and *time-unbounded* reachability. To solve both of them, we first give a characterization of $Prob(s, x, \Diamond^I at_F)$, namely, the probability of the set of paths which reach a set of goal states $F \subseteq S$ within time interval I starting from state s at time point x. This is done by resorting to a system of integral equations, which is a generalization of a similar characterization for CTMCs [3].

Proposition 1. *Let* $\mathcal{C} = (S, AP, L, \alpha, \mathbf{R}(t))$ *be an ICTMC with* $s \in S$, $x \in \mathbb{R}_{\geqslant 0}$, $F \subseteq S$ *and interval* $I \subseteq \mathbb{R}_{\geqslant 0}$ *with* $T_1 = \inf I$ *and* $T_2 = \sup I$. *The function* $S \times \mathbb{R}_{\geqslant 0} \times \mathcal{I} \to [0,1]$, $(s, x, I) \mapsto Prob(s, x, \Diamond^I at_F)$ *is the least fixed point of the operator*

$$\Omega : (S \times \mathbb{R}_{\geqslant 0} \times \mathcal{I} \to [0,1]) \to (S \times \mathbb{R}_{\geqslant 0} \times \mathcal{I} \to [0,1]) \ ,$$

where $\Omega(f)(s, x, I) =$

$$
\begin{cases}
\int_0^{T_2} \sum_{s' \in S} \mathbf{R}_{s,s'}(x + \tau) e^{-\int_0^\tau E_s(x+v)dv} \cdot f(s', x + \tau, I \ominus \tau)d\tau, & \text{if } s \notin F \ (1) \\[4mm]
e^{-\int_0^{T_1} E_s(x+v)dv} + \int_0^{T_1} \sum_{s' \in S} \mathbf{R}_{s,s'}(x+\tau) e^{-\int_0^\tau E_s(x+v)dv} \cdot f(s', x+\tau, I \ominus \tau)d\tau, & \text{if } s \in F \ (2)
\end{cases}
$$

3.1   Time-Bounded Reachability

We now solve the *time-bounded reachability* problem, i.e., given ICTMC $\mathcal{C}$, a set of goal states $F \subseteq S$ and a time bound $T \in \mathbb{R}_{\geqslant 0}$, to compute $Prob(s, x, \Diamond^{\leqslant T} at_F)$, the probability of $Paths(s, x, \Diamond^{\leqslant T} at_F)$ which is the set of paths that reach F within T time units given the initial time x. To accomplish this, we first compute $Prob(s, x, \Diamond^{=T} at_F)$, where the slightly different property $\Diamond^{=T} at_F$, in contrast to $\Diamond^{\leqslant T} at_F$, requires that states in F are reached at *exactly* time T. Note that $\Diamond^{\leqslant T} at_F$ and $\Diamond^{=T} at_F$ can also be written as $\Diamond^{[0,T]} at_F$ and $\Diamond^{[T,T]} at_F$, respectively, where $I = [0, T]$ or $I = [T, T]$ is a time interval. By instantiating (1), (2) in Prop. 1, we obtain that $Prob(s, x, \Diamond^{=T} at_F) =$

$$
\begin{cases}
\int_0^T \sum_{s' \in S} \mathbf{R}_{s,s'}(x + \tau) e^{-\int_0^\tau E_s(x+v)dv} \cdot Prob(s', x + \tau, \Diamond^{=T-\tau} at_F)d\tau, & \text{if } s \notin F \ (3) \\[4mm]
e^{-\int_0^T E_s(x+v)dv} + \int_0^T \sum_{s' \in S} \mathbf{R}_{s,s'}(x+\tau) e^{-\int_0^\tau E_s(x+v)dv} \cdot Prob(s', x+\tau, \Diamond^{=T-\tau} at_F)d\tau, & \text{if } s \in F \ (4)
\end{cases}
$$

Intuitively, (3) and (4) are justified as follows: If $s \notin F$, the probability of reaching an F-state from s after exactly T time units given the starting time x equals the probability of reaching some direct successor s' of s in τ time units, multiplied by the probability of reaching an F-state from s' in the remaining $T - \tau$ time units. If $s \in F$ at time x, then it can either stay in s (i.e., delay) for T time units (the first summand in (4)), or regard s as a non-F state and take a transition (the second summand in (4)).

We now address the problem of solving (3) and (4), read as a *system of integral equations*. We define $\mathbf{\Pi}(x, T)$ as the matrix with entries $\mathbf{\Pi}_{i,j}(x, T)$ denoting the probability of the set of paths starting from state i at time x and reaching state j at time $x + T$. For any ICTMC, the following equation holds:

$$
\mathbf{\Pi}(x, T) = \underbrace{\int_0^T \mathbf{M}(x, \tau)\mathbf{\Pi}(x + \tau, T - \tau)d\tau}_{\text{Markovian jump}} + \underbrace{\mathbf{D}(x, T)}_{\text{delay}} \tag{5}
$$

$\mathbf{M}(x, T)$ is the probability density matrix where $\mathbf{M}_{i,j}(x, T) = \mathbf{R}_{i,j}(x + T) \cdot e^{-\int_0^T E_i(x+v)dv}$ is the density to move from state i to j at exactly time T and $\mathbf{D}(x, T)$ is the diagonal delay probability matrix with $\mathbf{D}_{i,i}(x, T) = e^{-\int_0^T E_i(x+v)dv}$.

We note that $\mathbf{\Pi}(x, T)$ is actually the (equivalent) matrix form of (3) and (4). For (4), it follows directly that each of its summands has a counterpart in (5). For (3), note that $\mathbf{D}(x, T)$ is a diagonal matrix where all the off-diagonal elements are 0 and that (3) does not allow a delay transition from a non-F state. This correspondence builds a half-bridge between $Prob(s, x, \Diamond^{=T} at_F)$ and $\mathbf{\Pi}(x, T)$, whereas the following proposition completes the other half bridge between $\mathbf{\Pi}(x, T)$ and the *transient probability vector* $\pi(t)$ of ICTMCs:

Proposition 2. *Given* ICTMC $\mathcal{C}$ *with initial distribution* α *and rate matrix* $\mathbf{R}(t)$. *We have that* $\mathbf{\Pi}(0, t)$ *and* $\pi(t)$ *satisfy the following two equations:*

$$\pi(t) = \alpha \cdot \mathbf{\Pi}(0, t) \ , \tag{6}$$

$$\frac{d\pi(t)}{dt} = \pi(t) \cdot \mathbf{Q}(t), \ \pi(0) = \alpha \ , \tag{7}$$

where $\mathbf{Q}(t) = \mathbf{R}(t) - \mathbf{E}(t)$ *is the* infinitesimal generator *of* $\mathcal{C}$.

Intuitively, this proposition implies that solving the system of integral equations $\mathbf{\Pi}(x, t)$ boils down to computing the transient probability vector $\pi(t)$ with each element $\pi_s(t)$ indicating the probability to be in state s at time t given the initial probability distribution $\alpha = \pi(0)$. The transient probability is specified by a system of ODEs (7), the celebrated Chapman-Kolmogorov equations.

Given ICTMC $\mathcal{C}$, let $\mathcal{C}[F]$ be the ICTMC obtained by making the states in F absorbing in $\mathcal{C}$. We have the following theorem:

Theorem 1. *For any* ICTMC $\mathcal{C}$, $Prob^{\mathcal{C}}(s, x, \Diamond^{\leqslant T} at_F) = Prob^{\mathcal{C}[F]}(s, x, \Diamond^{=T} at_F)$.

To sum up, Proposition 1, 2 together with Theorem 1 suggest that computing time-bounded reachability probabilities in an ICTMC can be done, by first making the F states absorbing (and thus obtaining $\mathcal{C}[F]$) followed by solving a system of homogeneous ODEs (7) for $\mathcal{C}[F]$. By using standard numerical approaches, e.g., *Euler method* or *Runge-Kutta method* and their variants [16], this system of ODEs (i.e. the transient probability vector) can be solved.

3.2 Time-Unbounded Reachability

We then turn to the *time-unbounded reachability* problem, i.e., there are no constraints on the time to reach the F-states. Let $Prob(s, x, \Diamond\, at_F)$ denote the reachability probability from state s at time x to reach F within time interval $[0, \infty)$. Using Proposition 1, we can characterize $Prob(s, x, \Diamond\, at_F)$ as follows:

$$\begin{cases} \displaystyle\int_0^\infty \sum_{s' \in S} \mathbf{R}_{s,s'}(x + \tau) e^{-\int_0^\tau E_s(x+v)dv} \cdot Prob(s', x + \tau, \Diamond at_F)d\tau, & \text{if } s \notin F \quad (8) \\ 1, & \text{if } s \in F \quad (9) \end{cases}$$

The case $s \in F$ is derived from (2), where the probability to delay in an F-state for zero units of time is 1 and the probability to leave (i.e. taking a Markovian jump) an F-state in zero units of time is 0. When $s \notin F$, Eq. (8) is similar to (3) except that there is no bound on the time to leave a state $s \notin F$. Note that in contrast to the *time-bounded* case, in general it is not possible to reduce this system of integral equations to a system of ODEs. Since solving a system of integral equations is generally time consuming and numerically instable, we propose to investigate some special cases (subsets

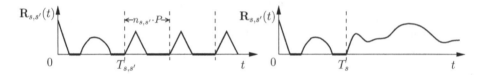

Fig. 1. Eventually periodic assumption (left) and eventually stable assumption (right)

of ICTMCs), for which the reduction to ODEs is possible. Here we consider two such classes, i.e. *eventually periodic* ICTMCs and *eventually uniform* ICTMCs. Their common feature is that rate functions of the given ICTMC exhibit regular behaviors after some time T. This allows for computing time-unbounded reachability probabilities efficiently (e.g., via DTMCs). Hence the problem turns out to be reducible to computing the time-bounded reachability probabilities with time bound T, which has been tackled in the previous section, and reachability probabilities for DTMCs. Both of them, fortunately, enjoy efficient computational methods.

Eventually periodic assumption. We consider *eventually periodic* ICTMCs.

Definition 4 (Eventually periodic assumption (EPA)). *An ICTMC $\mathcal{C}$ is* eventually periodic *if there exists some time $P \in \mathbb{R}_{>0}$ such that for any two states $s, s' \in S$, there exists some $T_{s,s'} \in \mathbb{R}_{\geqslant 0}$ and $n_{s,s'} \in \mathbb{N}$ such that*

$$\mathbf{R}_{s,s'}(t) = \begin{cases} \mathbf{R}^{(1)}_{s,s'}(t) & \text{if } t \leqslant T_{s,s'} \\ \mathbf{R}^{(2)}_{s,s'}(t) & \text{if } t > T_{s,s'} \end{cases}$$

where $\mathbf{R}^{(2)}_{s,s'}(t) = \mathbf{R}^{(2)}_{s,s'}(t + n_{s,s'} \cdot P)$.

An example rate function under the EPA is illustrated in Fig. 1 (left). After time point $T_{s,s'}$, the function $\mathbf{R}_{s,s'}(t)$ becomes periodic with the period $n_{s,s'} \cdot P$, where P is the "common factor" of all the periods of rate functions $\mathbf{R}_{s,s'}(t)$, for all $s, s' \in S$. For any ICTMC $\mathcal{C}$ satisfying EPA, let $T_{\text{EP}} = \max_{s,s' \in S} T_{s,s'}$ and $P_{\text{EP}} = (\gcd_{s,s' \in S} n_{s,s'}) \cdot P$. Intuitively, T_{EP} is the time since when all rate functions are periodic and P_{EP} is the period of all the periodic rate functions. For instance, suppose there are two rate functions with $\mathbf{R}^{(2)}_{s_1,s_2}(t) = 2 + \cos(\frac{1}{2}t)$ and $\mathbf{R}^{(2)}_{s_2,s_3}(t) = 3 - \sin(\frac{1}{3}t)$, and let $T_{s_1,s_2} = 10$, $T_{s_2,s_3} = 15$. Then $T_{\text{EP}} = \max\{10, 15\} = 15$, $P = \pi$, $n_{s_1,s_2} = 4$ and $n_{s_2,s_3} = 6$, and $P_{\text{EP}} = \gcd\{4, 6\} \cdot \pi = 12\pi$.

Time-unbounded reachability probabilities for an ICTMC under the EPA can be computed according to Alg. 1 and justified by Theorem 2. Let us explain it in more detail. Due to (9), once F states are reached, it is irrelevant how the paths continue. This justifies the model transformation from $\mathcal{C}$ to $\mathcal{C}[F]$. The reachability problem can be divided into two subproblems: (I) first to compute the probability to reach state $s' \in S$ at exactly time T_{EC} (the second *Prob* in (10), see below); and (II) then to compute the time-unbounded reachability from $s' \in S$ to F (the third *Prob* in (10)). In the following we will focus on (II): Recall that we denote $Prob(s, T_{\text{EP}}, \diamondsuit^{=P_{\text{EP}}} at_{s'})$ to be the probability to reach from s to s' after time P_{EP} starting from time point

T_{EP}. Since after time T_{EP} all rate functions are periodic with period P_{EP}, it holds that $Prob(s, T_{\text{EP}}, \Diamond^{=P_{\text{EP}}}at_{s'}) = Prob(s, T_{\text{EP}}+n\cdot P_{\text{EP}}, \Diamond^{=P_{\text{EP}}}at_{s'})$, for all $n \in \mathbb{N}$. It then suffices to compute $Prob(s, T_{\text{EP}}, \Diamond^{=P_{\text{EP}}}at_{s'})$ for any $s, s' \in S$. Given the ICTMC $\mathcal{C}$ with state space S, we build a DTMC $\mathcal{D}_{\mathcal{C}} = (S, \mathbf{P})$ with $\mathbf{P}_{s,s'} = Prob^{\mathcal{C}}(s, T_{\text{EP}}, \Diamond^{=P_{\text{EP}}}at_{s'})$. Intuitively, $\mathbf{P}_{s,s'}$ is the one-step probability (one-step here means one period) to move from s to s', and the problem (II) is now reduced to computing the reachability probability from s to F-states in arbitrarily many steps (since the time-unbounded case is considered), i.e., $Prob^{\mathcal{D}_{\mathcal{C}[F]}}(s, \Diamond \, at_F)$. This can be done by standard methods, e.g., *value iteration* or *solving a system of linear equations*, see, among others, [4] (Ch. 10).

Theorem 2. *Let* $\mathcal{C} = (S, \text{AP}, L, \alpha, \mathbf{R}(t))$ *be an* ICTMC *satisfying* EPA *with time* T_{EP} *and* P_{EP}, $s \in S$ *and* $F \subseteq S$. *Then:*

$$Prob^{\mathcal{C}}_{\text{EP}}(s, 0, \Diamond \, at_F) = \sum_{s' \in S} Prob^{\mathcal{C}[F]}(s, 0, \Diamond^{=T_{\text{EP}}} at_{s'}) \cdot Prob^{\mathcal{D}_{\mathcal{C}[F]}}(s', \Diamond \, at_F) \quad (10)$$

Remark 1. Sometimes we need to compute $Prob^{\mathcal{C}}_{\text{EP}}(s, x, \Diamond \, at_F)$ for ICTMC $\mathcal{C} = (S, \text{AP}, L, \alpha, \mathbf{R}(t))$, namely, the starting time is x instead of 0. To accomplish this, we define an ICTMC $\mathcal{C}' = (S, \text{AP}, L, \alpha, \mathbf{R}'(t))$ such that $\mathbf{R}'(t) = \mathbf{R}(t + x)$ and it follows that $\mathcal{C}'$ still satisfies EPA (with $T'_{\text{EP}} = T_{\text{EP}} - x$ if $x \leqslant T_{\text{EP}}$ and 0 otherwise; $P'_{\text{EP}} = P_{\text{EP}}$) and $Prob^{\mathcal{C}}_{\text{EP}}(s, x, \Diamond \, at_F) = Prob^{\mathcal{C}'}_{\text{EP}}(s, 0, \Diamond \, at_F)$.

Algorithm 1. Time-unbounded reachability for ICTMCs satisfying EPA

Require: ICTMC $\mathcal{C} = (S, \text{AP}, L, \alpha, \mathbf{R}(t))$, EPA time T_{EP}, period P_{EP}
Ensure: $Prob^{\mathcal{C}}_{\text{EP}}(s, 0, \Diamond \, at_F)$
1: For any two states $s, s' \in S$ in $\mathcal{C}[F]$, compute the *time-bounded reachability probability* with time bound T_{EP}, starting from time point x, i.e. $Prob^{\mathcal{C}[F]}(s, 0, \Diamond^{=T_{\text{EP}}} at_{s'})$;
2: For any two states $s, s' \in S$ in $\mathcal{C}[F]$, compute the *time-bounded reachability probability* with time bound P_{EP}, starting from time point T_{EP}, i.e. $Prob^{\mathcal{C}[F]}(s, T_{\text{EP}}, \Diamond^{=P_{\text{EP}}} at_{s'})$;
3: Construct a *discrete-time Markov chain* (DTMC for short) $\mathcal{D}_{\mathcal{C}[F]} = (S, \mathbf{P})$ with $\mathbf{P}_{s,s'} = Prob^{\mathcal{C}[F]}(s, T_{\text{EP}}, \Diamond^{=P_{\text{EP}}} at_{s'})$. We denote the *reachability probability* from s to F in $\mathcal{D}_{\mathcal{C}}$ by $Prob^{\mathcal{D}_{\mathcal{C}[F]}}(s, \Diamond \, at_F)$;
4: Return $\sum_{s' \in S} Prob^{\mathcal{C}[F]}(s, 0, \Diamond^{=T_{\text{EP}}} at_{s'}) \cdot Prob^{\mathcal{D}_{\mathcal{C}[F]}}(s', \Diamond \, at_F)$.

Eventually uniform assumption. The previous section has discussed rate functions enjoying a periodic behavior. A different class of rate functions are those which increase or decrease uniformly, e.g., an ICTMC in which all rates are a multiplicative of the *Weibull failure rate* which is characterized by the function $f(t) = \frac{\gamma}{\alpha}\left(\frac{t}{\alpha}\right)^{\gamma-1}$, where γ and α are the shape and scale parameters of the Weibull distribution, respectively. These distributions can e.g., characterize normal distributions, and are frequently used in reliability analysis. This suggests to investigate *eventually uniform* ICTMCs.

Definition 5 (Eventually uniform assumption (EUA)). *An* ICTMC $\mathcal{C}$ *is* eventually uniform *if there exists some time* $T_{\text{EU}} \in \mathbb{R}_{>0}$ *and an integrable function* $f(t) : \mathbb{R}_{>0} \to \mathbb{R}_{>0}$ *such that* $\lim_{t\to\infty} \int_{T_{\text{EU}}}^{t} f(\tau)d\tau \to \infty$ *and for any two states* $s, s' \in S$ *and* $t \geqslant T_{\text{EU}}$, $\mathbf{R}_{s,s'}(t) = f(t) \cdot \mathbf{R}^c_{s,s'}$, *where* $\mathbf{R}^c_{s,s'}$ *is a constant.*

In terms of the infinitesimal generator $\mathbf{Q}(t)$ of the ICTMC $\mathcal{C}$, EUA intuitively entails that there exists some function $f(t)$ and *constant* infinitesimal generator $\mathbf{Q}^c = \mathbf{R}^c - \mathbf{E}^c$ ($\mathbf{R}^c$ and $\mathbf{E}^c$ are the constant rate matrix and exit rate matrix, respectively) such that $\mathbf{Q}(t) = f(t){\cdot}\mathbf{Q}^c$ for all $t \geqslant T_{\mathrm{EU}}$. We also define the *constant transition probability matrix* $\mathbf{P}^c$ such that $\mathbf{P}^c_{s,s'} = \frac{\mathbf{R}^c_{s,s'}}{\mathbf{E}^c_s}$.

By restricting to the EUA, one can reduce the time-unbounded reachability problem for an ICTMC $\mathcal{C}$ to computing the time-bounded reachability probability with time bound T_{EU} and the reachability probability in a DTMC $\mathcal{D}^{\mathcal{C}}_{\mathrm{EU}}[F]$ with transition probability matrix $\mathbf{P}^c[F]$, where $\mathbf{P}^c[F]_{s,s'} = \mathbf{P}^c_{s,s'}$ for $s \notin F$; $\mathbf{P}^c[F]_{s,s} = 1$ and $\mathbf{P}^c[F]_{o,o'} = 0$, for $s \in F$ and $s' \neq s$. This is shown by the following theorem.

Theorem 3. *Let* $\mathcal{C} = (S, \mathrm{AP}, L, \alpha, \mathbf{R}(t))$ *be an* ICTMC *with* $s \in S$. *Given a set* F *of goal states and the* eventually uniform assumption *with the associated time* T_{EU} *and* DTMC $\mathcal{D}^{\mathcal{C}}_{\mathrm{EU}}$, *it holds that*

$$Prob^{\mathcal{C}}(s, 0, \Diamond\, at_F) = \sum_{s' \in S} Prob^{\mathcal{C}[F]}(s, 0, \Diamond^{=T_{\mathrm{EU}}}at_{s'}) \cdot Prob^{\mathcal{D}^{\mathcal{C}}_{\mathrm{EU}}[F]}(s', \Diamond\, at_F). \quad (11)$$

Remark 2. We note that the two assumptions, EUA and EPA are *incomparable*. There are rate functions (e.g. polynomials) which can *not* be represented as periodic functions but satisfy EUA; on the other hand, in case of EPA one can, for instance, assign the same sort of rate functions (e.g. sin) with different periods, and thus obtain an ICTMC which invalidates EUA.

4   LTL Model Checking

In this section, we tackle the problem of model checking properties specified by LTL formulae for ICTMCs. Model checking CTMCs against LTL is not very difficult, since one can easily extract the *embedded* DTMC of the given CTMC, and thus reduce the problem to the corresponding model checking problem of DTMCs, which is well-studied, see, e.g. [8]. However, this approach does *not* work for ICTMCs, since the rates of the ICTMC vary with time. Below we shall employ an automata-based approach. For this purpose, some basic definitions are in order.

Definition 6 (Generalized Büchi automata). *A generalized Büchi automaton (GBA) is a tuple* $\mathcal{A} = (\Sigma, Q, \Delta, Q_0, \mathcal{F})$, *where* Σ *is a finite alphabet;* Q *is a finite set of states;* $\Delta \subseteq Q \times \Sigma \times Q$ *is a transition relation;* $Q_0 \subseteq Q$ *is a set of initial states, and* $\mathcal{F} \subseteq 2^Q$ *is a set of acceptance sets.*

We sometimes write $q \xrightarrow{\sigma} q'$ if $(q, \sigma, q') \subseteq \Delta$ for simplicity. An infinite *word* $w \in \Sigma^\omega$ is accepted by $\mathcal{A}$, if there exists an infinite *run* $\theta \in Q^\omega$ such that $\theta[0] \in Q_0$, $(\theta[i], w[i], \theta[i+1]) \subseteq \Delta$ for $i \geqslant 0$ and for each $F \in \mathcal{F}$, there exist infinitely many indices $j \in \mathbb{N}$ such that $\theta[j] \in F$. Note that $w[i]$ (resp. $\theta[i]$) denotes the i-th letter (resp. state) on w (resp. θ). The accepted language of $\mathcal{A}$, denoted $\mathcal{L}(\mathcal{A})$, is the set of all words accepted by $\mathcal{A}$. Given a GBA $\mathcal{A}$ and state q, we denote by $\mathcal{A}[q]$ the automaton $\mathcal{A}$ with q as the unique initial state. Note that $\mathcal{L}(\mathcal{A}) = \bigcup_{q \in Q_0} \mathcal{L}(\mathcal{A}[q])$. A GBA $\mathcal{A}$ is *separated*, if for any two states q, q', $\mathcal{L}(\mathcal{A}[q']) \cap \mathcal{L}(\mathcal{A}[q'']) = \varnothing$.

It follows from [9] that the correspondence between LTL formulae and separated GBA can be established:

Theorem 4. *For any* LTL *formula* φ *over* AP, *there exists a separated GBA* $A_\varphi = (\Sigma, Q, \Delta, Q_0, \mathcal{F})$, *where* $\Sigma = 2^{AP}$ *and* $|Q| \leqslant 2^{\mathcal{O}(|\varphi|)}$, *such that* $\mathcal{L}(A_\varphi)$ *is the set of computations satisfying the formula* φ.

We note that the notion of *separated* is crucial for the remainder of this paper. A closely related notion, referred to as *unambiguous*, has been widely studied in automata and language theory, dating back to [1]. See also, among others, [5][13] for relevant literature. To the best of our knowledge, the notion of "separated" was firstly exploited in [9] for model checking DTMCs against LTL.

Definition 7 (Product). *Given an ICTMC* $\mathcal{C} = (S, \text{AP}, L, \alpha, \mathbf{R}(t))$ *and a separated GBA* $\mathcal{A} = (\Sigma, Q, \Delta, Q_0, \mathcal{F})$, *the product* $\mathcal{C} \otimes \mathcal{A}$ *is defined as*

$$\mathcal{C} \otimes \mathcal{A} = (Loc, \text{AP}, \tilde{L}, \tilde{\alpha}, \tilde{\mathbf{R}}(t)),$$

where $Loc = S \times Q$; $\tilde{L}(\langle s, q \rangle) = L(s)$; $\tilde{\alpha}(\langle s_0, q_0 \rangle) = \alpha(s_0)$ *if* $\alpha(s_0) > 0$ *and* $q_0 \in Q_0$, *and undefined elsewhere; and* $\tilde{\mathbf{R}}_{\langle s, q \rangle, \langle s', q' \rangle}(t) = \mathbf{R}_{s, s'}(t)$ *if* $q \xrightarrow{L(s)} q'$.

For the sake of clarity, we call the states of a product as *locations*.

Example 2. Given ICTMC $\mathcal{C}$ (Fig. 2(a)) and separated GBA $\mathcal{A}$ (Fig. 2(b)), the product $\mathcal{C} \otimes \mathcal{A}$ is shown in Fig. 2(c).

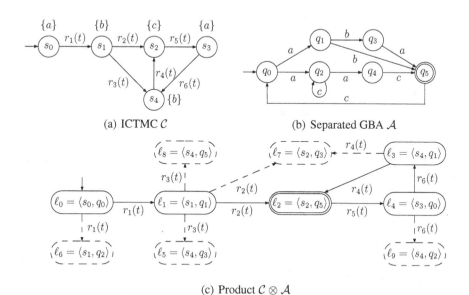

(a) ICTMC $\mathcal{C}$ (b) Separated GBA $\mathcal{A}$

(c) Product $\mathcal{C} \otimes \mathcal{A}$

Fig. 2. Example product construction of ICTMC $\mathcal{C}$ and separated GBA $\mathcal{A}$

Remark 3. Note that in general the product itself is *not* an ICTMC. The reason is two-fold: (1) If $|Q_0| > 1$, then $\tilde{\alpha}$ is *not* a distribution; (2) The sum of the rates of outgoing transitions from a location might exceed the exit rate of the location. For instance, in Example 2, the exit rate of ℓ_0, as defined, is $\tilde{E}_{\ell_0}(t) = E_{s_0}(t) = r_1(t)$; while the sum of the rates of its outgoing transitions is $2r_1(t)$. However, due to the fact that $\mathcal{A}$ is separated, as we will see later, it would not be a problem, cf. Proposition 3.

The generalized Büchi acceptance condition, roughly speaking, requires to visit some states infinitely often. As in the tradition of model checking Markovian models, we need to identify *bottom strongly connected components* (BSCCs) of the product (when read as a graph). A *strongly connected component* (SCC for short) of the product denotes a strongly connected set of locations such that no proper superset is strongly connected. A BSCC is an SCC from which no location outside is reachable. Unfortunately, generally in ICTMCs, there is no way to define a BSCC over the product since the rate of each transition is a *function* of time instead of a constant and thus a BSCC at time t might not be a BSCC at time t'. In other words, the topological structure (edge relation) of the product might change at any moment of time, which is one of the main difficulties of model checking ICTMCs.

To circumvent this problem, we make an (arguably mild) assumption, that is, we assume that ICTMCs are *eventually stable*, in the following sense.

Definition 8 (Eventually stable assumption (ESA)). *An ICTMC $\mathcal{C}$ is eventually stable if for each state $s \in S$, there exists some time T_s such that for any $t \geqslant T_s$ and $s' \in S$, either $\mathbf{R}_{s,s'}(t) > 0$ or $\mathbf{R}_{s,s'}(t) = 0$.*

W.l.o.g., we assume T_s is the smallest time point that the above assumption holds for state s. Let $T_{\mathrm{ES}} = \max_{s \in S} T_s$ be the smallest time point that an ICTMC is *stable*. Intuitively, an ICTMC is stable if its topological structure does *not* change any more. More specifically, transitions can alter their rates, but not from positive to zero or vice versa, i.e., no transitions will "disappear" or "newly created". An example rate function is illustrated in Fig. 1 (right), where after T_{ES} the rates keep strictly positive (note the particular value is irrelevant here). It turns out that ESA is essential for identifying stable BSCCs (also model checking LTL). A *stable* product as well as *stable* BSCC are defined in the same way, relative to the time point T_{ES}. *In the sequel, when we refer to BSCCs, we implicitly refer to the stable BSCCs in the stable product.* In accordance with this, we will sometimes write $s \mapsto s'$ for ICTMC $\mathcal{C}$ if $\mathbf{R}_{s,s'}(t) > 0$ with $t \geqslant T_{\mathrm{ES}}$; and similarly for $\ell \mapsto \ell'$ in the product.

Definition 9 (aBSCC). *Given the product $\mathcal{C} \otimes \mathcal{A}$ of an ICTMC $\mathcal{C} = (S, \mathrm{AP}, L, \alpha, \mathbf{R}(t))$ satisfying ESA and a GBA $\mathcal{A} = (\Sigma, Q, \Delta, Q_0, \mathcal{F})$, we define*

I. *a SCC is a set of locations $B \subseteq S \times Q$ such that (i) B is strongly connected meaning that for any two locations $\ell, \ell' \in B$, $\ell \mapsto^* \ell'$ where $\mapsto^*$ denotes the reflexive and transitive closure of $\mapsto$, and (ii) no proper superset of B is strongly connected;*

II. *a SCC B is accepting if $\forall F \in \mathcal{F}$, there exists some $\langle s, q \rangle \in B$ such that $q \in F$;*

III. *a SCC B is an accepting bottom SCC ($B \in$ aBSCC for short) if (i) B is accepting; (ii) for each location $\ell \in B$, there does not exist any location ℓ' such that*

$\ell \mapsto \ell'$ and ℓ' is in any other accepting SCC; (iii) for each location $\ell = \langle s, q \rangle \in B$, for any s' with $s \mapsto s'$, $\langle s', q' \rangle \in B$ for some q'.

As an example, we note, suppose that $r_4(t), r_5(t), r_6(t) > 0$ when $t \geqslant T_{\mathrm{ES}}$, that an accepting BSCC in the stable product in Fig. 2(c) is formed by ℓ_2, ℓ_3, ℓ_4. Note that $\{\ell_7\}$ is *not* an (accepting) SCC, so III(ii) is not violated. $\{\ell_8\}$ is not an SCC either, since we would require that $\ell_8 \mapsto^* \ell_8$ which fails to be.

Recall that given an LTL formula, one can obtain a corresponding *separated* automaton, which renders us very nice properties for the product defined in Definition 7. A couple of lemmas, dedicated to illustrate these properties are in order. The following two essentially exploit the fact that for each accepted word of a separated GBA, there is a unique accepting path.

Lemma 1. *Given the product* $C \otimes A$ *where* A *is separated. For any aBSCC* B *of the stable product* $C \otimes A$, *it cannot be the case that* $\langle s, q \rangle \mapsto \langle s', q' \rangle$ *and* $\langle s, q \rangle \mapsto \langle s', q'' \rangle$ *for any* $\langle s, q \rangle, \langle s', q' \rangle, \langle s', q'' \rangle$ *in* B *with* $q' \neq q''$.

We say that two locations $\langle s, q \rangle$ and $\langle s', q' \rangle$ in the product $C \otimes A$ are *connected*, if $q \xrightarrow{L(s)} q'^2$. We say that from location $\langle s, q \rangle$ there is a path leading to a BSCC B, if there is a sequence $\langle s_0, q_0 \rangle, \langle s_1, q_1 \rangle, \ldots, \langle s_n, q_n \rangle$ such that $\langle s, q \rangle = \langle s_0, q_0 \rangle$, $\langle s_i, q_i \rangle$ and $\langle s_{i+1}, q_{i+1} \rangle$ are connected for $0 \leqslant i < n$ and $\langle s_n, q_n \rangle \in B$.

Lemma 2. *Given the product* $C \otimes A$ *of an ICTMC* C *and a separated GBA* A, *it cannot be the case that there are two locations* $\langle s, q \rangle$ *and* $\langle s, q' \rangle$ *with* $q \neq q'$ *such that both of them have a path reaching an aBSCC.*

As said, given ICTMC C and separated GBA A, the product $C \otimes A$ itself is not an ICTMC (see Example 2). However, thanks to the fact that A is separated, we can transform $C \otimes A$ into an ICTMC. Lemma 1 and 2 entail that in the product $C \otimes A$, we can safely remove the locations which do not lead to an accepting BSCC, and thus obtain an ICTMC model, denoted $C\underline{\otimes}A$. Let us illustrate this by continuing Example 2. First note that the dashed locations are the trap locations from which the accepted location ℓ_2 cannot be reached. Those locations can safely be removed since the paths passing them will never be accepted. It is not a coincidence that at most one of the outgoing transitions from those "nondeterministic" locations (i.e., $\ell_0, \ell_1, \ell_3, \ell_4$) can reach the accepted locations. This is guaranteed by the separated property of the automaton (Lemma 2). By deleting all the dashed locations, we obtain $C\underline{\otimes}A$.

The following proposition claims that $C\underline{\otimes}A$ can be viewed as an ICTMC in the sense that it defines a stochastic process exactly as an ICTMC. The crucial point is that in $C\underline{\otimes}A$, for each location ℓ and time t, the sum of the rates of the emanating transitions from ℓ does *not* exceed the exit rate of ℓ. (Note that the sum could be strictly less than the exit rate as for ℓ_1 in Fig. 2(c), thus it is "substochastic".) With a little abusing of terms, we call this model an ICTMC.

Proposition 3. $C\underline{\otimes}A$ *is an ICTMC. Moreover, for each accepting cylinder set,* C *and* $C\underline{\otimes}A$ *give rise to the same probability.*

---

[2] Note that we do *not* require that $s \mapsto s'$. So "connected" is purely a graph-theoretic notion where the time is irrelevant.

Let $\mathcal{C} \otimes \mathcal{A}^{\star}$ be obtained from $\mathcal{C} \otimes \mathcal{A}$ by making each location in the aBSCCs absorbing, and define $F^{\star}$ as the set of locations in any aBSCC. Given an ICTMC $\mathcal{C}$ with eventually stable assumption (with T_{ES}) and an LTL formula φ, the probability of the set of paths of $\mathcal{C}$ satisfying φ, denoted $Prob_{\mathrm{ES}}^{\mathcal{C}}(\varphi)$, can be computed by Alg. 2.

Theorem 5. *For an* ICTMC $\mathcal{C}$ *with* T_{ES} *and an* LTL *formula* φ,

$$Prob_{\mathrm{ES}}^{\mathcal{C}}(\varphi) = \sum_{\tilde{\alpha}(\ell_0)>0} \sum_{\ell \in Loc} \tilde{\alpha}(\ell_0) \cdot Prob^{\mathcal{C}\otimes\mathcal{A}}(\ell_0, 0, \Diamond^{=T_{\mathrm{ES}}} at_{\ell}) \cdot Prob^{\mathcal{C}\otimes\mathcal{A}^{\star}}(\ell, T_{\mathrm{ES}}, \Diamond \, at_{F^{\star}}).$$

Algorithm 2. Model checking ICTMC against LTL

Require: ICTMC $\mathcal{C}$, LTL formula φ, ESA time T_{ES};
Ensure: $Prob_{\mathrm{ES}}^{\mathcal{C}}(\varphi)$
1: Transform φ to a separated generalized Büchi automaton $\mathcal{A}$;
2: Build the product $\mathcal{C} \otimes \mathcal{A} = (Loc, AP, \tilde{L}, \tilde{\alpha}, \tilde{\mathbf{R}}(t))$;
3: Find all *accepting* BSCCs in the (stable) product $\mathcal{C} \otimes \mathcal{A}$;
4: Remove all the trap locations yielding $\mathcal{C} \otimes \mathcal{A}$;
5: Compute the *time-bounded reachability* in $\mathcal{C} \otimes \mathcal{A}$ from initial location ℓ_0 to each $\ell \in Loc$, $Prob^{\mathcal{C}\otimes\mathcal{A}}(\ell_0, 0, \Diamond^{=T_{\mathrm{ES}}} at_{\ell})$;
6: Make each location in the aBSCCs absorbing, thus obtaining $\mathcal{C} \otimes \mathcal{A}^{\star}$ and $F^{\star}$;
7: Compute the *time-unbounded reachability probability* in $\mathcal{C} \otimes \mathcal{A}^{\star}$ from each $\ell \in Loc$ to $F^{\star}$, i.e., $Prob^{\mathcal{C}\otimes\mathcal{A}^{\star}}(\ell, T_{\mathrm{ES}}, \Diamond \, at_{F^{\star}})$;
8: $Prob_{\mathrm{ES}}^{\mathcal{C}}(\varphi) = \sum_{\tilde{\alpha}(\ell_0)>0} \sum_{\ell \in Loc} \tilde{\alpha}(\ell_0) \cdot Prob^{\mathcal{C}\otimes\mathcal{A}}(\ell_0, 0, \Diamond^{=T_{\mathrm{ES}}} at_{\ell}) \cdot Prob^{\mathcal{C}\otimes\mathcal{A}^{\star}}(\ell, T_{\mathrm{ES}}, \Diamond \, at_{F^{\star}})$.

Note that $Prob^{\mathcal{C}\otimes\mathcal{A}}(\ell_0, 0, \Diamond^{=T_{\mathrm{ES}}} at_{\ell})$ and $Prob^{\mathcal{C}\otimes\mathcal{A}^{\star}}(\ell, 0, \Diamond \, at_{\ell_{F^{\star}}})$ can be computed by the approaches in Section 3.1 and 3.2, respectively. Computing the former relies on solving a system of ODEs, whereas computing the latter, as stated in Section 3.2, one has to solve a system of integral equations in general.

Remark 4 (EPA, EUA and ESA). EPA and ESA are *incomparable*, i.e., there are ICTMCs that are eventually periodic but not stable (see e.g., the ICTMC with one rate function in Fig. 1 (left)), and vice versa (see, e.g., that in Fig. 1 (right)). When both assumptions are applied, we obtain ICTMCs that are "eventually positive periodic", i.e., eventually periodic and all rate function values in the periods are either strictly positive or being zero. For this subset of ICTMCs, one can resort to solving a system of ODEs and linear equations, as presented in Theorem 2 as well as Alg. 1.

EUA and ESA are *incomparable* as well. The counterexamples for both directions can be easily constructed. When both assumptions are applied, as in the previous case, the subset of ICTMCs (where $f(t)$ is eventually strictly positive) can be dealt with by solving a systems of ODEs and linear equations (Theorem 3).

The comparison of EPA and EUA can be found in Remark 2. We emphasize once again that ESA is of most importance in LTL model checking, in order to find stable BSCCs. However EPA or EUA are certain subsets of ICTMCs that we can efficiently deal with (meaning by solving a system of ODEs and linear equations). We mention that there are other approaches which can handle and solve the system of integral equations, e.g., approximation by truncating the infinite range of the integral.

Example 3. We continue Example 2 to show how to compute the set of paths of ICTMC $\mathcal{C}$ accepted by $\mathcal{A}$. Let the rate functions be defined as: $r_i(t) = i$ for $t \geqslant 0$ and $3 \leqslant i \leqslant 6$; and

$$r_1(t) = \begin{cases} t & x \in [0, 9.5) \\ 0 & x \in [9.5, 10) \\ 2 + \cos(\frac{1}{2}t) & x \in [10, \infty) \end{cases} \qquad r_2(t) = \begin{cases} 4.1 & x \in [0, 15) \\ 7.6 - \sin(\frac{1}{3}t) & x \in [15, \infty) \end{cases}$$

It is not difficult to see that this ICTMC satisfies both the ESA and EPA and $T_{ES} = 10$, $T_{EP} = 15$ and $P_{EP} = 12\pi$.

To compute $Prob_{ES}^{\mathcal{C}}(\mathcal{A})$, Alg. 2 is applied. Note that we omit the step of transforming an LTL formula to a GBA and the notation $Prob_{ES}^{\mathcal{C}}(\mathcal{A})$ is self-explanatory. We consider the first *Prob* appearing in step 8, namely, to compute $Prob^{\mathcal{C} \otimes \mathcal{A}}(\ell_0, 0, \Diamond^{=10} at_\ell)$ for all ℓ in $\mathcal{C} \otimes \mathcal{A}$. This is actually to compute the transient probability vector in $\mathcal{C} \otimes \mathcal{A}$ at time $T_{ES} = 10$, which can be done by solving a system of ODEs. We then consider the second *Prob* appearing in step 8, namely, to compute $Prob^{\mathcal{C} \otimes \mathcal{A}^*}(\ell, 10, \Diamond at_{\ell_2})$ (note that $F^* = \{\ell_2\}$). Finally, we wrap them up as follows:

$$Prob_{ES}^{\mathcal{C}}(\mathcal{A}) \overset{\Sigma}{=} \begin{cases} Prob^{\mathcal{C} \otimes \mathcal{A}}(\ell_0, 0, \Diamond^{=10} at_{\ell_0}) \cdot Prob^{\mathcal{C} \otimes \mathcal{A}^*}(\ell_0, 10, \Diamond at_{\ell_2}) \\ Prob^{\mathcal{C} \otimes \mathcal{A}}(\ell_0, 0, \Diamond^{=10} at_{\ell_1}) \cdot Prob^{\mathcal{C} \otimes \mathcal{A}^*}(\ell_1, 10, \Diamond at_{\ell_2}) \\ Prob^{\mathcal{C} \otimes \mathcal{A}}(\ell_0, 0, \Diamond^{=10} at_{\ell_2}) \cdot 1 \\ Prob^{\mathcal{C} \otimes \mathcal{A}}(\ell_0, 0, \Diamond^{=10} at_{\ell_3}) \cdot 1 \\ Prob^{\mathcal{C} \otimes \mathcal{A}}(\ell_0, 0, \Diamond^{=10} at_{\ell_4}) \cdot 1 \end{cases} \tag{12}$$

The left column of (12) is the transient probability vector; we then show how to compute the elements in the right column. For this purpose, generally we have to solve a system of integral equations. Here we obtain the following one:

$$\begin{cases} f_{\ell_0}(x) = \int_0^\infty r_1(x + \tau)e^{-\int_0^\tau r_1(x+v)dv} \cdot f_{\ell_1}(x + \tau)d\tau \\ f_{\ell_1}(x) = \int_0^\infty r_2(x + \tau)e^{-\int_0^\tau r_2(x+v)+r_3(x+v)dv} \cdot f_{\ell_2}(x + \tau)d\tau \\ f_{\ell_2}(x) = 1 \end{cases}$$

In this case, one obtains that $f_{\ell_2}(x) = 1$,

$$f_{\ell_1}(10) = \int_{10}^{15} 4.1 e^{-\int_{10}^\tau (4.1+3)dv} d\tau + \int_{15}^\infty (7.6 - \sin(\frac{1}{3}\tau)) \cdot e^{-\int_{10}^{15}(4.1+3)dv - \int_{15}^\tau (7.6-\sin(\frac{1}{3}(x+v))+3)dv} d\tau \ .$$

and $f_{\ell_0}(10)$ can be computed accordingly. It follows that $Prob^{\mathcal{C} \otimes \mathcal{A}^*}(\ell_0, 10, \Diamond at_{\ell_2}) = f_{\ell_0}(10)$ and $Prob^{\mathcal{C} \otimes \mathcal{A}^*}(\ell_1, 10, \Diamond at_{\ell_2}) = f_{\ell_1}(10)$. Hence (12) can be obtained.

Alternatively, let us note that fortunately in this case, the EPA is satisfied. So one can apply Alg. 1 to compute $Prob^{\mathcal{C} \otimes \mathcal{A}^*}(\ell, 10, \Diamond at_{\ell_2})$. Let us illustrate for the case that $\ell = \ell_0$. (The case that $\ell = \ell_1$ is similar.) For the first *Prob* in Alg. 1, step 4, it is again to compute the transient probability matrix $Prob^{\mathcal{C} \otimes \mathcal{A}^*}(\ell, 10, \Diamond^{=15-10} at_{\ell'})$, for $\ell, \ell' \in \{\ell_i \mid 1 \leqslant i \leqslant 4\}$ (note that ℓ_2 is already made absorbing in $\mathcal{C} \otimes \mathcal{A}^*$); and for the second *Prob*, we need to construct the DTMC $\mathcal{D}$ with $\mathbf{P}_{\ell, \ell'} = Prob^{\mathcal{C} \otimes \mathcal{A}^*}(\ell, 15, \Diamond^{=12\pi} at_{\ell'})$. It follows that

$$Prob_{EP}^{\mathcal{C} \otimes \mathcal{A}^*}(\ell_0, 10, \Diamond at_{\ell_2}) \overset{\Sigma}{=} \begin{cases} Prob^{\mathcal{C} \otimes \mathcal{A}^*}(\ell_0, 10, \Diamond^{=15-10} at_{\ell_0}) \cdot Prob^{\mathcal{D}}(\ell_0, \Diamond at_{\ell_2}) \\ Prob^{\mathcal{C} \otimes \mathcal{A}^*}(\ell_0, 10, \Diamond^{=15-10} at_{\ell_1}) \cdot Prob^{\mathcal{D}}(\ell_1, \Diamond at_{\ell_2}) \\ Prob^{\mathcal{C} \otimes \mathcal{A}^*}(\ell_0, 10, \Diamond^{=15-10} at_{\ell_2}) \cdot 1 \end{cases}$$

The **P** matrix of the DTMC $\mathcal{D}$ is as follows (let Θ denote $\mathcal{C} \underline{\otimes} \mathcal{A}^\star$):

$$\mathbf{P} = \begin{pmatrix} Prob^\Theta(\ell_0, 15, \Diamond^{=12\pi} \, at_{\ell_0}) & Prob^\Theta(\ell_0, 15, \Diamond^{=12\pi} \, at_{\ell_1}) & Prob^\Theta(\ell_0, 15, \Diamond^{=12\pi} \, at_{\ell_2}) \\ 0 & Prob^\Theta(\ell_1, 15, \Diamond^{=12\pi} \, at_{\ell_1}) & Prob^\Theta(\ell_1, 15, \Diamond^{=12\pi} \, at_{\ell_2}) \\ 0 & 0 & 1 \end{pmatrix}.$$

Hence $Prob_{\mathrm{EP}}^{\mathcal{C} \underline{\otimes} \mathcal{A}^\star}(\ell_0, 10, \Diamond \, at_{\ell_2})$ can be easily computed.

5   Conclusion

We have studied the problem of verifying linear-time properties against ICTMCs. Two variants of reachability problems, i.e. time-bounded and unbounded reachability, as well as LTL properties were considered. Future work consists of identifying more classes of ICTMCs for which efficient computational methods exist such that the approach studied in this paper can be applied. Other specifications like (D)TA, M(I)TL, will also be investigated.

References

1. Arnold, A.: Rational omega-languages are non-ambiguous. Theor. Comput. Sci. 26, 221–223 (1983)
2. Aziz, A., Sanwal, K., Singhal, V., Brayton, R.K.: Model-checking continous-time Markov chains. ACM Trans. Comput. Log. 1(1), 162–170 (2000)
3. Baier, C., Haverkort, B.R., Hermanns, H., Katoen, J.-P.: Model-checking algorithms for continuous-time Markov chains. IEEE Trans. Software Eng. 29(6), 524–541 (2003)
4. Baier, C., Katoen, J.-P.: Principles of Model Checking. MIT Press, Cambridge (2008)
5. Carton, O., Michel, M.: Unambiguous Büchi automata. Theor. Comput. Sci. 297(1-3), 37–81 (2003)
6. Chen, T., Han, T., Katoen, J.-P., Mereacre, A.: Quantitative model checking of continuous-time Markov chains against timed automata specification. In: LICS (to appear, 2009)
7. Cloth, L., Jongerden, M.R., Haverkort, B.R.: Computing battery lifetime distributions. In: DSN, pp. 780–789 (2007)
8. Courcoubetis, C., Yannakakis, M.: The complexity of probabilistic verification. J. ACM 42(4), 857–907 (1995)
9. Couvreur, J.-M., Saheb, N., Sutre, G.: An optimal automata approach to LTL model checking of probabilistic systems. In: Y. Vardi, M., Voronkov, A. (eds.) LPAR 2003. LNCS, vol. 2850, pp. 361–375. Springer, Heidelberg (2003)
10. Gokhale, S.S., Lyu, M.R., Trivedi, K.S.: Analysis of software fault removal policies using a non-homogeneous continuous time Markov chain. Software Quality Control 12(3), 211–230 (2004)
11. Hansson, H., Jonsson, B.: A logic for reasoning about time and reliability. Formal Asp. Comput. 6(5), 512–535 (1994)
12. Hinton, A., Kwiatkowska, M.Z., Norman, G., Parker, D.: Prism: A tool for automatic verification of probabilistic systems. In: Hermanns, H., Palsberg, J. (eds.) TACAS 2006. LNCS, vol. 3920, pp. 441–444. Springer, Heidelberg (2006)
13. Kähler, D., Wilke, T.: Complementation, disambiguation, and determinization of Büchi automata unified. In: Aceto, L., Damgård, I., Goldberg, L.A., Halldórsson, M.M., Ingólfsdóttir, A., Walukiewicz, I. (eds.) ICALP 2008, Part I. LNCS, vol. 5125, pp. 724–735. Springer, Heidelberg (2008)

14. Katoen, J.-P., Khattri, M., Zapreev, I.S.: A Markov reward model checker. In: QEST, pp. 243–244 (2005)
15. Katoen, J.-P., Mereacre, A.: Model checking HML on piecewise-constant inhomogeneous markov chains. In: Cassez, F., Jard, C. (eds.) FORMATS 2008. LNCS, vol. 5215, pp. 203–217. Springer, Heidelberg (2008)
16. Lambert, J.D.: Numerical Methods for Ordinary Differential Systems. John Wiley & Sons, Chichester (1991)
17. Rindos, A., Woolet, S.P., Viniotis, Y., Trivedi, K.S.: Exact methods for the transient analysis of non-homogeneous continuous-time Markov chains. In: Numerical Solution of Markov Chains (NSMC), pp. 121–134 (1995)

Statistical Model Checking Using Perfect Simulation*

Diana El Rabih and Nihal Pekergin

LACL, University of Paris-Est (Paris 12),
61 avenue Général de Gaulle 94010, Créteil, France
delrabih@univ-paris12.fr, nihal.pekergin@univ-paris12.fr

Abstract. We propose to perform statistical probabilistic model checking by using perfect simulation in order to verify steady-state and time unbounded until formulas over Markov chains. The model checking of probabilistic models by statistical methods has received increased attention in the last years since it provides an interesting alternative to numerical model checking which is poorly scalable with the increasing model size. In previous statistical model checking works, unbounded until formulas could not be efficiently verified, and steady-state formulas had not been considered due to the burn-in time problem to detect the steady-state. Perfect simulation is an extension of Markov Chain Monte Carlo (MCMC) methods that allows us to obtain exact steady-state samples of the underlying Markov chain, and thus it avoids the burn-in time problem to detect the steady-state. Therefore we suggest to verify time unbounded until and steady-state dependability properties for large Markov chains through statistical model checking by combining perfect simulation and statistical hypothesis testing.

1 Introduction

Probabilistic model checking is an extension of formal verification methods for systems exhibiting stochastic behavior. The system model is usually specified as a state transition system, with probabilities attached to transitions, for example Markov chains. From this model, a wide range of quantitative performance, reliability, and dependability measures of the original system can be computed. These measures can be specified using temporal logics as PCTL [5] for Discrete Time Markov Chains (DTMC) and CSL [2,3] for Continuous Time Markov Chains (CTMC). Most of the high level formalisms assume a CTMC as the underlying stochastic process. To perform probabilistic model checking there are two distinct approaches : numerical approach based on computation of transient-state or steady-state distribution of the underlying Markov chain and statistical approach based on hypothesis testing and on sampling by means of discrete event simulation or by measurement. The numerical approach is highly accurate but it suffers from the state space explosion problem. The statistical

---

* This work is supported by a french research project, ANR-06-SETI-002.

approach overcomes this problem but it does not guarantee that the verification result is correct. However it is possible to bound the probability of generating an incorrect answer so it provides probabilistic guarantees of correctness. Hence statistical model checking techniques constitute an interesting alternative to numerical techniques for large scale systems. A comparison of numerical and statistical approaches for probabilistic model checking has been done in [16]. Statistical approaches for model checking have received increasing attention in the last years [15,18,9,16,17]. Younes et al. have proposed a statistical approach based on hypothesis testing and discrete event simulation but with a focus on time bounded until formulas [15,18]. In [9] Sen et al. have proposed a statistical approach also based on hypothesis testing and discrete event simulation for verifying time unbounded until properties by introducing a stopping probability, p_s, which is the probability of terminating the generation of a trajectory after each state transition. This stopping probability must be extremely small to give correctness guarantees and the accuracy of their verification result would depend on the state space size, making the approach impractical, except for models with small state spaces. In fact, the steady-state formula was not studied before in any existing statistical approach and the unbounded until formula can not be checked efficiently by the existing approach [9] because of the steady-state detection problem (stopping probability problem). Thus we have proposed in [1] a novel approach to perform statistical model checking by combining perfect simulation and statistical hypothesis testing in order to check steady-state formulas and we have shown some preliminary results. Perfect simulation is an extension of MCMC methods allowing us to obtain exact steady-state samples of the underlying Markov chain and avoiding the burn-in time problem to detect the steady-state. Propp and Wilson have designed the algorithm of coupling from the past to perform perfect simulation [8]. A web page dedicated to this method is maintained by them (http://research.microsoft.com/en-us/um/people/dbwilson/exact/). As a perfect sampler, we use ψ^2 proposed in [12,10], designed for the steady-state evaluation of various monotone queueing networks (http://psi.gforge.inria.fr/website/Psi2-Unix-Website/). This tool permits to simulate a stationary distribution or directly a cost function or a reward of large Markov chains. An extension of this tool is proposed in [14] to study non monotone queueing networks.

In this paper, we extend our approach proposed in [1] by applying more efficient statistical hypothesis testing methods. Another extension is to design an algorithm to generate samples for the verification of time unbounded until formulas. Moreover, we integrate our proposed approach to the perfect sampler Ψ^2 [12], to be able to model check large performability and dependability models. Note that, the proposed approach is applicable both to monotone and to non-monotone systems, thus it allows us to generate samples for time unbounded until and steady-state formulas to perform statistical model checking. Moreover this approach is exteremely efficient for monotone systems and lets us overcome the state-space explosion problem. As application of our approach, we verify steady-state and time unbounded until dependability properties for a multistage interconnection queueing network illustrating its efficiency when considering very large models.

The rest of this paper is organised as follows: In section 2, we present some preliminaries on considered temporal logics CSL and PCTL and on the concept of statistical hypothesis testing. Section 3 is devoted to the perfect simulation. In section 4, we present our contribution for statistical probabilistic model checking using perfect simulation as well as the applicability and complexity of our proposed method. Section 5 presents the case study with experimental results. Finally, we conclude and present our future works in section 6.

2   Preliminaries

2.1   Temporal Logics for Markov Chains

In this subsection we give a brief introduction for the considered temporal logics operators. We consider essentially the until formulas for verification over execution paths and the steady-state operator for long run behaviours of the underlying model. The stochastic behaviour of the underlying system is described by a labelled Markov chain, $\mathcal{M}$, which may be in discrete or continuous time. These operators are defined in CSL defined over CTMCs [2,3] and in PCTL defined over DTMCs [5].

Let $\mathcal{M}$ take values in a finite set of states S, AP denote the finite set of atomic propositions. $L : S \rightarrow 2^{AP}$ is the labeling function which assigns to each state $s \in S$ the set $L(s)$ of atomic propositions $a \in AP$ those are valid in s. Let p be a probability, I a time interval, and $\bowtie$ a comparison operator: $\bowtie \in \{<, >, \leq, \geq\}$. The syntax is given as follows:

$$\varphi ::= true \mid a \mid \varphi \wedge \varphi \mid \neg \varphi \mid \mathcal{P}_{\bowtie \theta}(\varphi_1 \, \mathcal{U}^I \varphi_2) \mid \mathcal{P}_{\bowtie \theta}(\varphi_1 \, \mathcal{U} \varphi_2) \mid \mathcal{S}_{\bowtie \theta}(\varphi)$$

The satisfaction operator is denoted by $\models$, then for all states $s \in S$, $s \models true$. Atomic proposition a is satisfied by state s ($s \models a$) iff $a \in L(s)$. The logic operators are obtained using standard logic equivalence rules : $s \models \neg \varphi$ iff $s \not\models \varphi$, $s \models \varphi_1 \wedge \varphi_2$ iff $s \models \varphi_1 \wedge s \models \varphi_2$. Until formulas are evaluated over the paths initiated from a given initial state s. A state s satisfies $\mathcal{P}_{\bowtie \theta}(\varphi_1 \, \mathcal{U}^I \varphi_2)$, iff the sum of probability measures over paths starting from s, passing through only states satisfying φ_1 and reaching to a state satisfying φ_2 in time interval I meets the bound θ. The until formula without time interval is the time unbounded until formula which means that $I \in [0, \infty[$. The steady-state operator $\mathcal{S}_{\bowtie \theta}(\varphi)$ lets us to analyze the long-run behaviour of the system. If the sum of steady-state probabilities of states satisfying φ meets θ, this operator is satisfied. If $\mathcal{M}$ is ergodic, the steady-state distribution is independent of the initial state, then this formula is satisfied or not regardless of the initial state.

2.2   Statistical Hypothesis Testing

The probabilistic model checking consists in deciding whether the probability that the considered system satisfies the underlying property φ meets a given threshold

θ or not. Without loss of generality, we consider the case $\mathcal{P}_{\geq\theta}(\varphi)$ where φ is a path formula. Obviously, this is equivalent to verify $\neg\mathcal{P}_{<\theta}(\varphi)$. We can also consider the case $\mathcal{S}_{\geq\theta}(\varphi)$ where φ is a state formula. Obviously, this is equivalent to verify $\neg\mathcal{S}_{<\theta}(\varphi)$ and $\mathcal{S}_{\leq 1-\theta}(\neg\varphi)$. Let p be the probability that the system satisfies φ, then this verification problem $\mathcal{P}_{\geq\theta}(\varphi)$ (resp. $\mathcal{S}_{\geq\theta}(\varphi)$) can be formulated as an hypothesis testing: $H : p \geq \theta$ against the alternative hypothesis $K : p < \theta$. For solving statistical hypothesis testing problems it is not possible to guarantee a correct result but the probability to accept a false hypothesis can be bounded. The strength of the statistical test was determined by two parameters, α and β, where α is a bound on the probability of accepting K when H holds (known as a type I error, or false negative) and β is a bound on the probability of accepting H when K holds (a type II error, or false positive), where $\alpha + \beta \leq 1$. Thus the probability of accepting H can be determined for an hypothesis testing with ideal performance in the sense that the probability of a type I error is exactly α and the probability of a type II error is exactly β. The above formulation is problematic since it is impossible to control two probability errors independently. These conditions are relaxed by introducing an indifference region $]p_1, p_0[$ of width 2δ, where $p_0 = \theta + \delta$ and $p_1 = \theta - \delta$. Then, instead of testing $H : p \geq \theta$ against $K : p < \theta$, we test $H_0 : p \geq p_0$ against $H_1 : p \leq p_1$. The probability of accepting H is therefore at least $1 - \alpha$ if $p \geq \theta + \delta$ and at most β if $p \leq \theta - \delta$. For the indifference region $| p - \theta |< \delta$, the test gives no bound on the probability of accepting false hypothesis, thus we are indifferent whether H or K is accepted. Suppose that we have generated n samples (simulations), and a sample X_i is a positive sample ($X_i = 1$) if it satisfies φ and negative ($X_i = 0$) otherwise. X_i is a random variable with Bernoulli distribution with parameter p. Thus the probability to obtain a positive sample is p. There are mainly two methods for statistical hypothesis testing decision with constraints on error bounds [15,18,17]:

Single Sampling Plan (SSP). It is based on the acceptance sampling with fixed sample size and with a given acceptance strength (α, β). If $\sum_{i=1}^{n} X_i > m$, then H_0 is accepted otherwise H_1 is accepted, where m is the acceptance threshold. The hypothesis H_1 will be accepted with probability $F(m, n, p)$ and the null hypothesis H_0 will be accepted with the probability $1 - F(m, n, p)$, where $F(m, n, p)$ is a binomial distribution of $Y = \sum_{i=1}^{n} X_i : F(m, n, p) = Pr(Y \leq m) = \sum_{i=1}^{m} C(n, i)p^i(1 - p)^{n-i}$ with $C(n, i)$ is the combination of i from n. It is required that the probability of accepting H_1 when H_0 holds is at most α, and the probability of accepting H_0 when H_1 holds is at most β. These constraints can be illustrated as below:

- $\Pr[H_1$ is accepted $\mid H_0$ is true$] \leq \alpha$ which implies $F(m, n, p_0) \leq \alpha$ (C1)
- $\Pr[H_0$ is accepted $\mid H_1$ is true$] \leq \beta$ which implies $1 - F(m, n, p_1) \leq \beta$ (C2)

The sample size n and the acceptance threshold m must be chosen under these constraints and for optimal performance n must be minimised. The approximations formulas of n and m to optimise performance are given in [17,18].

Sequential Probability Ratio Test (SPRT). It is based on the sequential probability ratio test in which observations are taken into account in a sequential manner [18,17]. After making the ith simulation (generating the ith sample), one computes the following quotient:

$$q_i = \prod_{j=1}^{i} \frac{Pr[X_j = x_j \mid p = p_1]}{Pr[X_j = x_j \mid p = p_0]} = \frac{p_1^{d_i}(1-p_1)^{i-d_i}}{p_0^{d_i}(1-p_0)^{i-d_i}}$$

where $d_i = \sum_{j=1}^{i} X_j$ denoting the number of positive samples. H_0 is accepted if $q_i \leq B$, and H_1 is accepted if $q_i \geq A$. Finding A and B with a given strength (α, β) is non trivial, in practice A is chosen as $(1-\beta)/\alpha$ and B as $\beta/(1-\alpha)$. Then a new test whose strength is (α^*, β^*) is obtained, but such that $\alpha^* + \beta^* \leq \alpha + \beta$, meaning that either $\alpha^* \leq \alpha$ or $\beta^* \leq \beta$. In practice, it is often found that both inequalities hold.

The advantage of hypothesis testing over other statistical decision methods was demonstrated numerically in [17]. Note, also, that the SPRT method often can be used to improve efficiency for the approach based on hypothesis testing. In fact, if single sampling plan (SSP) method is used with strength (α, β) and indifference region of half-width δ, then the sample size n is roughly proportional to $\log \alpha$ and $\log \beta$ and inversely proportional to δ^2 [18]. Using the SPRT method instead of single sampling plan method can reduce the expected sample size by orders of magnitude in most cases, although the SPRT method is not guaranteed always to be more efficient.

3   Perfect Simulation

Let $\{X_i, i \geq 0\}$ be a time-homogeneous DTMC taking values in a finite set S. The dynamic of the chain can be defined by the following stochastic recursive function:

$$X_{n+1} = \eta(X_n, E_n) \tag{1}$$

where η is the system transition function, X_n is the nth observed state of the system, and $\{E_n\}$ an innovation process, $n \in N$. Clearly, if $\{E_n\}$ are independent and identically distributed then the stochastic process $\{X_i, i \geq 0\}$ defined by an initial value X_0 and recursive equations of Eq. 1 is a Markov chain [10]. In the sequel, we consider the notations of discrete event systems (the system is governed by a set of events) thus E_is in Eq. 1 are events $e \in \Sigma$ (Σ is the set of events). Conversely, given a transition probability matrix $\mathbf{P} = (p_{i,j})$, it is possible to find a function η such that Markov chain given by Eq. 1 has $\mathbf{P}$ as transition matrix: $p_{i,j} = \sum_{E_k \mid \eta(i, E_k) = j} \mathcal{P}(E_k)$. A natural way to construct the transition function η is to consider the inverse of the probability distribution function. Let us remark that this characterization is suitable for discrete event simulation. Practically, the sequence $\{E_i\}$ can be generated by a standard *random function* of programming languages which is uniformly distributed in the interval $[0, 1]$. Sample paths (trajectories) initiated from all possible initial values are generated with the same sequence of random numbers (events) by considering Eq. 1. If two sample paths reach to the same state, we say that they couple and then their trajectories will be the same. If the sample paths are generated beginning at time t=0 and evolving in the future $t = 1, 2, \ldots$ then it is called coupling in the future (forward coupling). It has been shown that if samples (observations) are constituted from states where all paths initiated at time 0 from all possible initial values are coupled, then this set of samples is not distributed according to the steady-state distribution [8]. Propp and Wilson [8] have ingeniously overcome this problem by reversing the time (by coming from the past to the present). In their algorithm called coupling from the past (backward coupling), they have shown that when trajectories start at time $-\infty$ and generated by coupling in the future, if all trajectories are coupled at time 0, it means that the steady-state behaviour has occured independently from initial states. Thus samples according to the steady-state distribution (if it exists) can be generated. We do not give here mathematical background but only present an intuitive sketch of proof to be able to explain its application for the verification of path formulas. In the case E_i are independently and identically distributed random variables, the evolution in n steps from time 0 to n or from time $-n$ to 0 are stochastically equivalent (they have the same distribution).

$$\eta(\cdots \eta(\eta(s_0, E_0), E_1), \cdots), E_{n-1}) =_{st} \eta(\cdots \eta(\eta(s_0, E_{-n+1}), E_{-n+2}), \cdots), E_0) \tag{2}$$

Let us suppose that all the trajectories initiated at time $-\tau$ from all initial values are coupled at time 0. Even if these trajectories have initiated earlier in the past, the coupling at time 0 would occur at the same state for identical $E_{-\tau}, E_{-\tau+1}, \cdots E_0$. Therefore if the coupling at time 0 occurs, then it can be also considered as the sample state when trajectories have initiated at time $-\infty$. This corresponds indeed to the stationary behavior due to Eq. 2. Thus we can generate samples according to the steady-state distribution by coupling from the past. We now present the algorithm given in [10], which is an adaptation of [8] from the implementation point of view. $Generate - event()$ is a function to generate the random events; $\eta(x, e) : S \times \Sigma \to S$ is the transition function of the considered system where x is a state of the state space S and e is an event in the set of events Σ. Thus $\eta(x, e)$ is the next state if event e occurs in state x. For

---

Algorithm 1. Backward coupling simulation

1: $t \leftarrow 1; E[1] \leftarrow Generate - event();$
2: **repeat**
3:     $t \leftarrow 2.t;$
4:     **for all** $x \in S$ **do**
5:         $y(x) \leftarrow x;$ {initialization of trajectories}
6:     **end for**
7:     **for** i=t downto t/2+1 **do**
8:         $E[i] \leftarrow Generate - event();$ {generation of new events from -t/2 +1 to -t}
9:     **end for**
10:     **for** i=t downto 1 **do**
11:         **for all** $x \in S$ **do**
12:             $y(x) \leftarrow \eta(y(x), E[i]);$ {generation of trajectories through events E[i], }
13:         **end for**
14:     **end for**
15: **until** all $y(x)$ are equal; {coupling of trajectories at time 0}
16: **return** $y(x)$ {that is the sample state reached at time 0 for the trajectory issued from x $\in S$ at time -t}

---

the first iteration the trajectories begin at time $t = -2$, if there is no coupling at time 0 (line 15), then $t = -4$ for the next iteration (line 3). Therefore if coupling exists, $\tau = -(2^i)$. The optimality of this doubling scheme (Algorithm 1) has been discussed in [8]. Let us remark that when one goes back more in the past, we keep already generated events (lines 7-8). Thus Algorithm 1 lets us generate the samples (line 16) of the stationary behavior (steady-state) of the Markov chain described by η (see Eq. 1).

Monotone perfect simulation. It has been shown that if the underlying model has monotone dynamic, it is sufficient to consider only trajectories issued from the set of minimal m and maximal M states since all other trajectories are evolved between them [8]. Obviously, this leads to a considerable reduction of the simulation time and the storage complexity. Moreover, it has been shown that many of the discrete event systems have a monotone dynamic [4,10]. Note that, a system is said to be monotone if all events e $\in \Sigma$ are monotone. Formally, an event e is said to be monotone if it preserves the partial ordering on the state space S $(x \leq y \Rightarrow \eta(x, e) \leq \eta(y, e))$. In fact, we consider only the set of maximal M and minimal m states as initial values among all states. So lines 4 and 11 of Algorithm 1 will be **4 and 11: for all x$\in$ M $\cup$ m** . In the sequel, we will call this algorithm as *Algorithm 1(monotone version)*.

Functional monotone perfect simulation. The backward simulation algorithm is improved by generating reward values at the steady state. Thus it will be sufficient to stop the backward simulation when all the trajectories collapse at time 0 on the same reward regardless the coupling state. Since the reward set is generally smaller than the state space, the coupling occurs more quickly in functional perfect simulation. Moreover, when rewards are monotone, then it will be sufficient to stop the backward simulation when the trajectories issued from all maximal M and minimal m states collapse at time 0 on the same reward. This may lead to an important reduction of the coupling time and the storage complexity [10]. Note that, a reward function r is said to be monotone if it satisfies $\forall$ (x, y) $\in S^2$, x $\leq$ y $\Rightarrow$ r(x) $\leq$ r(y). The functional monotone perfect simulation algorithm will be the same as Algorithm 1 apart from lines 4,11,15 and 16. **4 and 11: for all x$\in$ M $\cup$ m** , **15: until all** *reward(y(x))* **are equal** , **16: return** *reward(y(x))* . In the sequel, we will call this algorithm as *Algorithm 1(monotone functional version)*.

4   Statistical Probabilistic Model Checking Using Perfect Simulation

In this section, we present how sample paths are generated and tested for the verification of the steady-state formula $\psi = S_{\geq \theta}(\varphi)$ and the unbounded until formula $\phi = P_{\geq \theta}(\varphi_1 \, \mathcal{U} \varphi_2)$ through perfect simulation. This is equivalent to verify $\psi = S_{\leq 1-\theta}(\neg \varphi)$ or $\psi = \neg S_{<\theta}(\varphi)$ and $\phi = \neg P_{<\theta}(\varphi_1 \, \mathcal{U} \varphi_2)$. We propose our method by studying the two possible cases: The considered system can be either monotone or not. Once sample paths are generated, the statistical hypothesis testing can be applied on these observations (see section 2.2) for the decision procedure. Sample generation for the time bounded until is straightforward: starting from an initial state $X_0 = s_0$, the evolution in time interval I is generated by Eq. 1. Moreover, the case of nested formulas are not considered here and we refer to [15,18,17,9,16]. Let us remark here that the proposed sample paths generation is compatible with these proposed methods to check nested formulas either by combining numerical and statistical methods or by computing new precision bounds by applying only statistical method.

4.1   Decision Method

We will present now our chosen decision method when we perform our statistical hypothesis testing on generated samples for each one of the steady state and unbounded until cases. For these two cases, this decision method is derived from the application of one of SSP or SPRT methods for statistical hypothesis testing explained in section 2.2, by computing the sampling plan (n, m) having a fixed statistical strength (α, β) in the first method (SSP method) or by determining optimized sample size n having also strength (α, β) in the second method (SPRT method). In fact, in the first method the sample size n and the acceptance threshold m will be computed by using the approximation formulas given in [18,17]. Moreover, the labeled Markov Chain M, the threshold θ of the considered formula, the property φ (resp. $\varphi_1 \, \mathcal{U} \varphi_2$) (to be verified on each sample), and the indifference region parameter δ which is a function of θ are given as inputs. In fact, this decision method tests if φ (resp. $\varphi_1 \, \mathcal{U} \varphi_2$) is verified (positive sample) or not (negative sample) on each generated sample path, when counting the number of positive samples. For SSP method, it provides decision either *Yes* if the number of positive samples is greater or equal to m (ψ is satisfied) or *No* otherwise (ψ is not satisfied). For SPRT method, it provides decision either *Yes* if the ratio $q_i \leq \beta/(1\text{-}\alpha)$ (ψ is satisfied) or *No* if $q_i \geq (1\text{-}\beta)/\alpha$ (ψ is not satisfied).

4.2   Case of Steady State Operator

As it has been stated in Section 3, there are different cases to provide perfect samples depending on the monotonicity or not of the underlying model and depending also on the monotonicity or not of the associated reward in the case of monotone model. However the samples are generated essentially from perfect simulation Algorithm 1 with some modifications for each case, as explained in details in [1] (see also Section 4.4). In fact, in order to perform statistical model checking of the steady-state formula $\psi = S_{\geq \theta}(\varphi)$ by using monotone and/or functional perfect simulation, we need to test if the obtained steady-state samples satisfy φ or not. Thus we associate the reward $r_\varphi(x)$ to each state vector $x \in S$ for the given property φ:

$$r_\varphi(x) = 1, \quad \text{if } x \models \varphi \tag{3}$$
$$r_\varphi(x) = 0, \quad \text{otherwise } x \not\models \varphi$$

Therefore at time 0, we need indeed to test if the rewards are coupled at reward 0 or 1. In other words, we test if it is a positive or negative sample. Note that, we suppose in this case that the underlying markov chain is ergodic then the steady-state formula is satisfied regardless of the initial state.

4.3 Case of Unbounded Until Formula

The statistical checking principle of the time unbounded until formula $\mathcal{P}_{\geq\theta}(\varphi_1\,\mathcal{U}\varphi_2)$ consists of generating execution sample paths from an initial state s_0 and testing if each sample path verifies the property $\varphi_1\,\mathcal{U}\varphi_2$ or not.

We modify backward simulation algorithm to generate samples for the verification of unbounded until formula to design Algorithm 2. This algorithm is built by taking into account the fact that evolution in n steps from the past to present and from the present to the future are stochastically equivalent (see Eq. 2). There are three stopping conditions on each sample path generated from s_0:

1. the sample path reaches a φ_2 state, this path satisfies the property, we can conclude that it is a positive sample (lines 13 and 14 of Algorithm 2).
2. the sample path reaches a $\neg\varphi_1 \wedge \neg\varphi_2$ states, we can conclude that it is a negative sample (lines 15 and 16 of Algorithm 2).
3. the sample path visits always $\varphi_1 \wedge \neg\varphi_2$ states, it must be stopped when the steady-state is reached. If the steady-state is reached passing through φ_1 states without reaching a φ_2 state, then it is a negative one (lines 21 and 22 of Algorithm 2).

The states from which sample paths are initiated depend on monotonicity properties of the model. If the underlying model is monotone, the considered sample paths are generated by keeping only trajectories issued from the set of maximal and minimal states, then $S^* = Max \cup Min - s_0$ in the Algorithm 2. If the model is not monotone, then we consider all states $S^* = S - s_0$.

4.4 Applicability and Complexity of Proposed Approach

Perfect simulation can be applied to monotone systems as proposed in [10,12] and to non monotone systems as proposed in [14]. It can be applied to queuing networks, Markov chains [10,12] and to stochastic automata networks [13]. Therefore our proposed approach can be applied to monotone and to non monotone systems modeled by Markov chains, queuing networks or stochastic automata networks.

Monotone systems. In this case, we can apply *Algorithm 1 (monotone version)* if we don't need to compute steady state rewards. Otherwise we have two cases depending on the monotonicity of the reward function:

– Reward is monotone: *Algorithm 1 (monotone functional version)* can be applied in this case.
– Reward is not monotone: *Algorithm 1 (monotone version)* can be applied in this case.

Algorithm 2. Sample generation and testing for unbounded Until

---

1: $t \leftarrow 1$; $E[1] \leftarrow Generate - event()$; $STOP \leftarrow false$; $Result \leftarrow 0$;
2: **repeat**
3:    $t \leftarrow 2.t$;
4:    **for all** $x \in s_0 \cup S^*$ **do**
5:       $y(x) \leftarrow x$; {initialisation of trajectories}
6:    **end for**
7:    **for** i=t downto t/2+1 **do**
8:       E[i]=Generate-event() {generate new events from -t/2 +1 to -t}
9:    **end for**
10:   $i \leftarrow t$;
11:   **while** $(i \geq 1) \wedge \neg STOP$ **do**
12:      $y(s_0) \leftarrow \eta(y(x), E[i])$;
13:      **if** $y(s_0) \models \varphi_2$ **then**
14:         $STOP \leftarrow true$; $Result \leftarrow 1$; { a φ_2 state is reached}
15:      **else if** $y(s_0) \models \neg\varphi_1$ **then**
16:         $STOP \leftarrow true$; $Result \leftarrow 0$; {a $\neg\varphi_1 \wedge \neg\varphi_2$ state is reached}
17:      **else**
18:         **for all** $x \in S^*$ **do**
19:            $y(x) \leftarrow \eta(y(x), E[i])$;
20:         **end for**
21:         **if** all $y(x)$ are equal **then**
22:            $STOP \leftarrow true$; $Result \leftarrow 0$; {steady-state is reached}
23:         **end if**
24:      **end if**
25:      $i \leftarrow i - 1$;
26:   **end while**
27: **until** $STOP$
28: **return** $Result$

Non monotone systems. In this case, we can apply backward simulation algorithm *Algorithm 1* if we don't need to compute steady state rewards, otherwise *Algorithm 1 (functional version)* can be applied. The functional version is the same as *Algorithm 1* apart from lines 15 and 16 those are modified as lines 15 and 16 in *Algorithm 1 (monotone functional version)*.

The complexity of our approach is related to statistical model checking complexity which depends on the computed sample size, of the perfect simulation effort (or complexity) and of the trajectory length in case of path formulas. It has been shown that if the complexity of the backward simulation algorithm in the number of transition function evaluation is bounded by $|S|.(2.\mathbb{E}\tau^*)$ [10], then the mean time complexity $\mathbb{C}$ can be bounded by $\mathbb{C} \leq |S|.(2.\mathbb{E}\tau^*).c_\eta$ where τ^* is the coupling time of the backward scheme (coupling from the past scheme), $|S|$ is the state space size, c_η is the mean computation cost of $\eta(x,e)$. The memory complexity (storage of the set of generated events) is bounded by $2\mathbb{E}\tau^*$ and could be reduced to $\mathbb{E}\log_2\tau^* + 1$ [10]. Thus the complexity of the perfect simulation is clearly modest in case of monotone systems because we consider only maximal and minimal states as initial values among all states. In fact, the simulation time reduction is proportional to the size of the state space in this case [11], which is usually very large. It has been shown in [11] when studying coupling time distribution, that simulation times per sample for the studied queueing networks examples are just a few milli-seconds on a standard PC. In case of non monotone systems, it has been shown in [14] that there is only a need to compute two trajectories: an infimum and supremum envelopes, then the complexity of perfect simulation in this case will be also modest. Moreover, because of the independence of generated samples, the perfect simulation method can be parallelized efficiently [13].

5   Case Study and Experimental Results

As case study we present the dependability properties verification at long run of a multistage interconnection queueing network to illustrate the efficiency of our proposed method. In telecommunication networks, multistage models are used for modelling switches [7]. The considered model is a delta network with 4 stages and 8 buffers at each stage (see Fig. 1). Thus the total number of queues (buffer) is $n = 32$. With Markovian arrival and service hypothesis, the model can be defined as a CTMC with a state vector $(N_1 N_2 \cdots N_n)$ where N_i is the number of packets in the ith queue. The size of the state space is then $(N_{max} + 1)^{32}$, if the maximum queue size is N_{max}. We suppose homogeneous input traffic with arrival rate λ to the first stage and service rate $\mu = 1$ in each queue. The routing policy is rejection (packets are lost if the queue is full) and at the end of a service the routing probabilities are $1/2$ for both buffers in the next stage. There are 64 events (8 external arrivals at the 1st level + 8 departures at the 4th level + 2*8 routing events in first three levels). The monotonicity of these events (with respect to the component-wise order) and so the monotonicity of the model has been shown in [11].

The availability and saturation properties at long run of the considered model can be checked through the CSL steady-state and unbounded until formulas. State labels are defined through atomic propositions depending on the number of packets in queues. For a given $k \in \{0, \cdots, N_{max}\}$, $a_i(k)$ is true if $N_i \geq k$ and false otherwise. For example, $a_i (N_{max})$ is true if the ith buffer is full. The

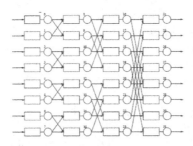

Fig. 1. Interconnection delta network

underlying CTMC is labelled with these atomic propositions depending on the considered property. It is then possible to express different interesting availability and reliability measures for the underlying system by means of these atomic propositions. Let φ_1 (resp. φ_2) be the state formula to specify if at least a queue (resp. all queues) at the fourth level is saturated, thus it is defined as the disjunction (resp. conjuction) of atomic propositions $a_i(N_{max})$, $24 \leq i \leq 31$. Steady-state formulas $\psi_1 = S_{<\theta_1}(\varphi_1)$, $\psi_2 = S_{<\theta_2}(\varphi_2)$ let us to study steady-state saturation or availability properties $(S_{>1-\theta_1}(\neg \varphi_1), S_{>1-\theta_2}(\neg \varphi_2))$. The properties on execution paths at long run can be studied by means of unbounded until formulas. Let φ_3 be the state formula to specify the saturation of at least a queue at the third level, thus it is defined by the disjunction of atomic propositions $a_i(N_{max})$, $16 \leq i \leq 23$. We consider $\psi_3 = P_{<\theta_1}(\neg\varphi_3 \, \mathcal{U} \, \varphi_1)$, $\psi_4 = P_{<\theta_2}(\neg\varphi_3 \, \mathcal{U} \, \varphi_2)$. Note that, $\neg\varphi_3$ represents the availability of all queues at the third level. Then ψ_3 (resp. ψ_4) checks if the probability of execution paths in which $\neg\varphi_3$ is verified until finding one state verifying φ_1 (resp. φ_2) meets the threshold θ or not. Since the underlying model is monotone, sample paths are generated by applying the monotone perfect simulation *(Algorithm 1 (monotone version))*. For steady-state formulas, in order to apply functional monotone perfect simulation *(Algorithm 1 (functional monotone version))*, it has been shown in [1] that the underlying reward r_φ is monotone. Contrary if the state formula is defined from $a_i(k)$ for some queues and $\neg a_i(k)$ for others, then we can only apply *(Algorithm 1 (monotone version))*, since the reward is not monotone. Thus the underlying formulas ψ_1 and ψ_2 can be checked by applying functional monotone perfect simulation, while ψ_3 and ψ_4 will be checked by only using monotone perfect simulation.

Now we suppose that $N_{max}=30$ and $\lambda=0.75$ at the first stage. Remark that the state space size is huge and intractable by conventional techniques ($31^{32} \simeq 5.10^{47}$). The perfect samples are generated by using tool Ψ^2 which provides monotone perfect samples [12]. For unbounded until generated sample paths we consider as initial state s_0 the state vector $(0 \ 0 \cdots 0)$ (all queues are empty).

We give in the Table 1 for different values of θ, δ, the decision for the considered steady-state and unbounded until formulas and the computed values of $(Nsamp, m)$ having statistical strength (α, β) by applying the SSP method of statistical hypothesis testing described in section 2.2. In the following tables, $Nsamp$ denotes the sample size, m is the acceptance threshold, $SMCD_1$: statistical model checking decision for the formula $S_{<\theta}(\varphi_1)$, $SMCD_2$: statistical model checking decision for the formula $S_{<\theta}(\varphi_2)$, $SMCD_3$: statistical model checking decision for the formula $P_{<\theta}(\neg\varphi_3 \, \mathcal{U} \, \varphi_1)$, $SMCD_4$: statistical model checking decision for the formula $P_{<\theta}(\neg\varphi_3 \, \mathcal{U} \, \varphi_2)$, α: the computed hypothesis testing Type I error(false negative), β: the computed hypothesis testing Type II error(false positive).

Next, we give in the Table 2 for different values of θ, δ, the decision for the considered steady-state and unbounded until formulas and the computed values of $Nsamp_1$ for statistical model checking of $S_{<\theta}(\varphi_1)$, $Nsamp_2$ for statistical model checking of $S_{<\theta}(\varphi_2)$, $Nsamp_3$ for statistical model checking of $P_{<\theta}(\neg\varphi_3 \, \mathcal{U} \, \varphi_1)$ and $Nsamp_4$ for statistical model checking of $P_{<\theta}(\neg\varphi_3 \, \mathcal{U} \, \varphi_2)$ having statistical

Table 1. SMC Decision for $S_{<\theta}(\varphi_1)$, $S_{<\theta}(\varphi_2)$, $P_{<\theta}(\neg\varphi_3\ \mathcal{U}\ \varphi_1)$ and $P_{<\theta}(\neg\varphi_3\ \mathcal{U}\ \varphi_2)$ with $\delta=\frac{\theta}{5}$ by using SSP

θ	$\alpha=\beta$	$Nsamp$	m	$SMCD_1$	$SMCD_2$	$SMCD_3$	$SMCD_4$
	10^{-2}	133944	132	Yes	Yes	No	Yes
10^{-3}	10^{-4}	342443	336	Yes	Yes	No	Yes
	10^{-6}	559235	548	Yes	Yes	No	Yes
	10^{-8}	779255	764	Yes	Yes	No	Yes
	10^{-2}	1340669	132	No	Yes	No	Yes
10^{-4}	10^{-4}	3427576	336	No	Yes	No	Yes
	10^{-6}	5597491	549	No	Yes	No	Yes
	10^{-8}	7799708	765	No	Yes	No	Yes
	10^{-2}	13407920	132	No	Yes	No	Yes
10^{-5}	10^{-4}	34278912	336	No	Yes	No	Yes
	10^{-6}	55980048	549	No	Yes	No	Yes
	10^{-8}	78004244	765	No	Yes	No	Yes

Table 2. SMC Decision for $S_{<\theta}(\varphi_1)$, $S_{<\theta}(\varphi_2)$, $P_{<\theta}(\neg\varphi_3\ \mathcal{U}\ \varphi_1)$ and $P_{<\theta}(\neg\varphi_3\ \mathcal{U}\ \varphi_2)$ with $\delta=\frac{\theta}{5}$ by using SPRT

θ	$\alpha=\beta$	$Nsamp_1$	$SMCD_1$	$Nsamp_2$	$SMCD_2$	$Nsamp_3$	$SMCD_3$	$Nsamp_4$	$SMCD_4$
	10^{-2}	13504	Yes	11477	Yes	1013	No	11477	Yes
10^{-3}	10^{-4}	34153	Yes	23003	Yes	1023	No	23003	Yes
	10^{-6}	46669	Yes	34505	Yes	1029	No	34505	Yes
	10^{-8}	68306	Yes	46006	Yes	1035	No	46006	Yes
	10^{-2}	57104	No	114870	Yes	10013	No	114870	Yes
10^{-4}	10^{-4}	85376	No	230234	Yes	10023	No	230234	Yes
	10^{-6}	117344	No	345354	Yes	10029	No	345354	Yes
	10^{-8}	144347	No	460472	Yes	10035	No	460472	Yes
	10^{-2}	34364	No	1148769	Yes	9013	No	1148769	Yes
10^{-5}	10^{-4}	70088	No	2302537	Yes	9023	No	2302537	Yes
	10^{-6}	92233	No	3453843	Yes	9029	No	3453843	Yes
	10^{-8}	117900	No	4605125	Yes	9035	No	4605125	Yes

strength (α, β) by applying the SPRT method of statistical hypothesis testing described in section 2.2.

We have verified properties on a very large system (state space 5.10^{47}) having threshold probabilities very close to zero with very small correctness bounds (α, β). The time per simulation (observation) is just a few milli-seconds on a standard PC, and it must be multiplied by the number of samples depending on the required correctness bounds. Our numerical results show that the computed sample size when applying SPRT is more optimised than the sample size obtained by applying SSP statistical solution method. Our main goal here is to illustrate the feasibility of the proposed approach for very large systems and rare events. Note that, for the steady-state operator the sample generation is stopped only when steady-state is reached while there are 3 stopping conditions for unbounded until formula. Moreover, for steady-state operator we have applied the functional monotone perfect simulation while for unbounded until formula we have applied monotone perfect simulation. Thus the time per simulation for steady-state operator is smaller than that of the unbounded until formula. Let us note that with $N_{max}=30$ and $\lambda = 0.75$ we can see that the mean queue length is relatively small, so saturation could be considered as a rare event, which explains our decision $SMCD_2$ and $SMCD_4$ about the probability of saturation of all queues at fourth stage to be always Yes. Finally, the monotone perfect sampling with statistical decision techniques provide a really interesting alternative for the probabilistic verification of large systems. Since the discrete event systems have in general monotone dynamics [4,10] this condition is not very restrictive hypothesis for real world models.

6   Conclusion and Future Works

We propose to do statistical model checking by combining perfect sampling and hypothesis testing. Therefore it will be possible to verify steady-state and unbounded time until formulas of temporal logics for Markov chains. In fact, the statistical model checking by Monte Carlo simulation has been already proposed for time bounded until formula [18]. However the steady-state operator had not been studied before and the unbounded until operator can not be efficiently checked by this approach because of stopping probability and steady-state detection problems [9]. Perfect simulation is a relatively recent extension of Monte Carlo simulation allowing to sample steady-state without any bias. We have integrated the proposed approach to the perfect sampler Ψ^2 [12], to be able to model check large performability and dependability models. We consider to apply our proposed approach to verify dependability properties specified by nested formulas composed of steady state and unbouned until formulas. The perfect sampler Ψ^2 is extended to study the non monotone models [14]. A new version of this perfect sampler is under implementation. Thus we plan to apply our proposed method to non monotone models using this updated version of Ψ^2. Another extension of our work will be to compare our statistical approach with the existing numerical approaches [6] those verify steady-state and unbounded until formulas as well as with the existing discrete event simulation based approaches, in terms of their complexity and efficiency. A comparison between numerical and statistical methods has been done in [16] showing that statistical method is more efficient for large scale systems but less accurate and less complex than numerical method.

Acknowledgment. The authors thank to Jean-Marc Vincent for fruitful discussions and for his help on Ψ^2 tool.

References

1. El Rabih, D., Pekergin, N.: Statistical model checking for steady state dependability verification. In: WIP paper in proceedings of 2nd International conference on Dependability. DEPEND 2009, IEEE CS proceedings, Athens, Greece (2009)

2. Aziz, A., Sanwal, K., Singhal, V., Brayton, R.: Model Checking Continuous Time Markov Chains. ACM Trans. on Comp. Logic 1(1), 162–170 (2000)
3. Baier, C., Haverkort, B., Hermanns, H., Katoen, J.P.: Model-Checking Algorithms for Continuous-Time Markov Chains. IEEE Trans. Software Eng. 29(6), 524–541 (2003)
4. Glasserman, P., Yao, D.: Monotone Structure in Discrete-Event Systems. John Wiley & Sons, Chichester (1994)
5. Hansson, H., Jonsson, B.: A logic for reasonning about time and reliability. Formal Aspects Compt. 6, 512–535 (1994)
6. Hinton, A., Kwiatkowska, M., Norman, G., Parker, D.: PRISM: A tool for automatic verification of probabilistic systems. In: Hermanns, H., Palsberg, J. (eds.) TACAS 2006. LNCS, vol. 3920, pp. 441–444. Springer, Heidelberg (2006)
7. Keshav, S.: An Engineering approach to computer networking. Addison Wesley, Reading (1997)
8. Propp, J.G., Wilson, D.B.: Exact sampling with coupled Markov chains and applications to statistical mechanics. Random Structures and Algorithms 9(1 and 2), 223–252 (1996)
9. Sen, K., Viswanathan, M., Agha, G.: On Statistical Model Checking of Stochastic Systems. In: Etessami, K., Rajamani, S.K. (eds.) CAV 2005. LNCS, vol. 3576, pp. 266–280. Springer, Heidelberg (2005)
10. Vincent, J.M., Marchand, C.: On the exact simulation of functionals of stationary Markov chains. Linear Algebra and its Applications 386, 285–310 (2004)
11. Vincent, J.-M., Vienne, J.: Perfect simulation of index based routing networks. Performance Evaluation Review 34(2), 24–25 (2006)
12. Vincent, J.-M., Vienne, J.: PSI2 a Software Tool for the Perfect Simulation of Finite Queuing Networks. In: QEST, Edinburgh (September 2007)
13. Fernandes, P., Vincent, J.-M., Webber, T.: Perfect Simulation of Stochastic Automata Networks. In: Al-Begain, K., Heindl, A., Telek, M. (eds.) ASMTA 2008. LNCS, vol. 5055, pp. 249–263. Springer, Heidelberg (2008)
14. Busic, A., Gaujal, B., Vincent, J.-M.: Perfect simulation and non-monotone (Markovian) systems. In: Proceedings of 3rd International Conference on Performance Evaluation Methodologies and Tools, VALUETOOLS 2008, Athens, Greece, October (2008)
15. Younes, H.L.S., Simmons, R.G.: Probabilistic verification of discrete event systems using acceptance sampling. In: Brinksma, E., Larsen, K.G. (eds.) CAV 2002. LNCS, vol. 2404, pp. 223–235. Springer, Heidelberg (2002)
16. Younes, H.L., Kwiatkowska, M., Norman, G., Parker, D.: Numerical vs. statistical probabilistic model checking. Software Tools for Technology Transfer 8(3), 216–228 (2006)
17. Younes, H.L.S.: Error Control for Probabilistic Model Checking. In: Emerson, E.A., Namjoshi, K.S. (eds.) VMCAI 2006. LNCS, vol. 3855, pp. 142–156. Springer, Heidelberg (2006)
18. Younes, H.L.S., Simmons, R.G.: Statistical probabilistic model checking with a focus on time-bounded properties. Information and Computation 204(9), 1368–1409 (2006)

Quantitative Analysis under Fairness Constraints

Christel Baier, Marcus Groesser, and Frank Ciesinski

Technische Universtät Dresden
Nöthnitzer Straße 46
01187 Dresden, Germany
{baier,groesser,ciesinsk}@tcs.inf.tu-dresden.de

Abstract. It is well-known that fairness assumptions can be crucial for verifying progress, reactivity or other liveness properties for interleaving models. This also applies to Markov decision processes as an operational model for concurrent probabilistic systems and the task to establish tight lower or upper probability bounds for events that are specified by liveness properties. In this paper, we study general notions of strong and weak fairness constraints for Markov decision processes, formalized in an action- or state-based setting. We present a polynomially time-bounded algorithm for the quantitative analysis of an MDP against ω-automata specifications under fair worst- or best-case scenarios. Furthermore, we discuss the treatment of strong and weak fairness and process fairness constraints in the context of partial order reduction techniques for Markov decision processes that have been realized in the model checker LiQuor and rely on a variant of Peled's ample set method.

1 Introduction

Markov decision processes (MDPs) are widely used as an operational model for randomized distributed algorithms, network protocols and systems with unreliable components. Several verification algorithms have been developed to reason about the (worst or best case) probabilities for temporal properties of systems specified by an MDP. In model checking of such systems as well as in the nonprobabilistic case, systems under consideration are often characterized by a component based view, e.g., systems of parallel processes [19,26,3], of modules [1,29], etc. that compete with each other for the resource of *action execution* in an abstract execution environment. Especially (but not only) when verifying liveness properties of such systems, the concept of fairness is very important. Without a sound notion of fairness there is almost always the unrealistic possibility of simply ignoring certain processes which trivially renders even simple liveness properties to not being satisfied. While in context of LTL verification incorporating fairness is an easy task - fairness conditions are essentially LTL conditions - for CTL a more sophisticated approach based on a tricky analysis of SCCs has to be applied [20,12]. Compared to models without fairness this leads to an increase of the complexity linear in the number of fairness conditions. For probabilistic systems the importance of fairness carries directly over. For Markov decision processes methods were proposed in principle (see related work below). The rough idea is a reduction to a probabilistic reachability problem (minimum and maximum probabilities) which is enabled by a graph based preanalysis that examines end components rather than SCCs.

Z. Liu and A.P. Ravn (Eds.): ATVA 2009, LNCS 5799, pp. 135–150, 2009.
© Springer-Verlag Berlin Heidelberg 2009

For this, however, no precise solutions for efficient algorithms were proposed yet. For example given k strong fairness assumptions of the form $\Box \Diamond H_i \rightarrow \Box \Diamond K_i$ for $1 \leq i \leq k$ there are (in addition to the fact that the number of end components in an MDP is exponential) 2^k "ways" to satisfy the fairness condition. Until now it remained unclear whether there is a polytime algorithm that solves this problem. We show here that given an arbitrary number of strong and weak fairness constraints the complexity of the preanalysis step in probabilistic model checking is increased only by a factor *linear* in the number of fairness constraints.

More precisely, the contributions of this paper are as follows. First, we provide algorithms for computing the probabilities for ω-regular properties in worst- or best-case scenarios when ranging over all fair schedulers, i.e., policies that ensure that almost surely the nondeterministic choices will be resolved in a fair way. The underlying fairness condition can be any mixture of strong and weak fairness constraints, formalized in an action- or state-based setting. The core of our approach relies on a recursive algorithm to compute end components [14,16,37] of appropriate sub-MDPs which serves to check the realizability of the given fairness condition where realizability means the existence of a fair scheduler. Compared to the quantitative analysis of MDPs against linear-time properties without fairness assumptions, the overhead of our algorithm is quadratic in the number of states and linear in the number of strong fairness conditions.

The second contribution of our paper is a discussion on the treatment of strong and weak process fairness in the context of partial order reduction for MDPs and stutter-invariant linear-time properties [6,15]. We will show that the current realization of the partial order reduction in the model checker LiQuor [4] is compatible with strong and weak process fairness in the sense that the extremal probabilities for stutter-invariant linear-time properties in the original MDP and the reduced MDP generated by LiQuor agree.

Related work. Fairness for probabilistic systems with nondeterminism has been first introduced by Hart, Sharir, Pnueli [24] and Rosier, Yen [37] to reason about almost-sure termination. Vardi [39] introduced the concept of fair schedulers of an MDP-like model for checking whether a given linear temporal formula holds with probability 1. The underlying notion of fairness for paths was strong fairness in the following sense: if some state s has been visited infinitely often then also all its successors. Following the approach of [39], we define a scheduler to be fair if almost all paths that can be generated by that scheduler are fair. However, our notion of fairness for paths is more general since we allow for any combination of strong and weak fairness constraints that might impose conditions on the states that are visited infinitely often (e.g., conditions on the current values of program or control variables or the enabledness of actions) or conditions on the actions that are taken infinitely often.

In the context of probabilistic branching time properties (formalized in the logic PCTL [9]) the concept of strong fairness has been discussed by Baier and Kwiatkowska in [8]. The paper [8] also contains a short remark on the treatment of PCTL* under strong fairness assumptions and provides a (rather complicated) characterization of certain sets of states that have to be computed when dealing with a fair semantics of PCTL*. Algorithms to compute these sets efficiently have not been discussed in [8]. Moreover, the notion of fairness studied in [8] is just a special case of strong fairness studied in this paper, while weak fairness has not been addressed in [8]. The textbook [7] briefly sketches how extremal probabilities for linear-time properties under strong fairness assumptions can be computed via an analysis of end components and a reduction to the maximal reachability probabilities, but does not provide algorithms for the required analysis of end components. The difficulty is that the relevant end components might be overlapping and therefore a naive approach that analyzes all end components will have exponential time complexity. In this paper we fill this gap by providing a polynomially time-bounded algorithm.

Different notions for the fairness of randomized schedulers of an MDP together with algorithms for extremal reachability probabilities and long-run averages have been presented by de Alfaro [18]. These notions impose lower probability bounds for the chosen actions rather than requiring that almost all generated paths are fair.

The concepts of α-fairness [35] or γ-fairness [2] have been introduced as sound and complete proof techniques to verify that a given linear-time property φ holds almost surely (called P-validity of φ in [2]) for an MDP-like model equipped with action-based strong and weak fairness constraints. The variants of α- and γ-fairness serve for reducing the question of the P-validity of φ to the question whether φ holds for all α- or γ-fair computations of $\mathcal{M}$, which can be checked by "non-probabilistic" methods. The concept of realizability is irrelevant for [35,2] (since the considered fairness constraints are trivially realizable). End components which are essential for our approach and quantitative properties are not considered in [35,2].

To the best of our knowledge, partial order reduction techniques for MDPs with fairness assumptions have not yet been considered in the literature. Our contribution relies on previous work on the ample set method for MDPs [6,15] and its realization in the probabilistic model checker LiQuor [4] which shares many concepts of the model checker SPIN [26]. Beside the differences that origin from the fact that we deal with probabilistic models and quantitative properties, while SPIN is a model checker for non-probabilistic systems, SPIN only supports weak fairness, whereas we deal here with strong and weak (process) fairness.

Organization. Section 2 summarizes the relevant concepts of Markov decision processes and explains our notations. Algorithms for the quantitative analysis of MDPs against automata-specifications under fairness assumptions are presented in Section 3. Section 4 explains the treatment of fairness assumptions within the partial order reduction framework for MDPs. Section 5 concludes the paper with some brief experimental results.

2   Preliminaries

The reader is assumed to be familiar with basic concepts of automata over infinite words and temporal logics (see e.g. [22,13,7]) and fairness for nondeterministic models (see e.g. [21,31,28]). We often use LTL- or CTL-like notations with the obvious meanings. E.g., if s is a state, T a set of states and H a set of actions then the notation $s \models \exists \Diamond T$ denotes that some state in T is reachable from s, while $\Box \Diamond H$ stands for the event "infinitely often an action in H is taken".

Markov decision processes (MDPs) are widely used as an operational interleaving model for programs consisting of concurrent probabilistic processes.

For the purposes of this paper, we use action names (which, among others, are needed to formalize process fairness and the ample set method) and labels for the states by sets of atomic propositions (which are used to specify path properties). In this section, we explain our notations and summarize the concepts that are relevant to present our results. For further details on MDPs see e.g. [36]. A *Markov decision process* (MDP) is a tuple $\mathcal{M} = (S, \mathsf{Act}, \delta, \mu, \mathsf{AP}, \mathfrak{L})$, where

- S is a finite nonempty set of states,
- Act is a finite nonempty set of actions,
- $\delta : S \times \mathsf{Act} \times S \rightarrow [0, 1]$ is a transition probability function such that $\sum_{t \in S} \delta(s, \alpha, t) \in \{0, 1\}$ for each $s \in S$ and $\alpha \in \mathsf{Act}$,
- $\mu : S \rightarrow [0, 1]$ is a probability distribution on S, called the initial distribution,
- AP is a finite set of atomic propositions and
- $\mathfrak{L} : S \rightarrow 2^{\mathsf{AP}}$ is a labelling function.

$\mathsf{Act}(s) \stackrel{\text{def}}{=} \{\alpha \in \mathsf{Act} : \exists t \in S : \delta(s, \alpha, t) > 0\}$ denotes the set of actions that are enabled in state s. We require that $\mathsf{Act}(s)$ is nonempty for each state $s \in S$. The intuitive operational behaviour of an MDP is as follows. If s is the current state, then at first one of the actions $\alpha \in \mathsf{Act}(s)$ is chosen nondeterministically. Secondly, action α is executed leading to state t with probability $\delta(s, \alpha, t)$.

An *infinite path* of an MDP is an alternating sequence $\pi = s_0 \, \alpha_1 \, s_1 \, \alpha_2 \ldots \in (S \times \mathsf{Act})^\omega$ of states and actions such that $\delta(s_i, \alpha_{i+1}, s_{i+1}) > 0$ for all $i \geq 0$. Paths are written in the form $\pi = s_0 \xrightarrow{\alpha_1} s_1 \xrightarrow{\alpha_2} s_2 \xrightarrow{\alpha_3} \ldots$. The *trace* of π is defined as the infinite word $\mathsf{trace}(\pi) \stackrel{\text{def}}{=} \mathfrak{L}(s_0)\mathfrak{L}(s_1)\mathfrak{L}(s_2) \ldots$ over the alphabet 2^{AP}. We define $\inf(\pi)$ to be the set of actions and state-labels (i.e., sets of atomic propositions) that appear infinitely often in π:

$$\inf(\pi) \stackrel{\text{def}}{=} \{\mathfrak{A} \in 2^{\mathsf{AP}} | \overset{\infty}{\exists} i \text{ s.t. } \mathfrak{L}(s_i) = \mathfrak{A}\} \cup \{\alpha \in \mathsf{Act} | \overset{\infty}{\exists} i \text{ s.t. } \alpha_i = \alpha\}.$$

A *finite path* is a finite prefix of an infinite path that ends in a state. We use the notation $\mathsf{last}(\pi)$ for the last state of a finite path π and $|\pi|$ for the length (number of actions) of a finite path. We denote by $\mathsf{Pathfin}$ (and $\mathsf{Pathinf}$) the set of all finite (infinite) paths of $\mathcal{M}$.

Schedulers. The concept of schedulers is needed to reason about probabilities for certain behaviors of an MDP. Schedulers are a means to resolve the nondeterminism in the states, and thus, yield a discrete Markov chain and a probability measure on the paths. Intuitively, a scheduler takes as input the "history" of a computation (formalized by a finite path π) and chooses the next action (resp. a distribution on actions). Formally, if $\mathcal{M}$ is an MDP as above a history-dependent randomized scheduler is a function $\mathcal{U} : \mathsf{Pathfin} \rightarrow \mathsf{Distr}(\mathsf{Act})$, such that $\{\alpha \in \mathsf{Act} : \mathcal{U}(\pi)(\alpha) > 0\} \subseteq \mathsf{Act}(\mathsf{last}(\pi))$ for each $\pi \in \mathsf{Pathfin}$. Here, $\mathsf{Distr}(\mathsf{Act})$ denotes the set of probability distributions on Act. A (finite or infinite) path $s_0 \xrightarrow{\alpha_1} s_1 \xrightarrow{\alpha_2} s_2 \ldots$ is called a $\mathcal{U}$-path, if $\mathcal{U}(s_0 \xrightarrow{\alpha_1} \ldots \xrightarrow{\alpha_i} s_i)(\alpha_{i+1}) > 0$ for every $0 \leq i < |\pi|$. Scheduler $\mathcal{U}$ is called *deterministic* if for each $\pi \in \mathsf{Pathfin}$ there exists an action α such that $\mathcal{U}(\pi)(\alpha) = 1$ (while $\mathcal{U}(\pi)(\beta) = 0$ for every other action $\beta \neq \alpha$). We simply treat deterministic schedulers as functions that map finite paths to actions. A *finite-memory* scheduler denotes a deterministic scheduler $\mathcal{U}$ that stores the information about the history in a finite-state automaton. Formally, finite-memory schedulers can be defined as tuples

$W = (\mathfrak{M}, \mathfrak{next}, \mathfrak{dec}, \mathfrak{m}_0)$ where $\mathfrak{M}$ is a finite set of modes, $\mathfrak{m}_0 \in \mathfrak{M}$ the initial mode, $\mathfrak{next} : \mathfrak{M} \times S \to \mathfrak{M}$ the next-mode function and $\mathfrak{dec} : \mathfrak{M} \times S \to \mathsf{Act}$ the decision function where $\mathfrak{dec}(\mathfrak{m}, s) \in \mathsf{Act}(s)$. Given a finite-memory scheduler W then the induced (history-dependent) deterministic scheduler $\mathcal{U}_W$ is given by $\mathcal{U}_W(\pi) = \mathfrak{dec}(\mathfrak{next}^*(\mathfrak{m}_0, \pi), \mathsf{last}(\pi))$ where $\mathfrak{next}^* : \mathfrak{M} \times \mathsf{Pathfin} \to \mathfrak{M}$ is defined inductively by $\mathfrak{next}^*(\mathfrak{m}, s) = \mathfrak{m}$, $\mathfrak{next}^*(\mathfrak{m}, s \xrightarrow{\alpha} \pi) = \mathfrak{next}^*(\mathfrak{next}(\mathfrak{m}, s), \pi)$ for all states s and finite paths π such that $\delta(s, \alpha, t) > 0$ if t is the first state of π. A *memoryless* scheduler is a finite-memory scheduler with a single mode. Memoryless schedulers can be specified as functions $W : S \to \mathsf{Act}$ such that $W(s) \in \mathsf{Act}(s)$. The set of all (history-dependent, randomized) schedulers for $\mathcal{M}$ is denoted by Sched. We write Sched_D (resp. Sched_{FM} or Sched_M) to denote the set of deterministic (finite-memory, memoryless) schedulers for $\mathcal{M}$. The behaviour of $\mathcal{M}$ under scheduler $\mathcal{U}$ can be formalized by a (possibly infinite-state) discrete Markov chain. $\mathsf{Pr}_s^\mathcal{U}$ denotes the standard probability measure on the σ-algebra of the infinite paths of $\mathcal{M}$ that is generated by the basic cylinders of finite paths starting in s. Given an ω-regular property E over AP (e.g., given by an LTL formula over AP or an ω-automaton with the alphabet 2^{AP}) then the set of paths π with $\mathsf{trace}(\pi)$ is measurable [39]. We write

$$\mathsf{Pr}^\mathcal{U}(s \models E) \overset{\text{def}}{=} \mathsf{Pr}_s^\mathcal{U}\{\pi \in \mathsf{Pathinf} : \mathsf{trace}(\pi) \in E\}$$

to denote the probability under scheduler $\mathcal{U}$ for state s to satisfy property E.

The probability measure induced by scheduler $\mathcal{U}$ for an MDP with initial distribution μ is denoted by $\mathsf{Pr}_\mathcal{M}^\mathcal{U}$ and given by $\sum_{s \in S} \mu(s) \cdot \mathsf{Pr}_s^\mathcal{U}$. Sometimes we add the symbol $\mathcal{M}$ also to other notations and write, e.g., $\mathsf{Pathinf}^\mathcal{M}$ or $\mathsf{Sched}^\mathcal{M}$, to make clear to which MDP the notations refer.

Subgraphs, end components, limit of paths. The key for the quantitative analysis of MDPs against ω-regular properties lies in the concept of end components [16,17,14,37] which can be seen as the MDP-counterpart to terminal strongly connected components in Markov chains. A *subgraph* of $\mathcal{M}$ is a pair (T, A) where $T \subseteq S$ and $A : T \to 2^{\mathsf{Act}}$ such that $A(t) \subseteq \mathsf{Act}(t)$ and $\{u \in S : \exists \alpha \in A(t) \text{ s. th. } \delta(t, \alpha, u) > 0\} \subseteq T$ for all $t \in T$. We often identify any subgraph (T, A) with the directed graph with the node-set T and an edge from state t to state u iff there exists an action $\alpha \in A(t)$ such $\delta(t, \alpha, u) > 0$. An *end component* of $\mathcal{M}$ is a nonempty strongly connected subgraph of $\mathcal{M}$. In particular, $A(t)$ is nonempty for all states $t \in T$ of an end component (T, A). An end component (T, A) is called a *subcomponent* of a subgraph (U, B) if $\emptyset \neq T \subseteq U$ and $A(t) \subseteq B(t)$ for all $t \in T$. An end component (T, A) is called *maximal* (in $\mathcal{M}$) if there is no end component $(V, C) \neq (T, A)$ of $\mathcal{M}$ such that (T, A) is a subcomponent of (V, C). Note that each state belongs to at most one maximal end component and that each state can be contained in several end components, but it can also happen that a certain state does not belong to any (maximal) end component. An end component (T, A) of a subgraph (U, B) is said to be maximal in (U, B) if if there is no subcomponent $(V, C) \neq (T, A)$ of (U, B) such that (T, A) is a subcomponent of (V, C).

Given an infinite path $\pi = s_0 \xrightarrow{\alpha_1} s_1 \xrightarrow{\alpha_2} s_2 \xrightarrow{\alpha_3} \ldots$, the *limit* of π, denoted $\mathsf{Lim}(\pi)$, is the pair (T, A) where $T = \mathsf{inf}(\pi) \cap S$ is the set of states in π that are visited infinitely often and $A : T \to 2^{\mathsf{Act}}$ is the function that assigns to any state

$t \in T$ the set of actions α such that $(s_i = t) \wedge (\alpha_{i+1} = \alpha)$ for infinitely many indices i. In particular, we have $\emptyset \neq A(t) \subseteq \inf(\pi) \cap \mathsf{Act}(t)$.

For each end component $\mathcal{E} = (T, A)$ there exists a finite-memory scheduler $\mathcal{U}_{\mathcal{E}}$ such that $\mathsf{Pr}_t^{\mathcal{U}_{\mathcal{E}}} \{\pi \in \mathsf{Pathinf} : \mathsf{Lim}(\pi) = \mathcal{E}\} = 1$ for all states $t \in T$. Such a finite-memory scheduler $\mathcal{U}_{\mathcal{E}}$ can be designed as follows. For $t \in T$ we pick an arbitrary enumeration $\alpha_{t,0}, \alpha_{t,1}, \ldots \alpha_{t,k_t}$ of the actions in $A(t)$. The modes of $\mathcal{U}_{\mathcal{E}}$ are the functions $\mathfrak{m} : T \to \mathbb{N}$ such that $0 \leq \mathfrak{m}(t) < k_t$ for all $t \in T$. The decision and next-mode function are defined by $\mathfrak{dec}(\mathfrak{m}, s) = \alpha_{s, \mathfrak{m}(s)}$ and $\mathfrak{next}(\mathfrak{m}, s) = \mathfrak{m}'$ where $\mathfrak{m}'(t) = \mathfrak{m}(t)$ if $t \in T \setminus \{s\}$ and $\mathfrak{m}'(s) = (\mathfrak{m}(s) + 1) \bmod k_s$. Vice versa, for each scheduler $\mathcal{U}$, the limit of almost all $\mathcal{U}$-paths of $\mathcal{M}$ consistutes an end component:

Lemma 1 ([16,17,14]). *For any given MDP $\mathcal{M}$ and scheduler $\mathcal{U}$ it holds that* $\mathsf{Pr}_s^{\mathcal{U}} \{\pi \in \mathsf{Pathinf} : \mathsf{Lim}(\pi)$ *is an end component* $\} = 1$.

Fairness. We deal here with the standard concept of strong and weak fairness [21,31,28] with a generic syntax that treats state- and action-based fairness in a uniform way. A *(single) fairness constraint* for $\mathcal{M}$ is a pair (H, K) such that $H, K \subseteq \mathsf{Act} \cup 2^{\mathsf{AP}}$ which can be treated as a weak or strong fairness constraint. Using LTL-like notations, (H, K) viewed as a strong fairness constraint stands for $\square\lozenge H \to \square\lozenge K$, while (H, K) treated as a weak fairness constraint means $\lozenge\square H \to \square\lozenge K$. This is formalized by two satisfaction relations $\vdash_{\mathsf{sfair}}$ and $\vdash_{\mathsf{wfair}}$. Given a set $X \subseteq \mathsf{Act} \cup 2^{\mathsf{AP}}$, we define:

$$X \vdash_{\mathsf{sfair}} (H, K) \quad \text{iff} \quad X \cap H = \emptyset \ \text{ or } \ X \cap K \neq \emptyset$$
$$X \vdash_{\mathsf{wfair}} (H, K) \quad \text{iff} \quad X \setminus H \neq \emptyset \ \text{ or } \ X \cap K \neq \emptyset .$$

For example, if $\mathcal{M}$ models the interleaving behavior of processes $\mathcal{P}_1, \ldots, \mathcal{P}_n$ and $\mathsf{Act}_\ell \subseteq \mathsf{Act}$ denotes the set of all actions of process $\mathcal{P}_\ell$ then (strong or weak) process fairness for process $\mathcal{P}_\ell$ can be formalized by the pair (H, K) where $H = \mathsf{Enabled}_\ell$ and $K = \mathsf{Act}_\ell$ with $\mathsf{Enabled}_\ell = \{\mathfrak{A} \in 2^{\mathsf{AP}} : \mathsf{enabled}_\ell \in \mathfrak{A}\}$ and $\mathsf{enabled}_\ell$ being an atomic proposition such that $\mathsf{enabled}_\ell \in \mathcal{L}(s)$ iff $\mathsf{Act}_\ell \cap \mathsf{Act}(s) \neq \emptyset$.

A *(general) fairness condition* for $\mathcal{M}$ is a pair $\mathcal{F} = (\mathcal{SF}, \mathcal{WF})$ where $\mathcal{SF}$ and $\mathcal{WF}$ are sets of (single) fairness constraints. Intuitively, $\mathcal{F}$ imposes strong fairness for all elements in $\mathcal{SF}$ and weak fairness for all elements in $\mathcal{WF}$. This is formalized by the satisfaction relation $\vdash_{\mathsf{fair}}$ which for $X \subseteq \mathsf{Act} \cup 2^{\mathsf{AP}}$ is given by:

$$X \vdash_{\mathsf{fair}} \mathcal{F} \quad \text{iff} \quad X \vdash_{\mathsf{sfair}} (H, K) \text{ for all } (H, K) \in \mathcal{SF} \ \text{ and}$$
$$X \vdash_{\mathsf{wfair}} (H, K) \text{ for all } (H, K) \in \mathcal{WF}.$$

We refer to the elements $\mathcal{SF}$ as strong fairness constraints and to the elements in $\mathcal{WF}$ as weak fairness constraints. An infinite path π in $\mathcal{M}$ is called *fair*, denoted $\pi \models \mathcal{F}$, if $\inf(\pi) \vdash_{\mathsf{fair}} \mathcal{F}$. A fairness condition $\mathcal{F}$ for $\mathcal{M}$ is called *realizable* if there exists a scheduler $\mathcal{U}$ such that $\mathsf{Pr}_s^{\mathcal{U}} \{\pi : \inf(\pi) \vdash_{\mathsf{fair}} \mathcal{F}\} = 1$ for all states $s \in S$. In this case, $\mathcal{U}$ is called a *fair scheduler.*

3   Quantitative Analysis under Fairness Assumptions

The standard automata-based approach (see e.g. [16,7]) to compute the maximal or minimal probabilities for a given ω-regular linear-time property E in an MDP

$\mathcal{M}$ relies on a representation of E by a deterministic ω-automaton $\mathcal{A}$. The product $\mathcal{M} \times \mathcal{A}$ can then be viewed as an MDP and the task is to compute minimal or maximal probabilities for the acceptance condition of $\mathcal{A}$ in the product. In what follows, we suppose that we are given an MDP $\mathcal{M} = (S, \mathsf{Act}, \delta, \mu, \mathsf{AP}, \mathfrak{L})$ (that might stand for the product) which is equipped with a fairness condition $\mathcal{F} = \langle \mathcal{SF}, \mathcal{WF} \rangle$ and a *Streett* or *Rabin* acceptance condition Acc, given by a set of pairs (H, K) where where $H, K \subseteq 2^{\mathsf{AP}}$. The goal of this section is to present algorithms for checking realizability of the given fairness condition $\mathcal{F}$ and for computing

$$\mathsf{Pr}_{\mathcal{F}}^{\mathsf{fairmax}}(s \models \mathsf{Acc}) \overset{\text{def}}{=} \sup_{\mathcal{U} \in \mathsf{FairSched}(\mathcal{F})} \mathsf{Pr}_s^{\mathcal{U}}\{\pi \in \mathsf{Pathinf} : \pi \models \mathsf{Acc}\}$$

where $s \in S$ and $\mathsf{FairSched}(\mathcal{F})$ denotes the set of all fair schedulers, i.e., schedulers $\mathcal{U}$ with $\mathsf{Pr}_s^{\mathcal{U}}\{\pi : \inf(\pi) \vdash_{\mathsf{fair}} \mathcal{F}\} = 1$ for all states s in $\mathcal{M}$.

We first address the problem of how to check whether the given fairness condition is *realizable*. A strong fairness constraint can hold in an end component $\mathcal{E}$, while it is violated in the maximal end component containing $\mathcal{E}$. Thus, the relevant end components might be non-maximal and the naive approach to consider all end components has exponential time complexity. Notice that any state can belong to many end components and the total number of end components can be exponentially in the number of states of $\mathcal{M}$. We now present a polynomially time-bounded algorithm for checking realizability which avoids the explicit consideration of all potential end components and relies on a recursive approach to compute maximal end components in $\mathcal{M}$ and certain subgraphs. An end component $\mathcal{E}$ of $\mathcal{M}$ is said to be *fair* iff all paths π with $\mathsf{Lim}(\pi) = \mathcal{E}$ are fair, i.e., $\mathcal{E}$ is fair iff $X_{\mathcal{E}} \vdash_{\mathsf{fair}} \mathcal{F}$ where $X_{\mathcal{E}}$ is the set $\{\mathfrak{L}(t) : t \in T\} \cup \bigcup_{t \in T} A(t)$. Let FMEC be the set of all states t such that $t \in T$ for some maximal end component (T, A) that contains a fair subcomponent. We then have:

Lemma 2. *There exists a finite-memory scheduler $\mathcal{W}$ such that*

$$\mathsf{Pr}_s^{\mathcal{W}}\{\pi \in \mathsf{Pathinf} : \pi \models \mathcal{F}\} = 1$$

for all states $s \in \mathsf{FMEC}$.

Theorem 1. *$\mathcal{F}$ is realizable iff $s \models \exists \Diamond \mathsf{FMEC}$ for all states $s \in S$.*

Proof. "$\Longrightarrow$": Suppose $\mathcal{F}$ is realizable. Let $\mathcal{U}$ be a fair scheduler and s a state. Lemma 1 yields the existence of some end component $\mathcal{E} = (T, A)$ such that $\mathsf{Pr}_s^{\mathcal{U}}\{\pi : \mathsf{Lim}(\pi) = \mathcal{E}\} > 0\}$. Since $\mathcal{U}$ is fair, this end component $\mathcal{E}$ must be fair. But then $T \subseteq \mathsf{FMEC}$ (as each end component is contained in some maximal end component). Thus, $\mathsf{Pr}_s^{\mathcal{U}}\{\pi : \pi \models \Diamond \mathsf{FMEC}\} > 0$ and therefore $s \models \exists \Diamond \mathsf{FMEC}$. "$\Longleftarrow$": Suppose $s \models \exists \Diamond \mathsf{FMEC}$ for all states s. For each state s we pick a shortest (finite) path π_s from s to some state in FMEC. Let $\mathcal{V}$ be a memoryless scheduler such that for $s \notin \mathsf{FMEC}$, action $\mathcal{V}(s)$ is the first action in π_s. Using standard arguments for finite Markov chains (note that the induced Markov chain of a memoryless scheduler is finite), we obtain that $\mathsf{Pr}_s^{\mathcal{V}}\{\pi : \pi \models \Diamond \mathsf{FMEC}\} = 1$ for all states s. We now can compose $\mathcal{V}$ and the finite-memory scheduler $\mathcal{W}$ of Lemma 2 to obtain a fair scheduler. Thus, $\mathcal{F}$ is realizable. ∎

The proof of Theorem 1 shows that realizability of $\mathcal{F}$ is equivalent to the existence of a fair finite-memory scheduler. Thanks to Theorem 1, realizability of a given fairness condition $\mathcal{F} = \langle \mathcal{SF}, \mathcal{WF} \rangle$ can be checked by the following procedure: (1)compute the maximal end components of $\mathcal{M}$, then (2) compute the set FMEC by checking for each maximal end component $\mathcal{E}$ of $\mathcal{M}$ whether $\mathcal{E}$ contains a fair sub-component. Finally (3) perform a reachability analysis in $\mathcal{M}$ to check whether FMEC is reachable from all states. In (1) we can apply the algorithm presented in [14,16] which relies on an iterative computation of SCCs and runs in time quadratic in the size of $\mathcal{M}$. Step (2) can be realized by the recursive algorithm check_fair$(\mathcal{E}, \mathcal{F})$ presented in Algorithm 1. In the initial calls from the main procedure (step (2) above), $\mathcal{E}$ is a maximal end component of $\mathcal{M}$. In the recursive calls, $\mathcal{E}$ is an maximal end component of some sub-MDP, that is, a possibly non-maximal end component of $\mathcal{M}$.

The considered sub-MDPs arise by removing certain states and/or actions. They have the form $\mathcal{E} \ominus H$ where $\mathcal{E} = (T, A)$ is an end component of $\mathcal{M}$ and $H \subseteq \mathsf{Act} \cup 2^{\mathsf{AP}}$. Then, $\mathcal{E} \ominus H$ denotes the subgraph (U, B) where $U = \{t \in T : \mathfrak{L}(t) \notin H\}$ and $B : U \to 2^{\mathsf{Act}}$, $B(t) = \{\alpha \in A(t) \setminus H : \sum_{u \in U} \delta(t, \alpha, u) = 1\}$ for all $t \in U$. The notation $\mathcal{E} \vdash_{\mathsf{sfair}} (H, K)$ for some strong fairness constraint (H, K) indicates that all paths π with $\mathsf{Lim}(\pi) = \mathcal{E}$ satisfy the strong fairness constraint (H, K). That is, $\mathcal{E} \vdash_{\mathsf{sfair}} (H, K)$ iff $X_{\mathcal{E}} \vdash_{\mathsf{sfair}} (H, K)$ where $X_{\mathcal{E}}$ is the union of the sets $\{\mathfrak{L}(t) : t \in T\}$ and $\bigcup_{t \in T} A(t)$. Similarly, $\mathcal{E} \vdash_{\mathsf{wfair}} (H, K)$ iff $X_{\mathcal{E}} \vdash_{\mathsf{wfair}} (H, K)$.

Algorithm 1. Recursive algorithm check_fair$(\mathcal{E}, \mathcal{F})$

Input: end component $\mathcal{E} = (T, A)$, fairness condition $\mathcal{F} = \langle \mathcal{SF}, \mathcal{WF} \rangle$

---

if $\mathcal{E} \not\vdash_{\mathsf{wfair}} (H, K)$ for some $(H, K) \in \mathcal{WF}$ **then** return "false" **end if**
if $\mathcal{E} \vdash_{\mathsf{sfair}} (H, K)$ for all $(H, K) \in \mathcal{SF}$ **then** return "true"
else
    pick $(H, K) \in \mathcal{SF}$ such that $\mathcal{E} \not\vdash_{\mathsf{sfair}} (H, K)$;
    compute the set of all maximal end components of the subgraph $\mathcal{E} \ominus H$;
    for all maximal end components $\mathcal{E}'$ of $\mathcal{E} \ominus H$
      if check_fair$(\mathcal{E}', \langle \mathcal{SF} \setminus \{(H, K)\}, \mathcal{WF} \rangle)$ **then** return "true" **end if**
    end for
    return "false"
end if

The soundness of Algorithm 1 can be shown (proof omitted), the recursion depth is bounded by the total number of strong fairness constraints. For each recursive call check_fair$(\mathcal{E}', \mathcal{F}')$ inside check_fair$(\mathcal{E}, \mathcal{F})$, $\mathcal{E}'$ is an end component of the subgraph $\mathcal{E} \ominus H$ of $\mathcal{E}$ where (H, K) is a strong fairness constraint such that $\mathcal{E} \not\vdash_{\mathsf{sfair}} (H, K)$. But then $X_{\mathcal{E}} \cap H \neq \emptyset$. Hence, $\mathsf{size}(\mathcal{E}') < \mathsf{size}(\mathcal{E})$ where the size of a subgraph (U, B) is defined by $\mathsf{size}(U, B) = |U| + |\{\alpha \in \mathsf{Act} : \alpha \in B(u) \text{ for some } u \in U\}|$. With n being the total size of an appropriate list representation for $\mathcal{M}$, an upper bound for asymptotic cost for step (2) can be provided by the recurrence

$$\mathcal{T}(n, f) = \mathcal{O}(n^2) + \max\{\mathcal{T}(n_1, f-1) + \ldots + \mathcal{T}(n_k, f-1) : (n_1, \ldots, n_k) \in \mathcal{N}(n)\}$$

where $\mathcal{N}(n)$ consists of all tuples $(n_1, \ldots, n_k) \in \mathbb{N}^k$ where $k \geq 1$, $n_1, \ldots, n_k \geq 1$ and $n_1 + \ldots + n_k < n$. The summand $\mathcal{O}(n^2)$ stands for the time required to compute the maximal end components of $\mathcal{M}$. We also assume that $|\mathcal{SF}| + |\mathcal{WF}| \leq n$. Then, the time required to check whether some weak or strong fairness constraint is violated is also covered by $\mathcal{O}(n^2)$. The terms $\mathcal{T}(n_i, f-1)$ stand for the cost that are caused by the recursive calls for the maximal end components of the subgraph $\mathcal{E} \ominus H$. If $\mathcal{E} \ominus H$ has k maximal end components and their sizes are $n_1, \ldots, n_k$ then $n_1 + \ldots + n_k$ is bounded by the size of $\mathcal{E} \ominus H$ which is at most $n-1$. The solution of this recurrence is $\mathcal{O}(n^2 \cdot f)$. Thus:

Theorem 2. *Checking realizablity of a fairness condition $\mathcal{F}$ in an MDP $\mathcal{M}$ is solvable by an algorithm that runs in time quadratic in the size of $\mathcal{M}$ and linear in the number of fairness constraints.*

For a given Streett or Rabin acceptance condition Acc, we can combine techniques that have been presented in the literature (see e.g. [7] for an explanation for Rabin acceptance) with our algorithm for checking realizability. For this some adaptions of Algorithm 1 can be used to compute the set AFMEC that results from the union of (the state-spaces of) all maximal end components that contain a fair subcomponent where Acc holds. Then, for $\mathcal{F}$ being realizable the problem of computing maximal probabilities to satisfy Acc under the given fairness condition $\mathcal{F}$ boils down to the problem of computing maximal reachability probabilities for AFMEC under all schedulers. This can be done by applying well-known techniques of linear programming or value/policy iteration (see e.g. [36]). If $\mathcal{F}$ is not realizable then $\mathrm{Pr}_{\mathcal{F}}^{\mathsf{fairmax}}(s \models \mathsf{Acc})$ can be computed by applying the above techniques to the sub-MDP $\mathcal{M}_{\mathcal{F}}$ that results from $\mathcal{M}$ by removing all states that cannot reach FMEC. Note that under any fair scheduler $\mathcal{U}$ for $\mathcal{M}$, the $\mathcal{U}$-paths will never enter a state s with $s \not\models \exists \Diamond \mathsf{FMEC}$. Thus, $\mathcal{M}$ and $\mathcal{M}_{\mathcal{F}}$ have the same fair schedulers. By Theorem 1, it is obvious that the given fairness condition $\mathcal{F}$ is realizable for $\mathcal{M}_{\mathcal{F}}$. Hence, we get:

Theorem 3. *The values $\mathrm{Pr}_{\mathcal{F}}^{\mathsf{fairmax}}(s \models \mathsf{Acc})$ can be computed in time polynomial in the size of $\mathcal{M}$ and linear in the number of fairness constraints and of (Streett or Rabin) acceptance pairs.*

4   Partial Order Reduction and Fairness

In this section we explain how to treat strong and weak process fairness in the context of partial order reduction (POR) for MDPs and stutter-invariant linear-time properties [6,15]. For partial order reduction the starting point is usually a description of an asynchronous parallel system by a representation of the subsystems that run in parallel, e.g., as in ProbMeLa, the input language of the model checker LiQuor. The rough idea behind partial order reduction is to construct a reduced system by abolishing redundancies in the MDP that originate from the interleaving of independent activities that are executed in parallel. For independent actions α and β, the interleaving semantics represents their parallel execution by the nondeterministic choice between the action sequences $\alpha\beta$ and $\beta\alpha$. If $\alpha\beta$ and $\beta\alpha$ have the same effect to the control and program variables, and thus lead to the same state distribution, the investigation of one order ($\alpha\beta$ or $\beta\alpha$) as a representative for both suffices under certain side conditions.

More general, instead of constructing the full system $\mathcal{M}$, the goal of partial order reduction is to generate an "equivalent" sub-system $\mathcal{M}_{\mathsf{red}}$ of the full transition system $\mathcal{M}$. We consider here a special instance of POR, namely the ample set method that has been developed for non-probabilistic systems [33,25,34] in the early 1990s and has been generalized to the probabilistic setting [6,15,5,23] in the last few years. The rough idea of the ample set method is to assign to any reachable state s of an MDP $\mathcal{M}$ an action-set $\mathsf{ample}(s) \subseteq \mathsf{Act}(s)$ and to construct a reduced system $\mathcal{M}_{\mathsf{red}}$ that results by using the action-sets $\mathsf{ample}(s)$ instead of $\mathsf{Act}(s)$. That is, starting from the initial states of $\mathcal{M}$, one builds up $\mathcal{M}_{\mathsf{red}}$ by only applying ample transitions. The reduced system should be equivalent to the original system in the desired sense, e.g., simulation equivalent or bisimulation equivalent, etc. Depending on the desired equivalence the defined ample sets have to fulfill certain conditions to ensure the equivalence. These equivalences typically identify those paths whose traces (i.e., words obtained from the paths by projection on the state labels) agree up to stuttering. In this context stuttering refers to the repetition of the same state labels. Two infinite paths π_1, π_2 are called *stutter equivalent*, denoted $\pi_1 \equiv_{\mathsf{st}} \pi_2$, iff there exists an infinite word $\mathfrak{A}_1\mathfrak{A}_2\mathfrak{A}_3 \ldots$ over 2^{AP} such that $\mathsf{trace}(\pi_1), \mathsf{trace}(\pi_2) \in \mathfrak{A}_1^+\mathfrak{A}_2^+\mathfrak{A}_3^+ \ldots$. An LT property over AP is called *stutter-invariant*, if it cannot distinguish between stutter equivalent paths, that is if for all stutter equivalent words $\varsigma_1, \varsigma_2 \in (2^{\mathsf{AP}})^\omega$ we have that $\varsigma_1 \in \mathsf{E}$ if and only if $\varsigma_2 \in \mathsf{E}$. An action α is called a *stutter action* if for each states s, t with $\delta(s, \alpha, t) > 0$ it holds that $\mathfrak{L}(s) = \mathfrak{L}(t)$. Given two MDPs $\mathcal{M}_1$, $\mathcal{M}_2$ with the same set of atomic propositions AP then $\mathcal{M}_1$ and $\mathcal{M}_2$ are called stutter-equivalent, denoted $\mathcal{M}_1 \equiv_{\mathsf{st}} \mathcal{M}_2$, if for each scheduler $\mathcal{U}_1$ of $\mathcal{M}_1$ there exists a scheduler $\mathcal{U}_2$ of $\mathcal{M}_2$ such $\mathsf{Pr}_{\mathcal{M}_1}^{\mathcal{U}_1}(\mathsf{E}) = \mathsf{Pr}_{\mathcal{M}_2}^{\mathcal{U}_2}(\mathsf{E})$ for all stutter-invariant measurable LT-properties $\mathsf{E} \subseteq (2^{\mathsf{AP}})^\omega$, and vice versa.

Theorem 4 ([6] Ample set method for MDPs). $\mathcal{M} = (S, \mathsf{Act}, \delta, \mu, \mathsf{AP}, \mathfrak{L})$ *be an MDP and* $\mathsf{ample} : S \to 2^{\mathsf{Act}}$ *a function satisfying the conditions proposed in [6]. Then,* $\mathcal{M} \equiv_{\mathsf{st}} \mathcal{M}_{\mathsf{red}}$. *Here,* $\mathcal{M}_{\mathsf{red}}$ *denotes the reduced MDP that emanates from the MDP* $\mathcal{M}$ *and the ample sets defined by the function* ample.

POR and fairness. We will now explain treating strong and weak (process) fairness in the context of partial order reduction for MDPs and stutter-invariant linear-time properties. In particular, we will show that any ample set conditions ensuring Theorem 4 are compatible with strong and weak LTL fairness conditions and that the implementation of the partial order reduction in LiQuor [4] (originally designed for nextfree LTL specifications and MDPs without fairness) is adequate for reasoning about extremal probabilities for stutter-invariant linear-time properties assuming strong or weak process fairness.

LTL fairness. We first observe that any fairness condition $\mathcal{F} = (\mathcal{SF}, \mathcal{WF})$, where $H, K \subseteq 2^{\mathsf{AP}}$ for all pairs $(H, K) \in \mathcal{SF} \cup \mathcal{WF}$ can be represented by a nextfree LTL formula

$$\varphi_{\mathcal{F}} = \bigwedge_{(H,K)\in\mathcal{SF}} (\Box\Diamond\phi_H \to \Box\Diamond\phi_K) \wedge \bigwedge_{(H,K)\in\mathcal{WF}} (\Diamond\Box\phi_H \to \Box\Diamond\phi_K)$$

where, for $J \subseteq 2^{\mathsf{AP}}$, ϕ_J denotes the formula $\bigvee_{\mathfrak{A}\in J} \psi_{\mathfrak{A}}$ and, for $\mathfrak{A} \subseteq \mathsf{AP}$, $\psi_{\mathfrak{A}}$ is the conjunction of the atomic propositions $a \in \mathfrak{A}$ and the literals $\neg a$ for $a \in \mathsf{AP} \setminus \mathfrak{A}$.

A well-known result [30] ensures that each nextfree LTL formula, and therefore $\mathcal{F}$, describes a stutter-invariant LT-property.

Theorem 5. *Let* $\mathcal{M} = (S, \mathsf{Act}, \delta, \mu, \mathsf{AP}, \mathfrak{L})$ *be an MDP,* $\mathcal{F}$ *an LTL fairness condition as above that uses only atomic propositions from* AP *and* $\mathsf{ample} : S \to 2^{\mathsf{Act}}$ *a function that assigns an ample-set to all states such that* $\mathcal{M} \equiv_{st} \mathcal{M}_{\mathsf{red}}$. *Then, for each stutter-invariant measurable LT property* $\mathsf{E} \subseteq (2^{\mathsf{AP}})^\omega$:

$$\sup_{\mathcal{U} \in \mathsf{FairSched}^{\mathcal{M}}(\mathcal{F})} \mathsf{Pr}^{\mathcal{U}}_{\mathcal{M}}(\mathsf{E}) = \sup_{\mathcal{U}' \in \mathsf{FairSched}^{\mathcal{M}_{\mathsf{red}}}(\mathcal{F})} \mathsf{Pr}^{\mathcal{U}'}_{\mathcal{M}_{\mathsf{red}}}(\mathsf{E})$$

Proof. "$\geq$" is obvious as $\mathcal{M}_{\mathsf{red}}$ is a sub-MDP of $\mathcal{M}$. To show "$\leq$" let $\mathcal{U}$ be a fair scheduler of $\mathcal{M}$. As $\mathcal{M}$ and $\mathcal{M}_{\mathsf{red}}$ are stutter-equivalent there exists a scheduler $\mathcal{U}'$ for $\mathcal{M}_{\mathsf{red}}$ such that $\mathsf{Pr}^{\mathcal{U}}_{\mathcal{M}}(\mathsf{E}) = \mathsf{Pr}^{\mathcal{U}'}_{\mathcal{M}_{\mathsf{red}}}(\mathsf{E})$ for all stutter-invariants measurable properties E. We have $\mathsf{Pr}^{\mathcal{U}'}_{\mathcal{M}_{\mathsf{red}}}(\mathcal{F}) = \mathsf{Pr}^{\mathcal{U}}_{\mathcal{M}}(\mathcal{F}) = 1$ as $\mathcal{F}$ describes a stutter-invariant LT property over AP. Thus, $\mathcal{U}'$ is a fair scheduler of $\mathcal{M}_{\mathsf{red}}$ and moreover $\mathsf{Pr}^{\mathcal{U}'}_{\mathcal{M}_{\mathsf{red}}}(\mathsf{E}) = \mathsf{Pr}^{\mathcal{U}}_{\mathcal{M}}(\mathsf{E})$ for each stutter-invariant measurable LT property $\mathsf{E} \subseteq (2^{\mathsf{AP}})^\omega$. ∎

Theorem 5 holds in the same way for the infimum instead of the supremum. It shows that with respect to LTL fairness conditions, the POR with the ample set conditions that are proposed in [6] is still applicable to fair quantitative model checking against nextfree LTL specifications. A disadvantage of this approach is that the atomic propositions from the fairness condition have to be taken into account for the notion of a stutter action and can therefore lead to a reduced MDP that is larger than the one obtained for the standard analysis (without fairness) against the same formula.

Process fairness. We will show that the current realization of the partial order reduction in the model checker `LiQuor` [4] – which has been designed for nextfree LTL specifications *without* fairness – is compatible with strong and weak process fairness in the sense that the extremal probabilities for stutter-invariant linear-time properties in the original MDP $\mathcal{M}$ and the reduced MDP $\mathcal{M}_{\mathsf{red}}$ generated by `LiQuor` agree. According to the input language `ProbMeLa` of `LiQuor` we consider a scenario of several probabilistic processes $\mathcal{P}_1, \ldots, \mathcal{P}_n$ that are executed in parallel. Thus the set of actions Act of the resulting MDP is the union of the set of actions Act_i of the processes $\mathcal{P}_i$. (The action sets $\mathsf{Act}_1, \ldots, \mathsf{Act}_n$ are supposed to be pairwise disjoint.) `ProbMeLa` [3] is a probabilistic variant of `ProMeLa` [26] which relies on an imperative guarded command language with Boolean guards that specify the enabledness of actions and a few probabilistic features (like probabilistic choice and lossy channels). In order to show our claim we now discuss the ample set conditions that have been implemented in `LiQuor`.

(A1) for all states s in $\mathcal{M}_{\mathsf{red}}$: $\mathsf{ample}(s) = \mathsf{Act}(s)$ or $\exists i : \mathsf{ample}(s) = \mathsf{Act}_i(s) = \{\alpha\}$, where α is a stutter action and for all $\beta \in \cup_{i \neq j}\mathsf{Act}_j$ it holds that the execution of α does not change the variables that are relevant for the guard of β, and vice versa.   **(A2)** Cycles $s_0 s_1 \ldots s_n s_0$ in $\mathcal{M}_{\mathsf{red}}$ contain a state s_i such that $\mathsf{ample}(s_i) = \mathsf{Act}(s_i)$.

The soundness of these conditions follows from the fact that these conditions are stronger than the conditions presented in [6]. The exact conditions from [6] are not relevant for the purpose of this paper and are therefore omitted here. In the sequel, we assume for each process $\mathcal{P}_i$ a fresh atomic proposition enabled$_i$ that serves to characterize the states where at least one action of process $\mathcal{P}_i$ (i.e., at least one action in Act$_i$) is enabled. We assume that enabled$_i$ is not contained in the original set AP and define $AP' = AP \cup \{\text{enabled}_i : 1 \leq i \leq n\}$. The labeling function of the MDP $\mathcal{M}$ is extended to a function $\mathfrak{L} : S \to 2^{AP'}$ by enabled$_i \in \mathfrak{L}(s)$ iff Act$_i \cap$ Act$(s) \neq \emptyset$. The original set AP provides the atoms to formalize the LT properties to be checked (e.g., by means of an LTL formula) and yields the basis for the notion of the stutter equivalence and stutter actions, while AP' serves to formalize process fairness. More precisely, we suppose that $\mathcal{M}$ posseses a fairness condition $\mathcal{F} = (\mathcal{SF}, \mathcal{WF})$ that imposes strong or weak fairness for processes, that is, for all $(H, K) \in \mathcal{SF} \cup \mathcal{WF}$ there is an index i such that $H = $ Enabled$_i$ and $K = $ Act$_i$ where Enabled$_i$ denotes the set of all subsets $\mathfrak{A}$ of AP' such that enabled$_i \in \mathfrak{A}$. Such a pair describes strong (resp. weak) fairness for process $\mathcal{P}_i$ such that if $\mathcal{P}_i$'s actions are infinitely often (resp. continuously from some moment) enabled then $\mathcal{P}_i$ performs infinitely many actions.

Theorem 6 (Soundness of (A1), (A2) for process fairness). *Let* $\mathcal{M} = (S, \text{Act}, \delta, \mu, \text{AP}, \mathfrak{L})$ *be an MDP,* $\mathcal{F}$ *a process fairness condition as above and* ample $: S \to 2^{\text{Act}}$ *a function satisfying conditions (A1) and (A2). Let* $\mathsf{E} \subseteq (2^{\text{AP}})^\omega$ *be a stutter-invariant measurable LT property. Then:*

$$\sup_{\mathcal{U} \in \mathsf{FairSched}^{\mathcal{M}}(\mathcal{F})} \mathsf{Pr}^{\mathcal{U}}_{\mathcal{M}}(\mathsf{E}) = \sup_{\mathcal{U}' \in \mathsf{FairSched}^{\mathcal{M}_{\text{red}}}(\mathcal{F})} \mathsf{Pr}^{\mathcal{U}'}_{\mathcal{M}_{\text{red}}}(\mathsf{E})$$

Proof. As in the proof of Theorem 5, it is sufficient to show "$\leq$". Given a fair scheduler $\mathcal{U}$ of $\mathcal{M}$, we apply the construction of [6,23] to obtain a corresponding scheduler $\mathcal{U}_{\text{red}}$ of $\mathcal{M}_{\text{red}}$ that yields the same probabilities for all stutter-invariant LT-properties. We now show that this scheduler $\mathcal{U}_{\text{red}}$ is fair. The precise construction of such a scheduler $\mathcal{U}_{\text{red}}$ has been presented in [23]. We will sketch here only the main ideas that are necessary for our argumentation. The construction of $\mathcal{U}_{\text{red}}$ relies on an iterative approach where an infinite sequence $\mathcal{U} = \mathcal{U}_0, \mathcal{U}_1, \mathcal{U}_2, \ldots$ of schedulers for $\mathcal{M}$ is constructed such that $\mathcal{U}_0, \ldots, \mathcal{U}_i$ agree on all finite paths of length $< i$. The scheduler $\mathcal{U}_{\text{red}}$ is then defined to be the "limit" of the schedulers $\mathcal{U}_i$. The transformations $\mathcal{U}_i \rightsquigarrow \mathcal{U}_{i+1}$ all rely on the same schema and we will sketch here the transformation for a single $\mathcal{U}_0$-path into a set of stutter-equivalent $\mathcal{U}_1$-paths. We will show that these $\mathcal{U}_1$-paths are fair w.r.t. $\mathcal{F}$ if π is fair w.r.t. $\mathcal{F}$.

Given a $\mathcal{U}_0$-path $\pi = s_0 \xrightarrow{\alpha_1} s_1 \xrightarrow{\alpha_2} s_2 \xrightarrow{\alpha_3} \ldots$ of $\mathcal{M}$, let n be the smallest number such that $\alpha_n \in$ ample(s). If no α_i is an ample-action of s_0, let n be ∞. Suppose first that n is finite. If $n = 1$ (e.g., if ample$(s_0) = $ Act(s_0)) then π stays unchanged. If $n > 1$ then condition (A1) ensures that α_n is enabled in each of the states $s_1, \ldots, s_{n-1}$. Indeed, assuming that $\{\alpha_n\} = $ Act$_j(s_0)$, for $1 \leq i \leq n-1$, $\alpha_i \notin$ Act$_j$ as `ProbMeLa` commands are executed consecutively. By (A1), the execution of the actions $\alpha_1, \ldots, \alpha_{n-1}$ does not change the variables that are relevant for the guard of α_n. Hence, α_n stays enabled in the states $s_1, \ldots, s_{n-1}$. Moreover, α_1 is enabled in every α_n-successor of s_0 and we can switch from the action sequence $\alpha_1 \alpha_2 \ldots \alpha_{n-1} \alpha_n$ to the action sequence $\alpha_n \alpha_1 \alpha_2 \ldots \alpha_{n-1}$. Both action sequences can be executed from state s_0 and yield the same distribution over the states that can be reached afterwards which leads to the following picture.

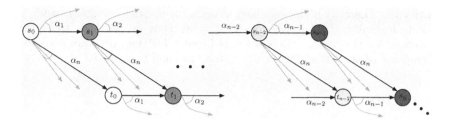

We define $\mathcal{U}_1$ such that $\pi_1 = s_0 \xrightarrow{\alpha_n} t_0 \xrightarrow{\alpha_1} \ldots \xrightarrow{\alpha_{n-2}} t_{n-2} \xrightarrow{\alpha_{n-1}} s_n \xrightarrow{\alpha_{n+1}} s_{n+1} \xrightarrow{\alpha_{n+2}} \ldots$ is a $\mathcal{U}_1$-path. Let us now suppose that $n = \infty$. By similar arguments, we define $\mathcal{U}_1$ such that $\pi_1 = s_0 \xrightarrow{\alpha} t_0 \xrightarrow{\alpha_1} t_1 \xrightarrow{\alpha_2} \ldots$ is a $\mathcal{U}_1$-path, where $\mathsf{ample}(s) = \{\alpha\}$. Moreover, $\mathcal{U}_1$ is defined in such a way that almost surely every $\mathcal{U}_1$-path originates from a $\mathcal{U}_0$-path via such a transformation. In summary, given a $\mathcal{U}$-path π starting in state s_0, the basic idea is to permute the first ample action of s that occurs along π to the beginning of the action sequence of π. If no such action exists, an arbitrary ample action of s is prepended to the action sequence of π. This step is then repeated ad infinitum to yield a scheduler $\mathcal{U}_{\mathsf{red}}$ of $\mathcal{M}_{\mathsf{red}}$.

Condition (A2) guarantees that each action of a $\mathcal{U}_0$-path π will almost surely be eventually executed by the "corresponding" $\mathcal{U}_{\mathsf{red}}$-path π_{red}. We therefore get that almost-surely

$$\inf(\pi) \cap \mathsf{Act} \subseteq \inf(\pi_{\mathsf{red}}) \cap \mathsf{Act}. \tag{1}$$

Moreover, we observe that if $n \neq \infty$ in the above described transformation, then π and π_1 share a common suffix. Thus:

$$\inf(\pi) = \inf(\pi_1). \tag{2}$$

If $n = \infty$ and $\mathsf{ample}(s_0) = \mathsf{Act}_j(s_0) = \{\alpha\}$ then

$$\mathsf{Act}_i(s_k) = \mathsf{Act}_i(t_k), \text{ for } i \neq j \text{ and } k \geq 0. \tag{3}$$

Indeed, condition (A1) ensures that the execution of α does not change the variables that are relevant for the execution of the actions $\beta \in \mathsf{Act}_i$ for $i \neq j$. As each t_k is an α-successor of s_k, equation (3) follows.

Let (H, K) be a fairness constraint stating fairness for process $\mathcal{P}_\ell$, i.e., $K = \mathsf{Act}_\ell$ and H consists of all subsets $\mathfrak{A}$ of AP' such that $\mathsf{enabled}_\ell \in \mathfrak{A}$. Let $\pi = s_0 \xrightarrow{\alpha_1} s_1 \xrightarrow{\alpha_2} s_2 \xrightarrow{\alpha_3} \ldots$ be a path in $\mathcal{M}$. If $\inf(\pi) \cap K \neq \emptyset$ then equation (1) ensures that $\inf(\pi_{\mathsf{red}}) \cap K \neq \emptyset$. Now assume that $\inf(\pi) \cap K = \emptyset$ and $\inf(\pi) \cap H = \emptyset$. If in the above described transformation from π to π_1, the index n is equal to ∞ then the chosen ample action α is not in Act_ℓ. Otherwise by (A1) α would be enabled in each state s_k for $k \geq 0$ (see the above picture), but then $\inf(\pi) \cap H \neq \emptyset$ which contradicts our assumption. Hence, if $n = \infty$, the chosen ample action is in some Act_j with $j \neq \ell$ and equation (3) ensures that $\mathsf{Act}_\ell(s_k) = \mathsf{Act}_\ell(t_k)$ for $k \geq 0$.

Altogether, equations (2) and (3) ensure that $(\inf(\pi) \cap K = \emptyset \wedge \inf(\pi) \cap H = \emptyset)$ implies that $\inf(\pi_1) \cap H = \emptyset$. Condition (A2) then ensures that almost surely $\mathcal{U}$-paths π with $\pi \vdash_{\mathsf{sfair}} (H, K)$ are transformed into $\mathcal{U}_{\mathsf{red}}$-paths π_{red} with $\pi_{\mathsf{red}} \vdash_{\mathsf{sfair}} (H, K)$. With similar arguments, we get that $\mathcal{U}$-paths π with $\pi \vdash_{\mathsf{wfair}} (H, K)$ transformed into $\mathcal{U}_{\mathsf{red}}$-paths π_{red} with $\pi_{\mathsf{red}} \vdash_{\mathsf{wfair}} (H, K)$. We conclude that for a fair scheduler $\mathcal{U}$ of $\mathcal{M}$, the scheduler $\mathcal{U}_{\mathsf{red}}$ of $\mathcal{M}_{\mathsf{red}}$ is also fair. ∎

Note that in Theorem 6 the auxiliary atomic propositions enabled$_i$ were only needed to formalize the fairness constraints, but they do not have to be taken into account for the construction of the reduced MDP, i.e., they are not used in the definition of stutter actions which is used in condition (A1).

5   Conclusion

In this paper we presented a solution to an important and so far unaddressed question in the context of calculating extremal probabilities for a Markov decision process satisfying a linear time property, namely the question of efficiently treating strong and weak fairness conditions. The presented approach increases the complexity only linear in the number of fairness constraints. It relies on a combination of ideas used in fair CTL model checking or checking emptiness for Streett automata with the concept of end components that yield the basis to reasoning about the limiting behavior of MDPs. We integrated algorithm 1 (page 142) in the model checker LiQuor [11] and analysed its performace in practise. The results suggest (see table below) that the use of process fairness (weak or strong) does not add a *significant* amount of time to the calculation times.

	MDP building			LP building (calculating the set FMEC)				
N	#states	#transitions	build	#max.ECs	#states in FMEC	unfair	weak	strong
(a) Randomized Gossiping, without Partial Order Reduction								
3	4015	5298	0.9s	321	3546	1.5s	1.7s	1.7s
4	488902	661307	4.4s	3438	353532	14.3s	16.7s	18.9s
5	n.a.	n.a	n.a.	n.a.	n.a.	n.a.	n.a.	n.a.
(b) Randomized Gossiping, reduced with partial order reduction								
3	403	488	0.6s	22	402	0.7s	0.8s	0.8s
4	4424	5380	1.3s	378	3652	1.9s	2.3s	2.9s
5	74485	90998	1.4s	3470	58372	2s	3.1s	4.7s
(c) Randomized Distributed Mutex protocol								
4	5535	25080	0.3s	1	5535	0.1s	0.2s	1s
5	47675	277820	3.1s	1	47675	0.5s	1.3s	2.4s
6	411255	2875896	37.5s	1	411255	5.6s	6.2s	8.6s
(d) Randomized Distributed Mutex protocol with partial order red.								
5	46046	180831	2.6s	1	46046	1.1s	1.5s	2.4s
6	385238	1625928	28.9s	1	385238	4.8s	6.1s	7.5s
7	3013345	15536978	330.3s	1	3013345	54.3s	106.2s	122.6s

For illustration we present results for two models: a version of the randomized gossiping protocol (a)-(b), see, [10] and a variant of the randomized dining philosophers [32] we called *randomized distributed mutex protocol (c)-(d)*. Column N denotes the number of processes. Both models represent two typical classes of models that are interesting in our context and were modelled in ProbMeLa. The first model contains many small maximal end components that have to be analysed seperately by the algorithm while the second model always consists of one maximal end component. The results indicate that even complex fairness conditions (e.g., strong fairness conditions that involve a fairness constraints for each process) can be handled efficiently in practise using the approach presented here. It is worth noting that due to the fact that models (c) and

(d) contain only one maximal end component the algorithm terminates early for the whole scenario, since only a single accepting fair subcomponent needs to be found.

References

1. Alur, R., Henzinger, T.A.: Reactive modules. Formal Methods in System Design: An International Journal 15(1), 7–48 (1999)
2. Arons, T., Pnueli, A., Zuck, L.: Parameterized verification by probabilistic abstraction. In: Gordon, A.D. (ed.) FOSSACS 2003. LNCS, vol. 2620, pp. 87–102. Springer, Heidelberg (2003)
3. Baier, C., Ciesinski, F., Größer, M.: Probmela: a modeling language for communicating probabilistic systems. In: Proc. MEMOCODE (2004)
4. Baier, C., Ciesinski, F., Grösser, M., Klein, J.: Reduction techniques for model checking markov decision processes. In: Proc.QEST 2008. IEEE CS Press, Los Alamitos (2008)
5. Baier, C., D'Argenio, P., Größer, M.: Partial order reduction for probabilistic branching time. In: Proc. QAPL. ENTCS, vol. 153(2) (2006)
6. Baier, C., Größer, M., Ciesinski, F.: Partial order reduction for probabilistic systems. In: Proc. QEST 2004. IEEE CS Press, Los Alamitos (2004)
7. Baier, C., Katoen, J.-P.: Principles of Model Checking. MIT Press, Cambridge (2008)
8. Baier, C., Kwiatkoswka, M.: Model checking for a probabilistic branching time logic with fairness. Distributed Computing 11(3) (1998)
9. Bianco, A., de Alfaro, L.: Model checking of probabilistic and nondeterministic systems. In: Thiagarajan, P.S. (ed.) FSTTCS 1995. LNCS, vol. 1026. Springer, Heidelberg (1995)
10. Chrobak, M., Gasieniec, L., Rytter, W.: A randomized algorithm for gossiping in radio networks. In: Wang, J. (ed.) COCOON 2001. LNCS, vol. 2108, p. 483. Springer, Heidelberg (2001)
11. Ciesinski, F., Baier, C.: LiQuor: a tool for qualitative and quantitative linear time analysis of reactive systems. In: Proc. QEST 2007. IEEE CS Press, Los Alamitos (2007)
12. Clarke, E., Emerson, E., Sistla, A.: Automatic verification of finite-state concurrent systems using temporal logic specifications. ACM TOPLAS 8(2) (1986)
13. Clarke, E., Grumberg, O., Peled, D.: Model Checking. MIT Press, Cambridge (1999)
14. Courcoubetis, C., Yannakakis, M.: The complexity of probabilistic verification. Journal of the ACM 42(4) (1995)
15. D'Argenio, P.R., Niebert, P.: Partial order reduction on concurrent probabilistic programs. In: Proc. QEST 2004. IEEE CS Press, Los Alamitos (2004)
16. de Alfaro, L.: Formal Verification of Probabilistic Systems. PhD thesis (1997)
17. de Alfaro, L.: Stochastic transition systems. In: Sangiorgi, D., de Simone, R. (eds.) CONCUR 1998. LNCS, vol. 1466, pp. 423–438. Springer, Heidelberg (1998)
18. de Alfaro, L.: From fairness to chance. In: Proc. PROBMIV. ENTCS, vol. 22 (1999)
19. Dijkstra, E.W.: Guarded commands, non-determinacy and the formal derivation of programs. Comm. ACM 18 (1975)
20. Allen Emerson, E., Lei, C.-L.: Modalities for model checking: branching time logic strikes back. Sci. Comput. Program 8(3) (1987)
21. Francez, N.: Fairness. Springer, Heidelberg (1986)
22. Grädel, E., Thomas, W., Wilke, T. (eds.): Automata, Logics, and Infinite Games. LNCS, vol. 2500. Springer, Heidelberg (2002)
23. Größer, M.: Reduction Methods for Probabilistic Model Checking. PhD thesis (2008)

24. Hart, S., Sharir, M., Pnueli, A.: Termination of probabilistic concurrent programs. ACM TOPLAS 5(3) (1983)
25. Holzmann, G., Peled, D.: An improvement in formal verification. In: Proc. FORTE. Chapman & Hall, Boca Raton (1994)
26. Holzmann, G.: The model checker SPIN. Software Engineering 23(5) (1997)
27. Klein, J., Baier, C.: On-the-fly stuttering in the construction of deterministic omega-automata. In: Holub, J., Žďárek, J. (eds.) CIAA 2007. LNCS, vol. 4783, pp. 51–61. Springer, Heidelberg (2007)
28. Kwiatkowska, M.: Survey of fairness notions. Inf. and Softw.Techn. 31(7) (1989)
29. Kwiatkowska, M., Norman, G., Parker, D.: PRISM: Probabilistic symbolic model checker. In: Field, T., Harrison, P.G., Bradley, J., Harder, U. (eds.) TOOLS 2002. LNCS, vol. 2324, p. 200. Springer, Heidelberg (2002)
30. Lamport, L.: Specifying concurrent program modules. TOPLAS 5(2) (1983)
31. Lehmann, D., Pnueli, A., Stavi, J.: Impartiality, justice and fairness: the ethics of concurrent termination. In: Even, S., Kariv, O. (eds.) ICALP 1981. LNCS, vol. 115, Springer, Heidelberg (1981)
32. Lehmann, D., Rabin, M.O.: On the advantage of free choice: A symmetric and fully distributed solution to the Dining Philosophers problem (extended abstract). In: Proc. POPL (1981)
33. Peled, D.: All from one, one for all: On model checking using representatives. In: Courcoubetis, C. (ed.) CAV 1993. LNCS, vol. 697. Springer, Heidelberg (1993)
34. Peled, D.: Partial order reduction: Linear and branching time logics and process algebras. In: Partial Order Methods in Verification, DIMACS, vol. 29(10) (1997)
35. Pnueli, A., Zuck, L.: Probabilistic verification. Information and Computation 103(1) (March 1993)
36. Puterman, M.: Markov Decision Processes: Discrete Stochastic Dynamic Programming. John Wiley & Sons, Inc., New York (1994)
37. Rosier, L.E., Yen, H.C.: On the complexity of deciding fair termination of probabilistic concurrent finite-state programs. Theoretical Computer Science (1988)
38. Schrijver, A.: Combinatorial Optimization: Polyhedra and Efficiency. Springer, Heidelberg (2003)
39. Vardi, M.: Automatic verification of probabilistic concurrent finite-state programs. In: Proc. FOCS (1985)

A Decompositional Proof Scheme for Automated Convergence Proofs of Stochastic Hybrid Systems*

Jens Oehlerking and Oliver Theel

Department of Computer Science
University of Oldenburg
26111 Oldenburg, Germany
{jens.oehlerking,oliver.theel}@informatik.uni-oldenburg.de

Abstract. In this paper, we describe a decompositional approach to convergence proofs for stochastic hybrid systems given as probabilistic hybrid automata. We focus on a concept called "stability in probability," which implies convergence of almost all trajectories of the stochastic hybrid system to a designated equilibrium point. By adapting classical Lyapunov function results to the stochastic hybrid case, we show how automatic stability proofs for such systems can be obtained with the help of numerical tools. To ease the load on the numerical solvers and to permit incremental construction of stable systems, we then propose an automatable Lyapunov-based decompositional framework for stochastic stability proofs. This framework allows conducting sub-proofs separately for different parts of the automaton, such that they still yield a proof for the entire system. Finally, we give an outline on how these decomposition results can be applied to conduct quantitative probabilistic convergence analysis, i.e., determining convergence probabilities below 1.

1 Introduction

During the previous decade, there has been significant progress in the field of automated stability proofs for feedback control systems. Most importantly, methods for the automatic computation of Lyapunov functions, serving as certificates of the stability property, have been developed [1,2,3,4]. A Lyapunov function can be seen as a type of generalized "energy function," ensuring that a system always makes some sort of progress while converging toward a desired equilibrium state. Central tools in this context are *semidefinite programming (SDP)* solvers, which numerically solve the constraint systems arising in Lyapunov function computation. These methods are, in theory, applicable to purely discrete-time (given as difference equations/inclusions or automata), purely continuous-time (given as differential equations/inclusions), and hybrid systems (given as a combination

---

* This work was partly supported by the German Research Foundation (DFG) as part of the Transregional Research Center "Automatic Verification and Analysis of Complex Systems" (SFB/TR 14/2 AVACS), www.avacs.org

Z. Liu and A.P. Ravn (Eds.): ATVA 2009, LNCS 5799, pp. 151–165, 2009.

of both). In the hybrid domain, the presence of both complex discrete structures and continuous dynamics given by differential equations makes the problem hard to solve in practice. In particular, the presence of complex discrete structures (i.e., large and irregular automata) often leads to problems with the numerical solvers: badly conditioned problems, rounding errors, and inaccuracies caused by the optimization algorithms themselves. Furthermore, it is difficult to design a stable hybrid system with complex discrete behavior, as existing analysis methods are only applicable to a complete model of the system. Consequently, they are of only limited help during the design process. Therefore, it is useful to decompose the problem of identifying a suitable Lyapunov function into SDP problems that are as small as possible, while still being able to conduct a convergence proof of the entire system. Apart from a decreased load on the numerical solver, arguments on parts of the hybrid system can be useful for successfully designing a system with the desired convergence property.

This paper extends the classes of hybrid systems that can be dealt with efficiently, by proposing such a decompositional approach for *probabilistic hybrid automata*, i.e., systems that contain probabilistic Markovian transitions between the discrete modes. We presented an automatable decompositional framework for systems without stochastic behavior in [5]. Here, we mainly focus on qualitative ("does a system converge with probability 1?") stability analysis, but also discuss the applicability of the results to quantitative ("with which probability is the system guaranteed to converge?") stability analysis. The result is an automatable decompositional framework allowing for the SDP-based computation of Lyapunov functions for the probabilistic case. As it turns out, probabilistic hybrid automata actually sometimes permit a stronger decomposition than their non-probabilistic counterparts. Furthermore, these results are also, to a certain extent, applicable to systems with *stochastic differential equations* instead of plain differential equations defining the continuous dynamics.

The paper is structured as follows: In Section 2, we formally define a probabilistic hybrid system model and probabilistic stability properties. Section 3 then states non-decompositional Lyapunov theorems that can be used to prove convergence, and details the computational procedure for computing such functions. In Section 4, we give decompositional techniques based on the computational method, yielding several theorems that allow the construction of a convergence proof from separate local computations. Section 5 shows the decomposition of a convergence proof for an example automaton. In Section 6, we discuss the exptension of these results for quantitative convergence analysis, i.e., for deriving stabilization properties that lie below probability 1. We then conclude in Section 7 with a discussion of the implications of our results.

2   Probabilistic Hybrid Systems

The system model we use in this paper is given next. It consists of standard hybrid automata, augmented with discrete probabilistic experiments tied to the discrete transitions. Whenever a transition is taken, we give a probability distribution over possible discrete successor states. Furthermore, we allow for differential inclusions in the mode dynamics instead of just differential equations.

Definition 1 (Probabilistic Hybrid Automaton). *Define $\mathcal{D}_n$ as the set of all n-dimensional, nonempty, convex, closed, and upper semicontinuous differential inclusions $\dot{x} \in F(x)$ on some state space $\mathcal{S}$. Here, $F(x)$ is a set-valued function mapping each x onto a set of possible values for the vector field direction $\dot{x}$.*

A hybrid automaton H *is a tuple* $(\mathcal{M}, \mathcal{S}, \mathcal{T}, Flow, Inv, Init)$, *where*

- $\mathcal{M}$ *is a finite set of* modes
- $\mathcal{S} = \mathbb{R}^n$ *is the* continuous state space
- $\mathcal{T}$ *is a set of* mode transitions *given as tuples* $(m, Target, G, Update)$, *where*
  - $m \in \mathcal{M}$ *is the* source mode
  - $Target: \mathcal{M} \to [0,1], \sum_{m \in \mathcal{M}} Target(m) = 1$ *is the* target mode mapping
  - $G \subseteq \mathcal{S}$ *is the* guard set
  - $Update: \mathcal{S} \to \mathcal{P}(\mathcal{S})$ *is the* update function *for the continuous state*
- $Flow: \mathcal{M} \to \mathcal{D}_n$ *is the* flow function, *mapping each mode onto a continuous evolution given as differential inclusion*
- $Inv: \mathcal{M} \to \mathcal{P}(\mathcal{S})$ *is the* invariant function, *mapping each mode onto a closed subset of the continuous state space*
- $Init \subseteq \mathcal{M} \times \mathcal{S}$ *is the set of combinations of initial discrete and continuous states*

Hybrid automata are finite automata where each node corresponds to a mode of the hybrid system and is labelled with a corresponding differential inclusion via the Flow function (see Figure 1). The continuous state must evolve according to this differential inclusion whenever the system is in this mode. Also, via Inv, each mode has an associated invariant set. A system may only stay in mode m if the current discrete state $x(t) \in \mathcal{S}$ is in Inv(m). Note that systems with only differential equations in the modes, instead of differential inclusions, are obtained by letting the $F(x)$ be singular sets.

Discrete transitions are driven by the following semantics: whenever the continuous state $x(t)$ reaches a guard set G of a mode transition with current mode m as source mode, the transition *can* be taken. As soon as the invariant set Inv(m) of the current mode m is left, m must be left immediately, i.e., some applicable transition *must* be taken. If this is not possible, then we will not consider the solution segment with respect to stability. These semantics permit non-deterministic switching in the sense that transitions can be specified to occur somewhere in a certain range of states. Whenever a transition is taken, the function Update is applied to the continuous state, and a new mode is chosen, based on the probability distribution given by Target.

Definition 2 (Trajectory). *A* trajectory *is a solution $x(t)$ for the hybrid automaton, considering only the evolution of the continuous state $x \in \mathcal{S}$. We only consider infinite, non-zeno solutions, i.e., $x(t)$ must be defined for all $t > 0$.[1] If*

---

[1] Finite solution segments can for instance occur if some invariant set is left, but no outgoing transition can be taken.

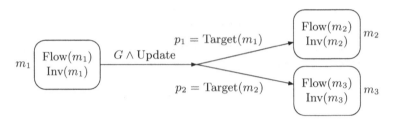

Fig. 1. Graphical representation of probabilistic hybrid automata

discrete updates of the continuous variables occur via Update functions at time t, then we consider x(t) as the state after all such updates. Similarly, m(t) is the discrete mode at time t. The (finite or infinite) mode sequence (m_i) lists all modes visited by a trajectory, in order.

The stability notion used in this paper is *global asymptotic stability in probability.* Informally, this term implies that each trajectory converges to an equilibrium point with probability 1, for all resolutions of possible non-determinism. Furthermore, a property similar to Lyapunov stability for the stochastic case is implied. Stronger stability definitions (e.g., almost sure stability), exist in the literature, but we chose global asymptotic stability in probability for two reasons: 1) it already implies convergence with probability 1, and 2) it blends in nicely with Lyapunov theory and allows the direct use of automatic Lyapunov function computation methods.

Definition 3 (Global Asymptotic Stability in Probability). *A probabilistic hybrid automaton H is globally stable in probability wrt. an equilibrium state x_e if for all trajectories x(t) of H*

$$\forall \epsilon, \epsilon' > 0 \, \exists \delta > 0 : ||x(0) - x_e|| < \delta \Rightarrow P(\exists t : ||x(t) - x_e|| > \epsilon') < \epsilon$$

and globally attractive in probability (GA-P) if for all trajectories x(t) of H

$$P(\lim_{t \to \infty} x(t) = x_e) = 1,$$

where 0 is the origin of $\mathbb{R}^n$. A system that is both globally stable in probability and globally attractive in probability is called globally asymptotically stable in probability (GAS-P).

3   Lyapunov Functions for Probabilistic Systems

Lyapunov functions are a central tool for proving stability properties for various kinds of dynamic systems. In the following, we present a theorem implying that the existence of a Lyapunov function whose value is *expected to decrease* at all time instants is sufficient for proving GAS-P for probabilistic hybrid automata.

Whenever a discrete transition is taken, it is permissible that the Lyapunov function increases, as long as this is not the expected behavior in the long run. Note that Lyapunov function computation, without loss of generality, assumes that the equilibrium of the system lies at the origin of the continuous state space. If one wants to show GAS-P wrt. some other equilibrium state, the system can be "shifted" accordingly.

Definition 4 (Definiteness). *A function $f : S \to \mathbb{R}, S \subseteq \mathbb{R}^n$ is called positive semidefinite, if for all $x \in S : f(x) \geq 0$, and positive definite, if it is positive semidefinite and $f(x) = 0 \Leftrightarrow x = 0$. A function f is called negative (semi)definite, if $-f$ is positive (semi)definite. A function $f : \mathbb{R}^n \to \mathbb{R}$ is called positive (semi)definite on a set $S \subset \mathbb{R}^n$, if the restricted function $f_{|S}$ is positive (semi)definite. This definition extends to negative (semi)definiteness accordingly.*

Theorem 1 (Discontinuous Lyapunov Functions for Probabilistic Hybrid Systems). *Let H be a probabilistic hybrid automaton. If for each $m \in \mathcal{M}$ there exists a continuously differentiable function $V_m : S \to \mathbb{R}$ such that*

(1) *$V_m(x) - \alpha ||x||$ is positive definite on $Inv(m)$ for some $\alpha > 0$,*
(2) *$\dot{V}_m(x) := \sup \left\{ \frac{dV_m}{dx} f(x) \,|\, f(x) \in F_m(x) \right\}$ is negative definite on $Inv(m)$, where F_m is the right hand side of the differential inclusion $Flow(m)$,*
(3) *for each mode transition $(m_1, Target, G, Update) \in \mathcal{T}$:*
    $x \in G \Rightarrow V_{m_1}(x) - \sum_{m \in \mathcal{M}} Target(m) \cdot V_m(Update(x)) \geq 0$,
(4) *for all $m : V_m(x) \to \infty$ as $||x|| \to \infty$,*

then H is GAS-P wrt. the equilibrium 0. The function V_m is called the local *Lyapunov function (LLF) of H for mode m. The family of the $V_m, m \in \mathcal{M}$ is called the* global (discontinuous) *Lyapunov function (GLF) of H.*

Proof. *Let $x(t)$ be a trajectory of H with switching times t_i and associated mode sequence (m_i). For ease of notation define $W(t) := V(x(t))$.*
Attractivity: *Per definition of the semantics for probabilistic hybrid automata and condition (2), for all $t_{i+1} \geq t \geq t_i$ the following holds:*

$$W(t) = W(t_i) + \int_{t_i}^{t} \dot{W}(\tau)d\tau \leq W(t_i).$$

This, together with condition (3), implies that, for all $t \geq 0$,

$$E(W(t)) = W(0) + E\left(\sum_i \int_{t_i}^{t_{i+1}} \dot{W}(\tau)d\tau\right) + E\left(\sum_i \Delta_i\right) \leq W(0),$$

where $\Delta_i = V_{m_i}(x(t_i)) - V_{m_{i+1}}(Update(x(t_i)))$. Therefore, for all $t \geq s \geq 0$, we obtain

$$E(W(t) \,|\, \{W(\tau) \,|\, \tau \leq s\}) \leq W(s),$$

i.e., $W(t)$ is a supermartingale[2] [6, p. 474]. Furthermore,

$$0 \leq E(W(t)) = W(0) + E\left(\sum_i \int_{t_i}^{t_{i+1}} \dot{W}(\tau)d\tau\right) + E\left(\sum_i \Delta_i\right) \leq W(0) < \infty.$$

Therefore, $E(|W(t)|) = E(W(t)) < \infty$ for all $t \geq 0$ and Doob's martingale convergence theorem [6, p. 505] can be applied, giving us

$$P(\exists x_0 : \lim_{t \to \infty} W(t) = x_0) = 1.$$

Condition (2) implies that $x_0 = 0$, therefore,

$$P(\lim_{t \to \infty} W(t) = 0) = 1,$$

and per conditions (1) and (4),

$$P(\lim_{t \to \infty} x(t) = 0) = 1.$$

Stability: Since $W(t)$ is a supermartingale, the following inequality holds for all $\tilde{\epsilon} > 0$:

$$P(\exists t : W(t) \geq \tilde{\epsilon}) \leq W(0)/\tilde{\epsilon}.$$

Let $\epsilon, \epsilon' > 0$. Choose $0 < \tilde{\epsilon} < \min\{\epsilon', 1/\epsilon\}$. Then

$$P(\exists t : W(t) > \epsilon') < \epsilon \cdot W(0).$$

Set $\delta := \inf\{||x|| \, | \, V_m(x) \geq 1, m \in \mathcal{M}\} > 0$, then $||x(0)|| < \delta$ implies that

$$P(\exists t : V(x(t)) > \epsilon') < \epsilon,$$

and therefore, per condition (1)

$$P(\exists t : ||x(t)|| > \epsilon') < \epsilon.$$

This theorem can also be adapted to the case where the differential inclusions per mode are replaced by stochastic differential equations $\dot{x} = f(x, \sigma)$. In this case, condition (2) can be replaced by

(2') $E\left(\frac{dV_m}{dx}f(x, \sigma)\right) = \frac{dV_m}{dx}E(f(x, \sigma))$ *is negative definite on $Inv(m)$*

For non-hybrid systems, a proof outline for this case based on results by Kushner [7] can be found in [8]. For the hybrid case, it can be combined with the proof for Theorem 1 to accommodate for stochastic differential equations in hybrid systems.

For linear dynamics and quadratic Lyapunov function candidates of the form $V(x) = x^T P x, P \in \mathbb{R}^n \times \mathbb{R}^n$, the conditions (1) to (4) can directly be mapped onto a *linear matrix inequality (LMI)* problem [9], which in turn can be solved

---

[2] *Supermartingales* are stochastic processes for which, given an evolution to time s, the expected value at time $t \geq s$ is never higher than the value at time s.

automatically with nonlinear optimization techniques [10]. The solution of such
an LMI problem consists of valuations of the entries of P and some auxiliary variables μ_m^i, ν_m^i, and η_e^i that are used to express the invariants and guards through
the so-called $\mathcal{S}$-procedure [10]. Invariants are encoded through an arbitrary number of matrices Q_m^i per mode m that satisfy $x \in Inv(m) \Rightarrow x^T Q_m^i x \geq 0$. The
same applies to the guard sets G and the matrices R_e^i. The $\mathcal{S}$-procedure always
results in correct over-approximations of invariant and guard sets, although it
can be conservative [2]. Denote "$x^T P x$ is positive semidefinite" as "$P \succeq 0$".
Assume the dynamics for each mode m are given as the conic hull of a family
of linear dynamics, i.e., $\dot{x} \in \text{cone}\{A_{m,1}x, \ldots, A_{m,k}x\}$. Then, the associated LMI
problem looks as follows.

Theorem 2 (LMI Formulation). *If the following LMI problem has a solution, then the system is GAS-P wrt. 0:*

Find $P_m \in \mathbb{R}^n \times \mathbb{R}^n, \alpha > 0, \mu_m^i \geq 0, \nu_m^i \geq 0, \eta_e^i \geq 0$, such that

$$\text{for each mode } m: P_m - \sum_i \mu_m^i Q_m^i - \alpha I \succeq 0 \tag{1}$$

$$\text{for each mode } m \text{ and each } j: -A_{m,j}^T P - P A_{m,j} - \sum_i \nu_m^i Q_m^i - \alpha I \succeq 0 \tag{2}$$

for each transition e and each target mode m' with $Target(m') > 0$:

$$P_m - \sum_{m'} Target(m') \cdot P_{m'} - \sum_i \eta_e^i R_e^i \succeq 0 \tag{3}$$

Conditions (1) to (3) directly map onto the same conditions of Theorem 1.
Condition (4) of Theorem 1 is already satisfied through the use of quadratic
function templates. If the system dynamics are not linear or a non-quadratic
Lyapunov function candidate is needed, then the *sums-of-squares decomposition*
[3] can be applied to transform the constraints into an LMI problem.

   LMI problems are a representation of semidefinite programming (SDP) problems, which in turn form a special class of convex optimization problems [10]
that can be solved with dedicated software, e.g., CSDP [11] or SeDuMi [12]. The
result of the computation – if it is successful – yields valuations of the matrix
variables P_m, and thereby a suitable discontinuous Lyapunov function, completing the stability proof. If no positive result is obtained, then no conclusion about
the stability or instability of the system can be drawn, and it is not easy to identify the cause of the problem. It is possible that the system is indeed unstable, or
that a different Lyapunov function parameterization (for instance applying the
sums-of-squares decomposition [3]) or a different hybrid automaton representation of the system might allow for a solution to the LMI problem. Moreover, the
computation might simply fail for numerical reasons, despite the existence of a
Lyapunov function. These problems are more likely to occur, the larger the LMI
problem grows, i.e., the more complex the hybrid automaton is.

   For this reason, we next turn to decompositional proofs of GAS-P, keeping the
LMI problems comparatively small, and in case of failure, giving constructive information about the part of the hybrid automaton that is most likely responsible

for the failure. Furthermore, decomposition can also be turned into composition, in the sense that a stable hybrid automaton can be designed step by step, by solving LMI problems for the different sub-automata. These sub-automata can then be composed according to the results in the next section, yielding a new stable automaton.

4   Decompositional Computation of Lyapunov Functions

This section deals with automaton-based decomposition of stability proofs, as opposed to techniques like the composition of input-to-state stable systems [4], which work on the continuous state space. The hybrid automaton is divided into sub-automata, for which LMI problems can either be solved completely independently, or sequentially, but with some information being passed from one computation to the next. In contrast to the non-stochastic setting covered in [5], it turned out that stochastic stability proofs allow for stronger decompositional results, which exploit the knowledge of transition properties. The different levels of decomposition are outlined in the following.

The decompositions take place on the graph structure defined by the automaton. Hence, we will apply graph-theoretic terms to the automaton by viewing the automaton as a hypergraph with some labels. The modes in the hybrid automaton are therefore sometimes referred to as *nodes*, and the transitions as *hyperedges*. Since one hybrid system can be represented by different hybrid automata with potentially different graph structures, some representations of the system might be more amenable to decomposition than others.

The first level of decomposition concerns the *strongly connected components* of the hybrid automaton.

Definition 5 (Strongly Connected Components). *A strongly connected component (SCC) of a hypergraph is a maximal subgraph G, such that each node in G is reachable from each other node.*

Note that, here, reachability is exclusively based on the graph structure: continuous dynamics, invariants, and guards are not taken into account. It is well known that every node of a hypergraph belongs to exactly one SCC, and that the reachability relation between the SCCs of a hypergraph forms an acyclic graph structure. This property can be exploited to allow for *completely independent* Lyapunov function computation for the SCCs of a hybrid automaton.

Theorem 3 (Decomposition into Strongly Connected Components). *Let H be a probabilistic hybrid automaton. If all sub-automata pertaining to the SCC of H are GAS-P wrt. 0, then so is H.*

The consequence of this theorem is that LMI problems as per Theorem 2 can be solved locally for each SCC, still yielding a proof of GAS-P for the entire system. The proof is a variant of the proof for non-probabilistic hybrid automata stated in [5]. The following corollary is a consequence of this property.

Corollary 1 (Multiple Equilibria). *If all SCCs of probabilistic hybrid automaton H are GA-P, but with respect to different equilibrium states, then each trajectory of H will converge to one of these states with probability 1.*

The second level of decomposition concerns cycles within an SCC and is also described in detail for non-probabilistic systems in [5]. Since it is based on the decompositional properties of Lyapunov functions, and not on the system itself, the result applies to both non-probabilistic and probabilistic hybrid automata. Therefore, we only give a brief summary of the decomposition technique.

These results are based on a theorem that allows the decomposition of LMI computations within an SCC. Consider an automaton consisting of two subgraphs C_1 and C_2, which overlap in exactly one node b (see Figure 2(a)). Again, LMI computations can be conducted separately for C_1 and C_2. However, the computations are not completely independent, but a conic predicate given by a family of local Lyapunov functions V_{b_i} for b is used to "connect" the two Lyapunov function computations for C_1 and C_2. First, a local LMI problem is solved for C_1, computing the V_{b_i} (see Figure 2(b)). These V_{b_i} have the property that, whenever the LLF for node b in a GLF for C_2 is a conic combination of the V_{b_i}, there exists a GLF for the entire system comprising both subgraphs. Therefore, this requirement on the LLF of b is added as an additional constraint to the LMI for C_2 (see Figure 2(c)). If there is a solution to this second local LMI problem, then the system is GAS-P. The probabilistic version of this theorem is given next. Again, a straightforward modification of the proof from [5] yields a variant for the probabilistic case.

Theorem 4 (Decomposition inside an SCC). *Let H be a probabilistic hybrid automaton consisting of two subgraphs C_1 and C_2 with a single common node b. Let $b, n_1, \ldots, n_j$ be the nodes of C_1 and $b, m_1, \ldots, m_k$ be the nodes of C_2. Let each $V_{b_1}, \ldots, V_{b_m}$ be a LLF for b belonging to a GLF $V_{b_i}, V_{n_1}^i, \ldots, V_{n_j}^i$ for the entire subgraph C_1. If there exists a GLF $V_b, V_{m_1}, \ldots, V_{m_k}$ for subgraph C_2 with $\exists \lambda_1, \ldots, \lambda_m > 0 : V_b = \sum_i \lambda_i V_{b_i}$, then H is GAS-P wrt. 0.*

We employ this theorem for cycle-based decomposition of the stability proof within an SCC. In a slight abuse of terminology, we will use the term "cycle" for the graphs generated by a cyclic path, as defined below.

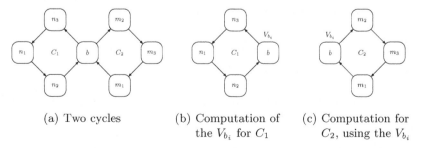

(a) Two cycles   (b) Computation of   (c) Computation for
                            the V_{b_i} for C_1 C_2, using the V_{b_i}

Fig. 2. Decomposition with separate computations for subgraphs C_1 and C_2

Definition 6 (Cycle). *A cycle of a hypergraph G is a subgraph G', such that there exists a closed path in G, covering all edges and nodes of G'. A cycle C is simple, if there exists such a path that only traverses each node once.*

Since each node inside an SCC is part of at least one simple cycle, this theorem allows for local LMI computations on a per-cycle basis. While solving the LMI problem for a cycle C, one can already compute adequate V_{b_i}, which are then taken into account for other cycles that intersect with C. Note, that this decomposition is in general conservative, i.e., some Lyapunov functions are lost in the computation of the V_{b_i}. It is, however, possible to approximate the real set of existing Lyapunov functions of the chosen parameterization arbitrarily close by increasing the number of computed V_{b_i}.

The previous two results stem from analysis of stability properties for non-probabilistic systems. We will now show another decompositional property that is only applicable to probabilistic hybrid automata. However, this decomposition will only preserve global attractivity in probability (GA-P), as opposed to global asymptotic stability in probability (GAS-P). Since attractivity (that is, convergence to the equilibrium) is usually the more interesting property, this is still a useful result.

If the automaton has certain local graph structures, then Lyapunov functions can sometimes be computed *completely independently per mode*, while still allowing for a proof of global attractivity in probability.

We first define *finiteness in probability*, a property of individual cycles. Informally, this property means that, with probability 1, it is only possible for a trajectory to traverse the cycle finitely long until the cycle is either not entered again or the trajectory ends up in a mode of the cycle which is not left any more.

Definition 7 (Finiteness in Probability). *A cycle C with node set V_C in a probabilistic hybrid automaton H is called* finite in probability *if for all trajectories of H with infinite mode sequences (m_i) the property $P(\exists m \in V_C \, \exists i_0 \, \forall i \geq i_0 : m_i \neq m) = 1$ holds.*

Finiteness in probability is a property that can often be derived directly from the graph structure, as stated by the following theorem (see also Figure 3).

Lemma 1 (Criterion for Finite in Probability Cycles). *Let C be a cycle in a probabilistic hybrid automaton H. If at least one edge in C belongs to a hyperedge e, such that there exists a mode m with $Target_e(m) > 0$ belonging to a different SCC, then C is finite in probability.*

Proof. Let (m_i) be an infinite mode sequence belonging to a trajectory of H. Let $\tilde{m}$ be the source mode of edge e. Show that $P(\exists i_0 \, \forall i \geq i_0 : m_i \neq \tilde{m}) = 1$.

Proof by contradiction. Assume that $P(\forall i_0 \, \exists i \geq i_0 : m_i = \tilde{m}) > 0$. Since edge e branches to another SCC with probability $p > 0$, this implies that $0 = \prod_{i=1}^{\infty}(1 - p) \geq P(\forall i_0 \, \exists i \geq i_0 : m_i = \tilde{m}) > 0$, which is a contradiction.

The consequence of this property for stability verification is as follows. A cycle that is finite in probability does not need to be mapped onto one LMI problem

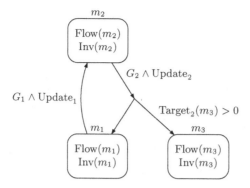

Fig. 3. Finite in probability cycle consisting of m_1 and m_2

for the entire cycle. Instead, it is sufficient to provide a local Lyapunov function for each mode of the cycle, with *no constraints spanning several modes*. The existence of such local Lyapunov functions ensures that the system will always stabilize, in case a trajectory "gets stuck in a mode". If it does not get stuck, then finiteness in probability ensures that the cycle is eventually left with probability 1. The following lemma breaks GA-P down into a probability on the cycles of the system and will be used to prove the decomposition theorem.

Lemma 2 (GA-P and Finite in Probability Cycles). *Let H be a probabilistic hybrid automaton. If for each cycle C of H one of the following two conditions holds, then H is GA-P wrt. 0:*

(1) C is finite in probability and for each $m \in C$ there exists a LLF V_m, or
(2) there exists a GLF for C

Proof. Case 1, (m_i) *is finite: Let m_n be the final element of (m_i). There either exists a LLF V_{m_n} for m_n per condition (1), or per condition (2) as part of a GLF. Therefore, $x(t) \to \infty$.*
Case 2, (m_i) *is infinite: Since (m_i) only contains modes belonging to a finite number of SCC $C_1, \ldots, C_m$, C_m cannot contain any finite in probability cycles. Therefore, per condition (2), there exists a GLF for C_m (which can be covered by a cycle) and therefore C_m is GA-P.*

By itself, this result is of limited use, because all cycles of the hybrid automaton need to be considered. However, it is used to prove the following theorem, which allows a further decomposition. It implies that nodes lying only on finite in probability *simple* cycles can be treated *completely separately* within an SCC.

Theorem 5 (Decomposition of Lyapunov Functions within an SCC). *Let C be an SCC of a probabilistic hybrid automaton. Let N be the set of modes that lie only on finite in probability simple cycles. Let C' be the hybrid automaton obtained by removing the modes of N and all incident transitions from C. If the following two conditions both hold, then C is GA-P wrt. 0:*

(1) for each $m \in N$ there exists a LLF V_m, and
(2) there exists a GLF for C'

Proof. We show that the prerequisites of Lemma 2 are always satisfied. Let D be a cycle in C as required by Lemma 2. There are three cases:

Case 1, D is simple and finite in probability: there exists a LLF for each node of D, either per condition (1) or as part of a GLF per condition (2). Therefore, condition (1) of Lemma 2 is satisfied for D.

Case 2, D is not simple, but finite in probability: D can be broken down into a family $D_1, \ldots, D_n$ of simple cycles. For each node in a D_i, there exists a LLF either per condition (1) or condition (2), and therefore for all nodes in D.

Case 3, D is not finite in probability: D cannot contain any simple subcycles that are finite in probability. Therefore, D is a subgraph of C', and a GLF exists for D per condition (2), implying condition (2) of Lemma 2.

To check whether a node is in N or not, an enumeration of only the simple cycles of the automaton is necessary. The result is, that nodes in N can each be treated separately, since they only require the existence of a local Lyapunov function. Once a LLF is found, they can be removed from the automaton, and the cycle-based decomposition procedure from Theorem 4 can be applied to the remainder of the SCC. Next, we will apply these decomposition results to an example automaton.

5   Example

As an example, we present a simple cruise controller system with a probabilistic transition (see Figure 4). The variable v models the difference between actual speed and desired speed v_0 (i.e., the system dynamics are shifted, such that $v = 0$ is the desired speed), and a models the acceleration. Mode $A1$ represents a saturation, enforcing a maximum acceleration, while mode $A2$ is the standard acceleration/deceleration mode that is active whenever a is below the saturation level and v is close to 0. $B1$ and $B2$ represent two different service brake modes, modeling different brake dynamics that are chosen probabilistically with probabilities $p_1 > 0$ and $p_2 > 0$ (for instance depending on the inclination of the track or the weather conditions, which are considered random in this model). Additionally, with a (small) probability $p_3 > 0$, the service brake system might fail altogether, activating an emergency brake mode F. From any mode except F, it is also possible that the vehicle is ordered to stop in a regular manner, e.g., because the destination has been reached. This is modeled in mode E.

By applying the theorems of Section 4, it is possible to decompose the stability proof for this system into a number of subproofs. We want to show that the system will either converge to $v = a = 0$, or the vehicle will come to a stop in modes E or F, which means convergence to $v = -v_0$, where v_0 is the desired speed. The modes E and F each form a separate SCC and can therefore be treated separately through Theorem 3 and Corollary 1. Since the cycles formed by $A2$ and $B1$ and by $A2$ and $B2$ are both finite in probability, the nodes $B1$

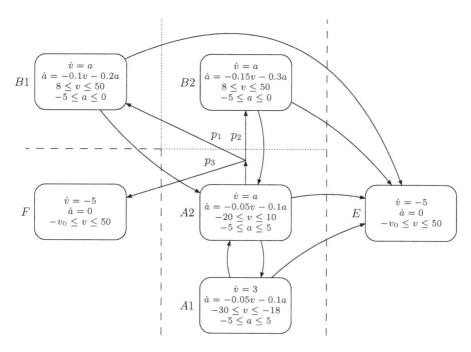

Fig. 4. Example automaton (guards and updates not pictured) and decomposition (dashed lines: Theorem 3, dotted lines: Theorem 5)

and $B2$ can also be analyzed separately per Theorem 5. This yields one LMI problem as per Theorem 2 for E, F, $B1$ and $B2$. Furthermore, one LMI problem for the cycle given by nodes $A1$ and $A2$ must be solved, including the two edges connecting them. If solutions for all of these independent LMI problems can be found, then all SCCs are GA-P, and all trajectories converge to either $v = a = 0$ or $v = -v_0$ with probability 1. In contrast, solving an LMI containing all constraints for all modes and transitions of the whole graph in one step is intractable in practice. The GLF for the SCC consisting of $A1$ and $A2$, as computed by an LMI solver, is given by $V_{A1} = 3.9804v^2 + 2.0001ta + 10.502a^2$ and $V_{A2} = 0.625v^2 + 2va + 10.5a^2$. Examples for LLF for the other nodes are $V_{B1} = 18.496v^2 + 26.314av + 100a^2$, $V_{B2} = 31.843v^2 + 40.98av + 100a^2$ and $V_E = V_F = v + v_0$.

6 Quantitative Analysis

In this section, we outline how the results of the previous section can be employed for quantitative stability analysis, i.e., the computation of convergence properties that lie below 1. Generally, this type of analysis is oriented along the SCCs of the hybrid system. If the convergence probability is strictly smaller than 1, then some trajectories need to reach a permanent decision point, where a stabilizing decision is taken with probability $p < 1$ and a non-stabilizing decision is taken with probability $1 - p$. The permanent decision points that are visible in the hybrid automaton are the transitions between SCCs: once an SCC is left, a return is impossible. Therefore, such a "decision" is irreversible for the trajectory. This leads to the conclusion that quantitative stability analysis can be conducted with help of SCCs: those that are "visible in the graph structure" and those that are "hidden in the guards and dynamics" and can be exposed by using alternate hybrid automaton representations of the system. First, we define global attractivity with probability of less than 1, and then we give a theorem on the SCCs that are visible in the graph structure.

Definition 8 (Global Attractivity with Probability $p < 1$). *A probabilistic hybrid automaton H is* globally attractive in probability with probability p (GA-P(p)) *with respect to an equilibrium state x_e, if for all trajectories $x(t)$ of H:* $P(\lim_{t \to \infty} x(t) = x_e) \geq p$.

Theorem 6 (Quantitative Analysis). *Let H be a probabilistic hybrid automaton, consisting of an SCC C, that is GA-P wrt. 0 and a number of SCC $C_1, \ldots, C_m$ that are successors of C. Assume that Init only contains hybrid states with nodes of C as their discrete state. Furthermore, assume that each C_i is known to be GA-P(p_i) wrt. 0 for some $0 \leq p_i \leq 1$. Let c_i be a lower bound on the probability that a trajectory of H ends up in C_i. Then, the sub-automaton of H consisting of C and the C_i is GA-P(p) wrt. 0, with $p = \sum c_i p_i$.*

Proof. Let (m_i) be a mode sequence belonging to a trajectory $x(t)$ of H. If (m_i) never leaves C, then $x(t)$ must converge to 0 with probability 1 since C is GA-P. If this is not the case, then (m_i) will enter SCC C_i with a probability of at least c_i. Since c_i is GA-P(p_i), $x(t)$ will then converge with probability p_i. Summing up over all C_i, we get a lower bound for the probability of convergence as $p = \sum c_i p_i$. Therefore, H is GA-P(p).

Lower bounds c_i can, for instance, be computed with the help of discrete time Markov decision processes, where the steady-state probability of ending up in an SCC is such a c_i. However, to obtain tight bounds on the stabilization property, it is necessary to have an automaton model of the system where all "branching points" are visible as transitions between SCC in the graph structure. At this point, methods for reachable set computation of hybrid systems can be employed to discover semantically equivalent automata (wrt. the continuous behavior) that have a "finer" SCC structure.

7   Conclusions

In this paper, we presented a scheme for decomposition of proofs of stability in probability for probabilistic hybrid automata. The decomposition results can be used to make automatic stability proofs through Lyapunov function computation more tractable in practice. Furthermore, the results give conditions, under which stability properties of sub-automata to be composed transfer to the newly obtained larger automaton. Therefore, stable automata can be designed step by step, applying Lyapunov function arguments that are local in the graph during the design process. Furthermore, failure of a Lyapunov function is now less problematic, since it will be visible which computational step – and therefore which part of the automaton – caused the problem. This knowledge allows for an easier diagnosis of the problem that prevented the stability proof from succeeding. In general, we postulate that decompositional reasoning makes it easier to see what makes or breaks stability properties in probabilistic hybrid automata.

References

1. Branicky, M.: Multiple Lyapunov functions and other analysis tools for switched and hybrid systems. IEEE Transactions on Automatic Control 43(4), 475–482 (1998)
2. Pettersson, S.: Analysis and Design of Hybrid Systems. PhD thesis, Chalmers University of Technology, Gothenburg (1999)
3. Parrilo, P.A.: Semidefinite programming relaxations for semialgebraic problems. Mathematical Programming, Series B (96), 293–320 (2003)
4. Heemels, M., Weiland, S., Juloski, A.: Input-to-state stability of discontinuous dynamical systems with an observer-based control application. In: Bemporad, A., Bicchi, A., Buttazzo, G. (eds.) HSCC 2007. LNCS, vol. 4416, pp. 259–272. Springer, Heidelberg (2007)
5. Oehlerking, J., Theel, O.: Decompositional construction of Lyapunov functions for hybrid systems. In: Majumdar, R., Tabuada, P. (eds.) HSCC 2009. LNCS, vol. 5469, pp. 276–290. Springer, Heidelberg (2009)
6. Shiryaev, A.N.: Probability, 2nd edn. Springer, Heidelberg (1996)
7. Kushner, H.J.: Stochastic stability. Lecture Notes in Mathematics, vol. (249), pp. 97–124 (1972)
8. Loparo, K.A., Feng, X.: Stability of stochastic systems. In: The Control Handbook, pp. 1105–1126. CRC Press, Boca Raton (1996)
9. Boyd, S., El Ghaoui, L., Feron, E., Balakrishnan, V.: Linear Matrix Inequalities in System and Control Theory. Society for Industrial and Applied Mathematics, SIAM (1994)
10. Boyd, S., Vandenberghe, L.: Convex Optimization. Cambridge University Press, Cambridge (2004)
11. Borchers, B.: CSDP, a C library for semidefinite programming. Optimization Methods and Software 10(1), 613–623 (1999), https://projects.coin-or.org/Csdp/
12. Romanko, O., Pólik, I., Sturm, J.F.: Using SeDuMi 1.02, a MATLAB toolbox for optimization over symmetric cones (1999), http://sedumi.ie.lehigh.edu

Memory Usage Verification Using Hip/Sleek

Guanhua He[1], Shengchao Qin[1], Chenguang Luo[1], and Wei-Ngan Chin[2]

[1] Durham University, Durham DH1 3LE, UK
[2] National University of Singapore
{guanhua.he,shengchao.qin,chenguang.luo}@durham.ac.uk,
chinwn@comp.nus.edu.sg

Abstract. Embedded systems often come with constrained memory footprints. It is therefore essential to ensure that software running on such platforms fulfils memory usage specifications at compile-time, to prevent memory-related software failure after deployment. Previous proposals on memory usage verification are not satisfactory as they usually can only handle restricted subsets of programs, especially when shared mutable data structures are involved. In this paper, we propose a simple but novel solution. We instrument programs with explicit memory operations so that memory usage verification can be done along with the verification of other properties, using an automated verification system Hip/Sleek developed recently by Chin et al. [10,19]. The instrumentation can be done automatically and is proven sound with respect to an underlying semantics. One immediate benefit is that we do not need to develop from scratch a specific system for memory usage verification. Another benefit is that we can verify more programs, especially those involving shared mutable data structures, which previous systems failed to handle, as evidenced by our experimental results.

1 Introduction

Ubiquitous embedded systems are often supplied with limited memory and computation resources due to various constraints on, e.g., product size, power consumption and manufacture cost. The consequences of violating memory safety requirements can be quite severe because of the close coupling of these systems with the physical world; in some cases, they can put human lives at risk. The Mars Rover's anomaly problem was actually due to a memory leak error and it took fifteen days to fix the problem and bring the Rover back to normal [21]. For applications running on resource-constrained platforms, a challenging problem would be how to make memory usage more predictable and how to ensure that memory usage fulfils the restricted memory requirements.

To tackle this challenge, a number of proposals have been reported on memory usage analysis and verification, with most of them focused on functional programs where data structures are mostly immutable and thus easier to handle [1,2,5,7,15,23]. Memory usage verification for imperative/OO languages can be more challenging due to mutability of states and object sharing. Existing solutions to this are mainly type-based [11,12,16]. Instead of capturing all aliasing

Z. Liu and A.P. Ravn (Eds.): ATVA 2009, LNCS 5799, pp. 166–181, 2009.

information, they impose restrictions on object mutability and sharing. Therefore, they can only handle limited subsets of programs manipulating shared mutable data structures.

The emergence of separation logic [17,22] promotes scalable reasoning via explicit separation of structural properties over the memory heap where recursive data structures are dynamically allocated. Since then, dramatic advances have been made in automated software verification via separation logic, e.g. the Smallfoot tool [3] and the Space Invader tool [6,13,24] for the analysis and verification on pointer safety (i.e. shape properties asserting that pointers cannot go wrong), the HIP/SLEEK tool [10,18,19] for the verification of more general properties involving both structural (shape) and numerical (size) information, the verification on termination [4], and the verification for object-oriented programs [9,14,20].

Given these significant advances in the field, a research question that we post to ourselves is: can we make use of some of these state-of-the-art verification tools to do a better job for memory usage verification, without the need of constructing a memory usage verifier from scratch? This paper addresses this question by proposing a simple but novel mechanism to memory usage verification using the HIP/SLEEK system developed by Chin et al. [10,19]. Separation logic offers a powerful and expressive mechanism to capture structural properties of shared mutable data structures including aliasing information. The specification mechanism in HIP/SLEEK leverages structural properties with numerical information and is readily capable for the use of memory usage specification.

Approach and contributions. Memory usage occur in both the heap and stack spaces. While heap space is used to store dynamically allocated data structures, stack memory is used for local variables as well as return addresses of method calls. On the specification side, we assume that two special global variables heap and stk of type int are reserved to represent respectively the available heap and stack memory in the pre-/post-conditions of each method. On the program side, we *instrument* the program to be verified with explicit operations over variables heap and stk using rewriting rules. We call the instrumented programs as *memory-aware programs*. The memory usage behaviour of the original program is now mimicked and made explicit in its memory-aware version via the newly introduced primitive operations over heap and stk. We also show that the original program and its memory-aware version are observationally equivalent modulo the behaviour of the latter on the special variables heap and stk as well as a fixed memory cost for storing the two global variables. Instead of constructing and implementing a fresh set of memory usage verification rules for the original program, we can now pass to HIP/SLEEK as inputs the corresponding memory-aware program together with the expected memory specification for automated memory usage verification.

In summary, this paper makes the following contributions:

– We propose a simple but novel solution to memory usage verification based on a verification tool HIP/SLEEK by first rewriting programs to their memory-aware counterparts.

- We demonstrate that the syntax-directed rewriting process is sound in the sense that the memory-aware programs are observationally equivalent to their original programs with respect to an instrumented operational semantics.
- We have integrated our solution with HIP/SLEEK and conducted some initial experiments. The experimental results confirm the viability of our solution and show that we can verify the memory safety of more programs compared with previous type-based approaches.

The rest of the paper is structured as follows. We introduce our programming and specification languages in Section 2. In Section 3 we present our approach to memory usage verification in HIP/SLEEK. Section 4 defines an underlying semantics for the programming language and formulates the soundness of our approach w.r.t. the semantics. Experimental results are shown in Section 5, followed by related work and concluding remarks afterwards.

2   Language and Specifications

In this section, we first introduce a core imperative language we use to demonstrate the work, and then depict the general specification mechanism used by HIP/SLEEK and show how memory usage specifications can be incorporated in.

2.1   Programming Language

To simplify presentation, we focus on a strongly-typed C-like imperative language in Figure 1.

A program P in our language consists of user-defined data types $tdecl$, global variables $gVar$ and method definitions $meth$. The notation $datat$ stands for the standard data type declaration used in programs, for example as below:

```
data node { int val; node next }
data node2 { int val; node2 prev; node2 next }
data node3 { int val; node3 left; node3 right; node3 parent }
```

The notation $spred$ denotes a user-defined predicate which may be recursively defined and can specify both structural and numerical properties of data structures involved. The syntax of $spred$ is given in Figure 2.

$$
\begin{array}{ll}
P & ::= tdecl^* \; gVar^* \; meth^* \qquad tdecl ::= datat \mid spred \\
datat & ::= \textbf{data} \; c \; \{ \; field^* \; \} \qquad field ::= t \; v \qquad t ::= c \mid \tau \\
\tau & ::= \textbf{int} \mid \textbf{bool} \mid \textbf{void} \qquad gVar ::= t \; v \\
meth & ::= t \; mn \; (([\textbf{ref}] \; t \; v)^*) \; mspec \; \{e\} \\
e & ::= \textbf{null} \mid k^\tau \mid v \mid v.f \mid v{:=}e \mid v_1.f{:=}v_2 \mid \textbf{new} \; c(v^*) \mid \textbf{free}(v) \\
& \quad \mid e_1; e_2 \mid t \; v; \; e \mid mn(v^*) \mid \textbf{if} \; v \; \textbf{then} \; e_1 \; \textbf{else} \; e_2
\end{array}
$$

Fig. 1. A Core (C-like) Imperative Language

Note that a parameter can be either pass-by-value or pass-by-reference, distinguished by the **ref** before a parameter definition. The method specification *mspec*, written in our specification language in Figure 2, specifies the expected behaviour of the method, including its memory usage behaviour. Our aim is to verify the method body against this specification. Our language is expression-oriented, so the body of a method is an expression composed of standard instructions and constructors of an imperative language. Note that the instructions **new** and **free** explicitly deal with memory allocation and deallocation, respectively. The term k^τ denotes a constant value of type τ. While loops are transformed to tail-recursive methods in a preprocessing step.

2.2   Specification Language

Our specification language is given in Figure 2. Note *spred* defines a new separation predicate c in terms of the formula Φ with a given pure invariant π. Such user-specified predicates can be used in the method specifications. The method specification *requires* Φ_{pr} *ensures* Φ_{po} comprises a precondition Φ_{pr} and a postcondition Φ_{po}.

The separation formula Φ, which appears in the predicate definition *spred* or in the pre-/post-conditions of a method, is in disjunctive normal form. Each disjunct consists of a $*$-separated heap constraint κ, referred to as *heap part*, and a heap-independent formula π, referred to as *pure part*. The pure part does not contain any heap nodes and is restricted to pointer equality/disequality γ and Presburger arithmetic ϕ. As we will see later, γ is used to capture the alias information of pointers during the verification, and ϕ is to record the numerical information of data structures, such as length of a list or height of a tree. Furthermore, Δ denotes a composite formula that could always be normalized into the Φ form [19].

The formula **emp** represents an empty heap. If c is a data node, the formula p::c$\langle v^* \rangle$ represents a singleton heap p$\mapsto$[(f : v)*] with f* as fields of data declaration c. For example, p::node$\langle 0, \text{null} \rangle$ denotes that p points to a **node** structure in the heap, whose fields have values 0 and **null**, respectively. If c is a (user-specified) predicate, p::c$\langle v^* \rangle$ stands for the formula c(p, v*) which signifies that

$$
\begin{array}{ll}
spred & ::= \mathbf{root}::c\langle v^* \rangle \equiv \Phi \ \mathbf{inv} \ \pi \\
mspec & ::= requires \ \Phi_{pr} \ ensures \ \Phi_{po} \\
\Phi & ::= \bigvee(\exists v^* \cdot \kappa \wedge \pi)^* \qquad \pi ::= \gamma \wedge \phi \\
\gamma & ::= v_1 = v_2 \mid v = \mathbf{null} \mid v_1 \neq v_2 \mid v \neq \mathbf{null} \mid \gamma_1 \wedge \gamma_2 \\
\kappa & ::= \mathbf{emp} \mid v::c\langle v^* \rangle \mid \kappa_1 * \kappa_2 \\
\Delta & ::= \Phi \mid \Delta_1 \vee \Delta_2 \mid \Delta \wedge \pi \mid \Delta_1 * \Delta_2 \mid \exists v \cdot \Delta \\
\phi & ::= b \mid a \mid \phi_1 \wedge \phi_2 \mid \phi_1 \vee \phi_2 \mid \neg \phi \mid \exists v \cdot \phi \mid \forall v \cdot \phi \\
b & ::= \mathbf{true} \mid \mathbf{false} \mid v \mid b_1 = b_2 \qquad a ::= s_1 = s_2 \mid s_1 \leq s_2 \\
s & ::= k^{\mathbf{int}} \mid v \mid k^{\mathbf{int}} \times s \mid s_1 + s_2 \mid -s \mid max(s_1, s_2) \mid min(s_1, s_2)
\end{array}
$$

Fig. 2. The Specification Language

the data structure pointed to by p has the shape c with parameters v*. As an example, one may define the following predicate for a singly linked list with length n:

$$\texttt{root::ll}\langle n \rangle \equiv (\texttt{root=null} \wedge n{=}0) \vee (\exists i, m, q \cdot \texttt{root::node}\langle i, q \rangle * \texttt{q::ll}\langle m \rangle \wedge n{=}m{+}1) \, \textbf{inv} \, n{\geq}0$$

The above definition asserts that an ll list either can be empty (the base case root=null where root is the "head pointer" pointing to the beginning of the whole structure described by ll), or consists of a head data node (specified by root::node⟨i, q⟩) and a separate tail data structure which is also an ll list (q::ll⟨m⟩ saying that q points to an ll list with length m). The separation conjunction * introduced in separation logic signifies that two heap portions are domain-disjoint. Therefore, in the inductive case of ll's definition, the separation conjunction ensures that the head node and the tail ll reside in disjoint heaps. A default invariant n≥0 is specified which holds for all ll lists. Existential quantifiers are for local values and pointers in the predicate, such as i, m and q.

A slightly more complicated shape, a doubly linked-list with length n, is described by:

$$\texttt{root::dll}\langle p, n \rangle \equiv (\texttt{root=null} \wedge n{=}0) \vee (\texttt{root::node2}\langle \_, p, q \rangle * \texttt{q::dll}\langle \texttt{root}, n{-}1 \rangle) \, \textbf{inv} \, n{\geq}0$$

The dll predicate has a parameter p to represent the prev field of the root node of the doubly linked list. This shape includes node root and all the nodes reachable through the next field starting from root, but not the ones reachable through prev from root. Here we also can see some shortcuts that underscore _ denotes an anonymous variable, and non-parameter variables in the right hand side of the shape definition, such as q, are implicitly existentially quantified.

As can be seen from the above, we can use κ to express the shape of heap and ϕ to express numerical information of data structures, such as length. This allows us to specify data structures with sophisticated invariants. For example, we may define a non-empty sorted list as below:

$$\texttt{root::sortl}\langle n, min \rangle \equiv (\texttt{root::node}\langle min, null \rangle \wedge n{=}1 \vee$$
$$(\texttt{root::node}\langle min, q \rangle * \texttt{q::sortl}\langle m, k \rangle \wedge n{=}m{+}1 \wedge min{\leq}k) \, \textbf{inv} \, n{\geq}0$$

The sortedness property is captured with the help of an additional parameter min denoting the minimum value stored in the list. The formula min≤k ensures the sortedness. With the aforesaid predicates, we can now specify the insertion-sort algorithm as follows:

node insert(node x, node vn)	node insertion_sort(node y)
requires x::sortl⟨n, min⟩ * vn::node⟨v, _⟩	*requires* y::ll⟨n⟩ ∧ n>0
ensures res::sortl⟨n+1, min(v, min)⟩;	*ensures* res::sortl⟨n, _⟩;
{···}	{···}

where a special identifier res is used in the postcondition to denote the result of a method. The postcondition of insertion_sort shows that the output list is sorted and has the same number of nodes. We can also specify that the input and output lists contain the same set of values by adding another parameter to the sort1 predicate to capture the bag of values stored in the list [10].

The semantics of our specification formula is similar to the model given for separation logic [22] except that we have extensions to handle user-defined shape predicates. We assume sets Loc of memory locations, Val of primitive values, with $0 \in$ Val denoting null, Var of variables (program and logical variables), and ObjVal of object values stored in the heap, with $c[f_1 \mapsto \nu_1, .., f_n \mapsto \nu_n]$ denoting an object value of data type c where $\nu_1, .., \nu_n$ are current values of the corresponding fields $f_1, .., f_n$. Let $s, h \models \Phi$ denote the model relation, i.e. the stack s and heap h satisfy Φ, with h, s from the following concrete domains:

$$h \in \text{Heaps} =_{df} \text{Loc} \rightharpoonup_{fin} \text{ObjVal} \qquad s \in \text{Stacks} =_{df} \text{Var} \rightarrow \text{Val} \cup \text{Loc}$$

Note that each heap h is a finite partial mapping while each stack s is a total mapping, as in the classical separation logic [17,22]. The detailed definitions of the model relation can be found in Chin et al. [10].

2.3 Memory Usage Specification

To incorporate memory usage into the specification mechanism of HIP/SLEEK, we employ two global variables heap and stk to represent the available heap and stack memory (in bytes). The memory requirement of a method can then be specified as a pure constraint over heap and stk in the precondition of the method. The remaining memory space upon the return from a method call can also be exhibited using a pure formula over heap$'$ and stk$'$ in the postcondition.[1] Due to perfect recovery of stack space upon return from a method call, stk$'$ in a method's postcondition will always be the same as its initial value stk. As an example, the method new_list(int n), which creates a singly linked list with length n, is given as follows together with its memory usage specification:

```
node new_list(int n)
    requires  heap≥8 * n ∧ n≥0 ∧ stk≥12 * n+4
    ensures   res::ll⟨n⟩ ∧ heap'=heap−8 * n ∧ stk'=stk
{ node r := null; if (n>0) { r := new_list(n−1); r := new node(n, r)}; r }
```

where the node was declared earlier in Sec 2.1. We assume that we use a 32-bit architecture; therefore, one node requires 8 bytes of memory. This assumption can be easily changed for a different architecture. The precondition specifies that the method requires at least $8 * n$ bytes of heap space and $12 * n + 4$ stack space before each execution with n denoting the size of the input.[2] After method

---

[1] A primed variable x$'$ in a specification formula denotes the latest value of variable x, with x representing its initial value.

[2] When a new local variable r is declared, 4 bytes of stack memory is consumed. Later when the method new_list is invoked recursively, its parameters, return address and local variables are all placed on top of the stack. This is why it requires at least $12 * n+4$ bytes of stack space.

execution, $8 * n$ bytes of heap memory is consumed by the returned list, but the stack space is fully recovered. This is reflected by the formula ($\text{heap}' = \text{heap} - 8 * n \wedge \text{stk}' = \text{stk}$) in the postcondition.

As another example, the following method free_list deallocates a list:

```
void free_list(node2 x)
   requires  x::dll⟨n⟩ ∧ heap≥0 ∧ stk≥12 ∗ n
   ensures   emp ∧ heap'=heap+12 ∗ n ∧ stk'=stk
{ if (x ≠ null) { node t := x; x := x.next; free(t); free_list(x) } }
```

We can see that $12 * n$ bytes of heap space is expected to be claimed back by the method as signified in the postcondition. Notice here the stack and heap memory are specified in terms of the logical variable n denoting the length of the list x, showing the possible close relation between the separation (shape and size) specification and the memory specification. Next we will show how to rewrite the program to its memory-aware version by using the two global variables heap and stk to mimic the memory behaviour, so that HIP/SLEEK can step in for memory usage verification.

3   Memory Usage Verification

In this section, we first present the instrumentation process which converts programs to be verified to memory-aware programs. We then briefly introduce the automated verification process in HIP/SLEEK.

3.1   The Instrumentation Process

The instrumentation process makes use of primitive operations over the global variables heap and stk to simulate the memory usage behaviour of the original program. It is conducted via the rewriting rules given in Figure 3.

These rewriting rules form a transformer $\mathcal{M}$ which takes in a program and returns its memory-aware version. Note that $\mathcal{M}$ conducts identical rewriting except for the following four cases: (1) heap allocation $\text{new } c(v^*)$; (2) heap deallocation $\text{free}(v)$; (3) local block $\{t \; v; \; e\}$; (4) method declaration $t_0 \; mn(t_1 \; v_1, .., t_n \; v_n)\{e\}$.

$$
\begin{array}{lll}
\mathcal{M}(E) & ::= & E \text{ where } E \in \{\text{null}, k^\tau, v, v.f, v_1.f:=v_2, mn(v^*)\} \\
\mathcal{M}(\text{new } c(v^*)) & ::= & dec\_hp(ssizeof(c)); \; \text{new } c(v^*) \\
\mathcal{M}(\text{free}(v)) & ::= & \text{free}(v); \; inc\_hp(ssizeof(type(v))) \\
\mathcal{M}(\{t \; v; e\}) & ::= & dec\_stk(sizeof(t)); \; \{t \; v; \; \mathcal{M}(e)\}; \; inc\_stk(sizeof(t)) \\
\mathcal{M}(v:=e) & ::= & v:=\mathcal{M}(e) \\
\mathcal{M}(e_1; e_2) & ::= & \mathcal{M}(e_1); \mathcal{M}(e_2) \\
\mathcal{M}(\text{if } v \text{ then } e_1 \text{ else } e_2) & ::= & \text{if } v \text{ then } \mathcal{M}(e_1) \text{ else } \mathcal{M}(e_2) \\
\mathcal{M}(t_0 \; mn(t_1 \; v_1, .., t_n \; v_n)\{e\}) & ::= & t_0 \; mn(t_1 \; v_1, .., t_n \; v_n)\{ \\
\multicolumn{3}{l}{\quad dec\_stk(sizeof(t_0, t_1, .., t_n)+4); \mathcal{M}(e); inc\_stk(sizeof(t_0, t_1, .., t_n)+4)\}}
\end{array}
$$

Fig. 3. Rewriting Rules for Instrumentation

To simulate the memory effect of **new** $c(v^*)$, we employ a primitive method over variable **heap**, called *dec_hp*, which is subject to the specification:

$$\text{void } dec\_hp(\text{int } n) \quad requires \; \text{heap} \geq n \wedge n \geq 0 \; ensures \; \text{heap}'=\text{heap}-n$$

To successfully call *dec_hp*(n), the variable **heap** must hold a value no less than the non-negative integer **n** at the call site. Upon return, the value of **heap** is decreased by **n**.

To simulate the memory effect of **free**(v), we employ a primitive method over **heap**, called *inc_hp*:

$$\text{void } inc\_hp(\text{int } n) \quad requires \; n \geq 0 \; ensures \; \text{heap}'=\text{heap}+n$$

The memory effect of local blocks and method bodies can be simulated in a similar way, and the difference is that they count on the stack instead of heap. For code blocks, we employ *dec_stk* to check the stack space is sufficient for the local variable to be declared, and decrease the stack space; meanwhile, at the end of the block, we recover such space by *inc_stk* due to the popping out of the local variables. As for method body, stack space is initially acquired (and later recovered) for method parameters and return address (four bytes), as the last rewriting rule suggests. The specifications for these two primitive methods are as follows:

$$\text{void } dec\_stk(\text{int } n) \quad requires \; \text{stk} \geq n \wedge n \geq 0 \; ensures \; \text{stk}'=\text{stk}-n$$
$$\text{void } inc\_stk(\text{int } n) \quad requires \; n \geq 0 \; ensures \; \text{stk}'=\text{stk}+n$$

Note that two different functions *sizeof* and *ssizeof* are used in the rewriting rules: *sizeof* is applied to both primitive and reference types, while *ssizeof* is applied to (user-defined) data types, by summing up the sizes of all declared fields' types obtained via *sizeof*. For example, *sizeof*(int) = 4, *sizeof*(**node**) = 4, and *ssizeof*(**node**) = 8, since the **node** data structure (defined in Section 2) contains an **int** field and a reference to another **node**. We also abuse these functions by applying them to a list of types, expecting them to return the sum of the results when applied to each type.

We present below the memory-aware versions for the two examples given in Section 2.

```
node new_list(int n)
  requires  emp ∧ heap≥8 * n∧
            n≥0 ∧ stk≥12 * n + 4
  ensures   res::ll⟨n⟩ ∧ stk'=stk∧
            heap'=heap−8 * n;
{ dec_stk(4);
  node r := null;
  if (n > 0) {
    dec_stk(8); r := new_list(n−1);
    inc_stk(8); dec_hp(8);
    r := new node(n, r) };
  inc_stk(4); r }
```

```
void free_list(node2 x)
  requires  x::dll⟨p, n⟩ ∧ heap≥0∧
            stk≥12 * n
  ensures   emp ∧ stk'=stk ∧
            heap'=heap+12 * n;
{ if (x ≠ null) {
    dec_stk(4);
    node2 t := x; x := x.next;
    free(t); inc_hp(12);
    dec_stk(8); free_list(x);
    inc_stk(8); inc_stk(4) }
}
```

Fig. 4. Example 1   **Fig. 5.** Example 2

Note that the memory effect is simulated via explicit calls to the afore-mentioned four primitive methods over **heap** and **stk**, which are highlighted in bold.

As one more example, we show in Figure 6 a program with more complicated memory usage behaviour. The program translates a doubly linked list (**node2**) into a singly linked list (**node**), by deallocating **node2** x and then creating a singly linked list with the same length and content. A heap memory of $4 * n$ bytes is reclaimed back since each **node2** object has one more field (which takes 4 bytes) than a **node** object.

```
node dl2sl(node2 x)
    requires  x::dll⟨_, n⟩ ∧ stk≥20∗n ∧ heap≥0
    ensures   res::ll⟨n⟩ ∧ stk'=stk ∧ heap'=heap+4∗n;
{ dec_stk(4); node r := null;
  if (x ≠ null) { dec_stk(4); int v := x.val; dec_stk(4);
      node2 t := x; x := x.next; free(t); inc_hp(12);
      dec_stk(8); r := dl2sl(x); inc_stk(8);
      dec_hp(8); r := new node(v, r); inc_stk(4); inc_stk(4) };
  inc_stk(4); r }
```

Fig. 6. Example 3

The instrumented programs are then passed to HIP/SLEEK for automated verification.

3.2   The Hip/Sleek Automated Verification System

An overview of the HIP/SLEEK automated verification system is given in Figure 7. The front-end of the system is a standard Hoare-style forward verifier HIP, which invokes the entailment prover SLEEK. The HIP verifier

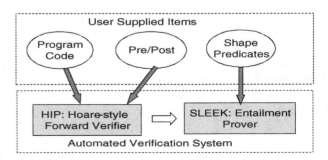

Fig. 7. The HIP/SLEEK Verification System

comprises a set of forward verification rules to systematically check that the precondition is satisfied at each call site, and that the declared postcondition is successfully verified (assuming the given precondition) for each method definition. The forward verification rules are of the form ⊢ $\{\Delta_1\}$ e $\{\Delta_2\}$ which expect the symbolic abstract state Δ_1 to be given before computing Δ_2. Given two separation formulas Δ_1 and Δ_2, the entailment prover SLEEK attempts to prove that Δ_1 entails Δ_2; if it succeeds, it returns a frame R such that $\Delta_1 \vdash \Delta_2 * R$. More details of the HIP and SLEEK provers can be found in Chin et al. [10].

4   Soundness

This section presents the soundness of our approach with respect to an underlying operational semantics given in Figure 8. Note that we instrument the state with memory size information, so a program state is represented by $\langle s, h, \sigma, \mu, e \rangle$, where s, h denote respectively the current stack and heap state as mentioned earlier, σ (μ) represents current available stack (heap) memory in bytes, and e is the program code to be executed. If the execution leads to an error, we denote the error state as er_1 if it is due to memory inadequacy, or as er_2 for all other errors (e.g. null pointer dereference). Note also that an intermediate construct $\mathtt{ret}(v^*, e)$ is introduced to denote the return value of call invocation and local blocks as in Chin et al. [10]. Later, we use $\hookrightarrow^*$ to denote the composition of any non-negative number of transitions, and $\uparrow$ for program divergence.

$$\langle s, h, \sigma, \mu, v \rangle \hookrightarrow \langle s, h, \sigma, \mu, s(v) \rangle \qquad \langle s, h, \sigma, \mu, k \rangle \hookrightarrow \langle s, h, \sigma, \mu, k \rangle$$

$$\langle s, h, \sigma, \mu, v := k \rangle \hookrightarrow \langle s[v \mapsto k], h, \sigma, \mu, () \rangle \qquad \langle s, h, \sigma, \mu, (); e \rangle \hookrightarrow \langle s, h, \sigma, \mu, e \rangle$$

$$\frac{s(v) \in dom(h)}{\langle s, h, \sigma, \mu, v.f \rangle \hookrightarrow \langle s, h, \sigma, \mu, h(s(v))(f) \rangle} \qquad \frac{s(v) \notin dom(h)}{\langle s, h, \sigma, \mu, v.f \rangle \hookrightarrow er_2}$$

$$\frac{\langle s, h, \sigma, \mu, e_1 \rangle \hookrightarrow \langle s_1, h_1, \sigma_1, \mu_1, e_3 \rangle}{\langle s, h, \sigma, \mu, e_1; e_2 \rangle \hookrightarrow \langle s_1, h_1, \sigma_1, \mu_1, e_3; e_2 \rangle} \qquad \frac{\langle s, h, \sigma, \mu, e \rangle \hookrightarrow \langle s_1, h_1, \sigma_1, \mu_1, e_1 \rangle}{\langle s, h, \sigma, \mu, v := e \rangle \hookrightarrow \langle s_1, h_1, \sigma_1, \mu_1, v := e_1 \rangle}$$

$$\frac{s(v) = \mathtt{true}}{\langle s, h, \sigma, \mu, \mathtt{if}\ v\ \mathtt{then}\ e_1\ \mathtt{else}\ e_2 \rangle \hookrightarrow \langle s, h, \sigma, \mu, e_1 \rangle}$$

$$\frac{s(v) = \mathtt{false}}{\langle s, h, \sigma, \mu, \mathtt{if}\ v\ \mathtt{then}\ e_1\ \mathtt{else}\ e_2 \rangle \hookrightarrow \langle s, h, \sigma, \mu, e_2 \rangle}$$

$$\frac{s(v_1) \in dom(h) \quad r = h(s(v_1))[f \mapsto s(v_2)] \quad h_1 = h[s(v_1) \mapsto r]}{\langle s, h, \sigma, \mu, v_1.f := v_2 \rangle \hookrightarrow \langle s, h_1, \sigma, \mu, () \rangle} \qquad \frac{s(v_1) \notin dom(h)}{\langle s, h, \sigma, \mu, v_1.f := v_2 \rangle \hookrightarrow er_2}$$

$$\frac{s(v) \mapsto l \in h \quad h_1 = h \backslash [s(v) \mapsto l] \quad \mu_1 = \mu + ssizeof(type(v))}{\langle s, h, \sigma, \mu, \mathtt{free}(v) \rangle \hookrightarrow \langle s, h_1, \sigma, \mu_1, () \rangle} \qquad \frac{s(v) \notin dom(h)}{\langle s, h, \sigma, \mu, \mathtt{free}(v) \rangle \hookrightarrow er_2}$$

$$\frac{\mathtt{data}\ c\ \{t_1\ f_1, .., t_n\ f_n\} \in P \quad \iota \notin dom(h)}{\mu \geq ssizeof(c) \quad \mu_1 = \mu - ssizeof(c) \quad r = c[f_i \mapsto s(v_i)]_{i=1}^n} \qquad \frac{\mu < ssizeof(c)}{\langle s, h, \sigma, \mu, \mathtt{new}\ c(v^*) \rangle \hookrightarrow \langle s, h + [\iota \mapsto r], \sigma, \mu_1, \iota \rangle} \qquad \frac{\mu < ssizeof(c)}{\langle s, h, \sigma, \mu, \mathtt{new}\ c(v^*) \rangle \hookrightarrow er_1}$$

$$\langle s, h, \sigma, \mu, \mathtt{ret}(v_1, .., v_n, k) \rangle \hookrightarrow \langle s - \{v_1, .., v_n\}, h, \sigma + sizeof(type(v_1), .., type(v_n)), \mu, k \rangle$$

$$\frac{\langle s, h, \sigma, \mu, e \rangle \hookrightarrow \langle s_1, h_1, \sigma_1, \mu_1, e_1 \rangle}{\langle s, h, \sigma, \mu, \mathtt{ret}(v^*, e) \rangle \hookrightarrow \langle s_1, h_1, \sigma_1, \mu_1, \mathtt{ret}(v^*, e_1) \rangle}$$

$$\frac{\sigma \geq sizeof(t) \quad \sigma_1 = \sigma - sizeof(t)}{\langle s, h, \sigma, \mu, \{t\ v;\ e\} \rangle \hookrightarrow \langle s + [v \mapsto \bot], h, \sigma_1, \mu, \mathtt{ret}(v, e) \rangle} \qquad \frac{\sigma < sizeof(t)}{\langle s, h, \sigma, \mu, \{t\ v;\ e\} \rangle \hookrightarrow er_1}$$

$$\frac{s_1 = s + [w_i \mapsto s(v_i)]_{i=m}^n}{\sigma \geq \Sigma_{i=m}^n sizeof(t_i) \quad \sigma_1 = \sigma - \Sigma_{i=m}^n sizeof(t_i)} \qquad \frac{\sigma < \Sigma_{i=m}^n sizeof(t_i)}{\langle s, h, \sigma, \mu, mn(v^*) \rangle \hookrightarrow er_1}$$

$$\frac{t_0\ mn((\mathtt{ref}\ t_i\ w_i)_{i=1}^{m-1}, (t_i\ w_i)_{i=m}^n)\ \{e\}}{\langle s, h, \sigma, \mu, mn(v_1, .., v_n) \rangle \hookrightarrow}$$
$$\langle s_1, h, \sigma_1, \mu, \mathtt{ret}(\{w_i\}_{i=m}^n, [v_i/w_i]_{i=1}^{m-1} e) \rangle$$

Fig. 8. Underlying Semantics

As shown in the transition rule, a successful execution of $\mathtt{free}(v)$ increases the heap size μ by $\mathit{ssizeof}(\mathit{type}(v))$. Note that we use $h \setminus [s(v){\mapsto}l]$ to erase $s(v)$ from h's domain. The execution of $\mathtt{new}\ c(v^*)$ first checks if the current heap space is sufficient for the allocation; if it succeeds, the heap size is decreased by $\mathit{ssizeof}(c)$. Here we adds $\iota \mapsto r$ into h by the notation $h + [\iota \mapsto r]$.

The stack space may be changed when the program enters into or exits from a local block $\{t\ v;\ e\}$, or invokes a method, or returns from a method call. Upon exit from a block or a method call, all local variables are popped out from the stack $(s - \{v_1, .., v_n\})$ and the corresponding stack space is recovered $(\sigma + \mathit{sizeof}(\mathit{type}(v_1), .., \mathit{type}(v_n)))$. Conversely, entering a block or invoking a method may require some stack space to store newly declared local variables or returning address of the method. So the relevant semantic rule first checks whether the stack space is sufficient to cater for a new block or a method invocation, if so, the program state is transformed. Otherwise a memory inadequacy error is reported.

Due to the recording of memory size information in program state, we need an extended model to link the underlying semantics with the separation formula, which is defined as follows:

$$s, h, \sigma, \mu \models \Phi \quad =_{def} \quad s, h \models [\sigma/\mathtt{stk}', \mu/\mathtt{heap}']\Phi$$

where $s, h \models \Phi$ was defined in Chin et al. [10].

Next, we show that the instrumented program $\mathcal{M}(e)$ is observationally equivalent to the original program e w.r.t. the semantics in Figure 8.

Theorem 1 (Observational Equivalence). *For any stack s, heap h, stack size σ, heap size μ, and program e and its instrumented version $\mathcal{M}(e)$, one and only one of the following cases holds:*

1. *$\exists s_1, h_1, \sigma_1, \mu_1 \cdot \langle s, h, \sigma, \mu, e \rangle \hookrightarrow^* \langle s_1, h_1, \sigma_1, \mu_1, \nu \rangle \iff \langle s[\mathtt{stk}{\mapsto}\sigma, \mathtt{heap}{\mapsto}\mu],$ $h, \sigma, \mu, \mathcal{M}(e) \rangle \hookrightarrow^* \langle s_1[\mathtt{stk}{\mapsto}\sigma_1, \mathtt{heap}{\mapsto}\mu_1], h_1, \sigma_1, \mu_1, \nu \rangle$ where value ν is the evaluation result of e;*
2. *$\langle s, h, \sigma, \mu, e \rangle \hookrightarrow^* er_1 \iff \langle s[\mathtt{stk}{\mapsto}\sigma, \mathtt{heap}{\mapsto}\mu], h, \sigma, \mu, \mathcal{M}(e) \rangle \hookrightarrow^* er_1;$*
3. *$\langle s, h, \sigma, \mu, e \rangle \hookrightarrow^* er_2 \iff \langle s[\mathtt{stk}{\mapsto}\sigma, \mathtt{heap}{\mapsto}\mu], h, \sigma, \mu, \mathcal{M}(e) \rangle \hookrightarrow^* er_2;$*
4. *$\langle s, h, \sigma, \mu, e \rangle \uparrow \iff \langle s[\mathtt{stk}{\mapsto}\sigma, \mathtt{heap}{\mapsto}\mu], h, \sigma, \mu, \mathcal{M}(e) \rangle \uparrow.$*

Note that the stack mapping $s[\mathtt{stk}{\mapsto}\sigma, \mathtt{heap}{\mapsto}\mu]$ is the same as s except that it maps $\mathtt{stk}$ to σ and $\mathtt{heap}$ to μ.

Proof. By structural induction over e. □

We assume that the global variables, such as $\mathtt{heap}$ and $\mathtt{stk}$, reside in the top frame of the run-time stack when a program starts to run. Note that invocations of the four primitive methods, namely $\mathit{inc\_hp}(\cdot)$, $\mathit{inc\_stk}(\cdot)$, $\mathit{dec\_hp}(\cdot)$ and $\mathit{dec\_stk}(\cdot)$, modify only the values of $\mathtt{heap}$ and $\mathtt{stk}$, but not the rest of the stack. Each invocation of these methods requires eight bytes of stack space, which is immediately recovered after the invocation.[3]

---

[3] Because of this, a memory-aware program may require an additional stack space of 8 bytes. For simplicity, we assume this has been taken into account implicitly.

Finally, the following theorem ensures the soundness of our memory usage verification:

Theorem 2. *For any method t mn $(([\mathtt{ref}] \; t \; v)^*)$ requires Φ_{pr} ensures Φ_{po} $\{e\}$, if we can verify $\mathcal{M}(e)$ against specification (Φ_{pr}, Φ_{po}), then we have $\forall s, h, \sigma, \mu \cdot (s, h, \sigma, \mu \models \Phi_{pr} \wedge \langle s, h, \sigma, \mu, e \rangle \hookrightarrow^* \langle s_1, h_1, \sigma_1, \mu_1, \nu \rangle) \implies s_1, h_1, \sigma_1, \mu_1 \models \Phi_{po}$.*

Proof. It follows from Theorem 1 and the soundness of the HIP/SLEEK verification process given in Chin et al. [10]. □

5   Experimental Results

We have implemented our proposal and integrated it with the HIP/SLEEK system to support memory usage verification. We have evaluated the system using a number of benchmarks, by first converting them to memory-aware programs and then passing them to the HIP/SLEEK system for memory usage verification (which is done as one pass along with the verification of other safety properties). One set of programs that we have tested are taken from Nguyen et al. [19]. Despite of small-size, these programs are composed of methods manipulating shared mutable data structures, such as (doubly) linked lists, cyclic linked lists, binary search trees, most of which cannot be handled by previous type-based memory usage verifiers. Another set of programs that we have tested are taken from the Olden Benchmark Suite [8]. These programs are of medium-size and quite often contain sophisticated memory usage behaviour. For all programs, we have manually supplied their memory specifications which are precise when validated through some sample runs. The initial experimental results have shown that the memory usage specification is expressive and the memory usage verification via HIP/SLEEK is powerful, especially in dealing with mutable data structures with sophisticated sharing.

Programs	Code (lines)	Verified Methods	Verification (in sec.)
Benchmark programs from Nguyen et al. [19]			
singly linked list	72	4/4	0.42
doubly linked list	104	4/4	1.20
binary search tree	62	2/2	0.32
cyclic linked list	78	2/2	0.48
Olden Benchmark suite			
treeadd	195	4/4	0.58
bisort	340	6/6	2.80
em3d	462	20/20	1.52
mst	473	22/22	1.64
tsp	545	9/9	3.44
health	562	15/15	7.35
power	765	19/19	5.17

Fig. 9. Experiment Results

Figure 9 summarises some statistics obtained during the experimental study. The statistics shows that our approach is general enough to handle many interesting data structures such as single linked lists, double linked lists, trees and cyclic linked lists. Column 4 shows the CPU times used (in seconds) for the verification. Our experiments were done under Linux platform on Intel Core Quad 2.66 GHz with 8 GB main memory. All programs take under 10 seconds to verify, even for medium-sized programs with sophisticated memory usage behaviour.

6   Related Work

Previous research on memory usage analysis and verification [1,2,5,7,15] mainly focuses on functional programs where data structures are mostly immutable and easier to deal with. Amadio et al. [1] define a simple stack machine for a first-order functional language and discuss the performance of type, size and termination verifications at bytecode level of the machine. Their contribution is to verify a system of annotations for the bytecode at loading time, and ensure both time and space resource bound required by its execution. Their work only takes into account stack bounds but not heap memory. Another related work is the research in the MRG (Mobile Resource Guarantees) project [2,5], which focuses on building a proof-carrying code system to guarantee that bytecode programs are free from run-time violations of resource bounds. The analysis is developed for a linearly typed bytecode language which is compiled from a first-order functional language, where the bounds are restricted to a linear form.

Hofmann and Jost [15] present a mechanism to obtain linear bounds on the heap space usage of first-order functional programs. It uses an amortised analysis by assigning hypothetical amounts of free space to data structures in proportion to their sizes. The analysis relies on a type system with resource annotations, and takes space reuse by explicit deallocation. With this approach, memory recovery can be supported within each function, but not across functions unless the dead objects are explicitly passed. Their analysis does not consider stack usage and is limited to a linear form without disjunction. Recently, Campbell [7] gives a type-based approach to stack space analysis. It uses the depth of data structures and adds extra structures to typing contexts to describe the form of the bounds. Heap memory is not considered in his work.

Previous works on memory usage verification [11,12,16] for imperative/OO programming languages mainly use type-based approaches. Chin et al. [12] propose a modular memory usage verification system for object-oriented programs. The system can check whether a certain amount of memory is adequate for safe execution of a given program. However, the verification framework requires alias control mechanism to overcome the mutability and sharing problems. Therefore, it can only handle restricted subsets of programs manipulating shared mutable data structures. Recently, Chin et al. [11] propose a memory bound analysis system for low-level programs. The system tries to infer both stack and heap space bounds, using fixpoint analyses for recursive methods and loops. However, the system does not handle shared objects. Hofmann and Jost [16] propose a type-based heap space analysis for Java style OO programs with explicit deallocation.

It uses an amortised analysis, and a potential is assigned to each datum according to its size and layout. Heap memory usage is calculated by an LP-solver based on function inputs during the type inference.

Different from previous works which try to build a memory usage verification system, we re-use a general-purpose verification system HIP/SLEEK for memory usage verification, where shape, size and alias information can be readily obtained from the specifications given in separation logic. With this tool, we can verify quite a number of programs that can not be handled by previous approaches, such as doubly linked lists, cyclic linked lists and binary trees.

7   Conclusion

In this paper we have proposed an approach to memory usage verification, by resorting to a general-purpose verification system HIP/SLEEK based on separation logic, where memory usage specifications can be depicted using two special variables **heap** and **stk**. Given a program to verify against its memory usage specifications, instead of constructing and implementing verification rules to conduct the verification, we rewrite the program to its memory-aware version where memory usage behaviours are mimicked by explicit operations over variables **heap** and **stk**. The obtained memory-aware program can then be passed to HIP/SLEEK for automated verification. Due to the fact that the memory-aware program is observationally equivalent to its original program, the memory safety for the original program follows directly from the memory safety proof of the instrumented program. We have implemented the rewriting process and integrated it with HIP/SLEEK. Our initial experimental study shows that we can verify quite a number of programs which can not be handled by previous memory usage verification systems mainly due to the manipulation of sophisticated shared mutable data structures.

As for future work, we aim to automatically infer memory usage specifications, where possible, to reduce the burden on users and also improve the level of automation for memory usage verification. We have just started another EPSRC-funded project aiming to automatically infer method specifications and loop invariants in a combined separation and numerical domain, which would benefit our memory usage analysis and verification.

Acknowledgement. This work was supported in part by the EPSRC projects [EP/E021948/1, EP/G042322/1] and the A*STAR grant R-252-000-233-305.

References

1. Amadio, R.M., Coupet-Grimal, S., Dal Zilio, S., Jakubiec, L.: A Functional Scenario for Bytecode Verification of Resource Bounds. In: Marcinkowski, J., Tarlecki, A. (eds.) CSL 2004. LNCS, vol. 3210, pp. 265–279. Springer, Heidelberg (2004)

2. Aspinall, D., Gilmore, S., Hofmann, M., Sannella, D., Stark, I.: Mobile resource guarantees for smart devices. In: Barthe, G., Burdy, L., Huisman, M., Lanet, J.-L., Muntean, T. (eds.) CASSIS 2004. LNCS, vol. 3362, pp. 1–26. Springer, Heidelberg (2005)

3. Berdine, J., Calcagno, C., O'Hearn, P.W.: Smallfoot: Modular automatic assertion checking with separation logic. In: de Boer, F.S., Bonsangue, M.M., Graf, S., de Roever, W.-P. (eds.) FMCO 2005. LNCS, vol. 4111, pp. 115–137. Springer, Heidelberg (2006)

4. Berdine, J., Cook, B., Distefano, D., O'Hearn, P.W.: Automatic termination proofs for programs with shape-shifting heaps. In: Ball, T., Jones, R.B. (eds.) CAV 2006. LNCS, vol. 4144, pp. 386–400. Springer, Heidelberg (2006)

5. Beringer, L., Hofmann, M., Momigliano, A., Shkaravska, O.: Automatic certification of heap consumption. In: Baader, F., Voronkov, A. (eds.) LPAR 2004. LNCS (LNAI), vol. 3452, pp. 347–362. Springer, Heidelberg (2005)

6. Calcagno, C., Distefano, D., O'Hearn, P.W., Yang, H.: Compositional shape analysis by means of bi-abduction. In: ACM POPL, pp. 289–300 (2009)

7. Campbell, B.: Amortised memory analysis using the depth of data structures. In: ESOP. LNCS, vol. 5502, pp. 190–204. Springer, Heidelberg (2009)

8. Carlisle, M.C., Rogers, A.: Software caching and computation migration in Olden. ACM SIGPLAN Notices 30(8), 29–38 (1995)

9. Chin, W.-N., David, C., Nguyen, H.H., Qin, S.: Enhancing modular oo verification with separation logic. In: ACM POPL, pp. 87–99 (2008)

10. Chin, W.-N., David, C., Nguyen, H.H., Qin, S.: Automated verification of shape, size and bag properties via user-defined predicates in separation logic. Under Consideration by Science of Computer Programming (2009), http://www.dur.ac.uk/shengchao.qin/papers/SCP-draft.pdf

11. Chin, W.-N., Nguyen, H.H., Popeea, C., Qin, S.: Analysing memory resource bounds for low-level programs. In: International Symposium on Memory Management (ISMM), pp. 151–160. ACM Press, New York (2008)

12. Chin, W.-N., Nguyen, H.H., Qin, S., Rinard, M.: Memory usage verification for oo Programs. In: Hankin, C., Siveroni, I. (eds.) SAS 2005. LNCS, vol. 3672, pp. 70–86. Springer, Heidelberg (2005)

13. Distefano, D., O'Hearn, P.W., Yang, H.: A local shape analysis based on separation logic. In: Hermanns, H., Palsberg, J. (eds.) TACAS 2006. LNCS, vol. 3920, pp. 287–302. Springer, Heidelberg (2006)

14. Distefano, D., Parkinson, M.J.: jStar: towards practical verification for Java. In: ACM OOPSLA, pp. 213–226 (2008)

15. Hofmann, M., Jost, S.: Static prediction of heap space usage for first order functional programs. In: ACM POPL, January 2003, pp. 185–197 (2003)

16. Hofmann, M., Jost, S.: Type-based amortised heap-space analysis. In: Sestoft, P. (ed.) ESOP 2006. LNCS, vol. 3924, pp. 22–37. Springer, Heidelberg (2006)

17. Ishtiaq, S., O'Hearn, P.W.: BI as an assertion language for mutable data structures. In: ACM POPL, January 2001, pp. 14–26 (2001)

18. Nguyen, H.H., Chin, W.-N.: Enhancing program verification with lemmas. In: Gupta, A., Malik, S. (eds.) CAV 2008. LNCS, vol. 5123, pp. 355–369. Springer, Heidelberg (2008)

19. Nguyen, H.H., David, C., Qin, S., Chin, W.-N.: Automated verification of shape and size properties via separation logic. In: Cook, B., Podelski, A. (eds.) VMCAI 2007. LNCS, vol. 4349, pp. 251–266. Springer, Heidelberg (2007)

20. Parkinson, M.J., Bierman, G.M.: Separation logic, abstraction and inheritance. In: ACM POPL, pp. 75–86 (2008)

21. Reeves, G., Neilson, T., Litwin, T.: Mars exploration rover spirit vehicle anomaly report. Jet Propulsion Laboratory Document No. D-22919 (July 2004)
22. Reynolds, J.: Separation logic: a logic for shared mutable data structures. In: IEEE LICS, July 2002, pp. 55–74 (2002)
23. Xi, H.: Imperative programming with dependent types. In: IEEE LICS, June 2000, pp. 375–387 (2000)
24. Yang, H., Lee, O., Berdine, J., Calcagno, C., Cook, B., Distefano, D., O'Hearn, P.W.: Scalable shape analysis for systems code. In: Gupta, A., Malik, S. (eds.) CAV 2008. LNCS, vol. 5123, pp. 385–398. Springer, Heidelberg (2008)

Solving Parity Games in Practice

Oliver Friedmann and Martin Lange

Dept. of Computer Science, University of Munich, Germany

Abstract. Parity games are 2-player games of perfect information and infinite duration that have important applications in automata theory and decision procedures (validity as well as model checking) for temporal logics. In this paper we investigate practical aspects of solving parity games. The main contribution is a suggestion on how to solve parity games efficiently in practice: we present a generic solver that intertwines optimisations with any of the existing parity game algorithms which is only called on parts of a game that cannot be solved faster by simpler methods. This approach is evaluated empirically on a series of benchmarking games from the aforementioned application domains, showing that using this approach vastly speeds up the solving process. As a side-effect we obtain the surprising observation that Zielonka's recursive algorithm is the best parity game solver in practice.

1 Introduction

Parity games are two-player games of perfect information played on directed graphs whose nodes are labeled with priorities. The winner of a play is determined by the parity (even or odd) of the *maximal* priority occurring infinitely often. Parity games have various applications in computer science, and the theory of formal languages and automata in particular. They are closely related to other games of infinite duration, in particular mean and discounted payoff as well as stochastic games [4,14]. An efficient parity game solver may be extendable to efficient solvers for those games as well.

Solving a parity game is equivalent (from a complexity-theoretic point of view) under linear-time reductions to the model checking problem for the modal μ-calculus [14]. Hence, any parity game solver is also a model checker for the μ-calculus (and vice-versa) and all its fragments like CTL, PDL, CTL*, etc. However, typical verification problems result in parity games with few priorities only for which specialised algorithms should be more efficient than a general solver.

Parity games also arise in decision procedures for temporal logics. While the satisfiability problem for linear-time logics like LTL, PSL or the linear-time μ-calculus reduces – in one form or the other – to the inclusion problem for non-deterministic Büchi automata (NBA) and therefore requires *complementation* thereof, branching-time logics require the determinisation of NBA in addition. So far, the only known constructions for determinising and complementing an NBA are Safra's [10], Piterman's [9], and Kähler and Wilke's [7]. The first one

Z. Liu and A.P. Ravn (Eds.): ATVA 2009, LNCS 5799, pp. 182–196, 2009.

yields a deterministic Streett automaton which is algorithmically not very easy to handle. The two others yield parity automata. Using these, the satisfiability (or validity) problem for branching-time logics not only reduces to the solving of parity games, there also does not seem to be a feasible alternative. The same holds for controller synthesis problems which are tackled by a reduction to the satisfiability problem of, typically, some branching-time logic like the modal μ-calculus [2]. Hence, being able to solve parity games well in practice is also vital for obtaining good satisfiability and controller synthesis tools.

A variety of algorithms for solving parity games has been invented so far. The most prominent deterministic ones are the constructive proof of memory-less determinacy by Zielonka [18] which yields a recursive algorithm, the local μ-calculus model checker by Stevens and Stirling [13], Jurdziński's small progress measures algorithm [5] with a symbolic version [8], the strategy improvement algorithm by Jurdziński and Vöge [17] with a locally optimal variation by Schewe [12], and the subexponential algorithm by Jurdziński, Paterson and Zwick [6] with a so-called big-step variant by Schewe [11]. This variety is owed to the theoretical challenge of answering the question whether parity games can be solved in polynomial time, rather than practical motivations. Nonetheless, a parity game solver that is efficient in practice is necessary for practical decision procedure for branching-time logics and for controller synthesis, and may even be used as a model checker. Van de Pol and Weber describe a parallel implementation of Jurdziński's small progress measures algorithm [16] but it turns out that in many cases, this algorithm is not the most efficient one. Also, their implementation does not feature known tricks that are supposed to be optimisations to any parity game solver.

The literature contains a few suggestions on how to tune a parity game solver. Jurdziński [5] mentions decomposition into SCCs and solving SCC-wise, removal of self-cycles on nodes, and priority compression. Huth et al. [1] mention the latter two and, in addition, priority propagation. In any case, these are suggested heuristics that have not been put to the test yet. While it is plausible that they are useful in speeding up parity game solvers in practice, no proper evidence of this has been given so far.

In this paper we present a rigorous empirical treatment of these optimisations. After recalling the theory of parity games in Sect. 2, we shortly describe such optimisations in Sect. 3 and devise a so-called generic solver. It is an algorithm which employs some of these optimisations in a certain order and fashion, and intertwines them with calls to a real algorithm for solving parity games. The choice of the optimisations and the design of the order etc. is motivated by common sense *and* experience in practice. Hence, this paper presents a particular way of employing particular optimisations that has turned out to be successful while others are less succesful (or even harmful). The success is quantified in Sect. 4 which examines the result that employing these optimisations has on the times needed to solve certain games. There are no families of games that people agree on as standard benchmarks. We therefore use hand-made games, some of which are taken from application domains listed above.

The approach presented in this paper is implemented in a publicly available tool which shows that parity games can – despite the lack of proof or fact about being polynomial-time solvable – be solved efficiently in practice. It also bears some surprises. All of the deterministic algorithms for solving parity games that have appeared in the literature so far have been implemented in the tool which therefore allows them to be compared w.r.t. their usability in practice. As a result, the small progress measures algorithm as well as the strategy improvement turn out to be generally slower than the recursive algorithm. This is a huge surprise since this algorithm was commonly accepted to be a constructive proof of determinacy but nothing more, in particular not to have any practical relevance at all. Furthermore, there are "optimisations" that have been suggested as a means for speeding up the solving which one should not employ because they turn out to slow down the solving.

The rest of the paper is organised as follows. Sect. 2 recalls parity games and necessary technicalities. Sect. 3 describes the aforementioned optimisations and presents the generic solver which is assembled out of these. Sect. 4 evaluates the solver empirically on some families of benchmarking games.

2   Preliminaries

A *parity game* is a tuple $G = (V, V_0, V_1, E, \Omega)$ where (V, E) forms a directed graph in which each node has at least one successor. The set of nodes is partitioned into $V = V_0 \cup V_1$ with $V_0 \cap V_1 = \emptyset$, and $\Omega : V \to \mathbb{N}$ is the *priority function* that assigns to each node a natural number called the *priority* of the node. We write $|\Omega|$ for the index of the parity game, that is the number of different priorities assigned to its nodes. The graph is required to be total, i.e. for every $v \in V$ there is a $w \in W$ s.t. $(v, w) \in E$. Here we only consider games based on finite graphs.

We also use infix notation vEw instead of $(v, w) \in E$ and define the set of all *successors* of v as $vE := \{w \mid vEw\}$, as well as the set of all *predecessors* of w as $Ew := \{v \mid vEw\}$. For a set $U \subseteq V$ and nodes $v, w \in V$ we will write $G \setminus U$ for the game that is obtained from G by eliminating all nodes in U, i.e. $(V \setminus U, V_0 \setminus U, V_1 \setminus U, E \setminus (V \times U \cup U \times V), \Omega)$ and $G \setminus \{(v, w)\}$ for the game that results from eliminating a possible edge between v and w – assuming that the result is still total – i.e. $(V, V_0, V_1, E \setminus \{(v, w)\}, \Omega)$.

The game is played between two players called 0 and 1 in the following way. Starting in a node $v_0 \in V$ they construct an infinite path through the graph as follows. If the construction so far has yielded a finite sequence $v_0 \ldots v_n$ and $v_n \in V_i$ then player i selects a $w \in v_n E$ and the play continues with the sequence $v_0 \ldots v_n w$.

Every play has a unique winner given by the *parity* of the greatest priority that occurs infinitely often in a play. The winner of the play $v_0 v_1 v_2 \ldots$ is player i iff $\max\{p \mid \forall j \in \mathbb{N} \, \exists k \geq j : \Omega(v_k) = p\} \equiv_2 i$ (where $i \equiv_2 j$ holds iff $|i - j|$ mod $2 = 0$). That is, player 0 tries to make an even priority occur infinitely often without any greater odd priorities occurring infinitely often, player 1 attempts the converse.

A *positional strategy* for player i in G is a – possibly partial – function $\sigma :$ $V_i \rightarrow V$. A play $v_0 v_1 \ldots$ *conforms* to a strategy σ for player i if for all $j \in \mathbb{N}$ we have: if $v_j \in V_i$ then $v_{j+1} = \sigma(v_j)$. Intuitively, conforming to a strategy means to always make those choices that are prescribed by the strategy. A strategy σ for player i is a *winning strategy* in node v if player i wins every play that begins in v and conforms to σ. We say that player i *wins* the game G starting in v iff he/she has a winning strategy for G starting in v.

With G we associate two sets $W_0, W_1 \subseteq V$; W_i is the set of all nodes v s.t. player i wins the game G starting in v. Here we restrict ourselves to positional strategies because it is well-known that a player has a (general) winning strategy iff she has a positional winning strategy for a given game. In fact, parity games enjoy positional determinacy meaning that for every node v in the game either $v \in W_0$ or $v \in W_1$ [3]. Furthermore, it is not difficult to show that, whenever player i has winning strategies σ_v for all $v \in U$ for some $U \subseteq V$, then there is also a single strategy σ that is winning for player i from every node in U.

The problem of solving a given parity game is to compute W_0 and W_1 as well as corresponding winning strategies σ_0 and σ_1 for the players on their respective winning regions. We will write $[]$ for the strategy with empty domain, and $\sigma[v \mapsto w]$ with vEw for the strategy that behaves like σ on all nodes in $V \setminus \{v\}$ and that maps v to w. Given two strategies σ, σ' for player i, we define their right-join $\sigma \twoheadleftarrow \sigma'$ as $(\sigma \twoheadleftarrow \sigma')(v) = \sigma(v)$ if $\sigma'(v)$ is undefined and $(\sigma \twoheadleftarrow \sigma')(v) = \sigma'(v)$ otherwise.

Let $U \subseteq V$ and $i \in \{0, 1\}$. The i-attractor of U contains all nodes from which player i can move "towards" U and player $1 - i$ must move "towards" U. Attractors will play an important role in the solving procedure described below because they can efficiently be computed using breadth-first search on the inverse graph underlying the game. At the same time, it is possible to construct an *attractor strategy* which is a positional strategy in a reachability game. Following this strategy guarantees player i to reach a node in U eventually, regardless of the opponent's choices. Define, for all $k \in \mathbb{N}$:

$$
\begin{aligned}
Attr_i^0(U) &:= U \\
Attr_i^{k+1}(U) &:= Attr_i^k(U) \cup \{v \in V_i \mid \exists w \in Attr_i^k(U) \text{ s.t. } vEw\} \\
&\quad \cup \{v \in V_{1-i} \mid \forall w : vEw \Rightarrow w \in Attr_i^k(U)\} \\
Attr_i(U) &:= \bigcup_{k \in \mathbb{N}} Attr_i^k(U)
\end{aligned}
$$

Note that any attractor on a finite game is necessarily finite, and the approximation defined above thus terminates after at most $|V|$ many steps. It is also not difficult to see that $Attr_i(U)$ can be computed in time $\mathcal{O}(|E|)$ for any i and U if the set operations take constant time only, using boolean arrays for example. The corresponding attractor strategy is defined as

$$
\sigma_i^{Attr}(v) := \begin{cases} w, & \text{if there is } k > 0 \text{ s.t. } v \in (V_i \cap Attr_i^k(U)) \setminus Attr_i^{k-1}(U) \\ & \text{and } w \in Attr_i^{k-1}(U) \cap vE \\ \bot, & \text{otherwise} \end{cases}
$$

Note that the choice of w is not unique, but any w with the prescribed property will suffice.

An important property that has been noted before [18,14] is that removing the i-attractor of any set of nodes from a game will still result in a total game graph.

3   Universal Optimisations and a Generic Solver

This section describes some universal optimisations – in the form of pre-transformations or incomplete solvers. These try to efficiently reduce the overall complexity of a given parity game in order to reduce the effort spent by any solver. Clearly, such optimisations have to ensure that a solution of the modified game can be effectively and efficiently translated back into a valid solution of the original game. Here we describe four: (1) SCC decomposition [5]; (2) detection of three special cases – two from [1]; (3) priority compression [5], and (4) priority propagation [1]. At the end we present a generic solver that makes use of most of them. The choice is motivated by two facts: their worst-case running time is low in comparison to that of a real solver: at most $\mathcal{O}(|\Omega| \cdot |E|)$, resp. $\mathcal{O}(|V| \log |V|)$. More importantly, they are empirically found to be beneficial.

3.1   SCC Decomposition

Let $G = (V, V_0, V_1, E, \Omega)$ be a parity game. A *strongly connected component* (SCC) is a non-empty set $C \subseteq V$ with the property that every node in C can reach every other node in C, i.e. uE^*v for all $u, v \in C$ (where E^* denotes the reflexive-transitive closure of E). We always assume SCCs to be maximal. We call an SCC C *proper* if $|C| > 1$ or $C = \{v\}$ for some v with vEv. Every parity game $G = (V, V_0, V_1, E, \Omega)$ can, in time $\mathcal{O}(|E|)$, be partitioned into SCCs $C_0, ..., C_n$ using Tarjan's algorithm for example [15].

There is a topological ordering $\rightarrow$ on these SCCs which is defined as $C_i \rightarrow C_j$ iff $i \neq j$ and there are $u \in C_i$, $v \in C_j$ with uEv. An SCC C is called *final* if there is no SCC C' s.t. $C \rightarrow C'$. Note that every finite graph must have at least one final SCC.

Parity games can be solved SCC-wise. Each play eventually gets trapped in an SCC, and the winner of the play is determined by the priorities of the nodes in this SCC alone, in particular not by priorities of nodes not in this SCC. Hence, an entire parity game can be solved by solving its SCCs starting with the final ones and working backwards in their order.

It is reasonable to assume that SCC decomposition speeds up the solving of a game. Suppose that the time it takes to solve a game G is $f(G)$, and that G can be decomposed into SCCs $C_0, \ldots, C_n$. Then solving SCC-wise will take time $f(C_1) + \ldots + f(C_n) + \mathcal{O}(|G|)$ which is asymptotically better than $f(G)$ if f is superlinear. Note that it takes at least linear time to solve a parity game because every node has to be visited at least once in order to determine which W_i it belongs to.

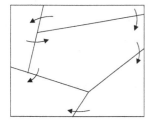 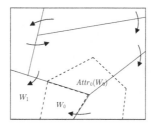 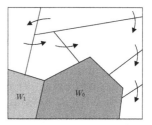

Fig. 1. Solving a game SCC-wise with refined decompositions

A naïve implementation of SCC-wise solving handles final SCCs and replaces the winning regions in those with two single self-looping nodes that are won by the respective players, and then continues with the next SCCs. A slightly more clever way is the following, as suggested by Jurdziński [5]. First, let W_i^G and σ_i^G be empty sets resp. strategies for the players $i \in \{0, 1\}$ on G.

1. Decompose G into SCCs $C_0, \ldots, C_n$. W.l.o.g. say that $C_0, \ldots, C_m$ are final for some $m \leq n$. Then one solves these obtaining winning regions W_i^j and strategies σ_i^j for $i \in \{0, 1\}$ and $j = 0, \ldots, m$. Add W_i^j to W_i^G for every i, j and add σ_i^j to σ_i^G via right-join.
2. Compute $A_i := Attr_i(W_i^0 \cup \ldots \cup W_i^m)$ for $i \in \{0, 1\}$ and corresponding attractor strategies σ_i which are also added to W_i^G and σ_i^G via right-join.
3. Repeat step 1 with $(G \setminus A_0) \setminus A_1$ until G is entirely solved.

Note that the attractors of the winning regions in some SCC can extend into SCCs further up, and eliminating them can result in a finer SCC structure than before. Hence, it suffices to decompose those of $C_{m+1}, \ldots, C_n$ that intersect with one of the attractors.

An example is depicted in Fig. 1. On the left it shows a parity game that is decomposed into 5 SCCs of which one is final. That is then solved using an arbitrary solver which partitions it into the winning regions W_0 and W_1. The middle then shows the attractor of W_0 reaching into other SCCs. On the right it shows the shaded regions already declared as winning for the respective players, and the two affected non-final SCCs being decomposed into SCCs again. This then yields a smaller parity game with 6 SCCs which can be solved iteratively until the winning regions partition the entire game.

3.2   Detection of Special Cases

There are certain games that can be solved very efficiently. W.l.o.g. we assume games to be proper and final SCCs. Note that non-proper SCCs are being solved using attractor computations in the procedure described above.

Self-cycle games. Suppose there is a node v such that vEv. Then there are two cases depending on the node's owner p and the parity of the node's priority. If

$\Omega(v) \not\equiv_2 p$ then taking the edge (v, v) is always a bad choice for player p and this edge can be removed from the game. If v is v's only successor then v itself can be removed and the process iterated in order to preserve totality. If $\Omega(v) \equiv_2 p$ then taking this edge is always good in the sense that the partial function $[v \mapsto v]$ is a winning strategy for player p on v. Hence, its attractor can be removed as described above. It is therefore possible to remove self-cycles from a game in time $\mathcal{O}(|E|)$, returning winning sets W_i and strategies σ_i for $i \in \{0, 1\}$ that result from the attractors of those nodes that are good for the respective players.

One-parity games. If all nodes in a proper SCC have the same parity the whole game is won by the corresponding player no matter which choice she makes. Hence, a winning strategy can be found by random choice in time $\mathcal{O}(|V|)$.

One-player games. A game G is a one-player game for player i iff for all $v \in V_{1-i}$ we have $|vE| = 1$. It can be solved in time $\mathcal{O}(|\Omega| \cdot |E|)$ as follows. Consider the largest priority p in G, and let $P := \{v \mid \Omega(v) = p\}$. There are two cases.

- If $p \equiv_2 i$ then player i wins the entire G because it is assumed to be a proper SCC and player $1 - i$ does not make any choices, so she can reach a node in P from any node in the game. A winning strategy can easily be constructed from an attractor strategy for P.
- If $p \not\equiv_2$ then let $A := Attr_{1-i}(P)$. Note that A consists of all nodes from which player i has to move through a node with priority p which is bad for her. Let $C_0, \ldots, C_m$ be a decomposition of $G \setminus A$ into SCCs. Now, player i wins from all nodes in G iff she wins from all nodes in one of $C_0, \ldots, C_m$, simply because they are part of the original SCC G in which player $1 - i$ does not move, so the attractor of any winning node is always the entire G.

This gives a simple recursive algorithm which considers the largest priority and either terminates or removes attractors, decomposes into SCCs and calls itself recursively on the sub-SCCs. If player $1 - i$ does not win on the entire G, then player $1 - i$ wins on the entire G, and this is the case if in all the recursive calls no sub-SCC is won by player i. Clearly, this can be realised in time $\mathcal{O}(|\Omega| \cdot |E|)$.

3.3 Priority Compression

The complexity of a parity game rises with $|\Omega|$. This optimisation step attempts to reduce this number. Note that it is not the actual values of priorities that determine the winner. It is rather their *parity* on the one hand and their *ordering* on the other. For instance, if there are two priorities $p_1 < p_2$ in a game with $p_1 \equiv_2 p_2$ but there is no p' such that $p_1 < p' < p_2$ and $p' \not\equiv_2 p_1$ then every occurrence of p_2 can be replaced by p_1.

The *compression* of G is a partial mapping $\omega : \mathbb{N} \to \mathbb{N}$ that is defined on all $\Omega(v)$ for any node v of the underlying game G; monotonic ($x \leq y$ implies $\omega(x) \leq \omega(y)$); decreasing ($\omega(x) \leq x$); parity-preserving ($\omega(x) \equiv_2 x$); dense ($\omega(x) < \omega(y) - 1$ implies $\exists z. \omega(x) < \omega(z) < \omega(y)$); and minimal ($\min\{\omega(x) \mid \omega(x) \neq \perp\} < 2$). Note that a compression of G is unique and can easily be computed in time $\mathcal{O}(|V|\log|V|)$: sort all nodes in ascending order of priority and then construct ω in a single sweep through this order, starting with 0 or 1 depending on the least priority in G.

If $G = (V, V_0, V_1, E, \Omega)$ and ω is its compression then $Comp(G) = (V, V_0, V_1, E, \omega \circ \Omega)$. It is the case that G and $Comp(G)$ have the same winning regions and strategies.

3.4 Priority Propagation

Suppose a play passes through a node v. Then it ultimately has to pass through *some* of its successors as well. If the priority of v is at most as high as that of all its successors, then one can replace the priority of v with the minimum of its successors' priorities without changing the winning regions and strategies. This is *backwards propagation*. Equally, in *forwards propagation* one replaces a node's priority with the minimum of the priorities of all its predecessors if that is greater than the current priority. This is sound because a node can only contribute to the determination of the winner of a play if it is visited repeatedly, i.e. if the play passes through one of its predecessors as well.

Technically, priority propagation on $G = (V, V_0, V_1, E, \Omega)$ computes a game $G = (V, V_0, V_1, E, \Omega')$ s.t. for all $v \in V$: $\Omega'(v) := \max\{\Omega(v), \min\{\Omega(w) \mid w \in U_v\}\}$ where $U_v = vE$ in case of backwards propagation and $U_v = Ev$ otherwise.

Note that propagation can be iterated, the forwards and backwards facets can be intertwined, and this process is guaranteed to terminate because priorities are at most increased but never beyond the maximal priority in G. Hence, the worst-case running time is $\mathcal{O}(|\Omega| \cdot |V| \cdot |E|)$, on average it will be much faster though.

Note that, even though priority propagation *increases* priorities, it *decreases* the range of priorities in a game, and is therefore supposedly beneficial to pre-ceed compression, because it allows for more compressed priorities. Empirically, however, the use of priority propagation turns out to be harmful. This is why it is not considered in the generic solver presented next.

3.5 A Generic Solver

We propose to solve parity games using the following generic algorithm which takes as parameter a real solver and applies it only where necessary. It relies heavily on SCC decomposition and attractor computations. Self-cycle elimination is done first because it can only be applied once and for all. Then the game is decomposed, and from then on, only final SCCs are being solved. Their priorities are being compressed – note that compression within an SCC rather than the entire game generally leads to better results – and are checked for being special cases. If this does not solve the SCC then the parameter solver is put to work on it. Finally, attractors of computed winning regions are formed, and the SCC decomposition is refined accordingly.

```
GenericSolver(G = (V, V_0, V_1, E, Ω), S) =
1        initialise empty winning regions W_0, W_1 and strategies σ_0, σ_1
2        eliminate self-cycles from G
3        while G is not empty do
4            decompose G into SCCs
5            for each final SCC C do
6                if C is a one-player-SCC then
7                    solve C directly
8                else
9                    if C is a one-parity-SCC then
10                       solve C directly
11                   else
12                       compress priorities on C
13                       solve C using S
14               compute and remove attractors of the winning regions in C
```

Here we assume that the procedures in lines 2,7,11 and 13 update the variables $W_0, W_1, \sigma_0, \sigma_1$ with the information about winning regions and strategies that they have found on parts of the game. Hence, the solution to the entire game is stored in these variables in the end. Note that this generic algorithm is sound whenever the backend S is sound, meaning that the answer it computes for a node is correct. It is complete – an answer is computed for every node – if the backend is complete. However, this is not necessary. In order to guarantee completeness one does not need completeness of the backend. Instead it suffices if the backend solves at least one node of a given game. Then the generic algorithm will eventually terminate with $W_0 \cup W_1 = V$.

4   Empirical Evaluation

The generic solver described above, together with 8 real solvers from the literature has been implemented in a tool called PGSOLVER[1]. The tool is written in OCaml; and it uses standard array representations for manipulating game graphs, in particular no symbolic methods.

Here we report on some of PGSOLVER's runtime result on benchmarking families of games. These benchmarks should cover typical applications of parity games, in particular games from the area of model checking and decision problems for branching-time logics. However, we remark that so far there is no standard collection of parity game benchmarks. Here we start with the following.

– *Decision procedures.* We apply to certain (hard) formulas the exponential reduction of the validity problem for the modal μ-calculus to the parity game problem using Piterman's determinisation procedure [9].
– *Model checking.* We encode two verification problems (fairness and reachability) as parity games.

---

[1] Publicly available via http://www.tcs.ifi.lmu.de/pgsolver

– *Random games.* Because of the absence of meaningful standardised parity game benchmarks we also evaluate the generic solver on random games.

The benchmarking games are presented in detail in the following. We only report on runtime results of the generic solver using the recursive algorithm, strategy improvement and the small progress measures algorithm as a backend because, on a separate note, these three algorithms turn out to be best in the sense that in general, they solve games faster than the other algorithms like the local model checker for example. This holds regardless of whether they are used directly or as a backend to the generic solver.

In order to exhibit the benefits of using the generic solver we present runtime results using various combinations of these optimisations: table columns labeled *all* contain running times obtained from the generic solver as presented above, i.e. using removal of self-cycles, SCC decomposition, priority compression and detection of special cases. Equally, columns *none* indicate using none of these, i.e. the entire game is solved by the backend. Columns labeled *scc* contain results from using SCC decomposition only, while *cyc* indicates the application of both SCC decomposition and removal of self-cycles. Finally, columns named *pcsg* imply the application of SCC decomposition, priority compression as well as detection of special cases. Note that the series presented in the tables to follow do not start with the smallest instances. We only present instances with non-negligable running times. On the other hand, the solving of larger instances not presented in the tables anymore has experienced time-outs after one hour, marked †, or the games were already to large to be stored in the heap space.

All tests have been carried out on a machine with two 2.4GHz Intel® Xeon™ processors and 4GB RAM space. The implementation does not (yet) support parallel computations, hence, each test is run on one processor only.

Decision Procedures. Consider the following μ-calculus formulas $\varphi_n := \psi_n \lor \neg\psi_n$, $n \in \mathbb{N}$, where

$$\psi_n := \mu X_1.\nu X_2 \ldots \sigma_n X_n.\left(q_1 \lor \Diamond\left(X_1 \land \left(q_2 \lor \Diamond(X_2 \land \ldots (q_n \lor \Diamond X_n))\right)\right)\right)$$

with $\sigma_n = \mu$ if n is odd, and $\sigma_n = \nu$ otherwise. Obviously, φ_n is valid. It has been chosen because of its high alternation depth which requires a relatively large NBA $\mathcal{A}_n$ that checks for the unfoldings of ν-formulas. The nodes of the parity game G_n resulting from φ_n are sets of subformulas of φ_n together with a state of a deterministic parity automaton $\mathcal{B}_n$ which is equivalent to $\mathcal{A}_n$ and which gives the game node its priority. The number of priorities in $\mathcal{B}_n$ depends on the size of $\mathcal{A}_n$ [9]. Hence, φ_n is chosen in order to yield games of large index.

Another family to be considered is the following μ-calculus formula

$$\varphi'_n := \nu X.\big(\underbrace{q \land \Diamond(q \land \Diamond(\ldots \Diamond(q}_{2n \text{ times}} \land \Diamond(\neg q \land \Diamond X))\ldots)))$$

$$\rightarrow \nu Z.\mu Y.(\neg q \land \Diamond Z) \lor (q \land \Diamond(q \land \Diamond Y))$$

which describes the language inclusion $((aa)^n b)^\omega \subseteq ((aa)^* b)^\omega$.

	n	nodes	sccs	Recursive Algorithm					Strategy Improvement					Small Progress Measures				
				all	cyc	pcsg	scc	none	all	cyc	pcsg	scc	none	all	cyc	pcsg	scc	none
φ_n	2	462	84	0.0s	0.0s	0.0s	0.0s	0.0s	0.0s	0.2s	0.0s	0.2s	1.0s	0.0s	0.1s	0.0s	0.1s	0.3s
	3	2.5K	219	0.0s	0.0s	0.0s	0.0s	0.5s	0.2s	5.8s	0.2s	6.2s	4.7m	0.2s	1.6s	0.2s	1.7s	4.6s
	4	14K	966	0.1s	0.1s	0.2s	0.2s	6.4s	7.4s	4.1m	8.1s	4.6m	†	0.6s	12s	0.8s	13s	39s
	5	58K	3.4K	0.6s	0.7s	1.2s	1.2s	53s	49s	33m	75s	40m	†	2.2s	56s	2.9s	60s	2.4m
	6	262K	15K	5.0s	5.2s	29s	29s	17m	12m	†	14m	†	†	5.1s	6.7m	32s	7.8m	†
	7	982K	55K	22s	25s	4.6m	5.2m	†	†	†	†	†	†	35s	42m	5.1m	44m	†
φ'_n	10	4.5K	1.1K	0.1s	0.1s	0.1s	0.2s	0.3s	0.1s	22m	0.1s	30m	†	0.0s	0.4s	0.0s	0.4s	0.9s
	50	21.5K	5.5K	0.5s	0.5s	3.3s	4.5s	7.8s	0.6s	†	6.5s	†	†	0.0s	13.6s	0.0s	15s	61s
	100	42.6K	10.8K	0.6s	0.7s	20s	20s	2.7m	1.1s	†	21s	†	†	0.1s	2.2m	0.2s	2.3m	6.5m
	500	211K	54.1K	5.4s	6.7s	13m	13m	29m	6.5s	†	11m	†	†	0.3s	†	5.1s	†	†
	1K	423K	108K	6.5s	7.6s	53m	54m	†	7.9s	†	43m	†	†	0.6s	†	17s	†	†
	2K	846K	216K	24s	27s	†	†	†	18s	†	†	†	†	1.4s	†	87s	†	†

Fig. 2. Runtime results on games from the decision procedures domain

The times needed to solve the resulting games as well as their sizes are presented in Fig. 2.

Model Checking I. We encode a simple fairness verification problem as a parity game. States of a transition system modelling an *elevator* for n floors are of type $\{1, \ldots, n\} \times \{\mathsf{o}, \mathsf{c}\} \times (\bigcup \{Perm(S) \mid S \subseteq \{1, \ldots, n\})$. The first component describes the current position of the elevator as one of the floors. The second component indicates whether the door is *open* or *closed*. The third component – a permutation of a subset of all available floors – holds the *requests*, i.e. those floors that should be served next. The transitions on these are as follows.

- At any moment, any request or none can be issued. For simplicity reasons, we assume that at most one floor is added to the requests per transition. Note that nondeterministically, no request can be issued, and a request for a certain floor that is already contained in the current requests does not change them.
- If the door is open then it is closed in the next step, the current floor does not change.
- If it is closed, the elevator moves one floor (up or down) into the direction of the first request. If the floor reached that way is among the requested ones, the door is opened and that floor is removed from the current requests. Otherwise, the door remains closed.

We consider two different implementations of this elevator model: the first one stores requests in FIFO style, the second in LIFO style. The games G_n (with FIFO), resp. G'_n (with LIFO) result from encoding the model checking problem for this transition system and the CTL* formula $\mathrm{A}(\mathsf{GF}isPressed \rightarrow \mathsf{GF}isAt)$ as a parity game [14]. Proposition *isPressed* holds in any state s.t. the request list contains the number n, and *isAt* holds in a state where the current floor is n. Hence, this formula requires all runs of the elevator to satisfy the following fairness property: if the top floor is requested infinitely often then it is being served infinitely often. It can easily be formulated in the modal μ-calculus using a formula of size 11 and alternation depth 2 (of type ν–μ–ν). Hence the resulting

	n	nodes	sccs	Recursive Algorithm					Strategy Improvement					Small Progress Measures				
				all	cyc	pcsg	scc	none	all	cyc	pcsg	scc	none	all	cyc	pcsg	scc	none
G_n	3	564	95	0.0s	0.0s	0.0s	0.0s	0.0s	0.0s	0.1s	0.0s	0.1s	0.10s	0.0s	0.0s	0.0s	0.0s	0.1s
	4	2.6K	449	0.1s	0.1s	0.1s	0.1s	0.2s	0.1s	1.8s	0.1s	2.0s	3.1s	0.1s	0.4s	0.1s	0.4s	0.4s
	5	15.6K	2.6K	0.4s	0.5s	0.6s	0.7s	1.4s	0.5s	2.0s	0.7s	2.2s	2.3s	0.5s	2.9s	0.7s	3.0s	3.9s
	6	108K	18K	3.1s	4.7s	4.9s	6.0s	11s	3.1s	†	4.5s	†	†	4.0s	33s	5.8s	33s	37s
	7	861K	143K	34s	44s	50s	73s	1.8m	36s	†	53s	†	†	39s	6.7m	59s	6.9m	7.6m
G'_n	3	588	99	0.0s	0.0s	0.0s	0.0s	0.0s	0.0s	0.0s	0.0s	0.0s	0.0s	0.0s	0.0s	0.0s	0.0s	0.0s
	4	2.8K	473	0.1s	0.1s	0.1s	0.1s	0.1s	0.1s	0.2s	0.1s	0.3s	0.7s	0.1s	0.2s	0.1s	0.2s	0.2s
	5	16.3K	2.7K	0.6s	0.7s	0.8s	0.9s	1.0s	0.6s	2.4s	0.8s	5.7s	13s	0.5s	1.3s	0.5s	1.5s	1.5s
	6	111K	18.5K	3.8s	4.3s	5.6s	6.0s	7.1s	3.8s	21s	8.7s	46s	5.3m	5.2s	20s	7.0s	24s	24s

Fig. 3. Runtime results on games from the elevator verification example

parity games have constant index 3. Note that G_n encodes a positive instance of the model checking problem whereas G'_n encodes a negative one. The times needed to solve them as well as their sizes are presented in Fig. 3. Larger instances caused out-of-memory failures due to the size of the underlying transition system.

Model Checking II. Typical verification problems often lead to special parity games for which there are specialised solvers. For instance, CTL model checking problems lead to alternation-free parity games, i.e. those in which every SCC is a single-parity SCC with index 0 or 1. We therefore consider a second set of benchmarks from the verification domain in the form of very special games. We model the well-known *Towers of Hanoi* represented as a transition system in which states consist of three stacks containing the numbers $\{1, \ldots, n\}$. The initial state is $([1, \ldots, n], [], [])$, and each state has up to 6 successors resulting from shifting the top element of one stack to another for as long as the top of that is not smaller.

The property to be tested is the CTL formula $\mathsf{EF}\textit{fin}$, where *fin* holds in the state $([], [1, \ldots, n], [])$ only. The resulting game $G_n = (V, V_0, V_1, E, \Omega)$ is special because $V_1 = \emptyset$ and only priorities 0 and 1 are being assigned to the states. The times needed to solve these games and their sizes are shown in Fig. 4. Note that the interesting part of solving the games of the former example is the computation of the winning *regions* which show those states from which the elevator has fair runs. Here, however, the interesting part is the computation of the winning *strategy* for player 0 since it represents a strategy for solving the Towers-of-Hanoi game.

Random Games. Finally, we evaluate the generic solver on random games. Note that the standard model of a random game which chooses, for each node, some d successors and randomly assigns priorities as well as node owners, leads to graphs which typically consist of one large SCC and several 1-node SCCs which have successors in the large one. Those do not add significantly to the runtime of the solving process which is predominantly determined by the large SCC. Hence, SCC decomposition would not necessarily prove to be useful in this random model. The truth, however, is that SCC decomposition is indeed useful in general but this random model creates special games on which it is not. While special

			Recursive Algorithm					Strategy Improvement					Small Progress Measures				
n	nodes	sccs	all	cyc	pcsg	scc	none	all	cyc	pcsg	scc	none	all	cyc	pcsg	scc	none
5	972	244	0.0s	0.0s	0.0s	0.0s	0.0s	0.0s	0.0s	0.0s	0.0s	0.9s	0.0s	0.0s	0.0s	0.0s	0.3s
6	2.9K	730	0.0s	0.0s	0.0s	0.0s	0.1s	0.0s	0.0s	0.0s	0.0s	15s	0.0s	0.0s	0.0s	0.0s	2.2s
7	8.7K	2.1K	0.1s	0.1s	0.1s	0.1s	0.2s	0.1s	0.1s	0.1s	0.1s	5.4m	0.1s	0.1s	0.1s	0.1s	13s
8	26K	6.5K	0.2s	0.2s	0.4s	0.4s	0.7s	0.2s	0.2s	0.4s	0.4s	†	0.2s	0.2s	0.4s	0.4s	77s
9	78K	19K	0.7s	0.7s	1.0s	1.0s	2.2s	0.7s	0.7s	1.0s	1.0s	†	0.7s	0.7s	1.0s	1.0s	9.9m
10	236K	59K	2.3s	2.3s	3.3s	3.3s	4.1s	2.3s	2.3s	3.3s	3.3s	†	2.3s	2.3s	3.3s	3.3s	37m
11	708K	177K	7.2s	7.2s	13s	13s	21s	7.2s	7.2s	13s	13s	†	7.2s	7.2s	13s	13s	†

Fig. 4. Runtime results on games from the Towers-of-Hanoi example

		Recursive Algorithm					Strategy Improvement					Small Progress Measures				
nodes	avg.sccs	all	cyc	pcsg	scc	none	all	cyc	pcsg	scc	none	all	cyc	pcsg	scc	none
1K	31	0.0s	0.0s	0.0s	0.0s	0.0s	0.0s	0.0s	0.3s	0.3s	1.2s	0.0s	0.0s	†	†	†
2K	71	0.0s	0.0s	0.0s	0.0s	0.1s	0.0s	0.0s	0.3s	0.3s	6.7s	0.0s	0.0s	†	†	†
5K	130	0.1s	0.1s	0.1s	0.1s	0.2s	0.1s	0.1s	0.7s	0.7s	61s	0.1s	0.1s	†	†	†
10K	244	0.2s	0.2s	0.2s	0.2s	0.5s	0.2s	0.2s	0.8s	0.9s	5.9m	0.4s	0.4s	†	†	†
20K	458	0.3s	0.4s	0.3s	0.4s	1.1s	0.4s	0.4s	2.7s	2.7s	32m	0.7s	0.7s	†	†	†
50K	1K	0.8s	1.1s	0.8s	1.1s	2.9s	1.1s	1.1s	3.7s	3.7s	†	1.7s	1.8s	†	†	†
100K	1.5K	2.7s	4.1s	2.9s	4.1s	6.3s	3.9s	4.0s	6.0s	11s	†	6.2s	6.5s	†	†	†
200K	2.3K	5.9s	8.4s	5.5s	8.4s	14s	8.4s	8.4s	16s	22s	†	13s	14s	†	†	†
500K	3.4K	16s	20s	18s	19s	60s	19s	20s	34s	34s	†	30s	31s	†	†	†
1M	12K	99s	2.1m	1.7m	2.3m	14m	1.7m	1.7m	13m	26m	†	2.8m	3.0m	†	†	†

Fig. 5. Runtime results on random games

games are important to consider, random games should be more general ones since a random model is typically employed in order to capture all sorts of other games. Thus, we enhance this simple random model in order to obtain more interesting games of size n: first, create clusters of sizes $< n$ according to this model, then combine these whilst adding random edges between the clusters. Fig. 5 presents the average number of SCCs that these random games posses, as well as the corresponding average runtime results. Each row represents 100 random games of corresponding size.

5   Conclusions

The previous section shows that it is possible to solve large parity games efficiently in practice. Contrary to common believe, even a large number of priorities does not necessarily pose a great difficulty in practice. All in all, there are five notable, maybe even surprising observations that can generally be made here.

(1) The recursive algorithm is much better than the other two algorithms if applied without any optimisation and preprocessing techniques. We believe that this is due to the nature of the recursive algorithm being itself based on a continuous decomposition of the game.

(2) SCC decomposition alone is highly profitable already, and in general even moreso when combined with any of the other optimisations, particularly the elimination of self-cycles.

(3) Not every optimisation speeds up all algorithms likewise. The recursive algorithm seems to profit more from self-cycle elimination than from priority compression and solving of special cases. This could be due to the fact that without eliminating self-cycles it expectedly requires a deep recursive descend in order to detect them by the recursion mechanism. On the other hand, the considered special cases can be solved quite fast by the recursive algorithm. Regarding strategy iteration and small progress measures iteration, it is the other way round: the detection of special cases as well as priority compression speed up the algorithms much more than treating self-cycles beforehand. The former is not surprising because both algorithms summarize nodes with the same priority and it is clear that the direct solution of special cases is faster than applying the iteration techniques to them. Finally it is also clear why the strategy iteration does not profit as much from elimination of self-cycles as the recursive algorithm since strategy iteration basically detects cycles and computes attractor-like strategies seeking cycles which is similar to the preprocessing technique that removes self-cycles. Similarly, the small progress measures algorithm easily detects self-cycles and back-propagates them through the graph which also corresponds to the computation of attractor-like strategies.

(4) There are even complex instances like the Towers-of-Hanoi example that are completely solved by the generic algorithm, i.e. without calling the backend even once. Obviously, generic optimisations as discussed in this paper have not at all the potential to give rise to a polynomial time algorithm that solves arbitrary parity games. But solving real-world parity game problems in practice can be heavily sped up by generic optimisation techniques.

(5) In general, it is advisable to enable all optimisations. Thus even an inexperienced user is on the safe side by activitating all of them. Also, using can cause tremendous speed-ups, which is witnessed for example in the drop of the average runtime from 14 to 1.5 minutes on random games with 1 million nodes using the recursive algorithm.

Despite developing additional universal optimisation techniques and parallelizing existing backend algorithms, there is another approach that should turn out to be of high value for practical solving: since it is very unlikely that one would ever find a real-world family of games on which *all* of the known backend algorithms show bad performance, there is an immediate improvement for the generic solver: it could take an arbitrary number of complete solvers as arguments and run them in parallel on those parts that cannot be solved by simpler methods. As soon as any of them provides a solution, the other computations can be killed.

References

1. Antonik, A., Charlton, N., Huth, M.: Polynomial-time under-approximation of winning regions in parity games. Technical report, Dept. of Computer Science, Imperial College London (2006)
2. Arnold, A., Vincent, A., Walukiewicz, I.: Games for synthesis of controllers with partial observation. Theor. Comput. Sci. 303(1), 7–34 (2003)

3. Emerson, E.A., Jutla, C.S.: Tree automata, μ-calculus and determinacy. In: Proc. 32nd Symp. on Foundations of Computer Science, San Juan, Puerto Rico, pp. 368–377. IEEE, Los Alamitos (1991)

4. Jurdziński, M.: Deciding the winner in parity games is in $UP \cap co\text{-}UP$. Inf. Process. Lett. 68(3), 119–124 (1998)

5. Jurdziński, M.: Small progress measures for solving parity games. In: Reichel, H., Tison, S. (eds.) STACS 2000. LNCS, vol. 1770, pp. 290–301. Springer, Heidelberg (2000)

6. Jurdziński, M., Paterson, M., Zwick, U.: A deterministic subexponential algorithm for solving parity games. In: Proc. ACM-SIAM Symp. on Discrete Algorithms, SODA 2006, pp. 114–123. ACM/SIAM (2006) (to appear)

7. Kähler, D., Wilke, T.: Complementation, disambiguation, and determinization of Büchi automata unified. In: Aceto, L., Damgård, I., Goldberg, L.A., Halldórsson, M.M., Ingólfsdóttir, A., Walukiewicz, I. (eds.) ICALP 2008, Part I. LNCS, vol. 5125, pp. 724–735. Springer, Heidelberg (2008)

8. Lange, M.: Solving parity games by a reduction to SAT. In: Majumdar, R., Jurdziński, M. (eds.) Proc. Int. Workshop on Games in Design and Verification, GDV 2005 (2005)

9. Piterman, N.: From nondeterministic Büchi and Streett automata to deterministic parity automata. In: Proc. 21st Symp. on Logic in Computer Science, LICS 2006, pp. 255–264. IEEE Computer Society, Los Alamitos (2006)

10. Safra, S.: On the complexity of ω-automata. In: Proc. 29th Symp. on Foundations of Computer Science, FOCS 1988, pp. 319–327. IEEE, Los Alamitos (1988)

11. Schewe, S.: Solving parity games in big steps. In: Arvind, V., Prasad, S. (eds.) FSTTCS 2007. LNCS, vol. 4855, pp. 449–460. Springer, Heidelberg (2007)

12. Schewe, S.: An optimal strategy improvement algorithm for solving parity and payoff games. In: Kaminski, M., Martini, S. (eds.) CSL 2008. LNCS, vol. 5213, pp. 369–384. Springer, Heidelberg (2008)

13. Stevens, P., Stirling, C.: Practical model-checking using games. In: Steffen, B. (ed.) TACAS 1998. LNCS, vol. 1384, pp. 85–101. Springer, Heidelberg (1998)

14. Stirling, C.: Local model checking games. In: Lee, I., Smolka, S.A. (eds.) CONCUR 1995. LNCS, vol. 962, pp. 1–11. Springer, Heidelberg (1995)

15. Tarjan, R.E.: Depth-first search and linear graph algorithms. SIAM J. Computing 1, 146–160 (1972)

16. van de Pol, J., Weber, M.: A multi-core solver for parity games. Electr. Notes Theor. Comput. Sci. 220(2), 19–34 (2008)

17. Vöge, J., Jurdziński, M.: A discrete strategy improvement algorithm for solving parity games. In: Emerson, E.A., Sistla, A.P. (eds.) CAV 2000. LNCS, vol. 1855, pp. 202–215. Springer, Heidelberg (2000)

18. Zielonka, W.: Infinite games on finitely coloured graphs with applications to automata on infinite trees. TCS 200(1–2), 135–183 (1998)

Automated Analysis of Data-Dependent Programs with Dynamic Memory

Parosh Aziz Abdulla[1], Muhsin Atto[2], Jonathan Cederberg[1], and Ran Ji[3]

[1] Uppsala University, Sweden
[2] University of Duhok, Kurdistan-Iraq
[3] Chalmers University of Technology, Gothenburg, Sweden

Abstract. We present a new approach for automatic verification of data-dependent programs manipulating dynamic heaps. A heap is encoded by a graph where the nodes represent the cells, and the edges reflect the pointer structure between the cells of the heap. Each cell contains a set of variables which range over the natural numbers. Our method relies on standard backward reachability analysis, where the main idea is to use a simple set of predicates, called *signatures*, in order to represent bad sets of heaps. Examples of bad heaps are those which contain either garbage, lists which are not well-formed, or lists which are not sorted. We present the results for the case of programs with a single next-selector, and where variables may be compared for (in)equality. This allows us to verify for instance that a program, like bubble sort or insertion sort, returns a list which is well-formed and sorted, or that the merging of two sorted lists is a new sorted list. We report on the result of running a prototype based on the method on a number of programs.

1 Introduction

We consider the automatic verification of data-dependent programs that manipulate dynamic linked lists. The contents of the linked lists, here refered to as a *heap*, is represented by a graph. The nodes of the graph represent the cells of the heap, while the edges reflect the pointer structure between the cells (see Figure 1 for a typical example).

The program has a dynamic behaviour in the sense that cells may be created and deleted; and that pointers

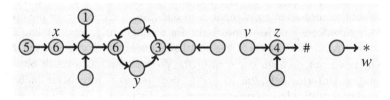

Fig. 1. A typical graph representing the heap

may be re-directed during the execution of the program. The program is also data-dependent since the cells contain variables, ranging over the natural numbers, that can be compared for (in)equality and whose values may be updated by the program. The values of the local variables are provided as attributes to the corresponding cells. Finally, we have a set of (pointer) variables which point to different cells inside the heap.

Z. Liu and A.P. Ravn (Eds.): ATVA 2009, LNCS 5799, pp. 197–212, 2009.

In this paper, we consider the case of programs with a single next-selector, i.e., where each cell has at most one successor. For this class of programs, we give a method for automatic verification of safety properties. Such properties can be either *structural properties* such as absence of garbage, sharing, and dangling pointers; or *data properties* such as sortedness and value uniqueness. We provide a simple symbolic representation, which we call *signatures*, for characterizing (infinite) sets of heaps. Signatures can also be represented by graphs. One difference, compared to the case of heaps, is that some parts may be *missing* from the graph of a signature. For instance, the absence of a pointer means that the pointer may point to an arbitrary cell inside a heap satisfying the signature. Another difference is that we only store information about the *ordering* on values of the local variables rather than their exact values. A signature can be interpreted as a *forbidden pattern* which should not occur inside the heap. The forbidden pattern is essentially a set of minimal conditions which should be satisfied by any heap in order for the heap to satisfy the signature. A heap satisfying the signature is considered to be *bad* in the sense that it contains a bad pattern which in turn implies that it violates one of the properties mentioned above. Examples of bad patterns in heaps are garbage, lists which are not well-formed, or lists which are not sorted. This means that checking a safety property amounts to checking the reachability of a finite set of signatures. We perform standard backward reachability analysis, using signatures as a symbolic representation, and starting from the set of bad signatures. We show how to perform the two basic operations needed for backward reachability analysis, namely checking entailment and computing predecessors on signatures.

For checking entailment, we define a pre-order $\sqsubseteq$ on signatures, where we view a signature as three separate graphs with identical sets of nodes. The edge relation in one of the three graphs reflects the structure of the heap graph, while the other two reflect the ordering on the values of the variables (equality resp. inequality). Given two signatures g_1 and g_2, we have $g_1 \sqsubseteq g_2$ if g_1 can be obtained from g_2 by a sequence of transformations consisting of either deleting an edge (in one of the three graphs), a variable, an isolated node, or contracting segments (i.e., sequence of nodes) without sharing in the structure graph. In fact, this ordering also induces an ordering on heaps where $h_1 \sqsubseteq h_2$ if, for all signatures g, h_2 satisfies g whenever h_1 satisfies g.

When performing backward reachability analysis, it is essential that the underlying symbolic representation, signatures in our case, is closed under the operation of computing predecessors. More precisely, for a signature g, let us define $Pre(g)$ to be the set of *predecessors* of g, i.e., the set of signatures which characterize those heaps from which we can perform one step of the program and as a result obtain a heap satisfying g. Unfortunately, the set $Pre(g)$ does not exist in general under the operational semantics of the class of programs we consider in this paper. Therefore, we consider an over-approximation of the transition relation where a heap h is allowed first to move to smaller heap (w.r.t. the ordering $\sqsubseteq$) before performing the transition. For the approximated transition relation, we show that the set $Pre(g)$ exists, and that it is finite and computable.

One advantage of using signatures is that it is quite straightforward to specify sets of bad heaps. For instance, forbidden patterns for the properties of list well-formedness and absence of garbage can each be described by 4-6 signatures, with 2-3 nodes in each signature. Also, the forbidden pattern for the property that a list is sorted consists of only one signature with two nodes. Furthermore, signatures offer a very compact symbolic representation of sets of bad heaps. In fact, when verifying our programs, the number of nodes in the signatures which arise in the analysis does not exceed ten. In addition, the rules for computing predecessors are *local* in the sense that they change only a small part of the graph (typically one or two nodes and edges). This makes it possible to check entailment and compute predecessors quite efficiently.

The whole verification process is fully automatic since both the approximation and the reachability analysis are carried out without user intervention. Notice that if we verify a safety property in the approximate transition system then this also implies its correctness in the original system. We have implemented a prototype based on our method, and carried out automatic verification of several programs such as insertion in a sorted lists, bubble sort, insertion sort, merging of sorted lists, list partitioning, reversing sorted lists, etc. Although the procedure is not guaranteed to terminate in general, our prototype terminates on all these examples.

Outline. In the next section, we describe our model of heaps, and introduce the programming language together with the induced transition system. In Section 3, we introduce the notion of signatures and the associated ordering. Section 4 describes how to specify sets of bad heaps using signatures. In Section 5 we give an overview of the backward reachability scheme, and show how to compute the predecessor and entailment relations on signatures. The experimental results are presented in Section 6. In Section 7 we give some conclusions and directions for future research. Finally, in Section 8, we give an overview of related approaches and the relationship to our work.

2   Heaps

In this section, we give some preliminaries on programs which manipulate heaps.

Let $\mathbb{N}$ be the set of natural numbers. For sets A and B, we write $f : A \rightarrow B$ to denote that f is a (possibly partial) function from A to B. We write $f(a) = \bot$ to denote that $f(a)$ is undefined. We use $f[a \leftarrow b]$ to denote the function f' such that $f'(a) = b$ and $f'(x) = f(x)$ if $x \neq a$. In particular, we use $f[a \leftarrow \bot]$ to denote the function f' which agrees on f on all arguments, except that $f'(a)$ is undefined.

Heaps. We consider programs which operate on dynamic data structures, here called *heaps*. A heap consists of a set of *memory cells* (*cells* for short), where each cell has one next-pointer. Examples of such heaps are singly liked lists and circular lists, possibly sharing their parts (see Figure 1). A cell in the heap may contain a datum which is a natural number. A program operating on a heap may use a finite set of *variables* representing *pointers* whose values are cells inside the heap. A pointer may have the special value null which represents a cell without successors. Furthermore, a pointer may be *dangling* which means that it does not point to any cell in the heap. Sometimes, we write the "*x*-cell" to refer to the the cell pointed to by the variable *x*. We also write "the value of the *x*-cell" to refer to the value stored inside the cell pointed to by *x*. A heap can naturally be encoded by a graph, as the one of Figure 1. A vertex in the graph represents a cell in the heap, while the edges reflect the successor (pointer) relation on the cells. A variable is attached to a vertex in the graph if the variable points to the corresponding cell in the heap. Cell values are written inside the nodes (absence of a number means that the value is undefined).

Assume a finite set X of variables. Formally, a *heap* is a tuple $(M, Succ, \lambda, Val)$ where

- M is a finite set of *(memory) cells*. We assume two special cells # and $*$ which represent the constant null and the *dangling* pointer value respectively. We define $M^{\bullet} := M \cup \{\#, *\}$.
- $Succ : M \to M^{\bullet}$. If $Succ(m_1) = m_2$ then the (only) pointer of the cell m_1 points to the cell m_2. The function $Succ$ is total which means that each cell in M has a successor (possibly # or $*$). Notice that the special cells # and $*$ have no successors.
- $\lambda : X \to M^{\bullet}$ defines the cells pointed to by the variables. The function λ is total, i.e., each variable points to one cell (possibly # or $*$).
- $Val : M \to \mathbb{N}$ is a partial function which gives the values of the cells.

In Figure 1, we have 17 cells of which 15 are in M, The set X is given by $\{x, y, z, v, w\}$. The successor of the z-cell is null. Variable w is attached to the cell $*$, which means that w is dangling (w does not point to any cell in the heap). Furthermore, the value of the x-cell is 6, the value of the y-cell is not defined, the value of the successor of the y-cell is 3, etc.

Remark. In fact, we can allow cells to contain multiple values. However, to simplify the presentation, we keep the assumption that a cell contains only one number. This will be sufficient for our purposes; and furthermore, all the definitions and methods we present in the paper can be extended in a straightforward manner to the general case. Also, we can use ordered domains other than the natural numbers such as the integers, rationals, or reals.

Programming Language. We define a simple programming language. To this end, we assume, together with the earlier mentioned set X of variables, the constant null where null $\notin X$. We define $X^{\#} := X \cup \{null\}$. A *program* P is a pair (Q, T) where Q is a finite set of *control states* and T is a finite set of *transitions*. The control states represent the locations of the program. A transition is a triple (q_1, op, q_2) where $q_1, q_2 \in Q$ are control states and op is an *operation*. In the transition, the program changes location from q_1 to q_2, while it checks and manipulates the heap according to the operation op. The operation op is of one of the following forms

- $x = y$ or $x \neq y$ where $x, y \in X^{\#}$. The program checks whether the x- and y-cells are identical or different.
- $x := y$ or $x.next := y$ where $x \in X$ and $y \in X^{\#}$. In the first operation, the program makes x point to the y-cell, while in the second operation it updates the successor of the x-cell, and makes it equal to the y-cell.
- $x := y.next$ where $x, y \in X$. The variable x will now point to the successor of the y-cell.
- $new(x)$, $delete(x)$, or $read(x)$, where $x \in X$. The first operation creates a new cell and makes x point to it; the second operation removes the x-cell from the heap; while the third operation reads a new value and assigns it to the x-cell.

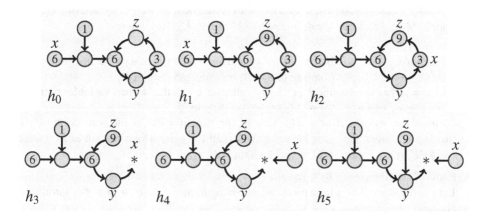

Fig. 2. Starting from the heap h_0, the heaps h_1, h_2, h_3, h_4, and h_5 are generated by performing the following sequence of operations: $z.num :> x.num$, $x := y.next$, $delete(x)$, $new(x)$, and $z.next := y$. To simplify the figures, we omit the special nodes # and $*$ unless one of the variables x, y, z is attached to them. For this reason the cell # is missing in all the heaps, and $*$ is present only in h_3, h_4, h_5.

- $x.num = y.num$, $x.num < y.num$, $x.num := y.num$, $x.num :> y.num$, or $x.num :<$ $y.num$, where $x, y \in X$. The first two operations compare the values of (number stored inside) the x- and y-cells. The third operation copies the value of the y-cell to the x-cell. The fourth (fifth) operation assigns non-deterministically a value to the x-cell which is larger (smaller) than that of the y-cell.

Figure 2 illustrates the effect of a sequence of operations of the forms described above on a number of heaps. Examples of some programs can be found in [2].

Transition System. We define the operational semantics of a program $P = (Q, T)$ by giving the transition system induced by P. In other words, we define the set of configurations and a transition relation on configurations. A *configuration* is a pair (q, h) where $q \in Q$ represents the location of the program, and h is a heap.

We define a transition relation (on configurations) that reflects the manner in which the instructions of the program change a given configuration. First, we define some operations on heaps. Fix a heap $h = (M, Succ, \lambda, Val)$. For $m_1, m_2 \in M$, we use $(h.Succ)[m_1 \leftarrow m_2]$ to denote the heap h' we obtain by updating the successor relation such that the cell m_2 now becomes the successor of m_1 (without changing anything else in h). Formally, $h' = (M, Succ', Val, \lambda)$ where $Succ' = Succ[m_1 \leftarrow m_2]$. Analogously, $(h.\lambda)[x \leftarrow m]$ is the heap we obtain by making x point to the cell m; and $(h.Val)[m \leftarrow i]$ is the heap we obtain by assigning the value i to the cell m. For instance, in Figure 2, let h_i be of the form $(M_i, Succ_i, Val_i, \lambda_i)$ for $i \in \{0, 1, 2, 3, 4, 5\}$. Then, we have $h_1 = (h_0.Val)[\lambda_0(z) \leftarrow 9]$ since we make the value of the z-cell equal to 9. Also, $h_2 = (h_1.\lambda_1)[x \leftarrow Succ_1(\lambda_1(y))]$ since we make x point to the successor of the y-cell. Furthermore, $h_5 = (h_4.Succ_4)[\lambda_4(z) \leftarrow \lambda_4(y)]$ since we make the y-cell the successor of the z-cell.

Consider a cell $m \in M$. We define $h \ominus m$ to be the heap h' we get by deleting the cell m from h. More precisely, we define $h' := (M', Succ', \lambda', Val')$ where

- $M' = M - \{m\}$.
- $Succ'(m') = Succ(m')$ if $Succ(m') \neq m$, and $Succ'(m') = *$ otherwise. In other words, the successor of cells pointing to m will become dangling in h'.
- $\lambda'(x) = *$ if $\lambda(x) = m$, and $\lambda'(x) = \lambda(x)$ otherwise. In other words, variables pointing to the same cell as x in h will become dangling in h'.
- $Val'(m') = Val(m')$ if $m' \in M'$. That is, the function Val' is the restriction of Val to M': it assigns the same values as Val to all the cells which remain in M' (since $m \notin M'$, it not meaningful to speak about $Val(m)$).

In Figure 2, we have $h_3 = h_2 \ominus \lambda_2(x)$.

Let $t = (q_1, op, q_2)$ be a transition and let $c = (q, h)$ and $c' = (q', h')$ be configurations. We write $c \xrightarrow{t} c'$ to denote that $q = q_1$, $q' = q_2$, and $h \xrightarrow{op} h'$, where $h \xrightarrow{op} h'$ holds if we obtain h' by performing the operation op on h. For brevity, we give the definition of the relation $\xrightarrow{op}$ for three types of operations. The rest of the cases can be found in [2].

- op is of the form $x := y.next$, $\lambda(y) \in M$, $Succ(\lambda(y)) \neq *$, and $h' = (h.\lambda)[x \leftarrow Succ(\lambda(y))]$.
- op is of the from $new(x)$, $M' = M \cup \{m\}$ for some $m \notin M$, $\lambda' = \lambda[x \leftarrow m]$, $Succ' = Succ[m \leftarrow *]$, $Val'(m') = Val(m')$ if $m' \neq m$, and $Val'(m) = \perp$. This operation creates a new cell and makes x point to it. The value of the new cell is not defined, while the successor is the special cell $*$. As an example of this operation, see the transition from h_3 to h_4 in Figure 2.
- op is of the form $x.num :> y.num$, $\lambda(x) \in M$, $\lambda(y) \in M$, $Val(\lambda(y)) \neq \perp$, and $h' = (h.Val)[\lambda(x) \leftarrow i]$, where $i > Val(\lambda(y))$.

We write $c \longrightarrow c'$ to denote that $c \xrightarrow{t} c'$ for some $t \in T$; and use $\xrightarrow{*}$ to denote the reflexive transitive closure of $\longrightarrow$. The relations $\longrightarrow$ and $\xrightarrow{*}$ are extended to sets of configurations in the obvious manner.

Remark. One could also allow deterministic assignment operations of the form $x.num := y.num + k$ or $x.num := y.num - k$ for some constant k. However, according the approximate transition relation which we define in Section 5, these operations will have identical interpretations as the non-deterministic operations given above.

3   Signatures

In this section, we introduce the notion of *signatures*. We will define an ordering on signatures from which we derive an ordering on heaps. We will then show how to use signatures as a symbolic representation of infinite sets of heaps.

Signatures. Roughly speaking, a signature is a graph which is "less concrete" than a heap in the following sense:

- We do not store the actual values of the cells in a signature. Instead, we define an ordering on the cells which reflects their values.
- The functions $Succ$ and λ in a signature are partial (in contrast to a heap in which these functions are total).

Formally, a signature g is a tuple of the form $(M, Succ, \lambda, Ord)$, where M, $Succ$, λ are defined in the same way as in heaps (Section 2), except that $Succ$ and λ are now *partial*. Furthermore, Ord is a partial function from $M \times M$ to the set $\{\prec, \equiv\}$. Intuitively, if $Succ(m) = \bot$ for some cell $m \in M$, then g puts no constraints on the successor of m, i.e., the successor of m can be any arbitrary cell. Analogously, if $\lambda(x) = \bot$, then x may point to any of the cells. The relation Ord constrains the ordering on the cell values. If $Ord(m_1, m_2) = \prec$ then the value of m_1 is strictly smaller than that of m_2; and if $Ord(m_1, m_2) = \equiv$ then their values are equal. This means that we abstract away the actual values of the cells, and only keep track of their ordering (and whether they are equal). For a cell m, we say that the value of m is *free* if $Ord(m, m') = \bot$ and $Ord(m', m) = \bot$ for all other cells m'. Abusing notation, we write $m_1 \prec m_2$ (resp. $m_1 \equiv m_2$) if $Ord(m_1, m_2) = \prec$ (resp. $Ord(m_1, m_2) = \equiv$).

We represent signatures graphically in a manner similar to that of heaps. Figure 3 shows graphical representations of six signatures $g_0, \ldots, g_5$ over the set of variables $\{x, y, z\}$. If a vertex in the graph has no successor, then the successor of the corresponding cell is not defined in g (e.g., the y-cell in g_4). Also, if a variable is missing in the graph, then this means that the cell to which the variable points is left unspecified (e.g., variable z in g_3). The ordering Ord on cells is illustrated by dashed arrows. A dashed single-headed arrow from a cell m_1 to a cell m_2 indicates that $m_1 \prec m_2$. A dashed double-headed arrow between m_1 and m_2 indicates that $m_1 \equiv m_2$. To simplify the figures, we omit self-loops indicating value reflexivity (i.e., $m \equiv m$). In this manner, we can view a signature as three graphs with a common set of vertices, and with three edge relations; where the first edge relation gives the graph structure, and the other two define the ordering on cell values (inequality resp. equality).

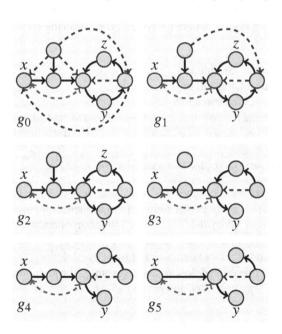

Fig. 3. Examples of signatures

In fact, each heap $h = (M, Succ, \lambda, Val)$ induces a unique signature which we denote by $sig(h)$. More precisely, $sig(h) := (M, Succ, \lambda, Ord)$ where, for all cells $m_1, m_2 \in M$, we have $m_1 \prec m_2$ iff $Val(m_1) < Val(m_2)$ and $m_1 \equiv m_2$ iff $Val(m_1) = Val(m_2)$. In other words, in the signature of h, we remove the concrete values in the cells and replace them by the ordering relation on the cell values. For example, in Figure 2 and Figure 3, we have $g_0 = sig(h_0)$.

Signature Ordering. We define an *entailment relation*, i.e., ordering $\sqsubseteq$ on signatures. The intuition is that each signature can be interpreted as a predicate which characterizes an infinite set of heaps. The ordering is then the inverse of implication: smaller signatures impose less restrictions and hence characterize larger sets of heaps. We derive a small signature from a larger one, by deleting cells, edges, variables in the graph of the signature, and by weakening the ordering requirements on the cells (the latter corresponds to deleting edges encoding the two relations on data values). To define the ordering, we give first definitions and describe some operations on signatures. Fix a signature $g = (M, Succ, \lambda, Ord)$.

A cell $m \in M$ is said to be *semi-isolated* if there is no $x \in X$ with $\lambda(x) = m$, the value of m is free, $Succ^{-1}(m) = \emptyset$, and either $Succ(m) = \bot$ or $Succ(m) = *$. In other words, m is not pointed to by any variables, its value is not related to that of any other cell, it has no predecessors, and it has no successors (except possibly $*$). We say that m is *isolated* if it is semi-isolated and in addition $Succ(m) = \bot$. A cell $m \in M$ is said to be *simple* if there is no $x \in X$ with $\lambda(x) = m$, the value of m is free, $|Succ^{-1}(m)| = 1$, and $Succ(m) \neq \bot$. In other words, m has exactly one predecessor, one successor and no label. In Figure 3, the topmost cell of g_3 is isolated, and the successor of the x-cell in g_4 is simple. In Figure 1, the cell to the left of the w-cell is semi-isolated in the signature of the heap.

The operations $(g.Succ)[m_1 \leftarrow m_2]$ and $(g.\lambda)[x \leftarrow m]$ are defined in identical fashion to the case of heaps. Furthermore, for cells m_1, m_2 and $\Box \in \{\prec, \equiv, \bot\}$, we define $(g.Ord)[(m_1, m_2) \leftarrow \Box]$ to be the signature g' we obtain from g by making the ordering relation between m_1 and m_2 equal to $\Box$. For a variable x, we define $g \ominus x$ to be the signature g' we get from g by deleting the variable x from the graph, i.e., $g' = (g.\lambda)[x \leftarrow \bot]$. For a cell m, we define the signature $g' = g \ominus m = (M', Succ', \lambda', Ord')$ in a manner similar to the case of heaps. The only difference is that Ord' (rather than Val') is the restriction of Ord to pairs of cells both of which are different from m.

Now, we are ready to define the ordering. For signatures $g = (M, Succ, \lambda, Ord)$ and $g' = (M', Succ', \lambda', Ord')$, we write that $g \lhd g'$ to denote that one of the following properties is satisfied:

- *Variable Deletion*: $g = g' \ominus x$ for some variable x,
- *Cell Deletion*: $g = g' \ominus m$ for some isolated cell $m \in M'$,
- *Edge Deletion*: $g = (g'.Succ)[m \leftarrow \bot]$ for some $m \in M'$,
- *Contraction*: there are cells $m_1, m_2, m_3 \in M'$ and a signature g_1 such that m_2 is simple, $Succ'(m_1) = m_2$, $Succ'(m_2) = m_3$, $g_1 = (g'.Succ)[m_1 \leftarrow m_3]$ and $g = g_1 \ominus m_2$, or
- *Order Deletion*: $g = (g'.Ord)[(m_1, m_2) \leftarrow \bot]$ for some cells $m_1, m_2 \in M'$.

We write $g \sqsubseteq g'$ to denote that there are $g_0 \lhd g_1 \lhd g_2 \lhd \cdots \lhd g_n$ with $n \geq 0$, $g_0 = g$, and $g_n = g'$. That is, we can obtain g from g' by performing a finite sequence of variable deletion, cell deletion, edge deletion, order deletion, and contraction operations. In Figure 3 we obtain: g_1 from g_0 through three order deletions; g_2 from g_1 through one order deletion; g_3 from g_2 through one variable deletion and two edge deletions; g_4 from g_3 through one node deletion and one edge deletion; and g_5 from g_4 through one contraction. It means that $g_5 \lhd g_4 \lhd g_3 \lhd g_2 \lhd g_1 \lhd g_0$ and hence $g_5 \sqsubseteq g_0$.

Heap Ordering

We define an ordering $\sqsubseteq$ on heaps such that $h \sqsubseteq h'$ iff $sig(h) \sqsubseteq sig(h')$. For a heap h and a signature g, we say that h *satisfies* g, denoted $h \models g$, if $g \sqsubseteq sig(h)$. In this manner, each signature characterizes an infinite set of heaps, namely the set $[\![g]\!] := \{h \mid h \models g\}$. Notice that $[\![g]\!]$ is upward closed w.r.t. the ordering $\sqsubseteq$ on heaps. We also observe that, for signatures g and g', we have that $g \sqsubseteq g'$ iff $[\![g']\!] \subseteq [\![g]\!]$. For a (finite) set G of signatures we define $[\![G]\!] := \bigcup_{g \in G} [\![g]\!]$. Considering the heaps of Figure 2 and the signatures of Figure 3, we have $h_1 \models g_0$, $h_2 \not\models g_0$, $h_0 \sqsubseteq h_1$, $h_0 \not\sqsubseteq h_2$, etc.

Remark. Our definition implies that signatures cannot specify "exact distances" between cells. For instance, we cannot specify the set of heaps in which the x-cell and the y-cell are exactly of distance one from each other. In fact, if such a heap is in the set then, since we allow contraction, heaps where the distance is larger than one will also be in the set. On the other hand, we can characterize sets of heaps where two cells are at distance at least k from each other for some $k \geq 1$.

4 Bad Configurations

In this section, we show how to use signatures in order to specify sets of *bad heaps* for programs which produce ordered linear lists. A signature is interpreted as a *forbidden pattern* which should not occur inside the heap. Typically, we would like such a program to produce a heap which is a linear list. Furthermore, the heap should not contain any garbage, and the output list should be ordered. For each of these three properties, we describe the corresponding forbidden patterns as a set of signatures which characterize exactly those heaps which violate the property. Later, we will collect all these signatures into a single set which exactly characterizes the set of bad configurations.

First, we give some definitions. Fix a heap $h = (M, Succ, \lambda, Val)$. A *loop* in h is a set $\{m_0, \ldots, m_n\}$ of cells such that $Succ(m_i) = m_{i+1}$ for all $i : 0 \leq i < n$, and $Succ(m_n) = m_0$. For cells $m, m' \in M$, we say that m' is *visible* from m if there are cells $m_0, m_1, \ldots, m_n$ for some $n \geq 0$ such that $m_0 = m$, $m_n = m'$, and $m_{i+1} = Succ(m_i)$ for all $i : 0 \leq i < n$. In other words, there is a (possibly empty) path in the graph leading from m to m'. We say that m' is *strictly visible* from m if $n > 0$ (i.e. the path is not empty). A set $M' \subseteq M$ is said to be *visible* from m if some $m' \in M'$ is visible from m.

Well-Formedness. We say that h is *well-formed* w.r.t a variable x if # is visible form the x-cell. Equivalently, neither the cell $*$ nor any loop is visible from the x-cell. Intuitively, if a heap satisfies this condition, then the part of the heap visible from the x-cell forms a linear list ending with #. For instance, the heap of Figure 1 is well-formed w.r.t. the variables v and z.

In Figure 2, h_0 is not well-formed w.r.t. the variables x and z (a loop is visible), and h_4 is not well-formed w.r.t. z (the cell $*$ is visible). The set of heaps violating well-formedness w.r.t. x are characterized by the four signatures in the figure to the right. The signatures b_1 and b_2 characterize (together) all heaps in which the cell $*$ is visible from the x-cell. The signatures b_3 and b_4 characterize (together) all heaps in which a loop is visible from the x-cell.

Garbage. We say that h contains *garbage* w.r.t a variable x if there is a cell $m \in M$ in h which is not visible from the x-cell. In Figure 2, the heap h_0 contains one cell which is garbage w.r.t. x, namely the cell with value 1. The figure to the right shows six signatures which together characterize the set of heaps which contain garbage w.r.t. x.

$b_5:$ $b_6:$

$b_7:$ $b_8:$

$b_9:$ $b_{10}:$

Sortedness. A heap is said to be *sorted* if it satisfies the condition that whenever a cell $m_1 \in M$ is visible from a cell $m_2 \in M$ then $Val(m_1) \leq Val(m_2)$. For instance, in Figure 2, only h_5 is sorted. The figure to the right shows a signature which characterizes all heaps which are not sorted.

$b_{11}:$

Putting Everything Together. Given a (reference) variable x, a configuration is considered to be *bad* w.r.t. x if it violates one of the conditions of being well-formed w.r.t. x, not containing garbage w.r.t. x, or being sorted. As explained above, the signatures $b_1, \ldots, b_{11}$ characterize the set of heaps which are bad w.r.t. x. We observe that $b_1 \sqsubseteq b_9$, $b_2 \sqsubseteq b_{10}, b_3 \sqsubseteq b_5$ and $b_4 \sqsubseteq b_6$, which means that the heaps $b_9.b_{10}, b_5, b_6$ can be discarded from the set above. Therefore, the set of bad configurations w.r.t. x is characterized by the set $\{b_1, b_2, b_3, b_4, b_7, b_8, b_{11}\}$.

Remark. Other types of bad patterns can be defined in a similar manner. Examples can be found in [2].

5 Reachability Analysis

In this section, we show how to check safety properties through backward reachability analysis. First, we give an abstract transition relation $\longrightarrow_A$ which is an over-approximation of the transition relation $\longrightarrow$. Then, we describe how to compute predecessors of signatures w.r.t. $\longrightarrow_A$; and how to check the entailment relation. Finally, we introduce sets of *initial* heaps (from which the program starts running), and describe how to check safety properties using backward reachability analysis.

Over-Approximation. The basic step in backward reachability analysis is to compute the set of predecessors of sets of heaps characterized by signatures. More precisely, for a signature g and an operation op, we would like to compute a finite set G of signatures such that $[\![G]\!] = \left\{ h \mid h \xrightarrow{op} [\![g]\!] \right\}$. Consider the signature g to the right. The set $[\![g]\!]$ contains exactly all heaps

$g:$ x, y

where x and y point to the same cell. Consider the operation op defined by $y := z.next$. The set H of heaps from which we can perform the operation and obtain a heap in $[\![g]\!]$ are all those where the x-cell is the immediate successor of the z-cell. Since signatures cannot capture the immediate successor relation (see the remark in the end of Section 3), the set H cannot be characterized by a set G of signatures, i.e., there is no G such that $[\![G]\!] = H$. To overcome this problem, we define an approximate transition relation $\longrightarrow_A$ which is an over-approximation of the relation $\longrightarrow$. More precisely, for heaps h and h', we have $h \xrightarrow{op}_A h'$ iff there is a heap h_1 such that $h_1 \sqsubseteq h$ and $h_1 \xrightarrow{op} h'$.

Computing Predecessors. We show that, for an operation op and a signature g, we can compute a finite set $Pre(op)(g)$ 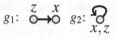 of signatures such that $[\![Pre(op)(g)]\!] = \left\{ h \mid h \xrightarrow{op}_A [\![g]\!] \right\}$. For instance in the above case the set $Pre(op)(g)$ is given by the $\{g_1, g_2\}$ shown in the figure to the right. Notice that $[\![\{g_1, g_2\}]\!]$ is the set of all heaps in which the x-cell is strictly visible from the z-cell. In fact, if we take any heap satisfying $[\![g_1]\!]$ or $[\![g_2]\!]$, then we can perform deletion and contraction operations (possibly several times) until the x-cell becomes the immediate successor of the z-cell, after which we can perform op thus obtaining a heap where x and y point to the same cell.

For each signature g and operation op, we show how to compute $Pre(op)(g)$ as a finite set of signatures. Due to lack of space, we show the definition only for the operation new. The definitions for the rest of the operations can be found in the [2]. For a cell $m \in M$ and a variable $x \in X$, we define m being x-*isolated* in a manner similar to m being *isolated*, except that we now allow m to be pointed to by x (and only x). More precisely, we say m is x-*isolated* if $\lambda(x) = m$, $\lambda(y) \neq m$ if $y \neq x$, the value of m is free, $Succ^{-1}(m) = \emptyset$, and $Succ(m) = \bot$. We define m being x-*semi-isolated* in a similar manner, i.e., by also allowing $*$ to be the successor of the x-cell. For instance, the leftmost cell of the signature b_1 in Section 4, and the x-cell in the signature $sig(h_5)$ in Figure 2 are x-semi-isolated.

We define $Pre(g)(new(x))$ to be the set of signatures g' such that one of the following conditions is satisfied:

– $\lambda(x)$ is x-semi-isolated, and there is a signature g_1 such that $g_1 = g \ominus \lambda(x)$ and $g' = g_1 \ominus x$.
– $\lambda(x) = \bot$ and $g' = g$ or $g' \in g \ominus m$ for some semi-isolated cell m.

Initial Heaps. A program starts running from a designated set H_{Init} of *initial heaps*. For instance, in a sorting program, H_{Init} is the set of well-formed lists which are (potentially) not sorted. Notice that this set is infinite since there is no bound on the lengths of the input lists. To deal with input lists, we follow the methodology of [7], and augment the program with an *initialization phase*. The program starts from an empty heap (denoted h_ε) and systematically (and non-deterministically) builds an arbitrary initial heap. In the case of sorting, the initial phase builds a well-formed list of an arbitrary length. We can now take the set H_{Init} to be the singleton containing the empty heap h_ε.

Checking Entailment. For signatures g and g', checking whether $g \sqsubseteq g'$ amounts to constructing an injection from the cells of g to those of g'. It turns out that a vast majority (more than 99%) of signatures, compared during the reachability analysis, are not related by entailment. Therefore, we have implemented a number of heuristics to detect negative answers as quickly as possible. An example is that a cell m in g should have (at most) the same labels as its image m' in g'; or that the in- and out-degrees of m are smaller than those of m'. The details of the entailment algorithm are included in [2].

Checking Safety Properties. To check a safety property, we start from the set G_{Bad} of bad signatures, and generate a sequence $G_0, G_1, G_2, \ldots$ of finite sets of signatures, where $G_0 = G_{Bad}$ and $G_{i+1} = \bigcup_{g \in G_i} Pre(g)$. Each time we generate a signature g such that $g' \sqsubseteq g$ for some already generated signature g', we discard g from the analysis.

We terminate the procedure when we reach a point where no new signatures can be added (all the new signatures are subsumed by existing ones). In such a case, we have generated a set G of signatures that characterize all heaps from which we can reach a bad heap through the approximate transition relation $\longrightarrow_A$. The program satisfies the safety property if $g \not\sqsubseteq sig(h_\varepsilon)$ for all $g \in G$.

6   Experimental Results

We have implemented the method described above in a prototype written in Java. We have run the tool on several examples, including all the benchmarks on singly linked lists with data known to us from the TVLA and PALE tools. Table 1 shows the results of our experiments. The column "#Sig." shows the total number of signatures that were computed throughout the analysis, the column "#Final" shows the number of signatures that remain in the visited set upon termination, the column "#Ent" shows the total number of calls to entailment that were made, and the last column shows the percentage of such calls that returned true. We have also considered buggy versions of some programs in which case the prototype reports an error.

All experiments were performed on a 2.2 GHz Intel Core 2 Duo with 4 GB of RAM. For each program, we verify well-formedness, absence of garbage, and sortedness. Also, in the case of the Partition program, we verify that the two resulting lists do not have common elements.

Table 1. Experimental results

Prog.	Time	#Sig.	#Final	#Ent	Ratio
EfficientInsert	0.1 s	44	40	1570	0.7%
NonDuplicateInsert	0.4 s	111	99	8165	0.2%
Insert	2.6 s	2343	1601	$2.2 \cdot 10^6$	0.03%
Insert (bug)	1.4 s	337	268	86000	0.09%
Merge	23.5 s	11910	5830	$3.6 \cdot 10^7$	0.017%
Reverse	1.5 s	435	261	70000	0.3%
ReverseCyclic	1.6 s	1031	574	375000	0.1%
Partition	2 m 49 s	21058	15072	$1.8 \cdot 10^8$	0.003%
BubbleSort	35.9 s	11023	10034	$7.5 \cdot 10^7$	0.001%
BubbleSortCyclic	36.6 s	11142	10143	$7.7 \cdot 10^7$	0.001%
BubbleSort (bug)	1.76 s	198	182	33500	0.07%
InsertionSort	11 m 53 s	34843	23324	$4.4 \cdot 10^8$	0.003%

7   Conclusions, Discussion, and Future Work

We have presented a method for automatic verification of safety properties for programs which manipulate heaps containing data. There are potentially two drawbacks of our method, namely the analysis is not guaranteed to *terminate*, and it may generate *false positives* (since we use an over-approximation). A sufficient condition for termination is *well quasi-ordering* of the entailment relation on signatures (see e.g. [3]). The only example known to us for *non-well-quasi-ordering* of this relation is based on a complicated sequence pattern by Nash-Williams (described in [13]) which shows non-well-quasi-ordering of permutations of sequences of natural numbers. Such artificial patterns are unlikely to ever appear in the analysis of typical pointer-manipulating programs. In fact, it is quite hard even to construct artificial programs for which the Nash-Williams pattern arises during backward reachability analysis. This is confirmed by the fact that our implementation terminates on all the given examples. As for false positives, the definition of the heap ordering $\sqsubseteq$ means that the abstract transition relation $\longrightarrow_A$ allows three types of imprecisions, namely it allows: (i) deleting garbage (nodes which are not visible from any variables), (ii) preforming contraction, and (iii) only storing the ordering on cell variables rather than their actual values. Program runs are not changed by (i) since we only delete nodes which are not accessible from the program pointers in the first place. Also, most program behaviors are not sensitive to the exact distances between nodes in a heap and therefore they are not affected by (ii). Finally, data-dependent programs (such as sorting or merge algorithms) check only ordering rather than complicated relations on data inside the heap cells. This explains why we do not get false positives on any of the examples on which we have run our implementation.

The experimental results are quite encouraging, especially considering the fact that our code is still highly unoptimized. For instance, most of the verification time is spent on checking entailment between signatures. We believe that adapting specialized algorithms, e.g. [20], for checking entailment will substantially improve performance of the tool.

Several extensions of our framework can be carried out by refining the considered preorder (and the abstraction it induces). For instance, if needed, our framework can be extended in a straightforward manner to handle arithmetical relations which are more complicated than simple ordering on data values such as *gap-order constraints* [17] or Presburger arithmetic. Given the fact that the analysis terminates on all benchmarks, it is tempting to characterize a class of programs which covers the current examples and for which termination is theoretically guaranteed. Another direction for future work is to consider more general classes of heaps with multiple selectors, and then study programs operating on data structures such as doubly-linked lists and trees both with and without data.

8   Related Work

Several works consider the verification of singly linked lists with data. The paper [14] presents a method for automatic verification of sorting programs that manipulate linked lists. The method is defined within the framework of TVLA which provides an abstract description of the heap structures in 3-valued logic [19]. The user may be required to provide *instrumentation predicates* in order to make the abstraction sufficiently precise. The analysis is performed in a forward manner. In contrast, the search procedure we describe in this paper is backward, and therefore also *property-driven*. Thus, the signatures obtained in the traversal do not need to express the state of the entire heap, but only those parts that contribute to the eventual failure. This makes the two methods conceptually and technically different. Furthermore, the difference in search strategy implies that forward and backward search procedures often offer varying degrees of efficiency in different contexts, which makes them complementary to each other in many cases. This has been observed also for other models such as parameterized systems, timed Petri nets, and lossy channel systems (see e.g. [4,9,1]).

Another approach to verification of linked lists with data is proposed in [6,7] based on *abstract regular model checking (ARMC)* [8]. In ARMC, finite-state automata are used as a symbolic representation of sets of heaps. This means that the ARMC-based approach needs the manipulation of quite complex encodings of the heap graphs into words or trees. In contrast, our symbolic representation uses signatures which provide a simpler and more natural representation of heaps as graphs. Furthermore, ARMC uses a sophisticated machinery for manipulating the heap encodings based on representing program statements as (word/tree) transducers. However, as mentioned above, our operations for computing predecessors are all *local* in the sense that they only update limited parts of the graph thus making it possible to have much more efficient implementations.

The paper [5] uses counter automata as abstract models of heaps which contain data from an ordered domain. The counters are used to keep track of lengths of list segments without sharing. The analysis reduces to manipulation of counter automata, and thus requires techniques and tools for these automata.

Recently, there has been an extensive work to use *separation logic* [18] for performing shape analysis of programs that manipulate pointer data structures (see e.g. [10,21]). The paper [16] describes how to use separation logic in order to provide a semi-automatic procedure for verifying data-dependent programs which manipulate heaps. In contrast, the approach we present here uses a built-in abstraction principle which is different from the ones used above and which makes the analysis fully automatic.

The tool PALE (Pointer Assertion Logic Engine) [15] checks automatically properties of programs manipulating pointers. The user is required to supply assertions expressed in the weak monadic second-order logic of graph types. This means that the verification procedure as a whole is only partially automatic. The tool MONA [11], which uses translations to finite-state automata, is employed to verify the provided assertions.

Recently, there have been several works which aim at algorithmic verification of systems whose configurations are finite graphs (e.g. [12,3]). These works may seem similar since they are all based on backward reachability using finite graphs as symbolic representations. However, they use different orderings on graphs which leads to entirely different methods for computing predecessor and entailment relations. In fact, the main challenge when designing verification algorithms on graphs, is to come up with the "right" notion of ordering: an ordering which allows computing entailment and predecessors, and which is sufficiently precise to avoid too many false positives. For instance, the *graph minor* ordering used in [12] to analyze distributed algorithms, is too weak to employ in shape analysis. The reason is that the contraction operation (in the case of the graph minor relation) is insensitive to the directions of the edges; and furthermore the ordering allows merging vertices which carry different labels (different variables), meaning that we would get false positives in almost all examples since they often rely tests like $x = y$ for termination. In our previous work [3], we combined abstraction with backward reachability analysis for verifying heap manipulating programs. However, the programs in [3] are restricted to be data-independent. The extension to the case of data-dependent programs requires a new ordering on graphs which involves an intricate treatment of structural and data properties. For instance, at the heap level, the data ordering amounts to keeping track of (in)equalities, while the structural ordering is defined in terms of garbage elimination and edge contractions (see the discussion in Section 7). This gives the two orderings entirely different characteristics when computing predecessors and entailment. Also, there is a non-trivial interaction between the structural and the data orderings. This is illustrated by the fact that even specifications of basic data-dependent properties like sortedness require forbidden patterns that contain edges from both orderings (see Section 4). Consequently, none of the programs we consider in this paper can be analyzed in the framework of [3]. In fact, since the programs here are data-dependent, the method of [3] may fail even to verify properties which are purely structural. For instance, the program EfficientInsert (described in [2]) gives a false non-well-formedness warning if data is abstracted away.

References

1. Abdulla, P.A., Annichini, A., Bouajjani, A.: Using forward reachability analysis for verification of lossy channel systems. Formal Methods in System Design (2004)
2. Abdulla, P.A., Atto, M., Cederberg, J., Ji, R.: Automated analysis of data-dependent programs with dynamic memory. Technical Report 2009-018, Dept. of Information Technology, Uppsala University, Sweden (2009),
   http://user.it.uu.se/~jonmo/datadependent.pdf
3. Abdulla, P.A., Bouajjani, A., Cederberg, J., Haziza, F., Rezine, A.: Monotonic abstraction for programs with dynamic memory heaps. In: Gupta, A., Malik, S. (eds.) CAV 2008. LNCS, vol. 5123, pp. 341–354. Springer, Heidelberg (2008)
4. Abdulla, P.A., Henda, N.B., Delzanno, G., Rezine, A.: Regular model checking without transducers (on efficient verification of parameterized systems). In: Grumberg, O., Huth, M. (eds.) TACAS 2007. LNCS, vol. 4424, pp. 721–736. Springer, Heidelberg (2007)
5. Bouajjani, A., Bozga, M., Habermehl, P., Iosif, R., Moro, P., Vojnar, T.: Programs with lists are counter automata. In: Ball, T., Jones, R.B. (eds.) CAV 2006. LNCS, vol. 4144, pp. 517–531. Springer, Heidelberg (2006)
6. Bouajjani, A., Habermehl, P., Moro, P., Vojnar, T.: Verifying programs with dynamic 1-selector-linked structures in regular model checking. In: Halbwachs, N., Zuck, L.D. (eds.) TACAS 2005. LNCS, vol. 3440, pp. 13–29. Springer, Heidelberg (2005)
7. Bouajjani, A., Habermehl, P., Rogalewicz, A., Vojnar, T.: Abstract tree regular model checking of complex dynamic data structures. In: Yi, K. (ed.) SAS 2006. LNCS, vol. 4134, pp. 52–70. Springer, Heidelberg (2006)
8. Bouajjani, A., Habermehl, P., Vojnar, T.: Abstract regular model checking. In: Alur, R., Peled, D.A. (eds.) CAV 2004. LNCS, vol. 3114, pp. 372–386. Springer, Heidelberg (2004)
9. Ganty, P., Raskin, J., Begin, L.V.: A complete abstract interpretation framework for coverability properties of wsts. In: Emerson, E.A., Namjoshi, K.S. (eds.) VMCAI 2006. LNCS, vol. 3855, pp. 49–64. Springer, Heidelberg (2006)
10. Guo, B., Vachharajani, N., August, D.I.: Shape analysis with inductive recursion synthesis. In: Proc. PLDI 2007, vol. 42 (2007)
11. Henriksen, J., Jensen, J., Jørgensen, M., Klarlund, N., Paige, B., Rauhe, T., Sandholm, A.: Mona: Monadic second-order logic in practice. In: Brinksma, E., Steffen, B., Cleaveland, W.R., Larsen, K.G., Margaria, T. (eds.) TACAS 1995. LNCS, vol. 1019. Springer, Heidelberg (1995)

12. Joshi, S., König, B.: Applying the graph minor theorem to the verification of graph transformation systems. In: Gupta, A., Malik, S. (eds.) CAV 2008. LNCS, vol. 5123, pp. 214–226. Springer, Heidelberg (2008)
13. Laver, R.: Well-quasi-orderings and sets of finite sequences. In: Mathematical Proceedings of the Cambridge Philosophical Society, vol. 79, pp. 1–10 (1976)
14. Lev-Ami, T., Reps, T.W., Sagiv, S., Wilhelm, R.: Putting static analysis to work for verification: A case study. In: Proc. ISSTA 2000 (2000)
15. Møller, A., Schwartzbach, M.I.: The pointer assertion logic engine. In: Proc. PLDI 2001, vol. 26, pp. 221–231 (2001)
16. Nguyen, H.H., David, C., Qin, S., Chin, W.-N.: Automated verification of shape and size properties via separation logic. In: Cook, B., Podelski, A. (eds.) VMCAI 2007. LNCS, vol. 4349, pp. 251–266. Springer, Heidelberg (2007)
17. Revesz, P.: Introduction to Constraint Databases. Springer, Heidelberg (2002)
18. Reynolds, J.C.: Separation logic: A logic for shared mutable data structures. In: Proc. LICS 2002 (2002)
19. Sagiv, S., Reps, T., Wilhelm, R.: Parametric shape analysis via 3-valued logic. ACM Trans. on Programming Languages and Systems 24(3), 217–298 (2002)
20. Valiente, G.: Constrained tree inclusion. J. Discrete Algorithms 3(2-4), 431–447 (2005)
21. Yang, H., Lee, O., Berdine, J., Calcagno, C., Cook, B., Distefano, D., O'Hearn, P.W.: Scalable shape analysis for systems code. In: Gupta, A., Malik, S. (eds.) CAV 2008. LNCS, vol. 5123, pp. 385–398. Springer, Heidelberg (2008)

On-the-fly Emptiness Check of Transition-Based Streett Automata

Alexandre Duret-Lutz[1], Denis Poitrenaud[2], and Jean-Michel Couvreur[3]

[1] EPITA Research and Development Laboratory (LRDE)
[2] Laboratoire d'Informatique de Paris 6 (LIP6)
[3] Laboratoire d'Informatique Fondamentale d'Orléans (LIFO)

Abstract. In the automata theoretic approach to model checking, checking a state-space S against a linear-time property φ can be done in $O(|S| \times 2^{O(|\varphi|)})$ time. When model checking under n strong fairness hypotheses expressed as a Generalized Büchi automaton, this complexity becomes $O(|S| \times 2^{O(|\varphi|+n)})$.

Here we describe an algorithm to check the emptiness of Streett automata, which allows model checking under n strong fairness hypotheses in $O(|S| \times 2^{O(|\varphi|)} \times n)$. We focus on transition-based Streett automata, because it allows us to express strong fairness hypotheses by injecting Streett acceptance conditions into the state-space without any blowup.

1   Introduction

The Automata Theoretic Approach to Model Checking [29, 28] is a way to check that a model M verifies some property expressed as a temporal logic formula φ, in other words: to check whether $M \models \varphi$. This verification is achieved in four steps, using automata over infinite words (ω-automata):

1. Computation of the state space of M. This graph can be seen as an ω-automaton A_M whose language $\mathscr{L}(A_M)$ is the set of all possible executions of M.
2. Translation of the temporal property φ into an ω-automaton $A_{\neg\varphi}$ whose language, $\mathscr{L}(A_{\neg\varphi})$, is the set of all executions that would invalidate φ.
3. Synchronized product of these two objects. This constructs an automaton $A_M \otimes A_{\neg\varphi}$ whose language is $\mathscr{L}(A_M) \cap \mathscr{L}(A_{\neg\varphi})$: the set of executions of the model M that invalidate the temporal property φ.
4. Emptiness check of this product. This operation tells whether $A_M \otimes A_{\neg\varphi}$ accepts an infinite word (a counterexample). The model M verifies φ iff $\mathscr{L}(A_M \otimes A_{\neg\varphi}) = \emptyset$.

On-the-fly algorithms. In practice the above steps are usually tightly tied by the implementation, due to transversal optimizations that forbid a sequential approach. One such optimization is the *on-the-fly model checking*, where the computation of the product, state space, and formula automaton are all driven by the progression of the emptiness check procedure: nothing is computed before it is required.

Being able to work on-the-fly has three practical advantages:

- Large parts of A_M may not need to be built because of the constraints of $A_{\neg\varphi}$.
- The emptiness check may find a counterexample without exploring (and thus constructing) the entire synchronized product.

Z. Liu and A.P. Ravn (Eds.): ATVA 2009, LNCS 5799, pp. 213–227, 2009.

– To save memory we can throw away states that have been constructed but are not actually needed. We would rebuild them later should they be needed again. [13]

From an implementation standpoint *on-the-fly model checking* puts requirements on the interface of the automata representing the product, the state graph, and the formula. For instance the interface used in Spot [8] amounts to two functions: one to obtain the initial state of the automata, another to get the successors of a given state. It is common to say that an emptiness check *is* on-the-fly when it is *compatible* with such an interface. For instance Kosaraju's algorithm [2, §23.5] for computing strongly connected components (SCC) will not work on-the-fly because it has to know the entire graph to transpose it. The algorithms of Tarjan [25] and Dijkstra [5, 6] are more suited to compute SCCs on-the-fly, because they perform a single depth-first search.

Fairness hypotheses [10] is a way to restrict the verification to a subset of "fair" executions of the model. For instance if we have a model of two concurrent processes running on the same host, we might want to assume that the scheduler is fair and that both processes will get slices of CPU-time infinitely often. When considering all the possible executions of the model, this hypothesis amounts to discarding all executions in which a process is stuck.

Transition-based Büchi and Streett automata. We shall consider two kinds of ω-automata that are expressively equivalent: Büchi automata and Streett automata. Büchi automata are more commonly used because there exist simple translations from LTL formulæ to Büchi automata and there exist many emptiness check algorithms for these automata [4]. Readers familiar with Büchi automata might be surprised that we use transition-based acceptance conditions rather than state-based ones. As noted by several authors [19, 3, 11, 12, 4, 26] this allows LTL formulæ to be translated into smaller automata, and for our purpose it will be useful to show why *weak* (resp. *strong*) *fairness hypotheses* can be added to a Büchi (resp. Streett) automaton without any blowup.

Streett Automata can also be used as intermediate steps in some methods to complement Büchi automata [27]. For instance in the automata theoretic approach to model checking, we could want to express a property P to verify, not as an LTL formula, but as a (more expressive) Büchi automaton A_P (or equivalently, an ω-regular expression). To ensure that $M \models A_P$ we should check that $\mathscr{L}(A_M \otimes \neg A_P) = \emptyset$. One way to compute $\neg A_P$ is to use Safra's construction [21] to construct a Streett automaton, and then convert this Streett automaton back into a Büchi automaton.

Our objective is to introduce an on-the-fly emptiness check for transition-based Streett automata, in order to efficiently verify linear-time properties under strong fairness hypotheses, or simply to check the emptiness of $A_M \otimes \neg A_P$ without the cost of converting $\neg A_p$ into a Büchi automaton. Existing emptiness checks for Streett automata [20, 15] share the same asymptotic complexity, but are state-based and will not work on-the-fly.

Outline. Section 2 briefly reviews LTL and transition-based Büchi automata. Section 3 then introduces fairness hypotheses and Streett automata. We recall that weak fairness hypotheses are free and show that strong fairness hypotheses are less costly to express with Streett automata. Finally section 4 gives an on-the-fly algorithm to check the emptiness of a Streett automaton in a way that is only linearly slower (in the number of acceptance conditions) than the emptiness check of a Büchi automaton.

2 Background

2.1 Linear-time Temporal Logic (LTL)

An LTL formula is constructed from a set AP of atomic propositions, the usual boolean operators ($\neg$, $\vee$, $\wedge$, $\rightarrow$) and some temporal operators: X (next), U (until), F (eventually), G (globally). An LTL formula can express a property on the execution of the system to be checked. Because we focus on fairness properties we shall not be concerned with the full semantics of LTL [1, 18], it is enough to describe the following two idioms:

- $G\,F\,p$ means that property p is true infinitely often (i.e., at any instant of the execution you can always find a later instant so that p is true),
- $F\,G p$ means that property p is eventually true continuously (i.e., at some instant in the future p will stay true for the remaining of the execution).

The size $|\varphi|$ of an LTL formula φ is its number of operators plus atomic propositions.

2.2 Büchi Automata

Definition 1. *(TGBA) A* Transition-based Generalized Büchi Automaton *[12]* over Σ *is a Büchi automaton with labels and generalized acceptance conditions on transitions. It can be defined as a tuple* $A = \langle \Sigma, \mathcal{Q}, q^0, \delta, \mathcal{F} \rangle$ *where* Σ *is an alphabet,* $\mathcal{Q}$ *is a finite set of states,* $q^0 \in \mathcal{Q}$ *is a distinguished initial state,* $\delta \subseteq \mathcal{Q} \times \Sigma \times \mathcal{Q}$ *is the (non-deterministic) transition relation,* $\mathcal{F} \subseteq 2^\delta$ *is a set of sets of accepting transitions.*

Graphically we represent the elements of $\mathcal{F}$ (which we call *acceptance conditions*) as small circles such as ● or ○ on Fig. 1a, 1b and 1d. We will also merge into a single transition all transitions between two states with identical acceptance conditions, as if the transition relation was actually in $\mathcal{Q} \times 2^\Sigma \times \mathcal{Q}$.[1]

For the purpose of model checking we have AP equal to the set of all atomic propositions that can characterize a configuration, and we use these automata with $\Sigma = 2^{AP}$ (i.e., each configuration of the system can be mapped into a letter of Σ). Graphically, with the aforementioned merging of transitions, it is therefore equivalent to label the transitions of the automata by propositional formulæ over AP.

An infinite word $\sigma = \sigma(0)\sigma(1) \cdots$ over the alphabet Σ is accepted by A if there exists an infinite sequence $\rho = (q_0, l_0, q_1)(q_1, l_1, q_2) \ldots$ of transitions of δ, starting at $q_0 = q^0$, and such that $\forall i \geqslant 0, \sigma(i) = l_i$, and $\forall f \in \mathcal{F}, \forall i \geqslant 0, \exists j \geqslant i, \rho(j) \in f$. That is, each letter of the word is recognized, and ρ traverses each acceptance condition infinitely often.

Given two TGBAs A and B, the synchronous product of A and B, denoted $A \otimes B$ is a TGBA that accepts only the words that are accepted by A and B. If we denote $|A|_s$ the number of accessible states of A, we have $|A \otimes B|_s \leq |A|_s \times |B|_s$. If we denote $|A|_t$ the number of transitions of A, we always have $|A|_t \leq |A|_s^2 \times |\Sigma|$. Also $|A \otimes B|_t \leq (|A|_s \times |B|_s)^2 \times |\Sigma| \leq |A|_t \times |B|_t$. Finally if a TGBA C has only one state and is deterministic, then $|A \otimes C|_s \leq |A|_s$ and $|A \otimes C|_t \leq |A|_t$.

---

[1] This optimization is pretty common in implementations; we only use it to simplify figures.

3   Coping with Fairness Hypotheses

Fairness hypotheses are a way to filter out certain behaviors of the model that are deemed irrelevant. For instance when modeling a communication between two processes over a lossy channel, we might want to assume that any message will eventually reach its destination after a finite number of retransmissions. Although there is one behavior of the model in which the retransmitted message is always lost, we may want to ignore this possibility during verification.

3.1   Weak and Strong Fairness

Let us give a definition of fairness involving a pair of events en and oc in a model M. An event could be the progress of some process, the execution of a particular instruction of the model, or even the fact that an instruction is enabled (i.e., could be executed).

Definition 2. *(Unconditional fairness) An event oc is* unconditionally fair *if it will happen infinitely often, i.e., if $M \models \mathsf{G}\,\mathsf{F}\,oc$.*

Definition 3. *(Weak fairness) A pair of events (en, oc) is* weakly fair *if whenever en occurs continuously, then oc will occur infinitely often: $M \models (\mathsf{F}\,\mathsf{G}\,en \to \mathsf{G}\,\mathsf{F}\,oc)$.*

Because we have $\mathsf{F}\,\mathsf{G}\,en \to \mathsf{G}\,\mathsf{F}\,oc \equiv \mathsf{G}\,\mathsf{F}((\neg en) \lor oc)$ weak fairness can be handled like unconditional fairness.

Fig. 1a shows an example of a 1-state TGBA recognizing $\mathsf{G}\,\mathsf{F}((\neg en) \lor oc)$. This TGBA is deterministic: for any configuration given by a set of truth values of en and oc, there is only one transition that can be followed. In fact, any formula of the form $\bigwedge_{i=1}^{n}(\mathsf{F}\,\mathsf{G}\,en_i \to \mathsf{G}\,\mathsf{F}\,oc_i)$, representing a combination of n weak (or unconditional)

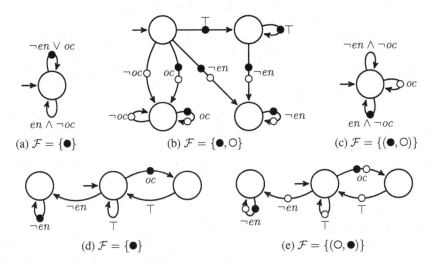

Fig. 1. (a) A TGBA equivalent to the LTL formula $\mathsf{G}\,\mathsf{F}((\neg en) \lor oc)$; (b),(d) two TGBAs equivalent to $\varphi = (\mathsf{G}\,\mathsf{F}\,en \to \mathsf{G}\,\mathsf{F}\,oc)$; (c),(e) two TSAs equivalent to φ. $\top$ denotes the *true* value.

fairness hypotheses, can be translated into a 1-state deterministic TGBA with 2^n transitions. Note that this "1-state determinism" property holds both because we are considering *generalized* automata and *transition-based* acceptance conditions, it would not not hold for *state-based* acceptance conditions.

Definition 4. *(Strong fairness) A pair of events* (en, oc) *is strongly fair if whenever* en *occurs infinitely often, then* oc *will occur infinitely often:* $M \models (\mathsf{G}\,\mathsf{F}\,en \to \mathsf{G}\,\mathsf{F}\,oc)$.

Fig. 1b and 1d show two TGBAs corresponding to the formula $\mathsf{G}\,\mathsf{F}\,en \to \mathsf{G}\,\mathsf{F}\,oc$. The first, bigger automaton is produced by LTL-to-Büchi translation algorithms such those of Couvreur [3] or Tauriainen [26]. The smaller one is a TGBA adaptation of an automaton shown by Kesten et al. [14]; we do not know of any general LTL-to-Büchi translation algorithm that would produce this automaton. Attempts to construct automata for conjunctions of strong fairness hypotheses, i.e. formulæ of the form $\bigwedge_{i=1}^{n}(\mathsf{G}\,\mathsf{F}\,en_i \to \mathsf{G}\,\mathsf{F}\,oc_i)$, will lead to a nondeterministic automaton that has either $3^n + 1$ or 3^n states depending on whether we base the construction on Fig. 1b or 1d. These automata have $2^{\mathrm{O}(n)}$ transitions.

3.2   Fairness in the Automata Theoretic Approach

Given a model M and an LTL formula φ, we can check whether $M \models \varphi$ by checking whether the automaton $A_M \otimes A_{\neg\varphi}$ accepts any infinite word (such a word would be a counterexample). Because $|A_{\neg\varphi}|_t = 2^{\mathrm{O}(|\varphi|)}$, we have $|A_M \otimes A_{\neg\varphi}|_t \le |A_M|_t \times 2^{\mathrm{O}(|\varphi|)}$. Checking the emptiness of a TGBA can be done in linear time with respect to its size, regardless of the number of acceptance conditions [4], so the whole verification process requires $\mathrm{O}(|A_M|_t \times 2^{\mathrm{O}(|\varphi|)})$ time.

Verifying φ under some fairness hypothesis represented as an LTL formula ψ amounts to checking whether $M \models (\psi \to \varphi)$, i.e., φ should hold only for the runs where ψ also holds. We can see that $A_M \otimes A_{\neg(\psi \to \varphi)} = A_M \otimes A_{\psi \wedge \neg\varphi} = A_M \otimes A_\psi \otimes A_{\neg\varphi}$. In other words, a fairness hypothesis could be represented by just an extra synchronized product before doing the emptiness check.

Weak fairness. We have seen that n weak fairness hypotheses can be represented by a 1-state deterministic TGBA. This means that the operation $A_M \otimes A_\psi$ is basically free: it will not add new states to those of A_M. In practice each transition of A_M would be labelled during its on-the-fly construction with the acceptance conditions of A_ψ. Model checking under n week fairness hypotheses is therefore independent of n^2 and requires $\mathrm{O}(|A_M|_t \times 2^{\mathrm{O}(|\varphi|)})$ time.

Strong fairness. Model checking under n strong fairness hypotheses is costly with Büchi automata: we have seen that these n hypotheses can be represented by a TGBA with $2^{\mathrm{O}(n)}$ transitions, the verification therefore requires $\mathrm{O}(|A_M|_t \times 2^{\mathrm{O}(|\varphi|+n)})$ time.

3.3   Streett Automata

Definition 5. *(TSA) A Transition-based Streett Automaton is a kind of TGBA in which acceptance conditions are paired. It can be also be defined as a tuple* $A = \langle \Sigma, \mathcal{Q}, q^0, \delta,$

---

[2] This is because we assume that we are using a generalized emptiness check [4].

$\mathcal{F}\rangle$ where $\mathcal{F} = \{(l_1, u_1), (l_2, u_2), \ldots, (l_r, u_r)\}$ is a set of pairs of acceptance conditions with $l_i \subseteq \delta$ and $u_i \subseteq \delta$.

The difference between TSA and TGBA lies in the interpretation of $\mathcal{F}$. An infinite word σ over the alphabet Σ is accepted by A if there exists an infinite sequence $\rho = (q_0, l_0, q_1)(q_1, l_1, q_2) \ldots$ of transitions of δ, starting at $q_0 = q^0$, and such that $\forall i \geqslant 0, \sigma(i) = l_i$, and $\forall (l, u) \in \mathcal{F}, (\forall i \geqslant 0, \exists j \geqslant i, \rho(j) \in l) \implies (\forall i \geqslant 0, \exists j \geqslant i, \rho(i) \in u)$. That is, each letter of the word is recognized, and for each pair (l, u) of acceptance conditions, if ρ encounters l infinitely often, then it encounters u infinitely often.

Given two TSA A and B, it is also possible to define their synchronous product $A \otimes B$ such that $|A \otimes B| = O(|A| \times |B|)$ and $\mathcal{L}(A \otimes B) = \mathcal{L}(A) \cap \mathcal{L}(B)$.

Büchi and Streett automata are known to be expressively equivalent [21]. Obviously a TGBA with acceptance conditions $\mathcal{F} = \{u_1, u_2, \ldots, u_n\}$ can be translated into an equivalent TSA without changing its structure: we simply use the acceptance conditions $\mathcal{F}' = \{(\mathcal{Q}, u_1), \ldots, (\mathcal{Q}, u_n)\}$. For instance Fig. 1e shows the TSA resulting from this rewriting applied to the TGBA of Fig. 1d.

The converse operation, translating Streett automata to Büchi, induces an exponential blowup of the number of states [22]. For instance Löding [16] shows how to translate a state-based Streett automaton of $|\mathcal{Q}|$ states and n pairs of acceptance conditions into a state-based Büchi automaton with $|\mathcal{Q}| \times (4^n - 3^n + 2)$ states (and 1 acceptance condition). The following construction shows how to translate a TSA of $|\mathcal{Q}|$ states and n pairs acceptance conditions of into a TGBA of $|\mathcal{Q}| \times (2^n + 1)$ states and n acceptance conditions. (The same construction could be achieved for state-based automata: here the gain is only due to the use of generalized acceptance conditions.)

Given a TSA $A = \langle \Sigma, \mathcal{Q}, q^0, \mathcal{F}, \delta \rangle$ with $\mathcal{F} = \{(l_1, u_1), (l_2, u_2), \ldots, (l_n, u_n)\}$, let $N = \{1, 2, \ldots, n\}$, and for any $(S, t) \in 2^N \times \delta$ let $pending(S, t) = (S \cup \{i \in N \mid t \in l_i\}) \setminus \{i \in N \mid t \in u_i\}$. Now define the TGBA $A' = \langle \Sigma, \mathcal{Q}', q^0, \delta', \mathcal{F}' \rangle$ where $\mathcal{Q}' = \mathcal{Q} \cup (\mathcal{Q} \times 2^N), \delta' = \delta \cup \{(s, g, (d, \emptyset)) \mid (s, g, d) \in \delta\} \cup \{((s, S), g, (d, pending(S, (s, g, d)))) \mid (s, g, d) \in \delta, S \in 2^N\}$, and $\mathcal{F}' = \{f_i \mid i \in 2^N\}$ with $f_i = \{((s, S), l, (d, D)) \in \delta' \mid N \setminus S = i\}$. Then $\mathcal{L}(A) = \mathcal{L}(A')$.

The justification behind this construction is that any run accepted by a Streett automaton can be split in two parts: a finite prefix, where any transition can occur, followed by a infinite suffix where it is guaranteed that any transition in l_i will be eventually followed by a transitions in u_i. The original TGBA is therefore cloned $2^n + 1$ times to construct the corresponding TSA. The first clone, using $\mathcal{Q}$ and δ, is where the prefix is read. From there the automaton can non-deterministically switch to the clone that is using states in $\mathcal{Q} \times \{\emptyset\}$. From now on the automaton has to remember which u_i it has to expect: this is the purpose of the extra set added to the state. An automaton is in state (s, S) that follows a transition in l_i will therefore reach state $(s, S \cup \{i\})$, and conversely, following a transition in u_i will reach state $(s, S \setminus \{i\})$. The function $pending(S, t)$ defined above computes those pending u_is. The acceptance conditions are defined to complement the set of pending u_is, to be sure they are eventually fulfilled.

3.4 Strong Fairness with Streett Automata

The TSA of Fig. 1e is however not the most compact way to translate a strong fairness formula: Fig. 1c shows how it can be done with a 1-state deterministic TSA.

Actually any LTL formula $\bigwedge_{i=1}^{n} \mathsf{G}\,\mathsf{F}\,en \rightarrow \mathsf{G}\,\mathsf{F}\,oc$ representing n strong fairness hypotheses can be translated into a 1-state deterministic TSA with n pairs of acceptance conditions and 4^n transitions. It is the TSA $A = \langle 2^{AP}, \{q\}, q, \delta, \mathcal{F} \rangle$ where $AP = \{oc_1, oc_2, \ldots, oc_n, en_1, en_2, \ldots en_n\}$, $\delta = \{\langle q, E, q \rangle \mid E \in 2^{AP}\}$, and $\mathcal{F} = \{(l_1, u_1), (l_2, u_2), \ldots, (l_n, u_n)\}$ with $l_i = \{(q, E, q) \in \delta \mid en_i \in E\}$ and $u_i = \{(q, E, q) \in \delta \mid oc_i \in E\}$. Again this "1-state determinism" would not hold for state-based Streett acceptance condition.

Combining this automaton with the construction of section 3.3, we can represent n strong fairness hypotheses using a TGBA of $2^n + 1$ states (and $4^n(2^n + 1)$ transitions). This is better than the TGBA of 3^n states presented in section 3.1, but the complexity of the verification would remain in $\mathrm{O}(|A_M|_t \times 2^{\mathrm{O}(|\varphi|+n)})$ time.

As when model checking under weak fairness hypotheses, the Streett acceptance conditions representing strong fairness hypotheses can be injected in the automaton A_M during its on-the-fly generation: any transition of A_M labelled by $E \in 2^{AP}$ receives the acceptance conditions $\alpha(E)$. The verification under n strong fairness hypotheses amounts to checking the emptiness of a TSA of size $\mathrm{O}(|A_M|_t \times 2^{\mathrm{O}(|\varphi|)})$, with n pairs of acceptance conditions.

We now show how to check this TSA emptiness in $\mathrm{O}(|A_M|_t \times n \times 2^{\mathrm{O}(|\varphi|)})$ time by adapting an algorithm by Couvreur [3, 4] that was originally designed for the emptiness check of TGBA.

4 Emptiness Check for Streett Automata

The behavior of the algorithm is illustrated on Fig. 2 on a TSA with 2 pairs of acceptance conditions: (●, ○) and (■, □). We are looking for runs that visit ○ (resp. □) infinitely often if they visit ● (resp. ■) infinitely often.

As its older brother (for TGBA [3, 4]) this algorithm performs a DFS to discover strongly connected components (SCC). Each SCC is labelled with the set of acceptance conditions that can be found on its edges, and will stop as soon as it finds an SCC whose label verifies (● → ○)∧(■ → □). Figures 2a–2f show the first steps until a terminal SCC (i.e. with no outgoing transition) is found. Let us denote $\mathcal{F} = \{(l_1, u_1), (l_2, u_2), \ldots, (l_n, u_n)\}$ the set of acceptance conditions of the Streett automaton, and $acc \subseteq \mathcal{F}$ the set of acceptance conditions of the terminal SCC encountered. When such a terminal SCC is found we can be in one of the three following cases.

1. Either the SCC is trivial (i.e. has no loops): it cannot be accepting and all its states can be ignored from now on.
2. Or the SCC is accepting: $\forall i, l_i \in acc \implies u_i \in acc$.
   In that case the algorithm terminates and reports the existence of an accepting run. It is better to check this condition any time a non-trivial SCC is formed, not only for terminal SCC: this gives the algorithm more chance to terminate early.
3. Or $\exists i, l_i \in acc \wedge u_i \notin acc$.
   In that case we cannot state whether the SCC is accepting or not. Maybe it contains an accepting run that does not use any transition of l_i. Fig. 2f is an instance of this case: $\mathcal{F} = \{(●, ○), (■, □)\}$ and $acc = \{●, ■, □\}$ so the algorithm cannot conclude immediately.

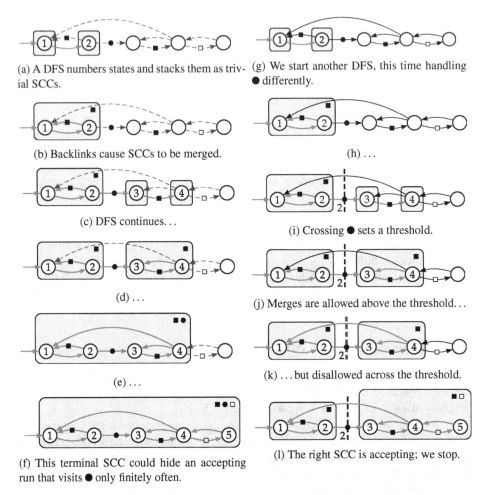

(a) A DFS numbers states and stacks them as trivial SCCs.

(b) Backlinks cause SCCs to be merged.

(c) DFS continues...

(d) ...

(e) ...

(f) This terminal SCC could hide an accepting run that visits ● only finitely often.

(g) We start another DFS, this time handling ● differently.

(h) ...

(i) Crossing ● sets a threshold.

(j) Merges are allowed above the threshold...

(k) ...but disallowed across the threshold.

(l) The right SCC is accepting; we stop.

Fig. 2. Running the emptiness check on a TSA with $\mathcal{F} = \{(\bullet,\bigcirc),(\blacksquare,\square)\}$

To solve third case, the algorithm will revisit the whole SCC, but avoiding transitions t such that $\exists i, t \in l_i \wedge u_i \notin acc$. Practically, we define the set $avoid = \{l_i \in acc \mid u_i \notin acc\}$ of l_i that cannot be satisfied, all the states from the SCC are removed from the hash table of visited states, and the algorithm makes another DFS with the following changes:

- amongst the outgoing transitions of a state, those who carry acceptance condition of $avoid$ are visited last
- crossing a transition labelled by an avoided acceptance condition sets up a threshold (denoted by a dashed vertical line on Fig. 2i)
- if a transition going out from a SCC goes back to another SCC in the search stack, then the two SCC will be merged only if the two SCC are behind the last threshold

set. Fig. 2j shows one case where merging has been allowed, while Fig 2k shows a forbidden attempt to merge two SCCs.

This new visit will construct smaller SCCs instead of the original terminal SCC. The only way to merge these smaller SCCs would be to accept a cycle using a transition from an acceptance condition (of $avoid$) that cannot be satisfied. For each of these smaller SCCs we can then decide whether they are trivial, accepting, or if they contain acceptance conditions (not already listed in $avoid$) that cannot be satisfied. In the latter case $avoid$ is augmented and the process is repeated. This recursion cannot exceed $|\mathcal{F}|$ levels since we complete $avoid$ at each step with at least one pair of $\mathcal{F}$.

Compared to the original emptiness check for TGBA that visits each state and transitions only once, this variant will in the worst case visit each state and transitions $|\mathcal{F}|+1$ times. On a TSA A this algorithm therefore works in $O(|A|_t \times |\mathcal{F}|)$ time.

```
1  Input: A Streett automaton A = ⟨Σ, Q, q⁰, δ, F⟩
2  Output: ⊤ iff ℒ(A) = ∅
3  Data: SCC: stack of
              ⟨state ∈ Q, root ∈ ℕ, la ⊆ F, acc ⊆ F, rem ⊆ Q, succ ⊆ δ, fsucc ⊆ δ⟩
          H: map of Q ↦ ℕ
          avoid: stack of ⟨root ∈ ℕ, acc ⊆ F⟩
          min: stack of ℕ
          max ← 0
4  begin
5   |   min.push(0)
6   |   avoid.push(⟨1, ∅⟩)
7   |   DFSpush(∅, q⁰)
8   |   while ¬SCC.empty() do
9   |   |   if SCC.top().succ = ∅ then
10  |   |   |   if SCC.top().fsucc ≠ ∅ then
11  |   |   |   |   swap(SCC.top().succ, SCC.top().fsucc)
12  |   |   |   |   min.push(max)
13  |   |   |   else
14  |   |   |   └   DFSpop()
15  |   |   else
16  |   |   |   pick one ⟨s, e, d⟩ off SCC.top().succ
17  |   |   |   a ← {f ∈ F | (s, e, d) ∈ f}
18  |   |   |   if d ∉ H then
19  |   |   |   |   DFSpush(a, d)
20  |   |   |   else if H[d] > min.top() then
21  |   |   |   |   merge(a, H[d])
22  |   |   |   |   acc ← SCC.top().acc
23  |   |   |   └   if ∀⟨l, u⟩ ∈ F, (l ∈ acc) ⟹ (u ∈ acc) then return ⊥
24  |   return ⊤
25 end
```

Fig. 3. Emptiness check of a Streett automaton

```
26 DFSpush(a ⊆ F, q ∈ Q)
27  │   max ← max + 1
28  │   H[q] ← max
29  │   SCC.push(⟨q, max, a, ∅, ∅, {⟨s, l, a, d⟩ ∈ δ | s = q, a ∩ avoid.top().acc = ∅},
                                    {⟨s, l, a, d⟩ ∈ δ | s = q, a ∩ avoid.top().acc ≠ ∅}⟩)
30 end
31 DFSpop()
32  │   ⟨q, n, la, acc, rem, _, _⟩ ← SCC.pop()
33  │   max ← n − 1
34  │   if n ≤ min.top() then
35  │    └  min.pop()
36  │   old_avoid ← avoid.top().acc
37  │   if n = avoid.top().root then
38  │    └  avoid.pop()
39  │   new_avoid ← old_avoid ∪ {l | ⟨l, u⟩ ∈ F, l ∩ acc ≠ ∅, u ∩ acc = ∅}
40  │   if new_avoid ≠ old_avoid then
41  │    │   foreach s ∈ rem do
42  │    │    └  delete H[s]
43  │    │   avoid.push(n, new_avoid)
44  │    │   DFSpush(la, q)
45  │   else
46  │    │   foreach s ∈ rem do
47  │    │    └  H[s] ← 0
48 end
49 merge(a ⊆ F, t ∈ ℕ)
50  │   r ← ∅
51  │   s ← ∅
52  │   f ← ∅
53  │   while t < SCC.top().root do
54  │    │   a ← a ∪ SCC.top().acc ∪ SCC.top().la
55  │    │   r ← r ∪ SCC.top().rem ∪ SCC.top().state
56  │    │   s ← s ∪ SCC.top().succ
57  │    │   f ← f ∪ SCC.top().fsucc
58  │    └  SCC.pop()
59  │   SCC.top().acc ← SCC.top().acc ∪ a
60  │   SCC.top().rem ← SCC.top().rem ∪ r
61  │   SCC.top().succ ← SCC.top().succ ∪ s
62  │   SCC.top().fsucc ← SCC.top().fsucc ∪ f
63 end
```

Fig. 3. (*Continued*)

Relation to other algorithms. The basic idea to using strongly connected components to check strong fairness is old [17, 9], and has been declined in a few algorithms to check the emptiness of (state-based) Streett automata [20, 15]. But these algorithms modify the graph before visiting it again, hindering on-the-fly computations.

At a high level, our algorithm is close to the one presented by Latvala and Heljanko [15], who suggests using any algorithm to compute SCCs. However we have more than implementation detail differences. Our algorithm is targeted to transition-based acceptance conditions, actually shows how to make the emptiness check on-the-fly, and uses two tricks that are dependent on the algorithm used to compute SCC. As mentioned in the introduction, there exists two similar algorithms to compute SCCs on-the-fly: Tarjan's [25] and Dijkstra's [5, 6]. The latter is less known, but better suited to model checking (it has less overhead and can abort earlier). Our trick to use a threshold to prevent SCC merges could work with either algorithms, but for the emptiness-check to be correct we also need to perform the DFS in terms on SCCs instead of working in terms of states. This ordering is possible with Dijkstra's algorithm, but not Tarjan's.

Implementation. Fig. 3 presents the algorithm. Its structure mimics that of the emptiness check for TGBA of Couvreur et al. [4], especially it profits from the idea of performing the DFS in terms of SCCs rather than states: the stack SCC serves both as a stack of connected components and as the DFS stack. The constituents of each entry are $state$ (the root state of the SCC), $root$ (its DFS number), la (the acceptance conditions of the incoming transition to $state$), acc (the acceptance conditions of the cycles inside the SCC), rem (the other states of the SCC), $succ$ and $fsucc$ (the unexplored successors of the SCC).

These unexplored successors are split into $succ$ and $fsucc$ to ensure a proper ordering with respect to avoided acceptance conditions. When a state is pushed down on SCC at line 29, $fsucc$ is loaded with all transitions in acceptance conditions that must be avoided, while $succ$ receive the others. The latter will be visited first: the algorithm always pick the next successor to visit from $succ$ (line 16) and will swap $fsucc$ and $succ$ once $succ$ is empty (lignes 9–11).

Thresholds, meant to prevent merging SCCs using a cycle that would use an unsatisfiable acceptance condition, are represented by the number (in DFS order) of the last state of the SCC from which the threshold transition is going out (that is 2 on our example). These numbers form the min stack; they are used line 20 before deciding whether to merge; they are pushed when $fsucc$ and $succ$ are swapped line 12, and are popped when the state of that number is removed line 35.

The acceptance conditions to avoid are pushed on top of a stack called $avoid$ which is completed anytime the algorithm needs to revisit an SCC (line 43). Each element of this stack is a pair $(ar, \overline{acc})$ where $root$ is the number of the first state of the SCC starting at which acceptance conditions in $\overline{acc}$ should be avoided. This stack is popped when the SCC rooted at $root$ has been visited and has to be removed (lines 37–38).

Correctness. Termination is guaranteed by the DFS and the fact that the number of avoided acceptance conditions cannot exceed $|\mathcal{F}|$. By lack of space, we only give the scheme of our proof that this algorithm will return $\perp$ if an accepting run exists in the input TSA, and will return $\top$ otherwise. (A complete proof is available in French [7].)

Let us use the following notations to describe the state of the algorithm:

$$SCC = \langle state_0, root_0, la_0, acc_0, rem_0, succ_0, fsucc_0 \rangle$$
$$\langle state_1, root_1, la_1, acc_1, rem_1, succ_1, fsucc_1 \rangle$$
$$\vdots$$
$$\langle state_n, root_n, la_n, acc_n, rem_n, succ_n, fsucc_n \rangle$$
$$min = min_0 min_1 \ldots min_p$$
$$avoid = \langle ar_0, \overline{acc_0} \rangle \langle ar_1, \overline{acc_1} \rangle \ldots \langle ar_r, \overline{acc_r} \rangle$$

Furthermore, let us denote $\mathfrak{S}_i$ the set of states represented by $SCC[i]$, and $\varphi(x)$ the index of the SCC containing the state numbered x:

$$\mathfrak{S}_i = \{s \in Q \mid root_i \leq H[s] < root_{i+1}\} \quad \text{for } 0 \leq i < n$$
$$\mathfrak{S}_n = \{s \in Q \mid root_n \leq H[s]\}$$
$$\varphi(x) = \max\{i \mid root_i \leq x\}$$

Lemma 1. *At any time between the execution of lines 8–23, for any pair $\langle ar_i, \overline{acc_i} \rangle$ on the avoid stack, there exists a unique entry $\langle state_j, root_j, la_j, acc_j, rem_j, succ_j, fsucc_j \rangle$ on the SCC stack such that $ar_i = root_j$. In other words, the avoid entries are always associated to roots of SCCs.*

Lemma 2. *When line 16 is run to pick a state amongst the successors of the top of SCC, the value of $\overline{acc_r}$ is the same as when this set of successors was created at line 29.*

Lemma 3. *The values of $(root_i)_{i \in [\![0,n]\!]}$ are strictly increasing and we have $root_n \leq max$ at all times between the execution of lines 8–23.*

Lemma 4. *Let us call n' the value of n at a moment right after lines 11–12 have been run. The sets $succ_{n'}$ and $fsucc_{n'}$ will never increase.*

Lemma 5. *The function g that to any $i \in \{0, ..., p\}$ associates $g(i) = \varphi(min_i)$ is injective. In other words, two states numbered min_{i_1} and min_{i_2} (with $i_1 \neq i_2$) cannot belong to the same SCC. Furthermore, if $n > min_p$, $root_{\varphi(min_p)+1} = min_p + 1$. In other words, min_p is the number of the last state of the SCC whose root has the number $root_{\varphi(min_p)}$. Finally, $root_{\varphi(min_p)} \leq min_p \leq max$.*

The state set Q of the TSA to check can be partitioned in three sets:

– *active states* are those which appear in H associated to a non-null value,
– *removed states* are those which appear in H with a null value,
– *unexplored states* are not yet in H.

The algorithm can move a state from the *unexplored* set to the *active* set, and from there it can move it either to the *removed* set or back to the *unexplored* set (lines 41–42).

The following invariants are preserved by all the lines of the main function (lines 8–23). They need to be proved together as their proofs are interdependent.

Invariant 1. *For all $i \leq n$, the subgraph induced by the states of $\mathfrak{S}_i$ is a SCC. Furthermore there exists a cycle in this SCC that visits all acceptance conditions of acc_i. Finally $\mathfrak{S}_0, \mathfrak{S}_1, \ldots, \mathfrak{S}_n$ is a partition of the set of active states.*

Invariant 2. $\forall i < n, \exists s \in \mathfrak{S}_i, \exists s' \in \mathfrak{S}_{i+1}, \exists p \in 2^{\Sigma}, \{f \in \mathcal{F} \mid (s, p, s') \in f\} = la_{i+1}$. *I.e., there exists a transition between the SCCs indexed by i and $i + 1$ that is in all that acceptance conditions of la_{i+1}.*

Invariant 3. *There is exactly max active states. No state of H is associated to a value greater than max. If two different states are associated to the same value in H, this value is 0. In particular, this means that for any value v between 1 and max, there exists a unique active state s such that $H[s] = v$.*

Invariant 4. *For all integer $i \leq n$, the set rem_i holds all the states of $\mathfrak{S}_i \setminus \{state_i\}$.*

Invariant 5. *Any removed state q cannot be part of an accepting run.*

Invariant 6. *There is no state accessible from $state_n$ from which we could find an accepting cycle using a transition in an acceptance condition from $\overline{acc_r}$.*

Invariant 7. *All transitions going from $\mathfrak{S}_{\varphi(min_p)}$ to $\mathfrak{S}_{\varphi(min_p)+1}$ are labelled by an acceptance condition of $\overline{acc_r}$. (In particular, $la_{\varphi(min_p)+1} \cap \overline{acc_r} \neq \emptyset$.)*

Invariant 8. $\forall j \geq \varphi(min_p), acc_j \cap \overline{acc_r} = \emptyset$ *and* $\forall j > \varphi(min_p) + 1, la_j \cap \overline{acc_r} = \emptyset$. *In other words, the SCC built after the last threshold, and the transitions between them, are not in acceptance conditions from $\overline{acc_r}$, except for the first transition visited after the last threshold (in $la_{\varphi(min_p)+1}$).*

The first two invariants imply that if the algorithm finds an i such that $\forall(l, u) \in \mathcal{F}, acc_i \in l \implies acc_i \in u$, then $SCC[i]$ is an accepting SCC (inv. 1) that is accessible (inv. 1 & 2), so the algorithm can terminate with $\perp$. Invariant 5 assures that no accepting run exists once all states have been *removed*: the algorithm therefore terminates with $\top$.

5 Conclusion

We have introduced a new algorithm for the on-the-fly emptiness check of transition-based Streett automata (TSA), that generalizes the algorithm for transition-based Büchi automata of Couvreur [3]. This algorithm checks the emptiness of a TSA A with $|A|_t$ transitions and $|\mathcal{F}|$ acceptance pairs in $O(|A|_t \times |\mathcal{F}|)$ time. We have seen that this algorithm allows us to check a linear-time property on a model A_M under n strong fairness hypotheses in $O(|A_M|_t \times 2^{O(|\varphi|)} \times n)$ time instead of the $O(|A_M|_t \times 2^{O(|\varphi|+n)})$ we would have using Büchi automata.

It should be noted that since Büchi automata can be seen as Streett automata without any structural change, this very same algorithm can also be used to check the emptiness of Büchi automata. In that case SCCs will never have to be revisited (the *avoid* stack stays empty) and the algorithms performs the same operations as the original algorithm for Büchi automata.

Using Streett automata could also be useful to translate some LTL properties that look like strong fairness properties. For instance Sebastiani et al. [24] give the following LTL formula as an example of a property that is hard to translate to Büchi automata (most of the tools blow up):

$$
\begin{aligned}
\Big((\mathsf{G}\,\mathsf{F}\,p_0 \to \mathsf{G}\,\mathsf{F}\,p_1) \wedge (\mathsf{G}\,\mathsf{F}\,p_2 \to \mathsf{G}\,\mathsf{F}\,p_0) \wedge \\
(\mathsf{G}\,\mathsf{F}\,p_3 \to \mathsf{G}\,\mathsf{F}\,p_2) \wedge (\mathsf{G}\,\mathsf{F}\,p_4 \to \mathsf{G}\,\mathsf{F}\,p_2) \wedge \\
(\mathsf{G}\,\mathsf{F}\,p_5 \to \mathsf{G}\,\mathsf{F}\,p_3) \wedge (\mathsf{G}\,\mathsf{F}\,p_6 \to \mathsf{G}\,\mathsf{F}(p_5 \vee p_4)) \wedge \\
(\mathsf{G}\,\mathsf{F}\,p_7 \to \mathsf{G}\,\mathsf{F}\,p_6) \wedge (\mathsf{G}\,\mathsf{F}\,p_1 \to \mathsf{G}\,\mathsf{F}\,p_7) \Big) \to \mathsf{G}\,\mathsf{F}\,p_8
\end{aligned}
$$

Spot's LTL-to-Büchi translator [8] produces a TGBA with 1731 states. With a dedicated algorithm Sebastiani et al. were able to produce a 1281-state Generalized Büchi automaton. However this formula has the form $\psi \to \varphi$ where ψ is a combinaison of 8 strong fairness hypotheses, and $\neg\varphi$ can be expressed as a Büchi automaton with 2 states and one acceptance condition. The whole formula can therefore be expressed as a transition-based Streett automaton with two states and 9 pairs of acceptance conditions.[3] This reduction should not be a surprise since Streett automata are exponentially more succinct than Büchi automata [23], however this example shows that it would be useful to have an efficient algorithm to translate LTL formulæ to Streett automata. Unfortunately we are not aware of any published work in this area.

References

[1] Clarke, E.M., Grumberg, O., Peled, D.A.: Model Checking. MIT Press, Cambridge (2000)
[2] Cormen, T.H., Leiserson, C.E., Rivest, R.L., Stein, C.: Introduction to Algorithms, 2nd edn. The MIT Press, Cambridge (2001)
[3] Couvreur, J.-M.: On-the-fly verification of temporal logic. In: Wing, J.M., Woodcock, J.C.P., Davies, J. (eds.) FM 1999. LNCS, vol. 1708, pp. 253–271. Springer, Heidelberg (1999)
[4] Couvreur, J.-M., Duret-Lutz, A., Poitrenaud, D.: On-the-fly emptiness checks for generalized Büchi automata. In: Godefroid, P. (ed.) SPIN 2005. LNCS, vol. 3639, pp. 169–184. Springer, Heidelberg (2005)
[5] Dijkstra, E.W.: EWD 376: Finding the maximum strong components in a directed graph (May 1973),
   http://www.cs.utexas.edu/users/EWD/ewd03xx/EWD376.PDF
[6] Dijkstra, E.W.: Finding the maximal strong components in a directed graph. In: A Discipline of Programming, ch. 25, pp. 192–200. Prentice-Hall, Englewood Cliffs (1976)
[7] Duret-Lutz, A.: Contributions à l'approche automate pour la vérification de propriétés de systèmes concurrents. PhD thesis, Université Pierre et Marie Curie (Paris 6) (July 2007)
[8] Duret-Lutz, A., Poitrenaud, D.: Spot: an extensible model checking library using transition-based generalized Büchi automata. In: Proc. MASCOTS 2004, Volendam, The Netherlands, October 2004, pp. 76–83. IEEE Computer Society, Los Alamitos (2004)

---

[3] Combining this with the TSA to TGBA construction from section 3.3 yields a TGBA of $2 \times (2^9 + 1) = 1026$ states that is even smaller than that of Sebastiani et al.

[9] Emerson, E.A., Lei, C.-L.: Modalities for model checking: Branching time logic strikes back. Science of Computer Programming 8(3), 275–306 (1987)

[10] Francez, N.: Fairness. Springer, Heidelberg (1986)

[11] Gastin, P., Oddoux, D.: Fast LTL to Büchi automata translation. In: Berry, G., Comon, H., Finkel, A. (eds.) CAV 2001. LNCS, vol. 2102, pp. 53–65. Springer, Heidelberg (2001)

[12] Giannakopoulou, D., Lerda, F.: From states to transitions: Improving translation of LTL formulæ to Büchi automata. In: Peled, D.A., Vardi, M.Y. (eds.) FORTE 2002. LNCS, vol. 2529, pp. 308–326. Springer, Heidelberg (2002)

[13] Godefroid, P., Holzmann, G., Pirottin, D.: State-space caching revisited. Formal Methods in System Design 7(3), 227–241 (1995)

[14] Kesten, Y., Pnueli, A., Vardi, M.Y.: Verification by augmented abstraction: The automata-theoretic view. Journal of Computer and System Sciences 62(4), 668–690 (2001)

[15] Latvala, T., Heljanko, K.: Coping with strong fairness. Fundamenta Informaticae 43(1–4), 1–19 (2000)

[16] Löding, C.: Methods for the transformation of ω-automata: Complexity and connection to second order logic. Diploma thesis, Institue of Computer Science and Applied Mathematics (1998)

[17] Lichtenstein, O., Pnueli, A.: Checking that finite state concurrent programs satisfy their linear specification. In: Proc. the 12th ACM Symposium on Principles of Programming Languages (POPL 1985), pp. 97–107. ACM, New York (1985)

[18] Merz, S.: Model checking: A tutorial overview. In: Cassez, F., Jard, C., Rozoy, B., Dermot, M. (eds.) MOVEP 2000. LNCS, vol. 2067, pp. 3–38. Springer, Heidelberg (2001)

[19] Michel, M.: Algèbre de machines et logique temporelle. In: Fontet, M., Mehlhorn, K. (eds.) STACS 1984. LNCS, vol. 166, pp. 287–298. Springer, Heidelberg (1984)

[20] Rauch Henzinger, M., Telle, J.A.: Faster algorithms for the nonemptiness of Streett automata and for communication protocol pruning. In: Karlsson, R., Lingas, A. (eds.) SWAT 1996. LNCS, vol. 1097, pp. 16–27. Springer, Heidelberg (1996)

[21] Safra, S.: Complexity of Automata on Infinite Objects. PhD thesis, The Weizmann Institute of Science, Rehovot, Israel (March 1989)

[22] Safra, S.: Exponential determinization for ω-automata with strong-fairness acceptance condition. In: Proc. STOC 1992. ACM, New York (1992)

[23] Safra, S., Vardi, M.Y.: On ω-automata and temporal logic (preliminary report). In: Proc. STOC 1989, pp. 127–137. ACM, New York (1989)

[24] Sebastiani, R., Tonetta, S., Vardi, M.Y.: Symbolic systems, explicit properties: on hybrid approches for LTL symbolic model checking. In: Etessami, K., Rajamani, S.K. (eds.) CAV 2005. LNCS, vol. 3576, pp. 350–363. Springer, Heidelberg (2005)

[25] Tarjan, R.: Depth-first search and linear graph algorithms. SIAM Journal on Computing 1(2), 146–160 (1972)

[26] Tauriainen, H.: Automata and Linear Temporal Logic: Translation with Transition-based Acceptance. PhD thesis, Helsinki University of Technology, Espoo, Finland (September 2006)

[27] Vardi, M.Y.: The Büchi complementation saga. In: Thomas, W., Weil, P. (eds.) STACS 2007. LNCS, vol. 4393, pp. 12–22. Springer, Heidelberg (2007)

[28] Vardi, M.Y.: Automata-theoretic model checking revisited (Invited paper.). In: Cook, B., Podelski, A. (eds.) VMCAI 2007. LNCS, vol. 4349, pp. 137–150. Springer, Heidelberg (2007)

[29] Vardi, M.Y.: An automata-theoretic approach to linear temporal logic. In: Moller, F., Birtwistle, G. (eds.) Logics for Concurrency. LNCS, vol. 1043, pp. 238–266. Springer, Heidelberg (1996)

On Minimal Odd Rankings for Büchi Complementation

Hrishikesh Karmarkar and Supratik Chakraborty

Department of Computer Science and Engineering
Indian Institute of Technology Bombay

Abstract. We study minimal odd rankings (as defined by Kupferman and Vardi[KV01]) for run-DAGs of words in the complement of a nondeterministic Büchi automaton. We present an optimized version of the ranking based complementation construction of Friedgut, Kupferman and Vardi [FKV06] and Schewe's[Sch09] variant of it, such that every accepting run of the complement automaton assigns a minimal odd ranking to the corresponding run-DAG. This allows us to determine minimally inessential ranks and redundant slices in ranking-based complementation constructions. We exploit this to reduce the size of the complement Büchi automaton by eliminating all redundant slices. We demonstrate the practical importance of this result through a set of experiments using the NuSMV model checker.

1 Introduction

The problem of complementing nondeterministic ω-word automata is fundamental in the theory of automata over infinite words. In addition to the theoretical aspects of the study of complementation techniques, efficient complementation techniques are extremely useful in practical applications as well. Vardi's excellent survey paper on the saga of Büchi complementation spanning more than 45 years provides a brief overview of various such applications of complementation techniques [Var07].

Various complementation constructions for nondeterministic Büchi automata on words (henceforth referred to as NBW) have been developed over the years, starting with Büchi [Büc62]. Büchi's algorithm resulted in a complement automaton with $2^{2^{O(n)}}$ states, starting from an NBW with n states. This upper bound was improved to $2^{O(n^2)}$ by Sistla et al [SVW87]. Safra [Saf88] provided the first asymptotically optimal $n^{O(n)}$ upper bound for complementation that passes through determinization. By a theorem of Michel [Mic88], it was known that Büchi complementation has a $n!$ lower-bound. With this, Löding [Löd99] showed that Safra's construction is asymptotically optimal for Büchi determinization, and hence for complementation. The $O(n!)$ (approximately $(0.36n)^n$) lower bound for Büchi complementation was recently sharpened to $(0.76n)^n$ by Yan [Yan08] using a full-automata technique. The complementation constructions of Klarlund [Kla91], Kupferman and Vardi [KV01] and Kähler and

Z. Liu and A.P. Ravn (Eds.): ATVA 2009, LNCS 5799, pp. 228–243, 2009.

Wilke [KW08] for nondeterministic Büchi automata are examples of determinization free (or *Safraless* as they are popularly called) complementation constructions for Büchi automata. The best known upper bound for the problem until
recently was $(0.97n)^n$, given by Kupferman and Vardi. This was recently sharpened by Schewe[Sch09] to an almost tight upper bound of $(0.76n)^n$ modulo a
factor of n^2.

NBW complementation techniques based on optimized versions of Safra's determinization construction (see, for example, Piterman's recent work [Pit07])
have been experimentally found to work well for automata of small sizes (typically $8 - 10$ states) [TCT+08]. However, these techniques are complex and
present fewer opportunities for optimized implementations. Ranking-based complementation constructions [KV01, FKV06, Sch09] are comparatively simpler
and appear more amenable to optimizations, especially when dealing with larger
automaton sizes. For example, several optimization techniques for ranking based
complementation constructions have been proposed recently [FKV06, GKSV03].
Similarly, language universality and containment checking techniques that use
the framework of ranking-based complementation but avoid explicit construction of complement automata have been successfully applied to NBW with more
than 100 states [DR09, FV09]. This leads us to believe that ranking-based complementation constructions hold much promise, and motivates our study of new
optimization techniques for such constructions.

The primary contributions of this paper can be summarized as follows : (i) We
present an improvement to the ranking based complementation constructions of
[FKV06] and [Sch09] for NBW. All accepting runs of our automaton on a word in
the complement language correspond to a minimal odd ranking of the run-DAG.
(ii) We show how to reduce the size of the complement automaton by efficiently
identifying and removing redundant slices without language containment checks.
(iii) We present an implementation of the proposed technique using the BDD-
based symbolic model checker NuSMV, and experimentally demonstrate the
advantages of our technique on a set of examples.

2 Ranking-Based NBW Complementation

Let $A = (Q, q_0, \Sigma, \delta, F)$ be an NBW, where Q is a set of states, $q_0 \in Q$ is an
initial state, Σ is an alphabet, $\delta : Q \times \Sigma \to 2^Q$ is a transition function, and
$F \in 2^Q$ is a set of accepting states. An NBW accepts a set of ω-words, where
an ω-word α is an infinite sequence $\alpha_0 \alpha_1 \ldots$, and $\alpha_i \in \Sigma$ for all $i \geq 0$. A run ρ
of A on α is an infinite sequence of states given by $\rho : \mathbb{N} \to Q$, where $\rho(0) = q_0$
and $\rho(i + 1) \in \delta(\rho(i), \alpha_i)$ for all $i \geq 0$. A run ρ of A on α is called *accepting*
if $inf(\rho) \cap F \neq \emptyset$, where $inf(\rho)$ is the set of states that appear infinitely often
along ρ. The run ρ is called *rejecting* if $inf(\rho) \cap F = \emptyset$. An ω-word α is accepted
by A if A has an accepting run on it, and is rejected otherwise. The set of all
words accepted by A is called the *language* of A, and is denoted $L(A)$. The
complementation problem for NBW is to construct an automaton A^c from a
given NBW A such that $L(A^c) = \Sigma^\omega \setminus L(A)$. We will henceforth denote the

complement language $\Sigma^\omega \setminus L(A)$ by $\overline{L(A)}$. An NBW is said to be in *initial normal form (INF)* if (i) the initial state is non-accepting and has a transition back to itself on every letter in Σ, and (ii) no other state has a transition to the initial state. An NBW is said to be *complete* if every state has at least one outgoing transition on every letter in Σ. Every NBW can be transformed to INF and made complete without changing the accepted language by adding at most one non-accepting initial state and at most one non-accepting "sink" state. All NBW considered in the remainder of this paper are assumed to be complete and in INF.

The (possibly infinite) set of all runs of an NBW $A = (Q, q_0, \Sigma, \delta, F)$ on a word α can be represented by a directed acyclic graph $G_\alpha = (V, E)$, where V is a subset of $Q \times \mathbb{N}$ and $E \subseteq V \times V$. The root vertex of the DAG is $(q_0, 0)$. For all $i > 0$, vertex $(q, i) \in V$ iff there is a run ρ of A on α such that $\rho(i) = q$. The set of edges of G_α is $E \subseteq V \times V$, where $((q, i), (q', j)) \in E$ iff both (q, i) and (q', j) are in V, $j = i + 1$ and $q' \in \delta(q, \alpha_i)$. Graph G_α is called the *run-DAG* of α in A. A vertex $(q, l) \in V$ is called an *F-vertex* if $q \in F$, i.e, q is a final state of A. A vertex (q, l) is said to be *F-free* if there is no F-vertex that is reachable from (q, l) in G_α. Furthermore, (q, l) is called *finite* if only finitely many vertices are reachable from (q, l) in G_α. For every $l \geq 0$, the set of vertices $\{(q, l) \mid (q, l) \in V\}$ constitutes *level* l of G_α. An accepting path in G_α is an infinite path $(q_0, 0), (q_{i_1}, 1), (q_{i_2}, 2) \ldots$ such that $q_0, q_{i_1}, \ldots$ is an accepting run of A. The run-DAG G_α is called rejecting if there is no accepting path in G_α. Otherwise, G_α is said to be accepting.

2.1   Ranking Functions and Complementation

Kupferman and Vardi [KV01] introduced the idea of assigning ranks to vertices of run-DAGs, and described a rank-based complementation construction for alternating Büchi automata. They also showed how this technique can be used to obtain a ranking-based complementation construction for NBW, that is easier to understand and implement than the complementation construction based on Safra's determinization construction[Saf88]. In this section, we briefly overview ranking-based complementation constructions for NBW.

Let $[k]$ denote the set $\{1, 2, \ldots, k\}$, and $[k]^{odd}$ (respectively $[k]^{even}$) denote the set of all odd (respectively even) numbers in the set $\{1, 2, \ldots, k\}$. Given an NBW A with n states and an ω-word α, let $G_\alpha = (V, E)$ be the run-DAG of α in A. A *ranking* r of G_α is a function $r : V \to [2n]$ that satisfies the following conditions: (i) for all vertices $(q, l) \in V$, if $r((q, l))$ is odd then $q \notin F$, and (ii) for all edges $((q, l), (q', l+1)) \in E$, we have $r((q', l+1)) \leq r((q, l))$. A ranking associates with every vertex in G_α a rank in $[2n]$ such that the ranks along every path in G_α are non-increasing, and vertices corresponding to final states always get even ranks. A ranking r is said to be *odd* if every infinite path in G_α eventually gets trapped in an odd rank. Otherwise, r is called an *even ranking*. We use $max\_odd(r)$ to denote the highest odd rank in the range of r.

A *level ranking* for A is a function $g : Q \to [2n] \cup \{\perp\}$ such that for every $q \in Q$, if $g(q) \in [2n]^{odd}$, then $q \notin F$. Let $\mathcal{L}$ be the set of all level rankings for

A. Given two level rankings $g, g' \in \mathcal{L}$, a set $S \subseteq Q$ and a letter σ, we say that g' covers (g, S, σ) if for all $q \in S$ and $q' \in \delta(q, \sigma)$, if $g(q) \neq \bot$, then $g'(q') \neq \bot$ and $g'(q') \leq g(q)$. For a level ranking g, we abuse notation and let $max\_odd(g)$ denote the highest odd rank in the range of g. A ranking r of G_α induces a level ranking for every level $l \geq 0$ of G_α. If $Q_l = \{q \mid (q, l) \in V\}$ denotes the set of states in level l of G_α, then the level ranking g induced by r for level l is as follows: $g(q) = r((q, l))$ for all $q \in Q_l$ and $g(q) = \bot$ otherwise. It is easy to see that if g and g' are level rankings induced for levels l and $l + 1$ respectively, then g' covers (g, Q_l, α_l), where α_l is the lth letter in the input word α. A level ranking g is said to be *tight* if the following conditions hold: (i) the highest rank in the range of g is odd, and (ii) for all $i \in [max\_odd(g)]^{odd}$, there is a state $q \in Q$ with $g(q) = i$.

Lemma 1 ([KV01]). *The following statements are equivalent:*

(P1) All paths of G_α see only finitely many F-vertices.
(P2) There is an odd ranking for G_α.

Kupferman and Vardi [KV01] provided a constructive proof of (P1) $\Rightarrow$ (P2) in the above Lemma. Their construction is important for some of our subsequent discussions, hence we outline it briefly here. Given an NBW A with n states, an ω-word $\alpha \in \overline{L(A)}$ and the run-DAG G_α of A on α, the proof in [KV01] inductively defines an infinite sequence of DAGs $G_0 \supseteq G_1 \supseteq \ldots$, where (i) $G_0 = G_\alpha$, (ii) $G_{2i+1} = G_{2i} \setminus \{(q, l) \mid (q, l) \text{ is finite in } G_{2i}\}$, and (iii) $G_{2i+2} = G_{2i+1} \setminus \{(q, l) \mid (q, l) \text{ is F-free in } G_{2i+1}\}$, for all $i \geq 0$. An interesting consequence of this definition is that for all $i \geq 0$, G_{2i+1} is either empty or has no finite vertices. It can be shown that if all paths in G_α see only finitely many F-vertices, then G_{2n-1} and all subsequent G_is must be empty. A ranking $r_{A,\alpha}^{KV}$ of G_α can therefore be defined as follows: for every vertex (q, l) of G_α, $r_{A,\alpha}^{KV}((q, l)) = 2i$ if (q, l) is finite in G_{2i}, and $r_{A,\alpha}^{KV}((q, l)) = 2i + 1$ if (q, l) is F-free in G_{2i+1}. Kupferman and Vardi showed that $r_{A,\alpha}^{KV}$ is an odd ranking [KV01]. Throughout this paper, we will use $r_{A,\alpha}^{KV}$ to denote the odd ranking computed by the above technique due to Kupferman and Vardi (hence KV in the superscript) for NBW A and $\alpha \in \overline{L(A)}$. When A and α are clear from the context, we will simply use r^{KV} for notational convenience.

The NBW complementation construction and upper size bound presented in [KV01] was subsequently tightened in [FKV06], where the following important observation was made.

Lemma 2 ([FKV06]). *Given a word $\alpha \in \overline{L(A)}$, there exists an odd ranking r of G_α and a level $l_{lim} \geq 0$, such that for all levels $l > l_{lim}$, the level ranking induced by r for l is tight.*

Lemma 2 led to a reduced upper bound for the size of ranking-based complementation constructions, since all non-tight level rankings could now be ignored after reading a finite prefix of the input word. Schewe[Sch09] tightened the construction and analysis further, resulting in a ranking-based complementation construction with an upper size bound that is within a factor of n^2 of the best known lower bound [Yan08]. Hence, Schewe's construction is currently the best known ranking-based construction for complementing NBW. Gurumurthy et al [GKSV03] presented a collection of practically useful optimization techniques for keeping the size of complement automata constructed using ranking techniques under control. Their experiments demonstrated the effectiveness of their optimizations for NBW with an average size of 6 states. Interestingly, their work also highlighted the difficulty of complementing NBW with tens of states in practice. Doyen and Raskin [DR09] have recently proposed powerful anti-chain optimizations in ranking-based techniques for checking universality $(L(A) =^? \Sigma^\omega)$ and language containment $(L(A) \subseteq^? L(B))$ of NBW. Fogarty and Vardi [FV09] have evaluated Doyen and Raskin's technique and also Ramsey-based containment checking techniques in the context of proving size-change termination (SCT) of programs. Their results bear testimony to the effectiveness of Doyen and Raskin's anti-chain optimizations for ranking-based complementation in SCT problems, especially when the original NBW is known to have *reverse-determinism* [FV09].

Given an NBW A, let KVF(A) be the complement NBW constructed using the Friedgut, Kupferman and Vardi construction with tight level rankings [KV01, FKV06]. For notational convenience, we will henceforth refer to this construction as *KVF-construction*. Similarly, let KVFS(A) be the complement automaton constructed using Schewe's variant[Sch09] of the KVF-construction. We will henceforth refer to this construction as *KVFS-construction*.

The work presented in this paper can be viewed as an optimized variant of Schewe's [Sch09] ranking-based complementation construction. The proposed method is distinct from other optimization techniques proposed in the literature (e.g. those in [GKSV03]), and adds to the repertoire of such techniques. We first show that for every NBW A and word $\alpha \in \overline{L(A)}$, the ranking r^{KV} is *minimal* in the following sense: if r is any odd ranking of G_α, then every vertex (q, l) in G_α satisfies $r^{KV}((q, l)) \leq r((q, l))$. We then describe how to restrict the transitions of the complement automaton obtained by the KVFS-construction, such that every accepting run of α assigns the same rank to all vertices in G_α as is assigned by r^{KV}. Thus, our construction ensures that acceptance of α happens only through minimal odd rankings. This allows us to partition the set of states of the complement automaton into *slices* such that for every word $\alpha \in \overline{L(A)}$, all its accepting runs lie in exactly one slice. Redundant slices can then be identified as those that never contribute to accepting any word in $\overline{L(A)}$. Removal of such redundant slices results in a reduced state count, while preserving the language of the complement automaton. The largest $k(> 0)$ such that there is a non-redundant slice with that assigns rank k to some vertex in the run-DAG gives the *rank of A*, as defined by [GKSV03]. Notice that our sliced view of the complement automaton is distinct from the notion of slices as used in [KW08].

Gurumurthy et al have shown [GKSV03] that for every NBW A, there exists an NBW B with $L(B) = L(A)$, such that both the KVF- and KVFS-constructions for B^c require at most 3 ranks. However, obtaining B from A is non-trivial, and requires an exponential blowup in the worst-case [FKV06]. Therefore, ranking-based complementation constructions typically focus on reducing the state count of the complement automaton starting from a given NBW A, instead of first computing B and then constructing B^c. We follow the same approach in this paper. Thus, we do not seek to obtain an NBW with the *minimum* rank for the complement of a given ω-regular language. Instead, we wish to reduce the state count of Kupferman and Vardi's rank-based complementation construction, starting from a given NBW A.

3   Minimal Odd Rankings

Given an NBW A and an ω-word $\alpha \in \overline{L(A)}$, an odd ranking r of G_α is said to be *minimal* if for every odd ranking r' of G_α, we have $r'((q,l)) \geq r((q,l))$ for all vertices (q,l) in G_α.

Theorem 1. *For every NBW A and ω-word $\alpha \in \overline{L(A)}$, the ranking $r^{KV}_{A,\alpha}$ is minimal.*

Proof. Let α be an ω-word in $\overline{L(A)}$. Since A and α are clear from the context, we will use the simpler notation r^{KV} to denote the ranking computed by Kupferman and Vardi's method. Let r be any (other) odd ranking of G_α, and let $V_{r,i}$ denote the set of vertices in G_α that are assigned the rank i by r. Since A is assumed to be a complete automaton, there are no finite vertices in G_α. Hence, by Kupferman and Vardi's construction, $V_{r^{KV},0} = \emptyset$. Note that this is consistent with our requirement that all ranking functions have range $[2n] = \{1, \ldots 2n\}$.

We will prove the theorem by showing that $V_{r,i} \subseteq \bigcup_{k=1}^{i} V_{r^{KV},k}$ for all $i > 0$. The proof proceeds by induction on i, and by following the construction of DAGs $G_0, G_1, \ldots$ in Kupferman and Vardi's proof of Lemma 1.

Base case: Consider $G_1 = G_0 \setminus \{(q',l') \mid (q',l') \text{ is finite in } G_0\} = G_\alpha \setminus \emptyset = G_\alpha$. Let (q_1,l_1) be a vertex in G_1 such that $r((q_1,l_1)) = 1$. Let (q_f,l_f) be an F-vertex reachable from (q_1,l_1) in G_α, if possible. By virtue of the requirements that F-vertices must get even ranks, and ranks cannot increase along any path, $r((q_f,l_f))$ must be < 1. However, this is impossible given that the range of r must be $[2n]$. Therefore, no F-vertex can be reachable from (q_1,l_1). In other words, (q_1,l_1) is F-free in G_1. Hence, by definition, we have $r^{KV}(q_1,l_1) = 1$. Thus, $V_{r,1} \subseteq V_{r^{KV},1}$.

Hypothesis: Assume that $V_{r,j} \subseteq \bigcup_{k=1}^{j} V_{r^{KV},k}$ for all $1 \leq j \leq i$.

Induction: By definition, $G_{i+1} = G_\alpha \setminus \bigcup_{s=1}^{i} V_{r^{KV},s}$. Let (q_{i+1},l_{i+1}) be a vertex in G_{i+1} such that $r((q_{i+1},l_{i+1})) = i + 1$. Since r is an odd ranking, all paths starting from (q_{i+1},l_{i+1}) must eventually get trapped in some odd rank $\leq i+1$ (assigned by r). We consider two cases.

- Suppose there are no infinite paths starting from (q_{i+1},l_{i+1}) in G_{i+1}. This implies (q_{i+1},l_{i+1}) is a finite vertex in G_{i+1}. We have seen earlier that for all $k \geq 0$, G_{2k+1} must be either empty or have no finite vertices. Therefore, $i + 1$ must be even, and $\mathsf{r}^{\mathsf{KV}}((q_{i+1}, l_{i+1})) = i + 1$ by Kupferman and Vardi's construction.

– There exists a non-empty set of infinite paths starting from (q_{i+1}, l_{i+1}) in G_{i+1}. Since $G_{i+1} = G_\alpha \setminus \bigcup_{s=1}^{i} V_{\mathsf{r}^{\mathsf{KV}}, s}$, none of these paths reach any vertex in $\bigcup_{s=1}^{i} V_{\mathsf{r}^{\mathsf{KV}}, s}$. Since $V_{r,j} \subseteq \bigcup_{k \in \{1,2,\ldots,j\}} V_{\mathsf{r}^{\mathsf{KV}}, k}$ for all $1 \leq j \leq i$, and since ranks cannot increase along any path, it follows that r must assign $i + 1$ to all vertices along each of the above paths. This, coupled with the fact that r is an odd ranking, implies that $i + 1$ is odd. Since F-vertices must be assigned even ranks by r, it follows from above that (q_{i+1}, l_{i+1}) is F-free in G_α. Therefore, $\mathsf{r}^{\mathsf{KV}}((q_{i+1}, l_{i+1})) = i + 1$ by Kupferman and Vardi's construction.

We have thus shown that all vertices in G_{i+1} that are assigned rank $i + 1$ by r must also be assigned rank $i+1$ by r^{KV}. Therefore, $V_{r,i+1} \setminus \bigcup_{j=1}^{i} V_{\mathsf{r}^{\mathsf{KV}}, j} \subseteq V_{\mathsf{r}^{\mathsf{KV}}, i+1}$. In other words, $V_{r,i+1} \subseteq \bigcup_{j=1}^{i+1} V_{\mathsf{r}^{\mathsf{KV}}, j}$.

By the principle of mathematical induction, it follows that $V_{r,i} \subseteq \bigcup_{k=1}^{i} V_{\mathsf{r}^{\mathsf{KV}}, k}$ for all $i > 0$. Thus, if a vertex is assigned rank i by r, it must be assigned a rank $\leq i$ by r^{KV}. Hence r^{KV} is minimal. $\quad\square$

Lemma 3. *For every $\alpha \in \overline{L(A)}$, the run-DAG G_α ranked by $\mathsf{r}^{\mathsf{KV}}_{A,\alpha}$ (or simply r^{KV}) satisfies the following properties.*

1. *For every vertex (q, l) that is not an F-vertex such that $\mathsf{r}^{\mathsf{KV}}((q, l)) = k$, there must be at least one immediate successor $(q', l+1)$ such that $\mathsf{r}^{\mathsf{KV}}((q', l+1)) = k$.*
2. *For every vertex (q, l) that is an F-vertex, such that $\mathsf{r}^{\mathsf{KV}}((q, l)) = k$, there must be atleast one immediate successor $(q', l+1)$ such that $\mathsf{r}^{\mathsf{KV}}((q', l+1)) = k$ or $\mathsf{r}^{\mathsf{KV}}((q', l+1)) = k - 1$*
3. *For every vertex (q, l) such that $\mathsf{r}^{\mathsf{KV}}((q, l)) = k$, where k is odd and > 1, there is a vertex (q', l') for $l' > l$ such that (q', l') is an F-vertex reachable from (q, l) and $\mathsf{r}^{\mathsf{KV}}((q', l')) = k - 1$.*
4. *For every vertex (q, l) such that $\mathsf{r}^{\mathsf{KV}}((q, l)) = k$, where k is even and > 0, every path starting at (q, l) eventually visits a vertex with rank less than k. Furthermore, there is a vertex (q', l') for $l' > l$ such that (q', l') is reachable from (q, l) and $\mathsf{r}^{\mathsf{KV}}((q', l')) = k - 1$.*

We omit the proof due to lack of space. The reader is referred to [KC09] for details of the proof.

4   A Motivating Example

We have seen above the KVFS-construction leads to almost tight worst case bounds for NBW complementation. This is a significant achievement considering the long history of Büchi complementation [Var07]. However, the KVFS-construction does not necessarily allow us to construct small complement automata for every NBW. Specifically, there exists a family of NBW

$\mathcal{A} = \{ A_3, A_5, \dots \}$ such that for every $i \in \{3, 5, \dots\}$: (i) A_i has i states, (ii) each of the ranking-based complementation constructions in [KV01], [FKV06] and [Sch09] produces a complement automaton with at least $\frac{i^{(\frac{i-1}{2})}}{e^i}$ states, and (iii) a ranking-based complementation construction that assigns minimal ranks to all run-DAGs results in a complement automaton with $\Theta(i)$ states.

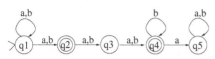

Fig. 1. Automaton A_5

Automata in the family $\mathcal{A}$ can be described as follows. Each A_i is an NBW $(Q_i, q_1, \Sigma, \delta_i, F_i)$, where $Q_i = \{q_1, q_2, \dots, q_i\}$, $\Sigma = \{a, b\}$, q_1 is the initial state and $F_i = \{q_j \mid q_j \in Q_i, j$ is even $\}$. The transition relation δ_i is given by: $\delta_i = \{(q_j, a, q_{j+1}), (q_j, b, q_{j+1}) \mid 1 \le j \le i - 2\} \cup \{(q_1, a, q_1), (q_1, b, q_1), (q_i, a, q_i), (q_i, b, q_i), (q_{i-1}, b, q_{i-1}), (q_{i-1}, a, q_i)\}$. Figure 1 shows the structure of automaton A_5 defined in this manner. Note that each $A_i \in \mathcal{A}$ is a complete automaton in INF. Furthermore, $b^\omega \in L(A_i)$ and $a^\omega \notin L(A_i)$ for each $A_i \in \mathcal{A}$. Let $\mathsf{KVF}(A_i)$ and $\mathsf{KVFS}(A_i)$ be the complement automata for A_i constructed using the KVF-construction and KVFS-construction respectively.

Lemma 4. *For every $A_i \in \mathcal{A}$, the number of states in $\mathsf{KVF}(A_i)$ and $\mathsf{KVFS}(A_i)$ is atleast $\frac{(i)^{(i-1)/2}}{e^i}$. Furthermore, there exists a ranking-based complementation construction for A_i that gives a complement automaton $A_i{}'$ with $\Theta(i)$ states.*

Proof sketch: The proof is obtained by considering the run-DAG for a^ω (which is $\in \overline{L(A_i)}$), and by showing that at least $\frac{(i)^{(i-1)/2}}{e^i}$ states are required in both the KVF- and KVFS-constructions in order to allow all possible consistent rank assignments to vertices of the run-DAG. On the other hand, a complementation construction that uses the ranking $f(q_i) = 1$, $f(q_1) = 3$ and $f(q_j) = 2$ for all $2 \le j \le i - 1$ at all levels of the run-DAG can be shown to accept $\overline{L(A)}$ with $\Theta(i)$ states. Details of the proof may be found in [KC09].

This discrepancy in the size of a sufficient rank set and the actual set of ranks used by the KVF- and KVFS-constructions motivates us to ask if we can devise a ranking-based complementation construction for NBW that uses the minimum number of ranks when accepting a word in the complement language. In this paper, we answer this question in the affirmative, by providing such a complementation construction.

5 Complementation with Minimal Ranks

Motivated by the example described in the previous section, we now describe an optimized ranking-based complementation construction for NBW. Given an NBW A, the complement automaton A' obtained using our construction has the special property that when it accepts an ω-word α, it assigns a rank r to G_α that agrees with the ranking $r_{A,\alpha}^{\mathsf{KV}}$ at every vertex in G_α. This is achieved by non-deterministically mimicking the process of rank assignment used to arrive at $r_{A,\alpha}^{\mathsf{KV}}$.

Our construction imposes additional constraints on the states and transitions of the complement automaton, beyond those in the KVF- and KVFS-constructions. For example, if k is the smallest rank that can be assigned to vertex (q, l), then the following conditions must hold: (i) if (q, l) is not an F-vertex then it must have a successor of the same rank at the next level, and (ii) if (q, l) is an F-vertex then it must have a successor at the next level with rank k or $k - 1$. The above observations are coded as conditions on the transitions of A', and are crucial if every accepting run of A' on $\alpha \in \overline{L(A)}$ must correspond to the unique ranking $r_{A,\alpha}^{KV}$ of G_α.

Recall that in [FKV06], a state of the automaton that tracks the ranking of the run-DAG vertices at the current level is represented as a triple (S, O, f), where S is a set of Büchi states reachable after reading a finite prefix of the word, f is a tight level ranking, and the O-set checks if all even ranked vertices in a (possibly previous) level of the run-DAG have moved to lower odd ranks. In our construction, we use a similar representation of states, although the O-set is much more versatile. Specifically, the O-set is populated turn-wise with states of the same rank k, for both odd and even k. This is a generalization of Schewe's technique that uses the O-set to check if even ranked states present at a particular level have moved to states with lower odd ranks. The O-set in our construction, however, does more. It checks if every state of rank k (whether even or odd) in an O-set eventually reaches a state with rank $k - 1$. If k is even. then it also checks if all runs starting at states in O eventually reach a state with rank $k - 1$. When all states in an O-set tracking rank 2 reach states with rank 1, the O-set is reset and loaded with states that have the maximal odd rank in the range of the current level ranking. The process of checking ranks is then re-started. This gives rise to the following construction for the complement automaton A'.

Let $A' = (Q', Q_0', \Sigma, \delta', F')$, where

- $Q' = \{2^Q \times 2^Q \times \mathcal{R}\}$ is the state set, such that if $(S, O, f) \in Q'$, then $S \subseteq Q$ and $S \neq \emptyset$, $f \in \mathcal{R}$ is a level ranking, $O \subseteq S$, and either $O = \emptyset$ or $\exists k \in [2n - 1]\ \forall q \in O,\ f(q) = k$.
- $Q_0' = \bigcup_{i \in [2n-1]^{odd}} \{(S, O, f) \mid S = \{q_0\},\ f(q_0) = i, O = \emptyset\}$ is the set of initial states.
- For every $\sigma \in \Sigma$, the transition function δ' is defined such that if $(S', O', f') \in \delta'((S, O, f), \sigma)$, the following conditions are satisfied.
  1. $S' = \delta(S, \sigma)$, f' covers (f, S, σ).
  2. For all $q \in S \setminus F$, there is a $q' \in \delta(q, \sigma)$ such that $f'(q') = f(q)$.
  3. For all $q \in S \cap F$ one of the following must hold
     (a) There is a $q' \in \delta(q, \sigma)$, such that $f'(q') = f(q)$.
     (b) There is a $q' \in \delta(q, \sigma)$, such that $f'(q') = f(q) - 1$.
  4. In addition, we have the following restrictions:
     (a) If f is not a tight level ranking, then $O' = O$
     (b) If f is a tight level ranking and $O \neq \emptyset$, then
        i. If for all $q \in O$, we have $f(q) = k$, where k is even, then
           • Let $O_1 = \delta(O, \sigma) \setminus \{q \mid f'(q) < k\}$.

- If $(O_1 = \emptyset)$ then $O' = \{q \mid q \in Q \land f'(q) = k - 1\}$, else
  $O' = O_1$.
  ii. If for all $q \in O$, we have $f(q) = k$, where k is odd, then
  - If $k = 1$ then $O' = \emptyset$
  - If $k > 1$ then let $O_2 = O \setminus \{q \mid \exists q' \in \delta(q, \sigma), (f'(q') = k - 1)\}$.
    - If $O_2 \neq \emptyset$ then $O' \subseteq \delta(O_2, \sigma)$ such that
      $\forall q \in O_2 \exists q' \in O', \ q' \in \delta(q, \sigma) \land f'(q') = k$.
    - If $O_2 = \emptyset$ then $O' = \{q \mid f'(q) = k - 1\}$.
  (c) If f is a tight level ranking and $O = \emptyset$, then $O' = \{q \mid f'(q) = max\_odd(f')\}$.
- As in the KVF- and KVFS-constructions, the set of accepting states of A'
  is $F' = \{(S, O, f) \mid f$ is a tight level ranking, and $O = \emptyset\}$

Note that unlike the KVF- and KVFS-constructions, the above construction does not have an initial phase of unranked subset construction, followed by a non-deterministic jump to ranked subset construction with tight level rankings. Instead, we start directly with ranked subsets of states, and the level rankings may indeed be non-tight for some finite prefix of an accepting run. The value of O is inconsequential until the level ranking becomes tight; hence it is kept as $\emptyset$ during this period. Note further that the above construction gives rise to multiple initial states in general. Since an NBW with multiple initial states can be easily converted to one with a single initial state without changing its language, this does not pose any problem, and we will not dwell on this issue any further.

Theorem 2. $L(A') = \overline{L(A)}$

The proof proceeds by establishing three sub-results: (i) every accepting run of A' on word α assigns an odd ranking to the run-DAG G_α and hence corresponds to an accepting run of $\mathsf{KVF}(A)$, (ii) the run corresponding to the ranking $r_{A,\alpha}^{KV}$ is an accepting run of A' on α, and (iii) $L(\mathsf{KVF}(A)) = \overline{L(A)}$[KV01]. Details of the proof may be found in [KC09].

Given an NBW A and the complement NBW A' constructed using the above algorithm, we now ask if A' has an accepting run on some $\alpha \in \overline{L(A)}$ that induces an odd ranking r different from $r_{A,\alpha}^{KV}$. We answer this question negatively in the following lemma.

Lemma 5. *Let $\alpha \in \overline{L(A)}$, and let r be the odd ranking corresponding to an accepting run of A' on α. Let $V_{r,i}$ (respectively, $V_{r_{A,\alpha}^{KV},i}$) be the set of vertices in G_α that are assigned rank i by r (respectively, $r_{A,\alpha}^{KV}$). Then $V_{r,i} = V_{r_{A,\alpha}^{KV},i}$ for all $i > 0$.*

Proof. We prove the claim by induction on the rank i. Since A and α are clear from the context, we will use r^{KV} in place of $r_{A,\alpha}^{KV}$ in the remainder of the proof.

Base case: Let $(q, l) \in V_{r^{KV},1}$. By definition, (q, l) is F-free. Suppose $r((q, l)) = m$, where $m > 1$, if possible. If m is even, the constraints embodied in steps (2), (3) and (4(b)i) of our complementation construction, coupled with the fact that the O-set becomes $\emptyset$ infinitely often, imply that (q, l) has an F-vertex descendant (q', l') in G_α. Therefore, (q, l) is not F-free – a contradiction! Hence m cannot be even.

Suppose m is odd and > 1. The constraint embodied in step (4(b)ii) of our construction, and the fact that the O-set becomes $\emptyset$ infinitely often imply that (q, l) has a descendant (q'', l'') that is assigned an even rank by r. The constraints embodied in steps (2), (3) and (4(b)i), coupled with the fact that the O-set becomes $\emptyset$ infinitely often, further imply that (q'', l'') has an F-vertex descendant in G_α. Hence (q, l) has an F-vertex descendant, and is not F-free. This leads to a contradiction again! Therefore, our assumption must have been incorrect, i.e. $r((q, l)) \leq 1$. Since 1 is the minimum rank in the range of r, we finally have $r((q, l)) = 1$. This shows that $V_{r^{KV}, 1} \subseteq V_{r, 1}$.

Now suppose $(q, l) \in V_{r, 1}$. Since r corresponds to an accepting run of A', it is an odd-ranking. This, coupled with the fact that ranks cannot increase along any path in G_α, imply that all descendants of (q, l) in G_α are assigned rank 1 by r. Since F-vertices must be assigned even ranks, this implies that (q, l) is F-free in G_α. It follows that $r^{KV}((q, l)) = 1$. Therefore, $V_{r, 1} \subseteq V_{r^{KV}, 1}$. From the above two results, we have $V_{r, 1} = V_{r^{KV}, 1}$.

Hypothesis: Assume that $V_{r, j} = V_{r^{KV}, j}$ for $1 \leq j \leq i$.

Induction: Let $(q, l) \in V_{r^{KV}, i+1}$. Then by the induction hypothesis, (q, l) cannot be in any $V_{r, j}$ for $j \leq i$. Suppose $r((q, l)) = m$, where $m > i + 1$, if possible. We have two cases.

1. $i + 1$ is odd: In this case, the constraints embodied in steps (2), (3), (4(b)i) and (4(b)ii) of our construction, coupled with the fact that the O-set becomes $\emptyset$ infinitely often, imply that vertex (q, l) has an F-vertex descendant (q', l') (possibly its own self) such that (i) $r((q', l')) = i + 2$, and (ii) vertex (q', l') in turn has a descendant (q'', l'') such that $r((q'', l'')) = i + 1$. The constraint embodied in (2) of our construction further implies that there must be an infinite path π starting from (q'', l'') in G_α such that every vertex on π is assigned rank $i + 1$ by r, and none of these are F-vertices. Since $r^{KV}((q, l)) = i + 1$ is odd, and since (q', l') is an F-vertex descendant of (q, l), we must have $r^{KV}((q', l')) \leq i$, where i is even. Furthermore, since r^{KV} is an odd ranking, every path in G_α must eventually get trapped in an odd rank assigned by r^{KV}. Hence, eventually every vertex on π is assigned an odd rank $< i$ by $r_{A, \alpha}^{KV}$. However, we already know that the vertices on π are eventually assigned the odd rank $i + 1$ by r. Hence $V_{r, j} \neq V_{r^{KV}, j}$ for some $j \in \{1, \ldots i\}$. This contradicts the inductive hypothesis!

2. $i + 1$ is even: In this case, the constraints embodied in steps (2), (3), (4(b)i) and (4(b)ii) of our construction, and the fact that the O-set becomes $\emptyset$ infinitely often, imply that (q, l) has a descendant (q', l') in G_α such that $r((q', l')) = i + 2$ (which is odd), and there is an infinite path π starting from (q', l') such that all vertices on π are assigned rank $i + 2$ by r. However, since r^{KV} is an odd ranking and since $r^{KV}((q, l)) = i + 1$ (which is even), vertices on π must eventually get trapped in an odd rank $\leq i$ assigned by r^{KV}. This

implies that $V_{r,j} \neq V_{r^{KV},j}$ for some $j \in \{1, \ldots i\}$. This violates the inductive hypothesis once again!

It follows from the above cases that $r((q,l)) \leq i + 1$. However, $(q,l) \notin V_{r^{KV},j}$ for $1 \leq j \leq i$ (since $(q,l) \in V_{r^{KV},i+1}$), and $V_{r,j} = V_{r^{KV},j}$ for $1 \leq j \leq i$ (by inductive hypothesis). Therefore, $(q,l) \notin V_{r,j}$ for $1 \leq j \leq i$. This implies that $r((q,l)) = i + 1$, completing the induction.

By the principle of mathematical induction, we $V_{r_{A,\alpha}^{KV},i} = V_{r,i}$ for all $i > 0$. □

Theorem 3. *Every accepting run of A' on $\alpha \in \overline{L(A)}$ induces the unique minimal ranking $r_{A,\alpha}^{KV}$.*

Proof. Follows from Lemma 5.

5.1 Size of Complement Automaton

The states of A' are those in the set $\{2^Q \times 2^Q \times \mathcal{R}\}$. While some of these states correspond to tight level rankings, others do not. We first use an extension of the idea in [Sch09] to encode a state (S, O, f) with tight level ranking f as a pair (g, i), where $g : Q \rightarrow \{1, \ldots, r\} \cup \{-1, -2\}$ and $r = max\_odd(f)$. Thus, for all $q \in Q$, we have $q \notin S$ iff $g(q) = -2$. If $q \in S$ and $q \notin O$, we have $g(q) = f(q)$. If $q \in O$ and $f(q)$ is even, then we let $g(q) = -1$ and $i = f(q)$. This part of the encoding is exactly as in [Sch09]. We extend this encoding to consider cases where $q \in O$ and $f(q) = k$ is odd. There are two sub cases to consider: (i) $O \subsetneq \{q \mid q \in S \wedge f(q) = k\}$, and (ii) $O = \{q \mid q \in S \wedge f(q) = k\}$. In the first case, we let $i = k$ and $g(q) = -1$ for all $q \in O$. In the second case, we let $i = k$ and $g(q) = f(q) = k$ for all $q \in O$. Since, f is a tight level ranking, the O-set cannot be empty when we check for states with an odd rank in our construction. Therefore, there is no ambiguity in identifying the set O in both cases (i) and (ii) above. It is now easy to see that g is always onto one of the three sets $\{1, 3, \ldots, r\}$, $\{-1\} \cup \{1, 3, \ldots, r\}$ or $\{-2\} \cup \{1, 3, \ldots, r\}$. By Schewe's analysis [Sch09], the total number of such (g, i) pairs is upper bounded by $O(tight(n + 1))$.

Now, let us consider states with non-tight level rankings. Our construction ensures that once an odd rank i appears in a level ranking g along a run ρ, all subsequent level rankings along ρ contain every rank in $\{i, i+2, \ldots max\_odd(g)\}$. The O-set in states with non-tight level ranking is inconsequential; hence we ignore this. Suppose a state with non-tight level ranking g contains the odd ranks $\{i, i-2, \ldots, j\}$, where $1 < j \leq i = max\_odd(g)$. To encode this state, we first replace g with a level ranking g' as follows. For all $k \in \{j, \ldots, i\}$ and $q \in Q$, if $g(q) = k$, then $g'(q) = k - j + c$, where $c = 0$ if j is even and 1 otherwise. Effectively, this transforms g to a tight level ranking g' by shifting all ranks down by $j - c$. The original state can now be represented as the pair $(g', -(j - c))$. Note that the second component of a state represented as (g, i) is always non-negative for states with tight level ranking, and always negative for states with non-tight level ranking. Hence, there is no ambiguity in decoding the state representation. Clearly, the total no. of states with non-tight rankings is $O(n.tight(n)) = O(tight(n+1))$. Hence, the size of A' is upper bounded by $O(tight(n+1))$ which differs from the lower bound of $\Omega(tight(n-1))$ given by [Yan08] by only a factor of n^2.

6   Slices of Complement Automaton

The transitions of the complement automaton A' obtained by our construction have the property that a state (S, O, f) has a transition to (S', O', f') only if $max\_odd(f) = max\_odd(f')$. Consequently, the set of states Q' can be partitioned into *slices* $Q_1, Q_3, \ldots, Q_{2n-1}$, where the set $Q_i = \{(S, O, f) | (S, O, f) \in Q' \wedge max\_odd(f) = i\}$ is called the ith slice of A'. It is easy to see that $Q' = \bigcup_{i \in [2n-1]^{odd}} Q_i$. Let ρ be an accepting run of A' on $\alpha \in \overline{L(A)}$. We say that ρ is *confined* to a slice Q_i of A' iff ρ sees only states from Q_i. If ρ is confined to slice i, and if r is the odd ranking induced by ρ, then $max\_odd(r) = i$.

Lemma 6. *All accepting runs of A' on $\alpha \in \overline{L(A)}$ are confined to the same slice.*

Proof. Follows from Theorem 3.   □

The above results indicate that if a word α is accepted by the ith slice of our automaton A', then it cannot be accepted by $\mathsf{KVF}(A)$ using a tight ranking with max odd rank $< i$. It is however possible that the same word is accepted by $\mathsf{KVF}(A)$ using a tight ranking with max odd rank $> i$. Figure 1 shows an example of such an automaton, where the word a^ω is accepted by $\mathsf{KVF}(A)$ using a tight ranking with max odd rank 5, as well as with a tight ranking with max odd rank 3. The same word is accepted by only the 3rd slice of our automaton A'. This motivates the definition of *minimally inessential ranks*. Given an NBW A with n states, odd rank i ($1 \leq i \leq 2n-1$) is said to be minimally inessential if every word α that is accepted by $\mathsf{KVF}(A)$ using a tight ranking with max odd rank i is also accepted by $\mathsf{KVF}(A)$ using a tight ranking with max odd rank $j < i$. An odd rank that is not minimally inessential is called minimally essential. As the example in Figure 1 shows, neither the KVF-construction nor the KVFS-construction allows us to detect minimally essential ranks in a straightforward way. Specifically, although the 5th slice of $\mathsf{KVF}(A)$ for this example accepts the word a^ω, 5 is not a minimally inessential rank. In order to determine if 5 is minimally inessential, we must isolate the 5th slice of $\mathsf{KVF}(A)$, and then check whether the language accepted by this slice is a subset of the language accepted by $\mathsf{KVF}(A)$ sans the 5th slice. This involves complementing $\mathsf{KVF}(A)$ sans the 5th slice, requiring a significant blowup. In contrast, the properties of our automaton A' allow us to detect minimally (in)essential ranks efficiently. Specifically, if we find that the ith slice of A' accepts a word α, we can infer than i is minimally essential. Once all minimally essential ranks have been identified in this manner, we can prune automaton A' to retain only those slices that correspond to minimally essential ranks. This gives us a way of eliminating redundant slices (and hence states) in $\mathsf{KVF}(A)$.

7 An Implementation of Our Algorithm

We have implemented the complementation algorithm presented in this paper as a facility on top of the BDD-based model checker NuSMV. In our implementation, states of the complement automaton are encoded as pairs (g, i), as

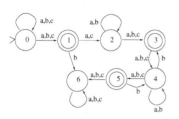

Fig. 2. Example automaton with gaps

explained in Section 5.1. Our tool takes as input an NBW A, and generates the state transition relation of the complement automaton A' using the above encoding in NuSMV's input format. Generating the NuSMV file from a given description of NBW takes negligible time (< 0.01s). The number of boolean constraints used in expressing the transition relation in NuSMV is quadratic in n. We use NuSMV's fair CTL model checking capability to check whether there exists an infinite path in a slice of A' (corresponding to a maximum odd rank k) that visits an accepting state infinitely often. If NuSMV responds negatively to such a query, we disable all transitions to and from states in this section of the NuSMV model. This allows us to effectively detect and eliminate redundant slices of our complement automaton, resulting in a reduction of the overall size of the automaton. For purposes of comparison, we have also implemented the algorithm presented in [Sch09] in a similar manner using a translation to NuSMV. We also compared the performance of our technique with those of Safra-Piterman [Saf88, Pit07] determinization based complementation technique and Kupferman-Vardi's ranking based complementation technique [KV01], as implemented in the GOAL tool [TCT$^+$08]. Table 1 shows the results of some of our experiments. We used the CUDD BDD library with NuSMV 2.4.3, and all our experiments were run

Table 1. Experimental Results. XX:timeout. (after 10 min)

Automaton (states,trans.,final)	KVFS algorithm States	MI Ranks	Our algorithm States	MI Ranks	GOAL WAA	SP
michel4 (6,15,1)	157	$\{9,7\}$	117	$\{9,7\}$	XX	105
g15 (6,17,1)	324	$\{9,7,5\}$	155	$\{9,7,5\}$	XX	39
g47 (6,13,3)	41	$\{5\}$	29	$\{5,3\}$	XX	28
ex4 (8,9,4)	3956	$\emptyset$	39	$\{7,5\}$	XX	7
ex16 (9,13,5)	10302	$\emptyset$	909	$\{7\}$	XX	30
ex18 (9,13,5)	63605	$\emptyset$	2886	$\emptyset$	XX	71
ex20 (9,12,5)	17405	$\emptyset$	156	$\{7\}$	XX	24
ex22 (11,18,7)	258	$\{7,5\}$	23	$\{7,5\}$	XX	6
ex24 (13,16,8)	4141300	$\emptyset$	19902	$\{9,7\}$	XX	51
ex26 (15,22,11)	1042840	$\emptyset$	57540	$\{7,5\}$	XX	XX
gap1 (15,22,11)	99	$\{5,1\}$	26	$\{5,1\}$	XX	16
gap2 (15,22,11)	532	$\{1\}$	80	$\{5,1\}$	XX	48

on an Intel Xeon 3GHz with 2 GB of memory and a timeout of 10 minutes. The entry for each automaton[1] lists the number of states, transitions and final states of the original automaton, the number of states of the complement automaton computed by the KVFS-construction and by our construction, and the set of minimally inessential ranks (denoted as "MI Ranks") identified by each of these techniques. In addition, each row also lists the number of states computed by the "Safra-Piterman" (denoted as "SP") technique and "Weak Alternating Automata" (denoted as "WAA") technique in GOAL.

A significant advantage of our construction is its ability to detect "gaps" in slices. As an example, the automaton in Figure (2) has ranks $1, 5$ as minimally inessential, while ranks 3 and 7 are minimally essential (see Table (1)). In this case, if we compute the *rank* of the NBW (as suggested in [GKSV03]) and then consider slices only upto this *rank*, we will fail to detect that rank 5 is minimally inessential. Therefore, eliminating redundant slices is a stronger optimization than identifying and eliminating states with ranks greater than the rank of the NBW.

8   Conclusion

In this paper, we presented a complementation algorithm for nondeterministic Büchi automata that is based on the idea of ranking functions introduced by Kupferman and Vardi[KV01]. We showed that the ranking assignment presented in [KV01] always results in a minimal odd ranking for run-DAGs of words in the complement language. We then described a complementation construction for NBW such that the complement NBW accepts only the run-DAG with the minimal odd ranking for every word in the complement. We observed that the states of the complement NBW are partioned into *slices*, and that each word in the complement is accepted by exactly one such slice. This allowed us to check for redundant slices and eliminate them, leading to a reduction the size of the complement NBW. It is noteworthy that this ability to reduce the size of the final complement NBW comes for free since the worst case bounds coincide with the worst case bounds of the best known NBW complementation construction. In the future, we wish to explore techniques to construct unambiguous automata and deterministic Rabin automata from NBW, building on the results presented here.

References

[Büc62]   Büchi, J.R.: On a decision method in restricted second order arithmetic. In: Proc. 1960 Int. Congr. for Logic, Methodology and Philosophy of Science, pp. 1–11. Stanford Univ. Press, Stanford (1962)

[DR09]   Doyen, L., Raskin, J.-F.: Antichains for the automata based approach to model checking. Logical Methods in Computer Science 5, 1–20 (2009)

---

[1] All example automata from this paper and the translator from automaton description to NuSMV are available at http://www.cfdvs.iitb.ac.in/reports/minrank

[FKV06]   Friedgut, E., Kupferman, O., Vardi, M.Y.: Büchi complementation made tighter. Int. J. Found. Comput. Sci. 17(4), 851–868 (2006)

[FV09]   Fogarty, S., Vardi., M.Y.: Büchi complementation and size-change termination. In: Proc. TACAS, pp. 16–30 (2009)

[GKSV03] Gurumurthy, S., Kupferman, O., Somenzi, F., Vardi, M.Y.: On complementing nondeterministic büchi automata. In: Geist, D., Tronci, E. (eds.) CHARME 2003. LNCS, vol. 2860, pp. 96–110. Springer, Heidelberg (2003)

[KC09]   Karmarkar, H., Chakraborty, S.: On minimal odd rankings for Büchi complementation (May 2009),
          http://www.cfdvs.iitb.ac.in/reports/index.php

[Kla91]   Klarlund, N.: Progress measures for complementation of ω-automata with applications to temporal logic. In: Proc. 32nd IEEE FOCS, San Juan, pp. 358–367 (1991)

[KV01]   Kupferman, O., Vardi, M.Y.: Weak alternating automata are not that weak. ACM Transactions on Computational Logic 2(3), 408–429 (2001)

[KW08]   Kähler, D., Wilke, T.: Complementation, disambiguation, and determinization of Büchi automata unified. In: Aceto, L., Damgård, I., Goldberg, L.A., Halldórsson, M.M., Ingólfsdóttir, A., Walukiewicz, I. (eds.) ICALP 2008, Part I. LNCS, vol. 5125, pp. 724–735. Springer, Heidelberg (2008)

[Löd99]   Löding, C.: Optimal bounds for transformations of ω-automata. In: Pandu Rangan, C., Raman, V., Sarukkai, S. (eds.) FST TCS 1999. LNCS, vol. 1738, pp. 97–109. Springer, Heidelberg (1999)

[Mic88]   Michel, M.: Complementation is more difficult with automata on infinite words. In: CNET, Paris (1988)

[Pit07]   Piterman, N.: From nondeterministic Büchi and Streett automata to deterministic Parity automata. Logical Methods in Computer Science 3(3:5), 1–217 (2007)

[Saf88]   Safra, S.: On the complexity of ω-automata. In: Proc. 29th IEEE FOCS, pp. 319–327 (1988)

[Sch09]   Schewe, S.: Büchi complementation made tight. In: Proc. STACS, pp. 661–672 (2009)

[SVW87]   Prasad Sistla, A., Vardi, M.Y., Wolper, P.: The complementation problem for Büchi automata with applications to temporal logic. Theoretical Computer Science 49, 217–237 (1987)

[TCT$^+$08] Tsay, Y.-K., Chen, Y.-F., Tsai, M.-H., Chan, W.-C., Luo, C.-J.: Goal extended: Towards a research tool for omega automata and temporal logic. In: Ramakrishnan, C.R., Rehof, J. (eds.) TACAS 2008. LNCS, vol. 4963, pp. 346–350. Springer, Heidelberg (2008)

[Var07]   Vardi, M.Y.: The Büchi complementation saga. In: Thomas, W., Weil, P. (eds.) STACS 2007. LNCS, vol. 4393, pp. 12–22. Springer, Heidelberg (2007)

[Yan08]   Yan, Q.: Lower bounds for complementation of omega-automata via the full automata technique. Logical Methods in Computer Science 4(1), 1–20 (2008)

Specification Languages for Stutter-Invariant Regular Properties⋆

Christian Dax[1], Felix Klaedtke[1], and Stefan Leue[2]

[1] ETH Zurich, Switzerland
[2] University of Konstanz, Germany

Abstract. We present specification languages that naturally capture exactly the regular and ω-regular properties that are stutter invariant. Our specification languages are variants of the classical regular expressions and of the core of PSL, a temporal logic, which is widely used in industry and which extends the classical linear-time temporal logic LTL by semi-extended regular expressions.

1 Introduction

Stutter-invariant specifications do not distinguish between system behaviors that differ from each other only by the number of consecutive repetitions of the observed system states. Stutter invariance is crucial for refining specifications and for modular reasoning [13]. Apart from these conceptual reasons for restricting oneself to stutter-invariant specifications, there is also a more practical motivation: stuttering invariance is an essential requirement for using partial-order reduction techniques (see, e.g., [2,11,15,16,20]) in finite-state model checking.

Unfortunately, checking whether an LTL formula or an automaton describes a stutter-invariant property is PSPACE-complete [18]. To leverage partial-order reduction techniques in finite-state model checking even when it is unknown whether the given property is stutter-invariant, Holzmann and Kupferman [12] suggested to use a stutter-invariant overapproximation of the given property. However, if the given property is not stutter-invariant, we might obtain counterexamples that are false positives. Moreover, the overapproximation of the property blows up the specification and decelerates the model-checking process.

Another approach for avoiding the expensive check whether a given property is stutter-invariant, is to use specification languages that only allow one to specify stutter-invariant properties. For instance, LTL without the next operator X, LTL_{-X} for short, captures exactly the stutter-invariant star-free properties [10, 17]. An advantage of such a syntactic characterization is that it yields a sufficient and easily checkable condition whether partial-order reduction techniques are applicable. However, LTL_{-X} is limited in its expressive power.

Independently, Etessami [9] and Rabinovich [19] gave similar syntactic characterizations of the stutter-invariant ω-regular properties. However, these characterizations are not satisfactory from a practical point of view. Both extend

---

⋆ Partly supported by the Swiss National Science Foundation.

Z. Liu and A.P. Ravn (Eds.): ATVA 2009, LNCS 5799, pp. 244–254, 2009.

fragments of LTL$_{-X}$ by allowing one to existentially quantify over propositions. To preserve stutter invariance the quantification is semantically restricted. Due to this restriction, the meaning of quantifying over propositions becomes unintuitive and expressing properties in the proposed temporal logics becomes difficult. Note that even the extension of LTL with the standard quantification over propositions is considered as difficult to use in practice [21]. Another practical drawback of the temporal logic in [19] is that the finite-state model-checking problem has a non-elementary worst-case complexity. The finite-state model-checking problem with the temporal logic in [9] remains in PSPACE, as for LTL. This upper bound on the complexity of the model-checking problem is achieved by additionally restricting syntactically the use of the non-standard quantification over propositions. The downside of this restriction is that the logic is not syntactically closed under negation anymore, which can make it more difficult or even impossible to express properties naturally and concisely in it. Expressing the complement of a property might lead to an exponential blow-up.

In this paper, we give another syntactic characterization in terms of a temporal logic of the ω-regular properties that are stutter invariant. Our characterization overcomes the limitations of the temporal logics from [9] and [19]. Namely, it is syntactically closed under negation, it is easy to use, and the finite-state model-checking problem with it is solvable in practice. Furthermore, we also present a syntactic characterization of the stutter-invariant regular properties. Our characterizations are given as variants of the classical regular expressions and the linear-time core of the industrial-strength temporal logic PSL [1], which extends LTL with semi-extended regular expressions (SEREs). We name our variants siSEREs and siPSL, respectively. Similar to PSL, siPSL extends LTL$_{-X}$ with siSEREs. For siSEREs, the use of the concatenation operator and the Kleene star is syntactically restricted. Moreover, siSEREs make use of a novel iteration operator, which is a variant of the Kleene star.

2   Preliminaries

Words. For an alphabet Σ, we denote the set of finite and infinite words by Σ^* and Σ^ω, respectively. Furthermore, we write $\Sigma^\infty := \Sigma^* \cup \Sigma^\omega$ and $\Sigma^+ := \Sigma^* \setminus \{\varepsilon\}$, where ε denotes the empty word. The concatenation of words is written as juxtaposition. The *concatenation* of the languages $K \subseteq \Sigma^*$ and $L \subseteq \Sigma^\infty$ is $K \, ; L := \{uv \, : \, u \in K \text{ and } v \in L\}$, and the *fusion* of K and L is $K : L := \{ubv \in \Sigma^\infty \, : \, b \in \Sigma, \; ub \in K, \text{ and } bv \in L\}$. Furthermore, for $L \subseteq \Sigma^*$, we define $L^* := \bigcup_{n \geq 0} L^n$ and $L^+ := \bigcup_{n \geq 1} L^n$ with $L^0 := \{\varepsilon\}$ and $L^{i+1} := L \, ; L^i$, for $i \in \mathbb{N}$. We write $|w|$ for the length of $w \in \Sigma^\infty$ and we denote the $(i+1)$st letter of w by $w(i)$, where we assume that $i < |w|$. For a word $w \in \Sigma^\omega$ and $i \geq 0$, we define $w^{\geq i} := w(i)w(i+1)\ldots$ and $w^{\leq i} := w(0)\ldots w(i)$.

Stutter-Invariant Languages. Let us recall the definition of stutter invariance from [18]. The *stutter-removal operator* $\sharp : \Sigma^\infty \to \Sigma^\infty$ maps a word $v \in \Sigma^\infty$ to the word that is obtained from v by replacing every maximal finite substring of identical letters by a single copy of the letter. For instance, $\sharp(aabbbccc) = abc$,

$\sharp(aab(bbc)^\omega) = a(bc)^\omega$, and $\sharp(aabbbccc^\omega) = abc^\omega$. A language $L \subseteq \Sigma^\infty$ is *stutter-invariant* if $u \in L \Leftrightarrow v \in L$, for all $u, v \in \Sigma^\infty$ with $\sharp(u) = \sharp(v)$. A word $w \in \Sigma^\infty$ is *stutter free* if $w = \sharp(w)$. For $L \subseteq \Sigma^\infty$, we define $L_\sharp := \{\sharp(w) : w \in L\}$.

Propositional Logic. For a set of propositions P, we denote the set of *Boolean formulas* over P by $\mathcal{B}(P)$, i.e., $\mathcal{B}(P)$ consists of the formulas that are inductively built from the propositions in P and the connectives $\wedge$ and $\neg$. For $M \subseteq P$ and $b \in \mathcal{B}(P)$, we write $M \models b$ iff b evaluates to true when assigning true to the propositions in M and false to the propositions in $P \setminus M$.

Semi-extended Regular Expressions. The syntax of *semi-extended regular expressions* (SEREs) over the proposition set P is defined by the grammar

$$r ::= \varepsilon \mid b \mid r^* \mid r\,;r \mid r:r \mid r \cup r \mid r \cap r,$$

where $b \in \mathcal{B}(P)$. We point out that in addition to the concatentation operator ;, SEREs have the operator : for expressing the fusion of two languages. The language of an SERE over P is inductively defined:

$$L(r) := \begin{cases} \{\varepsilon\} & \text{if } r = \varepsilon, \\ \{b \in 2^P : b \models r\} & \text{if } r \in \mathcal{B}(P), \\ L(s) \star L(t) & \text{if } r = s \star t, \\ (L(s))^* & \text{if } r = s^*, \end{cases}$$

where $\star \in \{;,:,\cup,\cap\}$. The *size* of an SERE is its syntactic length, i.e., $\|\varepsilon\| := 1$, $\|b\| := 1$, for $b \in \mathcal{B}(P)$, $\|r\star s\| := 1 + \|r\| + \|s\|$, for $\star \in \{\cup,\cap,;,:\}$, and $\|r^*\| := 1 + \|r\|$.

Propositional Temporal Logic. The core of the linear-time fragment of PSL [1] is as follows. Its syntax over the set P of propositions is given by the grammar

$$\varphi ::= p \mid \mathsf{cl}(r) \mid \neg\varphi \mid \varphi \wedge \varphi \mid \mathsf{X}\varphi \mid \varphi \,\mathsf{U}\, \varphi \mid r \diamond\!\!\rightarrow \varphi,$$

where $p \in P$ and r is an SERE over P. A PSL formula[1] over P is interpreted over an infinite word $w \in (2^P)^\omega$ as follows:

$w \models p$ iff $p \in w(0)$
$w \models \mathsf{cl}(r)$ iff $\exists k \geq 0: w^{\leq k} \in L(r)$ or $\forall k \geq 0: \exists v \in L(r): w^{\leq k}$ is a prefix of v
$w \models \varphi \wedge \psi$ iff $w \models \varphi$ and $w \models \psi$
$w \models \neg\varphi$ iff $w \not\models \varphi$
$w \models \mathsf{X}\varphi$ iff $w^{\geq 1} \models \varphi$
$w \models \varphi \,\mathsf{U}\, \psi$ iff $\exists k \geq 0: w^{\leq k} \models \psi$ and $\forall j < k: w^{\geq j} \models \varphi$
$w \models r \diamond\!\!\rightarrow \varphi$ iff $\exists k \geq 0: w^{\leq k} \in L(r)$ and $w^{\geq k} \models \varphi$

The *language* of a PSL formula φ is $L(\varphi) := \{w \in (2^P)^\omega : w \models \varphi\}$. As for SEREs, we define the *size* of a PSL formula as its syntactic length. That means, $\|p\| := 1$, $\|\mathsf{cl}(r)\| := 1 + \|r\|$, $\|\neg\varphi\| := \|\mathsf{X}\varphi\| := 1 + \|\varphi\|$, $\|\varphi \wedge \psi\| := \|\varphi \,\mathsf{U}\, \psi\| := 1 + \|\varphi\| + \|\psi\|$, and $\|r \diamond\!\!\rightarrow \varphi\| := 1 + \|r\| + \|\varphi\|$.

---

[1] For the ease of exposition, we identify PSL with its linear-time core.

Syntactic Sugar. We use the standard conventions to omit parenthesis, e.g., temporal operators bind stronger than Boolean connectives and the binary operators of the SEREs are left associative. We also use standard syntactic sugar for the Boolean values, the Boolean connectives, and the linear-time temporal operators: $\mathsf{ff} := p \wedge \neg p$, for some proposition $p \in P$, $\mathsf{tt} := \neg\mathsf{ff}$, $\varphi \vee \psi := \neg(\neg\varphi \wedge \neg\psi)$, $\varphi \to \psi := \neg\varphi \vee \psi$, $\mathsf{F}\varphi := \mathsf{tt}\,\mathsf{U}\,\varphi$, $\mathsf{G}\varphi := \neg\mathsf{F}\neg\varphi$, and $\varphi\,\mathsf{W}\,\psi := (\varphi\,\mathsf{U}\,\psi) \vee \mathsf{G}\varphi$, where φ and ψ are formulas. Moreover, $r \mathrel{\square\!\!\rightarrow} \varphi$ abbreviates $\neg(r \mathrel{\diamondsuit\!\!\rightarrow} \neg\varphi)$.

3   Stutter-Invariant Regular Properties

In this section, we present syntactic characterizations for stutter-invariant regular and ω-regular languages. In Section 3.1, we define a variant of SEREs that can describe only stutter-invariant languages. Furthermore, we show that this variant of SEREs is complete in the sense that any stutter-invariant regular language can be described by such an expression. Similarly, in Section 3.2, we present a variant of PSL for expressing stutter-invariant ω-regular languages. In Section 3.3, we give examples that illustrate the use of our stutter-invariant variant of PSL.

3.1   Stutter-Invariant SEREs

It is straightforward to see that stutter-invariant languages are not closed under the concatenation and the Kleene star. A perhaps surprising example is the SERE $p^+ \,;\, q^+$ over the proposition set $\{p, q\}$, which does not describe a stutter-invariant language, although $L(p^+)$ and $L(q^+)$ are stutter-invariant languages.[2] In our variant of SEREs, we restrict the use of concatenation and replace the Kleene star by an iteration operator, which uses the fusion instead of the concatenation for gluing words together. Namely, for a language L of finite words, we define $L^\oplus := \bigcup_{n \in \mathbb{N}} L_n$, where $L_0 := L$ and $L_{i+1} := L_i : L$, for $i \in \mathbb{N}$.

The following lemma summarizes some closure properties of the class of stutter-invariant languages.

Lemma 1. *Let $K \subseteq \Sigma^*$ and $L, L' \subseteq \Sigma^\infty$ be stutter-invariant languages. The languages $L \cap L'$, $L \cup L'$, $K : L$, and $K^\oplus$ are stutter-invariant. Furthermore, $\Sigma^* \setminus K$, $\Sigma^\omega \setminus L$, and $\Sigma^\infty \setminus L$ are stutter-invariant.*

Proof. We only show that the language $K : L$ is stutter-invariant. The other closure properties are similarly proved. Assume that $u \in K : L$ and $\sharp(u) = \sharp(v)$ for $u, v \in \Sigma^\infty$. Let $u = u'bu''$, for some $u' \in \Sigma^*$, $u'' \in \Sigma^\infty$, and $b \in \Sigma$ with $u'b \in K$ and $bu'' \in L$. Since K is stutter-invariant, we can assume without loss of generality that if u' is nonempty then $u'(|u'|-1) \neq b$. Since $\sharp(u) = \sharp(v)$, there are $v' \in \Sigma^*$ and $v'' \in \Sigma^\infty$ such that $v = v'bv''$, $\sharp(v') = \sharp(u')$, and $\sharp(bv'') = \sharp(bu'')$. From the stutter invariance of K and L, it follows that $v \in K : L$. $\square$

Our variant of SEREs is defined as follows.

---

[2] Note that the word $\{p,q\}\,\{p,q\}$ belongs to $L(p^+ \,;\, q^+)$ but the word $\{p,q\}$ does not.

Definition 1. *The syntax of* siSEREs *over the proposition set P is given by the grammar*

$$r ::= \varepsilon \mid b^+ \mid b^* ; r \mid r ; b^* \mid r : r \mid r \cup r \mid r \cap r \mid r^\oplus ,$$

where b ranges over the Boolean formulas in $\mathcal{B}(P)$. The language $L(r)$ of an siSERE r is defined as expected.

By an induction over the structure of siSEREs, which uses the closure properties from Lemma 1, we easily obtain the following theorem.

Theorem 1. *The language of every siSERE is stutter-invariant.*

In the remainder of this subsection, we show that any regular language that is stutter-invariant can be described by an siSERE. We prove this result by defining a function κ that maps SEREs to siSEREs. We show that it preserves the language if the given SERE describes a stutter-invariant language. The function κ is defined recursively over the structure of SEREs:

$$\kappa(\varepsilon) := \varepsilon$$
$$\kappa(b) := b^+$$
$$\kappa(s \cup t) := \kappa(s) \cup \kappa(t)$$
$$\kappa(s \cap t) := \kappa(s) \cap \kappa(t)$$
$$\kappa(s : t) := \kappa(s) : \kappa(t)$$
$$\kappa(s ; t) := \left(\kappa(s) : \bigcup_{a \in 2^P} \left(\hat{a}^+ : (\hat{a}^* ; \kappa(t)) \right) \right) \cup \begin{cases} \kappa(t) & \text{if } \varepsilon \in L(s) \\ \text{ff} & \text{otherwise} \end{cases}$$
$$\kappa(s^*) := \varepsilon \cup \kappa(s) \cup \left(\kappa(s) : \left(\bigcup_{a \in 2^P} \left(\hat{a}^+ : (\hat{a}^* ; \kappa(s)) \right) \right)^\oplus \right) ,$$

where $b \in \mathcal{B}(P)$, s, t are SEREs, and $\hat{a} := \bigwedge_{p \in a} p \wedge \bigwedge_{p \notin a} \neg p$, for $a \in 2^P$.

Lemma 2. *For every SERE r, the equality $L_\sharp(r) = L_\sharp(\kappa(r))$ holds.*

Proof. We show the lemma by induction over the structure of the SERE r. The base cases where r is ε or b with $b \in \mathcal{B}(P)$ are obvious. The step cases where r is of one of the forms $s \cup t$, $s \cap t$, or $s : t$ follow straightforwardly from the induction hypothesis.

Next, we prove the step case where r is of the form $s ; t$. For showing $L_\sharp(r) \subseteq L_\sharp(\kappa(r))$, assume that $u \in L_\sharp(r)$. There are words $x \in L(s)$ and $y \in L(t)$ such that $u = \sharp(xy)$. By induction hypothesis, we have that $\sharp(x) \in L_\sharp(\kappa(s))$ and $\sharp(y) \in L_\sharp(\kappa(t))$. The case where x the empty word is obvious. Assume that $x \neq \varepsilon$ and $a \in 2^P$ is the last letter of x. We have that $\sharp(xy) \in L_\sharp\big((\kappa(s) : \hat{a}) ; \kappa(t)\big)$ and

$$L_\sharp\big((\kappa(s) : \hat{a}) ; \kappa(t)\big) \subseteq L_\sharp\big((\kappa(s) : (\hat{a} ; \kappa(t)))\big) \subseteq L_\sharp\big(\kappa(s) : ((\hat{a} : \hat{a}) ; \kappa(t))\big)$$
$$\subseteq L_\sharp\big(\kappa(s) : (\hat{a}^+ : (\hat{a}^* ; \kappa(t)))\big) .$$

For showing $L_\sharp(r) \supseteq L_\sharp(\kappa(r))$, assume that $u \in L_\sharp(\kappa(r))$. We make a case split.

1. If $\varepsilon \in L(s)$ and $u \in L_\sharp(\kappa(t))$ then $u \in L_\sharp(t)$ by induction hypothesis. We conclude that $u \in L_\sharp(\varepsilon \, ; t) \subseteq L_\sharp(s \, ; t) = L_\sharp(r)$.
2. Assume that $u \in L_\sharp(\kappa(s) : \bigcup_{a \in 2^P} (\hat{a}^+ : (\hat{a}^* ; \kappa(t))))$. There is a letter $a \in 2^P$ such that $u \in L_\sharp(\kappa(s) : (\hat{a}^+ : (\hat{a}^* ; \kappa(t)))) = L_\sharp(\kappa(s) : (\hat{a} ; \kappa(t)))$. It follows that there are words x and y such that $u = xay$, $xa \in L_\sharp(\kappa(s))$, and $ay \in L_\sharp(\hat{a} ; \kappa(t))$. We have that either $ay \in L_\sharp(\kappa(t))$ or $y \in L_\sharp(\kappa(t))$. By induction hypothesis, we have that $xa \in L_\sharp(s)$ and either $ay \in L_\sharp(t)$ or $y \in L_\sharp(t)$. It follows that $u \in L_\sharp(r)$.

Finally, we prove the step case where r is of the form s^*. We first show $L_\sharp(r) \subseteq L_\sharp(\kappa(r))$. Assume that $u \in L_\sharp(s^*)$. If u is the empty word or $u \in L_\sharp(s)$ then there is nothing to prove. Assume that u is of the form $u_1 u_2 \ldots u_n$ with $u_i \in L_\sharp(s)$ and $u_i \neq \varepsilon$, for all $1 \leq i \leq n$. By induction hypothesis, we have that $u_i \in L_\sharp(\kappa(s))$. Let a_i be the last letter of u_i, for each $1 \leq i < n$, respectively. We have that $\sharp(a_{i-1} u_i) \in L_\sharp(\hat{a}_{i-1}^+ : (\hat{a}_{i-1}^* ; \kappa(s)))$, for all $1 < i \leq n$. It follows that $\sharp(u_1 a_1 u_2 \ldots a_{n-1} a_n) \in L(\kappa(s)) : L_\sharp(\hat{a}_1^+ : (\hat{a}_2^* ; \kappa(s))) : \ldots : L_\sharp(\hat{a}_{n-1}^+ : (\hat{a}_n^* ; \kappa(s)))$. Since $\sharp(u) = \sharp(u_1 a_1 u_2 \ldots a_{n-1} a_n)$, we conclude that $\sharp(u) \in L_\sharp(\kappa(r))$.

For showing $L_\sharp(r) \supseteq L_\sharp(\kappa(r))$, we assume that $u \in L_\sharp(\kappa(r))$. The cases $u = \varepsilon$ and $u \in L_\sharp(\kappa(s))$ are obvious. So, we assume that $u \in L_\sharp\big(\kappa(s) : \big(\bigcup_{a \in 2^P}(\hat{a}^+ : (\hat{a}^* ; \kappa(s)))\big)^\oplus\big) = L_\sharp\big(\kappa(s) : \big(\bigcup_{a \in 2^P}(\hat{a} ; \kappa(s))\big)^\oplus\big) = L_\sharp\big(s : \big(\bigcup_{a \in 2^P}(\hat{a} ; s)\big)^\oplus\big)$, where the last equality holds by induction hypothesis. There is an integer $n \geq 2$ and words $u_1, u_2, \ldots, u_n \in L(s)$ and letters $a_1, a_2, \ldots, a_{n-1} \in 2^P$ such that $u = \sharp(u_1 a_1 u_2 \ldots a_{n-1} u_n)$ and $\sharp(u_i) = \sharp(u_i a_i)$, for all $1 \leq i < n$. It follows that $u = \sharp(u_1 u_2 \ldots u_n) \in L_\sharp(s^*)$. □

A consequence of Lemma 2 is that the translated siSERE describes the minimal stutter-invariant language that overapproximates the language of the given SERE.

Lemma 3. *For every SERE r, $L(r) \subseteq L(\kappa(r))$ and if K is a stutter-invariant language with $L(r) \subseteq K$ then $L(\kappa(r)) \subseteq K$.*

Proof. Let K be a stutter-invariant language with $L(r) \subseteq K$ and let $w \in L(\kappa(r))$. We have to show that $w \in K$. Since $L(\kappa(r))$ is stutter-invariant, we have that $\sharp(w) \in L(\kappa(r))$. With Lemma 2, we conclude that $\sharp(w) \in L_\sharp(r)$. It follows that there is a word $u \in L(r)$ with $\sharp(u) = \sharp(w)$. Since $K \supseteq L(r)$, we have that $\sharp(w) \in K$ and thus, $w \in K$ since K is stutter-invariant.

It remains to be proven that $L(r) \subseteq L(\kappa(r))$. For $w \in L(r)$, we have that $\sharp(w) \in L_\sharp(r)$. By Lemma 2, we have that $\sharp(w) \in L_\sharp(\kappa(r))$. Since $L(\kappa(r))$ is stutter-invariant, we conclude that $w \in L(\kappa(r))$. □

From Lemma 3 we immediately obtain the following theorem.

Theorem 2. *For every stutter-invariant regular language L, there is an siSERE r such that $L(r) = L$.*

Note that the intersection and the fusion operation is not needed for SEREs to describe the class of regular languages. However, they are convenient for expressing regular languages naturally and concisely. It follows immediately from the definition of the function κ that siSEREs even without the intersection operation exactly capture the class of stutter-invariant regular languages. However, in contrast to the intersection operator, the fusion operator is essential for describing this class of languages with siSEREs.

Finally, we remark that when translating an SERE of the form $r \, ; \, s$ or s^*, we obtain an siSERE that contains a disjunction of all the letters in 2^P that contains $2^{|P|}$ copies of $\kappa(s)$. We conclude that in the worst case, the size of the siSERE $\kappa(r)$ for a given SERE r is exponential in $\|r\|$. It remains open whether for every SERE that describes a stutter-invariant regular language, there is a language-equivalent siSERE of polynomial size.

3.2   Stutter-Invariant PSL

Similar to the previous subsection, we define a variant of the core of PSL and show that this temporal logic describes exactly the class of stutter-invariant ω-regular languages.

Definition 2. *The syntax of* siPSL *formulas is similar to that of PSL formulas except that the formulas do not contain the temporal operator* X *and instead of SEREs they contain siSEREs. The semantics is defined as expected.*

By a straightforward induction over the structure of siPSL formulas and by using the closure properties from Lemma 1, we obtain the following theorem. Note that $L(r \Diamond\!\!\!\rightarrow \varphi) = L(r) \colon L(\varphi)$. Furthermore, it is easy to see that the language $L(\mathsf{cl}(r))$ is stutter-invariant if r is an SERE or siSERE that describes a stutter-invariant language.

Theorem 3. *The language of every siPSL formula is stutter-invariant.*

In the following, we show that every stutter-invariant ω-regular language can be described by an siPSL formula. We do this by extending the translations in [17] for eliminating the temporal operator X in LTL formulas to PSL formulas. We define the function τ that translates PSL formulas into siPSL formulas as follows. It is defined recursively over the formula structure and it uses the function κ from Section 3.1 for translating SEREs into siSEREs.

$$\tau(p) := p$$
$$\tau(\mathsf{cl}(r)) := \mathsf{cl}(\kappa(r))$$
$$\tau(\neg\varphi) := \neg\tau(\varphi)$$
$$\tau(\varphi \wedge \psi) := \tau(\varphi) \wedge \tau(\psi)$$
$$\tau(\varphi \, \mathsf{U} \, \psi) := \tau(\varphi) \, \mathsf{U} \, \tau(\psi)$$
$$\tau(r \Diamond\!\!\!\rightarrow \varphi) := \kappa(r) \Diamond\!\!\!\rightarrow \tau(\varphi)$$
$$\tau(\mathsf{X}\varphi) := \bigvee_{a \in 2^P} \left((\mathsf{G}\hat{a} \wedge \tau(\varphi)) \vee \bigvee_{b \in 2^P \setminus \{a\}} \left(\hat{a} \, \mathsf{U} \, (\hat{b} \wedge \tau(\varphi)) \right) \right)$$

The intuition of the elimination of the outermost operator X in a formula $\mathsf{X}\varphi$ is as follows: "the first time after now that some new event happens, φ must hold, or else, if nothing new ever happens, φ must hold right now."

Note that the size of the resulting siPSL formula is in the worst case exponential in the size of the given PSL formula. The sources of the blow-up are (1) the translation of the SEREs in the given PSL formula into siSEREs and (2) the elimination of the temporal operator X. We can improve the translation τ with respect to the size of the resulting formula by using the translation defined in [10] for eliminating the operator X in LTL formulas that describe stutter-invariant languages. The translation in [10] avoids the conjunctions over the letters in 2^P. Instead the conjunctions only range over the propositions in P. The elimination of an operator X is not exponential in $|P|$ anymore. However, the resulting translation for PSL into siPSL is still exponential in the worst case because of (1). The question whether the exponential blow-up can be avoided remains open.

The following lemma for τ is the analog of Lemma 2 for the function κ.

Lemma 4. *For every PSL formula* φ, *the equality* $L_\sharp(\varphi) = L_\sharp(\tau(\varphi))$ *holds.*

Similar to Lemma 3 for SEREs, we obtain that the function τ translates PSL formulas into siPSL formulas that minimally overapproximate the described languages with respect to stutter invariance.

Lemma 5. *For every PSL formula* φ, $L(\varphi) \subseteq L(\tau(\varphi))$ *and if* L *is a stutter-invariant language with* $L(\varphi) \subseteq L$ *then* $L(\tau(\varphi)) \subseteq L$.

From Lemma 5 we immediately obtain the following theorem.

Theorem 4. *For every stutter-invariant* ω-*regular language* L, *there is an siPSL formula* φ *such that* $L(\varphi) = L$.

We remark that the finite-state model-checking problem for PSL and siPSL fall into the same complexity classes. Namely, the finite-state model-checking problem for siPSL is EXPSPACE-complete and the problem becomes PSPACE-complete when the number of intersection operators in the given siPSL formulas is bounded. These complexity bounds can be easily established from the existing bounds on PSL, see [4] and [5,14]. Note that the automata-theoretic realization of the iteration operator $\oplus$ is similar to the one that handles the Kleene-star.

Recently, we proposed an extension of PSL with past operators [7]. As for LTL$_{-X}$ [17], we remark that our result on the stutter invariance of siPSL straightforwardly carries over to an extension of siPSL with past operators.

3.3   siPSL Examples

In the following, we illustrate that stutter-invariant ω-regular properties can be naturally expressed in siPSL. For comparison, we describe these properties in siPSL and other temporal logics that express stutter-invariant properties.

Star-Free Properties. Consider the following commonly used specification patterns taken from [8]:

(P1) *Absence:* p is false after q until r.
(P2) *Existence:* p becomes true between q and r.

Table 1. siPSL formulas and LTL$_{-X}$ formulas of the specification patterns

pattern	siPSL formula	LTL$_{-X}$ formula
P1	$G(q^+ : \neg r^+ \, \Box\!\!\mapsto \neg p)$	$G(q \wedge \neg r \rightarrow (\neg p) \, W \, r)$
P2	$G((q \wedge \neg r)^+ : (\neg p^* \, ; r^+) \, \Box\!\!\mapsto \mathrm{ff})$	$G(q \wedge \neg r \rightarrow (\neg r) \, W \, (p \wedge \neg r))$
P3	$G(q^+ : \neg r^+ : \neg p : (\neg r^*; r^+) \, \Box\!\!\mapsto \mathrm{ff})$	$G(q \wedge \neg r \wedge F r \rightarrow p \, U \, r)$
P4	$G(q^+ : (\neg r \wedge \neg s)^+ \, \Box\!\!\mapsto \neg p)$	$G(q \wedge \neg r \rightarrow (\neg p) \, W \, (s \vee r))$
P5	$G(q^+ : \neg r^+ : p \, \Box\!\!\mapsto (\neg r^+ : s^+ \, \Diamond\!\!\mapsto \mathrm{tt}))$	$G(q \wedge \neg r \rightarrow (p \rightarrow (\neg r) \, U \, (s \wedge \neg r)) \, W \, r)$

(P3) *Universality:* p is true between q and r.
(P4) *Precedence:* s precedes p, after q until r.
(P5) *Response:* s responds to p, after q until r.

Table 1 contains the formalization of these specification patterns in siPSL and LTL$_{-X}$. Note that any LTL$_{-X}$ is also an siPSL formula. However, since practitioners often find it easier to use (semi-extended) regular expressions than the temporal operators in LTL, we have used siSEREs in the siPSL formulas to formalize the patterns in siPSL. An advantage of siPSL over LTL$_{-X}$ is that one can choose between the two specifications styles and mix them.

Omega-regular Properties. We consider the stutter-invariant ω-regular language

$$L_n := \{w \in (2^{\{p\}})^\omega : \text{the number of occurrences of the subword } \{p\}\emptyset \text{ in } w$$
$$\text{is divisible by } n\},$$

for $n \geq 2$. The following siPSL formula describes the language L_n:

$$\mathsf{neverswitch} \vee \left(\left(\underbrace{((\neg p^* \, ; \mathsf{switch}) : \ldots : (\neg p^* \, ; \mathsf{switch}))}_{n \text{ times}} \right)^{\oplus} \Diamond\!\!\mapsto \mathsf{neverswitch} \right),$$

where $\mathsf{switch} := p^+ : (p^* \, ; \neg p^+)$ and $\mathsf{neverswitch} := (\neg p) \, W \, G p$.
Note that the language L_n is not star-free and thus, it cannot be described in LTL$_{-X}$. In the following, we compare our siPSL formalization of L_n with a formalization in the temporal logic SI-EQLTL from [9], which has the same expressive power as siPSL. We briefly recall the syntax and semantics of SI-EQLTL. The formulas in SI-EQLTL are of the form $\exists^h q_1 \ldots \exists^h q_n \varphi$, where φ is an LTL$_{-X}$ formula over a proposition set that contains the propositions $q_1, \ldots, q_n$. The semantics of the quantifier $\exists^h$ is as follows. Let P be a proposition set with $q \notin P$. The word $w \in (2^{P \cup \{q\}})^\omega$ is a *harmonious extension* of $v \in (2^P)^\omega$ if for all $i \in \mathbb{N}$, it holds that $v(i) = w(i) \cap P$ and if $v(i) = v(i+1)$ then $w(i) = w(i+1)$. For $v \in (2^P)^\omega$, we define $v \models \exists^h q \, \varphi$ iff $w \models \varphi$, for some harmonious extension $w \in (2^{P \cup \{q\}})^\omega$ of v.

For readability, we only state an SI-EQLTL formula that describes the language L_2 (the formula can be straightforwardly generalized for describing the language L_n with $n \geq 2$):

$$\exists^h q \big(q \wedge \mathsf{G}(q \rightarrow \mathsf{neverswitch} \vee \mathsf{switch}_2) \wedge \mathsf{F}\, \mathsf{neverswitch} \big),$$

where

$$\mathsf{switch}_2 := (\neg p \wedge q) \cup \Big((p \wedge q) \cup \big((\neg p \wedge \neg q) \cup ((p \wedge \neg q) \cup (\neg p \wedge q)) \big) \Big).$$

Intuitively, the subformula switch_2 matches subwords that contain two occurrences of $\{p\}\emptyset$. Furthermore, the harmoniously existentially quantified proposition q marks every position k of a word in L_2, where the number of occurrences of $\{p\}\emptyset$ in $w^{\leq k}$ is even.

We remark that we did not manage to come up with a simpler SI-EQLTL formula for describing the language L_n.[3] Nevertheless, we consider the SI-EQLTL formula for L_n still hard to read because of the harmonious quantified variable q and the nesting of the temporal operators, which is linear in n. Furthermore, note that the advantage of siPSL over LTL$_{-\mathsf{X}}$, namely, to mix different specification styles, is also an advantage of siPSL over SI-EQLTL.

4   Concluding Remarks

We have presented the specification languages siSEREs and siPSL, which capture exactly the classes of stutter-invariant regular and ω-regular languages, respectively. siSEREs are a variants of SEREs and siPSL is a variant of the temporal logic PSL [1], which is nowadays widely used in industry. siPSL inherits the following pleasant features from PSL. First, siPSL is easy to use. Second, the computational complexities for solving the finite-state model-checking problem with siPSL and fragments thereof are similar to the corresponding problems for PSL. Third, with only minor modifications we can use the existing tool support for PSL (like the model checker RuleBase [3], the formula translator into nondeterministic Büchi automata rtl2ba [7], or the translator used in [6] with all its optimizations) for siPSL. We only need to provide additional support for the new Kleene-star-like iteration operator $\oplus$ of the siSEREs.

References

1. IEEE standard for property specification language (PSL). IEEE Std 1850TM (October 2005)
2. Alur, R., Brayton, R.K., Henzinger, T.A., Qadeer, S., Rajamani, S.K.: Partial-order reduction in symbolic state-space exploration. Form. Method. Syst. Des. 18(2), 97–116 (2001)
3. Beer, I., Ben-David, S., Eisner, C., Geist, D., Gluhovsky, L., Heyman, T., Landver, A., Paanah, P., Rodeh, Y., Ronin, G., Wolfsthal, Y.: RuleBase: Model checking at IBM. In: Marie, R., Plateau, B., Calzarossa, M.C., Rubino, G.J. (eds.) TOOLS 1997. LNCS, vol. 1245, pp. 480–483. Springer, Heidelberg (1997)

---

[3] We encourage the reader to find a simpler SI-EQLTL formula that describes L_n.

4. Ben-David, S., Bloem, R., Fisman, D., Griesmayer, A., Pill, I., Ruah, S.: Automata construction algorithms optimized for PSL. Technical report, The Prosyd Project (2005), http://www.prosyd.org
5. Bustan, D., Havlicek, J.: Some complexity results for SystemVerilog assertions. In: Ball, T., Jones, R.B. (eds.) CAV 2006. LNCS, vol. 4144, pp. 205–218. Springer, Heidelberg (2006)
6. Cimatti, A., Roveri, M., Tonetta, S.: Symbolic compilation of PSL. IEEE Trans. on CAD of Integrated Circuits and Systems 27(10), 1737–1750 (2008)
7. Dax, C., Klaedtke, F., Lange, M.: On regular temporal logics with past. In: Proceedings of the 36th International Colloquium on Automata, Languages, and Programming, ICALP (to appear, 2009)
8. Dwyer, M.B., Avrunin, G.S., Corbett, J.C.: Patterns in property specifications for finite-state verification. In: Proceedings of the 21st International Conference on Software Engineering (ICSE), pp. 411–420 (1999), http://patterns.projects.cis.ksu.edu/
9. Etessami, K.: Stutter-invariant languages, ω-automata, and temporal logic. In: Halbwachs, N., Peled, D.A. (eds.) CAV 1999. LNCS, vol. 1633, pp. 236–248. Springer, Heidelberg (1999)
10. Etessami, K.: A note on a question of Peled and Wilke regarding stutter-invariant LTL. Inform. Process. Lett. 75(6), 261–263 (2000)
11. Godefroid, P., Wolper, P.: A partial approach to model checking. Inf. Comput. 110(2), 305–326 (1994)
12. Holzmann, G., Kupferman, O.: Not checking for closure under stuttering. In: Proceedings of the 2nd International Workshop on the SPIN Verification System. Series in Discrete Mathematics and Theoretical Computer Science, vol. 32, pp. 163–169 (1996)
13. Lamport, L.: What good is temporal logic? In: Proceedings of the 9th IFIP World Computer Congress. Information Processing, vol. 83, pp. 657–668 (1983)
14. Lange, M.: Linear time logics around PSL: Complexity, expressiveness, and a little bit of succinctness. In: Caires, L., Vasconcelos, V.T. (eds.) CONCUR 2007. LNCS, vol. 4703, pp. 90–104. Springer, Heidelberg (2007)
15. Peled, D.: Combining partial order reductions with on-the-fly model-checking. Form. Method. Syst. Des. 8(1), 39–64 (1996)
16. Peled, D.: Ten years of partial order reduction. In: Y. Vardi, M. (ed.) CAV 1998. LNCS, vol. 1427, pp. 17–28. Springer, Heidelberg (1998)
17. Peled, D., Wilke, T.: Stutter-invariant temporal properties are expressible without the next operator. Inform. Process. Lett. 63(5), 243–246 (1997)
18. Peled, D., Wilke, T., Wolper, P.: An algorithmic approach for checking closure properties of temporal logic specifications and ω-regular languages. Theoret. Comput. Sci. 195(2), 183–203 (1998)
19. Rabinovich, A.M.: Expressive completeness of temporal logic of action. In: Brim, L., Gruska, J., Zlatuška, J. (eds.) MFCS 1998. LNCS, vol. 1450, pp. 229–238. Springer, Heidelberg (1998)
20. Valmari, A.: A stubborn attack on state explosion. Form. Method. Syst. Des. 1(4), 297–322 (1992)
21. Vardi, M.Y.: From philosophical to industrial logics. In: Ramanujam, R., Sarukkai, S. (eds.) Logic and Its Applications. LNCS, vol. 5378, pp. 89–115. Springer, Heidelberg (2009)

Incremental False Path Elimination for Static Software Analysis

Ansgar Fehnker, Ralf Huuck, and Sean Seefried

National ICT Australia Ltd. (NICTA)*
Locked Bag 6016
University of New South Wales
Sydney NSW 1466, Australia

Abstract. In this work we introduce a novel approach for removing false positives in static program analysis. We present an incremental algorithm that investigates paths to failure locations with respect to feasibility. The feasibility test it done by interval constraint solving over a semantic abstraction of program paths. Sets of infeasible paths can be ruled out by enriching the analysis incrementally with observers. Much like counterexample guided abstraction refinement for software verification our approach enables to start static program analysis with a coarse syntactic abstraction and use richer semantic information to rule out false positives when necessary and possible. Moreover, we present our implementation in the Goanna static analyzer and compare it to other tools for C/C++ program analysis.

1 Introduction

One technique to find bugs in large industrial software packages is static program analysis. While it has been proven to be scalable and fast, it typically suffers to one degree or another from potential false positives. The main reason is that unlike software model checking, static program analysis typically works on a rather abstract level, such as control flow graphs (CFG) without any data abstraction. Therefore, a syntactic model of a program is a coarse abstraction, and reported error paths can be spurious, i.e. they may not correspond to an actual run in the concrete program.

In this paper we present an incremental algorithm that automatically investigates error paths and checks if they are infeasible. To do so, semantic information in the form of interval equations is automatically added to a previously purely syntactic model. This semantic information is only incorporated once a potential bug has been detected, i.e., a counterexample generated. While this ensures scalability and speed for the bug-free parts of a program, it allows to drill down further once a bug has been found.

---

* NICTA is funded by the Australian Government as represented by the Department of Broadband, Communications and the Digital Economy and the Australian Research Council through the ICT Centre of Excellence program.

Z. Liu and A.P. Ravn (Eds.): ATVA 2009, LNCS 5799, pp. 255–270, 2009.

The feasibility of a counterexample is analyzed using constraint solving over the interval domain, i.e., the possible ranges of all variables within a given path. A counterexample path is *spurious* if the least solution of a corresponding equation system is empty. The subset of equations responsible for an empty solution is called a *conflict*. In a second step we refine our syntactic model by a finite *observer* which excludes all paths that generate the same conflict. These steps are applied iteratively, until either no new counterexample can be found, or until a counterexample is found that cannot be proven to be spurious.

This approach is obviously inspired by counterexample guided abstraction refinement (CEGAR), as used in [1,2]. A main difference is the use of the *precise least solution* for interval equations [3] in the place of SAT-solving. This technique deals directly with loops, without the need to discover additional loop-predicates [2,4], or successive unrolling of the transition relation [5]. An alternative to SAT-based CEGAR in the context of static analysis, using polyhedral approximations, was proposed in [6,7]. Pre-image computations along the counterexamples are used to improve the accuracy of the polyhedral approximation. Our approach in contrast uses a *precise least solution* of an interval equation system, which is computationally faster, at the expense of precision. Our proposed approach combines nicely with the static analysis approach put forward in [8]. It defines, in contrast to semantic software model checking, syntactic properties on a syntactic abstraction of the program. The experimental results confirm that the proposed technique situates our tool in-between software model checking and static analysis tools. False positives are effectively reduced while interval solving converges quickly, even in the presence of loops.

The next section introduces preliminaries of labeled transition systems, interval solving and model checking for static properties. Section 3 introduces Interval Automata, the model we use to capture the program semantics. Section 4 presents the details of our approach. Implementation details and a comparison with other tools are given in Section 5.

2   Basic Definitions and Concepts

2.1   Labeled Transition Systems

This paper uses *labeled transition systems* (LTS) to describe the semantics of our abstract programs. An LTS is defined by (S, S_0, A, R, F) where S is a set of states, $S_0 \subseteq S$ is a sub-set of initial states, A is a set of actions and $R \subseteq S \times A \times S$ is a transition relation where each transition is labeled with an action $a \in A$, and $F \subseteq S$ is a set of final states. An LTS is *deterministic* if for every state $s \in S$ and action $a \in A$ there is at most one successor state such that $(s, a, s') \in R$.

The finite sequence $\rho = s_0 a_0 s_1 a_1 \ldots a_{n-1} s_n$ is an *execution* of an LTS $P = (S, S_0, A, R, F)$, if $s_0 \in S_o$ and $(s_i, a_i, s_{i+1}) \in R$ for all $i \geq 0$. An execution is *accepting* if $s_n \in F$. We say $w = a_0 \ldots a_{n-1} \in A^*$ *is a word in* P, if there exist s_i, $i \geq 0$, such that $s_0 a_0 s_1 a_1 \ldots a_{n-1} s_n$ form an execution in P. The *language* of P is defined by the set of all words for which there exists an accepting execution. We denote this language as $\mathcal{L}_P$.

The *product* of two labeled transition systems $P_1 = (S_1, S_{1_0}, A, R_1, F_1)$ and $P_2 = (S_2, S_{2_0}, A, R_2, F_2)$, denoted as $P_\times = P_1 \times P_2$, is defined as $P_\times = (S_1 \times S_2, S_{1_0} \times S_{1_0}, A, R_\times, F_1 \times F_2)$ where $((s_1, s_2), a, (s_1', s_2')) \in R_\times$ if and only if $(s_1, a, s_1') \in R_1$ and $(s_2, a, s_2') \in R_2$. The language of $P_\times$ is the *intersection* of the language defined by P_1 and P_2.

2.2   Interval Equation Systems

We define an *interval lattice* $\mathcal{I} = (I, \subseteq)$ by the set $I = \{\emptyset\} \cup \{[z_1, z_2] | z_1 \in \mathbb{Z} \cup \{-\infty\}, z_2 \in \mathbb{Z} \cup \{\infty\}, z_1 \leq z_2\}$ with the partial order implied by the *contained in* relation "$\subseteq$" , where a non-empty interval $[a, b]$ is *contained in* $[c, d]$, if $a \geq c$ and $b \leq d$. The empty element is the bottom element of this lattice, and $[-\infty, +\infty]$ the top element. Moreover, we consider the following operators on intervals: addition $(+)$, multiplication $(\cdot)$, union $\sqcup$, and intersection $\sqcap$ with the usual semantics $[\![.]\!]$ defined on them.

For a given finite set of variables $X = \{x_0, \dots, x_n\}$ over $\mathcal{I}$ we define an *interval expression* ϕ as follows:

$$\phi \doteq a \mid x \mid \phi \sqcup \phi \mid \phi \sqcap \phi \mid \phi + \phi \mid \phi \cdot \phi$$

where $x \in X$, and $a \in \mathcal{I}$. The set of all expression over X is denoted as $\mathcal{C}(X)$.

For all operation we have that $[\![\phi \circ \varphi]\!]$ is $[\![\phi]\!] \circ [\![\varphi]\!]$, where $\circ$ can be any of $\sqcup, \sqcap, +, \cdot$. A *valuation* is a mapping $v : X \to \mathcal{I}$ from an interval variable to an interval. Given an interval expression $\phi \in \mathcal{C}(X)$, and a valuation v, the $[\![\phi]\!]_v$ denoted the expression ϕ evaluated in v, i.e. it is defined to be the interval $[\![\phi[v(x_0)/x_0, \dots, v(x_n)/x_n]]\!]$, which is obtained by substituting each variable x_i with the corresponding interval $v(x_i)$.

An *interval equation system* is a mapping $IE : X \to \mathcal{C}(X)$ from interval variables to interval expressions. We also denote this by $x_i = \phi_i$ where $i \in 1, \dots, n$. The *solution* of such an interval equation system is a valuation satisfying all equations, i.e., $[\![x_i]\!] = [\![\phi_i]\!]_v$ for all $i \in 1, \dots, n$. As shown in [3] there always is a *precise least solution* which can be efficiently computed. By precise we mean precise with respect to the interval operators's semantics and without the use of additional widening techniques. Of course, from a program analysis point of view over-approximations are introduced, e.g., when joining two intervals $[1, 2] \sqcup [4, 5]$ results in $[1, 5]$. This, however, is due to the domain we have chosen.

2.3   Static Analysis by Model Checking

This work is based on an automata based static analysis framework as described in [8], which is related to [9,10,11]. The basic idea is to map a C/C++ program to its CFG, and to label it with occurrences of syntactic constructs of interest. The CFG together with the labels are mapped to, either a Kripke structure, or to the input language of a model checker, in our case NuSMV.

A simple example of this approach is shown in Fig. 1. Consider the contrived program foo which is allocating some memory, copying it a number of times

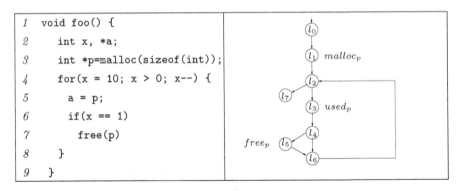

```
1   void foo() {
2       int x, *a;
3       int *p=malloc(sizeof(int));
4       for(x = 10; x > 0; x--) {
5           a = p;
6           if(x == 1)
7               free(p)
8       }
9   }
```

Fig. 1. Example program and labeled CFG for use-after-free check

to a, and freeing the memory in the last loop iteration. In our automata based approach we syntactically identify program locations that allocate, use, and free resource p. We automatically label the program's CFG with this information as shown on the right hand side of Fig. 1. To check whether after freeing some allocated resource, it is not used afterwards, we can check the CTL property:

$$AG \ (malloc_p \Rightarrow AG \ (free_p \Rightarrow \neg EF \ used_p)),$$

which means that whenever there is **free** after **malloc** for a resource p, there is no path such that p is used later on. Obviously, neglecting any further semantic information will lead to an alarm in this example, which is a false positive as p only gets freed in the last loop iteration.

3   Interval Automata

This section introduces *interval automata* (IA) which abstract programs and capture their operational semantics on the domain of intervals. We define an IA as an extended state machine where the control structure is a finite state machine, extended by a mapping from interval variables to interval expressions. We will show later how to translate a C/C++ program to an IA.

Definition 1 (Syntax). *An interval automaton is a tuple* $(L, l_0, X, E, update)$, *with*

- *a finite set of locations* L,
- *an initial location* l_0,
- *a set of interval variables* X,
- *a finite set of edges* $E \subseteq L \times L$, *and*
- *an effect function* update $: E \rightarrow (X \times \mathcal{C}(X))$.

The effect *update* assigns to each edge a pair of an interval variable and an interval expression. We will refer to the (left-hand side) variable part $update|_X$

as *lhs*, and to the (right-hand side) expression part $update|_{C(X)}$ as *rhsexpr*. The set of all variables that appear in *rhsexpr* will be denoted by *rhsvars*. Note, that only one variable is updated on each edge. This restriction is made for the sake of simplicity, but does not restrict the expressivity of an IA.

Definition 2 (Semantics). *The semantics of an IA $P = (L, l_0, X, E, update)$ are defined by a labeled transition system $LTS(P) = (S, S_0, A, R, F)$, such that*

- *the set of states S contains all states (l, v) with location l, and an interval valuation v.*
- *the set of initial states S_0 contains all states $s_0 = (l_0, v_0)$, with $v_0 \equiv [-\infty, \infty]$.*
- *the alphabet A is the set of edges E.*
- *the transition relation $R \subseteq S \times A \times S$ contains a triple $((l, v), (l, l'), (l', v'))$, i.e a transition from state (l, v) to (l', v') labeled (l, l'), if there exists a (l, l') in E, such that $v' = v[lhs(e) \leftarrow [\![rhsexpr(e)]\!]_v]$ and $[\![rhsexpr(e)]\!]_{v'} \neq \emptyset$.*
- *the set of final states $F = S$, i.e. all states are final states*

It might seem a bit awkward that the transitions in the LTS are labeled with the edges of the IA, but this will be used later to define the synchronous composition with an observer. Since each transition is labeled with its corresponding edge we obtain a deterministic system, i.e., for a given word there exists only one possible run. We identify a word $((l_0, l_1), (l_1, l_2), \ldots, (l_{m-1}, l_m))$ in the remainder by the sequence of locations $(l_0, \ldots, l_m)$.

Given an IA P. Its language $\mathcal{L}_P$ contains all sequences $(l_0, \ldots, l_n)$ which satisfy the following:

$$l_0 = l_0 \tag{1}$$

$$\wedge \; \forall i = 0, \ldots, n - 1. \; (l_i, l_{i+1}) \in E \tag{2}$$

$$\wedge \; v_0 \equiv [-\infty, +\infty] \wedge \exists v_1, \ldots, v_n. ([\![rhsexpr(l_i, l_{i+1})]\!]_{v_i} \neq \emptyset \tag{3}$$
$$\wedge \; v_{i+1} = v_i[lhs(l_i, l_{i+1}) \leftarrow [\![rhsexpr(l_i, l_{i+1})]\!]_{v_i}])$$

This mean that a word (1) starts in the initial location, (2) respects the edge relation E, and (3) that there exists a sequence of non-empty valuations that satisfies the updates associated with the edges. We use this characterization of words as satisfiability problem to generate systems of interval equations that have a non-empty solution only if a sequence $(l_0, \ldots, l_n)$ is a word. We will define for a given IA P and sequence w a *conflict* as an interval equation system with an empty least solution which proves that w cannot be a word of the IA P.

4 Path Reduction

The labeled CFG as defined in Section 2.3 is a coarse abstraction of the actual program. Like most static analysis techniques this approach suffers from false positives. In the context of this paper we define a property as a regular language, and satisfaction of a property as language inclusion. The program itself will be defined by an Interval Automaton P and its behavior is defined by the language of the corresponding $LTS(P)$. Since interval automata are infinite state systems, we do not check the IA itself but an abstraction $\hat{P}$. This abstraction is initially an annotated CFG as depicted in Fig. 1.

A *positive* is a word in the abstraction $\hat{P}$ that does not satisfy the property. A *false positive* is a positive that is not in the actual behavior of the program, i.e. it is not in the language of the $LTS(P)$. *Path reduction* is then defined as the iterative process that restricts the language of the abstraction, until either a true positive has been found, or until the reduced language satisfies the property.

4.1   Path Reduction Loop

Given an IA $P = (L, l_0, E, X, update)$ we define its finite abstraction $\hat{P}$ as follows: $\hat{P} = (L, l_0, E, E', L)$ is a labeled transition system with states L, initial state l_0, alphabet E, transition relation $E' = \{(l, (l, l'), l')|(l, l') \in E\}$, and the entire set L as final states. The LTS $\hat{P}$ is an abstraction of the $LTS(P)$, and it represents the finite control structure of P. The language of $\hat{P}$ will be denoted by $\mathcal{L}_{\hat{P}}$. Each word of $\hat{P}$ is by construction a word of $LTS(P)$. Let $\mathcal{L}_\phi$ be the language of the specification.

We assume to have a procedure that checks if the language of LTS $\mathcal{L}_{\hat{P}}$ is a subset of $\mathcal{L}_\phi$, and produces a counterexample if this is not the case (cf. Section 4.5). If it finds a word in $\mathcal{L}_{\hat{P}}$ that is not in $\mathcal{L}_\phi$, we have to check whether this word is in $\mathcal{L}_P$, i.e. we have to check whether it satisfies equation (1) to (3). Every word $w = (l_0, \ldots, l_m)$ in $\mathcal{L}_{\hat{P}}$ satisfies by construction (1) and (2). If a word $w = (l_0, \ldots, l_m)$ can be found such that there exists no solution for (3), it cannot be a word of $\mathcal{L}_P$. In this case we call the word *spurious*.

If we assume in addition to have a procedure to check whether a word is spurious (cf. Section 4.2), we can use these in an iterative loop to check if the infinite LTS of IA P satisfies the property, by checking a finite product of abstraction $\hat{P}$ with observers instead as follows:

1. Let $\hat{P}_0 := \hat{P}$, and $i = 0$.
2. Check if $w \in \mathcal{L}_{\hat{P}_i} \setminus \mathcal{L}_\phi$ exists. If such a w exists got to step 3, otherwise exit with "property satisfied".
3. Check if $w \in \mathcal{L}_P$. If $w \notin \mathcal{L}_P$ build observer Obs_w, otherwise exit with "property not satisfied". The observer (1) accepts w, and (2) satisfies that all accepted words w' are not in $\mathcal{L}_P$.
4. Let $\hat{P}_{i+1} := \hat{P}_i \times Obs_w^C$, with . $\hat{P}_i \times Obc_w^C$ is the synchronous composition of $\hat{P}_i$ and the complement of Obs_w. Increment i and goto step 3.

The remainder of this section explains how to check if a word is in $\mathcal{L}_P$, how to build a suitable observer, and how to combine it in a framework which uses NuSMV to model check the finite abstraction $\hat{P}_i$.

Example. The initial coarse abstraction as CFG in Fig. 1 loses the information that p cannot be used after it was freed. The shortest counterexample in Fig. 1 initializes x to 10 in line 4, enters the `for`-loop, takes the `if`-branch, frees p in line 7, decrements x, returns to the beginning of the `for`-loop, and then uses

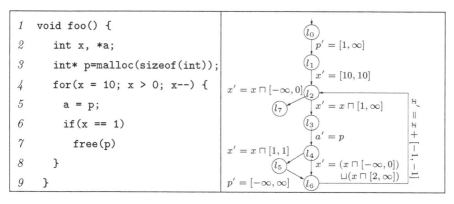

```
1   void foo() {

2       int x, *a;

3       int* p=malloc(sizeof(int));

4       for(x = 10; x > 0; x--) {

5           a = p;

6           if(x == 1)

7               free(p)

8       }

9   }
```

Fig. 2. Abstraction of the program as IA. Analysis of the syntactic properties of the annotated CFG in Fig.1 is combined with an analysis of the IA to the right.

p in line 5. This counterexample is obviously spurious. Firstly, because the if-branch with condition x == 1 at line 7 is not reachable while $x = 10$. Secondly, because if the programm could enter the if-loop, it would imply x == 1, and hence impossible to reenter the loop, given decrement x-- and condition x > 0.

4.2   Checking for Spurious Words

Every word $w = (l_0, \ldots, l_m)$ in $\mathcal{L}_{\hat{P}}$ satisfies by construction (1) and (2). It remains to be checked if condition (3) can be satisfied. A straightforward approach is to execute the trace on $LTS(P)$. However this can only determine if that particular word is spurious. Our proposed approach builds an equation system instead, which allows us to find a set of conflicting interval equations, which can in turn be used to show that an entire class of words is spurious. Another straightforward approach to build such an equation system is to introduce for each variable and edge in w an interval equation, and to use an interval solver to check if a solution to this system of interval equations exists. A drawback of this approach is that it introduces $(m + 1) \times n$ variables, and $m \times n$ equations. In the following we present an approach to construct an equation system with at most one equation and one variable for each edge in w.

Interval Equation System for a Sequence of Transitions. We describe how to obtain an equation system for a word $w \in \mathcal{L}_{\hat{P}}$, such that it has a non-empty least solution only if $w \in \mathcal{L}_P$. This system is generated in three steps:

I. Tracking variables. Let X_L be a set of fresh variables x_l. For each update of a variable, i.e. $x = lhs(l_{i-1}, l_i)$ we introduce a fresh variable x_{l_i}. We use the notation $x_{(i)}$ to refer to the last update of x before the i-th transition in $w = (l_0, \ldots, l_m)$. If no such update exist $x_{(i)}$ will be x_{l_0}.

w	var	$expr_w(i)$	IE_w	Reduced conflicts	
(l_0,l_1)	p_{l_1}	$[1,\infty]$			
(l_1,l_2)	x_{l_2}	$[10,10]$	$p_{l_1} = [1,\infty]$	$x_{l_2} = [10,10]$	conflict 1
(l_2,l_3)	x_{l_3}	$x_{l_2} \sqcap [1,\infty]$	$x_{l_2} = [10,10]\sqcup$	$x_{l_3} = x_{l_2} \sqcap [1,\infty]$	
(l_3,l_4)	a_{l_4}	p_{l_1}	$(x_{l_5} + [-1,-1])$	$x_{l_5} = x_{l_3} \sqcap [1,1]$	
(l_4,l_5)	x_{l_5}	$x_{l_3} \sqcap [1,1]$	$x_{l_3} = (x_{l_2} \sqcap [1,\infty])$		
(l_5,l_6)	p_{l_6}	$[-\infty,\infty]$	$a_{l_4} = p_{l_1} \sqcup p_{l_6}$	$x_{l_5} = [-\infty,\infty] \sqcap [1,1]$	conflict 2
(l_6,l_2)	x_{l_2}	$x_{l_5} + [-1,-1]$	$x_{l_5} = x_{l_3} \sqcap [1,1]$	$x_{l_2} = x_{l_5} + [-1,-1]$	
(l_2,l_3)	x_{l_3}	$x_{l_2} \sqcap [1,\infty]$	$p_{l_6} = [-\infty,\infty]$	$x_{l_3} = x_{l_2} \sqcap [1,\infty]$	
(l_3,l_4)	a_{l_4}	p_{l_6}			

Fig. 3. Equations for counterexample w of the IA depicted in Fig. 2

II. Generating equations. For each edge in w we generate an interval expression over X_L. We define $expr_w : \{0,\ldots,m\} \to \mathcal{C}(X_L)$ as follows:

$$expr_w(i) \mapsto rhsexpr(l_{i-1},l_i)[x_{(i-1)}/x]_{x\in rhsvars(l_{i-1},l_i)} \tag{4}$$

An expression $expr_w(i)$ is the right-hand side expression of the update on (l_{i-1},l_i), where all occuring variables are substituted by variables in X_L.

III. Generating equation system. Locations may occur more than once in a word, and variables maybe updated by multiple edges. Let $writes_w \subseteq X_L$ the set $\{x_l|\exists i \text{ s.t.} x = lhs(l_{i-1},l_i)\}$, and Ω_w be a mapping each $x_l \in writes_w$ the set $\{i|x = lhs(l_{i-1},l_i) \wedge l_i = l\}$. The system $IE_w : X_L \to \mathcal{C}(X_L)$ is defined as follows:

$$x_l \mapsto \begin{cases} \bigsqcup_{i\in\Omega_w(x_l)} expr_w(i) & \text{if } x_l \in writes_w \\ [-\infty,\infty] & \text{otherwise} \end{cases} \tag{5}$$

System IE_w assigns each variable $x_l \in writes_w$ to a union of expressions; one expression for each element in $\Omega_w(x,l)$.

Example. Fig. 3 depicts for word $w = (l_0,l_1,,l_2,l_3,l_4,l_5,l_6,l_2,l_3,l_4)$ how to generate IE_w. The first column gives the transitions in w. The second column gives the variable in $writes_w$. The variable p_{l_1}, for example, refers to the update of p on the first transition (l_0,l_1) of the IA in Fig. 2. We have that $x_{(5)} = x_{l_3}$, since the last update of x before (l_4,l_5) was on edge (l_2,l_3).

The third column gives the equations $expr_w(i)$. For example, the right-hand side $rhsexpr(l_4,l_5)$ is $x' = x \sqcap [1,1]$. Since $x_{(4)} = x_{l_3}$, we get that $expr_w(5)$ is $x_{l_3} \sqcap [1,1]$. The fourth column shows the equation system IE_w derived from the equations. We have, for example, that x is updated on (l_1,l_2), the second edge in w, and (l_6,l_2), the 8th edge. Hence, $\Omega_w(x_{l_2}) = \{2,8\}$. Equation $IE_w(x_{l_2})$ is then defined as the union of $expr_w(2)$, which is $[10,10]$, and $expr_w(8)$, which is $x_{l_5} + [-1,-1]$. The least solution of the equation system IE_w is $p_{l_1} = [1,\infty]$, $x_{l_2} = [10,10]$, $x_{l_3} = [10,10]$, $a_{l_4} = [-\infty,\infty]$, $x_{l_5} = \emptyset$, and $p_{l_6} = [-\infty,\infty]$. Since $x_{l_5} = \emptyset$, there exists no solution, and w is spurious. $\square$

Lemma 1. *Given a word $w \in \mathcal{L}_{\hat{P}}$. Then there exist a sequence of non-empty valuations $v_1, \ldots, v_m$ such that (3) holds for w only if IE_w has a non-empty least solution.*

Proof. Given solution to (3) we can construct non-empty solution of IE_w, which must be included in the least solution of IE_w.   □

An advantage of creating interval equations as described is that reason naturally over loops. A third or fourth repetition does not introduce new variable in $writes_w$, and neither new expressions. This means that the equation system for a word, which is a concatenation $\alpha\beta\beta\gamma$, has no non-empty solution, if the concatenation $\alpha\beta\gamma$ has. The least solution will be the same.

4.3   Conflict Discovery

The previous subsection described how to check if a given word $w \in \mathcal{L}_{\hat{P}}$ is spurious. Interval solving, however, leads to an over-approximation, mostly due to the ⊔-operation. This subsection describes how to reduce the numbers of (non-trivial) equations in a conflict and at the same time the over-approximation error, by restricting conflicts to fragments and cone-of-influence.

For CEGAR approaches for infinite-state systems it has been observed that it is sufficient and often more efficient to find a spurious fragments of a counterexample, rather than a spurious counterexample [12,13]. The effect is similar to small or minimal predicates in SAT-based approaches. The difference between a word and a fragment in our context is that a fragment may start in any location.

Given a word $w = (l_0, \ldots, l_m)$ a fragment $w' = (l'_0, \ldots, l'_{m'})$ is a subsequence of w. For fragment w' of a word w we can show the analog of Lemma 1. If the least solution of $IE_{w'}$ is empty, i.e. if the fragment w' is spurious, then the word w is spurious. If there exists a sequence of non-empty valuations $v_1, \ldots, v_m$ for w, then they also define a non-empty subsequence of valuations for w', and these have to be contained in the least solution of $IE_{w'}$.

A word of length $m - 1$ has $m^2/2$ fragments. Rather than checking all of these we can rule out most of these based on two observations. To be useful at least the last edge of a fragment has to result in an empty solution. An *update* in (3) can only result in an empty solution, if there exist an element in $\mathcal{I}$ that is mapped to the empty set by *update*. We call such updates *restricting*. An example of such updates are intersections with constants such as $x' = x \sqcap [1, \infty]$. We can omit all (l_{i-1}, l_i) after the last last restricting update in w'. Similarly, we find that edges with updates that map valuation $v \equiv [-\infty, \infty]$ to $[-\infty, \infty]$, can be omitted from the beginning of a fragment.

Given thus reduced fragment w', we can reduce $IE_{w'}$ further, by omitting all equations that are not in the cone-of-influence of the last restricting update. We refer to the resulting system of equations as $\overline{IE}_{w'}$. In the remainder we will refer to $\overline{IE}_{w'}$ as the *reduced conflict*, which is uniquely determined by the fragment w'. The reduction to the cone-of-influence, guarantees that $IE_{w'}$ has an empty least solution if $\overline{IE}_{w'}$ has. The converse is not true. However, since we consider all possible fragments, it is guaranteed that if a set of removed equations result in a conflict, these will appear as reduced conflict of another fragment.

Example. There are two conflicts among the candidate fragments in Fig. 3. Conflict 1, for fragment $(l_1, l_2, l_3, l_4, l_5)$, has as least solution $x_{l_2} = [10, 10], x_{l_3} = [10, 10], x_{l_5} = \emptyset$. Conflict 2, for fragment $(l_4, l_5, l_6, l_2, l_3)$, has as least solution $x_{l_5} = [1, 1], x_{l_2} = [0, 0], x_{l_3} = \emptyset$. The equation was p_{l_6} was not included in the second conflict, as it is not in the cone-of-influence of x_{l_3}. Note, that variable x in equation $\overline{IE}(x_{l_5})$ was substituted by $[-\infty, \infty]$. This expression was generated by the first edge (l_4, l_5) of the fragment $(l_4, l_5, l_6, l_2, l_3)$. The last update before this edge is outside of the scope of the fragment, and hence x was assumed to be $[-\infty, \infty]$, which is a conservative over-approximation.

4.4   Conflict Observer

Given a reduced conflict $\overline{IE}_w$ for a fragment $w = (l_0, \ldots, l_m)$, we construct an observer such that if a word $w' \in \mathcal{L}_{\hat{P}}$ is accepted, then $w' \notin \mathcal{L}_P$. The observer is a LTS over the same alphabet E as $LTS(P)$ and $\hat{P}$.

Definition 3. *Given IA $P = (L, l_0, E, X, update)$ and reduced conflict $\overline{IE}_w$ for a fragment $w = (l_0, \ldots, l_m)$, define X_w as the set of all variables $x \in X$ such that $x = lhs(l_{i-1}, l_i)$, for some edge (l_{i-1}, l_i) in w. Observer Obs_w is a LTS with*

- *set S_{Obs} of states (current, eqn, conflict) with valuation current : $X_w \to L$, valuation eqn : $writes_w \to \{unsat, sat\}$, and location conflict $\in \{all, some, none\}$.*
- *initial state $(write_0, eqn_0, loc_0)$ with $current_0 \equiv l_0$, $eqn_0 \equiv unsat$, and $conflict_0 = none$.*
- *alphabet E*
- *transition relation $S_{Obs} \times E \times S_{Obs}$.*
- *a set final states F. A state is final if conflict = all.*

Due to the limited space we give an informal definition of the transition relation. The detailed formal definition can be found on [14].

- Variable *conflict* changes its state based on the next state of *eqn*. We have that $conflict'(x_l)$ is *all, some, none*, if $eqn'(x_l) = sat$ for all, some or no $x_l \in writes_w$, respectively. Once *conflict* is in *all* it remains there forever.
- Variable *eqn* represents $\overline{IE}_w(x_l)$ for $x_l \in writes_w$. The successor $eqn'(x_l)$ will change if $x = lhs(\lambda, \lambda')$ and $\lambda' = l$. If substituting variables x by $x_{current(x)}$ in $rhserpr(\lambda, \lambda')$, results in an expression that does not appear in $\overline{IE}_w(x_l)$, for any x_l, then $eqn'(x_l) = unsat$ for all x_l. Otherwise, the successor $eqn'(x_l)$ is *sat* for matching variables x_l, and remains unchanged for all others. This is a simple syntactic match, achieved by comparing the indices and variables that appear in $\overline{IE}_w(x_l)$ with the values of $current(x)$.
- Variable *current* is used to record for each variable the location of the last update. If *conflict'* is none, then $current'(x) = l_0$. Otherwise, if (λ, λ') is in w, and $x = lhs(\lambda, \lambda')$, then $current'(x) = \lambda'$. Otherwise, it remains unchanged.

The interaction between *current*, *eqn*, and *conflict* is somewhat subtle. The idea is that the observer is initially in *conflict = none*. If an edge is observed such

which generates an expression $expr(i)$ that appears in $\overline{IE}_w(x_l)$, with $i \in \Omega_w(x_l)$ (see Eq. (5)), then $conflict' = some$, and the corresponding $eqn(x_l) = sat$. It can be deduced $\overline{IE}_w(x_l)$ is satisfied, unless another expression is encountered that might enlarge the fix-point. This is the case when an expression for x_l will generated, that does not appear in $\overline{IE}_w(x_l)$. It is conservatively assumed that this expression increases the fixpoint solution.

If $conflict = all$ it can be deduced that the observed edges produce an equation system $\overline{IE}_{w'}$ that has a non-empty solution only if $\overline{IE}_w$ has a non-empty solution. And from the assumption we know that $\overline{IE}_w$ has an empty-solution, and thus also $\overline{IE}_{w'}$. Which implies that the currently observed run is infeasible and cannot satisfy Eq. 3.

Given a reduced conflict $\overline{IE}_w$ for fragment w we have two properties.

- If a word $w' \in \mathcal{L}_{\hat{P}}$ is accepted by Obs_w, then $w \notin \mathcal{L}_P$.
- Given a fragment w' such that $\overline{IE}_{w'} = \overline{IE}_w$, and a word w'' such that w' is a subsequence, then w'' is accepted by Obs_w.

The first property states that the language of $\hat{P}' = \hat{P} \times Obs_w^C$ contains $\mathcal{L}_P$. The second ensures that each observer is only constructed once. This is needed to ensure termination. Each observer is uniquely determined by the finite set expressions that appear in it, and since X_L and E are finite, there exists only a finite set of possible expressions that may appear in (4). Consequently, there can only exist a finite set of conflicts as defined by (5).

Example. The observer for the first conflict in Fig. 3 accepts a word if a fragment generates conflict $x_{l_2} \mapsto [10, 10], x_{l_3} \mapsto x_{l_2} \sqcap [1, \infty], x_{l_5} \mapsto x_{l_3} \sqcap [1, 1]$. This is the case if it observes edge (l_1, l_2), edge (l_2, l_3) with a last write to x at l_2, and edge (l_4, l_5) with a last write to x at l_3. All other edges are irrelevant, as long as they do not write to x_2, x_3 or x_5, and change the solution. This would be, for example, the case for (l_2, l_3) if $current(x) \neq l_2$. This would create an expression different from $x_{l_2} \sqcap [1, \infty]$, and thus potentially enlarge the solution set.

The observer for the other conflicts is constructed similarly. The complement of these observers are obtained by labeling all states in $S \setminus F$ as final. The product of the complemented observers with the annotated CFG in Fig.1 removes all potential counterexamples. The observer for the first conflict prunes all runs that enter the `for`-loop once, and then immediately enter the `if`-branch. The observer for the second conflict prunes all words that enter the `if`-branch and return into the loop.

4.5   Path Reduction with NuSMV

The previous subsections assumed a checker for language inclusion for LTS. In practice we use however the CTL model checker NuSMV. The product of $\hat{P}$ with the complement of the observers is by construction proper a abstractions of $LTS(P)$. The results language inclusion would therefore extend also to invariant checking, path inclusion, LTL and ACTL model checking. For pragmatic reasons we do not restrict ourselves to any of these, but use full CTL and LTL[1].

---

[1] NuSMV 2.x supports LTL as well.

Whenever NuSMV produces a counterexample path, we use interval solving as described before to determine if this path is spurious.

Note, that path reduction can also be used to check witnesses, for example for reachability properties. In this case path reduction will check if a property which is true on the level of abstraction is indeed satisfied by the program.

The abstraction $\hat{P}$ and the observers are composed synchronously in NuSMV. The observer synchronizes on the current and next location of $\hat{P}$. The property is defined as a CTL property of $\hat{P}$. The acceptance condition of the complements of observers is modeled as LTL fairness condition $G\neg(conflict = all)$.

5   Implementation and Experiments

5.1   C to Interval Equations

This section describes how to abstract a C/C++ program to a set of interval equations, and covers briefly expression statements, condition statements as well as the control structures.

Expressions statements involving simple operations such as addition and multiplication are directly mapped to interval equations. E.g., an expression statement x=(x+y)*5 is represented as $x_{i+1} = (x_i + y_i) * [5, 5]$. Subtraction such as $x = x - y$ can be easily expressed as $x_{i+1} = x_i + ([-1, -1] * y_i)$.

Condition statements occur in constructs such as if-then-else, for-loops, while-loops etc. For every condition such as x<5 we introduce two equations, one for the true-case and one for the false-case. Condition x<5 has two possible outcomes $x_{tt} = x \sqcap [-\infty, 4]$ and $x_{ff} = x \sqcap [5, \infty]$. More complex conditions involving more than one variable can also be approximated and we refer the interested reader to [15].

Joins are introduced where control from two different branches can merge. For instance, let x_i be the last *lhs*-variable in the if-branch of an if-then-else, and let x_j be the last *lhs*-variables in the else-branch. The values after the if-then-else is then the union of both possible values, i.e., $x_k = x_i \sqcup x_j$.

For all other operations which we cannot accurately cover we simply over-approximate their possible effect. Function calls, for example, are handled as conservatively as possible, i.e., x=foo() is abstracted as $x_i = [-\infty, +\infty]$. The same holds for most of pointer arithmetic, floating point operations and division.

It should be noted that infeasible paths mostly depend on combinations of conditions which cannot be satisfied. Typically, condition expressions and the operations having an effect on them are rather simple. Therefore, it is a sufficient first approach to over-approximate most but the aforementioned constructs.

5.2   Comparison

To evaluate our path reduction approach we added it to our static checker Goanna, and compared its results with three other static analysis tools, and three software model checkers. One of the static analyzers is a commercial tool. We applied these tools to five programs.[2]

P1 The first program is the one discussed throughout the paper. It is similar to the example discussed in [4].

P2 The second program is identical, except that the loop is initialized to x=100.

P3 The third program tests how different tools deal with unrelated clutter. The correctness depends on two if-conditions: the first sets a flag, and the second assigns a value to a variable only if the first is set. In between the two if-blocks is some unrelated code, in this case a simple if-then-else.

P4 The fourth program is similar to the third, except that a for-loop counting up to 10 was inserted in-between the two relevant if-blocks .

P5 The last one is similar to the first program. This program uses however two counter-variables x and y. The correctness of the programm depends on the loop-invariant $x = y$. It is similar to the examples presented in [16].

For each of the programs we constructed one instance with a bug, and one without. For the first program P1, e.g. the loop condition was changed to x>=0. Since not all tools check for the same properties, we introduced slightly different bugs for the different tools, which however all depended on the same paths.

The results in Table 1 show the static analysis tools often fail to produce correct warnings. Splint, for example, produces for the instances with and without a bug the same warnings, which is only correct in half of the cases. The software model checking tools in contrast always give the correct result. Our proposed path reduction produces one false positive, for program P5. The least solution of the interval equation shows that both variables take values in the same interval, but the solver is unable to infer the stronger invariant $x = y$.

The experiments were performed on a DELL PowerEdge SC1425 server, with an Intel Xeon processor running at 3.4 GHz, 2 MiB L2 cache and 1.5 GiB DDR-2 400 MHz ECC memory. The following table gives the maximal, minimal, mean and median run-times in seconds:

Table 1. The table on the left-hand side shows for each tool if it found a true positive/negative "+" or a false positive/negative "-". Entries "(-)" and "(+)" refer to warnings that there *may* be an error. The table on the right-hand-side compares the number of iterations of the three software model checkers with Goanna.

	no violation					violation				
	P1	P2	P3	P4	P5	P1	P2	P3	P4	P5
Splint	+	+	-	-	-	-	-	+	+	+
UNO	(-)	(-)	(-)	(-)	-	(+)	(+)	+	+	+
com. tool	+	+	+	+	-	-	-	+	+	+
Goanna	+	+	+	+	-	+	+	+	+	+
Blast	+	+	+	+	+	+	+	+	+	+
Satabs	+	+	+	+	+	+	+	+	+	+
CBMC	+	+	+	+	+	+	+	+	+	+

	no violation					violation				
	P1	P2	P3	P4	P5	P1	P2	P3	P4	P5
Goanna	2	2	3	2	1	2	2	4	3	2
Blast	3	3	4	12	12	11	101	5	12	10
Satabs	4	4	1	1	21	10	100	3	1	19
CBMC	10	100	1	10	10	11	101	1	10	11

---

[2] These can be found on http://www.cse.unsw.edu.au/~ansgar/fpe/

	max	min	mean	median
Splint	0.012	0.011	0.012	0.012
UNO	0.032	0.025	0.028	0.025
com. tool	0.003	0.002	0.003	0.003
Goanna	0.272	0.143	0.217	0.226
Blast	58.770	0.126	6.371	0.529
Satabs	5374.037	0.076	539.694	0.336
CBMC	0.221	0.079	0.137	0.121

The static analysis tools are overall fast, and their run times are almost independent of the example program. For test programs as small at these the run-time reflect mostly the time for overhead and setup. The run-times for the model checkers vary more, the maximum is attained for the instance of program P2 (x=100) that contains a bug. Satabs in particular showed exponential run times. The default for Satabs is to abort after 50 iterations. It takes about 460 seconds to reach this limit. After doubling the maximal number of iterations to 100, the runtime increases more than 10 times. Memory is not a problem, as Satabs never exceeds 5% of the available memory. Blast shows also exponential runtimes, but less pronounced. The run-times for CBMC, in contrast, grow about linearly with an increasing number of iterations. When the loop is initialized to x=1000 it takes, for example, about 2.4 sec to complete all 1000 iterations. With Goanna the run time for program P1 and P2 are independent of the number of loops, as expected. Goanna benefits from the fact that interval solving deals efficiently with loops without unrolling [3].

6   Conclusions

In this work we presented an approach to enhance static program analysis with counterexample guided path reduction to eliminate false positives. While by default we investigate programs on a purely syntactic level, once we find a potential counterexample, it is mapped to an interval equation system. In case that the least solution of this system is empty, we know that the counterexample is spurious and identify a subset of equations which caused the conflict. We create an observer for the conflict, augment our syntactic model with this observer, re-run the analysis with the new model and keep repeating this iterative process until no more counterexamples occur or none can be ruled out anymore.

One of the advantages of our approach is that we do not require to unroll loops or to detect loop predicates as done in some CEGAR approaches. In fact, path-based interval solving is insensitive to loop bounds, and handles loops just like any other construct. However, path-based interval solving adds precision to standard abstract interpretation interval analysis. Moreover, we only use one data abstraction, namely a simple interval semantics for C/C++ programs.

We implemented our approach in our static analysis tool Goanna and compared it for a set of examples to existing software model checkers and static program analyzers. This demonstrated that Goanna is typically more precise than standard program analyzers and almost as precise as static model checkers. Of course, the design and strength of software model checkers is to check for a much richer class of properties.

Future work is to evaluate our approach further on real life software to identify a typical false alarm reduction ratio. Given that static analysis typically turns up a few bugs per 1000 lines of code, this will require some extensive testing. Moreover, we like to explore if slightly richer domains can be used to get additional precision without a signification increase in computation time and, most importantly, if this makes any significant difference for real life software.

References

1. Henzinger, T.A., Jhala, R., Majumdar, R., Sutre, G.: Software verification with BLAST. In: Ball, T., Rajamani, S.K. (eds.) SPIN 2003. LNCS, vol. 2648, pp. 235–239. Springer, Heidelberg (2003)
2. Clarke, E., Kroening, D., Sharygina, N., Yorav, K.: SATABS: SAT-based predicate abstraction for ANSI-C. In: Halbwachs, N., Zuck, L.D. (eds.) TACAS 2005. LNCS, vol. 3440, pp. 570–574. Springer, Heidelberg (2005)
3. Gawlitza, T., Seidl, H.: Precise fixpoint computation through strategy iteration. In: De Nicola, R. (ed.) ESOP 2007. LNCS, vol. 4421, pp. 300–315. Springer, Heidelberg (2007)
4. Kroening, D., Weissenbacher, G.: Counterexamples with loops for predicate abstraction. In: Ball, T., Jones, R.B. (eds.) CAV 2006. LNCS, vol. 4144, pp. 152–165. Springer, Heidelberg (2006)
5. Clarke, E., Kroening, D., Lerda, F.: A tool for checking ANSI-C programs. In: Jensen, K., Podelski, A. (eds.) TACAS 2004. LNCS, vol. 2988, pp. 168–176. Springer, Heidelberg (2004)
6. Gulavani, B., Rajamani, S.: Counterexample driven refinement for abstract interpretation. In: Hermanns, H., Palsberg, J. (eds.) TACAS 2006. LNCS, vol. 3920, pp. 474–488. Springer, Heidelberg (2006)
7. Wang, C., Yang, Z., Gupta, A., Ivancic, F.: Using counterexamples for improving the precision of reachability computation with polyhedra. In: Damm, W., Hermanns, H. (eds.) CAV 2007. LNCS, vol. 4590, pp. 352–365. Springer, Heidelberg (2007)
8. Fehnker, A., Huuck, R., Jayet, P., Lussenburg, M., Rauch, F.: Model checking software at compile time. In: Proc. TASE 2007. IEEE Computer Society, Los Alamitos (2007)
9. Holzmann, G.: Static source code checking for user-defined properties. In: Proc. IDPT 2002, Pasadena, CA, USA (June 2002)
10. Dams, D.R., Namjoshi, K.S.: Orion: High-precision methods for static error analysis of C and C++ programs. In: de Boer, F.S., Bonsangue, M.M., Graf, S., de Roever, W.-P. (eds.) FMCO 2005. LNCS, vol. 4111, pp. 138–160. Springer, Heidelberg (2006)
11. Schmidt, D.A., Steffen, B.: Program analysis as model checking of abstract interpretations. In: Levi, G. (ed.) SAS 1998. LNCS, vol. 1503, pp. 351–380. Springer, Heidelberg (1998)
12. Fehnker, A., Clarke, E., Jha, S., Krogh, B.: Refining abstractions of hybrid systems using counterexample fragments. In: Morari, M., Thiele, L. (eds.) HSCC 2005. LNCS, vol. 3414, pp. 242–257. Springer, Heidelberg (2005)
13. Jha, S.K., Krogh, B., Clarke, E., Weimer, J., Palkar, A.: Iterative relaxation abstraction for linear hybrid automata. In: Proc. HSCC 2007. LNCS (2007)

14. Fehnker, A., Huuck, R., Rauch, F., Seefried, S.: Counterexample guided path reduction. Technical Report (number to be assigned), NICTA (January 2008)
15. Ermedahl, A., Sjödin, M.: Interval analysis of C-variables using abstract interpretation. Technical report, Uppsala University (December 1996)
16. Jhala, R., McMillan, K.L.: A practical and complete approach to predicate refinement. In: Hermanns, H., Palsberg, J. (eds.) TACAS 2006. LNCS, vol. 3920, pp. 459–473. Springer, Heidelberg (2006)

A Framework for Compositional Verification of Multi-valued Systems via Abstraction-Refinement*

Yael Meller, Orna Grumberg, and Sharon Shoham

Computer Science Department, Technion, Haifa, Israel
{ymeller,orna,sharonsh}@cs.technion.ac.il

Abstract. We present a framework for fully automated compositional verification of μ-calculus specifications over multi-valued systems, based on multi-valued abstraction and refinement.

Multi-valued models are widely used in many applications of model checking. They enable a more precise modeling of systems by distinguishing several levels of uncertainty and inconsistency. Successful verification tools such as STE (for hardware) and YASM (for software) are based on multi-valued models.

Our compositional approach model checks individual components of a system. Only if all individual checks return *indefinite* values, the *parts of the components* which are responsible for these values, are composed and checked. Thus the construction of the full system is avoided. If the latter check is still indefinite, then a *refinement* is needed.

We formalize our framework based on bilattices, consisting of a truth lattice and an information lattice. Formulas interpreted over a multi-valued model are evaluated w.r.t. to the truth lattice. On the other hand, refinement is now aimed at increasing the information level of model details, thus also increasing the information level of the model checking result. Based on the two lattices, we suggest how multi-valued models should be composed, checked, and refined.

1 Introduction

Model checking [8] is a successful technique which is widely used for hardware and software verification. It is limited, however, by its high memory requirement, referred to as the *state explosion problem*. Two of the most successful approaches for fighting this problem are abstraction and compositional verification. In [21] the two approaches are joined in the context of 3-valued abstraction. There, each component M_i of a composed system M is lifted into a 3-valued model $M_i \uparrow$ which forms an abstraction of M. Model checking a formula φ on $M_i \uparrow$ can result in either a definite value *true* or *false*, or an *indefinite* value. In the former case, it is guaranteed that the result is also the value of φ on M. In the latter case, however, nothing can be deduced about the composed system. If the checks of all individual components return *indefinite* values, then the *parts of the components* which are responsible for these values are identified, composed, and model checked. Thus, the construction of the full composed system is avoided. Finally, if the latter check is still indefinite then a *refinement* is applied to each component separately.

---

* An extended version including full proofs is published as a technical report in [19].

Z. Liu and A.P. Ravn (Eds.): ATVA 2009, LNCS 5799, pp. 271–288, 2009.

In this work we present a framework generalizing the compositional approach in [21] to general multi-valued models. Our interest in such a framework stems from the fact that multi-valued modeling is widely used in many applications of model checking. It is used to model concrete systems more precisely and to define abstract models.

Multi-valued models enable a more precise modeling of systems by distinguishing several levels of uncertainty and inconsistency. For example, 3-valued models are used to describe models with partial information [3]. 4-valued models can model disagreement and their generalizations are used to handle inconsistent views of a system [10,16]. Temporal logic query checking [6,5] can also be reduced to multi-valued model checking. Multi-valued models have been widely used for abstraction as well: 3-valued (abstract) models allow proving truth as well as falsity of formulas for the concrete models they represent [13]. The 6-valued models in [1] are tuned to better achieving proofs of falsification. 4-valued models extend 3-valued abstractions by enabling to capture inconsistencies in software [14] and hardware (in STE) [20]. Tools to provide multi-valued verification such as YASM ([14]) and STE ([20]) were developed and successfully applied to software and hardware verification.

Multi-valued models may still suffer from the state explosion problem. Thus, a compositional approach may enhance the verification of larger systems.

The first step we take in formalizing a compositional multi-valued framework is to introduce bilattices [11]. A bilattice defines two lattices over a given set of elements: the *truth lattice* and the *information lattice*, each accompanied with an order. Formulas interpreted over a multi-valued model are evaluated w.r.t. the truth lattice. On the other hand, the relation of "more abstract" over models is based on the information lattice: Roughly, a model M_2 is more abstract than a model M_1 if values of atomic propositions and transitions in M_2 are smaller or equal by the information order than the corresponding values in M_1. Consequently, the valuation of a formula in M_2 will be smaller or equal by the information order than its value in M_1. In fact, since we consider the full μ-calculus, a bidirectional correspondence between transitions of M_1 and M_2 is needed. To capture this, we define a mixed-simulation relation, based on the information lattice, which turns out to be nontrivial.

Bilattices provide a natural way to identify lattice elements that are *consistent*, meaning they represent some concrete elements of the bilattice (to be formalized later). We can also identify *definite* elements. Those are elements that need not be refined. For simplicity, in the rest of the paper we restrict the discussion to Consistent Partial Distributive Bilattices (CPDB), which consist of exactly all the consistent elements.

Once we establish our setting by means of bilattices, we can fill in the rest of the framework's ingredients. First, we define the notion of *composition* of multi-valued systems. Next, we use the model checking algorithm for multi-valued systems and the alternation-free μ-calculus, suggested in [22]. We also show, in case the checks on individual components are indefinite, how to identify, compose, and check the parts of the models that are needed for the evaluation of the checked formula. As we exemplify later, the resulting composed system is often much smaller than the full composed system. Finally, we develop a heuristics for finding a *criterion for refinement*, in case the result of model checking the composed system is indefinite.

In the framework above we do not discuss the construction of multi-valued abstract models. This is investigated for instance in [15], which presents a methodology for a systematic construction of an abstract model for a given concrete one.

Other works deal with several aspects of multi-valued model checking, but none investigate a compositional approach. Multi-valued symbolic model checking is described in [7]. An alternative definition of (bi)simulation is suggested in [18]. However, there, the relation returns a value, indicating how "close" the models are. Our mixed simulation, on the other hand, returns either true or false, indicating whether one model is an abstraction of the other. A relation similar to our mixed simulation is defined in [1]. Preservation of formulas via simulation is described there in terms of information order. However, they handle a 6-valued framework, rather then a general multi-valued one. Also, they suggest refinement only if the result is the smallest element in the information order, $\perp$. In contrast, we allow refinement for any indefinite value in the bilattice. Bilattices are used also in [15]. However, they are not exploited there for refinement.

To summarize, the main contributions of this paper are:

– We present a framework for fully automated compositional verification of multi-valued systems w.r.t. μ-calculus specifications. The framework is based on multi-valued abstraction-refinement. To the best of our knowledge, this is the first compositional approach for multi-valued model checking.
– We apply our framework to the alternation-free μ-calculus model checking algorithm. In particular, we develop an algorithm for refinement in this context.
– We formalize our framework based on bilattices. This allows to naturally define the consistent and definite elements in the bilattice. It also provides a clear definition of abstraction and refinement in the multi-valued context. It thus provides a better understanding of the multi-valued framework.
– Based on the information order of a bilattice, we define a mixed simulation relation over multi-valued models, preserving μ-calculus specifications.

2 Preliminaries

In this section we introduce the concepts of lattices, multi-valued Kripke models, μ-calculus and multi-valued model checking graphs.

Definition 1. *A lattice $\mathcal{L} = (L, \leq)$ consists of a set L with a partial order $\leq$ over L, where every finite subset B of L has a least upper bound, join, denoted $\sqcup B$, and a greatest lower bound, meet, denoted $\sqcap B$, both in L. A lattice is distributive if $\sqcup$ and $\sqcap$ distribute over each other.*

Examples of lattices are shown in Fig. 1(a),(b),(c) and (e).

Definition 2. $\mathcal{D} = (L, \leq, \neg)$ *is a* De Morgan algebra *if $(L, \leq)$ is a finite distributive lattice, $\neg : L \to L$ is a negation function s.t. $\forall a, b$: $\neg\neg a = a$, $a \leq b \Leftrightarrow \neg b \leq \neg a$, and De Morgan laws are satisfied.*

All De Morgan algebras have a greatest (top) element, denoted $true$, and a least (bottom) element, denoted $false$.

2.1 Multi-valued Models and μ-Calculus

Definition 3. *A* Multi-Valued Kripke model *is a 6-tuple* $M = \langle \mathcal{L}, AP, S, s_0, R, \Theta \rangle$, *where* $\mathcal{L} = (L, \leq, \neg)$ *is a De Morgan algebra, AP is a set of atomic propositions, S is a finite set of states, s_0 is the initial state, $R : S \times S \to L$ is a mapping of transitions to values in L, and $\Theta : AP \to (S \to L)$ associates with each atomic proposition p, a mapping from S to L, describing the truth value of p in each state.*

Definition 4. *Let AP be a set of atomic propositions and Var a set of propositional variables, s.t. $p \in AP$ and $Z \in Var$. The μ-calculus in negation normal form is defined by:*

$$\varphi ::= p \mid \neg p \mid Z \mid \psi \vee \psi' \mid \psi \wedge \psi' \mid \Box \psi \mid \Diamond \psi \mid \mu Z.\psi \mid \nu Z.\psi$$

Let L_μ denote the set of all formulas generated by the above grammar. Fixpoint quantifiers μ and ν are variable binders. We write η for either μ or ν. We assume formulas are well-named, i.e. no variable is bound more than once in any formula. Thus for a *closed* formula $\varphi \in L_\mu$, every variable Z identifies a unique subformula $fp(Z) = \eta Z.\psi$ of φ. The set $Sub(\varphi)$ includes all subformulas of φ.

An *environment* $\mathcal{V} : Var \to (S \to L)$ defines the meaning of free variables. For a variable $Z \in Var$ and a mapping $l : S \to L$, we write $\mathcal{V}[Z = l]$ for the environment that agrees with $\mathcal{V}$ except that it maps Z to l.

The multi-valued semantics $\|\varphi\|_{\mathcal{V}}^M$ of a μ-calculus formula φ w.r.t. a multi-valued Kripke model M and an environment $\mathcal{V}$ [4] is given as a mapping $S \to L$, in which each state s of M is mapped to a value in L describing the truth value of φ in s. In the following, lfp, gfp stand for least and greatest fixpoints, respectively, which exist based on [23]. $\|\varphi\|_{\mathcal{V}}^M$ is defined by:

$$\|p\|_{\mathcal{V}}^M = \lambda s.\Theta(p)(s) \qquad\qquad\qquad \|\neg p\|_{\mathcal{V}}^M = \lambda s.\neg\Theta(p)(s)$$

$$\|\varphi_1 \vee \varphi_2\|_{\mathcal{V}}^M = \lambda s.\|\varphi_1\|_{\mathcal{V}}^M \vee \|\varphi_2\|_{\mathcal{V}}^M \qquad \|\varphi_1 \wedge \varphi_2\|_{\mathcal{V}}^M = \lambda s.\|\varphi_1\|_{\mathcal{V}}^M \wedge \|\varphi_2\|_{\mathcal{V}}^M$$

$$\|\Diamond\varphi\|_{\mathcal{V}}^M = \lambda s.\bigvee_{s' \in S}(R(s, s') \wedge \|\varphi\|_{\mathcal{V}}^M(s')) \quad \|\Box\varphi\|_{\mathcal{V}}^M = \lambda s.\bigwedge_{s' \in S}(\neg R(s, s') \vee \|\varphi\|_{\mathcal{V}}^M(s'))$$

$$\|Z\|_{\mathcal{V}}^M = \mathcal{V}(Z) \qquad \|\nu Z.\varphi\|_{\mathcal{V}}^M = \text{gfp}(\lambda g.\|\varphi\|_{\mathcal{V}[Z=g]}^M) \qquad \|\mu Z.\varphi\|_{\mathcal{V}}^M = \text{lfp}(\lambda g.\|\varphi\|_{\mathcal{V}[Z=g]}^M)$$

For closed formulas we drop the environment, and refer to $\|\varphi\|^M$.

2.2 Multi-valued Model-Checking Algorithm

A multi-valued model checking algorithm for a closed L_μ formula over a multi-valued Kripke model is suggested in [22]. There, multi-valued games are introduced, and a multi-valued model checking problem is translated into a problem of finding the value of a multi-valued game. In this work, we only use the model checking graph (further referred to as *mc-graph*) defined in [22], with its connections to the model checking algorithm.

Let M be a multi-valued Kripke model over $\mathcal{L} = (L, \leq, \neg)$ and φ_0 a closed L_μ formula. The *mc-graph* is defined by $G(M, \varphi_0) = (n^0, N, E)$, where N is a set of nodes, $E \subseteq N \times N$ is a set of edges in the graph and $n^0 \in N$ is the initial node. Nodes in the mc-graph are elements of $S \times Sub(\varphi_0)$, denoted $t \vdash \psi$, and $n^0 = s_0 \vdash \varphi_0$. Nodes of type $s \vdash \varphi_0 \vee \varphi_1$ or $s \vdash \Diamond\varphi$ are considered $\vee$-nodes, whereas nodes of type $s \vdash \varphi_0 \wedge \varphi_1$

or $s \vdash \Box\varphi$ are $\wedge$-nodes. Nodes of type $s \vdash Z$ or $s \vdash \eta Z.\varphi$ can be either $\vee$-nodes or $\wedge$-nodes. The edges of the mc-graph are defined by the following rules.

$$\frac{s \vdash \varphi_0 \vee \varphi_1}{s \vdash \varphi_i} \, i \in \{0, 1\} \qquad \frac{s \vdash \eta Z.\varphi}{s \vdash Z} \qquad \frac{s \vdash \Diamond\varphi}{t \vdash \varphi} \, R(s, t) \neq false$$

$$\frac{s \vdash \varphi_0 \wedge \varphi_1}{s \vdash \varphi_i} \, i \in \{0, 1\} \qquad \frac{s \vdash Z}{s \vdash \varphi} \text{ if } fp(Z) = \eta Z.\varphi \qquad \frac{s \vdash \Box\varphi}{t \vdash \varphi} \, R(s, t) \neq false$$

Every edge $(n, n') \in E$ corresponds to a rule where n, n' are of the form of the upper, respectively lower, part of the rule. If no rule is defined from some node n, then there are no outgoing edges from n in the mc-graph. This happens in terminal nodes of the form $t \vdash p$ or $t \vdash \neg p$, or in terminal nodes of the form $t \vdash \Diamond\varphi$ or $t \vdash \Box\varphi$ where there are no transitions from the state t in the Kripke model.

Each edge in E is associated with a value from L: edges that refer to a transition of the model get the value of that transition. The rest get the value $true$. By abuse of notation we use $R(n, n')$ to refer to the value of an edge $(n, n') \in E$.

Definition 5. *([22]) Let $n \in G$ be a terminal node, $val(n)$ is defined as follows. $val(t \vdash q) = \Theta(q)(t)$, $val(t \vdash \neg q) = \neg\Theta(q)(t)$, $val(t \vdash \Diamond\varphi) = false$ and $val(t \vdash \Box\varphi) = true$.*

In [22] an algorithm for computing a value of nodes on a mc-graph is presented. The algorithm handles the *alternation-free* fragment of L_μ, where no nesting of fixpoints is allowed. Given a mc-graph $G(M, \varphi_0) = (n^0, N, E)$ and a function $val : N \to L$ which maps terminal nodes in G to values in L (Def. 5), the algorithm returns a mc-function $\chi : N \to L$ that maps each node to a value from L.

Algorithm 1 (mc-algorithm [22]). *G is partitioned to Maximal Strongly Connected Components (MSCCs) and a (total) order on them is determined, reflected by their numbers: $Q_1,...,Q_k$. The order fulfills the rule that if $i < j$ then there are no edges from Q_i to Q_j. The components are handled by increasing values of i. Consider a single Q_i. Each node $n \in Q_i$ is associated with a value $\chi(n)$ as follows. For a terminal node n, $\chi(n) = val(n)$. For a $\vee$-node n we set $\chi(n)$ to be $\bigvee\{R(n, n') \wedge \chi(n')|R(n, n') \neq false\}$. Similarly, if n is a $\wedge$-node then $\chi(n) = \bigwedge\{\neg R(n, n') \vee \chi(n')|R(n, n') \neq false\}$. If Q_i is a non-trivial MSCC then it contains exactly one fixpoint variable Z. In this case, first label the nodes in Q_i with temporary values, $temp(n)$, that are updated iteratively. For nodes of the form $n = s \vdash Z$, initialize $temp(n)$ to true if Z is of type ν, or to false if Z is of type μ (the rest remain uninitialized). Then apply the previous rules for $\vee, \wedge$-nodes until the temporary values do not change anymore. Finally, set $\chi(n) = temp(n)$ for every node n in Q_i. Return χ as the mc-function.*

In [22], the connection between χ and the model checking problem is proved, by showing that $\chi(n^0) = \|\varphi_0\|^M(s_0)$. In the context of this work we will be interested also in the internal nodes of G. We therefore generalize the correspondence between χ and the multi-valued semantics to *all* nodes in G.

For $\psi \in Sub(\varphi_0)$, ψ^* denotes the result of replacing every free occurrence of $Z \in Var$ in ψ by $fp(Z)$. Note that ψ^* is a closed formula, and if ψ is closed then $\psi^* = \psi$.

Theorem 1. *Let $G(M, \varphi_0)$ be a mc-graph, s.t. φ_0 is an alternation-free closed L_μ formula. Let χ be the mc-function returned by the **mc-algorithm**, then for every $s \vdash \psi \in N$, $\chi(s \vdash \psi) = \|\psi^*\|^M(s)$.*

3   Bilattices and Partial Bilattices

In this section we introduce bilattices, consider several of their attributes, and define the notion of partial bilattices.

Definition 6. *[11] A distributive bilattice is a structure $\mathcal{B} = (B, \leq_i, \leq_t, \neg)$ s.t.: (1) $\mathcal{B}_i = (B, \leq_i)$ is a lattice, $\mathcal{B}_t = (B, \leq_t, \neg)$ is a De Morgan algebra; (2) meet($\otimes$), join($\oplus$) of $\mathcal{B}_i$, and meet($\wedge$), join($\vee$) of $\mathcal{B}_t$ are monotone w.r.t. both $\leq_i$ and $\leq_t$; (3) all meets and joins distribute over each other; and (4) negation ($\neg$) is $\leq_i$ monotone.*

The bilattices considered in this work are distributive, thus the use of the term bilattice refers to distributive bilattice. In our context, the relation $\leq_t$ is an order on the "degree of truth". The bottom in this order is denoted by $false$ and the top by $true$. The relation $\leq_i$ is an order on the "degree of information". Thus, if $x \leq_i y$, y gives us at least as much information as x (and possibly more). The bottom in the information order is denoted by $\bot$ and the top by $\top$.

Theorem 2. *[11] Let $\mathcal{D} = (D, \leq, \neg)$ be a De Morgan algebra, and $\mathcal{B}(\mathcal{D})$ be a structure $(D \times D, \leq_i, \leq_t, \neg)$ s.t. (1) $\langle a, b \rangle \leq_i \langle c, d \rangle \triangleq a \leq c$ and $b \leq d$; (2) $\langle a, b \rangle \leq_t \langle c, d \rangle \triangleq a \leq c$ and $d \leq b$; and (3) $\neg \langle a, b \rangle \triangleq \langle b, a \rangle$. Then, $\mathcal{B}(\mathcal{D})$ is a distributive bilattice. Furthermore, every distributive bilattice is isomorphic to $\mathcal{B}(\mathcal{D})$ for some De Morgan algebra $\mathcal{D}$.*

Intuitively, for a De Morgan algebra $\mathcal{D}$, an element $\langle x, y \rangle$ of $\mathcal{B}(\mathcal{D})$ is interpreted as a value whose "degree of truth" is x and "degree of falsity" is y. If we view $\mathcal{D}$ as a concrete truth domain, $\mathcal{B}(\mathcal{D})$ can be viewed as its abstract truth domain. Given an element $c \in D$, $\langle x, y \rangle \in D \times D$ approximates c if x is no more true than c, and y is no more false than c. Thus, $\langle c, \neg c \rangle$ is the best approximation of c, and $\langle x, y \rangle$ approximates c if $\langle x, y \rangle \leq_i \langle c, \neg c \rangle$. We say that $\langle x, y \rangle \in D \times D$ is *consistent* if $\langle x, y \rangle \leq_i \langle c, \neg c \rangle$ for some $c \in D$. Thus $\langle x, y \rangle$ is consistent iff $y \leq \neg x$ (defined similarly in [15]). We say that $\langle x, y \rangle \in D \times D$ is *definite* if $\langle c, \neg c \rangle \leq_i \langle x, y \rangle$ for some $c \in D$. Thus $\langle x, y \rangle$ is definite iff $y \geq \neg x$. If $\langle x, y \rangle \in D \times D$ is definite and consistent, then $\langle x, y \rangle = \langle c, \neg c \rangle$ for some $c \in D$.

Example 1. Fig. 1(a),(b) present an example of the distributive bilattice for the 4-valued Belnap structure ([2]). This bilattice is isomorphic to the bilattice $\mathcal{B}(\mathcal{D})$ created from the 2-valued De Morgan algebra $\mathcal{D} = (\{T, F\}, \leq, \neg)$, where $F \leq T$, $\neg T = F$. Thus, $t \triangleq \langle T, F \rangle$, $f \triangleq \langle F, T \rangle$, $\top \triangleq \langle T, T \rangle$ and $\bot \triangleq \langle F, F \rangle$. t, f are best approximations of T, resp. F. $\top$, representing maximal degree of truth and falsity, is inconsistent. t, f and $\top$ are definite elements. $\bot$ is indefinite.

When referring to a bilattice $\mathcal{B}$, we sometimes implicitly refer to the structure $\mathcal{B}(\mathcal{D})$ isomorphic to $\mathcal{B}$ (which exists by Thm. 2). In particular, we use '$\leq$' to denote the order on the elements in the De Morgan algebra $\mathcal{D}$ of $\mathcal{B}(\mathcal{D})$.

Definition 7. $\mathcal{P} = (B, \leq)$ *is a* partial lattice *if it is a lattice, except that join is not always defined. A* partial distributive bilattice *is a structure* $\mathcal{P} = (B, \leq_i, \leq_t, \neg)$ *defined similarly to a distributive bilattice (Def. 6), except that* $\mathcal{P}_i = (B, \leq_i)$ *is a partial lattice, and requirements (2) and (3) hold for join of* $\mathcal{P}_i$ *only if it is defined.*

Definition 8. *Let* $\mathcal{B}(\mathcal{D}) = \langle D \times D, \leq_i, \leq_t, \neg \rangle$ *be a bilattice, and let* $P \subseteq D \times D$ *be the set of all consistent elements in* $\mathcal{B}(\mathcal{D})$. *Then* $\mathcal{P}(\mathcal{B}) = \langle P, \leq_i, \leq_t, \neg \rangle$ *is the* consistent structure induced *by* $\mathcal{B}(\mathcal{D})$, *where* $\leq_t$, $\leq_i$ *and* $\neg$ *in* $\mathcal{P}(\mathcal{B})$ *are as in* $\mathcal{B}(\mathcal{D})$, *restricted to* P.

Theorem 3. *Let* $\mathcal{B}(\mathcal{D}) = \langle D \times D, \leq_i, \leq_t, \neg \rangle$ *be a bilattice, and let* $\mathcal{P}(\mathcal{B}) = \langle P, \leq_i, \leq_t, \neg \rangle$ *be the consistent structure induced by it, then* $\mathcal{P}(\mathcal{B})$ *is a partial distributive bilattice.*

We refer to consistent structures, which, by Thm. 3, are also partial distributive bilattices, as *consistent partial distributive bilattices* (CPDB). Note that in CPDBs we do not have $\top$. $\bot$, *true* and *false* always exist. Note further that for CPDBs, the set of maximal elements w.r.t. $\leq_i$ is exactly the set of definite elements, all of the form $\langle c, \neg c \rangle$ for some $c \in D$.

Theorem 4. *Let* $\mathcal{B} = \langle B, \leq_i, \leq_t \ \neg \rangle$ *be either a distributive bilattice or a CPDB, and let* $a, b \in B$ *be definite values. Then* $a \wedge b$, $a \vee b$ *and* $\neg a$ *are definite as well.*

Example 2. Examples of CPDBs appear in Fig. 1. The CPDB induced by the bilattice of the Belnap structure is described in Fig. 1(a) and (b), as the un-boxed elements, which are all the consistent elements. This CPDB is isomorphic to the standard 3-valued structure, where $? \triangleq \bot$, $T \triangleq t$ and $F \triangleq f$. The structure 3×3 is defined by the CPDB in Fig. 1(e) and (f). This CPDB is isomorphic to the CPDB induced by the bilattice $\mathcal{B}(\mathcal{D})$ created from the 2-views De Morgan algebra $\mathcal{D} = (\{T, F\} \times \{T, F\}, \leq, \neg)$, where $\leq$ and $\neg$ are defined bitwise. That is, for $a_1 a_2, b_1 b_2 \in \{T, F\} \times \{T, F\}$, $a_1 a_2 \leq b_1 b_2$ iff $a_1 \leq b_1$ and $a_2 \leq b_2$. Also, $\neg a_1 a_2 \triangleq \neg a_1 \neg a_2$. The 3×3 structure represents two different views, which may be contradictory (e.g. TF). However, such elements should not be confused with inconsistent elements in $\mathcal{B}(\mathcal{D})$ such as $\langle TT, TT \rangle$.

The consistent elements of $\mathcal{B}(\mathcal{D})$ are mapped into pairs over $\{T, F, ?\}$ in the 3×3 structure. E.g., $\langle TF, FF \rangle$ is represented by T? and $\langle TT, FF \rangle$ is represented by TT. The resulting structure contains both representations of the elements of the concrete 2-views domain (e.g. TT), and their approximations (e.g. T?).

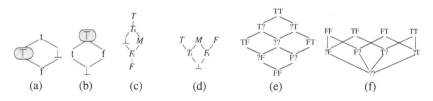

(a)   (b)   (c)   (d)   (e)   (f)

Fig. 1. Truth (a) and information (b) orders of 4-valued Belnap structure; Truth (c) and information (d) orders of 6-valued structure; Truth (e) and information (f) orders of 3×3 structure; Boxed nodes are inconsistent

Multi-valued Kripke models as well as the semantics of L_μ formulas and mc-graphs are defined over a De Morgan algebra $\mathcal{L}$. These definitions can easily be extended to a multi-valued structure, which is either a distributive bilattice or a CPDB. Thus, we have both information and truth lattices. In this case, the lattice $\mathcal{L}$ used in the multi-valued semantics is the truth lattice. For simplicity, in the rest of this work we use CPDBs.

4   Mixed Simulation and Refinement of Multi-valued Models

In this section we define a mixed simulation relation between two multi-valued Kripke models M_1 and M_2, and present a refinement algorithm based on the multi-valued model checking algorithm. We first define a relation between two multi-valued Kripke models, both defined over the same CPDB $\mathcal{B}$, which guarantees preservation of L_μ formulas w.r.t the multi-valued semantics. The relation is defined by means of the information order. Intuitively, it identifies the fact that M_2 contains less information than M_1. Thus, M_2 is an abstraction of M_1.

Definition 9. *Let* $M_i = \langle \mathcal{B}, AP, S_i, s_0^i, R_i, \Theta_i \rangle$ *for* $i \in \{1, 2\}$ *be multi-valued Kripke models.* $H \subseteq S_1 \times S_2$ *is a* mixed simulation *from* M_1 *to* M_2 *if* $(s_1, s_2) \in H$ *implies:*

1. $\forall p \in AP : \Theta_2(p)(s_2) \leq_i \Theta_1(p)(s_1)$.
2. $\forall t_1 \in S_1$ *s.t.* $R_1(s_1, t_1) \neq false \ \exists t_2 \in S_2$ *s.t.* $(t_1, t_2) \in H$ *and* $R_2(s_2, t_2) \leq_i R_1(s_1, t_1)$.
3. $\forall t_2 \in S_2$ *s.t.* $R_2(s_2, t_2) \not\leq_i false \ \exists t_1 \in S_1$ *s.t.* $(t_1, t_2) \in H$ *and* $R_2(s_2, t_2) \leq_i R_1(s_1, t_1)$.

If exists a mixed simulation H *s.t.* $(s_0^1, s_0^2) \in H$, *then* M_2 abstracts M_1, *denoted* $M_1 \preceq M_2$.

Note that requirements (2) and (3) are not symmetrical. By requirement (2), every transition in M_1 has a representation in M_2, whereas by requirement (3), only transitions in M_2 s.t. $R_2(s_2, t_2) \not\leq_i false$ have a representation in M_1. These requirements are similar to the requirements of mixed simulation in the 3-valued case ([12,9]). There, every *may* transition in M_1 has a representation in M_2, and every *must* transition in M_2 has a representation in M_1. In the multi-valued case transitions which are may and not must are transitions s.t. $R(s, t) \leq_i false$.

Theorem 5. *Let* $H \subseteq S_1 \times S_2$ *be a mixed simulation relation from* M_1 *to* M_2, *and let* φ *be a closed* L_μ *formula. Then for every* $(s_1, s_2) \in H$, $\|\varphi\|^{M_2}(s_2) \leq_i \|\varphi\|^{M_1}(s_1)$.

The mixed simulation relation can be used to describe the relation between a concrete model, M_c, and its abstraction, M_A: $M_c \preceq M_A$, where M_c is defined over $\mathcal{D}$ and M_A is defined over $\mathcal{P}(\mathcal{B}(\mathcal{D}))$. This is because M_c can be interpreted as a model over $\mathcal{P}(\mathcal{B}(\mathcal{D}))$, where the values are all definite (by Thm. 4 the semantics is maintained).

Given an abstract model, the information order enables us to capture the notion of a model checking result being "not good enough", namely, a result that needs to be refined. This is a result that does not give us the most information possible. That is, it is indefinite.

Let M_c be a concrete model over $\mathcal{D}$, and let M_A be an abstract model for it over $\mathcal{P}(\mathcal{B}(\mathcal{D}))$, i.e. $M_c \preceq M_A$, s.t. M_A should be refined. Our refinement consists of two parts. First, we choose a criterion for model refinement. Then, based on the criterion, the model is refined by either increasing the information level of some transition or of an atomic proposition in some state, or by splitting states. These refinement steps are similar to the refinement steps in [17]. The refinement is applied directly on the mc-graph. In fact, it suffices to refine the indefinite subgraph, where the mc-graph is pruned in definite nodes.

In the rest of the section we study choosing a criterion for model refinement. For a mc-function $\chi : N \to L$, given that $\chi(n^0)$ is indefinite, our goal in the refinement is to find and eliminate at least one of the reasons of the indefinite result. The criterion for the refinement is obtained from a failure node. This is a node $n = s \vdash \varphi \in N$ s.t. (1) $\chi(n)$ is indefinite; (2) $\chi(n)$ affects $\chi(n_0)$; and (3) $\chi(n)$ can be changed by increasing the information level of either an atomic proposition in s or some transition from s. (3) means that n *itself* is responsible for introducing (some) uncertainty. (1) and (2) require that this uncertainty is relevant to $\chi(n^0)$.

We adapt the **mc-algorithm** (Algo. 1) to remember for each node whose value is indefinite a failure node and a failure reason. The failure node and reason of n^0 will be used for refining the model. For a terminal node n, if $\chi(n)$ is indefinite, the failure node and reason attached to it are the node itself. To handle nonterminal nodes, we define an auxiliary function $f : N \to L$ that keeps for each node $n \in N$ its most updated value in the algorithm: If $\chi(n)$ is already defined, then $f(n) = \chi(n)$. Otherwise, if $temp(n)$ is defined, then $f(n) = temp(n)$.

Let n be a node for which $f(n)$ has been updated last. If $f(n)$ is definite, then no failure node and reason are attached to it. If $f(n)$ is indefinite, do the following:

1. If n is a $\vee$-node, find node n' with $R(n, n') \neq false$, for which the following hold:
   (a) $\forall n'' \in N$ where $n' \neq n''$ and $R(n, n'') \neq false$, $(R(n, n'') \wedge f(n'')) \leq_t (R(n, n') \wedge f(n'))$ or $(R(n, n'') \wedge f(n''))$ and $(R(n, n') \wedge f(n'))$ are uncomparable.
   (b) $R(n, n') \wedge f(n')$ is indefinite.
   Intuitively, for some n', if requirement (a) holds then $R(n, n') \wedge f(n')$ is maximal, and thus affects $f(n)$. Requirement (b) ensures that it is possible to refine $R(n, n')$ or $f(n')$. For the given node n and a chosen node n' satisfying (a),(b) define a failure node and reason for n as follows:
      i   If $f(n')$ is definite or $R(n, n') \lneq_t f(n')$, then n is the failure node, and the edge (n, n') is the failure reason.
      ii If $R(n, n')$ is definite or $f(n') \lneq_t R(n, n')$, then the failure node and reason of n are those of n'.
      iii Otherwise, arbitrarily choose either n as a failure node and the edge as a failure reason, or the failure node and reason of n' as the failure node and reason of n.
2. The case where n is a $\wedge$-node is dual, where instead of searching for a maximal $R(n, n') \wedge f(n')$, we now try to find a minimal $\neg R(n, n') \vee f(n')$.

Definite values are closed under $\neg$, $\wedge$ and $\vee$ (Thm. 4), thus if a node is given an indefinite value, this indefinite value results from an indefinite value of either a son n' of n, or an edge from n. For example, consider case 1(i). If $f(n')$ is definite, then $R(n, n')$ is necessarily indefinite (Thm. 4). Similarly, if $R(n, n') \lneq_t f(n')$, then $R(n, n') \wedge f(n') = R(n, n')$, which again, means that $R(n, n')$ is indefinite. Either way, $R(n, n')$ can be refined and is therefore a failure reason. The correctness of the failure search is formalized by the following lemma.

Lemma 1. *For every node n, if $f(n)$ is given an indefinite value, then there exists n' s.t. $R(n, n') \neq false$, which satisfies requirements (a),(b). Furthermore, $f(n')$ is already defined at that time. In addition, if the updating of failure node and reason of n is based on n', then n' also has a failure node and reason.*

A failure node and reason for n is updated *every time* $f(n)$ is updated. Thus, when the **mc-algorithm** terminates, for every n, if $\chi(n)$ is indefinite, then the failure node and reason for n is based on χ. Altogether there are two cases in which we consider the node itself as a failure node. The first case is when the node is a terminal node whose value is indefinite, for which the failure reason is clear. The second case is when the node has an indefinite edge to n' which is the failure reason. In this case n is the failure node since refining the value of the edge may change the value of n. The failure reason translates to an atomic proposition with an indefinite value in the first case, and to an indefinite transition in the second case. Note that the algorithm is heuristic in the sense that it does not guarantee that all possible refinements of the failure node and reason will increase the information level of the result. It greedily searches for a failure node and reason which is most likely to increase the result w.r.t. the information order.

Example 3. Consider the mc-graph in Fig. 3(b). For the node n_0 marked $(s_2, t_2) \vdash \Diamond o$ there are three possible failure nodes and reasons. The first is n_0 itself being the failure node and the edge to node n_3 marked $(s_3, t_2) \vdash o$ being the reason. The second is node n_1 marked $(s_2, t_2) \vdash o$ being the failure node and reason, and the third is node n_0 itself and the edge to n_1 being the reason.

Recall that refinement is done by either increasing the information level of some transition or atomic proposition, or by splitting states. The information lattice of the underlying multi-valued structure is finite. Thus, if the underlying concrete model is finite, then there is a finite number of refinement steps possible. We conclude:

Lemma 2. *If M_c is finite then in a finite number of refinement steps the model checking result will be the same as the one in the underlying concrete model, M_c.*

5   Partial Model Checking and Subgraphs

In this section we investigate properties of the **mc-algorithm** (Algo. 1). In particular, we present sufficient conditions under which a subgraph of a mc-graph can be valuated "correctly" (to be formally defined later) without considering the full mc-graph. In the rest of the section, G denotes a multi-valued mc-graph over $\mathcal{B} = (L, \leq_i, \leq_t, \neg)$.

Definition 10. *Let G be a mc-graph and let $f : N \to L$ be a function. For a non-terminal node $n \in G$, and two nodes n', n'' sons of n, n' covers n'' under f w.r.t n, if one of the following holds:*

- *n is a $\wedge$-node and: (1) $(\neg R(n, n') \vee f(n')) \leq_t (\neg R(n, n'') \vee f(n''))$; and (2) $\forall v', v'' \in L$: if $f(n') \leq_i v'$ and $f(n'') \leq_i v''$ then $(\neg R(n, n') \vee v') \leq_t (\neg R(n, n'') \vee v'')$.*
- *n is a $\vee$-node and: (1) $(R(n, n'') \wedge f(n'')) \leq_t (R(n, n') \wedge f(n'))$; and (2) $\forall v', v'' \in L$: if $f(n') \leq_i v'$ and $f(n'') \leq_i v''$ then $(R(n, n'') \wedge v'') \leq_t (R(n, n') \wedge v')$.*

Intuitively, a son n' covers a son n'' in the sense that if f defines the value of the sons, then it suffices to take into account n' (and ignore n'') in order to determine the value of the node n. In our setting, f will sometimes only provide a lower bound w.r.t. $\leq_i$ on the value of the nodes. However, the second requirement ensures that the covering holds for every $f' \geq_i f$ as well. Note that the notion of covering defines a partial order on the nodes of the mc-graph. As a result, for every covered node n'' there exists a covering node n' s.t. n' is non-covered.

Example 4. Consider the mc-graph in Fig. 3(b). Assume the underlying structure is the 3×3 structure (Fig. 1(e), (f)). The values of the edges are $R(n_0, n_1) = ?T$ and $R(n_0, n_2) = ??$. Let $f(n_1) = ?T$ and $f(n_2) = F?$. We show that n_2 is covered by n_1 under f. Clearly, requirement (1) holds ($F?\wedge?? \leq_t ?T\wedge?T$). For requirement (2), we need to show that $\forall v_1, v_2 \in L$: if $f(n_1) \leq_i v_2$ and $f(n_2) \leq_i v_2$ then $(R(n_0, n_2) \wedge v_2) \leq_t (R(n_0, n_1)\wedge v_1)$. Specifically, we need to show that $\forall v_1 \in \{?T, TT, FT\}, \forall v_2 \in \{F?, FF, FT\}$: $v_2\wedge?? \leq_t v_1\wedge?T$, which obviously holds.

In the example, the value given to n_0 based on all its sons is the same as if the son n_2 had not been considered. We will next exploit this property.

Definition 11. *Let G be a mc-graph and χ its mc-function. A subgraph G' of G is closed if every node n in G' is either terminal in G', or G' contains all non-covered sons of n under χ and corresponding edges.*

Let G be a mc-graph, χ its mc-function, and $\chi_I : N \to L$ a partial mc-function. χ_I is *correct w.r.t. χ* if for every $n \in G$, if $\chi_I(n)$ is defined, then $\chi_I(n) = \chi(n)$.

Theorem 6. *Let G be a mc-graph and χ its mc-function. Consider a closed subgraph G' of G with a partial mc-function χ_I which is correct w.r.t. χ and defined over (at least) all terminal nodes in G'. Then applying the **mc-algorithm** on G' with χ_I as an initial valuation (replacing val) results in a mc-function χ' of G' s.t. for every n in G', $\chi'(n) = \chi(n)$.*

6 Compositional Model Checking

In this section we define the composition of two models, and describe an algorithm for model checking the composed system, without fully constructing it.

In compositional model checking the goal is to verify a formula φ on a composed system $M_1 \| M_2$. In our setting M_1 and M_2 are multi-valued Kripke models defined over the same CPDB $\mathcal{B} = (L, \leq_i, \leq_t, \neg)$. The models synchronize on the joint labelling of the states. In the following, for $i \in \{1, 2\}$ we assume that every (abstract) model M_i has an underlying concrete model M_i^c s.t. $M_i^c \preceq M_i$. Let $M_i = \langle \mathcal{B}, AP_i, S_i, s_0^i, R_i, \Theta_i \rangle$, we use $\bar{i}$ to denote the remaining index in $\{1, 2\} \setminus \{i\}$.

Definition 12. *Let $s_1 \in S_1$, $s_2 \in S_2$ be states in M_1 and M_2 resp. Then, s_1, s_2 are weakly composable if for every $p \in AP_1 \cap AP_2 : \Theta_1(p)(s_1) \oplus \Theta_2(p)(s_2)$ is defined.*

Note that $\oplus$ might be undefined since $\mathcal{B}$ is a CPDB (Def. 8). Intuitively, if $\oplus$ is defined, then the composition of the states is consistent on all atomic propositions.

Definition 13. *States $s_1 \in S_1$, $s_2 \in S_2$ are* composable *if they are weakly composable, and for every $p \in AP_1 \cap AP_2 : \Theta_1(p)(s_1)$ and $\Theta_2(p)(s_2)$ are definite.*

In fact, since the definite values in CPDB are highest in the information order, if s_1 and s_2 are composable, then for every $p \in AP_1 \cap AP_2$, $\Theta_1(p)(s_1) = \Theta_2(p)(s_2)$.

We say that M_1 and M_2 are *composable* if their initial states are composable.

Definition 14. *Let M_1 and M_2 be composable models. Their composition, denoted $M_1\|M_2$, is the multi-valued Kripke model $M = \langle \mathcal{B}, AP, S, s_0, R, \Theta \rangle$, where $AP = AP_1 \cup AP_2$, $s_0 = (s_0^1, s_0^2)$, $S = \{(s_1, s_2) \in S_1 \times S_2 | s_1, s_2$ are weakly composable$\}$. For each $(s_1, s_2), (t_1, t_2) \in S$: If t_1, t_2 are composable, $R((s_1, s_2), (t_1, t_2)) = R_1(s_1, t_1) \wedge R_2(s_2, t_2)$. Otherwise, if t_1, t_2 are weakly composable, $R((s_1, s_2), (t_1, t_2)) = R_1(s_1, t_1) \wedge R_2(s_2, t_2) \wedge \bot$. For each $(s_1, s_2) \in S$ and $p \in AP$: if $p \in AP_1 \cap AP_2$ then $\Theta(p)(s_1, s_2) = \Theta_1(p)(s_1) \oplus \Theta_2(p)(s_2)$, if $p \in AP_i \setminus AP_{\bar{i}}$ then $\Theta(p)(s_1, s_2) = \Theta_i(p)(s_i)$.*

The definition of the states in the composed model enables composition of states that are weakly composable but not composable. Such states do not exist in a composed concrete model (since the values of all atomic propositions in a concrete model are maximal w.r.t. $\leq_i$). However, they might exist when considering a composed *abstract* model. Unlike composable states, the weakly composable states in a composed abstract model might not have any corresponding state in the underlying concrete model. This is because in the concrete model, where the information level of some atomic propositions increases, the states might disagree on some p in their joint labelling.

Even though we are enabling weakly composable states which might not exist in the underlying concrete model, we want the abstract composed model to be an abstraction of the concrete composed model (i.e., we want to maintain a mixed simulation relation between these models). This is done with the definition of R. In the case where the target states are composable, the definition of R is immediate. If the target states are weakly composable but not composable, then we want to take into account the possibility that the transition does not exist. Defining its value to be $\bot$ achieves this goal. However, we can in fact guarantee more than that (in terms of the information order) by taking the meet w.r.t. $\leq_t$ with $\bot$. This ensures that the value of the composed transition is no "more true" than $\bot$, but may be "more false" than $\bot$ and thus more informative. More precisely, consider the CPDB $\mathcal{P}(\mathcal{B}(\mathcal{D}))$ isomorphic to $\mathcal{B}$, where $\mathcal{D} = (D, \leq, \neg)$ is a De Morgan algebra. Then $\bot$ is defined as $\langle d_\bot, d_\bot \rangle \in D \times D$ where for every $a \in D.d_\bot \leq a$. Thus, for every $\langle a, b \rangle \in D \times D$, $\langle a, b \rangle \wedge \bot = \langle d_\bot, b \rangle$, which means that the falsity level of $\langle a, b \rangle$ is preserved, whereas the truth level is minimal.

Allowing weakly composable states gives freedom to the user when abstracting each of the models, as all atomic propositions can be abstracted. In contrast, in [21], where composition of 3-valued models is discussed, joint labelling cannot be abstracted, thus all composable states in the abstract model represent composable states in the concrete model. There is a tradeoff presented with this freedom. On the one hand, the user can define a very coarse abstraction in each of the separate models. On the other hand, the abstract composed model might now include more states that do not represent any state in the concrete model.

From now on we fix AP to be $AP_1 \cup AP_2$.

Next, we define *lifting* of models for the purpose of compositional verification. The idea is to view each model M_i as an abstraction of $M_1||M_2$.

Definition 15. *The lifted model of* $M_i = \langle \mathcal{B}, AP_i, S_i, s_0^i, R_i, \Theta_i \rangle$ *is* $M_i \!\uparrow = \langle \mathcal{B}, AP, S_i, s_0^i, R_i \!\uparrow, \Theta_i \!\uparrow \rangle$ *where: for every* $s_i, t_i \in S_i$: $R_i \!\uparrow (s_i, t_i) = R_i(s_i, t_i) \wedge \bot$. *For every* $s_i \in S_i$, $p \in AP$: *if* $p \in AP_i$ *then* $\Theta_i \!\uparrow (p)(s_i) = \Theta_i(p)(s_i)$. *If* $p \in AP \setminus AP_i$ *then* $\Theta_i \!\uparrow (p)(s_i) = \bot$.

The value of each literal over $AP \setminus AP_i$ in each state of $M_i \!\uparrow$ is minimal w.r.t. the $\leq_i$ order ($\bot$). Indeed, its value in M will be determined by $M_{\bar{i}}$. In addition, each transition of M_i is also uncertain, in the sense that it cannot be "more true" than $\bot$. This is because in the composition it might be removed if a matching transition does not exist in $M_{\bar{i}}$.

Theorem 7. *For every* $i \in \{1,2\}$, $M_1||M_2 \preceq M_i \!\uparrow$. *The mixed simulation relation* $H \subseteq S \times S_i$ *is given by* $\{((s_1, s_2), s_i)|(s_1, s_2) \in S\}$.

Since each $M_i \!\uparrow$ abstracts $M_1||M_2$, we are able to first consider each component separately: Theorem 5 ensures that for every closed L_μ formula φ, $\|\varphi\|^{M_i\uparrow} \leq_i \|\varphi\|^{M_1||M_2}$. In particular, $\|\varphi\|^{M_1\uparrow} \oplus \|\varphi\|^{M_2\uparrow}$ is defined, and a definite result on one of the components suffices to determine a definite value on $M_1||M_2$. Note that a definite value on $M_1||M_2$ can be achieved even if both $\|\varphi\|^{M_i\uparrow}$ are indefinite, but $\|\varphi\|^{M_1\uparrow} \oplus \|\varphi\|^{M_2\uparrow}$ is definite.

A more typical case is when the valuation of φ on both $M_1 \!\uparrow$ and $M_2 \!\uparrow$ is indefinite. This reflects the fact that φ depends on both components and on their synchronization. Typically, such a result requires some refinement of the abstract model. Considering the composition of the two components is a refinement of the lifted models. Still, having considered each component separately can guide us into focusing on the places where we indeed need to consider the composition of the components.

We use the mc-graphs of $M_1 \!\uparrow$ and $M_2 \!\uparrow$ for building a subgraph for $M_1||M_2$, and by that avoid building the full composed model. The mc-graphs of the two components present all the information gained from model checking each component. To resolve the indefinite result, we first try to compose the parts of the mc-graphs which might be needed to determine the value of the formula.

Definition 16. *For every* $i \in \{1,2\}$ *let* $G_i = (n_i^0, N_i, E_i)$ *be the mc-graph of* $M_i \!\uparrow$, *with* χ_i *its mc-function.* $\chi_f : N_1 \times N_2 \to L$ *is defined by* $\chi_f(n_1, n_2) = \chi_1(n_1) \oplus \chi_2(n_2)$. $E_f : (N_1 \times N_2) \times (N_1 \times N_2) \to L$ *is defined as follows. Let* $n_i' = (s_i' \vdash \varphi') \in N_i$, *then* $E_f((n_1, n_2), (n_1', n_2')) = R_1(s_1, s_1') \wedge R_2(s_2, s_2')$ *if* s_1' *and* s_2' *are composable, and* $E_f((n_1, n_2), (n_1', n_2')) = R_1(s_1, s_1') \wedge R_2(s_2, s_2') \wedge \bot$ *if* s_1' *and* s_2' *are weakly composable but not composable.*

Let $G = (n^0, N, E)$ be a mc-graph and let $f : N \to L$ and $e : N \times N \to L$ be two functions. For a non-terminal node n in G, and two nodes n' and n'' which are sons of n, we abuse the notion of covering (Def. 10) and say that n' *covers* n'' *under* f *and* e w.r.t. n, if n' covers n'' under f w.r.t. n when e replaces the transition relation R.

Definition 17. (Product Graph) *For every* $i \in \{1,2\}$ *let* $G_i = (n_i^0, N_i, E_i)$ *be the mc-graph of* $M_i \!\uparrow$, *with an initial node* $n_i^0 = (s_i^0 \vdash \varphi) \in N_i$. *Also let* χ_i *be the mc-function of*

G_i. *The product graph of G_1 and G_2, denoted $G_\| = (n_\|^0, N_\|, E_\|)$, is defined as the least graph that obeys the following:*

- $n_\|^0 = (s_1^0, s_2^0) \vdash \varphi$ *is the initial node in $G_\|$.*
- *Let $n_1 = s_1 \vdash \psi$, $n_2 = s_2 \vdash \psi$ be s.t. $(n_1, n_2) \in N_\|$, and $\chi_f(n_1, n_2)$ is indefinite. Then for every $n_1' = (s_1' \vdash \psi') \in N_1$ and $n_2' = (s_2' \vdash \psi') \in N_2$, if the following holds: (1) s_1', s_2' are weakly composable; (2) $E_1(n_1, n_1') \neq false$ and $E_2(n_2, n_2') \neq false$; and (3) (n_1', n_2') is not covered under χ_f and E_f w.r.t. (n_1, n_2). Then: (a) $(n_1', n_2') \in N_\|$; and (b) $E_\|((n_1, n_2), (n_1', n_2')) = E_f((n_1, n_2), (n_1', n_2'))$.*

Lemma 3. *Let $G_\|$ be the product graph defined above. $\forall n \in N_\|$, $\chi_f(n)$ is defined.*

Note that the value of the edges in $G_\|$ is identical to their value in the composed model. This is because the product graph already refers to the complete system $M_1 \| M_2$. In contrast, the values of the edges in the mc-graphs of each component are all smaller or equal by truth order than $\bot$.

The product graph is constructed by a top-down traversal on the mc-graphs of the two models, where, starting from the initial node, nodes that share the same formulas and whose states are weakly composable, will be considered. Whenever two non-terminal nodes n_1, n_2 are composed, if $\chi_f(n_1, n_2)$ is indefinite, then the outgoing edges are computed as the product of their outgoing edges, restricted to weakly composable nodes. In particular, this means that if a node in one mc-graph has no matching node in the other, then it will be omitted from the product graph. After computing all legal sons based on the outgoing edges, the nodes which are covered under χ_f will be removed, leaving as outgoing edges and nodes only nodes which are not covered under χ_f. In addition, when a terminal node of one mc-graph is composed with a non-terminal node of the other, the resulting node is a terminal node in $G_\|$. Note that we compute χ_f and E_f only by need. In fact, when constructing $G_\|$ it suffices to consider the indefinite subgraphs $G_1^?$ and $G_2^?$ of G_1 and G_2 resp. (pruned in definite nodes). This is because whenever a definite node is composed with another node (definite or not), χ_f of the resulting node is definite, which makes it a terminal node.

We accompany $G_\|$ with an initial mc-function, χ_I, for its terminal nodes, based on the mc-functions of the two mc-graphs. We use the following observation:

Let $n = (s_1, s_2) \vdash \psi$ be a terminal node in $G_\|$. Then at least one of the following holds. Either (a) at least one of $s_1 \vdash \psi$ and $s_2 \vdash \psi$ is a terminal node in its mc-graph; Or (b) $\chi_f(s_1 \vdash \psi, s_2 \vdash \psi)$ is definite; Or (c) both $s_1 \vdash \psi$ and $s_2 \vdash \psi$ are non-terminal but no outgoing edges were left in their composition.

Definition 18. *The initial mc-function χ_I of $G_\|$ is defined as follows. Let $n = (s_1, s_2) \vdash \psi \in N_\|$ be a terminal node. If it fulfills case (a) or (b), then $\chi_I(n) = \chi_1(s_1 \vdash \psi) \oplus \chi_2(s_2 \vdash \psi)$. If it fulfills case (c), then $\chi_I(n) = true$ if n is a $\wedge$-node, and $\chi_I(n) = false$ if n is a $\vee$-node. χ_I is undefined for the rest of the nodes.*

Theorem 8. *The resulting product graph $G_\|$ is a closed subgraph of G, the mc-graph over $M_1 \| M_2$ with a mc-function χ. In addition, χ_I is defined over all the terminal nodes of $G_\|$, and is correct w.r.t. χ.*

Theorems 6 and 8 imply that applying the **mc-algorithm** on $G_{\parallel}$ with χ_I results in a correct mc-function χ w.r.t. $G_{\parallel}$. Thus, $\chi(n_{\parallel}^0)$ is the value of the model checking of φ in $M_1 \| M_2$. As a result, to model check φ on $M_1 \| M_2$ it remains to model check $G_{\parallel}$. Note that the full graph for $M_1 \| M_2$ is not constructed.

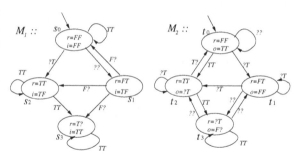

Fig. 2. Components M_1 and M_2

If the model checking result is indefinite (which is only possible if $M_1 \| M_2$ is abstract), then refinement is performed on each component separately, as described in the following steps, which summarize our compositional algorithm for checking an alternation-free L_μ formula φ on $M_1 \| M_2$.

Step 1: Model check each $M_i \uparrow$ separately (for $i \in \{1, 2\}$):
1. Construct the mc-graph G_i for φ and $M_i \uparrow$.
2. Apply multi-valued model checking on G_i. Let χ_i be the resulting mc-function.
If $\chi_1(n_1^0)$ or $\chi_2(n_2^0)$ is definite, return the corresp. model checking result for $M_1 \| M_2$.

Step 2: Consider the composition $M_1 \| M_2$:
1. Construct the product graph $G_{\parallel}$ of the mc-graphs $G_1^?$ and $G_2^?$.
2. Apply multi-valued model checking on $G_{\parallel}$ (with the initial mc-function).
If $\chi_{\parallel}(n_{\parallel}^0)$ is definite, return the corresp. model checking result for $M_1 \| M_2$.

Step 3: Refine: Consider the failure node and reason returned by model checking $G_{\parallel}$ (where $\chi_{\parallel}(n_{\parallel}^0)$ is indefinite). If it is p for some $p \in AP_i$, then refine $G_i^?$;
Else let it be a transition $((s_1, s_2), (s_1', s_2'))$. Then:
1. If s_1', s_2' are weakly composable but not composable, refine both $G_1^?$ and $G_2^?$ according to $AP_1 \cap AP_2$.
2. If $R_i(s_i, s_i') \leq_t R_{\bar{i}}(s_{\bar{i}}, s_{\bar{i}}')$, refine the transition $R_i(s_i, s_i')$ in $G_i^?$.
3. If $R_i(s_i, s_i')$ and $R_{\bar{i}}(s_{\bar{i}}, s_{\bar{i}}')$ are uncomparable, refine the subgraph(s) in which the transition is indefinite.
Go to Step 1(2) with the refined indefinite subgraphs.

Theorem 9. *For finite components, the compositional algorithm is guaranteed to terminate with a definite answer.*

Example 5. An example for the algorithm is given in Fig. 2,3. The two (abstract) components are described in Fig. 2. The underlying multi-valued structure is the 3×3 structure (described in Fig. 1(e), (f)). The atomic proposition o is local to M_1, i is local to M_2, and r is a joint atomic proposition that M_1 and M_2 synchronize on. We wish to verify the property $\Box(\neg i \vee \Diamond o)$. The mc-graph of the lifted model $M_1 \uparrow$ is described in Fig. 3(a). The mc-graph of $M_2 \uparrow$ can be created similarly. Note that the edges of the mc-graph get a different value than their value in the model, as this is a mc-graph of the lifted model, thus we can no longer guarantee the existence of these edges. The model checking on each of the models does not result in a definite answer, and we need to

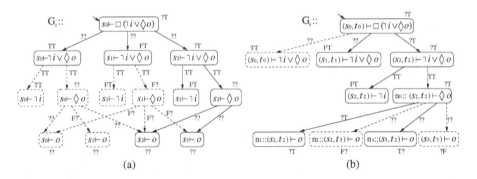

Fig. 3. (a) mc-graph of $M_1 \uparrow$; (b) the product graph. Dashed nodes are covered. Solid lines mark actual product graph.

consider their composition. The parts that are actually composed are marked with solid lines in Fig. 3(a). The product graph and its model checking is shown in Fig. 3(b), where the edges get their actual value. The nodes which are covered are marked with dashed lines. These nodes are created and removed on-the-fly, since they are covered. The actual nodes that compose the product graph are marked with solid lines. The property is still not verified in the composed model, thus a refinement is needed. Note that the product graph considers only a small part of the compound system, as it takes advantage of the information from model checking the separate components.

7   Discussion

This paper describes a *framework* for multi-valued model checking of L_μ formulas w.r.t. systems composed of several components. The framework is described as follows.

- Lift each individual component M_i into a component $M_i \uparrow$ s.t. $M_1 \| M_2 \preceq M_i \uparrow$.
- Model check each of the lifted models separately. If the result is definite, then this also holds for the full system.
- Construct the product graph of the individual mc-graphs; model check it correctly.
- If the result on the product graph is definite, then this result holds for the full system. Otherwise, refine the components as needed.

We showed how our framework can be implemented for model checking of CPDBs, and alternation-free L_μ formulas. We applied a specific model checking and reason finding algorithm (Algo. 1, Sec. 4), but these can be replaced by other algorithms.

Our framework is suitable for full L_μ, provided that the model checking and reason finding algorithm can handle the full L_μ. Examples of such algorithms for a 3-valued structure can be found in [13]. Indeed, in [21] a compositional framework such as ours, but with the 3-valued semantics, has been presented for the full L_μ.

Our framework can also be used for logics other than the μ-calculus. For example, the *full-PML* logic, which extends the modal operators with past operators, AY and EY, is used in [1], along with a 6-valued structure (described in Fig. 1(c),(d)). The structure is a CPDB, but since they use a logic with significantly different semantics, specific adaptations in some of the framework stages should be done.

References

1. Ball, T., Kupferman, O., Yorsh, G.: Abstraction for falsification. In: Etessami, K., Rajamani, S.K. (eds.) CAV 2005. LNCS, vol. 3576, pp. 67–81. Springer, Heidelberg (2005)
2. Belnap, N.D.: A useful four-valued logic. In: Modern uses of multiple valued logics (1977)
3. Bruns, G., Godefroid, P.: Model checking partial state spaces with 3-valued temporal logics. In: Halbwachs, N., Peled, D.A. (eds.) CAV 1999. LNCS, vol. 1633, pp. 274–287. Springer, Heidelberg (1999)
4. Bruns, G., Godefroid, P.: Model checking with multi-valued logics. In: Díaz, J., Karhumäki, J., Lepistö, A., Sannella, D. (eds.) ICALP 2004. LNCS, vol. 3142, pp. 281–293. Springer, Heidelberg (2004)
5. Bruns, G., Godefroid, P.: Temporal logic query checking. In: LICS 2001 (2001)
6. Chan, W.: Temporal-logic queries. In: Emerson, E.A., Sistla, A.P. (eds.) CAV 2000. LNCS, vol. 1855, pp. 450–463. Springer, Heidelberg (2000)
7. Chechik, M., Devereux, B., Easterbrook, S.M., Gurfinkel, A.: Multi-valued symbolic model-checking. In: ACM Transactions on Software Engineering and Methodology, vol. 12 (2003)
8. Clarke, E.M., Grumberg, O., Peled, D.A.: Model Checking. MIT Press, Cambridge (1999)
9. Dams, D., Gerth, R., Grumberg, O.: Abstract interpretation of reactive systems. ACM Trans. Program. Lang. Syst. 19(2) (1997)
10. Easterbrook, S.M., Chechik, M.: A framework for multi-valued reasoning over inconsistent viewpoints. In: ICSE 2001 (2001)
11. Fitting, M.: Bilattices are nice things. In: Self-Reference (2002)
12. Godefroid, P., Jagadeesan, R.: Automatic abstraction using generalized model checking. In: Brinksma, E., Larsen, K.G. (eds.) CAV 2002. LNCS, vol. 2404, p. 137. Springer, Heidelberg (2002)
13. Grumberg, O., Lange, M., Leucker, M., Shoham, S.: When not losing is better than winning: Abstraction and refinement for the full μ-calculus. Information and Computation 205(8) (2007)
14. Gurfinkel, A., Chechik, M.: Why waste a perfectly good abstraction? In: Hermanns, H., Palsberg, J. (eds.) TACAS 2006. LNCS, vol. 3920, pp. 212–226. Springer, Heidelberg (2006)
15. Gurfinkel, A., Wei, O., Chechik, M.: Systematic construction of abstractions for model-checking. In: Emerson, E.A., Namjoshi, K.S. (eds.) VMCAI 2006. LNCS, vol. 3855, pp. 381–397. Springer, Heidelberg (2006)
16. Huth, M.L., Pradhan, S.: Lifting assertion and consistency checkers from single to multiple viewpoints. In: TR 2002/11, Dept. of Computing. Imperial College, London (2002)
17. Jain, H., Kroening, D., Sharygina, N., Clarke, E.M.: Word level predicate abstraction and refinement for verifying RTL Verilog. In: DAC 2005 (2005)
18. Kupferman, O., Lustig, Y.: Latticed simulation relations and games. In: Namjoshi, K.S., Yoneda, T., Higashino, T., Okamura, Y. (eds.) ATVA 2007. LNCS, vol. 4762, pp. 316–330. Springer, Heidelberg (2007)
19. Meller, Y., Grumberg, O., Shoham, S.: A framework for compositional verification of multi-valued systems via abstraction-refinement. In: TR CS-2009-14, Dept. of Computer Science. Technion – Israel Institute of Technology (2009)

20. Seger, C.-J.H., Bryant, R.E.: Formal verification by symbolic evaluation of partially-ordered trajectories. Formal Methods in System Design 6(2) (1995)
21. Shoham, S., Grumberg, O.: Compositional verification and 3-valued abstractions join forces. In: Riis Nielson, H., Filé, G. (eds.) SAS 2007. LNCS, vol. 4634, pp. 69–86. Springer, Heidelberg (2007)
22. Shoham, S., Grumberg, O.: Multi-valued model checking games. In: Peled, D.A., Tsay, Y.-K. (eds.) ATVA 2005. LNCS, vol. 3707, pp. 354–369. Springer, Heidelberg (2005)
23. Tarski, A.: A lattice-theoretical fixpoint theorem and its applications. Pacific J. Math. 5 (1955)

Don't Know for Multi-valued Systems

Alarico Campetelli, Alexander Gruler, Martin Leucker, and Daniel Thoma

Institut für Informatik, Technische Universität München, Germany

Abstract. This paper studies abstraction and refinement techniques in the setting of multi-valued model checking for the μ-calculus. Two dimensions of abstractions are identified and studied: Abstraction by joining states of the underlying multi-valued Kripke structure as well as abstraction of truth values, for each following both an *optimistic* and *pessimistic* account. It is shown that our notion of abstraction is *conservative* in the following sense: The truth value in a concrete system is "between" the optimistic and pessimistic assessment. Moreover, model checking of abstracted systems is shown to be again a multi-valued model checking problem, allowing to reuse multi-valued model checking engines. Finally, whenever the optimistic and pessimistic model checking result differ, the *cause* for such an assessment is identified, allowing the abstraction to be refined to eventually yield a result for which both the optimistic and pessimistic assessment coincide.

1 Introduction

In multi-valued logics, a formula evaluates no longer to just *true* or *false* but to one of many *truth values*. This allows to express to which *extent* a property is considered satisfied by a program, or, in the setting of *trust models, how much* a person can be trusted [1]. The main motivation of this work is, however, inspired by our study of software product lines (or software product families). Within software product lines [2] a set of similar systems, called *products*, is modelled explicitly expressing their commonalities and differences. We have shown in [3] that a software product family can conveniently be modeled as one *single* multi-valued system, in which each value corresponds to a subset of products. Thus, the question of *which* products of the product line satisfy a certain property corresponds to the truth value of the formula encoding the property with respect to the multi-valued system.

As explained in [4,5], a Kripke structure (KS) can be extended to the multi-valued setting by assigning to each proposition in each state one of many (truth) *values* and likewise to each transition also a value, resulting in the notion of a multi-valued Kripke structure (mv-KS). A value of some proposition might then be interpreted as to which extend a proposition holds, a person may be trusted initially, or in which products of a product line a certain proposition holds. Similarly, the value of a transition might identify to which amount a transition might influence the truth value, might modify the trust value of some person when taking the transition, or, in which products the transition is actually present.

In model checking, a temporal or modal logic is typically used to specify (intended) properties of a given mv-KS. As such a logic typically ranges over atomic proposition,

Z. Liu and A.P. Ravn (Eds.): ATVA 2009, LNCS 5799, pp. 289–305, 2009.

Boolean combinations, and temporal or modal operators, it is helpful to consider values from a *lattice*, where *meet* ($\sqcap$) and *join* ($\sqcup$) naturally yield a semantics for conjunction and disjunction, respectively. The meaning of temporal or modal operators is adjusted appropriately. Then, the semantics of a formula with respect to a mv-KS is one element of the lattice, denoting either the extent to which the formula holds, the trust value of some person performing actions, or the set of all products satisfying the formula. Model Checking multi-valued versions of the classical logics LTL, CTL, CTL*, and the μ-calculus has the been extensively studied already, for example in [6,4,5,7].

The state explosion problem in (two-valued) model checking—complicating its practical application—does, of course, not vanish in the multi-valued setting. Therefore, it is important to study abstraction techniques also for multi-valued model checking. This paper studies abstraction and refinement techniques in the setting of multi-valued model checking for the μ-calculus as introduced in [5].

We identify and study two orthogonal forms of abstractions for mv-KS: Firstly, we consider abstractions of mv-KS induced by joining states to form abstract states, as it is typically considered also in the two-valued setting. In this setting, a meanwhile popular form of abstraction is to consider structures that are simultaneously an *over* as well as *under*-approximation of a system, as introduced in [8] in the setting of the μ-calculus. To this end, Larsen's and Thomsen's Kripke modal transition systems are used to describe abstract systems in which a transition can be *may*, denoting an over-approximation, or *must*, denoting an under-approximation [9]. This, essentially leads to *three* possible values for a transition: It is there for sure, it is not there for sure, or it may be there. This explains that three-valued settings are themselves often used for abstractions [10]. In this paper, however, we study abstraction *of* rather than abstraction *by* mv-KS. Over-approximation can be intuitively explained as an *optimistic* account of the system's transitions, while we consider an under-approximation a *pessimistic* account. We then transfer this understanding to the multi-valued setting to obtain notions of abstractions. A first, interesting result is that an abstract mv-KS can be again considered as a mv-KS, yet over a richer lattice, which we call the op-lattice. This allows to reuse multi-valued model checking engines also for abstraction.

The second source of abstraction that we study is that by abstracting values. Especially in the setting of product lines, in which a family of N products gives rise to the powerset lattice with 2^N elements, it is essential to also abstract lattice elements, practically say by identifying different products, hereby reducing N. To follow both the optimistic and pessimistic view, we need, however, *two* abstractions for the lattice elements, here given as usual in abstract interpretation by (two) Galois connections [11]. We introduce a simulation relation and show that in the presence of such a relation the actual model checking values lies "between" the optimistic and pessimistic one that is based on the abstract system. Note that in [12] the concept of a *latticed simulation* is introduced, which, however, does not allow to combine a pessimistic and optimistic view into one abstraction.

Finally, whenever the optimistic and pessimistic model checking result differ, the *cause* for such an assessment is identified. We explain how to compute the cause based on the structure of the formula to be checked. Knowing causes allows to refine the abstraction to eventually yield a result for which both the optimistic and pessimistic assessment coincide.

2 Preliminaries

Lattices. An algebraic structure $(\mathcal{L}, \sqcap, \sqcup)$ consisting of a set $\mathcal{L}$, a binary operation $\sqcap : \mathcal{L} \times \mathcal{L} \rightarrow \mathcal{L}$ called *meet* and a binary operation $\sqcup : \mathcal{L} \times \mathcal{L} \rightarrow \mathcal{L}$ called *join* is a *lattice* if it satisfies the following equations for all elements $x, y, z \in \mathcal{L}$: (i) $x \sqcap y = y \sqcap x$ and $x \sqcup y = y \sqcup x$, (ii) $x \sqcap (y \sqcap z) = (x \sqcap y) \sqcap z$ and $x \sqcup (y \sqcup z) = (x \sqcup y) \sqcup z$, (iii) $x \sqcap (y \sqcup x) = x$ and $x \sqcup (y \sqcap x) = x$, and (iv) $x \sqcap x = x$ and $x \sqcup x = x$. Equivalently to the definition as an algebraic structure, a lattice can be defined as a partially ordered set $(\mathcal{L}, \sqsubseteq)$ where for each $x, y \in \mathcal{L}$, there exists (i) a unique *greatest lower bound* (glb), which is called the *meet* of x and y, denoted by $x \sqcap y$, (ii) and a unique *least upper bound* (lub), which is called the *join* of x and y, denoted by $x \sqcup y$. Depending on the application, in the following we use one or the other form for dealing with lattices.

The definitions of glb and lub extend to finite sets of elements $A \subseteq \mathcal{L}$ as expected, which are then denoted by $\bigsqcap A$ and $\bigsqcup A$, respectively. A lattice is called *finite* iff $\mathcal{L}$ is finite. Every finite lattice has a least element, called *bottom*, denoted by $\bot$, and a greatest element, called *top*, denoted by $\top$. A lattice is *distributive*, iff $x \sqcap (y \sqcup z) = (x \sqcap y) \sqcup (x \sqcap z)$, and, dually, $x \sqcup (y \sqcap z) = (x \sqcup y) \sqcap (x \sqcup z)$. In a *de Morgan* lattice, every element x has a unique *dual* element $\neg x$, such that $\neg\neg x = x$ and $x \sqsubseteq y$ implies $\neg y \sqsubseteq \neg x$. Typically, we denote a de Morgan lattice as a quadruple $(\mathcal{L}, \sqcap, \sqcup, \neg)$.

A complete distributive lattice is called *Boolean* iff for all elements $x \in \mathcal{L}$ we have $x \sqcup \neg x = \top$ and $x \sqcap \neg x = \bot$. A typical Boolean lattice is the one induced by the power of some non-empty finite set $\{1, \ldots, N\}$, for $N \in \mathbb{N}$: $(2^N, \subseteq)$ where meet, join, and dual of elements, are given by set intersection, set union, and complement of sets, respectively. For example, Figure 4(a) shows the powerset lattice for $N = 3$.

Multi-valued Kripke Structures. Let $\mathcal{P}$ be a set of propositional constants. A *multi-valued Kripke structure* (mv-KS) is a tuple $\mathcal{K} = (S, \mathcal{L}, \mathcal{R}, L)$ where S is a set of states, $\mathcal{L}$ is a de Morgan lattice, $\mathcal{R} : S \times S \rightarrow \mathcal{L}$ is a transition function associating an element of the lattice to each pair of states, and $L : S \rightarrow (\mathcal{P} \rightarrow \mathcal{L})$ is yields for a proposition in each state an element of the lattice. With $\mathcal{MK}$ we denote the set of all mv-KS.

A Kripke structure in the usual sense can be seen as a mv-KS with values over the two element lattice consisting of a bottom $\bot$ and a top $\top$ element, ordered as shown in Figure 3(a). Value $\top$ then means that the property holds in the considered state while $\bot$ means that it does not hold. Similarly, $\mathcal{R}(s, s') = \top$ reads as there is a corresponding transition while $\mathcal{R}(s, s') = \bot$ means there is no transition between the states s and s'.

Multi-valued modal μ-calculus. In the following we introduce a *multi-valued modal version* of the μ-calculus along the lines of [7]. Let $\mathcal{V}$ be a set of propositional variables. Formulae of the *multi-valued modal μ-calculus* are given by

$$\varphi ::= \mathit{true} \mid \mathit{false} \mid q \mid \neg\varphi \mid Z \mid \varphi \vee \varphi \mid \varphi \wedge \varphi \mid \Diamond\varphi \mid \Box\varphi \mid \mu Z.\varphi \mid \nu Z.\varphi$$

where $q \in \mathcal{P}$, and $Z \in \mathcal{V}$. Let $mv\text{-}\mathfrak{L}_\mu$ denote the set of *closed* formulae generated by the above grammar, where the fixpoint quantifiers μ and ν are variable binders. The

$$
\begin{array}{rcl}
[\![true]\!]_\rho & := & \lambda s.\top \\
[\![false]\!]_\rho & := & \lambda s.\bot \\
[\![q]\!]_\rho & := & \lambda s.L(s)(q) \\
[\![\neg\varphi]\!]_\rho & := & \lambda s.\neg[\![\varphi]\!]_\rho(s) \\
[\![Z]\!]_\rho & := & \rho(Z)
\end{array}
\qquad
\begin{array}{rcl}
[\![\varphi \vee \psi]\!]_\rho & := & [\![\varphi]\!]_\rho \sqcup [\![\psi]\!]_\rho \\
[\![\varphi \wedge \psi]\!]_\rho & := & [\![\varphi]\!]_\rho \sqcap [\![\psi]\!]_\rho \\
[\![\Diamond\varphi]\!]_\rho & := & \lambda s.\bigsqcup\{\mathcal{R}(s,s') \sqcap [\![\varphi]\!]_\rho(s')\} \\
[\![\Box\varphi]\!]_\rho & := & \lambda s.\bigsqcap\{\neg\mathcal{R}(s,s') \sqcup [\![\varphi]\!]_\rho(s')\} \\
[\![\mu Z.\varphi]\!]_\rho & := & \bigsqcap\{f \mid [\![\varphi]\!]_{\rho[Z\mapsto f]} \sqsubseteq f\} \\
[\![\nu Z.\varphi]\!]_\rho & := & \bigsqcup\{f \mid f \sqsubseteq [\![\varphi]\!]_{\rho[Z\mapsto f]}\}
\end{array}
$$

Fig. 1. Semantics of $mv\text{-}\mathfrak{L}_\mu$ formulae

semantics of a $mv\text{-}\mathfrak{L}_\mu$ formula is an element of $\mathcal{L}^S$, i.e., a function from S to $\mathcal{L}$ yielding for the formula at hand and a given state its *satisfaction value* measured in terms of the lattice. In the setting of software product lines, for example, this is the set of all products for which the formula holds in the given state. More precisely, the *semantics* $[\![\varphi]\!]_\rho^{\mathcal{K}}$ of a $mv\text{-}\mathfrak{L}_\mu$ formula φ with respect to a mv-KS $\mathcal{K}$ and an *environment* $\rho : \mathcal{V} \to \mathcal{L}^S$, which explains the meaning of free variables in φ, is defined as shown in Figure 1, where $\rho[Z \mapsto f]$ denotes the environment that maps Z to f and agrees with ρ on all other arguments. When clear from the context, we drop indices $\mathcal{K}$ and ρ.

Regarding motivation, consider the $\Diamond$-operator as an example: $\Diamond\varphi$ is classically supposed to hold in states that have a successor satisfying φ. In a multi-valued version, we first take the value of a transition and reduce it (meet it) with the value of φ in that successor. As there might be transitions to different successors, we take the best value.

The functionals $\lambda f.[\![\varphi]\!]_{\rho[Z\mapsto f]} : \mathcal{L}^S \to \mathcal{L}^S$ are monotone wrt. $\sqsubseteq$ for any Z, φ and S. By [13], least and greatest fixpoints of these functionals exist. *Approximants* of $mv\text{-}\mathfrak{L}_\mu$ formulae are defined as usual: if $fp(Z) = \mu Z.\varphi$ then $Z^0 := \lambda s.\bot$, $Z^{n+1} := [\![\varphi]\!]_{\rho[Z\mapsto Z^n]}$ for any ordinal n and any environment ρ, and $Z^\lambda := \bigsqcap_{n<\lambda} Z^n$ for a limit ordinal λ. Dually, if $fp(Z) = \nu Z.\varphi$ then $Z^0 := \lambda s.\top$, $Z^{n+1} := [\![\varphi]\!]_{\rho[Z\mapsto Z^n]}$, and $Z^\lambda := \bigsqcup_{n<\lambda} Z^n$.

3 Conservative Abstractions for MV-Kripke Structures

In this section we introduce two different kinds of abstractions for multi-valued Kripke structures, both motivated by practical applications, and made explicit by respective abstraction operators. As we show, the combined application of both abstraction operations (i) yields again a mv-KS, which means that we can technically deal with the abstracted system in the same way as with the concrete system, i. e. in particular, we can apply the same model checking techniques, and (ii) that it is conservative in the sense that the result of evaluating any $mv\text{-}\mathfrak{L}_\mu$ formulae on the abstract system is always a conservative abstraction of the evaluation on the concrete system.

Abstraction by joining states. Consider the part of a mv-KS shown in Figure 2(a). A standard idea of abstraction, which we follow as our first approach, is to join states in a concrete system to form combined *abstract states* in the abstract system. For example,

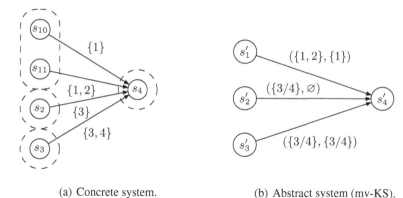

(a) Concrete system.   (b) Abstract system (mv-KS).

Fig. 2. An Example of a combined abstraction. The abstraction joined states as indicated by the dashed lines, e. g. s_{10} and s_{11}, and does additionally abstract the original lattice elements 3 and 4 with one abstract element denoted by 3/4.

the concrete states s_{10} and s_{11} in Figure 2(a) are joined (indicated by the dashed line) to form the abstract state s'_1 in Figure 2(b).[1]

Regarding transitions, we label the abstract transitions with values representing over- and under-approximation of the corresponding concrete (original) transitions. More specifically, the two transitions from the concrete states s_{10} and s_{11} to s_4, respectively, are over-approximated by the label $\{1, 2\}$ and under-approximated with $\{1\}$, in the abstraction. We combine this approximation information to label the corresponding transition in the abstract system with a *tuple* consisting of the over- and under-approximation. This results again in a lattice $\mathcal{L}_{op}$ of tuples based on the lattice $\mathcal{L}$ used to label transitions in the concrete system as follows:

Definition 1 (op-lattice). *Let $\mathcal{L}$ be a de Morgan lattice. The lattice*

$$\mathcal{L}_{op} = (\{(m_1, m_2) \in \mathcal{L} \times \mathcal{L} \mid m_1 \sqsupseteq m_2\}, \sqcap_{op}, \sqcup_{op}, \neg_{op})$$

with the operations $\sqcap_{op}, \sqcup_{op}, \neg_{op}$ given by

$$(m_1, m_2) \sqcap_{op} (m'_1, m'_2) := (m_1 \sqcap m'_1, m_2 \sqcap m'_2)$$
$$(m_1, m_2) \sqcup_{op} (m'_1, m'_2) := (m_1 \sqcup m'_1, m_2 \sqcup m'_2)$$
$$\neg_{op}(m_1, m_2) := (\neg m_2, \neg m_1)$$

is called the optimistic-pessimistic lattice (op-lattice) *for $\mathcal{L}$.*

We called $\mathcal{L}_{op}$ an *optimistic-pessimistic* lattice as its elements embody these two kinds of views—regardless whether we interpret its elements as degrees of truth or configurations of a software product line: The first entry of the tuple represents the best case, e. g. the "highest" truth value or the largest set of configurations of a software product family, while the second entry represents the (worst) case which is achieved at the least, e. g.

---
[1] Please ignore the transitions from s'_2 and s'_3 to s'_4 for the moment.

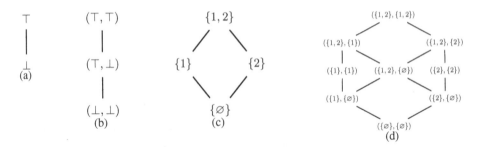

Fig. 3. In (b) true, false and don't know lattice for the two-element lattice (a), in (c) lattice for two product lines and corresponding op-lattice in (d)

the "lowest" guaranteed truth value or the (smallest) set of configurations which still guarantees a certain property. The op-lattice of the two valued and four valued Boolean lattices shown in Figures 3(a) and 3(c) are given in Figures 3(b) and 3(d), respectively. Observe that Figure 3(b) shows the three-valued lattices commonly used for abstraction in the setting of the μ-calculus [14].

Let us formalize the abstraction process motivated before. To this end, we define what it means to combine concrete states and abstract them to an abstract state in an abstract system. Let the function $\gamma : S_A \rightarrow \mathcal{P}(S_C)$ be a mapping which identifies (i) which concrete states in S_C are combined, (ii) and to which abstract state in S_A they are abstracted. We require γ to be *abstraction complete* , i.e., for all $s_C \in S_C$ there is $s_A \in S_A$ with $s_C \in \gamma(s_A)$. Thus each concrete state is accounted by at least one abstract state. Now, we are prepared to define an abstraction operator abs_S which represents the act of abstracting by joining states.

Definition 2 (State Abstraction Operator). *We call the function abs_S yielding the abstract mv-KS $abs_S ((S_C, \mathcal{L}_C, \mathcal{R}_C, L_C), \gamma) = (S_A, \mathcal{L}_A, \mathcal{R}_A, L_A)$ of the concrete mv-KS $(S_C, \mathcal{L}_C, \mathcal{R}_C, L_C)$ by joining states according to the abstraction complete function γ the* state abstraction operator, *where the set S_A of abstract states is implicitly given by γ, the lattice $\mathcal{L}_A$ is the op-lattice of $\mathcal{L}_C$ and*

$$\mathcal{R}_A(s_A, s'_A) = \left(\bigsqcup_{s_C \in \gamma(s_A)} \bigsqcup_{s'_C \in \gamma(s'_A)} \mathcal{R}_C(s_C, s'_C) , \bigsqcap_{s_C \in \gamma(s_A)} \bigsqcup_{s'_C \in \gamma(s'_A)} \mathcal{R}_C(s_C, s'_C) \right)$$

$$L_A(s_A, p) = \left(\bigsqcup_{s_C \in \gamma(s_A)} L_C(s_C, p) , \bigsqcap_{s_C \in \gamma(s_A)} L(s_C, p) \right)$$

The function abs_S maps a mv-KS representing a concrete system to a mv-KS which representing its abstraction by combining states via function γ. For the pessimistic view, it takes the worst of the (best) combinations of states. For example, the lattice shown in Figure 3(d) is the op-lattice which defines the transition labels for an abstract mv-KS which is constructed by abstracting from a concrete mv-KS where the transitions were labeled with elements of the lattice shown in Figure 3(c). Also note, that following our construction we exactly get the usual three-valued lattice (cf. Figure 3(b)) if we abstract a (two-valued) Kripke structure, where the existence and missing of transitions is equal to labeling the transitions with the two-valued *Boolean lattice* as shown in Figure 3(a) [14].

Abstraction of lattices elements. The abstraction of states as performed by our first abstraction operation abs_S reduces the state space by joining states. Thus, the abstract system usually also has significantly fewer transitions. To further reduce the abstract system, we may want to identify some elements of the lattice. Therefore, we also consider abstractions of the original lattice. In the following we introduce such a kind of abstraction and provide a definition of a second abstraction operator, correspondingly. Note, that the first abstraction operator yields a mv-KS labeled with an op-lattice, on which we can apply the second abstraction operator subsequently.

Consider again Figure 2(b): Assume that we no longer want to differ between the two lattice elements 3 and 4. Thus, we abstract these elements to a single element—denoted by 3/4—in the abstract lattice. Being the only abstraction of lattice elements we make, the resulting abstract lattice consists of the three elements $\{1, 2, 3/4\}$, which may now be used to label transitions in the abstract system. The effect of this abstraction is shown in Figure 2(b): Since we abstract 3 and 4 together, whenever 3 and 4 occur apart from each other in the concrete system, this asks for an optimistic and a pessimistic view in the abstract system, represented by the transition $s'_2 \xrightarrow{(3/4, \emptyset)} s'_4$: There is no transition in the pessimistic case (entry $\emptyset$ of the tuple), yet a transition for the element 3/4 in the optimistic view.

In order to formalize such an abstraction from lattices we use the concept of Galois connections which is well know in the area of abstract interpretation.

Definition 3 (Galois Connection [11]). *Let $\mathcal{L}_1$ and $\mathcal{L}_2$ be lattices. A pair $(\uparrow, \downarrow)$ of monotone functions $\uparrow : \mathcal{L}_1 \to \mathcal{L}_2$ and $\downarrow : \mathcal{L}_2 \to \mathcal{L}_1$ is a* Galois connection *from $\mathcal{L}_1$ to $\mathcal{L}_2$, if $\forall l \in \mathcal{L}_1 : l \sqsubseteq \downarrow(\uparrow(l))$ and $\forall a \in \mathcal{L}_2 : \uparrow(\downarrow(a)) \sqsubseteq a$.*

For the soundness proof of our approach we depend on some of the common properties of Galois connections. In particular, any Galois connection $(\uparrow, \downarrow)$ from $\mathcal{L}_1$ to $\mathcal{L}_2$ fulfills (i) $\uparrow(l) \sqsubseteq m \Leftrightarrow l \sqsubseteq \downarrow(m)$, (ii) $\uparrow(\bigsqcup L) = \bigsqcup_{l \in L} \uparrow(l)$, and (iii) $\downarrow(\bigsqcap M) = \bigsqcap_{m \in M} \downarrow(m)$. Figure 4 shows an example of a Galois connection between two lattices which illustrates these properties. The abstraction combines the (concrete) elements 1 and 2 of the lattice $\mathcal{L}_1$ (cf. Figure 4(a)) to the single element 1/2 in the lattice $\mathcal{L}_2$. The solid line shows an example of how the Galois connection $(\uparrow, \downarrow)$ works: We abstract $(\uparrow)$ element $\{2\}$ to $\{1/2\}$ and concretize $(\downarrow)$ then back to the $\{1, 2\}$. This is an optimistic approximation as $\{2\} \sqsubseteq \{1, 2\}$. In particular, properties (i)-(iii) are fulfilled.

Usually Galois connections are applied for abstractions by using $\uparrow$ as the abstraction function and $\downarrow$ as the concretization function. Since by definition $l \sqsubseteq \downarrow(\uparrow(l))$ holds, this abstraction yields an over-approximation, or an optimistic approximation in our terminology. For our approach we additionally need a pessimistic approximation (under-approximation). We define the pessimistic approximation using a second Galois connection and swapping the interpretation of the mapping functions: For the pessimistic case we use $\downarrow$ as an abstraction function and $\uparrow$ as a concretization function.

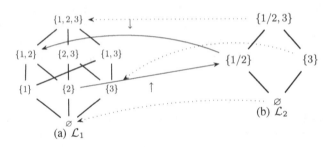

Fig. 4. A galois connection allows to interpret the lattice $\mathcal{L}_2$ as an abstraction of $\mathcal{L}_1$, where the (concrete) lattice elements 1 and 2 are abstracted to a single element in $\mathcal{L}_2$, denoted by $1/2$. Dashed and solid lines illustrate a part of the galois connection $(\uparrow, \downarrow)$.

We now define the lattice to label our abstract systems. We call it the *abstract op-lattice*. It is based on the original lattice from which we abstract elements and two Galois connections which define our optimistic and pessimistic view. Since we now use different lattices for the optimistic and pessimistic approximation, it is no longer possible to define negation for the elements of the abstract lattice directly. Therefore we additionally require two negation functions, that map between the optimistic and pessimistic view appropriately.

Definition 4 (aop-lattice). *Let $\mathcal{L}_C$ be a de Morgan lattice and $\mathcal{L}_o$ and $\mathcal{L}_p$ be lattices. Let $(\uparrow_o, \downarrow_o)$ with $\uparrow_o : \mathcal{L}_C \to \mathcal{L}_o$ and $\downarrow_o : \mathcal{L}_o \to \mathcal{L}_C$ and $(\uparrow_p, \downarrow_p)$ with $\uparrow_p : \mathcal{L}_p \to \mathcal{L}_C$ and $\downarrow_p : \mathcal{L}_C \to \mathcal{L}_p$ be Galois connections. Furthermore, let $\mathcal{L}_o$ and $\mathcal{L}_p$ be connected by two anti-monotone negation functions $\neg_o : \mathcal{L}_o \to \mathcal{L}_p$ and $\neg_p : \mathcal{L}_p \to \mathcal{L}_o$ with $\neg_o \uparrow_o(x) \sqsubseteq \downarrow_p(\neg x)$ and $\uparrow_o(\neg x) \sqsubseteq \neg_p \downarrow_p(x)$. We call the lattice*

$$\mathcal{L}_{aop} = \left(\{ (m_o, m_p) \in \mathcal{L}_o \times \mathcal{L}_p \mid \downarrow_o(m_o) \sqsupseteq \uparrow_p(m_p) \}, \sqcap_{aop}, \sqcup_{aop}, \neg_{aop} \right)$$

with the operations given by

$$(m_o, m_p) \sqcap_{aop} (m'_o, m'_p) := (m_o \sqcap m'_o \,,\, m_p \sqcap m'_p)$$
$$(m_o, m_p) \sqcup_{aop} (m'_o, m'_p) := (m_o \sqcup m'_o \,,\, m_p \sqcup m'_p)$$
$$\neg_{aop}(m_o, m_p) := (\neg_p m_p \,,\, \neg_o m_o)$$

the abstract optimistic-pessimistic lattice (aop-lattice) for the lattice $\mathcal{L}_C$.

Using the properties of Galois connections and the definition of the negation functions, we easily see:

Proposition 1 (aop-lattice is well-defined). *For all lattice values $x \in \mathcal{L}_C$ it holds that $(\uparrow_o(x), \downarrow_p(x)) \in \mathcal{L}_{aop}$ and that $\sqcup_{aop}, \sqcap_{aop}, \neg_{aop}$ are well-defined and in the sense that they preserve the condition $\downarrow_o(m_o) \sqsupseteq \uparrow_p(m_p)$.*

Negation on an aop-lattice always yields an over- and under-approximation of a corresponding concrete element. But it also allows for the loss of information, since the

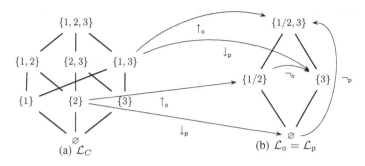

Fig. 5. Illustration of the negation function(s) in a aop-lattice

result of negation in the concrete might not be representable "exactly" in the abstract. Figure 5 illustrates such a situation. It shows the lattice $\mathcal{L}_C$ that we consider for the concrete system, whereas for the abstraction, the same lattices $\mathcal{L}_o = \mathcal{L}_p$ for the optimistic and pessimistic case are used. Consider the concrete element $x = \{2\}$ and its negation $\neg x = \{1, 3\}$ (in the concrete system). Following the arrows shows $\neg_o \uparrow_o (x) = \{3\} \sqsubseteq \{3\} = \downarrow_p(\neg x)$ and $\uparrow_o(\neg x) = \{1/2, 3\} \sqsubseteq \{1/2, 3\} = \neg_p \downarrow_p(x)$. This means that the negation of the optimistic-pessimistic tuple encloses the actually correct negation result.

An aop-lattice is obviously distributive, but the preceding discussion shows that it is not a de Morgan lattice. However, our whole theory and model checking machinery can be extended to non-de Morgan lattices. In particular, Theorem 1 also holds for non de Morgan lattices. Nevertheless, using the same lattice for the over and underapproximation (cf. Theorem 2) yields an aop-lattice which *is* a de Morgan lattice. Thus, to simplify presentation, we silently assume that an aop-lattice is indeed a de Morgan lattice. Note, that if using the state abstraction operator only, we get an op-lattice which also *is* a de Morgan lattice.

Now we make precise the idea of abstraction by abstracting the lattice and provide a suitable abstraction operator abs_L.

Definition 5 (Lattice Abstraction Operator). *Let $(S_A, \mathcal{L}_A, \mathcal{R}_A, L_A)$ be a mv-KS, and $\uparrow_o, \downarrow_p$ be two Galois connections with corresponding negation functions $\neg_o, \neg_p$. Then, the* lattice abstraction operator abs_L *yields an abstracted mv-KS*

$$abs_L \left((S_A, \mathcal{L}_A, \mathcal{R}_A, L_A), \uparrow_o, \downarrow_p, \neg_o, \neg_p \right) = (S'_A, \mathcal{L}'_A, \mathcal{R}'_A, L'_A)$$

labeled with an aop-lattice $\mathcal{L}'_A$, where $S'_A = S_A$ and

$$\mathcal{R}'_A(s, s') = \left(\uparrow_o ((\mathcal{R}_A(s, s'))_1) , \downarrow_p ((\mathcal{R}_A(s, s'))_2) \right)$$
$$L'_A(s, p) = \left(\uparrow_o ((L_A(s, p))_1) , \downarrow_p ((L_A(s, p))_2) \right)$$

This completes our idea of abstraction: For any concrete mv-KS, the subsequent application of both abstraction operators—abs_L after abs_S—yields a mv-KS labeled with an aop-lattice representing the combination of both kinds of abstractions.

While we have provided two abstraction operators to exemplify our ideas of abstraction, we show that model checking the abstract system yields conservative results for the concrete system by means of a *conservative abstraction*.

Definition 6 (Conservative Abstraction). *Let $\mathcal{L}_C$ be a de Morgan lattice and $\mathcal{L}_A$ an aop-lattice with the Galois connections $(\uparrow_o, \downarrow_o)$ from $\mathcal{L}_C$ to $\mathcal{L}_o$ and $(\uparrow_p, \downarrow_p)$ from $\mathcal{L}_p$ to $\mathcal{L}_C$ with the negation functions $\neg_o$ and $\neg_p$. Let $\mathcal{K}_C = (S_C, \mathcal{L}_C, \mathcal{R}_C, L_C)$ be the concrete and $\mathcal{K}_A = (S_A, \mathcal{L}_A, \mathcal{R}_A, L_A)$ the abstract multi-valued Kripke-structure. Furthermore, let γ be an abstraction complete function which specifies how to abstract concrete states. Then, we call $\mathcal{K}_A$ a conservative abstraction of $\mathcal{K}_C$, if the following conditions hold:*

$$\uparrow_p((L_A(s_A, p))_2) \sqsubseteq \bigsqcap_{s_C \in \gamma(s_A)} L(s_C, p) \qquad \text{(ca-lab (i))}$$

$$\downarrow_o((L_A(s_A, p))_1) \sqsupseteq \bigsqcup_{s_C \in \gamma(s_A)} L(s_C, p) \qquad \text{(ca-lab (ii))}$$

$$\uparrow_p((\mathcal{R}_A(s_A, s_A'))_2) \sqsubseteq \bigsqcap_{s_C \in \gamma(s_A)} \bigsqcup_{s_C' \in \gamma(s_A')} \mathcal{R}_C(s_C, s_C') \qquad \text{(ca-trans (i))}$$

$$\downarrow_o((\mathcal{R}_A(s_A, s_A'))_1) \sqsupseteq \bigsqcup_{s_C \in \gamma(s_A)} \bigsqcup_{s_C' \in \gamma(s_A')} \mathcal{R}_C(s_C, s_C') \qquad \text{(ca-trans (ii))}$$

Note that both abstraction operators as well as their concatenation induce conservative abstractions. A conservative abstraction is exactly that kind of abstract mv-KS which we require such that the evaluation of a formula $\varphi \in mv\text{-}\mathfrak{L}_\mu$ (cf. Section 2) yields useful results. More precisely, evaluating a $mv\text{-}\mathfrak{L}_\mu$ formula on a conservative abstraction of a concrete system $\mathcal{K}_C$ always yields a tuple representing the optimistic and pessimistic approximation of the result that would be produced when evaluating the formula on $\mathcal{K}_C$ directly. Theorem 1 states this correctness result in a formal manner.

Theorem 1 (Correctness of abstraction). *Let $\mathcal{K}_C = (S_C, \mathcal{L}_C, \mathcal{R}_C, L_C)$ be the concrete multi-valued Kripke-structure and $\mathcal{K}_A = (S_A, \mathcal{L}_A, \mathcal{R}_A, L_A)$ be a conservative abstraction of $\mathcal{K}_A$. Let the corresponding Galois connections $(\uparrow_o, \downarrow_o)$, $(\uparrow_p, \downarrow_p)$, and the abstraction function γ be defined as in Definition 6. Then for all $s_A \in S_A$, for all $s_C \in \gamma(s_A)$ and for all formulae $\varphi \in mv\text{-}\mathfrak{L}_\mu$ it holds that:*

$$\uparrow_p(m_p) \sqsubseteq [\![\varphi]\!]_\varnothing^{\mathcal{K}_C}(s_C) \sqsubseteq \downarrow_o(m_o)$$

where $(m_o, m_p) = [\![\varphi]\!]_\varnothing^{\mathcal{K}_A}(s_A)$ is the result of the evaluation of φ on $\mathcal{K}_A$.

Proof. The proof is carried out by induction over the structure of a μ-calculus formula. To demonstrate the central ideas, we explain the induction step for the $\Diamond$-operator. We confine ourselves to the correctness of the under-approximation as the over-approximation can be proved in an similar, slightly simpler way.

Let $(\_)_2$ denote the second, pessimistic entry of an aop-lattice tuple. We want to prove, that $\uparrow_p(([\![\Diamond\varphi]\!](s_A))_2)$ yields an under-approximation for each concrete state $s_C \in \gamma(s_A)$ of the evaluation of the same formula on the concrete system. By semantics of the $\Diamond$-operator we obtain $\uparrow_p(\bigsqcup_{s_A'}\{(\mathcal{R}(s_A, s_A'))_2 \sqcap ([\![\varphi]\!](s_A'))_2\})$. By induction we know that $([\![\varphi]\!](s_A'))_2 \sqsubseteq \downarrow_p(\bigsqcap_{\hat{s}_C' \in \gamma(s_A')} [\![\varphi]\!](\hat{s}_C'))$. This yields an upper bound for our under-approximation:

$$\uparrow_{\mathsf{p}}(\bigsqcup\{\downarrow_{\mathsf{p}}(\bigsqcap_{\tilde{s}_C\in\gamma(s_A)}\bigsqcup_{\tilde{s}'_C\in\gamma(s'_A)}\mathcal{R}(\tilde{s}_C,\tilde{s}'_C))\sqcap\downarrow_{\mathsf{p}}(\bigsqcap_{\hat{s}'_C\in\gamma(s'_A)}[\![\varphi]\!](\hat{s}'_C))\})$$

Now we can apply Galois connection properties and choose $\tilde{s}_C = s_C$ and thus obtain a weaker upper bound $\bigsqcup_{s'_A}\{\bigsqcup_{\tilde{s}'_C\in\gamma(s'_A)}\mathcal{R}(s_C,\tilde{s}'_C)\sqcap\bigsqcap_{\hat{s}'_C\in\gamma(s'_A)}[\![\varphi]\!](\hat{s}'_C)\}$. By exploiting distributivity of $\sqcap$ and $\sqcup$ this can be simplified to:

$$\bigsqcup_{s'_A}\bigsqcup_{\tilde{s}'_C\in\gamma(s'_A)}\bigsqcap_{\hat{s}'_C\in\gamma(s'_A)}\{\mathcal{R}(s_C,\tilde{s}'_C)\sqcap[\![\varphi]\!](\hat{s}'_C)\}$$

We can now choose $\hat{s}'_C = \tilde{s}'_C$ and obtain once again a weaker upper bound:

$$\bigsqcup_{s'_C}\{\mathcal{R}(s_C,s'_C)\sqcap[\![\varphi]\!](s'_C)\} = [\![\Diamond\varphi]\!](s_C)$$

This least upper bound is identical to the definition of the $\Diamond$-operator semantics and thus completes the proof.   □

So far, we have presented the most general setting, in which we used different lattices for the optimistic and pessimistic approximation, respectively. However, it may usually be more convenient to use the same (de Morgan) lattice for both kinds of approximation. Doing so allows to define one of the two required Galois connections in terms of the other one and to use the negation defined on the lattice instead of the two negation functions mapping between separated lattices:

Theorem 2 (Simplification). *Let $\mathcal{L}_C$ be a lattice and $\mathcal{L}_{op}$ be a de Morgan lattice. Let $(\uparrow_{\mathsf{o}},\downarrow_{\mathsf{o}})$ be a Galois connection from $\mathcal{L}_C$ to $\mathcal{L}_{op}$. This Galois connection induces two other functions $\uparrow_{\mathsf{p}} : x \mapsto \neg\downarrow_{\mathsf{o}}(\neg x)$ and $\downarrow_{\mathsf{p}} : x \mapsto \neg\uparrow_{\mathsf{o}}(\neg x)$ which also define a Galois connection $(\uparrow_{\mathsf{p}},\downarrow_{\mathsf{p}})$ from $\mathcal{L}_{op}$ to $\mathcal{L}_C$. Together with the negation functions $\neg_{\mathsf{o}}(x) = \neg_{\mathsf{p}}(x) = \neg x$ we obtain an aop-lattice for $\mathcal{L}_C$.*

We can prove this theorem by showing that $(\uparrow_{\mathsf{p}},\downarrow_{\mathsf{p}})$ fulfills the Galois connection properties and that the conditions for the negation functions stated in Definition 4 hold. If not stated differently we will work with such a simple form of abstraction.

4   Causes for Indefinite Results and Refinement

Whenever the optimistic and pessimistic assessment of a formula evaluated on the abstract system differ, we might be interested in refining (one of) the abstractions, to eventually obtain a result that coincides with that for the concrete system. While we leave precise ideas of refinement for future work, we elaborate a function *causes* that returns the *causes* of why the semantics of a formula interpreted over a mv-Kripke structure using the aop-lattice is a tuple in which the left and right components differ. To determine the causes, we analyze the results of the required steps to compute the semantics of a formula by means of a standard fixpoint computation. Revisit Figure 1, in which the semantics of a mv-$\mathcal{L}_\mu$ formula is given. Since the semantics of μ-calculus fixpoint operators can be computed in an iterative manner [13], they do not have to be treated explicitly. The semantics of the □- and ◇-operators is given by means of transitions and meet and join operators. Thus, a relevant computation step for determining causes is basically one of (i) the evaluation of the labeling function L for some atomic proposition p and state s (ii) the evaluation of the transition relation function $\mathcal{R}$ for two states s and s', (iii) the computation of negation, or (iv) the computation of meet and join. In the latter case, the meet and join operators may be indexed by state variables iterating over the states of the Kripke structure needed to compute the semantics of the □- and ◇-operator. Therefore, to describe a computation, we define a formula language $\mathfrak{L}_\Phi$ with state variables s_i by the following grammar:

$$\Phi := \neg\Phi \mid \Phi \sqcap \Phi \mid \Phi \sqcup \Phi \mid \bigsqcap_{s_i} \Phi \mid \bigsqcup_{s_i} \Phi \mid L(s_i, p) \mid \mathcal{R}(s_i, s_j)$$

Before we give a precise definition of causes, we present the intuition behind this notion. At first, let us discuss in which way the abstraction from lattices (the shift from op-lattice to aop-lattice) gives rise to imprecision. Consider the optimistic and pessimistic abstraction of the powerset lattice over the elements $1, \ldots, 5$ shown in Figures 6(a) and 6(b), respectively, in which abstract elements are named according to their concrete counter parts. Now, consider a meet of the elements $\{1, 2, 3, 4\}$ and $\{2, 3, 4, 5\}$ within the pessimistic lattice. As there is no element $\{2, 3, 4\}$, the result is $\varnothing$. Thus, the computation of a pessimistic value might be more pessimistic just because of the lattice abstraction. To identify the situations that pessimistic as well as optimistic values are diluted by such meet and join operations, we consider causes as elements in the *concrete* rather than the abstract lattice.

The other source for different optimistic and pessimistic assessment is due to abstraction by joining states. More precisely, propositions and transitions may be assessed with differing optimistic and pessimistic values. However, combining such imprecise verdicts by meet and join may actually eliminate certain imprecision: Take for example the three-valued lattice in which $(\top, \bot) \sqcap (\bot, \bot)$ yields the precise verdict $(\bot, \bot)$, thus eliminating any cause for refinement.

Hence, we should study in which way meet, join, and negation operators actually modify causes for why the respective subformulae have a differing verdict, both due to the fact that imprecision determined for subformulae may be eliminated by meet and join but also introduced due to the lattice abstraction.

We are now set to introduce our ideas formally. Let $\mathcal{L}_o$ be the lattice for the optimistic and $\mathcal{L}_p$ for the pessimistic view as introduced in Definition 4. The function *causes* that returns the set of causes for one computation step from a causes domain $\mathfrak{c}$ made precise below uses the result of the present computation step, the results of the directly preceding computation steps, and the causes computed for the preceding steps (its subformulae). Thus, the function *causes* has the type:

$$causes : (\mathfrak{L}_\Phi \times \mathcal{L}_o \times \mathcal{L}_p) \times ((\mathfrak{L}_\Phi \to \mathcal{L}_o) \times (\mathfrak{L}_\Phi \to \mathcal{L}_p)) \times (\mathfrak{L}_\Phi \to \mathfrak{c}) \to \mathfrak{c}$$

Let us now elaborate on the causes domain: We consider a cause to be a pair (m_o, m_p) of elements of the concrete lattice $\mathcal{L}_C$, which limit the possible range of values for the semantics, together with a *context*, describing the qualitative origin of the different assessment. More specifically, a context could denote one of (i) a proposition in some

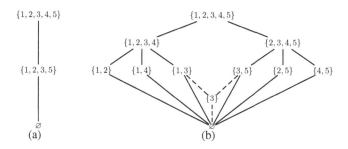

Fig. 6. An optimistic lattice $\mathcal{L}_o$ and a pessimistic lattice $\mathcal{L}_p$, where $\{3\}$ is added during refinement

state, (ii) some transition, (iii) or o/p identifying the lattices $\mathcal{L}_p$ or $\mathcal{L}_o$. The latter symbols are used to indicate the situation that the results are diluted due to abstraction of lattices. Consequently, we define the domain of causes as $\mathfrak{c} := \mathcal{L}_C \times \mathfrak{k}$ and the set of contexts as $\mathfrak{k} := (S \times P) \cup (S \times S) \cup \{o, p\}$, where (i) $S \times P$ refers to a label of a state, (ii) $S \times S$ to a transition, and (iii) $\{o, p\}$ to the optimistic or pessimistic lattice $\mathcal{L}_o$ or $\mathcal{L}_p$.

In the following we will use as names for the function parameters m_o for the optimistic and m_p for the pessimistic result, ξ_o (ξ_p) for the function mapping preceding computations to their optimistic (pessimistic, resp.) results and $\zeta \subseteq \mathfrak{c}$ to their causes. We give the definition of *causes* in an inductive fashion.

Atomic propositions. For an atomic proposition p a cause is just the pair of concrete lattice elements, for which the proposition is undetermined for some state s:

$$causes(p(s), m_o, m_p, \xi_o, \xi_p, \zeta) = \{(s, p, (\downarrow_o(m_o), \uparrow_p(m_p)))\}$$

For example, if an atomic proposition p evaluates to $\{1, 2, 3, 4, 5\}$ in the optimistic and to $\{2, 3, 4, 5\}$ in the pessimistic account, the cause is $(s, p, (\{1, 2, 3, 4, 5\}, \{2, 3, 4, 5\}))$.

Transitions. Causes for transitions are similarly defined as for atomic propositions:

$$causes(\mathcal{R}(s, s'), m_o, m_p, \xi_o, \xi_p, \zeta) = \{(s, s', (\downarrow_o(m_o), \uparrow_p(m_p)))\}$$

Let us illustrate the causes for transitions, which may be raised by two different reasons: Several states could have been joined and therefore differently labeled transitions (or propositions respectively) could have been merged as shown in Figure 7(a) or information could have been lost due to the abstraction from the concrete lattice as shown in Figure 7(b). A combination of both cases is likewise possible as shown in Figure 7(c), where the example is driven over the powerset lattice of three elements.

Negation. When using different lattices for the optimistic and pessimistic view, negation results in a loss of precision if the complement of an element of one lattice is not exactly representable in the other lattice. A cause in this case expresses, that in one of the abstract lattices a given element is missing. Since negation never increases precision, causes for preceding computations can just be passed on. Figure 8 shows how information can be lost due to negation.

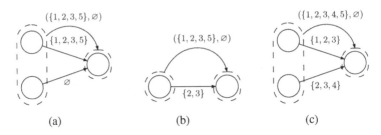

Fig. 7. Imprecision due to joining states 7(a), to lattice abstraction 7(b), and to both 7(c)

To define the cause for negation formally, let us consider
one case: Recall that $m_p =$
$\neg\xi_o(\varphi(s))$. If this computation
would have been carried out in
the concrete lattice, we would
have obtained $\downarrow_o(\xi_o(\varphi(s)))$. If
the negation of the latter value
is different from $\uparrow_p(m_p)$, we
have a further imprecision due
to the lattice abstraction. Other-

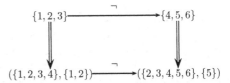

Fig. 8. Information loss due to negation. Negating
$\{1, 2, 3\}$ results in $\{4, 5, 6\}$. Negating the abstraction
$\{1, 2, 3, 4\}, \{1, 2\}$ could yield $(\{3, 4, 5, 6\}, \{5, 6\})$ but
the result in this example is even less precise.

wise, the only imprecision is due to the so far accounted ones denoted by ζ. Thus, we
define *causes* as follows:

$$causes((\neg\varphi)(s), m_o, m_p, \xi_o, \xi_p, \zeta) =$$

$$\zeta(\varphi(s)) \cup \begin{cases} \{(\neg\downarrow_o(\xi_o(\varphi(s))), \uparrow_p(m_p))\} & \text{if components differ} \\ \{(\uparrow_p(\xi_p(\varphi(s))), \neg\downarrow_o(m_o))\} & \text{if components differ} \end{cases}$$

Meet and join. Let us consider the case of a meet operation. The treatment of the join
operator is dual and omitted here. Let (m_o, m_p) be obtained by $((\xi_o^1 \sqcap \xi_o^2), (\xi_p^1 \sqcap \xi_p^2))$,
where $\xi_\sigma^j = \xi_\sigma(\varphi_j(s))$, for $j \in \{1, 2\}$, $\sigma \in \{o, p\}$.

As with negation calculating the meet can, on one hand, result in further imprecision
(because of the lattice abstraction). However, due to the properties of Galois connections both operations are exact on either the optimistic or the pessimistic view. Therefore we can only lose informations because of missing elements in one of the abstract
lattices. So, as seen below, we add, similarly as in the case of negation, causes.

On the other hand, a meet may result in a gain of information due to the meet in
the pessimistic view. The additional information can be used to remove or reduce the
imprecision listed in causes of preceding computation steps. To illustrate the idea, consider the meet of $\xi^1 = (\{2, 3\}, \{2, 3\})$ and $\xi^2 = (\{1, 2, 3\}, \{3\})$, which results into
$(m_o, m_p) = (\{2, 3\}, \{3\})$. Note that ξ^2, in the product line interpretation, denotes that
no precise information about products 1 and 2 is available, while ξ^1 represents a precise
result. Now, considering the result $(\{2, 3\}, \{3\})$, we observe that the imprecision about
product 1 is no longer a concern, while that for product 2 is still of interest. Practically,

the result may be expressed by taking the cause based on $\xi^2 = (\xi_o^2, \xi_p^2)$ and adjusting its components by the result m_o and m_p as follows: $(\xi_o^2 \sqcap m_o, (\xi_p^2 \sqcup m_p) \sqcap (\xi_o^2 \sqcap m_o))$, where the meet in the second component with the first component is only to make sure that the second component is smaller than the first component. This modification is expressed by the following operator *fil*, that takes an optimistic result m_o, a pessimistic result m_p and a cause:

$$fil(m_o, m_p, (k, (l_o, l_p))) = (k, l_o \sqcap \downarrow_o(m_o), (l_p \sqcup \uparrow_p(m_p)) \sqcap (l_o \sqcap \downarrow_o(m_o)))$$

Then we are ready to define the function causes for a meet operation as:

$$causes((\varphi_1 \sqcap \varphi_2)(s), m_o, m_p, \xi_o, \xi_p, \zeta) =$$
$$\{(\downarrow_o(\xi_o(\varphi_1(s))) \sqcap \downarrow_o(\xi_o(\varphi_2(s)))), \uparrow_p(m_p))\} \text{ if components differ}$$
$$\cup \bigcup_{c \in \zeta(\varphi_1(s)) \cup \zeta(\varphi(s))} fil(m_o, m_p, c)$$

Example 1. For a better understanding of the propagation of causes we consider as example the meet of $(\{1, 2, 3, 4, 5\}, \{1, 2, 3, 4\})$ and $(\{1, 2, 3, 4, 5\}, \{2, 3, 4, 5\})$. Using the lattices in Figures 6(a) and 6(b) for the optimistic respectively pessimistic view, this results in $(\{1, 2, 3, 4, 5\}, \varnothing)$. Calculating the meet in an exact manner would have resulted in $(\{1, 2, 3, 4, 5\}, \{2, 3, 4\})$. We therefore *obtain* the cause $(p, (\{2, 3, 4\}, \varnothing))$.

Now, let us assume that the fixpoint computation (expressed by a formula of the grammar introduced above) requires to join the previous result $(\{1, 2, 3, 4, 5\}, \varnothing)$ with the pair $(\{1, 2, 3, 4, 5\}, \{1, 2\})$ which results in $(\{1, 2, 3, 4, 5\}, \{1, 2\})$. Since we now have information about 2, we can *modify* the cause to $(p, (\{2, 3, 4\} \sqcap \{1, 2, 3, 4, 5\}, (\varnothing \sqcup \{1, 2\}) \sqcap \{2, 3, 4\}))$, resulting in $(p, (\{2, 3, 4\}, \{2\})$.

As next step we take the meet of $(\{1, 2, 3, 4, 5\}, \{1, 2\})$ and $(\{1, 2, 3, 5\}, \{1, 2\})$ which results in $(\{1, 2, 3, 5\}, \{1, 2\})$. Since we obtained information about 4, the cause is further simplified to $(p, (\{2, 3\}, \{2\})$. We can now modify the lattice for the pessimistic view $\mathcal{L}_p$ by adding an element for 3 as shown in Figure 6(b). Repeating the computation results in $(\{1, 2, 3, 5\}, \{1, 2, 3\})$ and thus yield the same imprecision as we started the computation with.

Note that the treatment of causes as pairs (m_o, m_p) can be simplified in Boolean lattices to a single value $m_o \sqcap \neg m_p$ actually representing set difference.

The computation of causes can be interweaved with the computation of the semantics. In case of a *don't know result*, meaning that the optimistic and pessimistic assessment differ, a cause can be picked according to a meaningful heuristics, whose discussion is beyond the scope of this paper, and a suitable refinement may be accomplished. Reassessment of the semantics eventually yields a precise model checking result.

5   Conclusion

In this paper we have introduced abstraction techniques for multi-valued Kripke structures. More precisely, we have given two different kinds of abstraction: The first kind abstracts by joining states, in the usual way. The second kind of abstraction combines lattice elements realizing the idea of not differing between certain concrete products (of a software product line) or truth values in the abstract anymore. The combination of both abstractions yields again a multi-valued Kripke structure which represents the abstract system. Here, the transitions are labeled with a tuple representing the optimistic and pessimistic assessment of this transition.

On such an abstract multi-valued Kripke structure we can evaluate properties using the existing multi-valued model checking machinery. More importantly, we have shown that the result of evaluating a $mv\text{-}\mathfrak{L}_\mu$ formula on the abstract system always yields the optimistic and pessimistic limits, in which the concrete value is located for sure.

To eventually obtain a model checking result for which the optimistic and pessimistic assessment coincide, refinement of abstractions in needed. Therefore, we have introduced the notion of causes: Whenever the optimistic and pessimistic assessment differ, a cause guides us during the process of concretization and gives us those states in the abstract, which we have to concretize first.

References

1. Sassone, V., Krukow, K., Nielsen, M.: Towards a formal framework for computational trust. In: de Boer, F.S., Bonsangue, M.M., Graf, S., de Roever, W.-P. (eds.) FMCO 2006. LNCS, vol. 4709, pp. 175–184. Springer, Heidelberg (2007)
2. Clements, P.C., Northrop, L.: Software Product Lines: Practices and Patterns. SEI Series in Software Engineering. Addison-Wesley, Reading (2001)
3. Gruler, A., Leucker, M., Scheidemann, K.D.: Modeling and model checking software product lines. In: Barthe, G., de Boer, F.S. (eds.) FMOODS 2008. LNCS, vol. 5051, pp. 113–131. Springer, Heidelberg (2008)
4. Chechik, M., Easterbrook, S.M., Petrovykh, V.: Model-checking over multi-valued logics. In: Oliveira, J.N., Zave, P. (eds.) FME 2001. LNCS, vol. 2021, pp. 72–98. Springer, Heidelberg (2001)
5. Bruns, G., Godefroid, P.: Model checking with multi-valued logics. In: Díaz, J., Karhumäki, J., Lepistö, A., Sannella, D. (eds.) ICALP 2004. LNCS, vol. 3142, pp. 281–293. Springer, Heidelberg (2004)
6. Chechik, M., Devereux, B., Gurfinkel, A.: Model-checking infinite state-space systems with fine-grained abstractions using spin. In: Dwyer, M.B. (ed.) SPIN 2001. LNCS, vol. 2057, pp. 16–36. Springer, Heidelberg (2001)
7. Shoham, S., Grumberg, O.: Multi-valued model checking games. In: Peled, D.A., Tsay, Y.-K. (eds.) ATVA 2005. LNCS, vol. 3707, pp. 354–369. Springer, Heidelberg (2005)
8. Bruns, G., Godefroid, P.: Model checking partial state spaces with 3-valued temporal logics. In: Halbwachs, N., Peled, D.A. (eds.) CAV 1999. LNCS, vol. 1633, pp. 274–287. Springer, Heidelberg (1999)
9. Larsen, K.G., Thomsen, B.: A modal process logic. In: LICS, pp. 203–210. IEEE Computer Society, Los Alamitos (1988)
10. Godefroid, P., Huth, M., Jagadeesan, R.: Abstraction-based model checking using modal transition systems. In: Larsen, K.G., Nielsen, M. (eds.) CONCUR 2001. LNCS, vol. 2154, pp. 426–440. Springer, Heidelberg (2001)
11. Cousot, P., Cousot, R.: Abstract interpretation: A unified model for static analysis of programs by construction or approximation of fixpoints. In: Proc.4th ACM Symp. on Principles of Programming Languages, pp. 238–252 (1977)

12. Kupferman, O., Lustig, Y.: Latticed simulation relations and games. In: Namjoshi, K.S., Yoneda, T., Higashino, T., Okamura, Y. (eds.) ATVA 2007. LNCS, vol. 4762, pp. 316–330. Springer, Heidelberg (2007)

13. Tarski, A.: A lattice-theoretical fixpoint theorem and its application. Pacific J. Math. 5, 285–309 (1955)

14. Grumberg, O., Lange, M., Leucker, M., Shoham, S.: Don't know in the μ-calculus. In: Cousot, R. (ed.) VMCAI 2005. LNCS, vol. 3385, pp. 233–249. Springer, Heidelberg (2005)

Logahedra: A New Weakly Relational Domain

Jacob M. Howe[1] and Andy King[2,3]

[1] Department of Computing, City University London, EC1V 0HB, UK
[2] Portcullis Computer Security Limited, Pinner, HA5 2EX, UK
[3] Computing Laboratory, University of Kent, Canterbury, CT2 7NF, UK

Abstract. Weakly relational numeric domains express restricted classes of linear inequalities that strike a balance between what can be described and what can be efficiently computed. Popular weakly relational domains such as bounded differences and octagons have found application in model checking and abstract interpretation. This paper introduces logahedra, which are more expressiveness than octagons, but less expressive than arbitrary systems of two variable per inequality constraints. Logahedra allow coefficients of inequalities to be powers of two whilst retaining many of the desirable algorithmic properties of octagons.

1 Introduction

Polyhedra are used in abstract interpretation [4] and model checking real-time [9] and hybrid systems [7]. The domain operations of general polyhedra can be prohibitively expensive, thus there has been much recent interest in so-called weakly relational domains that seek to balance expressivity and cost by imposing restrictions on the class of inequalities that can be represented. For example, octagons [11] restrict polyhedra [4] to inequalities of at most two variables where the coefficients are -1, 0 or 1 and thereby obtain (at worst) cubic domain operations. Other weakly relational domains whose operations reside in low complexity classes are pentagons [10], two variable per inequality (TVPI) constraints [17] and bounded differences [9]. Domains that do not impose the two variable per inequality restriction include octahedra [3] and template constraints [14].

This paper introduces a new class of weakly relational domain called logahedra. A logahedron is a system of implicitly conjoined two variable inequalities where the coefficients are constrained to be powers of two (or zero). Such coefficients naturally arise because the size of primitive types. For instance, suppose an array of 32-bit integers was dynamically allocated with, say, $\mathsf{malloc}(n)$ where n is the size of the memory block in bytes. Then an array index i is in range iff the logahedral inequalities $0 \leq i$ and $4i+4 \leq n$ are satisfied. Logahedra are proposed as a solution to two problems arising in program analysis. The first problem is that octagons, whilst having good computational properties, are restricted in what they can describe. The second problem is that when the coefficients of inequalities are not constrained (as they are for octagons), for example in general polyhedra or TVPI, the coefficients can easily become very large, requiring multiple precision libraries for their storage and manipulation. This can be prohibitively costly [16]. Logahedra address the first problem by allowing a greater

Z. Liu and A.P. Ravn (Eds.): ATVA 2009, LNCS 5799, pp. 306–320, 2009.

variety of constraints to be expressible than octagons, whilst retaining octagons' good computational properties (indeed, logahedra are a true generalisation of octagons; logahedra are strictly more expressive, with octagons being a special case). They address the second problem by restricting the possible coefficients of inequalities; further, since the allowable coefficients are powers of two, they can be represented by their exponents rather than by the number itself, allowing very large coefficients to be represented using machine integers.

Logahedra are themselves a strict subset of TVPI constraints and inherit many of their domain operations. Yet the most important domain operation, (full) completion, has the same complexity as for octagons hence is more efficient than for TVPI, being (truly) cubic. The most complicated domain operation, as with TVPI, is incremental completion. This is the operation of adding a single constraint to an already complete system to give an updated complete system. Incrementally adding constraints is more in tune with the needs of analysis than full completion, therefore incremental completion is arguably the key operation. This operation is also the most complicated and is synthesised from the way new inequalities can be derived in the act of completing a system. This result is applicable to arbitrary two variable systems, not just logahedra. The paper advances the theory of weakly relation domains by making the following contributions:

- The class of logahedral constraints is introduced and it is argued that they have representational advantages over TVPI constraints, whilst being more expressive than octagons.
- A parameterised subclass of logahedra, bounded logahedra, is defined that is a generalisation of octagons in that octagons are a special case of bounded logahedra. Bounded logahedra are more expressive than octagons, whilst retaining their asymptotic complexity.
- Domain operations for both logahedral and bounded logahedral constraints are defined and algorithms for the operations are presented. In part, these build on TVPI operations and include original approaches to completion and abstraction that are applicable to other weakly relational domains.
- Preliminary experiments (and an example) indicate that logahedra have the potential to significantly increase the power of analysis.

2   Logahedral Constraints

Logahedra fall between octagons [11] and TVPI [17] in that octagonal constraints can be expressed as logahedral constraints which, in turn, can be expressed as TVPI constraints, that are themselves two variable restrictions of polyhedral constraints. These classes are defined over a set of (indexed) variables X:

Definition 1. $\mathsf{Oct} = \{ax + by \leq d \mid x, y \in X \wedge a, b \in \{-1, 0, 1\} \wedge d \in \mathbb{Q}\}$

Definition 2. $\mathsf{Log} = \{ax + by \leq d \mid x, y \in X \wedge a, b \in \{-2^n, 0, 2^n \mid n \in \mathbb{Z}\} \wedge d \in \mathbb{Q}\}$

Definition 3. $\mathsf{TVPI} = \{ax + by \leq d \mid x, y \in X \wedge a, b, d \in \mathbb{Q}\}$

Definition 4. $\text{Poly} = \{\sum_{i=1}^{|X|} a_i x_i \leq d \mid x_i \in X \wedge a_i, d \in \mathbb{Q}\}$

Both Oct and TVPI, like Poly, are closed under variable elimination, that is, if $y \in X$ and $S \subseteq \text{Oct}$ (respectively $S \subseteq \text{TVPI}$) then $\exists y.S \in \text{Oct}$ (respectively $\exists y.S \in \text{TVPI}$). For instance, if $S = \{x - 2y \leq 5, 3y + z \leq 7, 5y - u \leq 0\} \subseteq \text{TVPI}$ then $\exists y.S$ can be derived by combing pairs of inequality with opposing signs for y to obtain $\exists y.S = \{3x + 2z \leq 29, -2u + 5x \leq 25\}$ which is indeed in TVPI. Variable elimination (projection) is an important operation in program analysis and an abstract domain should ideally be closed under it so as to minimise the loss of information; Log possesses this property. Furthermore, as well as being more expressive than Oct, Log has representational advantages over TVPI. This makes Log a natural object for study.

2.1 Representation of Coefficients

The representational advantages of logahedra are hinted at by their name. Since the absolute value of the coefficients are powers of two, it suffices to represent the logarithm of the value, rather than the value itself. This allows coefficients to be presented by their exponents in machine words, thereby avoiding the computational burden of large coefficients.

As with TVPI inequalities, a logahedral inequality can be binary, that is, involve two variables, when $a \neq 0$ and $b \neq 0$; or be unary, when either $a = 0$ or $b = 0$ (but not both); or be constant when $a = b = 0$. Constant constraints are written as either *true* or *false*. A dense representation for the binary case can be achieved by observing that $ax + by \leq d$ can be expressed as $x + (b/a)y \leq d/a$ if $a > 0$ and $-x - (b/a)y \leq -d/a$ otherwise. Thus to represent $ax + by \leq d$ it is sufficient to distinguish the variables x and y, represent the signs of a and b (as two bits) and then either represent $\lg |b/a|$ and d/a or $\lg |b/a|$ and $-d/a$. A unary inequality such as $ax \leq d$ can be expressed as $x \leq d/a$ if $a > 0$ and $-x \leq -d/a$ otherwise, therefore it is not even necessary to represent a logarithm. Henceforth, without loss of generality, all logahedra will be represented with first coefficient of -1, 0 or 1.

2.2 Representation of Constants

Unlike TVPI, that can alternatively be defined with $a, b, d \in \mathbb{Z}$, the constant d is required to be rational, even without a restriction on the first coefficient. Consider, for example, $4x - 2y \leq 2/3$. This has no equivalent logahedral representation with an integer constant. Furthermore, rational constants are required for closure under variable elimination. Consider eliminating y from a system such as $\{x - 2y \leq 3, x + 4y \leq -1\}$ which yields the single inequality $3x \leq 5$. This, in itself, is not logahedral but the constraint can be equivalently expressed as $x \leq 5/3$ which is logahedral.

2.3 Bounded Logahedra and Their Representation

The Log class contains an unbounded number of inequalities for each two variable pair. The Oct class, however, is bounded since the size of the coefficients is bounded. Therefore it is worth considering restricting the coefficients of logahedra to within a bound:

Definition 5. $\mathsf{Log}_k = \{ax + by \leq d \mid x, y \in X \wedge a \in \{-1, 0, 1\} \wedge b \in C_k \wedge d \in \mathbb{Q}\}$ where $C_k = \{-2^n, 0, 2^n \mid n \in \mathbb{Z} \wedge -k \leq n \leq k\}$, $k \in \mathbb{N}$.

Notice that $\mathsf{Oct} = \mathsf{Log}_0$. An alternative definition would restrict the first coefficient to be a power of two rather than a unit. However, it is curious to observe that the class Log_3 is not expressible with the alternative definition.

The case for Log_k is further motivated by considering the inequalities required to describe relationships between values stored in machine integers. The following proposition states that inside a bounded box (induced by the size of the type) the set of integer points described by a Log constraint can also be described by a Log_k constraint where k is determined by the size of the bounding box.

Proposition 1. Suppose $ax + by \leq d \in \mathsf{Log}$ and $\mathsf{Box}_k = ([-2^k, 2^k - 1] \cap \mathbb{Z})^2$. Then there exists $ax + b'y \leq d' \in \mathsf{Log}_{k+1}$ such that $\{\langle x, y \rangle \in \mathsf{Box}_k \mid ax + by \leq d\} = \{\langle x, y \rangle \in \mathsf{Box}_k \mid ax + b'y \leq d'\}$

Proof. Wlog suppose $c \equiv ax + by \leq d \in \mathsf{Log}$ where $a \in \{-1, 1\}$ and $b \notin C_{k+1}$.

Find $\langle x^*, y^* \rangle \in \mathbb{Z}^2$ that maximises $ax + by$ subject to $ax + by \leq d$, $-2^k \leq x \leq 2^k - 1$ and $-2^k \leq y \leq 2^k - 1$. (This can be achieved in $O(\lg |b|)$ time [5].) The Log constraint $ax + by \leq d'$, where $d' = ax^* + by^*$, describes the same set of integer points in Box_k as c. Put $s = \mathsf{sign}(b)$, $l = lg(|b|)$, $k' = \mathsf{sign}(l)(k+1)$ and $b' = s2^{k'}$. Then $c' := (ax + b'y \leq d') \in \mathsf{Log}_{k+1}$.

If $b' = s2^{k+1}$ then c' adds no new integer solutions since Box_k has height $2^{k+1} - 1$ and c' passes through $\langle x^*, y^* \rangle$. Likewise, if $b' = s2^{-(k+1)}$ then again c' adds no new solutions since Box_k has width $2^{k+1} - 1$ and c' passes through $\langle x^*, y^* \rangle$. The result follows.

The Log_k class has $4(2k + 1)$ binary and 4 unary inequalities for each pair of variables, therefore, for fixed k, the domain is bounded. The force of the proposition is that for an signed integer representation of, say, 32 bits, it is sufficient to restrict attention to Log_{33}. For unsigned integers analogous results hold. Importantly, observe that for any given Box_k, the domain Log_{k+1} retains closure under variable elimination. This is because, by proposition 1, any inequality (obtained by combining a pair of inequalities) that falls outside Log_{k+1} can be replaced with another drawn from Log_{k+1} without loss of information. A final observation that is potentially exploitable is that for a given Box_k and a pair of coefficients, there is a maximum value for the constant beyond which the inequality does not restrict the box. For example, $x + y \leq d$ is vacuous if $2^{k+1} - 2 \leq d$.

3   Worked Example

This section contains an example to demonstrate the use of logahedra in value range analysis. It serves to illustrate the domain operations required, for which definitions and algorithms will be given in the next section. In addition, the example illustrates the expressivity of logahedra versus octagons.

In the following C program, read_value() reads a value from a file. The objective of the analysis is to verify the safety of the array access in line 5, no matter what values are read. To this end, the set of $\langle x, y \rangle$ values that can arise immediately after executing lines (1) ... (6) are over-approximated by the logahedra $P_1, \ldots, P_6$. Each of the these logahedra are defined by a separate equation. The set P_2' over-approximates the set of $\langle x, y \rangle$ values occurring immediately before line 2. P_2' differs from P_2 in that P_2 assumes that the loop condition holds. The updates at lines (3), (4) and (6) are modelled as translations. Since the value read_value() is not known at analysis time, the values of $\langle x, y \rangle$ at line (5) can be either that at line (3) or (4). P_5 is thus defined as the join of P_3 and P_4. P_2' is also formulated as the join of P_1 and P_6, but also applies widening, ∇.

(1) int x = 0, y = 0, array[8];	$P_1 = \{\langle 0, 0 \rangle\}$
(2) while (x < 4)	$P_2' = P_2'\nabla(P_1 \sqcup P_6)$ $P_2 = P_2' \sqcap \{\langle x, y \rangle \mid x < 4\}$
{ if (read_value() == 0)	
(3) y = y+2;	$P_3 = \{\langle x, y + 2 \rangle \mid \langle x, y \rangle \in P_2\}$
else	
(4) y = y+1;	$P_4 = \{\langle x, y + 1 \rangle \mid \langle x, y \rangle \in P_2\}$
(5) array[y] = y;	$P_5 = P_3 \sqcup P_4$
(6) x = x+1; }	$P_6 = \{\langle x + 1, y \rangle \mid \langle x, y \rangle \in P_5\}$

Solutions to the equations, or at least upper-approximations to them, can be found by repeatedly applying the equations until a fixpoint is reached. As in other polyhedral analyses [4], widening is introduced to enforce convergence since $P_1, P_2', \ldots, P_6$ grow as the equations are reapplied. To obtain convergence, it is sufficient to put $Q_1 \nabla Q_2 = Q_1 \sqcup Q_2$ if Q_1 and Q_2 differ in dimension; otherwise $Q_1 \nabla Q_2$ is defined as the (non-redundant) inequalities of Q_1 that hold for Q_2. This removes unstable bounds from Q_1 whilst ensuring $Q_1 \sqcup Q_2 \subseteq Q_1 \nabla Q_2$ [6].

The diagrams in Fig. 1 show how $P_1, P_2', \ldots, P_6$ develop during the fixpoint calculation from their initial values of $\emptyset$. Diagram (a) shows how P_1 is changed by the first equation; thereafter P_1 is stable. Initially $P_6 = \emptyset$ so that $P_1 \sqcup P_6 = P_1$.

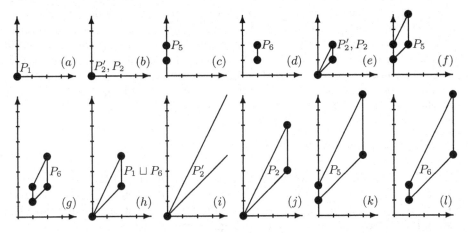

Fig. 1. Logahedra P_1, P_2', P_2, P_5 and P_6 (P_3 and P_4 are omitted)

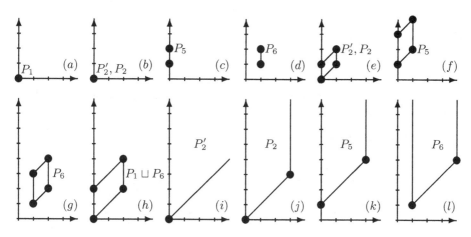

Fig. 2. Octagons P_1, P_2', P_2, P_5 and P_6 (P_3 and P_4 are omitted)

Since $P_2' = \emptyset$ differs in dimension from P_1, the second equation assigns P_1 to P_2'. Diagram (c) illustrates P_5, which is a line segment, that is the join of P_3 and P_4 which are themselves translations of P_2. P_6 in diagram (d) is a translation of P_5. When reapplying the second equation, P_2' and $P_1 \sqcup P_6$ again differ in dimension so that P_2' is updated to the solid triangle depicted in diagram (e). Diagrams (f) and (g) illustrate the effect of translations and a join, P_5, and another translation, P_6. On the third application of the second equation, P_2' and $P_1 \sqcup P_6$ are 2 dimensional, hence P_2' is updated to just retain the two stable inequalities, as illustrated in (i). Diagram (j) shows how the loop condition is reinserted. P_2' remains unchanged when its equation is applied a fourth time. The $\langle x, y \rangle$ values summarised by P_5 in diagram (k) show that y can possibly take a value of 8, indicating a possibly erroneous array access. The analysis shows that enlarging the array by one element alleviates the problem. For this example, the analysis would terminate without widening, though this is not always so.

Fig. 2 repeats the analysis with octagons. Diagrams (e) and (h) show that the upper bound on y is unstable since the domain cannot express $y \leq 2x$. Hence, in diagram (i), P_2' loses crucial information on the maximal values of y. Moreover, if widening was not applied, then the upper bound of y would grow indefinitely. Thus the loss of information cannot be remedied by more sophisticated widening. Curiously, the example was not manufactured to show the benefits of logahedra, but rather to illustrate polyhedral analysis to a lay audience.

4 Logahedral Domain Operations

This section details the domain operations previously introduced. These operate on finite sets of inequalities, such as $\wp^f(\mathsf{Log})$ and $\wp^f(\mathsf{Log}_k)$, where $\wp^f(S)$ denote the set of finite subsets of a given set S. The *entailment* ordering on $\wp^f(\mathsf{Poly})$, and its subdomains $\wp^f(\mathsf{TVPI})$, $\wp^f(\mathsf{Log})$ and $\wp^f(\mathsf{Log}_k)$, is given by $I_1 \models I_2$ iff any assignment that satisfies each inequality $c_1 \in I_1$ also satisfies each $c_2 \in I_2$. *Equivalence* is defined as $I \equiv I'$ iff $I \models I'$ and $I' \models I$.

Example 1. If $I = \{x - 2y \le 7, y \le 2\}$ and $I' = \{x \le 12\}$ then $I \models I'$ since every assignment to x and y satisfying I also satisfies I'. But $I' \not\models I$. If $c := 3x \le 2$ and $c' := x \le 2/3$ then $\{c\} \equiv \{c'\}$ and indeed c and c' are multiples of one another.

4.1   Completion

The algorithms for many operations on logahedra (and other weakly relational domains) require implied inequalities to be made explicit. The process of inferring all implied constraints is called completion and is the dominating computational expense in the operations of which it forms a part. Therefore a clear understanding of how completion is applied, along with efficient algorithms, is essential. Completion is formalised in terms of syntactic projection:

Definition 6. If $Y \subseteq X$ then *syntactic projection* onto Y is defined $\pi_Y(S) = \{c \in S \mid \mathsf{vars}(c) \subseteq Y\}$, where $\mathsf{vars}(c)$ is the set of variables occurring in c.

Definition 7. The set of logahedral inequalities $I \subseteq \mathsf{Log}$ is *complete* iff for all $c \in \mathsf{Log}$ it holds that if $I \models c$ then $\pi_{\mathsf{vars}(c)}(I) \models c$.

Example 2. Let $I_0 = \{x - y \le 0, 2x + y \le 1\}$. I_0 is not complete because $I_0 \models x \le 1/3$ but $\pi_{\{x\}}(I_0) = \emptyset \not\models x \le 1/3$. Put $I_1 = I_0 \cup \{x \le 1/3\}$. The constant constraint *true* does not compromise completion since $\pi_\emptyset(I_1) = \emptyset \models true$.

Example 3. Suppose $I_0 = \{x - y \le -1, y - z \le -1, z - x \le -1\}$. I_0 is not complete since $\pi_{\{x,z\}}(I_0) \not\models x - z \le -2$ and $\pi_{\{x,y\}}(I_0) \not\models y - x \le -2$. Put $I_1 = I_0 \cup \{x - z \le -2, y - x \le -2\}$. I_1 is still not complete since $\pi_\emptyset(I_1) \models false$ (I_0 is unsatisfiable). Put $I_2 = I_1 \cup \{false\}$. Then I_2 is complete.

The action of deriving implied inequalities, or computing resultants to use the terminology of Nelson [12], is formalised below:

Definition 8. If $c = ax + by \le d$, $c' = a'x + b'z \le d'$ and $a.a' < 0$ then $\mathsf{result}(c, c', x) = |a'|by + |a|b'z \le |a'|d + |a|d'$ otherwise $\mathsf{result}(c, c', x) = \bot$.

The operation $\mathsf{result}(c, c', x)$ is analogously defined when $c := ax \le d$ or $c' := a'x \le d'$. Note that it is necessary to stipulate which variable is eliminated because a single pair of inequalities may possess two resultants, as is illustrated by the pair $c := x + y \le 1$, $c' := -2x - 3y \le 1$ for which $\mathsf{result}(c, c', x) = -y \le 3$ and $\mathsf{result}(c, c', y) = x \le 4$. The resultant operator lifts to sets of inequalities:

Definition 9. If $I_1, I_2 \subseteq \mathsf{TVPI}$ then

$$\mathsf{result}(I_1, I_2) = \{c \mid c_i \in I_i \wedge x \in \mathsf{vars}(c_1) \cap \mathsf{vars}(c_2) \wedge c = \mathsf{result}(c_1, c_2, x) \ne \bot\}$$

Full Completion. Completing a set of inequalities I [17] amounts to repeatedly augmenting I with $\mathsf{result}(I, I)$ until an I' is obtained such that no further (non-redundant) inequalities can be added to $\pi_Y(I')$ for any $Y \subseteq X$. During completion, the computation of resultants is interleaved with the removal of redundant inequalities. An inequality c is considered to be redundant in I iff $\pi_{\mathsf{vars}(c)}(I) \setminus \{c\} \models c$, that is, c is redundant in its syntactic projection $\pi_{\mathsf{vars}(c)}(I)$. To remove such constraints from I, the existence of an operator $\mathsf{filter}_Y(I) = I'$ is assumed for each $Y \subseteq X$ such that $|Y| \leq 2$. The operator is assumed to satisfy the three conditions that $I' \subseteq I$, $I' \equiv I$ and $I'' \not\equiv I$ for all $I'' \subset I'$. Such an operator can be constructed straightforwardly, and resides in $O(|I|)$ when I is ordered [8, section 2]. With filter_Y in place, it is possible to filter an entire system $I \subseteq \mathsf{Log}$ by computing $\mathsf{filter}(I) = \cup\{\mathsf{filter}_Y(\pi_Y(I)) \mid Y \subseteq X \wedge |Y| = 2\}$.

Definition 10. The (full) completion operator $\mathsf{complete} : \wp(\mathsf{Log}) \to \wp(\mathsf{Log})$ is defined: $\mathsf{complete}(I) = \cup_{i \geq 0} I_i$ where $I_0 = I$ and $I_{i+1} = \mathsf{filter}(I_i \cup \mathsf{result}(I_i, I_i))$.

Nelson [12], working over TVPI, used a divide and conquer argument to bound the number of iterations that need be computed before stability is achieved:

Lemma 1. $\mathsf{complete}(I) = I_m$ where $m = \lceil \lg(|X|) \rceil$ and I_m is defined as above.

This result becomes more intruiging when the domain is Log_k. Completion can be calculated in a semi-naive fashion by defining $I_0 = I$ and $\delta_0 = I$ and computing $I_{i+1} = \mathsf{filter}(I_i \cup \mathsf{result}(\delta_i, I_i))$ and $\delta_{i+1} = I_{i+1} \setminus I_i$ for $i \in [0, m-1]$. Since $|\cup_{i=0}^m \delta_i|$ is in $O(|X|^2)$ it follows that the cumulative running time of $\mathsf{result}(\delta_i, I_i)$ is $O(|X|^3)$. Since each invocation of filter resides in $O(|X|^2)$ and it is called $m-1$ times, it follows that the running time of completion is $O(|X|^3)$. Hence, like Oct, but unlike TVPI, Log_k comes with a (full) completion operation that resides in $O(|X|^3)$. It is conceivable that this result extends to other subclasses of TVPI that also retain closure under variable elimination.

Incremental Completion. During analysis inequalities are encountered one by one. Thus an important addition to full completion is *incremental completion* that takes a complete system, augments it with an additional inequality and returns the completion of the augmented system. Such an algorithm has been proposed for TVPI [15, Algorithm 7], together with a sketched correctness proof. Given the importance of completion, the following proposition, whose proof is given in [8], provides a rigorous foundation for an incremental algorithm.

Proposition 2. If $c' \in \mathsf{Log}$, $I \subseteq \mathsf{Log}$ is complete and $c \in \mathsf{complete}(I \cup \{c'\})$ then one of the following holds:

- $c \in I \cup \{c'\}$
- $c \in \mathsf{result}(c', c_0)$ where $c_0 \in I$
- $c \in \mathsf{result}(\mathsf{result}(c', c_0), \{c_1\})$ where $c_0, c_1 \in I$

$I \cup \{c'\}$ can thus be completed by computing $I_2 = \mathsf{filter}(I_1 \cup \mathsf{result}(I_1 \setminus \{c'\}, I_1 \setminus I))$ where $I_1 = \mathsf{filter}(I \cup \{c'\} \cup \mathsf{result}(I, \{c'\}))$. Nelson showed that if $J_1, J_2 \subseteq \mathsf{TVPI}$

where $\mathsf{vars}(J_1) = \{x, y\}$ and $\mathsf{vars}(J_2) = \{y, z\}$ then $|\mathsf{result}(J_1, J_2)| \leq 2|J_1| + 2|J_2|$ [12, section 3]. It follows that $|I_1| \leq 3|I| + 3$ and $|I_2| \leq 13|I| + 13$, thus although computing I_2 for Log takes $O(|I|^2)$ time it requires $O(|I|)$ space overall. For Log_k with fixed k, computing I_1 and I_2 both reside in $O(|X|^2)$. This squares with incremental closure for octagons which is also in $O(|X|^2)$.

4.2 Entailment

The value of completeness is that it simplifies other operations. To illustrate, consider the problem of detecting if a fixpoint has been reached, that is, deciding whether $I_1 \models I_2$ for $I_1, I_2 \in \wp^f(\mathsf{Log})$. Suppose I_1 is complete. If $false \in I_1$ then it follows $I_1 \models I_2$. Otherwise $I_1 \models I_2$ iff $\pi_Y(I_1) \models \pi_Y(I_2)$ for all $Y \subseteq X$ and $|Y| = 2$. Moreover, recall that inequalities $ax + by \leq d$ are maintained in the form $a \in \{-1, 0, 1\}$ and suppose $b \in \{-1, 1\}$ if $a = 0$. Then the planar entailment check $\pi_Y(I_1) \models \pi_Y(I_2)$ can be decided by testing $\mathsf{filter}_Y(\pi_Y(I_1) \cup \pi_Y(I_2)) = \pi_Y(I_1)$.

4.3 Variable Elimination

Variable elimination (projection) is required to remove out of scope variables, and all information pertaining to them, from a logahedral abstraction. Fourier-Motzkin can be applied to eliminate a variable x from $I \in \wp^f(\mathsf{Log})$ which amounts to computing $\exists x.I = \cup\{c \mid c = \mathsf{result}(c_1, c_2, x) \wedge c_1, c_2 \in I \wedge c \neq \bot\}$. However if I is complete then $\exists x.I = \cup\{\pi_Y(I) \mid Y \subseteq X \setminus \{x\} \wedge |Y| \leq 2\}$. If I were incomplete then $\exists x.I$ may lose some information as is witnessed by $I = \{w - x \leq 0, \, x - y \leq 0\}$. Then $\cup\{\pi_Y(I) \mid Y \subseteq X \setminus \{x\} \wedge |Y| \leq 2\} = \emptyset$ yet $\exists x.I \models w - y \leq 0$.

Projection also provides a way to realise translations induced by assignments of the form $x = x + c$ where $c \in \mathbb{Z}$. If I describes the state prior to the assignment, then the state after is described by $\exists x'.(\{x = x'\} \cup \exists x.(I \cup \{x' = x + c\}))$.

4.4 Abstraction

This section explains how to approximate a finite set of arbitrary Poly constraints by a finite set of Log constraints. Abstraction is employed as a component of join but is also used to translate program statements, for example, loop conditions, into logahedral inequalities. Approximation has two stages: projection onto planar sets of TVPI constraints and relaxation of these to logahedral constraints. Consider the latter step first, and suppose $I \subseteq \mathsf{TVPI}$ is finite and that $\mathsf{vars}(I) \subseteq Y$ where $|Y| = 2$. Suppose $I = \{c_0, ..., c_{n-1}\}$ is non-redundant and ordered by orientation. This can be achieved in $O(|I| \lg |I|)$ time. Wlog each c_i is assumed to take the form $a_i x + b_i y \leq d_i$ where $a_i \in \{-1, 0, 1\}$. Let $c_1 \angle c_2$ be a predicate that holds when $a_1 b_2 - a_2 b_1 < 0$, that is, that c_1 is oriented before c_2 in a clockwise relative order by angle. Suppose also that $c_{-1} = c_{n-1}$ and $c_n = c_0$. If c_i and c_{i+1} do not intersect at a vertex let $p_i = \bot$, otherwise let $p_i = (\psi_i, \phi_i)$ be this vertex, which can be calculated in constant time. If $b_i = 0$ then put $l_i = u_i = 0$, otherwise define $l_i = \mathsf{sign}(b_i) 2^{\lfloor \lg(|b_i|) \rfloor}$ and $u_i = \mathsf{sign}(b_i) 2^{\lceil \lg(|b_i|) \rceil}$. For each $i \in [0, n-1]$ put $c'_i = \bot$ if $p_{i-1} = \bot$ otherwise define

$$c_i' = \begin{cases} a_i x + u_i y \le a_i \psi_{i-1} + u_i \phi_{i-1} & \text{if } a_i = \text{sign}(b_i) \\ a_i x + l_i y \le a_i \psi_{i-1} + l_i \phi_{i-1} & \text{if } a_i \ne \text{sign}(b_i) \end{cases}$$

Likewise if $p_i = \bot$ put $c_i'' = \bot$ otherwise define

$$c_i'' = \begin{cases} a_i x + l_i y \le a_i \psi_i + l_i \phi_i & \text{if } a_i = \text{sign}(b_i) \\ a_i x + u_i y \le a_i \psi_i + u_i \phi_i & \text{if } a_i \ne \text{sign}(b_i) \end{cases}$$

The $a_i = \text{sign}(b_i)$ test determines whether the inequalities resulting from the upper and lower approximations of $|b_i|$ support p_{i-1} or p_i. Some of the logahedral constraints c_i', c_i'' may be too strong in that $I \not\models c_i'$ or $I \not\models c_i''$ and these, with the $\bot$ constraints, are filtered out to abstract I as follows:

Definition 11. Let $\alpha_Y(I) = \{c_i' \mid c_i' \ne \bot \wedge c_{i-1} \angle c_i'\} \cup \{c_i'' \mid c_i'' \ne \bot \wedge c_i'' \angle c_{i+1}\}$ where c_i', c_i'' are defined as above for finite $I \subseteq \text{TVPI}$, $\text{vars}(I) \subseteq Y$ and $|Y| = 2$.

Note that the filtering test amounts to an $O(1)$ orientation check. The angular test guarantees that the retained inequalities are supporting.

Example 4. The example illustrates the approximation of two constraints from a larger system I. Suppose $c_{i-1} := -x \le 0$, $c_i := -x + (3/2)y \le 0$, $c_{i+1} := -x + (5/2)y \le 2$ and $p_{i+1} = \bot$. The logahedral approximation is illustrated in Fig. 3. Observe $p_{i-1} = (0,0)$ and $p_i = (3,2)$. Since $l_i = 2^{\lfloor \lg(3/2) \rfloor} = 1$, $u_i = 2^{\lceil \lg(3/2) \rceil} = 2$, $a_i \ne \text{sign}(b_i)$, $p_{i-1} \ne \bot$ and $p_i \ne \bot$ it can be seen that $c_i' := -x + y \le 0$ and $c_i'' := -x + 2y \le 1$. Moreover, since $l_{i+1} = 2^{\lfloor \lg(5/2) \rfloor} = 2$, $u_{i+1} = 2^{\lceil \lg(5/2) \rceil} = 4$, $a_{i+1} \ne \text{sign}(b_{i+1})$, $p_i \ne \bot$ and $p_{i+1} = \bot$ it follows $c_{i+1}' := -x + 2y \le 1$ and $c_{i+1}'' := \bot$.

Now suppose instead, $c_{i+1} := -x + (7/4)y \le 1/2$, which preserves $p_i = (3,2)$. Then $I \not\models c_i''$ and c_i'' is not an approximating constraint. But $c_i'' \angle c_{i+1}$ does not hold since $(-1.7/4) - (-1.2) > 0$, hence $c_i'' \notin \alpha_Y(I)$. Likewise $c_{i+1}' \notin \alpha_Y(I)$.

Although α_Y is partial, it can be used to abstract arbitrary TVPI systems:

Definition 12. The abstraction map $\alpha : \wp^f(\text{TVPI}) \to \wp^f(\text{Log})$ is given by $\alpha(I) = \cup \{\alpha_Y(\exists Y.I) \mid Y \subseteq X \wedge |Y| = 2\}$

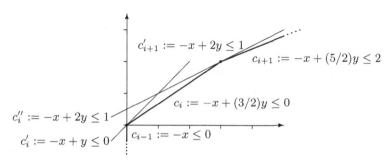

Fig. 3. Approximation with logahedral constraints

In the above $\exists Y.I$ denotes project I onto Y, that is, the repeated application of Fourier-Motzkin to elimination of all variables $x \in X \setminus Y$ from I. However, if I is complete then $\alpha(I) = \cup\{\pi_Y(I) \mid Y \subseteq X \wedge |Y| = 2\}$. Interestingly, α can be immediately lifted to $\alpha : \wp^f(\mathsf{Poly}) \to \wp^f(\mathsf{Log})$ since if I is a finite set then $\exists Y.I$ is a finite set. The symbol α hints at the existence of a Galois connection between $\langle \wp^f(\mathsf{Poly}), \models \rangle$ and $\langle \wp^f(\mathsf{Log}), \models \rangle$, and indeed α is monotonic. But such a structure can only be obtained by quotienting $\wp^f(\mathsf{Poly})$ and $\wp^f(\mathsf{Log})$ by $\equiv$ to obtain posets. The upper adjoint of α is the identity.

To abstract the inequalities I or $I \cup \mathsf{Box}_k$ to Log_k put $c'_i := \mathsf{sign}(b_i)y \leq \mathsf{sign}(b_i)\phi_{i-1}$ and $c''_i := a_i x + \mathsf{sign}(b_i)2^k y \leq a_i \psi_i + \mathsf{sign}(b_i)2^k \phi_i$ if $a_i = \mathsf{sign}(b_i)$ and $k < \lceil \lg(|b_i|) \rceil$. Likewise, if $\lfloor \lg(|b_i|) \rfloor < -k$ then put $c'_i := a_i x + \mathsf{sign}(b_i)2^{-k}y \leq a_i \psi_{i-1} + \mathsf{sign}(b_i)2^{-k}\phi_{i-1}$ and $c''_i := a_i x \leq a_i \psi_i$. Similarly for $a_i \neq \mathsf{sign}(b_i)$.

4.5   Meet and Abstraction

Meet over $\langle \wp^f(\mathsf{Log}), \models \rangle$ can be defined by $[I_1]_{\equiv} \sqcap [I_2]_{\equiv} = [I_1 \cup I_2]_{\equiv}$. Thus, meet reduces to set union when a class $[I]_{\equiv}$ is represented by a set I. Henceforth quotienting will be omitted, for brevity, and to reflect implementation.

A less trivial problem is that of computing $\alpha(I_1 \cup I_2)$ where $I_1 \in \wp^f(\mathsf{Log})$ and $I_2 \in \wp^f(\mathsf{Poly})$. This arises as a special case when a statement is encountered, such as a loop condition $x \leq y+z$ or an assignment $x = y+z$, that cannot be expressed logahedrally. If these statements are described respectively by $I_2 = \{x \leq y + z\}$ and $I_2 = \{y+z \leq x, x \leq y+z\}$, and I_1 is a logahedral description of the program state, then the subsequent state is described by $\alpha(I_1 \cup I_2)$. Thus, in an analysis, $\alpha(I_1 \cup I_2)$ performs the role of meet when I_2 is not logahedral.

This problem has been tackled using linear programming [15]. To illustrate, suppose $I_2 = \{c'\}$ where $c' := \sum_{k=1}^{n} a'_k x_k \leq d'$. Let $i, j \in [1, n]$ where $i \neq j$ and minimise $\sum_{k\neq i, k\neq j} a'_k x_k$ subject to I_1 and c'. If a minimum $d_{i,j}$ exists then it follows $I_1 \cup \{c'\} \models a'_i x_i + a'_j x_j \leq d' - d_{i,j}$. TVPI inequalities found this way are added to I_1. An alternative and potentially more precise approach, which is applicable to both TVPI and logahedra, is based on extending the resultant operator to polyhedral inequalities in the following fashion:

Definition 13. If $c := a_i x_i + a_j x_j \leq d \in \mathsf{TVPI}$, $c' := \sum_{k=1}^{n} a'_k x_k \leq d' \in \mathsf{Poly}$, $a'_j \neq 0$ and $a_i.a'_i < 0$ then $\mathsf{result}(c, c', x_i) = (|a'_i|a_j + |a_i|a'_j)x_j + |a_i| \sum_{k \notin \{i,j\}} a'_k x_k \leq |a'_i|d + |a_i|d'$ otherwise $\mathsf{result}(c, c', x_i) = \bot$.

The $a'_j \neq 0$ condition ensures $|\mathsf{vars}(\mathsf{result}(c, c', x_i))| < |\mathsf{vars}(c')|$. Thus if c' is ternary then $\mathsf{result}(c, c', x_i)$ is either binary or undefined. The partial result map can be lifted to a total map $\mathsf{result}(I_1, I_2)$ for $I_1 \subseteq \mathsf{TVPI}$ and $I_2 \subseteq \mathsf{Poly}$ by analogy with definition 9. With this in place, an operator $\mathsf{extend}(I_1, I_2)$ is introduced, designed so that $\alpha(I_1 \cup I_2) \models \mathsf{extend}(I_1, I_2)$.

Definition 14. The map $\mathsf{extend} : \wp^f(\mathsf{TVPI}) \times \wp^f(\mathsf{Poly}) \to \wp^f(\mathsf{TVPI})$ is defined $\mathsf{extend}(I, \delta) = \cup_{i\geq 0} I_i$ where $I_0 = \mathsf{complete}(I \cup (\delta \cap \mathsf{TVPI}))$, $\delta_0 = \delta \setminus \mathsf{TVPI}$, $R_{i+1} = \mathsf{result}(I_i, \delta_i)$, $I_{i+1} = \mathsf{complete}(I_i \cup (R_{i+1} \cap \mathsf{TVPI}))$ and $\delta_{i+1} = R_{i+1} \setminus I_{i+1}$.

If δ is comprised of ternary constraints, which is the dominating case [15], then result is applied once. If desired, incremental closure can be used to compute complete($I_i \cup (R_{i+1} \cap \text{TVPI})$), since proposition 2 extends to TVPI [8]. If extend(I, δ) is not logahedral, then α must subsequently be applied.

Example 5. Consider augmenting $I = \{x - y \leq 0, -x + y \leq 0\}$ with $c' := x - 2y + z \leq 0$. Then $I_0 = I$ and $\delta_0 = \{c'\}$. Thus $R_1 = \text{result}(I_0, \delta_0) = \{y + z \leq 0\}$ whence $\delta_1 = \emptyset$ and $I_1 = \text{complete}(I_0 \cup R_1) = I \cup \{y + z \leq 0, x + z \leq 0\}$. These inequalities cannot be inferred with the linear programming technique of [15].

Example 6. Let $I = \{w - x \leq 0, y - z \leq 0\}$ and $c' := w + x + y + z \leq 1$. Then $I_0 = \text{complete}(I) = I$ and $\delta_0 = \{c'\}$. Thus $R_1 = \text{result}(I_0, \delta_0) = \{2w + y + z \leq 1, x + w + 2y \leq 1\}$, $I_1 = I_0$ and $\delta_1 = R_1$. Next $R_2 = \text{result}(I_2, \delta_1) = \{2w + 2y \leq 1\}$, $I_2 = \text{complete}(I_1 \cup R_2) = I_1 \cup R_2 = I \cup \{w + y \leq 1/2\}$ and $\delta_2 = \emptyset$.

4.6 Join

Join is required to merge abstractions on different paths, as is shown with P_5 in section 3. If quotienting is omitted, then join over $\wp^f(\text{Log})$ can be defined $I_1 \sqcup I_2 = \cup \{\overline{\exists} Y.I_1 \sqcup_Y \overline{\exists} Y.I_2 \mid Y \subseteq X \land |Y| = 2\}$ where $J_1 \sqcup_Y J_2 = \alpha_Y(J_1 \lor J_2)$ and $\lor$ is join (planar convex hull) for TVPI [15]. Join also benefits from completeness since if I_i is complete then $\overline{\exists} Y.I_i = \pi_Y(I_i)$. The TVPI operation $\lor$ is $O(n \lg n)$ where $n = |J_1| + |J_2|$, hence the overall cost of $\sqcup$ is dominated by completion.

With $\sqcap$ and $\sqcup$ thus defined, $\langle \wp^f(\text{Log}), \models, \sqcap, \sqcup \rangle$ forms a lattice. Furthermore, Log_k has additional structure since C_k is finite (see definition 5). In particular, if $I \subseteq \text{Log}_k$ then there exists a finite $K \subseteq I$ such that $I \equiv K$. As a consequence $\langle \wp^f(\text{Log}_k), \models, \sqcap, \sqcup \rangle$ is a complete lattice.

Widening [6] is often applied with join in order to enforce termination. As has been explained elsewhere [11,15], care must be taken not to reintroduce inequalities through completion that have been deliberately discarded in widening.

5 Logahedra versus Octagons and TVPI

Logahedra are theoretically well motivated and their representational advantages, as a generalisation of octagons, are of interest. To provide preliminary data on the power of bounded logahedra two sets of experiments were performed.

In the first experiment sets of integer points, $\{\langle x, y \rangle \mid x, y \in [-32, 32]\}$ were randomly selected. For each set, between 1 and 63 points were generated. The best $\text{Oct} = \text{Log}_0$ and Log_k (for $k \in [1, 5]$) abstractions were computed and compared with the best TVPI abstraction. The comparison is based on the number of integer points in the abstractions. For example, one set of 23 points had 7 extreme points. The Oct, the five Log and the TVPI descriptions were satisfied by 3221, 3027, 2881, 2843, 2835, 2819, 2701 integer points. Thus the precision loss incurred by Oct over TVPI is $(3321 - 2701)/2701 = 0.230$. Likewise the losses for Log relative to TVPI are 0.121, 0.067, 0.053, 0.050 and 0.044. This was done

Table 1. Precision comparison of Oct and Log_k against TVPI on random data

vertices	sets	Oct	Log_k k=1	k=2	k=3	k=4	k=5
1	2044	0.000	0.000	0.000	0.000	0.000	0.000
2	2958	82.640	43.941	30.675	26.396	25.024	24.481
3	5923	1.874	0.998	0.700	0.611	0.584	0.576
4	10423	0.557	0.294	0.195	0.163	0.153	0.149
5	14217	0.352	0.192	0.125	0.100	0.092	0.089
6	13550	0.276	0.152	0.097	0.075	0.067	0.064
7	9058	0.234	0.131	0.081	0.061	0.054	0.051
8	4345	0.205	0.115	0.071	0.053	0.046	0.043
9	1508	0.188	0.105	0.064	0.047	0.040	0.038
10	398	0.171	0.096	0.058	0.042	0.035	0.033
11	64	0.165	0.095	0.054	0.037	0.031	0.029
12	6	0.179	0.107	0.06	0.045	0.038	0.036

for 64K sets and the results are summarised in Table 1. The table presents the mean precision loss where the sets are grouped by their number of vertices.

The data reveals that describing exactly two points is by far the most inaccurate scenario for Oct and Log_k; if the angle between the points is suitably acute then the TVPI constraints are satisfied by just the two points whereas the Oct and Log_k constraints can be satisfied by a band of integral points. Precision loss decreases beyond this two point case. Enlarging the sample space does not noticeably effect the relative precision loss other than accentuating the two point case. Observe that the relative precision loss declines as k increases, suggesting that logahedra can offer a significant precision improvement over octagons.

The second set of experiments compares the abstractions of two variable projections of the results of a polyhedral analysis tightened to integer points for a series of benchmarks [1,2,13]. As in the first experiment, comparisons are made between the number of points in the TVPI, Oct and Log_k abstractions. Table 2 details benchmarks, their number of variables, the pair of variables in the projection, the number of integer points in the TVPI abstraction and the number of additional points for Oct and Log_k abstractions. Benchmarks and projections where Oct and TVPI give the same abstraction are omitted from the table. This was the case for the additional 12 programs in the benchmark suite.

The data illustrates the power of octagons, with the majority of two variable projections being octagonal (indeed, many of these were intervals). It also illustrates that there are cases when non-octagonal constraints occur, with (as in the first experiment) Log_k precision improving as k increases.

Together, the results motivate further study. The random data demonstrates that logahedra have the potential to deliver precision gains over octagons, however, the analysis data adds a note of caution. It is not surprising that many program invariants can be described by intervals, nor that many of the remainder are octagonal. The data (and the example in section 3) shows that the descriptive power of logahedra can improve analysis, leaving open the question of whether

Table 2. Precision comparison of Oct and Log_k against TVPI on analysis data

fixpoint	*vars*	*project*	Oct	Log_k k=1	k=2	k=3	k=4	k=5	TVPI
cars.inv	5	(4, 5)	312	234	78	54	54	54	3640
efm1.inv	6	(3, 6)	1	0	0	0	0	0	128
heap.inv	5	(1, 2)	1056	0	0	0	0	0	33
heap.inv	5	(3, 4)	465	0	0	0	0	0	1055
heap.inv	5	(3, 5)	465	0	0	0	0	0	1055
robot.inv	3	(1, 2)	528	0	0	0	0	0	1089
scheduler-2p.invl1	7	(3, 6)	135	120	90	30	18	18	180
scheduler-2p.invl1	7	(4, 6)	115	100	70	20	12	12	260
scheduler-2p.invl1	7	(6, 7)	135	120	90	30	18	18	180
scheduler-2p.invl2	7	(4, 6)	189	168	126	42	26	26	245
scheduler-2p.invl2	7	(6, 7)	90	80	60	20	12	12	215
scheduler-3p.invl1	10	(4, 9)	264	198	66	45	45	45	390
scheduler-3p.invl1	10	(9, 10)	264	198	66	45	45	45	390
scheduler-3p.invl3	10	(4, 8)	312	234	78	54	54	54	455
scheduler-3p.invl3	10	(8, 9)	144	108	36	24	24	24	405
scheduler-3p.invl3	10	(9, 10)	534	128	128	128	128	128	1725
see-saw.inv	2	(1, 2)	990	231	110	110	110	110	2454
swim-pool-1.inv	9	(4, 6)	62	61	59	55	47	31	4162

the additional cost (a higher constant in the complexity) pays for itself with improved accuracy. The answer to this question is in part application specific.

6 Conclusion

This paper has introduced logahedra, a new weakly relational abstract domain. A variant of logahedra, bounded logahedra Log_k, where k is the maximum exponent is also introduced. Logahedra lie strictly between octagons and TVPI in terms of expressive power, with octagons forming a special case, $\text{Oct} = \text{Log}_0$. Bounded logahedra retain the good computational properties of octagons, whilst being less restrictive. The theory for the abstract domain has been given, along with algorithms for each domain operation. Logahedra have the further advantage that their variable coefficients can be represented by their exponents, mitigating the problem of large coefficients that arise when using polyhedra or TVPI. A preliminary investigation into the expressive power of logahedra, plus a worked example, suggests that they can lead to more accurate analysis, but cautions that many invariants can be described using intervals and octagons. Future work will further investigate the application of logahedra in verification.

Acknowledgements. The authors thank Phil Charles, Tim Hopkins, Stefan Kahrs and Axel Simon for useful discussions. The work was supported by EPSRC projects EP/E033105/1 and EP/E034519/1. The authors would like to thank the University of St Andrews and the Royal Society for their generous support.

References

1. Bardin, S., Finkel, A., Leroux, J., Petrucci, L.: FAST: Fast Acceleration of Symbolic Transition Systems. In: Hunt Jr., W.A., Somenzi, F. (eds.) CAV 2003. LNCS, vol. 2725, pp. 118–121. Springer, Heidelberg (2003)
2. Charles, P.J., Howe, J.M., King, A.: Integer Polyhedra for Program Analysis. In: AAIM. LNCS, vol. 5564, pp. 85–99. Springer, Heidelberg (2009)
3. Clarisó, R., Cortadella, J.: The Octahedron Abstract Domain. Science of Computer Programming 64, 115–139 (2007)
4. Cousot, P., Halbwachs, N.: Automatic Discovery of Linear Restraints among Variables of a Program. In: POPL, pp. 84–97. ACM Press, New York (1978)
5. Eisenbrand, F., Laue, S.: A Linear Algorithm for Integer Programming in the Plane. Mathematical Programming 102(2), 249–259 (2005)
6. Halbwachs, N.: Détermination Automatique de Relations Linéaires Vérifiées par les Variables d'un Programme. PhD thesis, Université Scientifique et Médicale de Grenoble (1979)
7. Henzinger, T.A., Ho, P.-H., Wong-Toi, H.: HyTech: A Model Checker for Hybrid Systems. Software Tools for Technology Transfer 1, 110–122 (1997)
8. Howe, J.M., King, A.: Closure Algorithms for Domains with Two Variables per Inequality. Technical Report TR/2009/DOC/01, School of Informatics, City University London (2009),
   http://www.soi.city.ac.uk/organisation/doc/research/tech_reports/
9. Larsen, K.G., Larsson, F., Pettersson, P., Yi, W.: Efficient Verification of Real-time Systems: Compact Data Structure and State-space Reduction. In: IEEE Real-Time Systems Symposium, pp. 14–24. IEEE Computer Society, Los Alamitos (1997)
10. Logozzo, F., Fähndrich, M.: Pentagons: a Weakly Relational Abstract Domain for the Efficient Validation of Array Accesses. In: ACM Symposium on Applied Computing, pp. 184–188. ACM Press, New York (2008)
11. Miné, A.: The Octagon Abstract Domain. Higher-Order and Symbolic Computation 19(1), 31–100 (2006)
12. Nelson, C.G.: An $n^{\lg n}$ Algorithm for the Two-Variable-Per-Constraint Linear Programming Satisfiability Problem. Technical Report STAN-CS-78-689, Stanford University, Computer Science Department (1978)
13. Sankaranarayanan, S., Sipma, H.B., Manna, Z.: Constraint Based Linear Relations Analysis. In: Giacobazzi, R. (ed.) SAS 2004. LNCS, vol. 3148, pp. 53–68. Springer, Heidelberg (2004)
14. Sankaranarayanan, S., Sipma, H.B., Manna, Z.: Scalable Analysis of Linear Systems Using Mathematical Programming. In: Cousot, R. (ed.) VMCAI 2005. LNCS, vol. 3385, pp. 25–41. Springer, Heidelberg (2005)
15. Simon, A.: Value-Range Analysis of C Programs: Towards Proving the Absence of Buffer Overflow Vulnerabilities. Springer, Heidelberg (2008)
16. Simon, A., King, A.: Exploiting Sparsity in Polyhedral Analysis. In: Hankin, C., Siveroni, I. (eds.) SAS 2005. LNCS, vol. 3672, pp. 336–351. Springer, Heidelberg (2005)
17. Simon, A., King, A., Howe, J.M.: Two Variables per Linear Inequality as an Abstract Domain. In: Leuschel, M. (ed.) LOPSTR 2002. LNCS, vol. 2664, pp. 71–89. Springer, Heidelberg (2003)

Synthesis of Fault-Tolerant Distributed Systems*

Rayna Dimitrova** and Bernd Finkbeiner

Saarland University, Germany

Abstract. A distributed system is fault-tolerant if it continues to perform correctly even when a subset of the processes becomes faulty. Fault-
tolerance is highly desirable but often difficult to implement. In this
paper, we investigate fault-tolerant *synthesis*, i.e., the problem of determining whether a given temporal specification can be implemented as
a fault-tolerant distributed system. As in standard distributed synthesis, we assume that the specification of the correct behaviors is given
as a temporal formula over the externally visible variables. Additionally,
we introduce the *fault-tolerance specification*, a CTL* formula describing
the effects and the duration of faults. If, at some point in time, a process
becomes faulty, it becomes part of the external environment and its further behavior is only restricted by the fault-tolerance specification. This
allows us to model a large variety of fault types. Our method accounts
for the effect of faults on the values communicated by the processes, and,
hence, on the information available to the non-faulty processes. We prove
that for fully connected system architectures, i.e., for systems where each
pair of processes is connected by a communication link, the fault-tolerant
synthesis problem from CTL* specifications is **2EXPTIME**-complete.

1 Introduction

Fault-tolerance is an important design consideration in distributed systems.
A fault-tolerant system is able to withstand situations where a subset of its
components breaks: depending on the chosen type of fault-tolerance, the system
may completely mask the fault, return to correct behavior after a finite amount
of time, or switch to a behavior that is still safe but possibly less performant.
Fault-tolerance is highly desirable but often difficult to implement. Thus, formal
methods for verification [7] and synthesis [10] of fault-tolerance are necessary.

Traditionally, fault-tolerance requirements are chosen manually. While it is
obviously desirable to stay as close as possible to the normal behavior, the question which type of fault-tolerance can be realized in a given system is difficult to
decide and requires a careful analysis of both the desired system functionality
and the possible faults. In this paper, we develop algorithmic support for this

* This work was partly supported by the German Research Foundation (DFG) as
  part of the Transregional Collaborative Research Center Automatic Verification and
  Analysis of Complex Systems (SFB/TR 14 AVACS).
** Supported by a Microsoft Research European PhD Scholarship.

Z. Liu and A.P. Ravn (Eds.): ATVA 2009, LNCS 5799, pp. 321–336, 2009.

design step. We present a synthesis algorithm that determines if a given temporal specification has a fault-tolerant implementation, and, in case the answer is positive, automatically derives such an implementation.

Our goal is thus more ambitious than previous approaches (cf. [10, 2, 4]) to fault-tolerant synthesis, which transform an existing fault-intolerant implementation into a fault-tolerant version. While such approaches are often able to deliver fault-tolerant systems, they are inherently incomplete, and can therefore not be used to *decide* whether a given fault-tolerance requirement can be realized. In order to obtain a decision procedure, we cannot treat the implementation of the system functionality and the implementation of its fault-tolerance as two separate tasks, but must rather extend the synthesis algorithm to address both concerns at once. In the restricted setting of closed systems, i.e., of systems without input, such a combination has already been carried out: Attie et al. [1] represent faults by a finite set of fault actions that may be carried out by a malicious environment. Their method then synthesizes a program that is correct with respect to a specified set of such possible environments.

The key challenge in moving from simple closed systems to general distributed systems is to account for the incomplete information available to the individual processes. Faults may affect the communication between processes, which affects the information the non-faulty processes have. Our setting builds on that of standard distributed synthesis [6], where the communication links between the processes are described as a directed graph, called the *system architecture*. We assume the architecture is *fully connected* and the system specification is *external* [13, 8], i.e., it does not refer to the internal variables. For standard synthesis, this case is known to be decidable: while the processes may read different inputs, they can simply transmit all information to the other processes through the internal communication links. The distributed system thus resembles a monolithic program in the sense that all processes are aware of the global state.

The situation is more difficult in a fault-tolerant system, since, when a fault occurs in some process, the process essentially becomes part of the hostile environment and the remaining processes can no longer rely on receiving accurate information about the external input at its site. We present a synthesis algorithm for CTL* specifications that accounts for the resulting incomplete information. The given CTL* specification is a *fault-tolerance specification* which encodes the effects and the durations of the faults and the desired type of tolerance.

Our algorithm is based on a transformation of the architecture and of the fault-tolerance specification. The architecture transformation changes the set of external input variables by introducing a new input variable for each process and making the original input variables unobservable for all processes in the architecture. The transformation of the specification establishes the relation between the original input of a process and the new *faulty input*. The two inputs are constrained to be the same during the normal operation of the corresponding process, which guarantees the correctness of the transformation, and may differ when the process is faulty, which allows us to assume that in the transformed architecture the faults do not affect the transmission of external input. Thus, we can reduce the distributed synthesis problem for the original architecture and fault-tolerance specification to the one of finding a monolithic implementation that satisfies the transformed specification in the presence of faults.

We hence establish that the synthesis of fault-tolerant distributed systems with fully connected system architectures and external specifications is decidable. In fact, the problem is no more expensive than standard synthesis: fault-tolerant distributed synthesis from CTL* specifications is 2EXPTIME-complete.

2   Modelling Fault-Tolerant Systems

2.1   Faults and Fault-Tolerance

Types of Faults. In the field of fault-tolerant distributed computing faults are categorized in a variety of ways. The categorization of faults according to the behavior they cause, results in several standard classes [3, 1]. *Stuck-at* faults can, for example, cause a component or a wire to be stuck in some state. If a process is affected by a *fail-stop* or a *crash* fault, it stops (potentially permanently) executing any actions before it violates its input-output specification. In both cases the process is uncorrectably corrupted, but while fail-stop faults are *detectable*, that is, other processes are explicitly notified of the fault, crash stops are *undetectable*. If a process fails to respond to an input from another component, i.e., some action is omitted, it is said to exhibit an *omission fault*. Omission faults are a subset of the class of *timing faults* that cause the component to respond with the correct value but outside the required time interval. The most general class of *Byzantine faults* encompasses all possible faults, including arbitrary and even malicious behavior of the affected process, and are in general undetectable.

According to their duration, faults can be *permanent, transient,* or *intermittent.* In the latter two cases, upon recovery the affected process returns to normal operation from the arbitrary state it has reached in the presence of the fault.

Fault-Tolerance Requirements. Usually the system is not required to satisfy the original specification after a fault occurs, but instead comply with some fault-tolerance policy. Fault-tolerance properties are generally classified according to whether and how they respect the safety and liveness parts of the original specification. This classification yields three main types of tolerance. *Masking tolerance* always respects both safety and liveness. In *non-masking tolerance,* however, the safety property might be temporarily violated, but is guaranteed to be eventually restored, while the liveness part is again always respected. A third type is *fail-safe tolerance.* When formalizing fail-safe tolerance it is assumed that the original specification is given as conjunction of a safety and a liveness specifications [12], and after fault occurrence only the safety conjunct has to be satisfied.

2.2   Architectures for Fault-Tolerant Synthesis

An architecture describes the communication between the processes in a distributed system and their interaction with the external environment. We model the occurrence of a fault as an action of the environment. In the following, we assume that faults are *detectable*, that is there exists a reliable unit of the external environment that notifies all processes immediately when a fault occurs in some of them, and also informs them exactly which processes were faulty in the previous execution step. To this end, we consider architectures with a distinguished set of external input *fault-notification variables*, which all processes in the system are allowed to read. Alternatively, the fault-notification variables could be made invisible to the system processes, in which case finding the fault-detection mechanism would be part of the synthesis problem.

An *architecture* $A = (env, P, Ext, C, (D(v))_{v \in Ext}, (In(p), Out(p))_{p \in P})$ is a tuple that consists of: environment env, a finite set of processes P, a set Ext of *external variables* together with a finite domain $D(v)$ for each $v \in Ext$, a set C (disjoint from Ext) of *internal variables*, and read and write permissions for each $p \in P$. The set Ext is the union of the disjoint sets I, O, H and N, where:

- The set I consists of the *external input variables* whose values are supplied by the environment env. The set I is the union of the sets I_p, where for each process p, I_p is a set of external input variables, this process can read. Each variable in I is read by at least one (possibly several) processes in P.
- The set O consists of the *external output variables*, via which the processes provide their output to the environment env. The set O is the union of the *disjoint* sets O_p, where for each process p, O_p is the set of external output variables written by that process, which no other process in P can read.
- The set H consists of the *external private environment variables* written by the environment env, and which none of the processes in P can read.
- The set $N = \{n_p, m_p \mid p \in P\}$ of external input variables for *fault notification* contains one variable n_p for each process p that is used by the environment to notify all processes for a fault occurrence in p and a variable m_p that indicates whether p was faulty in the previous execution step. The variables in N can be read by all processes and are written only by the environment. The domain $D(n_p)$ of n_p is a finite subset of $\mathbb{N}$ that consists of the different faults that can occur in process p, where 0 indicates normal operation. Similarly for m_p.

The set C consists of the variables used for *internal communication* between the processes. It is the union of the *disjoint* sets C_p, where for each process p, C_p is the set of internal variables written by p via which it communicates to the other processes. We denote with V the set of all variables in an architecture A.

For a process p, the set $In(p)$ consists of all variables (internal or external) this process is allowed to read and $Out(p) = C_p \cup O_p$ consists of all variables that this process is allowed to write. By definition, the sets $Out(p)$ are disjoint.

The architecture associates with each external variable $v \in Ext$ a finite nonempty domain $D(v)$ together with some designated element $d_0(v) \in D(v)$. The domains of the internal variables are unconstrained by the architecture, and hence the capacity of the communication channels is not limited a priori.

Consider some nonempty finite domains $D(v)_{v \in C}$ for the internal variables in A. For a subset $U \subseteq V$, we denote with $D(U)$ the Cartesian product $\prod_{u \in U} D(u)$ and with $d_0(U)$ the tuple $(d_0(u))_{u \in U}$. For $d \in D(U)$, $u \in U$ and $U' \subseteq U$, $d\langle u \rangle$ and

$d\langle U'\rangle$ denote the projections of d on the variable u and on the subset of variables U', respectively. For a finite or infinite sequence $\sigma = d_0 d_1 d_2 \ldots$ of elements of $D(U)$ and $j \geq 0$, we denote by $\sigma[j]$ the element d_j and with $\sigma(j)$ the prefix of length j of σ (if $j = 0$, then $\sigma(j) = \varepsilon$). Projection trivially extends to sequences and prefixes. When σ is finite, we denote with $|\sigma|$ the number of elements of σ.

We consider synchronous communication with delay: at each step, each process reads its current external input and the output of the processes in P delayed by one step. For a *global computation history* $\sigma \in D(V)^*$ we have that $\sigma[0] = d_0(V)$ and for every $j \geq 1$, $\sigma[j]\langle I \cup H \cup N\rangle$ is the input provided by the environment at step j and $\sigma[j]\langle V \setminus (I \cup H \cup N)\rangle$ is the output of the processes at step $j - 1$, i.e., the history reflects the delay. Thus, for simplicity of the presentation we have assumed that the delay of each variable $v \in V \setminus (I \cup H \cup N)$ is 1. Our results can be easily extended to the case of arbitrary *a priori fixed* delays.

Fully Connected Architectures. An architecture A is *fully connected* if every pair of processes is connected via a communication link with sufficient capacity.

From now on, we consider only fully connected architectures and w.l.o.g. assume that $C = \{c_p, t_p \mid p \in P\}$, where for each process p, the variables c_p and t_p are written by p and read by all processes, and the domain of c_p is fixed to be $D(I_p)$. Thus, process p can use c_p to communicate its input. We denote with c_p^v the component of the variable c_p used for the transmission of $v \in I_p$. The domains of the variables t_p for $p \in P$ are left unspecified in the architecture.

2.3   The Specification Language CTL*

Syntax. Let AP be a finite set of atomic propositions. The logic CTL* distinguishes state and path formulas. State formulas are called *CTL* formulas*.

State formulas over AP are formed according to the following grammar, where $p \in AP$ and θ stands for a path formula: $\varphi ::= true \mid p \mid \neg\varphi \mid \varphi_1 \wedge \varphi_2 \mid \mathsf{E}\theta$. Path formulas are formed according to the following grammar, where φ is a state formula and θ, θ_1 and θ_2 are path formulas: $\theta ::= \varphi \mid \neg\theta \mid \theta_1 \wedge \theta_2 \mid \mathsf{X}\theta \mid \theta_1 \,\mathcal{U}\, \theta_2$.

As abbreviations we can define the remaining usual boolean operators over state and path formulas. For a path formula θ, we define the state formula $\mathsf{A}\theta$ as $\neg\mathsf{E}\neg\theta$, the path formula $\mathsf{F}\theta$ as $true \,\mathcal{U}\, \theta$ and the path formula $\mathsf{G}\theta$ as $\neg\mathsf{F}\neg\theta$.

Trees. As usual, for a finite set X, an X-tree is a prefix-closed subset $T \subseteq X^*$ of finite words over X. The direction of every nonempty node $\sigma \cdot x \in X^+$ is defined as $dir(\sigma \cdot x) = x$, and for ε, $dir(\varepsilon) = x_0$ where $x_0 \in X$ is some designated root direction. A X-tree T is called *total* if $\varepsilon \in T$ and for every $\sigma \in T$ there exists at least one successor $\sigma \cdot x \in T$, $x \in X$. If $T = X^*$, then T is called *full*. For a given finite set Y, a Y-labeled X-tree is a pair $\langle T, l\rangle$, where T is an X-tree and $l : T \to Y$ is a labelling function that maps each node in T to an element of Y.

Semantics. Consider a set of variables V with $D(V)$ being the Cartesian product of their domains. Let AP be a finite set of atomic propositions over V. A CTL* formula φ over AP can then be interpreted over total $D(V)$-labeled trees according to the standard semantics [5] of CTL*. A total $D(V)$-labeled tree $\langle T, l \rangle$ is a model of φ, written $\langle T, l \rangle \models \varphi$, iff the root node of $\langle T, l \rangle$ satisfies φ.

2.4 Specifying Fault-Tolerance

The *system specification* describes the desired input-output behavior of the system in the absence of faults and leaves the internal communication unconstrained. That is, we are given an *external specification* as a CTL* formula φ over atomic propositions from the set $AP = \{v = a \mid v \in Ext \setminus N, a \in D(v)\}$, i.e., about external variables. The models of φ are total $D(Ext)$-labeled $D(Ext)$-trees.

In the presence of faults, the system need not satisfy the original specification, but instead comply with some (possibly weaker) *fault-tolerance specification*. An external specification for an architecture A can refer to the fault notification variables in N. This allows for specifying the intended fault-tolerance policy as well as encoding the effects and durations of faults in the input CTL* formula.

Given the original specification φ, we first construct a formula Φ_{TOL} according to the required type of fault-tolerance. The user can describe manually as a CTL* formula the desired properties of the behavior of the system in the presence of particular faults in particular processes and combinations thereof. Of course, classical fault-tolerance requirements, such as masking, non-masking or fail-safe, can be also specified (for masking tolerance it suffices to leave the specification unchanged). Moreover, in the case of simple specifications such as *invariants*, i.e., of the form $\mathsf{AG}\psi$, this compilation can be done *automatically*: For fail-safe and non-masking tolerance, the tolerance properties are respectively $\mathsf{AG}(\psi \vee (\textit{fault-present} \wedge \psi_{safe}))$ and $\mathsf{AG}(\psi \vee (\textit{fault-present} \wedge \mathsf{AFAG}\psi))$, where $\textit{fault-present} = \bigvee_{p \in P} \neg(n_p = 0)$ and ψ_{safe} is the safety conjunct of ψ.

In our model, the occurrence of a fault causes the affected process to behave in an arbitrary way, i.e., it exhibits maximal behavior. However, by constraining this behavior in the fault-tolerance specification, we can model several of the fault types mentioned in the beginning of this section, as well as many more.

Given a set of faults with their effects on the behavior of a process and their durations, we transform the formula φ_{TOL} into the *fault-tolerance specification* Φ^t, by relativizing the path quantifiers in the formula φ_{TOL} w.r.t. the corresponding assumptions on the environment. These assumptions are encoded in the formulas *fault-behavior*, *fault-duration*, and *fault-distribution*, whose construction we discuss below. Thus, the fault-tolerance specification Φ^t is obtained from the formula φ_{TOL} by substituting each occurrence of $\mathsf{A}\theta$ by $\mathsf{A}((\textit{fault-behavior} \wedge \textit{fault-duration} \wedge \textit{fault-distribution}) \rightarrow \theta)$, and each occurrence of $\mathsf{E}\theta$ by $\mathsf{E}(\textit{fault-behavior} \wedge \textit{fault-duration} \wedge \textit{fault-distribution} \wedge \theta)$.

The formula *fault-behavior* describes the possible behaviors of the processes in the presence of each of the given faults. Let $\textit{faulty-output}(d, p)$ be a state formula describing the possible outputs of process p when affected by the fault of type d (we can assume that a stopped process outputs some default element $\perp$). Then, $\textit{fault-behavior} = \mathsf{G} \bigwedge_{p \in P} \bigwedge_{d \in D(n_p)} (n_p = d \rightarrow \mathsf{X}(\textit{faulty-output}(d, p)))$.

The formula *fault-duration* constrains the duration of faults. Let $D'(n_p)$ and $D''(n_p)$ be the subsets of $D(n_p)$ consisting of the permanent and the transient faults, respectively, for a process $p \in P$. For each $d \in D''(n_p)$, we assume the existence of a boolean variable r_p^d in H, where r_p^d being true means that process p has recovered from d. The path formulas $permanent(d,p) = \mathsf{G}((n_p = d) \rightarrow \mathsf{G}(n_p = d))$ and $transient(d,p) = \mathsf{G}(((n_p = d) \rightarrow (n_p = d \, \mathcal{U} \, r_p^d)) \wedge (r_p^d \rightarrow (\neg(n_p = d) \wedge \mathsf{G}r_p^d)))$ state that the occurrence of fault of type d in process p is permanent, respectively transient (i.e., the duration of the fault is finite and the recovered process cannot perturb again, cf. [7]). Finally, we define the formula $fault\text{-}duration = \bigwedge_{p \in P}((\bigwedge_{d \in D'(n_p)} permanent(d,p)) \wedge (\bigwedge_{d \in D''(n_p)} transient(d,p)))$.

The user can also provide a path formula $fault\text{-}distribution$ that constrains the number of faulty processes in the considered system during the execution, e.g., there is at most one faulty process at every point of the execution.

To avoid restriction to only memoryless implementations, we assume that at every point of the system's execution at least one process is not faulty, i.e., the synthesized system is designed to tolerate up to $n - 1$ simultaneously faulty processes, where n is the total number of processes. Thus, we assume that the formula $fault\text{-}distribution$ is a conjunction of the user specified requirements and: the formula $\mathsf{G} \bigvee_{p \in P}(n_p = 0)$ which guarantees that there is at least one non-faulty process at every point, and the formula $\mathsf{G} \bigwedge_{p \in P}(n_p = d \rightarrow \mathsf{X}(m_p = d))$, which states that the values of the variables m_p and n_p are correctly related.

Note that for common fault types such as fail-stop or stuck-at, as well as for the usual constraints on the duration of faults, the fault-tolerance specification can be compiled automatically from the original specification. The user can also specify customized requirements expressible in CTL*. From now on, we assume that the fault-tolerance specification is given as input to our algorithm.

Example (Reliable Broadcast). In a broadcast protocol, the environment consists of n clients $E_1, \ldots, E_n$, which broadcast messages. The system consists of n servers, $S_1, \ldots, S_n$ that correspond to the processes $p_1, \ldots, p_n$, which deliver the messages to the clients. Each client E_j communicates only with the corresponding server S_j and we assume that each message sent by a client is unique.

A system with 3 servers is depicted on Fig. 1, where we have omitted the internal communication variables. Let M be the finite set of possible message contents. The domain of each input, output or communication variable $v \in \{i_j, o_j, c_j \mid j = 1, 2, 3\}$ is $D(v) = \{(m, j) \mid m \in M, j \in \{1, 2, 3\}\} \cup \{\bot\}$, where j denotes the broadcaster's name and $\bot$ indicates the absence of message.

In the absence of faults, the correctness can be specified by the following standard requirements: (1) If a client E_j broadcasts a message m, then the server S_j eventually delivers m; (2) If a server delivers a message m, then all

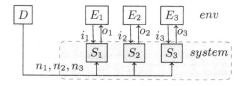

Fig. 1. Architecture of a distributed server

servers eventually deliver m; (3) For every message m, every server delivers (m, l) at most once and does so only if m was previously broadcast by the client E_l.

The environment component D notifies all servers when a fault in server j occurs, by setting n_j to 1. A faulty server sends arbitrary messages to the corresponding client and to the other servers. The duration of faults is unconstrained. Thus, both formulas *fault-behavior* and *fault-duration* are equivalent to *true*.

We specify the fault-tolerance requirement as follows. We replace each requirement that a server eventually delivers a message m by the weaker requirement that it has to eventually deliver a message, provided that from that point on it is never faulty. The safety property that the servers do not invent messages is also weakened to hold only for non-faulty processes. Thus, we obtain a variation of the standard requirements for reliable broadcast from [9].

Validity: *If a client E_j broadcasts a message m and the corresponding server S_j is never faulty from that point on, then S_j eventually delivers m.*

$$\varphi_j^V = \mathsf{AG} \bigwedge_{m \in M} ((i_j = (m, j) \wedge \mathsf{G}(n_j = 0)) \to \mathsf{F}(o_j = (m, j)))$$

Agreement: *If a non-faulty server E_j delivers a message (m, l), then all servers that are non-faulty from that point on eventually deliver (m, l).*

$$\varphi_j^A = \mathsf{AG} \bigwedge_{m \in M, l \in P} (o_j = (m, l) \wedge n_j = 0 \to \bigwedge_{p \in P} (\mathsf{G}(n_p = 0) \to \mathsf{F}(o_p = (m, l))))$$

Integrity: *For every message m, every non-faulty server E_j delivers (m, l) at most once and does so only if m was previously broadcast by the client E_l.*

$$\varphi_j^I = \mathsf{AG} \bigwedge_{m \in M, l \in P} ((n_j = 0 \wedge o_j = (m, l)) \to \mathsf{X}\mathsf{G}(n_j = 0 \to \neg(o_j = (m, l)))) \wedge$$
$$\mathsf{AG} \bigwedge_{m \in M, l \in P} \neg((\neg i_l = (m, l)) \, \mathcal{U} \, (o_j = (m, l) \wedge n_j = 0 \wedge \neg i_l = (m, l)))$$

2.5   The Fault-Tolerant Synthesis Problem

Let $A = (env, P, Ext, C, (D(v))_{v \in Ext}, (In(p), Out(p))_{p \in P})$ be a fully connected architecture. A *distributed implementation* for the architecture A consists of a tuple $(D(v))_{v \in C}$ of sets defining domains for the internal variables and a tuple $\hat{s} = (s_p)_{p \in P}$ of implementations for the processes in P, where an *implementation* for a process p is a function (strategy) $s_p : D(In(p))^* \to D(Out(p))$ which maps each *local input history* for p to an assignment to the variables written by p. A distributed implementation $\hat{s}$ is *finite-state* if for each process p, the domain $D(C_p)$ is finite and the strategy s_p can be represented by a finite automaton.

In the absence of faults, a distributed implementation $\hat{s} = (s_p)_{p \in P}$ defines a *computation tree* $CT(\hat{s}) = \langle T, dir \rangle$, where $T \subseteq D(V)^*$ is the greatest total tree such that for all $\sigma \in D(V)^*$ and all $d \in D(V)$, if $\sigma \cdot d \in T$, then $\sigma \in T$ and for every $p \in P$ it holds that $d\langle Out(p) \rangle = s_p(\sigma \langle In(p) \rangle)$. Recall that the *realizability problem* for an architecture A with fixed finite domains for all variables and a CTL* specification φ over $Ext \setminus N$ is to decide whether there exists a finite-state distributed implementation $\hat{s}$ for A such that $CT(\hat{s}) \models \varphi$. The *distributed synthesis problem* requires finding such an implementation if one exists.

In the presence of faults, a distributed implementation $\hat{s} = (s_p)_{p \in P}$ defines a *fault computation tree* $FCT(\hat{s}) = \langle T, dir \rangle$, where $T \subseteq D(V)^*$ is the greatest total tree such that for all $\sigma \in D(V)^*$ and $d \in D(V)$, if $\sigma \cdot d \in T$, then $\sigma \in T$ and *for every* $p \in P$ *such that* $dir(\sigma)\langle n_p \rangle = 0$ it holds that $d\langle Out(p)\rangle = s_p(\sigma\langle In(p)\rangle)$, i.e., the output of only non-faulty processes determines the successors of a node.

The implementations for the processes in P should be independent of information about the external environment the processes do not have. Consider an external input variable $v \in I$ and assume that at some point all processes allowed to read v are faulty. The behavior of the (non-faulty) processes in P at this and at later points of the execution of the system should not depend on the value of v at that moment, because the faulty processes may communicate the value incorrectly and their states may be arbitrarily perturbed. Thus, we say that two local histories for a process p are *equivalent up to faults* if they differ only in the values of external input variables at points when all processes reading them were faulty. A distributed implementation is *consistent w.r.t. faults* if all strategies produce the same output for histories that are equivalent up to faults.

Note that for an implementation that is consistent w.r.t. faults, the output of a strategy for a process p is allowed to depend on the value of a variable $v \in I_p$ from points in the history in which process p was faulty, as long as some process allowed to read v was not faulty. Thus, provided that at each point of the execution of the system there exists at least one process that is not faulty (an assumption that can be specified in the fault-tolerance specification as shown above), a recovered process is allowed to depend on the history up to equivalence w.r.t. faults. This is possible since in a fully connected architecture a process can, upon recovery from a fault, receive information about the current state of the system from another process that was not faulty at the previous step.

Definition 1 (Equivalence up to faults). *For a process* $p \in P$, *we define the equivalence relation* $\equiv_p^f$ *on* $D(In(p))^*$ *in the architecture A as follows. For* $\sigma_1 \in D(In(p))^*$ *and* $\sigma_2 \in D(In(p))^*$, *we have* $\sigma_1 \equiv_p^f \sigma_2$ *if and only if* $|\sigma_1| = |\sigma_2|$, $\sigma_1[|\sigma_1| - 1] = \sigma_2[|\sigma_2| - 1]$ *and for every* $0 \leq j < |\sigma_1| - 1$ *it holds that: (1)* $\sigma_1[j]\langle In(p) \setminus I_p \rangle = \sigma_2[j]\langle In(p) \setminus I_p \rangle$ *and (2) for every* $v \in I_p$, *if there exists a process* $q \in P$ *with* $v \in I_q$ *and* $\sigma[j]\langle n_q \rangle = 0$, *then it holds that* $\sigma_1[j]\langle v \rangle = \sigma_2[j]\langle v \rangle$.

Definition 2 (Consistency w.r.t. faults). *We say that a distributed strategy* $\hat{s}$ *for the architecture A is* consistent w.r.t. faults *if for every* $p \in P$ *and for every* σ_1 *and* σ_2 *in* $D(In(p))^*$ *with* $\sigma_1 \equiv_p^f \sigma_2$ *it holds that* $s_p(\sigma_1) = s_p(\sigma_2)$.

Definition 3 (Fault-Tolerant Synthesis Problem). *The* fault-tolerant realizability problem *for an architecture A and a CTL^* fault-tolerance specification* Φ^t *is to decide whether there exists a finite-state distributed implementation $\hat{s}$ for A that is consistent w.r.t. faults and such that* $\mathcal{F}CT(\hat{s}) \models \Phi^t$. *The* fault-tolerant synthesis problem *requires finding such an implementation if the answer is yes.*

3   Synthesis

Our synthesis algorithm builds on that of single-process synthesis under incomplete information [11], via a standard reduction for fully connected architectures and external specifications [8]. We now provide the necessary preliminaries based on the classical synthesis case and in the next sections we present the methodology we developed to employ a similar approach in the fault-tolerant setting.

3.1 Synthesis for Fully Connected Architectures

Transmission Delay. In a fully connected architecture, the output of every process p may depend, with a certain delay, on all external input variables in $I \cup N$. The delay, $delay(v, p)$, of the transmission of an external input variable v to a process p in a fully connected architecture is 0 if $v \in I_p \cup N$ and 1 otherwise.

Input-Output Functions. An *input-output function* for a process p is a function $g_p : D(I \cup N)^* \to D(O_p)$ which based on the *global input history* assigns values to the variables in O_p. A *global input-output function* $g : D(I \cup N)^* \to D(O)$ assigns values to all external output variables, based on the global input history. An input-output function g_p is *delay-compatible* if for each $\sigma_1, \sigma_2 \in D(I \cup N)^*$, for which for every $v \in I \cup N$ it holds that $\sigma_1\langle v\rangle(|\sigma_1| - delay(v, p)) = \sigma_2\langle v\rangle(|\sigma_2| - delay(v, p))$, it holds that $g_p(\sigma_1) = g_p(\sigma_2)$. A global input-output function g is *delay-compatible* iff so is the projection of g on O_p, for every process $p \in P$.

Routing Strategies. Given a nonempty set $D(v)$ for each $v \in C$, a *routing* $\hat{r} = (r_p)_{p \in P}$ for an architecture A is a tuple of local *memoryless* strategies, called *routing strategies*, where for each $p \in P$, $r_p : D(In(p)) \to D(C_p)$ is a function that given values for the variables in $In(p)$, assigns values to the variables in C_p.

In a fully connected architecture A, each process p can transmit the values of I_p to the other processes via the variable c_p. A *simple routing* $\hat{r} = (r_p)_{p \in P}$ is one for which $r_p(d)\langle c_p\rangle = d\langle I_p\rangle$ and it allows every process to trivially reconstruct the value of every variable in I. A distributed implementation $\hat{s}$ for A *has simple routing* if for every $\sigma \in D(V)^*$ and $p \in P$ it holds that $s_p(\sigma\langle In(p)\rangle)\langle c_p\rangle = dir(\sigma)\langle I_p\rangle$, i.e., the strategies directly forward the external input. For fully connected architectures it suffices to consider only implementations with simple routing.

Synthesis for Fully Connected Architectures and External Specifications. In [8] it was shown that the distributed synthesis problem is decidable for uniformly well-connected architectures with linearly preordered information and external specifications, and it can be reduced to finding a collection of delay-compatible input-output functions for the processes in P. Fully connected architectures are a special case of uniformly well-connected architectures in which all processes have the same information and hence fall in this class. Moreover, in order to find such a collection of input-output functions, it suffices to find a delay-compatible global input-output function and use projection to obtain functions for the processes in P. Thus, the problem reduces to the single-process synthesis problem under incomplete information with the additional requirement of delay-compatibility.

3.2 Single-Process Synthesis under Incomplete Information

Let $A = (env, \{p\}, Ext, \emptyset, (D(v))_{v \in Ext}, (I \cup N, O))$ be a single-process architecture and ψ be a CTL* specification over the variables in $V = I \cup H \cup N \cup O$.

Tree Automata. An *alternating parity tree automaton* is a tuple $\mathcal{A} = (Y, X, Q, q_0, \delta, \alpha)$, where Y is a finite alphabet, X is a finite set of directions, Q is a finite set of states, $q_0 \in Q$ is the initial state, $\delta : Q \times Y \to \mathbb{B}^+(Q \times X)$ is a transition function that maps a state and an input letter to a positive boolean combination of pairs of states and directions, and a coloring function $\alpha : Q \to Col \subset \mathbb{N}$ that maps each state to some color from a finite set Col. An alternating automaton runs on full Y-labeled X-trees. A *run tree* on a given full Y-labeled X-tree $\langle X^*, l \rangle$ is a $Q \times X^*$-labeled tree where the root is labeled with (q, ε) and where for every node ρ with label (q, σ) the set of children K of ρ satisfies the following properties: (1) for every $\rho' \in K$, the label of ρ' is $(q', \sigma \cdot x)$ for some $q' \in Q$ and $x \in X$ such that (q', x') is an atom of $\delta(q, l(\sigma))$, and (2) the set of atoms defined by the set of children K satisfies $\delta(q, l(\sigma))$. An infinite path fulfills the *parity condition* if the maximal color of the states appearing infinitely often is even. A run tree is accepting if all infinite paths fulfill the parity condition. A full Y-labeled X-tree is *accepted* if it has an accepting run tree. A *nondeterministic automaton* is an alternating automaton, in which, in the DNF of each transition every disjunct contains exactly one (q, x) for every $x \in X$.

Symmetric alternating automata are a variant of alternating automata that run on total Y-labeled X-trees. For a symmetric alternating automaton $\mathcal{S} = (Y, Q, q_0, \delta, \alpha)$, Q, q_0, and α are as above, but the transition function $\delta : Q \times Y \to \mathbb{B}^+(Q \times \{\Box, \Diamond\})$ maps a state and an input letter to a positive boolean combination over atoms that refer to *some*($\Diamond$) or *all*($\Box$) successors in the tree. A *run tree* on a given Y-labeled X-tree $\langle T, l \rangle$ is a $Q \times X^*$-labeled tree where the root is labeled with (q, ε) and where for every node ρ with label (q, σ) the set of children K of ρ satisfies the following properties: (1) for every $\rho' \in K$, the label of ρ' is $(q', \sigma \cdot x)$ for some $q' \in Q$, $x \in X$ and $\sigma \cdot x \in T$ such that $(q', \Box)$ or $(q', \Diamond)$ is an atom of $\delta(q, l(\sigma))$, and (2) interpreting each occurrence of $(q', \Box)$ as $\bigwedge_{x \in X, \sigma \cdot x \in T}(q', x)$ and each occurrence of $(q', \Diamond)$ as $\bigvee_{x \in X, \sigma \cdot x \in T}(q', x)$, the set of atoms defined by the set of children K satisfies $\delta(q, l(\sigma))$.

Automata-Theoretic Solution. For a CTL* formula ψ one can construct an alternating parity tree automaton $\mathcal{A}_\psi$ with $2^{O(|\psi|)}$ states that accepts exactly the models of ψ [11]. Via the automata transformations described in [11], the realizability problem for the single process architecture A and the specification ψ can be reduced to the nonemptiness of an alternating tree automaton $\mathcal{C}_\psi$ that is obtained from $\mathcal{A}_\psi$ and that has the same number of states as $\mathcal{A}_\psi$.

Theorem 1 (from [11]). *The single-process synthesis problem for CTL* with incomplete information is 2EXPTIME-complete.*

4   Encoding Fault-Tolerant Realizability

In this section we present a transformation of the architecture and the fault-tolerance specification to an architecture and a specification for which the distributed fault-tolerant synthesis problem can be reduced to single-process synthesis under incomplete information. The key challenge is to account for the fact, that the non-faulty processes cannot rely on receiving accurate information about the external input of a faulty process. We describe how we model the effect of a fault occurrence on the informedness of the non-faulty processes. We show that the described transformations do not affect fault-tolerant realizability.

Architecture Transformation. To circumvent the change of informedness of the processes in the architecture caused by the occurrences of faults, and yet allow a faulty process to communicate incorrectly its external input to the other processes, we introduce a *faulty copy of the external input of each process.*

Formally, we transform the architecture A into an architecture A^f defined as follows: $A^f = (env, P, Ext^f, C, (D(v))_{v \in Ext^f}, (In^f(p), Out(p))_{p \in P})$, where V^f is partitioned into $I^f = F$, $H^f = H \cup I$, N, C and O. The new set of variables $F = \{f_p \mid p \in P\}$ consists of the *external faulty-input variables*, one for each process p in P, whose values are supplied by the environment. For $p \in P$ we have $In^f(p) = (In(p) \setminus I_p) \cup \{f_p\}$. The domain of each f_p is $D(I_p)$ and we denote with f_p^v the component of f_p that corresponds to a variable $v \in I_p$.

In the architecture A^f, none of the processes is allowed to read the values of the original input variables in I and thus, a routing strategy for process p can only transmit the value of the faulty-input variable f_p to the other processes.

Specification Transformation. The relation between the correct and the faulty input in normal execution and after the occurrence of a fault is established by an assumption on the environment introduced in the specification: While the tuple of values given by the environment to the input variables of a process p and the value given to the corresponding faulty-input variable for that process are constrained to be the same during the normal execution of process p, during the time process p is faulty this may not be the case. Formally, the assumption is $faulty\text{-}input = \mathsf{G} \bigwedge_{p \in P, v \in I_p} (n_p = 0 \rightarrow f_p^v = v)$. Then the formula Φ^f is obtained by substituting in the fault-tolerance specification Φ^t each occurrence of $\mathsf{A}\theta$ by $\mathsf{A}(faulty\text{-}input \rightarrow \theta)$ and each occurrence of $\mathsf{E}\theta$ by $\mathsf{E}(faulty\text{-}input \wedge \theta)$.

For implementations for the architecture A^f we assume that faults do not affect the forwarding of external input by a faulty process. This results in the fault computation tree $\mathcal{FCT}^f(\hat{s}) = \langle T, dir \rangle$, where $T \subseteq D(V^f)^*$ is the greatest total tree such that for all $\sigma \in D(V^f)^*$ and all $d \in D(V^f)$, if $\sigma \cdot d \in T$, then $\sigma \in T$ and *for every* $p \in P$ it holds that $d\langle c_p \rangle = s_p(\sigma \langle In^f(p) \rangle)\langle c_p \rangle$ and if $dir(\sigma)\langle n_p \rangle = 0$ then $d\langle Out(p) \rangle = s_p(\sigma \langle In^f(p) \rangle)\langle Out(p) \rangle$. The following theorem establishes the connection between the fault computation trees for the implementations for the architecture A^f and the implementations for the original architecture A.

Theorem 2. *There exists a finite-state distributed implementation $\hat{s}$ with simple routing for the architecture A that is consistent w.r.t. faults and such that the fault computation tree $\mathcal{FCT}(\hat{s})$ is a model of Φ^t iff there exist a finite-state distributed implementation $\hat{s}^f$ with simple routing for the architecture A^f such that the fault computation tree $\mathcal{FCT}^f(\hat{s}^f)$ is a model of Φ^f.*

Proof (Idea). We define mappings from local input histories for a process $p \in P$ in the architecture A to local input histories for p in A^f and vice versa. An element of $D(In(p))^*$ is mapped to an element of $D(In^f(p))^*$, where the value of f_p in a state of the image prefix is the value of c_p from the next state in the original prefix, if such a state exists, and is equal to the tuple of values for I_p in the corresponding state of the original prefix otherwise. When mapping $D(In^f(p))^*$ to $D(In(p))^*$, the value of a variable $v \in I_p$ in a state of the image prefix is the same as the value of c_q^v from the next state in the original prefix, if such a state exists and there exists a process q with $v \in I_q$ that is not faulty in the corresponding state of the original prefix, and is the value of f_p^v from the corresponding state in the original prefix otherwise. Based on these mappings we define the respective strategies and show that they have the required properties. The formal definitions and proof can be found in the full version of this paper.

5   From Fault Input-Output Trees to Full Trees

We now present a modification of the classical construction that transforms an automaton on total trees into one that accepts full trees. Our construction accounts for the shape of the total tree resulting from the occurrences of faults.

Consider the architecture A^f and the formula Φ^f obtained as described in Sect. 4 from the architecture A and the fault-tolerance specification Φ^t.

For a global input-output function g for A^f, we define a *fault input-output tree* $\mathcal{FOT}(g) = \langle T, dir \rangle$ similarly to fault computation trees: $T \subseteq D(Ext^f)^*$ is the greatest total tree such that for all $\sigma \in D(Ext^f)^*$ and all $d \in D(Ext^f)$, if $\sigma \cdot d \in T$, then $\sigma \in T$ and for all $p \in P$ with $dir(\sigma)\langle n_p \rangle = 0$ it holds that $d\langle O_p \rangle = g(\sigma\langle I^f \rangle)\langle O_p \rangle$. The tree $\mathcal{FOT}(g)$, which is a total $D(Ext^f)$-labeled $D(Ext^f)$-tree, can be represented as a full $D(Ext^f) \times D(O)$-labeled $D(Ext^f)$-tree where the nodes are labeled additionally with the output of g that determines the enabled directions. Given a full $D(Ext^f) \times D(O)$-labeled $D(Ext^f)$-tree $\mathcal{T}$, we can determine the corresponding total *characteristic tree under faults*, $char_F(\mathcal{T})$.

Definition 4. *Let $\langle D(Ext^f)^*, l \rangle$ be a full $D(Ext^f) \times D(O)$-labeled $D(Ext^f)$-tree. We define the characteristic tree under faults as the total $D(Ext^f)$-labeled $D(Ext^f)$-tree $\langle T, dir \rangle = char_F(\langle D(Ext^f)^*, l \rangle)$ as follows: $T \subseteq D(Ext^f)^*$ is the greatest total tree such that for all $\sigma \in D(Ext^f)^*$ and all $d' \in D(Ext^f)$, if $\sigma \cdot d' \in T$, then $\sigma \in T$ and the condition $(*)$ below holds:*

$(*)$ *for every $p \in P$, if $d\langle n_p \rangle = 0$, then $d'\langle O_p \rangle = d_o\langle O_p \rangle$, where $l(\sigma) = \langle d, d_o \rangle$.*

For the CTL* formula Φ^f, we can construct [11] a symmetric parity automaton $\mathcal{S}_\Phi$ that accepts exactly the models of Φ^f. This automaton runs on total $D(Ext^f)$-labeled trees, has $2^{O(|\Phi^f|)}$ states and five colors. Since automata transformations are simpler for automata running on full trees, from the symmetric automaton $\mathcal{S}_\Phi$ we construct the alternating parity automaton $\mathcal{A}_\Phi$ that accepts a full tree iff its characteristic tree under faults is a model of Φ^f. The transition function of $\mathcal{A}_\Phi$ uses the information about enabled successors given in the labels: Where $\mathcal{S}_\Phi$ sends a copy to all successors (some successor), $\mathcal{A}_\Phi$ sends a copy to all enabled successors (some enabled successor). However, here the enabled successors are determined only according to the output of the processes that are non-faulty according to the node's label.

Theorem 3. *If $\mathcal{S}_\Phi$ is a symmetric automaton over $D(Ext^f)$-labeled $D(Ext^f)$-trees, we can construct an alternating parity automaton $\mathcal{A}_\Phi$ such that $\mathcal{A}_\Phi$ accepts a $D(Ext^f) \times D(O)$-labeled $D(Ext^f)$-tree $\mathcal{T}$ iff $\mathcal{S}_\Phi$ accepts $char_F(\mathcal{T})$. The automaton $\mathcal{A}_\Phi$ has the same state space and acceptance condition as $\mathcal{S}_\Phi$.*

6   Synthesis of Fault-Tolerant Systems

We reduced the fault-tolerant synthesis problem for the architecture A and the formula Φ^t to the corresponding problem for the architecture A^f and Φ^f. In A^f we can assume that faults do not affect the routing of input and therefore we can reduce the problem to finding delay-compatible input-output functions.

Delay-Compatible Global Input-Output Functions for A^f. From a symmetric automaton $\mathcal{S}_\Phi$ that accepts exactly the total $D(Ext^f)$-labeled $D(Ext^f)$-trees that are models of Φ^f, we construct, as explained in the previous section, an alternating parity tree automaton $\mathcal{A}_\Phi$ that accepts a full $D(Ext^f) \times D(O)$-labeled $D(Ext^f)$-tree $\mathcal{T}$ iff $char_F(\mathcal{T})$ is a model of Φ^f. Via standard transformations we obtain from $\mathcal{A}_\Phi$ a nondeterministic automaton $\mathcal{N}_\Phi$ with number of states doubly exponential in the size of Φ^f that accepts a $D(O)$-labeled $D(I^f \cup N)$-tree $\mathcal{T}$ iff $\mathcal{T}$ corresponds to a global input-output function for A whose fault input-output tree is a model of Φ^f. Via a construction similar to the one in [8], we transform $\mathcal{N}_\Phi$ into a nondeterministic tree automaton $\mathcal{D}_\Phi$ that accepts exactly the labeled trees accepted by $\mathcal{N}_\Phi$ that correspond to delay-compatible global input-output functions. The size of $\mathcal{D}_\Phi$ is linear in the size of $\mathcal{N}_\Phi$. If the language of $\mathcal{D}_\Phi$ is nonempty the nonemptiness test produces a finite-state delay-compatible global input-output function $g : D(I^f \cup N)^* \to D(O)$ for A^f for which $\mathcal{FOT}(g) \models \Phi^f$.

From Global Input-Output Functions to Distributed Implementations. By projecting a finite-state delay-compatible global input-output function g for A^f on the sets O_p of variables we obtain a set of delay-compatible input-output functions $(g_p)_{p \in P}$ for the processes in A^f. These functions are represented as finite automata, which have the same set of states Q_g, which are labeled by elements of $D(O_p)$, and the same deterministic transition function δ_g. For each variable $t_p \in C$, we define $D(t_p) = Q_g \cup \{\bot\}$, $d_0(t_p) = \bot$ and for each $c_p \in C$ we have $D(c_p) = D(I_p^f)$. Then, we define a simple routing $\hat{r} = (r_p)_{p \in P}$ as follows. For every process p and $d \in D(In^f(p))$, the value assigned to t_p by r_p is determined as follows. If $d\langle t_q \rangle = \bot$ for all q, this value is q_g^0 (the initial state). Otherwise, the value is $\delta_g(t, d')$, where $t = d\langle t_q \rangle$ for some process q with $d\langle m_q \rangle = 0$ if one exists, or some fixed process q otherwise, and for every $f_q \in I^f$, $d'\langle f_q \rangle = d\langle c_q \rangle$.

Combining the functions $(g_p)_{p \in P}$ with this simple routing we obtain a finite-state distributed implementation $\hat{s}^f = (s_p^f)_{p \in P}$ for A^f. If the tree $\mathcal{FOT}(g)$ is a model of Φ^f, then so is the tree $\mathcal{FCT}^f(\hat{s}^f)$.

Clearly, vice versa, if there exists a distributed implementation $\hat{s}$ for A^f with $\mathcal{FCT}^f(\hat{s}^f) \models \Phi^f$, then there exists a delay-compatible global input-output function g with $\mathcal{FOT}(g) \models \Phi^f$ and hence the language of $\mathcal{D}_\Phi$ is not empty.

Recalling the relation between the implementations in the architectures A and A^f we established in Sect. 4, we obtain the following result.

Theorem 4. *The fault-tolerant distributed synthesis problem is 2EXPTIME-complete for fully connected architectures and external specifications.*

7 Conclusion

We have presented a synthesis algorithm that determines for a fully connected architecture and a temporal specification whether a fault-tolerant implementation exists, and, in case the answer is positive, automatically derives such an implementation. We demonstrated that the framework of incomplete information is well-suited for encoding the effects of faults on the informedness of individual processes in a distributed system. This allowed us to reduce the fault-tolerant distributed synthesis problem to single-process synthesis with incomplete information for a modified specification. We thus showed that the fault-tolerance synthesis problem is decidable and no more expensive than standard synthesis. Establishing general decidability criteria for architectures that are not fully connected as well as extending the scope to broader fault types such as Byzantine faults are two open problems that deserve further study.

References

[1] Attie, P.C., Arora, A., Emerson, E.A.: Synthesis of fault-tolerant concurrent programs. ACM Trans. Program. Lang. Syst. 26(1), 125–185 (2004)

[2] Bonakdarpour, B., Kulkarni, S.S., Abujarad, F.: Distributed synthesis of fault-tolerant programs in the high atomicity model. In: Masuzawa, T., Tixeuil, S. (eds.) SSS 2007. LNCS, vol. 4838, pp. 21–36. Springer, Heidelberg (2007)

[3] Dolev, D., Strong, H.R.: A simple model for agreement in distributed systems. In: Simons, B., Spector, A.Z. (eds.) Fault-Tolerant Distributed Computing. LNCS, vol. 448, pp. 42–50. Springer, Heidelberg (1990)

[4] Ebnenasir, A., Kulkarni, S.S., Arora, A.: FTSyn: a framework for automatic synthesis of fault-tolerance. STTT 10(5), 455–471 (2008)

[5] Emerson, E.A.: Temporal and modal logic. In: Handbook of Theoretical Computer Science. Formal Models and Sematics (B), vol. B, pp. 995–1072 (1990)

[6] Finkbeiner, B., Schewe, S.: Uniform distributed synthesis. In: Proc. LICS 2005, June 2005, pp. 321–330 (2005)

[7] Fisman, D., Kupferman, O., Lustig, Y.: On verifying fault tolerance of distributed protocols. In: Ramakrishnan, C.R., Rehof, J. (eds.) TACAS 2008. LNCS, vol. 4963, pp. 315–331. Springer, Heidelberg (2008)

[8] Gastin, P., Sznajder, N., Zeitoun, M.: Distributed synthesis for well-connected architectures. In: Arun-Kumar, S., Garg, N. (eds.) FSTTCS 2006. LNCS, vol. 4337, pp. 321–332. Springer, Heidelberg (2006)

[9] Hadzilacos, V., Toueg, S.: A modular approach to fault-tolerant broadcasts and related problems. In: Distributed Systems, 2nd edn., Addison-Wesley, Reading (1993)

[10] Kulkarni, S.S., Arora, A.: Automating the addition of fault-tolerance. In: Formal Techniques in Real-Time and Fault-Tolerant Systems, pp. 82–93 (2000)

[11] Kupferman, O., Vardi, M.Y.: Church's problem revisited. Bulletin of Symbolic Logic 5(2), 245–263 (1999)
[12] Manolios, P., Trefler, R.: Safety and liveness in branching time. In: Proc. LICS, pp. 366–374. IEEE Computer Society Press, Los Alamitos (2001)
[13] Pnueli, A., Rosner, R.: Distributed reactive systems are hard to synthesize. In: Proc. FOCS, vol. II, pp. 746–757. IEEE, Los Alamitos (1990)

Formal Verification for High-Assurance Behavioral Synthesis*

Sandip Ray[1], Kecheng Hao[2], Yan Chen[3], Fei Xie[2], and Jin Yang[4]

[1] Department of Computer Sciences, University of Texas at Austin, Austin, TX 78712
[2] Department of Computer Science, Portland State University, Portland, OR 97207
[3] Toyota Technological Institute at Chicago, Chicago, IL 60637**
[4] Strategic CAD Labs, Intel Corporation, Hillsboro, OR 97124

Abstract. We present a framework for certifying hardware designs generated through behavioral synthesis, by using formal verification to certify the associated synthesis transformations. We show how to decompose this certification into two components, which can be respectively handled by the complementary verification techniques, theorem proving and model checking. The approach produces a certified reference flow, composed of transformations distilled from production synthesis tools but represented as transformations on graphs with an associated formal semantics. This tool-independent abstraction disentangles our framework from the inner workings of specific synthesis tools while permitting certification of hardware designs generated from a broad class of behavioral descriptions. We provide experimental results suggesting the scalability on practical designs.

1 Introduction

Recent years have seen high complexity in hardware designs, making it challenging to develop reliable, high-quality systems through hand-crafted Register Transfer Level (RTL) or gate-level implementations. This has motivated a gradual migration away from RTL towards Electronic System Level (ESL) designs which permit description of design functionality abstractly in high-level languages, *e.g.*, SystemC. However, the ESL approach crucially depends on reliable tools for *behavioral synthesis*, that is, automated synthesis of a hardware circuit from its ESL description. Behavioral synthesis tools apply a sequence of transformations to compile the ESL description to an RTL design.

Several behavioral synthesis tools are available today [1,2,3,4]. Nevertheless, and despite its great need, behavioral synthesis has not yet found wide acceptance in industrial practice. A major barrier to its adoption is the lack of designers' confidence in correctness of synthesis tools themselves. The difference in abstraction level between a synthesized design and the ESL description puts the onus on behavioral synthesis to ensure that the synthesized design indeed conforms to the description. On the other hand, synthesis transformations necessary to produce designs satisfying the growing demands of performance and power include complex and aggressive optimizations which must respect subtle invariants. Consequently, synthesis tools are often either (a) error-prone or (b) overly conservative, producing circuits of poor quality and performance [4,5].

---

* This research was partially supported by a grant from Intel Corporation.
** Yan Chen was a M.S. student at Portland State University when he participated in this research.

Z. Liu and A.P. Ravn (Eds.): ATVA 2009, LNCS 5799, pp. 337–351, 2009.

In this paper, we develop a scalable, mechanized framework for certifying behavioral synthesis flows. Certification of a synthesis flow amounts to the guarantee that its output preserves the semantics of its input description; thus, the question of correctness of the synthesized design is reduced to the question of analysis of the behavioral description. Our approach is distinguished by two key features:

- Our framework is *independent* of the inner workings of a specific tool, and can be applied to certify designs synthesized by different tools from a broad class of ESL descriptions. This makes our approach particularly suitable for certifying security-critical hardware which are often synthesized from domain-specific languages [6].
- The approach produces a certified *reference flow*, which makes explicit generic invariants that must be preserved by different transformations. The reference flow serves as a formal specification for reliable, aggressive synthesis transformations.

Formal verification has enjoyed significant successes in the analysis of industrial hardware designs [7,8]. Nevertheless, applying formal verification directly to certify a *synthesized* design is undesirable for two reasons. First, it defeats the very purpose of behavioral synthesis as a vehicle for raising design abstraction since it requires reasoning at the level of the synthesized design rather than the behavioral description. Second, the cost of analyzing a complex design is substantial and the cost must be incurred for each design certification. Instead, our approach targets the *synthesis flow*, thereby raising the level of abstraction necessary for design certification.

In the remainder of this section, we first provide a brief overview of behavioral synthesis with an illustrative example; we then describe our approach in greater detail.

1.1   Behavioral Synthesis and an Illustrative Example

A behavioral synthesis tool accepts a design description and a library of hardware resources; it performs a sequence of transformations on the description to generate RTL. The transformations are roughly partitioned into the following three phases.

- **Compiler transformations.** These include loop unrolling, common subexpression elimination, copy propagation, code motion, etc. Furthermore, expensive operations (*e.g.*, division) are often replaced with simpler ones (*e.g.*, subtraction).
- **Scheduling.** This phase determines the clock step for each operation. The ordering between operations is constrained by the data and control dependencies. Scheduling transformations include chaining operations across conditional blocks and decomposing one operation into a sequence of multi-cycle operations based on resource constraints. Furthermore, several compiler transformations are employed, exploiting (and creating opportunities for) operation decomposition and code motions.
- **Resource binding and control synthesis.** This phase binds operations to functional units, allocates and binds registers, and generates the control circuit to implement the schedule.

After these transformations, the design can be expressed as RTL. This design is subjected to further manual optimizations to fine-tune for performance and power.

Each synthesis transformation is non-trivial. The consequence of their composition is a significant difference in abstraction from the original description. To illustrate this,

```
void encrypt (uint32_t* v, uint32_t* k) {
    /* set up */
    uint32_t v0=v[0], v1=v[1], sum=0, i;
    /* a key schedule constant */
    uint32_t delta=0x9e3779b9;
    /* cache key */
    uint32_t k0=k[0], k1=k[1],
             k2=k[2], k3=k[3];

    /* basic cycle start */
    for (i=0; i < 32; i++) {
        sum += delta;
        v0 += ((v1<<4)+k0)^(v1 + sum)
              ^((v1>>5)+k1);
        v1 += ((v0<<4)+k2)^(v0 + sum)
              ^((v0>>5)+k3);
    }

    /* end cycle */
    v[0]=v0; v[1]=v1;
}
```

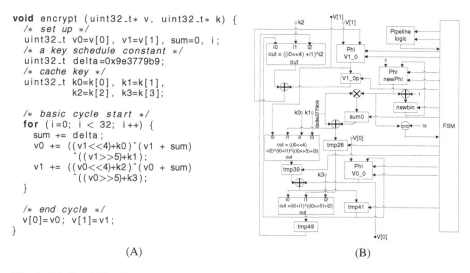

(A)   (B)

Fig. 1. (A) C code for TEA encryption function. (B) Schema of RTL synthesized by AutoPilot.

consider the synthesis of the Tiny Encryption Algorithm (TEA) [9]. Fig. 1 shows a C implementation and the circuit synthesized by the AutoPilot behavioral synthesis tool [10]. The following transformations are involved in the synthesis of the circuit.

- In the first phase, constant propagation removes unnecessary variables.
- In the second phase, the key scheduling transformation performed is *pipelining*, to enable overlapping execution of operations from different loop iterations.
- In the third phase, operations are bound to hardware resources (*e.g.*, "+" operation to an adder), and the FSM module is generated to schedule circuit operations.

Each transformation must respect subtle design invariants. For instance, paralleling operations from different loop iterations must avoid race conditions, and scheduling must respect data dependencies. Since such considerations are entangled with low-level heuristics, it is easy to have errors in the synthesis tool implementation, resulting in buggy designs [5]. However, the difference in abstraction level makes direct comparison between the C and RTL descriptions impractical; performing such comparison through sequential equivalence checking [11] requires cost-prohibitive symbolic co-simulation to check input/output correspondence.

1.2 Approach Overview

We address the above issue by breaking the certification of behavioral synthesis transformations into two components, **verified** and **verifying**.[1] Fig. 2 illustrates our framework. A **verified** transformation is formally certified once and for all using theorem

---

[1] The terms "*verified*" and "*verifying*" as used here are borrowed from analogous notions in the compiler certification literature.

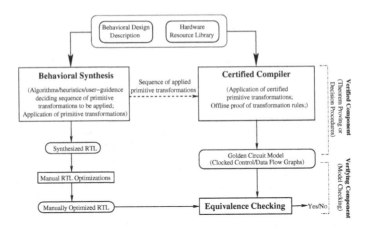

Fig. 2. Framework for certification of behavioral synthesis flows

proving; a *verifying* transformation is not itself verified, but each instance is accompanied by a verification of correspondence between input and output. The viability of decomposition is justified by the nature of behavioral synthesis. Transformations applied at the higher level, (*e.g.*, compiler and scheduling transformations) are generic. The cost of a monolithic proof is therefore mitigated by the reusability of the transformation over different designs. Such transformations make up the *verified* component. On the other hand, the optimizations performed at the lower levels are unique to the design being synthesized; these transformations constitute the *verifying* component. Since the verification is discharged per instance, it must be fully automatic. However, these transformations tend to be localized and independent of global invariants, making it tractable to verify them automatically by sequential equivalence checking.

1.3   Golden Circuit Model and Synthesis Certification

In a practical synthesis tool, transformations are implemented with low-level, optimized code. A naive approach for the *verified* component, *e.g.*, to formally verify such a tool with all optimizations would be prohibitive. Furthermore, such an approach would tie the framework to a single tool, limiting reusability.

  To mitigate this challenge, we develop a formal, graph-based abstraction called *clocked control/data flow graph* (CCDFG), which serves as the universal golden circuit model. We discuss our formalization of CCDFG in Section 2. CCDFG is an abstraction of the control/data flow graph (CDFG) — used as an intermediate representation in most synthesis tools — augmented with a schedule. The close connection between the formal abstraction and the representation used in a synthesis flow enables us to view synthesis transformations as transformations on CCDFG, while obviating a morass of tool-specific details. We construct a *reference flow* as a sequence of CCDFG transformations as follows: each transformation generates a CCDFG that is guaranteed to preserve semantic correspondence with its input. A production transformation is decomposed into *primitive transformations*, together with algorithms/heuristics that determine the application sequence of these transformations. Once the primitive transformations are certified, the algorithms or heuristics do not affect the correctness of a transformation sequence, only the performance. The reference flow requires no knowledge about the algorithms/heuristics which are often confidential to a synthesis tool.

Given a synthesized hardware design $\mathcal{D}$ and its corresponding behavioral description, the certification of the hardware can be mechanically performed as follows.

- Extract the CCDFG $\mathcal{C}$ from the behavioral description.
- Apply the certified primitive transformations from the reference flow, following the application sequence provided by the synthesis tool. The result is a CCDFG $\mathcal{C}'$ that is close to to $\mathcal{D}$ in abstraction level.
- Apply equivalence checking to guarantee correspondence between $\mathcal{C}'$ and $\mathcal{D}$.

The overall correctness of this certification is justified by the correctness of the **verified** and **verifying** components and their coupling through the CCDFG $\mathcal{C}'$.

How does the approach disentangle the certification of a synthesized hardware from the inner workings of the synthesis tool? Although each certified transformation mimics a corresponding transformation applied by the tool, from the perspective of *certifying* the hardware they are merely heuristic guides transforming CCDFGs to facilitate equivalence checking: certification of the synthesized hardware reduces to checking that the *initial* CCDFG reflects the design intent. The initial CCDFG can be automatically extracted from the synthesis tools' initial internal representation.[2] Furthermore, the framework abstracts low-level optimizations making the verification problem tractable.

The rest of the paper is organized as follows. In Section 2 we present the semantics of CCDFG. In Section 3 we discuss how to use theorem proving to verify the correctness of generic CCDFG transformations. In Section 4 we present our equivalence checking procedure. We provide initial experimental results in Section 5, discuss related work in Section 6, and conclude in Section 7.

2   Clocked Control/Data Flow Graphs

A CCDFG can be viewed as a formal *control/data flow graph* (CDFG) — used as internal representation in most synthesis tools including Spark and Autopilot — augmented with a schedule. Fig. 3 shows two CCDFGs for the TEA encryption. The semantics of CCDFG are formalized in the logic of the ACL2 theorem prover [12]. This section briefly discusses the formulation of a CCDFG; for a more complete account, see [13].

The formalization of CCDFG assumes that the underlying language provides the semantics for a collection *ops* of *primitive operations*. The primitive operations in Fig. 1 include comparison and arithmetic operations. We also assume a partition of design variables into *state variables* and *input variables*. Variable assignments are assumed to be in a Static in Single Static Assignment (SSA) form. Design descriptions are assumed to be amenable to control and data flow analysis. Control flow is broken up into basic

---

[2] Since the input description is normally unclocked, the initial CCDFG does not contain schedule information, and can be viewed as a CDFG. Schedules are generated by synthesis transformations that turn the unclocked representation to a clocked one.

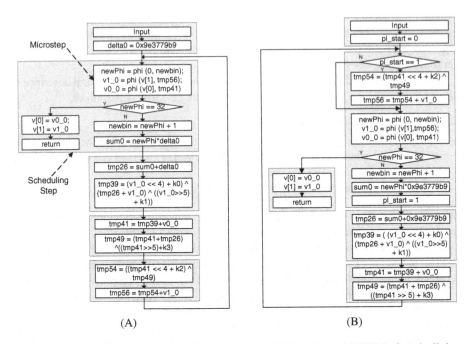

Fig. 3. (A) Initial CCDFG of TEA encryption function. (B) Transformed CCDFG after pipelining. The shaded regions represent scheduling steps, and white boxes represent microsteps. For brevity, only the control flow is shown; data flow is omitted. Although the underlying operations are assumed to be in SSA form, the diagrams aggregate several single assignments for simplicity.

blocks. Data dependency is given by "read after write" paradigm: op_j is data dependent on op_i if op_j occurs after op_i in some control flow path and computes an expression over some state variable v that is assigned most recently by op_i in the path. The language is assumed to disallow circular data dependencies.

Definition 1 (Control and Data Flow Graphs). *Let* $ops \triangleq \{op_1, \ldots, op_n\}$ *be a set of operations over some set* V *of (state and input) variables, and* bb *be a set of basic blocks each consisting of a sequence of operations. A* data flow graph G_D *over ops is a directed acyclic graph with vertex set ops. A* control flow graph G_C *is a graph with vertex set bb and each edge labeled with an assertion over* V.

An edge in G_D from op_i to op_j represents data dependency, and an edge in G_C from bb_i to bb_j indicates that bb_i is a direct predecessor of bb_j in the control flow of. An assertion on an edge holds whenever program control makes the corresponding transition.

Definition 2 (CDFG). *Let* $ops \triangleq \{op_1, \ldots, op_m\}$ *be a set of operations over a set of variables* V, $bb \triangleq \{bb_1, \ldots, bb_n\}$ *be a set of basic blocks over ops,* G_D *and* G_C *are data and control flow graphs over ops and bb respectively. A* CDFG *is the tuple* $G_{CD} \triangleq \langle G_D, G_C, H \rangle$, *where* H *is a mapping* $H : ops \to bb$ *such that* $H(op_i) = bb_j$ *iff* op_i *occurs in* bb_j.

The execution order of operations in a CDFG is irrelevant as long as control and data dependencies are respected. The definition of *microsteps* makes this notion explicit.

Definition 3 (Microstep Ordering and Partition). *Let $G_{CD} \triangleq \langle G_C, G_D, H \rangle$, where the set of vertices of G_C is $bb \triangleq \{bb_1, \ldots, bb_l\}$, and the set of vertices in G_D is ops $\triangleq \{op_1, \ldots, op_n\}$. For each $bb_k \in bb$, a* microstep ordering *is a relation $\prec_k$ over $ops(bb_k) \triangleq \{op_i : H(op_i) = bb_k\}$ such that $op_a \prec_k op_b$ if and only if there is a path from op_a to op_b in the subgraph $G_{D,k}$ of G_D induced by $ops(bb_k)$. A* microstep partition *of bb_k under $\prec_k$ is a partition M_k of $ops(bb_k)$ satisfying the following two conditions. (1) For each $p \in M_k$, if $op_a, op_b \in p$ then $op_a \not\prec op_b$ and $op_b \not\prec_k op_a$. (2) If $p, q \in M_k$ with $p \neq q$, $op_a \in p$, $op_b \in q$, and $op_a \prec_k op_b$, then for each $op_{a'} \in p$ and $op_{b'} \in q$ $op_{b'} \not\prec_k op_{a'}$. A* microstep partition *of G_{CD} is a set M containing each microstep partition M_k.*

If op_a and op_b are in the same partition, their order of execution does not matter; if p and q are two microsteps where $p \prec_k q$, the operations in p must be executed before q to respect the data dependencies. Note that we treat different instances of the same operation as different (with same semantics); this permits stipulation of H as a function instead of a relation, and simplifies the formalization. In Fig. 3, each white box corresponds to a microstep partition. Since G_D is acyclic, $\prec_k$ is an irreflexive partial order on $ops(bb_k)$ and the notion of microstep partition is well-defined. Given a microstep partition $M \triangleq \{m_0, m_1, \ldots\}$ of G_{CD} each m_i is called a *microstep* of G_{CD}. It is convenient to view $\prec_k$ as a partial order over the microsteps of bb_k.

CCDFGs are formalized by augmenting a CDFG with a schedule. Consider a microstep partition M of G_{CD}. A *schedule* T of M is a partition or *grouping* of M; for $m_1, m_2 \in M$, if m_1 and m_2 are in the same group in T, we say that they belong to the same scheduling step. Informally, if two microsteps in M are in the same group in T then they are executed within the same clock cycle.

Definition 4 (CCDFG). *A CCDFG is a tuple $G \triangleq \langle G_{CD}, M, T \rangle$, where G_{CD} is a CDFG, M is a microstep partition of G_{CD}, and T is a schedule of M.*

We formalize CCDFG executions through a state-based semantics. A *CCDFG state* is a valuation of state variables, and a *CCDFG input* is a valuation of input variables. We also assume a well-defined *initial state*. Given a sequence $\mathcal{I}$ of inputs, an *execution* of a CCDFG $G = \langle G_{CD}, M, T \rangle$ is a sequence of CCDFG states that corresponds to an evaluation of the microsteps in M respecting T.

Finally, we consider *outputs* and *observation*. An *output* of a CCDFG G is some computable function f of (a subset of) state variables of G; informally, f corresponds to some output signal in the circuit synthesized from G. To formalize this in ACL2's first order logic, the output is restricted to a Boolean expression of the state variables; the domain of each state variable itself is unrestricted, which enables us to represent programs such as the Greatest Common Divider (GCD) algorithm that do not return Boolean values. For each state s of G, the *observation* corresponding to an output f at state s is the valuation of f under s. Given a set F of output functions, any sequence $\mathcal{E}$ of states of G induces a sequence of observations $\mathcal{O}$; we refer to $\mathcal{O}$ as the *observable behavior* of $\mathcal{E}$ under F.

3   Certified Compilation

Certifying a transformation T requires showing that if the application of T on a CCDFG G generates a new CCDFG G', then there is provable correspondence between the executions of G and G'. The certification process crucially depends on a formal notion of correspondence to relate the executions of G and G'. Note that the notion must comprehend differences between execution order of operations as long as the sequence of observations is unaffected. The notion we use is loosely based on *stuttering trace containment* [14,15]. Roughly, a CCDFG G' *refines* G if for each execution of G' there is an execution of G that produces the same observable behavior up to stuttering. We formalize this notion below.

Definition 5 (Compressed Execution). *Let $\mathcal{E} \triangleq s_0, s_1, \ldots$ be an execution of CCDFG G and F be a set of output functions over G. The* compression *of $\mathcal{E}$ under F is the subsequence of $\mathcal{E}$ obtained by removing each s_i such that $f(s_i) = f(s_{i+1})$ for every $f \in F$.*

Definition 6 (Trace Equivalence). *Let G and G' be two CCDFGs on the same set of state and input variables, $\mathcal{E}$ and $\mathcal{E}'$ be executions of G and G' respectively, and F be a set of output functions. We say that $\mathcal{E}$ is* trace equivalent *to $\mathcal{E}'$ if the observable behavior of the compression of $\mathcal{E}$ under F is the same as the observable behavior of the compression of $\mathcal{E}'$ under F.*

Definition 7 (CCDFG Refinement). *We say that a CCDFG G' refines G if for each execution $\mathcal{E}'$ of G' there is an execution $\mathcal{E}$ of G such that $\mathcal{E}$ is trace equivalent to $\mathcal{E}'$.*

Remark 1. For the **verified** component, we use refinement instead of full equivalence as a notion of correspondence between CCDFGs, to permit connecting the same ESL description with a number of different concrete implementations. In the **verifying** framework, we will use a stronger notion of equivalence (and indeed, equivalence without stuttering), to facilitate sequential equivalence checking.

In addition to showing that a transformation on a CCDFG G produces a refinement of G, we must account for the possibility that a transformation may be applicable to G only if G has a specific structural characteristic; furthermore the result of application might produce a CCDFG with a characteristic to facilitate a subsequent transformation. To make explicit the notion of applicability of a transformation, we view a transformation as a "guarded command" $\tau \triangleq \langle pre, T, post \rangle$: τ is applicable to a CCDFG which satisfies *pre* and produces a CCDFG which satisfies *post*.

Definition 8 (Transformation Correctness). *A transformation $\tau \triangleq \langle pre, T, post \rangle$ is* correct *if the result of applying T to any CCDFG G satisfying pre refines G and satisfies post.*

The following theorem is trivial by induction on the sequence of transformations. Here $[T_0, \ldots, T_n]$ represents the composition of $T_0, \ldots, T_n$.

Theorem 1 (Correctness of Transformation Sequences). *Let $\tau_0, \ldots, \tau_n$ be some sequence of correct transformations, where $\tau_i \triangleq \langle pre_i, T_i, post_i \rangle$, Let $post_i \Rightarrow pre_{i+1}$, $1 \leq i < n$. Then the transformation $\langle pre_1, [T_0, T_1, \ldots, T_n], post_n \rangle$ is correct.*

Theorem 1 justifies decomposition of a transformation into a sequence of primitive transformations. Note that the proof of Theorem 1 is independent of a specific transformation. We thus construct a *reference flow* as follows. (1) Identify and distill a sequence $\tau_0, \ldots, \tau_n$ of primitive transformations; (2) verify τ_i individually; and (3) check that for each $0 \leq i < n$, $post_i \Rightarrow pre_{i+1}$. Theorem 1 guarantees the correctness of the flow.

Verifying the correctness of individual guarded transformations using theorem proving might involve significant manual effort. To ameliorate this cost, we identify and derive *generic theorems* that can certify a class of similar transformations. As a simple example, consider any transformation that refines the schedule. The following theorem states that each such transformation is correct.

Theorem 2 (Correctness of Schedule Refinement). *Let* $G \triangleq \langle G_{CD}, M, T \rangle$ *and* $G' \triangleq \langle G_{CD}, M, T' \rangle$ *be CCDFGs such that for any two microsteps* $m_i, m_j \in M$ *if* T' *assigns* m_i *and* m_j *the same group then so does* T. *Then* G' *is a refinement of* G.

Theorem 2 is admittedly trivial; it is only shown here for illustration purposes. However, the same approach can verify more complex transformations. For example, consider the constant propagation and pipelining transformations shown in Figure 3 for our TEA example. The implementations of these transformations involve significant heuristics, for instance, to determine whether to apply the transformations in a specific case, how many iterations of the loop should be pipelined, etc. However, from the perspective of correctness, the only relevant conditions about the two transformations are: (1) if a variable v is assigned a constant c, then v can be eliminated by replacing each occurrence with c; and (2) a microstep m_i can be overlapped with microstep m_j from a subsequent iteration if for each $op_i \in m_i$ and $op_j \in m_j$, $op_j \not\prec op_i$ in G. Since these conditions are independent of a specific design (*e.g.*, TEA) to which the transformation is applied, the same certification can be used to justify its applicability for diverse designs. The approach is viable because we employ theorem proving which supports an expressive logic, thereby permitting stipulation of the general conditions above as formal predicates in the logic. For example, as we show in previous work [16], we can make use of first-order quantification to formalize a generic refinement proof of arbitrary pipelines, which is directly reusable for verification of the pipeline transformation in our framework. Another generic transformation that is widely employed in behavioral synthesis is *operation balancing*; its correctness depends only on the fact that the operations involved are associative and commutative and can be proven for CCDFGs containing arbitrary associative-commutative operations.

We end the discussion of the **verified** framework with another observation. Since the logic of ACL2 is executable, *pre* and *post* can be efficiently executed for a given concrete transformation. Thus, a transformation $\tau \triangleq \langle pre, T, post \rangle$ can be applied *even before verification* by using *pre* and *post* for runtime checks: if a CCDFG G indeed satisfies *pre* and the application of τ on G results in a CCDFG satisfying *post* then the *instance* of application of τ on G can be composed with other compiler transformations; furthermore, the expense of the runtime assertion checking can be alleviated by generating a *proof obligation for a specific instance*, which is normally more tractable than a monolithic generic proof of the correctness of τ. This provides a trade-off between the computational expense of runtime checks and verification of individual instances with a (perhaps deep) one-time proof of the correctness of a transformation.

4 Equivalence Checking

We now discuss how to check equivalence between a CCDFG and its synthesized circuit. The *verified* component facilitates close correspondence between the transformed CCDFG and the synthesized circuit, critical to the scalability of equivalence checking.

4.1 Circuit Model

We represent a circuit as a Mealy machine specifying the updates to the state elements (latches) in each clock cycle. Our formalization of circuits is typical in traditional hardware verification, but we make combinational nodes explicit to facilitate the correspondence with CCDFGs.

Definition 9 (Circuit). *A circuit is a tuple* $M = \langle I, N, F \rangle$ *where I is a vector of inputs; N is a pair $\langle N_c, N_d \rangle$ where N_c is a set of combinational nodes and N_d is a set of latches; and F is a pair $\langle F_c, F_d \rangle$ where F_c maps each combinational node $c \in N_c$ to an expression over $N_c \cup N_d \cup I$ and for each latch $d \in N_d$, F_d maps each latch d to $n \in N_c \cup N_d \cup I$ where F_d is a delay function which takes the current value of n to be the next-state value of d.*

A *circuit state* is an assignment to the latches in N_d. Given a sequence of valuations to the inputs $i_0, i_1, \ldots,$ a *circuit trace* of M is the sequence of states $s_0, s_1, \ldots,$ where (1) s_0 is the initial state and (2) for each $j > 0$, the state s_j is obtained by updating the elements in N_d given the state valuation s_{j-1} and input valuation i_{j-1}. The *observable behavior* of the circuit is the sequence of valuations of the *outputs* which are a subset of latches and combinational nodes.

4.2 Correspondence between CCDFGs and Circuits

Given a CCDFG G and a synthesized circuit M, it is tempting to define a notion of correspondence as follows: (1) Establish a fixed mapping between the state variables of G and the latches in M, and (2) stipulate an execution of G to be equivalent to an execution of M if they have the same observable behavior. However, this does not work in general since the mappings between state variables and latches may be different in each clock cycle. To address this, we introduce $EMap : ops \rightarrow N_c$, mapping CCDFG *operations* to the combinational nodes in the circuit: each operation is mapped to the combinational node that implements the operation; the mapping is independent of clock cycles. Fig. 4 shows the mapping for the synthesized circuit of TEA. Recall from Section 1.1 that the FSM decides the *control signals* for the circuit; the FSM is thus excluded from the mapping. We now define the equivalence between G and M.

Definition 10. *A CCDFG state x of G is equivalent to a circuit state s of M with respect to an input i and a microstep partition t, if for each operation op in t, the inputs to op according to x and i are equivalent to the inputs to $EMap(op)$ according to s and $EMap(i)$, i.e., the values of each input to op and the corresponding input to $EMap(op)$ are equivalent, and the outputs of op are equivalent to the outputs of $EMap(op)$.*

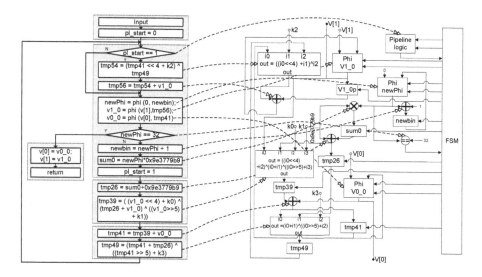

Fig. 4. Synthesized circuit for TEA and the corresponding operation mapping with pipelined CCDFG; dotted lines represent mapping from CCDFG operations to combinational circuit nodes

Definition 11. *Given a CCDFG G and a circuit M, G is equivalent to M if and only if for any execution $[x_0, x_1, x_2, \ldots]$ of G generated by an input sequence $[i_0, i_1, i_2, \ldots]$ and by microstep partition $[t_0, t_1, \ldots]$ of G, and the state sequence $[s_0, s_1, s_2, \ldots]$ of M generated by the input sequence $[EMap(i_0), EMap(i_1), EMap(i_2), \ldots]$, x_k and s_k are equivalent with respect to t_k under i_k, $k \geq 0$.*

4.3 Dual-Rail Simulation for Equivalence Checking

We check equivalence between CCDFG G and circuit M by dual-rail symbolic simulation (Fig. 5); the two rails simulate G and M respectively, and are synchronized by clock cycle. The equivalence checking in clock cycle k is conducted as follows:

1. The current CCDFG state x_k and circuit state s_k are checked to see whether for the input i_k, the inputs to each operation op in the scheduling step t_k are equivalent to the inputs to $EMap(op)$. If yes, continue; otherwise, report inequivalence.
2. G is simulated by executing t_k on x_k under i_k to compute x_{k+1} and recording the outputs of each $op \in t_k$. M is simulated for one clock cycle from s_k under input $EMap(i_k)$ to compute s_{k+1}. The outputs for each op are checked for equivalence with the outputs of $EMap(op)$. If yes, continue; otherwise, report inequivalence.
3. The next scheduling step t_{k+1} is determined from control flow. If t_k has multiple outgoing control edges, the last microstep of t_k executed is identified. The outgoing control edge from this microstep whose condition evaluates to true leads to t_{k+1}.

We permit both bounded and unbounded (fixed-point) simulations. In particular, the simulation proceeds until (i) the equivalence check fails, (ii) the end of a bounded input sequence is reached, or (iii) a fixed point is reached for an unbounded input sequence.

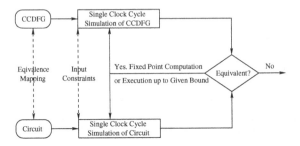

Fig. 5. Dual-Rail simulation scheme for equivalence checking between CCDFG and circuit

We have implemented the dual-rail scheme on the bit level in the Intel *Forte* environment [17], where symbolic states are represented using BDDs. We have also implemented the scheme on the word level with several built-in optimizations, using Satisfiability Modulo Theories (SMT); this is viable since word-level mappings between operations and circuit nodes are explicit. We use bit-vectors to encode the variables in the CCDFG and the circuit; the SMT engine checks input/output equivalence and determines control paths. Our word-level checker is based on the CVC3 SMT engine [18].

The bit-level and word-level checkers are complementary. The bit-level checker ensures that the equivalence checking is decidable, while the word-level checker provides the optimizations crucial to scalability. The word-level checker can make effective use of results from bit-level checking in many cases. One typical scenario is as follows. Suppose M is a design module of modest complexity but is awkward to check at word-level. Then the bit-level checker is used to check the equivalence of the CCDFG of M with its circuit implementation; when the word-level checker is used for equivalence checking of a module that calls M, it skips the check of M, treating the CCDFG of M and its circuit implementation as equivalent black boxes.

5   Experimental Results

We used the bit-level checker on a set of CCDFGs for GCD and the corresponding circuits synthesized by AutoPilot. The experiments were conducted on a workstation with 3GHz Intel Xeon processor with 2GB memory. Table 1 shows the statistics before and after schedule refinement (Theorem 2). Since we bit-blast all CCDFG operations, the running time grows exponentially with the bit width; for 8-bit GCD, checking requires about 2 hours. It is interesting to understand how schedule refinement affects the performance of equivalence checking. Schedule refinement partitions operations in the loop body into two clock cycles. This does not change fixed-point computation; however, the number of cycles for which the circuit is simulated doubles. For small bit-widths, the running time after schedule refinement is about two times slower than that before. However, for large bit widths, the running time is dominated by the complexity of the CCDFG simulation instead of the circuit simulation. The decrease in time with the increase in bit width from 7 to 8 is likely due to BDD variable reordering.

Table 1. Bit-level equivalence checking statistics

Circuit		Before schedule refinement		After schedule refinement	
Bit Width	# of Nodes	Time (Sec.)	BDD Nodes	Time (Sec.)	BDD Nodes
2	96	0.02	503	0.02	783
3	164	0.05	4772	0.07	11113
4	246	0.11	42831	0.24	20937
5	342	0.59	16244	1.93	99723
6	452	12.50	39968	27.27	118346
7	576	369.31	220891	383.98	164613
8	714	6850.56	1197604	3471.74	581655

Table 2. Word-level equivalence checking statistics

Design	GCD	TEA	DCT	3DES	3DES_key
C Code Size (# of Lines)	14	12	52	325	412
RTL Size (# of Lines)	364	1001	688	18053	79976
Time (Seconds)	2	15.6	30.1	355.7	2351.7
Memory (Megabytes)	4.1	24.6	49.2	59.4	307.2

Using our word-level checker, we have checked several RTL designs synthesized by AutoPilot with CCDFGs derived from AutoPilot's intermediate representations; the statistics are shown in Table 2. The designs illustrate different facets of the framework. GCD contains a loop whose number of iterations depends on the inputs. TEA has an explicitly bounded loop. DCT contains sequential computation without loop. 3DES represents a practical design of significant size. 3DES_key is included to illustrate the scalability of our approach on relatively large synthesized designs. The results demonstrate the efficacy of our word-level equivalence checking. In contrast, full word-level symbolic simulation comparing the input/output relations of C and RTL runs out of memory on all the designs but DCT (for which it needs twice as much time and memory).

6 Related Work

An early effort [19] on verification of high-level synthesis targets the behavioral portion of VHDL [20]. A translation from behavioral VHDL to dependence flow graphs [21] was verified by structural induction based on the CSP [22] semantics. Recently, there has been research on certified synthesis of hardware from formal languages such as HOL [23] in which a compiler that automatically translates recursive function definitions in HOL to clocked synchronous hardware has been developed. A certified hardware synthesis from programs in Esterel, a synchronous design language, has been also been developed [24] in which a variant of Esterel was embedded in HOL.

Dave [25] provides a comprehensive bibliography of compiler verification. One of the earliest work on compiler verification was the Piton project [26], which verified a simple assembly language compiler. Compiler certification forms a critical component of the Verisoft project [27], aiming at correctness of implementations of computing systems with both hardware and software components. The Verifix [28] and CompCert [29] projects have explored a general framework for certification of compilers for various C subsets [30,31]. There has also been work on a *verifying* compiler, where each instance of a transformation generates a proof obligation discharged by a theorem prover [32].

There has been much research on sequential equivalence checking (SEC) between RTL and gate-level hardware designs [33,34]. Research has also be done on combinational equivalence checking between high-level designs in software-like languages (*e.g.*, SystemC) and RTL-level designs [11]. There has also been effort for SEC between software specifications and hardware implementations [35]: GSTE assertion graphs [36] were extended so that an assertion graph edge have pre and post condition labels, and also associated assignments that update state variables. There has also been work on equivalence checking with other graph representations, *e.g.*, Signal Flow Graph [37].

7   Conclusion

We have presented a framework for certifying behavioral synthesis flows. The framework includes a combination of *verified* and *verifying* paradigms: high-level transformations are certified once and for all by theorem proving, while low-level tweaks and optimizations can be handled through model checking. We demonstrated the use of the CCDFG structure as an interface between the two components. Certification of different compiler transformations is uniformly specified by viewing them as manipulation of CCDFGs. The transformed CCDFG can then be used for equivalence checking with the synthesized design. One key benefit of the approach is that it obviates the need for developing formal semantics for each different intermediate representation generated by the compiler. Furthermore, the low-level optimizations implemented in a synthesis tool are abstracted from the reasoning framework without weakening the formal guarantee on the synthesized design. Our experimental results indicate that the approach scales to verification of realistic designs synthesized by production synthesis tools.

In future work, we will make further improvements to improve scalability. In the *verified* component, we are formalizing other generic transformations *e.g.*, code motion across loop iterations. In the *verifying* component, we are considering the use of theorem proving to partition a CCDFG into smaller subgraphs for compositional certification. We are also exploring ways to tolerate limited perturbations in mappings between CCDFGs and circuits (*e.g.*, due to manual RTL tweaks) in their equivalence checking.

References

1. Forte Design Systems: Behavioral Design Suite, http://www.forteds.com
2. Celoxica: DK Design Suite, http://www.celoxica.com
3. Cong, J., Fan, Y., Han, G., Jiang, W., Zhang, Z.: Behavioral and Communication Co-Optimizations for Systems with Sequential Communication Media. In: DAC (2006)
4. Gajski, D., Dutt, N.D., Wu, A., Lin, S.: High Level Synthesis: Introduction to Chip and System Design. Kluwer Academic Publishers, Dordrecht (1993)
5. Kundu, S., Lerner, S., Gupta, R.: Validating High-Level Synthesis. In: Gupta, A., Malik, S. (eds.) CAV 2008. LNCS, vol. 5123, pp. 459–472. Springer, Heidelberg (2008)
6. Galois, Inc.: Cryptol: The Language of Cryptography (2007)

7. Russinoff, D.: A Mechanically Checked Proof of IEEE Compliance of a Register-Transfer-Level Specification of the AMD-K7 Floating-point Multiplication, Division, and Square Root Instructions. JCM 1 (1998)
8. O'Leary, J., Zhao, X., Gerth, R., Seger, C.J.H.: Formally Verifying IEEE Compliance of Floating-point Hardware. Intel Technology Journal Q1 (1999)
9. Wheeler, D.J., Needham, R.M.: Tea, a tiny encryption algorithm. In: Fast Software Encryption (1994)
10. AutoESL: AutoPilot Reference Manual. AutoESL (2008)
11. Hu, A.J.: High-level vs. RTL combinational equivalence: An introduction. In: ICCD (2006)
12. Kaufmann, M., Manolios, P., Moore, J.S.: Computer-Aided Reasoning: An Approach. Kluwer Academic Publishers, Boston (2000)
13. Ray, S., Chen, Y., Xie, F., Yang, J.: Combining theorem proving and model checking for certification of behavioral synthesis flows. Technical Report TR-08-48, University of Texas at Austin (2008)
14. Abadi, M., Lamport, L.: The Existence of Refinement Mappings. TCS 82(2) (1991)
15. Lamport, L.: What Good is Temporal Logic? Information Processing 83 (1983)
16. Ray, S., Hunt Jr., W.A.: Deductive Verification of Pipelined Machines Using First-Order Quantification. In: Alur, R., Peled, D.A. (eds.) CAV 2004. LNCS, vol. 3114, pp. 31–43. Springer, Heidelberg (2004)
17. Seger, C.J.H., Jones, R., O'Leary, J., Melham, T., Aagaard, M., Barrett, C., Syme, D.: An industrially effective environment for formal hardware verification. TCAD 24(9) (2005)
18. Barrett, C., Tinelli, C.: CVC3. In: Damm, W., Hermanns, H. (eds.) CAV 2007. LNCS, vol. 4590, pp. 298–302. Springer, Heidelberg (2007)
19. Chapman, R.O.: Verified high-level synthesis. PhD thesis, Ithaca, NY, USA (1994)
20. IEEE: IEEE Std 1076: IEEE standards VHDL language reference manual
21. Johnson, R., Pingali, K.: Dependence-based program analysis. In: PLDI (1993)
22. Hoare, C.A.R.: Communicating Sequential Processes. Prentice-Hall, Englewood Cliffs (1985)
23. Gordon, M., Iyoda, J., Owens, S., Slind, K.: Automatic formal synthesis of hardware from higher order logic. TCS 145 (2006)
24. Schneider, K.: A verified hardware synthesis for Esterel. In: DIPES (2000)
25. Dave, M.A.: Compiler verification: a bibliography. SIGSOFT SEN 28(6) (2003)
26. Moore, J.S.: Piton: A Mechanically Verified Assembly Language. Kluwer Academic Publishers, Dordrecht (1996)
27. Verisoft Project: http://www.verisoft.de
28. Verifix Project: http://www.info.uni-karlsruhe.de/~verifix
29. CompCert Project: http://pauillac.inria.fr/~xleroy/compcert
30. Leinenbach, D., Paul, W.J., Petrova, E.: Towards the formal verification of a C0 compiler: Code generation and implementation correctness. In: SEFM (2005)
31. Leroy, X.: Formal certification of a compiler back-end or: programming a compiler with a proof assistant. In: POPL (2006)
32. Pike, L., Shields, M., Matthews, J.: A Verifying Core for a Cryptographic Language Compiler. In: ACL2 (2006)
33. Baumgartner, J., Mony, H., Paruthi, V., Kanzelman, R., Janssen, G.: Scalable sequential equivalence checking across arbitrary design transformations. In: ICCD (2006)
34. Kaiss, D., Goldenberg, S., Hanna, Z., Khasidashvili, Z.: Seqver: A sequential equivalence verifier for hardware designs. In: ICCD (2006)
35. Feng, X., Hu, A.J., Yang, J.: Partitioned model checking from software specifications. In: ASP-DAC (2005)
36. Yang, J., Seger, C.J.H.: Introduction to generalized symbolic trajectory evaluation. TVLSI 11(3) (2003)
37. Claesen, L., Genoe, M., Verlind, E.: Implementation/specification verification by means of SFG-Tracing. In: CHARME (1993)

Dynamic Observers for the Synthesis
of Opaque Systems

Franck Cassez[1,*], Jérémy Dubreil[2,**], and Hervé Marchand[2,**]

[1] National ICT Australia & CNRS, Sydney, Australia
[2] INRIA Rennes - Bretagne Atlantique, Campus de Beaulieu, Rennes, France

Abstract. In this paper, we address the problem of synthesizing *opaque* systems by selecting the set of observable events. We first investigate the case of *static* observability where the set of observable events is fixed a priori. In this context, we show that checking whether a system is opaque and computing an optimal static observer ensuring opacity are both PSPACE-complete problems. Next, we introduce *dynamic* partial observability where the set of observable events can change over time. We show how to check that a system is opaque w.r.t. a dynamic observer and also address the corresponding synthesis problem: given a system G and secret states S, compute the set of dynamic observers under which S is opaque. Our main result is that the synthesis problem can be solved in EXPTIME.

1 Introduction

Security is one of the most important and challenging aspects in designing services deployed on large open networks like Internet or mobile phones, e-voting systems etc. For such services, naturally subject to malicious attacks, methods to certify their security are crucial. In this context there has been a lot of research to develop formal methods for the design of secure systems and a growing interest in the formal verification of security properties [1,2,3] and in their model-based testing [4,5,6,7,8]. Security properties are generally divided into three categories: *integrity*, *availability* and *confidentiality*. We focus here on confidentiality and especially information flow properties. We use the notion of *opacity* defined in [9] formalizing the absence of information flow, or more precisely, the impossibility for an attacker to infer the truth of a predicate (it could be the occurrence in the system of some particular sequences of events, or the fact that the system is in some particular configurations). Consider a predicate φ over the runs of a system G and an attacker observing only a subset of the events of G. We assume that the attacker knows the model G. In this context, the attacker should not be able to infer that a run of G satisfies φ. The secret φ is opaque for G with respect to a given partial observation if for every run of G that satisfies φ, there exists a run, observationally equivalent from the attacker's point of view, that does not satisfy φ. In such a case, the attacker can never be sure that a run of G satisfying φ has occurred. In the sequel, we shall consider a secret φ corresponding to a set of secret states. Finally, note that

---

* Author supported by a Marie Curie International Outgoing Fellowship within the 7th European Community Framework Programme.
** Authors partially supported by the Politess RNRT project.

Z. Liu and A.P. Ravn (Eds.): ATVA 2009, LNCS 5799, pp. 352–367, 2009.

the definition of opacity is general enough to define other notions of information flow like trace-based non-interference and anonymity (see [9]). Note also that *secrecy* [10] can be handled as a particular case of opacity (see Section 3) and thus our framework applies to secrecy as well.

Related Work. Methods for the synthesis of opaque systems have already been investigated from the supervisory control point of view. In these frameworks, some of the events are uncontrollable and the set of events an external attacker can observe is fixed. If the system is G, the approach is then to *restrict* G (remove some of its behaviors) using a supervisor (or controller) C, in order to render a secret φ opaque in the supervised system $C(G)$. In [11], the authors consider several secrets and attackers with different sets of observable events. They provide sufficient conditions to compute an optimal controller preserving all secrets assuming that the controller has complete knowledge of the system and full control on it. In [12,13], the authors consider a control problem under partial observation and provide algorithms to compute the optimal controller ensuring the opacity of one secret against one attacker. Other works on the enforcement of opacity by means of controllers can be found in [14]. Note that these approaches are intrusive in the sense that the system G has to be modified.

Our Contribution. In this paper, instead of restricting the behavior of the system by means of a controller C which disables some actions, we consider *dynamic* observers that will dynamically change the set of observable events in order to ensure opacity. Compared to the previous approaches related to the supervisory control theory, this approach is not intrusive in the sense that it does not restrict G but only hides some events at different points in the course of the execution of the system. Indeed, one can think of a dynamic observer as a *filter* (See Figure 1) which is added on top of G.

Fig. 1. Architecture Filtering out Sequences of Events in G

The main contributions of this paper are two-fold. First, we extend the notion of opacity for static observers (i.e., the natural projection) to dynamic observers.[1] We show how to check opacity when the dynamic observer is given by a finite automaton. Second we give an algorithm to compute the set of all dynamic observers which can ensure opacity of a secret φ for a given system G. Finally we consider an optimization problem which is to compute a least expensive dynamic observer.

The notion of *dynamic observers* was already introduced in [15] for the fault diagnosis problem. Notice that the fault diagnosis problem and the opacity problems are not reducible one to the other and thus we have to design new algorithms to solve the opacity problems under dynamic observations.

Organization of the Paper. In Section 2 we introduce some notations for words, languages and finite automata. In Section 3 we define the notion of opacity with static

---

[1] At this point, it should be mentioned that we assume the attacker has not only a perfect knowledge of the system but also of the observer.

observers and show that deciding opacity for finite automata is PSPACE-complete. We also consider the optimization problem of computing a largest set (cardinality-wise) of observable events to ensure opacity and we show that this problem is PSPACE-complete as well. Section 4 is the core of the paper and considers dynamic observers for ensuring opacity. We prove that the set of all observers that ensure opacity can be computed in EXPTIME. In Section 5 we briefly discuss how to compute optimal dynamic observers. Omitted proofs and details are given in Appendix or available in the extended version of this paper [16].

2   Notation and Preliminaries

Let Σ be a finite alphabet. Σ^* is the set of finite words over Σ and contains the *empty word* ε. A *language* L is any subset of Σ^*. Given two words $u \in \Sigma^*$ and $v \in \Sigma^*$, we denote $u.v$ the concatenation of u and v which is defined in the usual way. $|u|$ stands for the length of the word u (the length of the empty word is zero). We let Σ^n with $n \in \mathbb{N}$ denote the set of words of length n over Σ. Given $\Sigma_1 \subseteq \Sigma$, we define the *projection* operator on finite words, $P_{\Sigma_1} : \Sigma^* \to \Sigma_1^*$, that removes in a sequence of Σ^* all the events that do not belong to Σ_1. Formally, P_{Σ_1} is recursively defined as follows: $P_{\Sigma_1}(\varepsilon) = \varepsilon$ and for $\lambda \in \Sigma, s \in \Sigma^*$, $P_{\Sigma_1}(s.\lambda) = P_{\Sigma_1}(s).\lambda$ if $\lambda \in \Sigma_1$ and $P_{\Sigma_1}(s)$ otherwise. Let $K \subseteq \Sigma^*$ be a language. The definition of projection for words extends to languages: $P_{\Sigma_1}(K) = \{P_{\Sigma_1}(s) \mid s \in K\}$. Conversely, let $K \subseteq \Sigma_1^*$. The *inverse projection* of K is $P_{\Sigma,\Sigma_1}^{-1}(K) = \{s \in \Sigma^* \mid P_{\Sigma_1}(s) \in K\}$. We omit the subscript Σ_1 in the sequel when it is clear from the context.

We assume that the system is given by an *automaton* G which is a tuple $(Q, q_0, \Sigma, \delta, F)$ with Q a set of states, $q_0 \in Q$ is the initial state, $\delta : Q \times \Sigma \to 2^Q$ is the transition relation and $F \subseteq Q$ is the set of *accepting* states. If Q is finite, G is a *finite automaton* (FA). We write $q \xrightarrow{\lambda}$ whenever $\delta(q, \lambda) \neq \emptyset$. An automaton is *complete* if for each $\lambda \in \Sigma$ and each $q \in Q, q \xrightarrow{\lambda}$. G is *deterministic* if for all $q \in Q, \lambda \in \Sigma, |\delta(q, \lambda)| \leq 1$.

A *run* ρ from state q_0 in G is a finite sequence of transitions $q_0 \xrightarrow{\lambda_1} q_1 \xrightarrow{\lambda_2} q_2 \cdots q_{i-1} \xrightarrow{\lambda_i} q_i \cdots q_{n-1} \xrightarrow{\lambda_n} q_n$ s.t. $\lambda_{i+1} \in \Sigma$ and $q_{i+1} \in \delta(q_i, \lambda_{i+1})$ for $0 \leq i \leq n - 1$. The *trace* of the run ρ is $tr(\rho) = \lambda_1.\lambda_2 \cdots \lambda_n$. We let $last(\rho) = q_n$, and the length of ρ, denoted $|\rho|$, is n. For $i \leq n$ we denote by $\rho[i]$ the prefix of the run ρ truncated at state q_i, i.e., $\rho(i) = q_0 \xrightarrow{\lambda_1} q_1 \cdots q_{i-1} \xrightarrow{\lambda_i} q_i$. The set of finite runs from q_0 in G is denoted $Runs(G)$. A word $u \in \Sigma^*$ is *generated* by G if $u = tr(\rho)$ for some $\rho \in Runs(G)$. Let $L(G)$ be the set of words generated by G. The word $u \in \Sigma^*$ is *accepted* by G if $u = tr(\rho)$ for some $\rho \in Runs(G)$ with $last(\rho) \in F$. The *language of (finite) words* $L_F(G)$ of G is the set of words accepted by G. If G is a FA such that $F = Q$ we simply omit F in the tuple that defines G.

In the sequel we shall use the *Post* operator defined by: let $X \subseteq Q, Post(X, \varepsilon) = X$ and for $u \in \Sigma^*, \lambda \in \Sigma, Post(X, u.\lambda) = \cup_{q \in Post(X,u)} \delta(q, \lambda)$. We also let $Post(X, L) = \cup_{u \in L} Post(X, u)$ for a non empty language L.

The product of automata is defined in the usual way: the product automaton represents the concurrent behavior of the automata with synchronization on the common events. Given $G_1 = (Q_1, q_0^1, \Sigma_1, \delta_1, F_1)$ and $G_2 = (Q_2, q_0^2, \Sigma_2, \delta_2, F_2)$ we denote $G_1 \times G_2$ the product of G_1 and G_2.

3   Opacity with Static Projections

In the sequel, we let $G = (Q, q_0, \Sigma, \delta, F)$ be a non-deterministic automaton over Σ and $\Sigma_o \subseteq \Sigma$. Enforcing opacity aims at preventing an attacker $\mathcal{U}$, from deducing confidential information on the execution of a system from the observation of the events in Σ_o. Given a run of G with trace u, the observation of the attacker $\mathcal{U}$ is given by the static natural projection $P_{\Sigma_o}(u)$ following the architecture of Figure 1 with $D(u) = P_{\Sigma_o}(u)$. In this paper, we shall consider that the confidential information is directly encoded in the system by means of a set of states F[2]. If the current trace of a run is $u \in L(G)$, the attacker should not be able to deduce, from the knowledge of $P_{\Sigma_o}(u)$ and the structure of G, that the current state of the system is in F. As stressed earlier, the attacker $\mathcal{U}$ has full knowledge of the structure of G (he can perform computations using G like subset constructions) but only has a partial observation upon its behaviors, namely the observed traces in Σ_o^*. The set of Σ_o-traces of G is $Tr_{\Sigma_o}(G) = P_{\Sigma_o}(L(G))$. We define the operator $[\![\cdot]\!]_{\Sigma_o}$ by: $[\![\varepsilon]\!]_{\Sigma_o} = \{\varepsilon\}$ and for $\mu \in \Sigma_o^*$ and $\lambda \in \Sigma_o$, $[\![\mu.\lambda]\!]_{\Sigma_o} = P_{\Sigma}^{-1}(\mu).\lambda \cap L(G)$. In other words, $u \in [\![\mu.\lambda]\!]_{\Sigma_o}$ iff (1) the projection of u is $\mu.\lambda$ and (2) the sequence u ends with an observable "λ" event and (3) $u \in L(G)$.

Remark 1. We suppose that $\mathcal{U}$ is reacting faster than the system. Therefore, when an observable event occurs, $\mathcal{U}$ can compute the possible set of states of G before G moves even if G can do an unobservable action.   ◇

Next we introduce the notion of opacity defined in [9]. Intuitively, a set of states F is said to be *opaque* with respect to a pair (G, Σ_o) if the attacker $\mathcal{U}$ can never be sure that the current state of G is in the set F.

Definition 1 (State Based Opacity). *Let $F \subseteq Q$. The secret F is* opaque *with respect to (G, Σ_o) if for all $\mu \in Tr_{\Sigma_o}(G)$, $Post(\{q_0\}, [\![\mu]\!]_{\Sigma_o}) \not\subseteq F$.*

We can extend Definition 1 to a (finite) family of sets $\mathcal{F} = \{F_1, F_2, \cdots, F_k\}$: the secret $\mathcal{F}$ is *opaque* with respect to (G, Σ_o) if for each $F \in \mathcal{F}$, F is opaque w.r.t. (G, Σ_o). This can be used to express other kinds of confidentiality properties. For example, [10] introduced the notion of *secrecy* of a set of states F. Intuitively, F is not *secret* w.r.t. G and Σ_o whenever after an observation μ, the attacker either knows that the system is in F or knows that it is not in F. Secrecy can thus be handled considering the opacity w.r.t. a family $\{F, Q \setminus F\}$. In the sequel we consider only one set of states F and, when necessary,

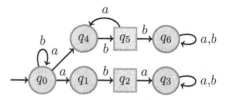

Fig. 2. State based opacity illustration

we point out what has to be done for solving the problems with family of sets.

---

[2] Equivalently, the secret can be given by a regular language over Σ^*, see [16].

Example 1. Consider the automaton G of Figure 2, with $\Sigma_o = \Sigma = \{a, b\}$. The secret is given by the states $F = \{q_2, q_5\}$. The secret F is certainly not opaque with respect to (G, Σ), as by observing a trace $b^*.a.b$, the attacker $\mathcal{U}$ knows that the system is in a secret state. Note that he does not know whether it is q_2 or q_5 but still he knows that the state of the system is in F.   □

In the sequel we shall focus on variations of the State Based Opacity Problem:

Problem 1 (Static State Based Opacity Problem).
INPUT: A non-deterministic FA $G = (Q, q_0, \Sigma, \delta, F)$ and $\Sigma_o \subseteq \Sigma$.
PROBLEM: Is F opaque w.r.t. (G, Σ_o) ?

3.1   Checking State Based Opacity

In order to check for the opacity of F w.r.t. (G, Σ_o), we first introduce the classical notion of determinization via subset construction adapted to our definition of opacity: $Det_o(G) = (\mathcal{X}, X_0, \Sigma_o, \Delta, F_o)$ denotes the deterministic automaton given by:

- $\mathcal{X} \subseteq 2^Q \setminus \emptyset$, $X_0 = \{q_0\}$ and $F_o = 2^F$,
- given $\lambda \in \Sigma_o$, if $X' = Post(X, (\Sigma \setminus \Sigma_o)^*.\lambda) \neq \emptyset$ then $\Delta(X, \lambda) = X'$.

Checking whether F is opaque w.r.t. (G, Σ_o) amounts to checking whether a state in F_o is reachable. To check opacity for a family $\{F_1, F_2, \cdots, F_k\}$, we define F_o to be the set $2^{F_1} \cup 2^{F_2} \cup \cdots \cup 2^{F_k}$ (as pointed out before, this enables us to handle secrecy).

The previous construction shows that opacity on non-deterministic FA can be checked in exponential time. Actually, checking state based opacity for (non-deterministic) FA is PSPACE-complete. Given a FA G over Σ and F the set of accepting states, the (language) universality problem is to decide whether $L_F(G) = \Sigma^*$. If not, then G is not universal. Checking language universality for non-deterministic FA is PSPACE-complete [17] and Problem 1 is equivalent to universality.

Theorem 1. *Problem 1 is PSPACE-complete for non-deterministic FA.*

Proof. We assume that G is complete i.e., $L(G) = \Sigma^*$. Note that $[\![u]\!]_\Sigma = u$. Now, G is not universal iff there exists $u \in \Sigma^*$ such that $Post(\{q_0\}, [\![u]\!]_\Sigma) \subseteq Q \setminus F$. With the definition of state based opacity, taking $\Sigma_o = \Sigma$, we have:

$$Q \setminus F \text{ is not opaque w.r.t. } (G, \Sigma) \iff \exists \mu \in \Sigma^* s.t. Post(\{q_0\}, [\![\mu]\!]_\Sigma) \subseteq Q \setminus F. \quad \square$$

PSPACE-easiness was already known and follows from a result in [18]: the model-checking problem for a temporal logics which can specify security properties is proved to be PSPACE-complete.

3.2   Maximum Cardinality for Static Projections

If a secret is opaque w.r.t. a set of observable events Σ_o, it is worthwhile noticing that it will still be opaque w.r.t. any subset of Σ_o. It might be of interest to hide as few events as possible from the attacker still preserving opacity of a secret. Indeed, hiding an event can be seen as energy consuming or as limiting the interactions or visibility for users of the system (and some of them are not malicious attackers) and thus should be avoided. Given the set of events Σ of G, we can check whether the secret is opaque w.r.t. $\Sigma_o \subseteq \Sigma$. In that case, we may increase the number of visible letters and check again if the secret remains opaque. This suggests the following optimization problem:

Problem 2 (Maximum Cardinality of Observable Events).
INPUT: A non-deterministic FA $G = (Q, q_0, \Sigma, \delta, F)$ and $n \in \mathbb{N}$ s.t. $n \leq |\Sigma|$.
PROBLEMS:

(A) Is there any $\Sigma_o \subseteq \Sigma$ with $|\Sigma_o| = n$, such that F is opaque w.r.t. (G, Σ_o) ?
(B) If the answer to (A) is "yes", find the maximum n_0 such that there exists $\Sigma_o \subseteq \Sigma$ with $|\Sigma_o| = n_0$ and F is opaque w.r.t. (G, Σ_o).

Theorem 2. *Problem 2.(A) and Problem 2.(B) are PSPACE-complete.*

Proof. PSPACE-easiness follows directly as we can guess a set Σ_o with $|\Sigma_o| = n$ and check in PSPACE whether F is opaque w.r.t. (G, Σ_o). Thus Problem 2.(A) is in NPSPACE and thus in PSPACE. PSPACE-hardness is also easy because taking $n = |\Sigma|$ amounts to checking that F is opaque w.r.t. (G, Σ) which has been shown equivalent to the universality problem (proof of Theorem 1).

To solve Problem 2.(B) it suffices to iterate a binary search and thus Problem 2.(B) is also in PSPACE. To see it is PSPACE-complete, to check whether F is opaque w.r.t. (G, Σ), it suffices to solve Problem 2.(B) and then check whether $n_0 = |\Sigma|$.   □

4   Opacity with Dynamic Projection

So far, we have assumed that the observability of events is given a priori and this is why we used the term static projections. We generalize this approach by considering the notion of *dynamic projections* encoded by means of *dynamic observers* as introduced in [15]. Dynamic projection allows us to render unobservable some events after a given observed trace (for example, some outputs of the system). To illustrate the benefits of such projections, we consider the following example:

Example 2. Consider again the automaton G of Example 1, Figure 2, where F = $\{q_2, q_5\}$. With $\Sigma_o = \Sigma = \{a, b\}$, F is not opaque. If either $\Sigma_o = \{a\}$ or $\Sigma_o = \{b\}$, then the secret becomes opaque. Thus if we have to define static sets of observable events, at least one event will have to be permanently unobservable. However, the less you hide, the more important is the observable behavior of the system. Thus, we should try to reduce as much as possible the hiding of events. We can be more efficient by us-ing a dynamic projection that will render unobservable an event only when necessary. Indeed, after observing b^*, the attacker knows that the system is in the initial state. However, if a subsequent "a" follows, then the attacker should not be able to observe "b" as in this case it could know the system is in a secret state. We can then design a dynamic events's hider as follows: at the beginning, everything is observable; when an "a" occurs, the observer hides any subsequent "b" occurrences and permits only the observation of "a". Once an "a" has been observed, the observer releases its hiding by letting both "a" and "b" be observable again.   ◇

4.1   Opacity Generalized to Dynamic Projection

We now define the notion of dynamic projection and its associated dynamic observer.

Dynamic Projections and Observers. A dynamic projection is a function that will decide to let an event be observable or to hide it, thus playing the role of a filter between the system and the attacker to prevent information flow (see Figure 1).

Definition 2. *A* dynamic observability choice *is a mapping* $T : \Sigma^* \to 2^\Sigma$. *The (observation-based)* dynamic projection *induced by T is the mapping $D : \Sigma^* \to \Sigma^*$ defined by $D(\varepsilon) = \varepsilon$, and for all $u \in \Sigma^*$ and all $\lambda \in \Sigma$,*

$$D(u.\lambda) = D(u).\lambda \ \text{ if } \ \lambda \in T(D(u)) \ \text{ and } \ D(u.\lambda) = D(u) \ \text{ otherwise.} \tag{1}$$

Assuming that $u \in \Sigma^*$ occurred in the system and $\mu \in \Sigma^*$ has been observed by the attacker i.e., $\mu = D(u)$, then the events of $T(\mu)$ are the ones currently observable. Note that this choice does not change until an observable event occurs. Given $\mu \in \Sigma^*$, $D^{-1}(\mu) = \{u \in \Sigma^* \mid D(u) = \mu\}$ is the set of sequences that project onto μ.

Example 3. A dynamic projection $D : \Sigma^* \to \Sigma^*$ corresponding to the one of Example 2 can be induced by the dynamic observability choice T defined by $T(u) = \{a\}$ for all $u \in b^*.a$ and $T(u) = \{a, b\}$ for all the other sequences $u \in \Sigma^*$. ◇

Given a FA G and a dynamic projection D, we denote by $Tr_D(G) = D(L(G))$, the set of observed traces. Conversely, given $\mu \in Tr_D(G)$, the set of words $[\![\mu]\!]_D$ of G that are compatible with μ is defined by:

$$[\![\varepsilon]\!]_D = \{\varepsilon\} \quad \text{and for } \mu \in \Sigma^*, \ \lambda \in \Sigma : [\![\mu.\lambda]\!]_D = D^{-1}(\mu).\lambda \cap L(G).$$

Given two different dynamic projections D_1 and D_2 and a system G over Σ, we say that D_1 and D_2 are *G-equivalent*, denoted $D_1 \sim_G D_2$, whenever for all $u \in L(G)$, $D_1(u) = D_2(u)$. The relation $\sim_G$ identifies two dynamic projections when they agree on $L(G)$; they can disagree on other words in Σ^* but since they will not be generated by G, it will not make any difference from the attacker point of view. In the sequel we will be interested in computing the interesting part of dynamic projections given G, and thus will compute one dynamic projection in each class.

Opacity with Dynamic Projection. We generalize Definition 1 by taking into account the new observation interface given by D.

Definition 3. *Given a FA $G = (Q, q_0, \Sigma, \delta, F)$, F is opaque with respect to (G, D) if*

$$\forall \mu \in Tr_D(G), \ Post(\{q_0\}, [\![\mu]\!]_D) \not\subseteq F. \tag{2}$$

Again, this definition extends to family of sets. We say that D is a *valid* dynamic projection if (2) is satisfied (i.e., whenever F is opaque w.r.t. (G, D)) and we denote by $\mathcal{D}$ the set of valid dynamic projections. Obviously if $D_1 \sim_G D_2$, then D_1 is valid if and only if D_2 is valid. We denote by $\mathcal{D}_{\sim_G}$ the quotient set of $\mathcal{D}$ by $\sim_G$.

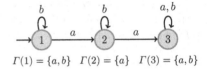

$\Gamma(1) = \{a, b\}$ $\Gamma(2) = \{a\}$ $\Gamma(3) = \{a, b\}$

Fig. 3. Example of a Dynamic Observer

Remark 2. Let $\Sigma_o \subseteq \Sigma$, then if D is a dynamic projection that defines a constant mapping making actions in Σ_o always observable (and the others always unobservable), we have $D(u) = P_{\Sigma_o}(u)$ and we retrieve Definition 1. The property of secrecy can be extended as well using dynamic projection.   ⬦

In the sequel, we shall be interested in checking the opacity of F w.r.t. (G, D) or to synthesize such a dynamic projection D ensuring this property. In Section 3, the dynamic projection was merely the natural projection and computing the observational behavior of G was easy. Here, we need to find a characterization of these dynamic projections that can be used to check opacity or to enforce it. To do so, we introduce the notion of dynamic observer [15] that will encode a dynamic projection in terms of automata.

Definition 4 (Dynamic observer). *A dynamic observer is a complete deterministic labeled automaton $\mathcal{O} = (X, x_0, \Sigma, \delta_o, \Gamma)$ where X is a (possibly infinite) set of states, $x_0 \in X$ is the initial state, Σ is the set of input events, $\delta_o : X \times \Sigma \to X$ is the transition function (a total function), and $\Gamma : X \to 2^{\Sigma}$ is a labeling function that specifies the set of events that the observer keeps observable at state x. We require that for all $x \in X$ and for all $\lambda \in \Sigma$, if $\lambda \notin \Gamma(x)$, then $\delta_o(x, \lambda) = x$, i.e., if the observer does not want an event to be observed, it does not change its state when such an event occurs.*

We extend δ_o to words of Σ^* by: $\delta_o(q, \varepsilon) = q$ and for $u \in \Sigma^*, \lambda \in \Sigma, \delta_o(q, u.\lambda) = \delta_o(\delta_o(q, u), \lambda)$. Assuming that the observer is at state x and an event λ occurs, it outputs λ whenever $\lambda \in \Gamma(x)$ or nothing (ε) if $\lambda \notin \Gamma(x)$ and moves to state $\delta_o(x, \lambda)$. An observer can be interpreted as a functional transducer taking a string $u \in \Sigma^*$ as input, and producing the output which corresponds to the successive events it has chosen to keep observable. An example of dynamic observer is given in Figure 3. We now relate the notion of dynamic observer to the one of dynamic projection.

Proposition 1. *Let $\mathcal{O} = (X, x_0, \Sigma, \delta_o, \Gamma)$ be an observer and define $D_{\mathcal{O}}$ by: $D_{\mathcal{O}}(\varepsilon) = \varepsilon$, and for all $u \in \Sigma^*$, $D_{\mathcal{O}}(u.\lambda) = D_{\mathcal{O}}(u).\lambda$ if $\lambda \in \Gamma(\delta_o(x_0, u))$ and $D_{\mathcal{O}}(u)$ otherwise. Then $D_{\mathcal{O}}$ is a dynamic projection. In the sequel, we write $[\![\mu]\!]_{\mathcal{O}}$ for $[\![\mu]\!]_{D_{\mathcal{O}}}$.*

Proof. To prove that $D_{\mathcal{O}}$ defined above is a dynamic projection, it is sufficient to exhibit a dynamic observability choice $T : \Sigma^* \to 2^{\Sigma}$ and to show that (1) holds. Let $T(u) = \Gamma(\delta_o(x_0, D_{\mathcal{O}}(u)))$. It is easy to show by induction that $\delta_o(x_0, u) = \delta_o(x_0, D_{\mathcal{O}}(u))$ because $\delta_o(x, \lambda) = x$ when $\lambda \notin \Gamma(x)$. We can then define $T(u) = \Gamma(\delta_o(x_0, u))$ and the result follows from this remark.   □

Proposition 2. *Given a dynamic projection D induced by T, let $\mathcal{O}_D = (\Sigma^*, \varepsilon, \Sigma, \delta_D, T)$ where $\delta_D(w, \lambda) = D(w.\lambda)$. Then $\mathcal{O}_D$ is a dynamic observer.*

Proof. $\mathcal{O}_D$ is complete and deterministic by construction. Moreover after a sequence u if $D(u.\lambda) = D(u)$ then $\delta_D(u, \lambda) = u$.   □

Note that there might exist several equivalent observers that encode the same dynamic projection. For example, the observer depicted in Figure 3 is one observer that encodes the dynamic projection described in Example 3. But, one can consider other observers obtained by unfolding an arbitrary number of times the self-loops in states 1 or 3. Finally, to mimic the language theory terminology, we will say that a dynamic projection D is *regular* whenever there exists a finite state dynamic observer $\mathcal{O}$ such that $D_{\mathcal{O}} = D$.

To summarize this part, we can state that with each dynamic projection D, we can associate a dynamic observer $\mathcal{O}_D$ such that $D = D_{\mathcal{O}_D}$. In other words, we can consider a dynamic projection or one of its associated dynamic observers whenever one representation is more convenient than the other. If the dynamic projection D derived from $\mathcal{O}$ is valid, we say that $\mathcal{O}$ is a *valid* dynamic observer. In that case, we will say that F is opaque w.r.t. $(G, \mathcal{O})$ and we denote by $\mathcal{OBS}(G)$ the set of all valid dynamic observers.

4.2   Checking Opacity with Dynamic Observers

The first problem we are going to address consists in checking whether a given dynamic projection ensures opacity. To do so, we assume given a dynamic observer which defines this projection map. The problem, we are interested in, is then the following:

Problem 3 (Dynamic State Based Opacity Problem).
INPUT: A non-deterministic FA $G = (Q, q_0, \Sigma, \delta, F)$ and a dynamic observer
$\quad \mathcal{O} = (X, x_0, \Sigma, \delta_o, \Gamma)$.
PROBLEM: Is F opaque w.r.t. $(G, \mathcal{O})$?

We first construct an automaton which represents what an attacker will see under the dynamic choices of observable events made by $\mathcal{O}$. To do so, we define the automaton $G \otimes \mathcal{O} = (Q \times X, (q_0, x_0), \Sigma \cup \{\tau\}, \delta, F \times X)$ where τ is a fresh letter not in Σ and δ is defined for each $\lambda \in \Sigma \cup \{\tau\}$, and $(q, x) \in Q \times X$ by:

 – $\delta((q, x), \lambda) = \delta_G(q, \lambda) \times \{\delta_o(x, \lambda)\}$ if $\lambda \in \Gamma(x)$;
 – $\delta((q, x), \tau) = \left(\cup_{\lambda \in \Sigma \setminus \Gamma(x)} \delta_G(q, \lambda)\right) \times \{x\}$.

Proposition 3. *F is opaque w.r.t. $(G, \mathcal{O})$ iff $F \times X$ is opaque w.r.t. $(G \otimes \mathcal{O}, \Sigma)$.*

Proof. Let $\mu \in Tr_{\mathcal{O}}(G)$ be a trace observed by the attacker. We prove the following by induction on the length of μ:

$$q \in Post_G(\{q_0\}, \llbracket \mu \rrbracket_{\mathcal{O}}) \iff (q, x) \in Post_{G \otimes \mathcal{O}}(\{(q_0, x_0)\}, \llbracket \mu \rrbracket_{\Sigma}) \text{ for some } x \in X.$$

If $\mu = \varepsilon$, the result is immediate. Assume that $\mu' = \mu.\lambda$. Let $q \in Post_G(\{q_0\}, \llbracket \mu' \rrbracket_{\mathcal{O}})$. By definition of $\llbracket \mu' \rrbracket_{\mathcal{O}}$ we have $q_0 \xrightarrow{u} q' \xrightarrow{v} q'' \xrightarrow{\lambda} q$ with $u \in \llbracket \mu \rrbracket_{\mathcal{O}}$, $u.v.\lambda \in \llbracket \mu.\lambda \rrbracket_{\mathcal{O}}$. By induction hypothesis, it follows that $(q', \delta_o(x_0, u)) \in Post_{G \otimes \mathcal{O}}(\{(q_0, x_0)\}, \llbracket \mu \rrbracket_{\Sigma})$ where $\delta_o(x_0, u)$ is the (unique) state of $\mathcal{O}$ after reading u. Then, there exists a word $w \in (\Sigma \cup \{\tau\})^*$ such that $P_{\Sigma}(w) = \mu$ and $(q_0, x_0) \xrightarrow{w} (q', \delta_o(x_0, u))$ is a run of $G \otimes \mathcal{O}$. Assume $v = v_1.v_2.\cdots.v_k, k \geq 0$. As $\mathcal{O}(u.v) = \mathcal{O}(u)$, we must have $v_i \notin \Gamma(\delta_o(x_0, u.v_1.\cdots.v_i))$ when $1 \leq i \leq k$. Hence, by construction of $G \otimes \mathcal{O}$, there is a sequence of transitions in $G \otimes \mathcal{O}$ of the form

$$(q', \delta_o(x_0, u)) \xrightarrow{\tau} \delta_o(x_0, u.v_1) \xrightarrow{\tau} \quad \cdots \quad \xrightarrow{\tau} (q'', \delta_o(x_0, u.v))$$

with $\lambda \in \Gamma(\delta_o(x_0, u.v))$. Thus, $(q_0, x_0) \xrightarrow{w} (q', \delta_o(x_0, u)) \xrightarrow{\tau^k.\lambda} (q, \delta_o(u.v.\lambda))$ is a run of $G \otimes \mathcal{O}$ with $P_{\Sigma}(w.\tau^k.\lambda) = \mu.\lambda = \mu'$. This implies $(q, \delta_o(x_0, u.v.\lambda)) \in Post_{G \otimes \mathcal{O}}(\{(q_0, x_0)\}, \llbracket \mu' \rrbracket_{\Sigma})$. For the converse if we have a sequence of τ transitions in $G \otimes \mathcal{O}$, they must originate from actions in G which are not observable. $\square$

The previous result is general, and if $\mathcal{O}$ is a FA we obtain the following theorem:

Theorem 3. *For finite state observers, Problem 3 is PSPACE-complete.*

Proof. As the size of the product $G \otimes \mathcal{O}$ is the product of the size of G and the size of $\mathcal{O}$ and opacity can be checked in PSPACE, PSPACE-easiness follows. Now, checking state based opacity with respect to (G, Σ) can be done using a simple observer with one state which always let Σ observable and PSPACE-hardness follows.   □

As Proposition 3 reduces the problem of checking opacity with dynamic observers to the problem of checking opacity with static observers, Theorem 3 extends to family of sets (and thus to secrecy).

4.3   Enforcing Opacity with Dynamic Projections

So far, we have assumed that the dynamic projection/observer was given. Next we will be interested in *synthesizing* one in such a way that the secret becomes opaque w.r.t. the system and this observer.

Problem 4 (Dynamic Observer Synthesis Problem).
INPUT: A non-deterministic FA $G = (Q, q_0, \Sigma, \delta, F)$.
PROBLEM: Compute the set of valid dynamic observers $\mathcal{OBS}(G)^3$.

Deciding the existence of a valid observer is trivial: it is sufficient to check whether always hiding Σ is a solution. Moreover, note that $\mathcal{OBS}(G)$ can be infinite. To solve Problem 4, we reduce it to a safety 2-player game. Player 1 will play the role of an observer and Player 2 what the attacker observes. Assume the automaton G can be in any of the states $s = \{q_1, q_2, \cdots, q_n\}$, after a sequence of actions occurred. A round of the game is: given s, Player 1 chooses which letters should be observable next i.e., a set $t \subseteq \Sigma$; then it hands it over to Player 2 who picks up an observable letter $\lambda \in t$; this determines a new set of states G can be in after λ, and the turn is back to Player 1. The goal of the Players are defined by:

- The goal of Player 2 is to pick up a sequence of letters such that the set of states that can be reached after this sequence is included in F. If Player 2 can do this, then it can infer the secret F. Player 2 thus plays a *reachability game* trying to enforce a particular set of states, say Bad (the states in which the secret is disclosed).
- The goal of Player 1 is opposite: it must keep the game in a safe set of states where the secret is not disclosed. Thus Player 1 plays a *safety game* trying to keep the game in the complement set of Bad.

As we are playing a (finite) turn-based game, Player 2 has a strategy to enforce Bad iff Player 1 has no strategy to keep the game in the complement set of Bad (turn-based finite games are *determined* [19]).

We now formally define the 2-player game and show it allows us to obtain a finite representation of all the valid dynamic observers. Let $H = (S_1 \cup S_2, s_0, M_1 \cup M_2, \delta_H)$ be the deterministic game automaton derived from G and given by:

---

[3] Our aim is actually to be able to generate at least one observer for each representative of $\mathcal{D}_{\sim_G}$, thus capturing all the interesting dynamical projections.

- $S_1 = 2^Q$ is the set of Player 1 states and $S_2 = 2^Q \times 2^\Sigma$ the set of Player 2 states;
- the initial state of the game is the Player 1 state $s_0 = \{q_0\}$;
- Player 1 will choose a set of events to hide in Σ, then Player 1 actions are in the alphabet $M_1 = 2^\Sigma$ and Player 2 actions are in $M_2 = \Sigma$;
- the transition relation $\delta_H \subseteq (S_1 \times M_1 \times S_2) \cup (S_2 \times M_2 \times S_1)$ is given by:
  - Player 1 moves (observable events): if $s \in S_1, t \subseteq \Sigma$, then $\delta_H(s, t) = (s, t)$;
  - Player 2 moves (observed events): if $(s, t) \in S_2, \lambda \in t$ and $s' = Post(s, (\Sigma \setminus t)^*.\lambda) \neq \emptyset$, then $\delta_H((s, t), \lambda) = s'$.

Remark 3. If we want to exclude the possibility of hiding everything for Player 1, it suffices to build the game H with this constraint on Player 1 moves i.e., $\forall s \in S_1$, and $t \neq \emptyset, \delta_H(s, t) = (s, t)$. ◇

We define the set of *Bad* states to be the set of Player 1 states s s.t. $s \subseteq F$. For a family of sets $F_1, F_2, \cdots, F_k$, *Bad* is the set of states $2^{F_1} \cup 2^{F_2} \cup \cdots \cup 2^{F_k}$. Let $Runs_i(H), i = 1, 2$ be the set of runs of H that end in a Player i state. A *strategy* for Player i is a mapping $f_i : Runs_i(H) \rightarrow M_i$ that associates with each run that ends in a Player i state, the new choice of Player i. Given two strategies f_1, f_2, the game H generates the set of runs $Outcome(f_1, f_2, H)$ combining the choices of Players 1 and 2 w.r.t. f_1 and f_2. f_1 is a *winning strategy* for Playing 1 in H for avoiding *Bad* if for all Player 2 strategies f_2, no run of $Outcome(f_1, f_2, H)$ contains a *Bad* state. A winning strategy for Player 2 is a strategy f_2 s.t. for all strategy f_1 of Player 1, $Outcome(f_1, f_2, H)$ reaches a *Bad* state. As turn-based games are determined, either Player 1 has a winning strategy or Player 2 has a winning strategy.

We now relate the set of winning strategies for Player 1 in H to the set of valid dynamic projections. Let $P_{M_2}(\varrho) = P_\Sigma(tr(\varrho))$ for a run ϱ of H. The proof of the following Proposition 4 is given in Appendix.

Definition 5. *Given a dynamic projection D, we define the strategy f_D such that for every $\varrho \in Runs_1(H)$, $f_D(\varrho) = T_D(P_{M_2}(\varrho))$.*

Proposition 4. *Let D be a dynamic projection. D is valid if and only if f_D is a winning strategy for Player 1 in H.*

Given a strategy f for Player 1 in H, for all $\mu \in \Sigma^*$, there exists at most one run $\varrho_\mu \in Outcome_1(f, H)$ such that $P_{M_2}(tr(\varrho_\mu)) = \mu$.

Definition 6. *Let f be a strategy for Player 1 in H. We define the dynamic projection D_f induced by the dynamic observability choice $T_f : \Sigma^* \rightarrow 2^\Sigma$ given by: $T_f(\mu) = f(\varrho_\mu)$ if ϱ_μ is in $Outcome(f, H)$ and $T_f(\mu) = \Sigma$ otherwise.*

Notice that when ϱ_μ is not in $Outcome(f, H)$, it does not really matter how we define T_f because there is no word $w \in L(G)$ s.t. $\mu = D_f(w)$.

Proposition 5. *If f is a winning strategy for Player 1 in H, then D_f is a valid dynamic projection.*

Proof. Applying the construction of Definition 5 yields $f_{D_f} = f$. Since f is a winning strategy, by Proposition 4, we get that D_f is a valid dynamic projection. □

Notice that we only generate a representative for each of the equivalence classes induced by $\sim_G$. However, an immediate consequence of the two previous propositions is that there is a bijection between the set of winning strategies of Player 1 and $\mathcal{D}_{\sim_G}$.

4.4   Most Permissive Dynamic Observer

We now define the notion of *most permissive* valid dynamic observers. For an observer $\mathcal{O} = (X, x_o, \Sigma, \delta_o, \Gamma)$ and $w \in \Sigma^*$, recall that $\Gamma(\delta_o(x_o, w))$ is the set of events that $\mathcal{O}$ chooses to render observable after observing w. Assume that $w = \lambda_1 \lambda_2 \cdots \lambda_k$. Let $\overline{w} = \Gamma(x_o).\lambda_1.\Gamma(\delta_o(x_o, w[1])).\lambda_2.\Gamma(\delta_o(x_o, w[2])) \cdots \lambda_k.\Gamma(\delta_o(x_o, w[k]))$ i.e., $\overline{w}$ contains the history of what $\mathcal{O}$ has chosen to observe at each step and the next observable event that occurred after each choice.

Definition 7. *Let* $\mathcal{O}^* : (2^\Sigma.\Sigma)^* \rightarrow 2^{2^\Sigma}$. *The mapping* $\mathcal{O}^*$ *is the* most permissive valid dynamic observer[4] *ensuring the opacity of F if the following holds:*

$$\mathcal{O} = (X, x_o, \Sigma, \delta_o, \Gamma) \text{ is a valid observer} \iff \forall w \in L(G), \ \Gamma(\delta_o(x_o, w)) \in \mathcal{O}^*(\overline{w}).$$

The definition of the most permissive valid observer states that any valid observer $\mathcal{O}$ must choose a set of observable events in $\mathcal{O}^*(\overline{w})$ on input w; if an observer chooses its set of observable events in $\mathcal{O}^*(\overline{w})$ on input w, then it is a valid observer.

Theorem 4. *The most permissive valid observer* $\mathcal{O}^*$ *can be computed in EXPTIME.*

Proof. The detailed proof is given in Appendix. For a sketch, the most permissive valid dynamic observer is obtained using the most permissive winning strategy in the game H. It is well-known result [20] that for a finite game, if there is a winning strategy, there is a memoryless most permissive one. Moreover whether there is a winning strategy can be decided in linear time in the size of the game. As the size of H is exponential in the size of G and Σ the result follows.   ☐

We let $\mathcal{F}_H$ be the automaton representing the most permissive observer. Theorem 4 states that $\mathcal{F}_H$ can be used to generate any valid observer. In particular, given a finite-memory winning strategy, the corresponding valid observer is finite and thus its associated dynamic projection is regular. An immediate corollary of Theorem 4 is the following:

Corollary 1. *Problem 4 is in EXPTIME.*

Example 4. To illustrate this section, we consider the following small example. The system is depicted by the automaton in Figure 4(a). The set of secret states is reduced to the state (2). Figure 4(b) represents the associated game automaton. The states of Player 1 are represented by circles whereas the ones of Player 2 are represented by squares. The only bad states is the state (2). The most permissive valid dynamic observer is obtained when Player 1 does not allow transition $\{a, b\}$ to be triggered in state (1) (otherwise,

---

[4] Strictly speaking $\mathcal{O}^*$ is not an observer because it maps to sets of sets of events whereas observers map to sets of events. Still we use this term because it is the usual terminology in the literature.

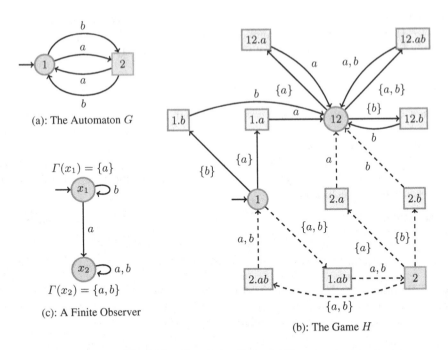

(a): The Automaton G

(c): A Finite Observer

(b): The Game H

Fig. 4. Most Permissive Dynamic Observer

Player 2 could choose to observe either event a or b and in this case the game will evolve into state (2) and the secret will be revealed). The dashed lines represents the transitions that are removed from the game automaton to obtain the most permissive observer. Finally, Figure 4(c) represents a valid observer $\mathcal{O}$ generated from the most permissive observer with the memoryless strategy $f(1) = \{a\}$ and $f(12) = \{a, b\}$. ◇

5   Optimal Dynamic Observer

Among all the possible observers that ensure the opacity of the secret, it is worthwhile noticing that some are better (in some sense) than other: they hide less events on *average*. We here define a notion of cost for observers which captures this intuitive notion. We first introduce a general cost function and we show how to compute the cost of a given pair $(G, \mathcal{O})$ where G is a system and $\mathcal{O}$ a finite state observer. Second, we show that among all the valid observers (that ensure opacity), there is an optimal cost, and we can compute an observer which ensures this cost. The problems in this section and the solutions are closely related to the results in [15] and use the same tools: Karp's mean-weight algorithm [21] and a result of Zwick and Paterson [22]. We want to define a notion of cost which takes into account the set of events the observer chooses to hide and also how long it hides them. We assume that the observer is a finite automaton $\mathcal{O} = (X, x_0, \Sigma, \delta_o, \Gamma)$. With each set of observable events $\Sigma' \in 2^{\Sigma}$ we associate a *cost of hiding* $\Sigma \setminus \Sigma'$ which is a positive integer. We denote

$Cost : 2^{\Sigma} \to \mathbb{N}$ this function. Now, if $\mathcal{O}$ is in state x, the current cost per time unit is $Cost(\Gamma(x))$. Let $Runs^n(G)$ be the set of runs of length n in $Runs(G)$. Given a run $\rho = q_0 \xrightarrow{\lambda_1} q_1 \cdots q_{n-1} \xrightarrow{\lambda_n} q_n \in Runs^n(G)$, let $x_i = \delta_o(x_0, w_i)$ with $w_i = tr(\rho[i])$. The *cost* associated with $\rho \in Runs^n(G)$ is defined by:

$$Cost(\rho, G, \mathcal{O}) = \frac{1}{n+1} \cdot \sum_{i=0..n} Cost(\Gamma(x_i)).$$

Notice that the time basis we take is the number of steps which occurred in G. Thus if the observer is in state x, and chooses to observe $\Gamma(x)$ at steps i and $i+1$, $Cost(\Gamma(x))$ will be counted twice: at steps i and $i+1$. The definition of the cost of a run corresponds to the average cost per time unit, the time unit being the number of steps of the run in G. Define the cost of the set of runs of length n that belongs to $Runs^n(G)$ by: $Cost(n, G, \mathcal{O}) = \max\{Cost(\rho, G, \mathcal{O}) \mid \rho \in Runs^n(G)\}$. The *cost of an observer* with respect to a system G is

$$Cost(G, \mathcal{O}) = \limsup_{n \to \infty} Cost(n, G, \mathcal{O}) \qquad (3)$$

(notice that the limit may not exist whereas the limit sup is always defined.) To compute the cost of a given observer, we can use a similar algorithm as the one given in [15], and using Karps's maximum mean-weight cycle algorithm [21]:

Theorem 5. *Computing $Cost(G, \mathcal{O})$ is in PTIME.*

Proof. We can prove that the cost of an observer is equal to the maximum mean-weight cycle in $G \otimes \mathcal{O}$. The size of $G \otimes \mathcal{O}$ is polynomial in the size of G and $\mathcal{O}$. Computing the maximum mean-weight cycle can be done in linear time w.r.t. the size of $G \otimes \mathcal{O}$. $\square$

Finally we can solve the following optimization problem:

Problem 5 (Bounded Cost Observer).
INPUTS: an automaton $G = (Q, q_0, \Sigma, \delta, F)$ and an integer $k \in \mathbb{N}$.
PROBLEMS:
(A) Is there any $\mathcal{O} \in \mathcal{OBS}(G)$ s.t. F is opaque w.r.t. $(G, \mathcal{O})$ and $Cost(G, \mathcal{O}) \leq k$?
(B) If the answer to (A) is "yes", compute a witness observer $\mathcal{O}$ s.t. $Cost(G, \mathcal{O}) \leq k$.

To solve this problem we use a result from Zwick and Paterson [22], which is an extension of Karp's algorithm for finite state games.

Theorem 6. *Problem 5 can be solved in EXPTIME.*

The solution to this problem is the same as the one given in [15], and the proof for the opacity problem is detailed in [16]. The key result is Theorem 4, which enables us to represent all the winning strategies in H as a finite automaton. Synchronizing G and the most permissive valid dynamic observer $\mathcal{F}_H$ produces a *weighted game*, the optimal value of which can be computed in PTIME (in the size of the product) using the algorithm in [22]. The optimal strategies can be computed in PTIME as well. As $G \times \mathcal{F}_H$ has size exponential in G and Σ, the result follows.

6 Conclusion

In this paper, we have investigated the synthesis of opaque systems. In the context of static observers, where the observability of events is fixed a priori, we provided an algorithm (PSPACE-complete) to compute a maximal subalphabet of observable actions ensuring opacity. We have also defined a model of dynamic observers determining whether an event is observable after a given observed trace. We proved that the synthesis of dynamic observers can be solved in EXPTIME, and EXPTIME-hardness is left open.

We assumed that the dynamic observers can change the set observable events only after an observable event has occurred. This assumption should fit most applications since the knowledge of the attacker also depends on observed traces. It would be interesting to investigate also the case where this decision depends on the word executed by the system. The case where the observability depends on the state of the system should also be considered as it would be easy to implement in practice. Finally, the notion of semantics of an observed trace used throughout this article is based on the assumption that the attacker can react, i.e., acquire knowledge, faster than the system's evolution. It would be interesting to adapt this work to other types of semantics.

References

1. Lowe, G.: Towards a completeness result for model checking of security protocols. Journal of Computer Security 7(2-3), 89–146 (1999)
2. Blanchet, B., Abadi, M., Fournet, C.: Automated Verification of Selected Equivalences for Security Protocols. In: 20th IEEE Symposium on Logic in Computer Science (LICS 2005), Chicago, IL, pp. 331–340. IEEE Computer Society, Los Alamitos (2005)
3. Hadj-Alouane, N., Lafrance, S., Lin, F., Mullins, J., Yeddes, M.: On the verification of intransitive noninterference in mulitlevel security. IEEE Transaction On Systems, Man, And Cybernetics—Part B: Cybernetics 35(5), 948–957 (2005)
4. Schneider, F.B.: Enforceable security policies. ACM Trans. Inf. Syst. Secur. 3(1), 30–50 (2000)
5. Ligatti, J., Bauer, L., Walker, D.: Edit automata: enforcement mechanisms for run-time security policies. Int. J. Inf. Sec. 4(1-2), 2–16 (2005)
6. Darmaillacq, V., Fernandez, J.C., Groz, R., Mounier, L., Richier, J.L.: Test generation for network security rules. In: Uyar, M.Ü., Duale, A.Y., Fecko, M.A. (eds.) TestCom 2006. LNCS, vol. 3964, pp. 341–356. Springer, Heidelberg (2006)
7. Le Guernic, G.: Information flow testing - the third path towards confidentiality guarantee. In: Cervesato, I. (ed.) ASIAN 2007. LNCS, vol. 4846, pp. 33–47. Springer, Heidelberg (2007)
8. Dubreil, J., Jéron, T., Marchand, H.: Monitoring information flow by diagnosis techniques. Technical Report 1901, IRISA (August 2008)
9. Bryans, J., Koutny, M., Mazaré, L., Ryan, P.: Opacity generalised to transition systems. International Journal of Information Security 7(6), 421–435 (2008)
10. Alur, R., Černý, P., Zdancewic, S.: Preserving secrecy under refinement. In: Bugliesi, M., Preneel, B., Sassone, V., Wegener, I. (eds.) ICALP 2006. LNCS, vol. 4052, pp. 107–118. Springer, Heidelberg (2006)
11. Badouel, E., Bednarczyk, M., Borzyszkowski, A., Caillaud, B., Darondeau, P.: Concurrent secrets. Discrete Event Dynamic Systems 17, 425–446 (2007)
12. Dubreil, J., Darondeau, P., Marchand, H.: Opacity enforcing control synthesis. In: Proceedings of the 9th International Workshop on Discrete Event Systems (WODES 2008), Göteborg, Sweden, May 2008, pp. 28–35 (2008)

13. Dubreil, J., Darondeau, P., Marchand, H.: Opacity enforcing control synthesis. Technical Report 1921, IRISA (February 2009)
14. Takai, S., Oka, Y.: A formula for the supremal controllable and opaque sublanguage arising in supervisory control. SICE Journal of Control, Measurement, and System Integration 1(4), 307–312 (2008)
15. Cassez, F., Tripakis, S.: Fault diagnosis with static or dynamic diagnosers. Fundamenta Informatica 88(4), 497–540 (2008)
16. Cassez, F., Dubreil, J., Marchand, H.: Dynamic Observers for the Synthesis of Opaque Systems. Technical Report 1930, IRISA (May 2009)
17. Stockmeyer, L.J., Meyer, A.R.: Word problems requiring exponential time: Preliminary report. In: STOC, pp. 1–9. ACM, New York (1973)
18. Alur, R., Cerný, P., Chaudhuri, S.: Model checking on trees with path equivalences. In: Grumberg, O., Huth, M. (eds.) TACAS 2007. LNCS, vol. 4424, pp. 664–678. Springer, Heidelberg (2007)
19. Martin, D.A.: Borel determinacy. Annals of Mathematics 102(2), 363–371 (1975)
20. Thomas, W.: On the synthesis of strategies in infinite games. In: Mayr, E.W., Puech, C. (eds.) STACS 1995. LNCS, vol. 900, pp. 1–13. Springer, Heidelberg (1995), Invited talk
21. Karp, R.: A characterization of the minimum mean cycle in a digraph. Discrete Mathematics 23, 309–311 (1978)
22. Zwick, U., Paterson, M.: The complexity of mean payoff games on graphs. Theoretical Computer Science 158(1–2), 343–359 (1996)

Symbolic CTL Model Checking of Asynchronous Systems Using Constrained Saturation*

Yang Zhao and Gianfranco Ciardo

Department of Computer Science and Engineering
University of California, Riverside
{zhaoy,ciardo}@cs.ucr.edu

Abstract. The saturation state-space generation algorithm has demonstrated clear improvements over state-of-the-art symbolic methods for asynchronous systems. This work is motivated by efficiently applying saturation to CTL model checking. First, we introduce a new "constrained saturation" algorithm which constrains state exploration to a set of states satisfying given properties. This algorithm avoids the expensive after-the-fact intersection operations and retains the advantages of saturation, namely, exploiting event locality and benefiting from recursive local fixpoint computations. Then, we employ constrained saturation to build the set of states satisfying EU and EG properties for asynchronous systems. The new algorithm can achieve orders-of-magnitude reduction in runtime and memory consumption with respect to methods based on breath-first search, and even with a previously-proposed hybrid approach that alternates between "safe" saturation and "unsafe" breadth-first searches. Furthermore, the new approch is fully general, as it does not require the next-state function to be expressable in Kronecker form. We conclude this paper with a discussion of some possible future work, such as building the set of states belonging to strongly connected components.

1 Introduction

CTL model checking is an important state-of-the-art approach in formal verification. Paired with the use of BDDs [2], which provide a time and space efficient data structure to perform operations such as union, intersection, and relational product over sets of states, symbolic model checking [13] is one of the most successful techniques to verify industrial hardware and embedded software systems.

Most current symbolic model checkers, such as NuSMV [12], employ methods based on breath-first search (BFS). The saturation algorithm [7] employs a very different philosophy, recursively computing "local fixpoints". A series of publications has proven the clear advantages of saturation for state-space generation over traditional symbolic approaches [6,8,9,14], while extending its applicability to increasingly general settings. However, our previous attempts to apply saturation to CTL model checking have been only partially successful [10].

---

* Work supported in part by the National Science Foundation under grant CCF-0848463.

Z. Liu and A.P. Ravn (Eds.): ATVA 2009, LNCS 5799, pp. 368–381, 2009.

This paper addresses CTL model checking for asynchronous systems by proposing an extended *constrained saturation* algorithm. This algorithm constrains the saturation-based state-space exploration to a given set of states without explicitly executing the expensive intersection operations normally required to implement CTL operators. Furthermore, unlike the original approach [10] where the next-state function had to satisfy a Kronecker expression, the proposed algorithm is fully general, as it employs a disjunctive-then-conjunctive encoding that exploits the common characteristics of asynchronous systems. Constrained saturation can be used to compute the set of states satisfying an EU formula as well as to efficiently compute the *backward reachability relation*, which we in turn use for a new algorithm to compute the set of states satisfying an EG formula.

The remainder of this paper is organized as follows. Section 2 introduces the relevant background on MDDs and the saturation algorithm. Section 3 introduces constrained saturation and new EU computation algorithm. Section 4 proposes a new EG computation algorithm based on the backward reachability relation. We conclude this paper and outline future work in the last section.

2   Preliminaries

Consider a discrete-state model $(\mathcal{S}, \mathcal{S}_{init}, \mathcal{E}, \mathcal{N})$ where the state space $\mathcal{S}$ is given by the product $\mathcal{S}_L \times \cdots \times \mathcal{S}_1$ of local state spaces of L submodels, that is, each (global) state $\mathbf{i}$ is a tuple $(i_L, \cdots, i_1)$, where $i_k \in \mathcal{S}_k$, for $L \geq k \geq 1$; the set of initial states is $\mathcal{S}_{init} \subseteq \mathcal{S}$; the set of (asynchronous) events is $\mathcal{E}$; the next-state function $\mathcal{N} : \mathcal{S} \to 2^{\mathcal{S}}$ is described in disjunctively partitioned form as $\mathcal{N} = \bigcup_{\alpha \in \mathcal{E}} \mathcal{N}_\alpha$, where $\mathcal{N}_\alpha(\mathbf{i})$ is the set of states that can be reached in one step when α occurs, or fires, in state $\mathbf{i}$. We say that α is *enabled* in state $\mathbf{i}$ if $\mathcal{N}_\alpha(\mathbf{i}) \neq \emptyset$. Correspondingly, $\mathcal{N}^{-1}$ and $\mathcal{N}_\alpha^{-1}$ denote the inverse next-state functions, e.g., $\mathcal{N}_\alpha^{-1}(\mathbf{i})$ is the set of states that can reach $\mathbf{i}$ in one step by firing event α.

For high-level models, the generation of the state space $\mathcal{S}$ is an important and interesting problem in itself. This is particularly true for models such as Petri nets, where the sets $\mathcal{S}_k$ might not be known a priori. However, using the saturation algorithm, the state spaces of complex models can usually be generated in acceptable runtime, so we now assume that state-space generation is a preprocessing step that has been already performed prior to model checking. Consequently, the sets $\mathcal{S}_k$, their sizes n_k, and the reachable state space $\mathcal{S}_{rch} \subseteq \mathcal{S}$ are assumed known in the following discussion, and we let $\mathcal{S}_k = \{0, ..., n_k - 1\}$, without loss of generality. More details about our state-space generation algorithm are reviewed in Section 2.3.

2.1   Symbolic Encoding of Sets of States

Binary decision diagrams (BDDs) [2] are the most widely used data structure to store and manipulate sets of states. Instead of BDDs, we employ *multi-way decision diagrams* (MDDs) to encode sets of states. MDDs extend BDDs by allowing integer-valued variables, so that the choices for nodes at level k naturally correspond to the local states of submodel k.

Definition 1. A *quasi-reduced* MDD is an acyclic directed edge-labeled graph where:

- Each node a belongs to a level in $\{L, \cdots, 1, 0\}$, denoted by $a.lvl$.
- There is a single root node.
- The only terminal nodes are **0** and **1**, and are at level 0.
- A nonterminal node a at level k, with $L \geq k \geq 1$, has n_k outgoing edges labeled with a different integer in $\{0, ..., n_k - 1\}$. The node pointed by the edge labeled with i_k is denoted $a[i_k]$, and, if not **0**, it must be at level $k - 1$.

The set encoded by MDD node a at level $k > 1$ is then recursively defined as

$$\mathcal{B}(a) = \bigcup_{i_k \in \mathcal{S}_k} \{i_k\} \times \mathcal{B}(a[i_k]).$$

with terminal cases $\mathcal{B}(\mathbf{0}) = \emptyset$ and $\mathcal{B}(a) = \{i_1 \in \mathcal{S}_1 : a[i_1] = \mathbf{1}\}$ if $a.lvl = 1$.

2.2 Symbolic Encoding of the Next-State Functions

In a traditional symbolic approach, the next-state function $\mathcal{N}$ is encoded using a $2L$-level BDD or MDD, with levels ordered as $L, L', ..., 1, 1', 0$, where levels L through 1, corresponding to the "from" states, and levels L' through $1'$, corresponding to the "to" states, are *interleaved*. Given a next-state function $\mathcal{N}$ and a set of states $\mathcal{X}$, the image computation or *relational product* builds the set $\mathcal{N}(\mathcal{X}) = \{\mathbf{j} : \exists \mathbf{i} \in \mathcal{X}, (\mathbf{i}, \mathbf{j}) \in \mathcal{N}\}$.

A commonly employed technique is to conjunctively or disjunctively partition the next-state function encoded by a monolithic MDD into several MDDs [3,11]. For asynchronous systems, it is natural to disjunctively store each next-state function $\mathcal{N}_\alpha$, for each event $\alpha \in \mathcal{E}$, so that the overall next-state function $\mathcal{N} = \bigcup_{\alpha \in \mathcal{E}} \mathcal{N}_\alpha$ is actually never stored as a single MDD.

Locality is a fundamental property enjoyed by most asynchronous systems: an event α is *independent* of the kth submodel (or, briefly, of k) if its enabling does not depend on i_k and its firing does not change the value of i_k. A level k belongs to the *support* set of event α, denoted $supp(\alpha)$, if α is not independent of k. We define $Top(\alpha)$ and $Bot(\alpha)$ to be the maximum and minimum levels in $supp(\alpha)$, and $\mathcal{E}_k$ to be the set of events $\{\alpha \in \mathcal{E} : Top(\alpha) = k\}$. Also, we let $\mathcal{N}_k$ be the next-state function corresponding to all events in $\mathcal{E}_k$, i.e., $\mathcal{N}_k = \bigcup_{Top(\alpha)=k} \mathcal{N}_\alpha$.

In previous work [9], the locality of events is indicated by the presence of identity matrices in a *Kronecker* description of the model's next-state function. However, while the existence of a Kronecker description is not a restriction for some formalisms (e.g., ordinary Petri nets, even if extended with inhibitor and reset arcs), it does impose constraints on the decomposition granularity in others (e.g., Petri nets with arbitrary marking-dependent arc cardinalities or transition guards). [11] proposes a new encoding for the transition relation based on a disjunctive-conjunctive partition and a *fully-identity* reduction rule for MDDs. [14] compares several possible MDD reduction rules and finally adopts the *quasi-identity-fully (QIF)* reduction rule for MDDs encoding next-state functions. This

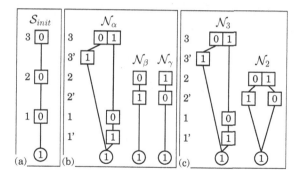

Fig. 1. An example of set and next-state function encoding using MDDs

encoding is successfully applied to saturation and allows for complex variable dependencies in asynchronous systems. A $2L$-level MDD encoding next-state function $\mathcal{N}_\alpha$ with this QIF reduction rule satisfies the following:

- The root node is at level $Top(\alpha)$, an unprimed level.
- (Interleaving) Level k is immediately followed by level k', for $L \geq k \geq 1$.
- (Quasi-reduced rule) If $k \in supp(\alpha)$, level k is present on every path in the MDD encoding $\mathcal{N}_\alpha$.
- (Identity-reduced rule) If $k \in supp(\alpha)$, level k' can be present on a path in the MDD encoding $\mathcal{N}_\alpha$, or it can be absent. In the latter case, the meaning of an edge $a[i_k] = b$, with $a.lvl = k > b.lvl$ is that a *singular* node c at level k' has been skipped, i.e., a node with $c[i_k] = b$ and $c[j_k] = \mathbf{0}$ for $j_k \in \mathcal{S}_k \setminus \{i_k\}$.
- (Fully-reduced rule) If $k \notin supp(\alpha)$, level k is absent on every path in the MDD encoding $\mathcal{N}_\alpha$. The meaning of an edge $a[i_l] = b$, with $a.lvl > k > b.lvl$ is that a *redundant* node c at level k has been skipped, i.e., a node with $c[i_k] = b$ for every $i_k \in \mathcal{S}_k$.
- (Fully-identity-reduced pattern) This is really a combination of the two preceding cases. The interpretation of an edge skipping levels k and k' (or of the root being at a level below k') is that α is independent of i_k, i.e., event α is enabled when the kth local state is i_k, for any $i_k \in \mathcal{S}_k$, and that, if α fires, the kth local state remains equal to i_k in the new state.

Figure 1(a) shows a 3-level MDD encoding an initial set of states containing a single state, $\mathcal{S}_{init} = \{000\}$. Figure 1(b) shows three MDDs encoding next-state functions for events α, β, and γ, respectively. Figure 1(c) shows the next-state functions merged by levels, $\mathcal{N}_3 = \mathcal{N}_\alpha$, $\mathcal{N}_2 = \mathcal{N}_\beta \cup \mathcal{N}_\gamma$, and $\mathcal{N}_1 = \emptyset$ (not shown). Note, for example, that $\mathcal{N}_2$ does not depend on level 1 and that the node at level $3'$ for the 1-child of the root of $\mathcal{N}_3$ is skipped due to the identity-reduced rule.

2.3   State Space Generation

All symbolic approaches to state-space generation use some variant of symbolic image computation. The simplest approach is a breadth-first iteration, directly implementing the definition of the state space $\mathcal{S}_{rch}$ as the fixpoint of the expression $\mathcal{S}_{init} \cup \mathcal{N}(\mathcal{S}_{init}) \cup \mathcal{N}^2(\mathcal{S}_{init}) \cup \mathcal{N}^3(\mathcal{S}_{init}) \cup \cdots$.

Locality and disjunctive partition of the next-state function form instead the basis is for the saturation algorithm. The key idea is to fire events node-wise, bottom-up, and exhaustively, instead of level-wise and exactly once per iteration. A node a is *saturated* if it is a fixpoint with respect to firing any event that is independent of all levels above k:

$$\forall h, k \geq h \geq 1, \forall \alpha \in \mathcal{E}_h, \mathcal{S}_L \times \cdots \times \mathcal{S}_{k+1} \times \mathcal{B}(a) \supseteq \mathcal{N}_\alpha(\mathcal{S}_L \times \cdots \times \mathcal{S}_{k+1} \times \mathcal{B}(a))$$

Starting from the MDD encoding the initial states, the nodes in the MDD are saturated in order, from the bottom level to the top level. Of course, one of the advantages of saturation is that, given the QIF reduction, the application of $\mathcal{N}_\alpha$ needs to start at level $Top(\alpha)$, and not all the way up, at the root of entire MDD. Every node is saturated before being checked in the unique table, including nodes newly created when firing an event on a node at a higher level.

2.4   CTL Model Checking

CTL is a widely used temporal logic to describe the system properties because of its simple yet expressive syntax. All CTL properties are state properties and can be checked by manipulating sets of states. It is well-known that $\{\mathsf{EX}, \mathsf{EU}, \mathsf{EG}\}$ is a complete set of operators for CTL, that is, it can be used to express any other CTL operator (for example, the EF operator is a special case of EU, since $\mathsf{EF}p \equiv \mathsf{E}true\mathsf{U}p$). The $\mathsf{EX}p$ operator can be easily computed as the relational product $\mathcal{N}^{-1}(\mathcal{P})$, where $\mathcal{P}$ is the set of states satisfying property p. Building the set of states satisfying $\mathsf{EF}p$ is instead essentially the same process as state-space generation, the only differences being that we start from $\mathcal{P}$ instead of $\mathcal{S}_{init}$ and that we go backwards instead of forwards, thus we use $\mathcal{N}^{-1}$ (or $\mathcal{N}_\alpha^{-1}$, or $\mathcal{N}_k^{-1}$, as appropriate) instead of $\mathcal{N}$.

The traditional algorithm to obtain the set of states satisfying $\mathsf{E}p\mathsf{U}q$ computes a least fixpoint (see *EUtrad* in Figure 2; all sets of states and relations over states in our pseudocode are encoded using MDDs, of course). Starting from $\mathcal{Q}$, the set of states satisfying q, it computes the intersection of the preimage of the explored states, $\mathcal{X}$, with the states in $\mathcal{P}$. The newly computed states are added to the explored states, for the next iteration. The number of iterations is thus equal to the longest path of states in $\mathcal{P} \setminus \mathcal{Q}$ reaching a state in $\mathcal{Q}$.

A saturation-based EU computation algorithm was instead proposed in [10] (see *EUsat* in Figure 2). First, it partitions the set $\mathcal{E}$ of events into safe, $\mathcal{E}_S$, and unsafe, $\mathcal{E}_U = \mathcal{E} \setminus \mathcal{E}_S$, where $\alpha \in \mathcal{E}$ is safe iff $\mathcal{N}_\alpha^{-1}(\mathcal{P} \cup \mathcal{Q}) \subseteq \mathcal{P}$, i.e., it is such that, following its firing backwards, we can only find states in $\mathcal{P}$ (alternatively, we can restrict all sets by intersecting them with the reachable states $\mathcal{S}_{rch}$ in the above test). The algorithm iteratively (1) saturates the MDD encoding the set of explored states using only safe events, then (2) fires each unsafe event once using $\mathcal{N}_U^{-1} = \bigcup_{\alpha \in \mathcal{E}_U} \mathcal{N}_\alpha^{-1}$ in breadth-first fashion, then (3) intersects the result with $\mathcal{P}$, and finally (4) adds the result to the working set $\mathcal{X}$.

$EUtrad(in\ \mathcal{P}, \mathcal{Q})$: set of state	$EUsat(in\ \mathcal{P}, \mathcal{Q})$: set of state
1 declare $\mathcal{X}$: set of states	1 declare $\mathcal{X}, \mathcal{Y}$: set of state;
2 $\mathcal{X} \leftarrow \mathcal{Q}$;	2 declare $\mathcal{E}_U, \mathcal{E}_S$: set of event;
3 repeat	3 $ClassifyEvents(\mathcal{P} \cup \mathcal{Q}, \mathcal{E}_U, \mathcal{E}_S)$
4 $\mathcal{X} \leftarrow \mathcal{X} \cup (\mathcal{N}^{-1}(\mathcal{X}) \cap \mathcal{P})$;	4 $\mathcal{X} \leftarrow \mathcal{Q}$;
5 until $\mathcal{X}$ does not change;	5 $Saturate(\mathcal{X}, \mathcal{E}_S)$
6 return $\mathcal{X}$;	6 repeat
	7 $\mathcal{Y} \leftarrow \mathcal{X}$;
$EGtrad(in\ \mathcal{P})$: set of state	8 $\mathcal{X} \leftarrow \mathcal{X} \cup (\mathcal{N}_U^{-1}(\mathcal{X}) \cap (\mathcal{P} \cup \mathcal{Q}))$
1 declare $\mathcal{X}$: set of states	9 if $\mathcal{X} \neq \mathcal{Y}$ then
2 $\mathcal{X} \leftarrow \mathcal{P}$;	10 $Saturate(\mathcal{X}, \mathcal{E}_S)$
3 repeat	11 until $\mathcal{X} = \mathcal{Y}$;
4 $\mathcal{X} \leftarrow \mathcal{X} \cap \mathcal{N}^{-1}(\mathcal{X})$;	12 return $\mathcal{X}$;
5 until $\mathcal{X}$ does not change;	
6 return $\mathcal{X}$;	

Fig. 2. Traditional and saturation-based CTL model checking algorithms

The traditional EG algorithm (see *EGtrad* in Figure 2) computes a greatest fixpoint by iteratively eliminating states without successors in the working set $\mathcal{X}$. [10] also attempts to compute set of states satisfying EGp using forward and backward EU saturation from a single state in $\mathcal{P}$. However, this approach is more efficient than the traditional algorithm only in very special cases.

3   Constrained Saturation for the **EU** Operator

The set of states satisfying EpUq is a least fixpoint, where the saturation algorithm could be efficiently employed. However, the challenge arises from the need to "filter out" the states not in $\mathcal{P}$ before exploring their predecessors. Failure to do so can results in paths which temporarily go out of $\mathcal{P}$, so that the result may include some states not satisfying EpUq. The saturation algorithm does not find states in breadth-first-search order, as the process of saturating a node often consists of firing a series of events. Performing an expensive intersection operation *after each firing* would be enormously less time and memory efficient.

The advantage of Algorithm *EUsat* [10] over *EUtrad* depends on the structure of the model. If there are no safe events with respect to a given property p, *EUsat* degrades to the simple breadth-first exploration of *EUtrad*. To overcome this difficulty, we propose two approaches, both aimed at exploring only states in $\mathcal{P}$ without requiring an expensive intersection operation after each firing.

1. Saturation with Constrained Next-State Functions. For each $\mathcal{N}_k^{-1}$, we build a *constrained inverse next-state function* $\mathcal{N}_{k,\mathcal{P}}^{-1}$ such that

$$\mathbf{j} \in \mathcal{N}_{k,\mathcal{P}}^{-1}(\mathbf{i}) \Longleftrightarrow (\mathbf{j} \in \mathcal{P}) \wedge \mathbf{j} \in \mathcal{N}_k^{-1}(\mathbf{i}).$$

Algorithm *ConsNSF* in Figure 3 builds the MDD representation of $\mathcal{N}_{\alpha,\mathcal{P}}^{-1}$.

2. Constrained Saturation. This is the main contribution of our paper. We do not explicitly constrain the next-state functions, but perform instead a "check-and-fire" step when computing the constrained preimage (function *ConsRelProd* in the pseudocode of Figure 3), based on the following observation:

$$\mathcal{B}(t) = RelProd(s,r) \cap \mathcal{B}(a) \iff \mathcal{B}(t[i']) = \bigcup_{i \in \mathcal{S}_l} RelProd(s[i], r[i][i']) \cap \mathcal{B}(a[i']), \quad (1)$$

where t and s are L-level MDDs encoding sets of states, $l = s.lvl$, and r is a $2L$-level encoding a next-state function. This can be considered as a form of *ITE* operator [2], widely used in BDD operations, but extended from boolean to integer variables. The overall process of EU computation based on constrained saturation is then shown in Figure 3. The key differences from the saturation algorithm in [9] are marked with a "⋆".

The idea of the first approach is straightforward: all constrained next-state functions $\mathcal{N}_{\alpha,\mathcal{P}}^{-1}$ are forced to be safe by definition. According to the saturation-based EU computation algorithm in Figure 2, the result is obtained in a single iteration (a single call to *Saturate*). The downside of this approach is a possible decrease in locality. A property p is *dependent* on level k if the value of i_k affects the satisfiability of p, i.e., if the (fully-reduced) encoding of p has nodes at level k. After constraining a next-state function $\mathcal{N}_\alpha$ with p, the levels on which p depends become part of the support, thus, $Top(\mathcal{N}_{\alpha,\mathcal{P}}^{-1}) = \max\{Top(\mathcal{P}), Top(\mathcal{N}_\alpha^{-1})\}$. If $\mathcal{P}$ depends on level L, all the constrained next-state functions belong to $\mathcal{E}_L^{-1}$ and the saturation algorithm degrades to BFS, losing its advantages.

The second approach, constrained saturation, does not modify the transition relation explicitly, but constrains the state exploration "on-the-fly" following the "check-and-fire" policy. This policy guarantees that the state exploration is constrained to set $\mathcal{P}$. At the same time, it retains the advantages of saturation due to exploiting event locality and employing recursive local fixpoint computations. In the pseudocode shown in the right portion of Figure 3, the "check-and-fire" policy can be summarized into two cases:

1. If $p[i] = \mathbf{0}$, $s[i]$ is kept unchanged without adding new states (line 4 in function *ConsSaturate*).
2. When computing the relational product, check whether the newly generated local state is included in p on each level (line 7 in function *ConsSaturate* and line 5 in function *ConsRelProd*). If instead $p[i'] = \mathbf{0}$ in formula (1), the relational product stops the recursive execution and returns $\mathbf{0}$.

Another tradeoff affecting efficiency is how to select the set of states $\mathcal{P}$ when checking $\mathsf{E}p\mathsf{U}q$. In high-level models, $\mathcal{P}$ is often associated with an atomic property, e.g., "place a of the Petri Net is empty" or a "localized" property dependent on just a few levels. There are then two reasonable choices to define $\mathcal{P}$:

- $\mathcal{P} = \mathcal{P}_{pot}$: include all states in the potential state space $\mathcal{S}$ that satisfy the given property, even if they are not reachable (recall that the potential state space is finite because the bound for each local state space $\mathcal{S}_k$ is known).

---

mdd $EUsatConsNSF(mdd$ $\mathcal{P},$ mdd $\mathcal{Q})$

1 foreach $\alpha \in \mathcal{E}$ do $\mathcal{N}^{-1}_{\alpha,\mathcal{P}} \leftarrow ConsNSF(\mathcal{P}, \mathcal{N}^{-1}_{\alpha})$;
2 mdd $s \leftarrow Saturate(\mathcal{Q})$;
3 $s \leftarrow intersection(s, \mathcal{S}_{rch})$;
4 return s;

---

mdd $ConsNSF(mdd$ a, mdd $r)$

1 if $a = 1$ and $r = 1$ then return 1;
2 if $InCache_{ConsNSF}(a,r,t)$ then return t;
3 mdd $t \leftarrow 0$;   level $lr \leftarrow r.lvl$;   level $la \leftarrow a.lvl$;
4 if $lr < la$ then
5   foreach $i \in \mathcal{S}_{la}$ s.t. $a[i] \neq 0$ do $t[i][i] \leftarrow ConsNSF(a[i], r)$;
6 else if $lr > la$ then
7   foreach $i, i' \in \mathcal{S}_{lr}$ s.t. $r[i][i'] \neq 0$ do $t[i][i'] \leftarrow ConsNSF(a, r[i][i'])$;
8 else   • $lr = la$
9   foreach $i, i' \in \mathcal{S}_{lr}$ s.t. $r[i][i'] \neq 0$ and $a[i'] \neq 0$ do $t[i][i'] \leftarrow ConsNSF(a[i'], r[i][i'])$;
10 $CacheAdd_{ConsNSF}(a, r, t)$;
11 return t;

---

mdd $EUconsSat(mdd$ a, mdd $b)$ • a: the constraint; b: the set being saturated

1 mdd $s \leftarrow ConsSaturate(a, b)$;
2 $s \leftarrow intersection(s, \mathcal{S}_{rch})$;
3 return s;

---

mdd $ConsSaturate(mdd$ a, mdd $s)$ • a: the constraint; s: the set being saturated

1 if $InCache_{ConsSaturate}(a, s, t)$ then return t;
2 level $l \leftarrow s.lvl$; mdd $t \leftarrow NewNode(l)$; mdd $r \leftarrow \mathcal{N}^{-1}_l$;
3 foreach $i \in \mathcal{S}_l$ s.t. $s[i] \neq 0$ do
4★   if $a[i'] \neq 0$ then $t[i] \leftarrow ConsSaturate(a[i], s[i])$;   else $t[i] \leftarrow s[i]$;
5 repeat
6   foreach $i, i' \in \mathcal{S}_l$ s.t. $r[i][i'] \neq 0$ do
7★   if $a[i'] \neq 0$ then
8   mdd $u \leftarrow ConsRelProd(a[i'], t[i], r[i][i'])$; $t[i'] \leftarrow Or(t[i'], u)$;
9 until t does not change;
10 $t \leftarrow UniqueTablePut(t)$; $CacheAdd_{ConsSaturate}(a, s, t)$;
11 return t;

---

mdd $ConsRelProd(mdd$ a, mdd s, mdd $r)$

1 if $s = 1$ and $r = 1$ then return 1;
2 if $InCache_{ConsRelProd}(a, s, r, t)$ then return t;
3 level $l \leftarrow s.lvl$; mdd $t \leftarrow 0$;
4 foreach $i, i' \in \mathcal{S}_l$ s.t. $r[i][i'] \neq 0$ do
5★   if $a[i'] \neq 0$ then
6★ mdd $u \leftarrow ConsRelProd(a[i'], s[i], r[i][i'])$;
7★   if $u \neq 0$ then
8★   if $t = 0$ then $t \leftarrow NewNode(l)$;
9★ $t[i'] \leftarrow Or(t[i'], u)$;
10 $t \leftarrow ConsSaturate(a, UniqueTablePut(t))$; $CacheAdd_{ConsRelProd}(a, s, r, t)$;
11 return t;

Fig. 3. EU computation: saturation using a constrained next-state function ($EUsatConsNSF$) and constrained saturation ($EUconsSat$)

– $\mathcal{P} = \mathcal{P}_{rch}$: include in $\mathcal{P}$ only the *reachable* states that satisfy the given property, $\mathcal{P}_{rch} = \mathcal{P}_{pot} \cap \mathcal{S}_{rch}$.

We are normally only interested in reachable states and, of course, backward state exploration from unreachable states can only lead to more unreachable states; all these unreachable states can be filtered out *after* saturation, without affecting the correctness of the result (unlike the discussion at the beginning of this section, pertaining to filtering out states not in $\mathcal{P}$). Exploration including the unreachable states might result in greater time and memory requirements, in which case using $\mathcal{P}_{rch}$ is preferable for algorithmic efficiency. On the other hand, $\mathcal{P}_{pot}$ is often dependent on very few levels, while, for most models, $\mathcal{P}_{rch}$ is a strict subset of $\mathcal{S}$, thus depends on many levels, and this increases the complexity of algorithm, especially for the first approach. In the ideal case, we can constrain the state exploration to $\mathcal{P}_{rch}$ with an acceptable overhead.

The experimental results in Section 5 demonstrate that constrained saturation using $\mathcal{P}_{rch}$ tends to perform much better than saturation with constrained next-state functions in both runtime and memory consumption. We select it as our main method to compute the EU operator, as well as the reachability relation, which we introduce in the next section.

4   Reachability Relation and the EG Operator

The EGp property describes the existence of a path in $\mathcal{P}$ from a state leading to a nontrivial strongly-connected component (SCC), where p holds in all states along the path and in the SCC. In this section, we propose a new EGp computation algorithm based on the reachability relation, built using constrained saturation.

The following defines the (backward) *reachability relation* of a set of states $\mathcal{X}$ within $\mathcal{P}$, denoted with $(\mathcal{N}_{\mathcal{X},\mathcal{P}}^{-1})^+$.

Definition 2. *Given a state* $\mathbf{i} \in \mathcal{X}$, $\mathbf{j} \in (\mathcal{N}_{\mathcal{X},\mathcal{P}}^{-1})^+(\mathbf{i})$ *iff there exists a nontrivial (i.e., positive length) forward path* π *from* $\mathbf{j}$ *to* $\mathbf{i}$ *and all states in* π *belong to* $\mathcal{P}$.

If $\mathbf{j} \in (\mathcal{N}_{\mathcal{X},\mathcal{P}}^{-1})^+(\mathbf{i})$, we know that $\mathbf{j}$ is in $\mathcal{P}$. Since it is not always necessary to compute the reachability relation for all $\mathbf{i} \in \mathcal{S}$, we can build the reachability relation starting only from states in $\mathcal{X}$, to reduce time and memory consumption.

Claim 1. If $\mathbf{j} \in (\mathcal{N}_{\mathcal{S},\mathcal{P}}^{-1})^+(\mathbf{i})$, then $\exists \mathbf{i}' \in \mathcal{N}^{-1}(\mathbf{i}) \cap \mathcal{P}$ s.t. $\mathbf{j} \in ConsSaturate(\mathcal{P}, \{\mathbf{i}'\})$.

This claim comes from the definition of constrained saturation and derives a way of building the reachability relation efficiently. Starting from the MDD encoding $\mathcal{N}^{-1}$, appropriately restricted to a set of states (e.g., $\mathcal{P}$), we compute the constrained saturation for states encoded at the primed levels. Analogous to constrained saturation, this process can be performed bottom-up recursively on each level.

Claim 2. EGp holds in state $\mathbf{j}$ iff $\exists \mathbf{i} \in \mathcal{P}$ s.t. $\mathbf{i} \in (\mathcal{N}_{\mathcal{P},\mathcal{P}}^{-1})^+(\mathbf{i})$ and $\mathbf{j} \in (\mathcal{N}_{\mathcal{P},\mathcal{P}}^{-1})^+(\mathbf{i})$.

From this claim, we can obtain an algorithm to compute the set of states satisfying EGp. Given a 2L-level MDD encoding the reachability relation, it is easy to obtain the set of states $\mathcal{S}_{scc} = \{\mathbf{i} : \mathbf{i} \in (\mathcal{N}_{\mathcal{P},\mathcal{P}}^{-1})^+(\mathbf{i})\}$. These states belong to SCCs where property $\mathcal{P}$ holds continuously. Then, the result of EGp can be obtained computing $RelProd(\mathcal{S}_{scc}, (\mathcal{N}_{\mathcal{P},\mathcal{P}}^{-1})^+)$.

Building the reachability relation is a time and memory intensive task, constituting the bottleneck for our new EG algorithm. On the other hand, the reachability relation contains more information than the basic EG property and has further applications. We discuss one of them: EG computation under a weak fairness constraint. Fairness is widely used in formal specification of protocols; in particular, weak fairness specifies that there is an infinite execution on which some states, say in $\mathcal{F}$, appear infinitely often. The difficulty lies in that the fact that executions in SCCs which do not contains states in $\mathcal{F}$ must be eliminated to guarantee the fairness, and the traditional EG algorithm cannot handle this problem. However, this extension is easy in our framework, as discussed next.

Claim 3. EGp under weak a fairness constraint $\mathcal{F}$ holds in state $\mathbf{j}$ iff $\exists \mathbf{i} \in \mathcal{F}$ s.t. $\mathbf{i} \in (\mathcal{N}_{\mathcal{F}\cap\mathcal{P},\mathcal{P}}^{-1})^+(\mathbf{i})$ and $\mathbf{j} \in (\mathcal{N}_{\mathcal{F}\cap\mathcal{P},\mathcal{P}}^{-1})^+(\mathbf{i})$.

Since $\mathbf{i} \in \mathcal{F}$, the SCCs containing such a state satisfy the fairness constraint. We only need to build reachability relation on these states. An interesting point is that many fewer state pairs are in $(\mathcal{N}_{\mathcal{F}\cap\mathcal{P},\mathcal{P}}^{-1})^+$ than in $(\mathcal{N}_{\mathcal{P},\mathcal{P}}^{-1})^+$. Although, in symbolic approaches, fewer states do not always lead to smaller MDDs, thus lower time and memory requirements, it is often the case in our framework that considering fairness will reduce the runtime, which is quite the opposite than in traditional approaches.

5   Experimental Results

We implemented the proposed approach in SMART [5] and report on experiments run on an Intel Xeon 3.0Ghz workstation with 3GB RAM under SuSE Linux 9.1. Detailed descriptions of the models we use in the experiments can be found in the SMART User Manual [4]. The state space size for each model is controlled by a parameter N. For comparison, we study each model in both SMART and NuSMV version 2.4.3 [1].

5.1   Results for the EU Computation

Table 1 shows the results for each EU query. The runtime (seconds), final (mem-f) and peak memory (mem-p) consumption (Kbytes) required by NuSMV, the old version of SMART [10], and our new approach are shown in the corresponding columns, fo reach model. We compare the following five approaches:

- *BFS*: the traditional EU algorithm implemented in SMART
- *ConNSFSat-$\mathcal{P}_{pot}$*: Saturation using constrained next-state functions, where the next-state functions are constrained using $\mathcal{P}_{pot}$
- *ConNSFSat-$\mathcal{P}_{rch}$*: Saturation using constrained next-state functions, where the next-state functions are constrained using $\mathcal{P}_{rch}$.
- *ConSat-$\mathcal{P}_{pot}$*: Constrained saturation with $\mathcal{P}_{pot}$.
- *ConSat-$\mathcal{P}_{rch}$*: Constrained saturation with $\mathcal{P}_{rch}$.

Table 1. Results for the EU computation

| | NuSMV [1] | | OldSmart [10] | | | BFS | | | SMART | | | | | | | | | | | |
| | | | | | | | | | ConsNSFSat-P_{pot} | | | ConsNSFSat-P_{rch} | | | ConsSat-P_{pot} | | | ConsSat-P_{rch} | | |
Model	sec	KB(f)	sec	KB(f)	KB(p)	sec	KB(f)	KB(p)	sec	KB(f)	KB(p)	sec	KB(f)	KB(p)	sec	KB(f)	KB(p)	sec	KB(f)	KB(p)
leader									$E(pref_1 = 0)U(status_0 = leader)$											
5	44.1	62,057	9.8	163	6,998	1.6	3,112	6,539	28.8	632	809	1.1	1,351	2,375	17.6	544	776	1.2	602	728
6	304.8	180,988	296.1	463	40,429	8.3	12,175	24,080	2,022.5	1,283	2,328	19.8	3,153	8,046	1,032.9	1,473	2,284	14.9	1,054	1,337
7	1,791.5	666,779	—			39.8	44,551	91,466	—			347.3	8,726	23,332	—			114.9	2,078	2,616
8	—		—			371.5	171,867	277,649	—			—			—			4,058.2	4,110	5,139
phil.									$E(phil_1 \neq eat)U(phil_0 = eat)$											
50	1,644.2	75,282	< 0.1	73	287	4.7	3,248	4,586	< 0.1	464	465	0.2	1,117	1,591	0.2	436	436	< 0.1	435	435
100			0.2	147	872	60.6	7,141	16,446	0.2	861	864	0.8	3,119	4,907	0.4	817	843	0.3	816	841
500			2.9	740	16,082	—			0.3	3,837	3,870	160.7	52,447	87,791	0.7	3,856	3,885	0.4	3,850	3,876
1,000			4.1	1,036	30,707	—			0.6	5,262	5,269	1,228.2	100,516	164,137	4.8	7,589	7,697	0.8	5,253	5,271
robin									$E(p_1 \neq load)U(p_0 = send)$											
10	29.2	70,583	5.1	186	4,447	0.1	494	574	< 0.1	92	92	< 0.1	204	204	< 0.1	90	90	< 0.1	64	64
20						1.4	3,088	3,738	< 0.1	283	317	< 0.1	598	659	0.1	312	312	< 0.1	166	166
100						—			5.7	14,272	14,274	636.1	17,398	30,833	3.6	15,899	15,907	< 0.1	4,269	4,298
200						—			163.1	105,787	105,788	—			111.6	119,988	119,988	0.4	28,781	28,790
fms									$E(M_1 > 0)U(P_1s = P_2s = P_3s = N)$											
10	578.9	181,353	0.1	27	628	5.2	35,979	35,980	0.4	407	477	43.2	993	2,965	< 0.1	257	288	< 0.1	256	286
25			1.6	155	8,223	—			31.5	638	1,362	—			1.8	981	1,107	1.9	977	1,104
50			24.0	812	75,884	—			2,566.3	1,449	6,972	—			39.1	1,247	6,018	40.5	1,246	6,006
100						—			—			—			1,128.0	4,302	40,588	1,200.9	4,299	40,504
queens									$E(p[N-1][N]=1)U(p[N-1][N]=0)$											
10	15.3	77,861				1.1	9,744	9,744	< 0.1	2,728	2,728	< 0.1	1,899	1,899	0.2	3,532	3,532	< 0.1	1,841	1,841
11	84.0	327,907				7.2	41,252	41,252	0.5	12,445	12,445	0.1	7,289	7,312	1.6	15,877	15,877	< 0.1	7,043	7,062
12	595.1	1,355,128				237.2	186,360	186,360	2.3	52,764	52,765	0.7	80,785	80,859	9.1	75,347	75,347	< 0.1	29,714	29,763
13						—			10.9	236,501	236,506	6.1	166,711	166,837	86.9	337,265	337,265	< 0.1	133,121	133,121

Our main method, constrained saturation using $\mathcal{P}_{rch}$, outperforms (sometimes by orders-of-magnitude) NuSMV and other methods in both time and memory. In comparison with NuSMV, the saturation-based methods excel because of the local fixpoint iteration scheme. The improvement of our new work over our old approach [10] can be attributed to both the MDD encoding of the next-state function and the more advanced saturation schemes.

Overall, *ConSat* requires less runtime as well as memory than *ConNSFSat*, because the constrained next-state functions often impose overhead on relational product operations. The difference between the results of *ConNSFSat*-$\mathcal{P}_{pot}$ and *ConNSFSat*-$\mathcal{P}_{rch}$ shows the tradeoff discussed at the end of Section 3. *ConSat* constrained with $\mathcal{P}_{rch}$ is more advantageous than with $\mathcal{P}_{pot}$ because *ConSat* is not sensitive to the complexity of the constraint set due to our lightweight "check-and-fire" policy. The reduction in state exploration becomes the dominant factor for efficiency.

5.2   Results for the **EG** Computation

Table 2 compares the results of NuSMV, BFS (SMART-BFS) and the method in Section 4 (SMART-RchRel) for EG computation with or without fairness constraints. For BFS, the number of iterations is listed in column *itr*.

Without fairness, traditional BFS (in NuSMV or SMART-BFS) is often orders-of-magnitude faster than our algorithm based on the reachability relation. This result is not surprising due to the time and memory complexity of building the reachability relation, even if this is done using saturation.

Another experiment is provided to show the merit of our algorithm. We build a simple model with a long path from an SCC where EGp holds to a terminal state, with p holding on every state on this path. We parameterize the length of

Table 2. Results for the EG computation

Model	EG query									Fairness				
	NuSMV			SMART-BFS			SMART-RchRel			NuSMV		SMART-RchRel		
	sec	KB(f)	itr	sec	KB(f)	KB(p)	sec	KB(f)	KB(p)	sec	KB	sec	KB(f)	KB(p)
leader	EG($status_0 \neq leader$)									$pref_0 = 1$				
3	0.2	9,308	14	0.1	139	196	4.9	934	1,115	0.6	11,428	0.02	266	268
4	3.0	50,187	18	<0.1	400	436	791.6	5,999	7,225	11.2	49,655	207.4	5,271	6,394
phil.	EG($phil_0 \neq eat$)									$phil_0 = has\_left\_fork$				
10	0.1	7,193	4	<0.1	95	95	0.1	170	170	0.2	8,447	<0.1	113	113
50	3.0	50,187	4	<0.1	220	241	0.2	682	682	1,244.5	75,274	<0.1	393	399
100	–	–	4	0.1	444	562	1.1	1,180	1,191	–	–	0.1	704	705
robin	EG($true$)									$p1 = Ask$				
10	2.3	70,581	1	<0.1	86	86	0.1	437	437	73.5	73,145	<0.1	222	222
50	–	–	1	0.1	1,263	1,263	4.8	15,676	15,676	–	–	0.3	1,902	1,902
100	–	–	1	1.0	7,688	7,688	53.9	100,719	102,941	–	–	1.5	9,317	9,317
fms	EG¬($P_1s = P_2s = P_3s = N$)									$P_1s = N$				
5	0.8	18,474	1	<0.1	61	135	1.9	1,022	1,024	2.5	35,238	0.27	419	475
10	16.5	60,559	1	<0.1	128	220	1,062.4	4,338	6,231	191.8	62,188	77.7	607	1,050
kanban	EG($P_1out > 0 \vee P_2out > 0 \vee P_3out > 0 \vee P_4out > 0$)									$P_1out = N$				
8	2.1	42,925	1	<0.1	279	415	1,131.1	1,949	2,714	2.2	43,511	6.2	1,303	1,486
10	4.4	58,693	1	<0.1	529	930	–	–	–	4.6	58,705	27.0	2,507	2,939

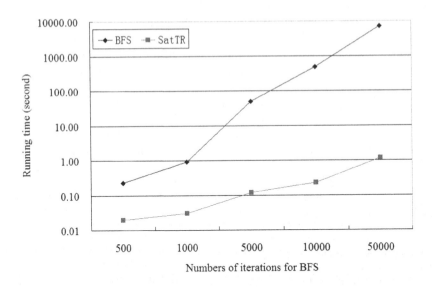

Fig. 4. EG computation based on BFS v.s. reachability relation

the path to control the number of iterations which a traditional EG algorithm will require to reach the fixpoint. For different numbers of iterations, from 500 to 50,000, we compare the runtimes (in seconds) of traditional (BFS) search and our algorithm (SatTR) in Figure 4. As the number of iterations grows, the runtime of our algorithm grows much slower than that of the traditional algorithm, due to the efficient state exploration scheme in constrained saturation.

If we consider fairness, as discussed in Section 4, the time and memory complexity of building the reachability relation is often reduced, while that of the traditional algorithm in NuSMV increases. The advantage of our algorithm is observable in this case, especially for some complex models which are not manageable in NuSMV.

6   Conclusion and Future Work

In this paper, we focus on symbolic CTL model checking based on the idea of the saturation algorithm. To constrain state exploration in a given set of states, we present a constrained saturation algorithm. The "check-and-fire" policy filters out the states not in the given set when saturating MDD nodes recursively. For the EG operator, we first symbolically build the reachability relation, using constrained saturation, then compute the set of states satisfying EGp. We discuss desirable properties of our new EU and EG algorithms and analyze a set of experimental results.

Constrained saturation enables building the reachability relation for some complex systems. The application of the reachability relation can be further extended to SCC construction, a basic problem in emptiness checking for Büchi automata. Another future work is to reduce the cost of building the reachability relation. For SCC enumeration, $\mathcal{X}$ in $R_{\mathcal{X},\mathcal{S}}^{+}$ can be refined to reduce the computation complexity.

References

1. NuSMV: a new symbolic model checker, `http://nusmv.irst.itc.it/`
2. Bryant, R.E.: Graph-based algorithms for boolean function manipulation. IEEE Transactions on Computers 35(8), 677–691 (1986)
3. Burch, J.R., Clarke, E.M., Long, D.E.: Symbolic model checking with partitioned transition relations. In: Halaas, A., Denyer, P.B. (eds.) Int. Conference on Very Large Scale Integration, Edinburgh, Scotland, August 1991. IFIP Transactions, pp. 49–58. North-Holland, Amsterdam (1991)
4. Ciardo, G., et al.: SMART: Stochastic Model checking Analyzer for Reliability and Timing, User Manual, `http://www.cs.ucr.edu/~ciardo/SMART/`
5. Ciardo, G., Jones, R.L., Miner, A.S., Siminiceanu, R.: Logical and stochastic modeling with SMART. Perf. Eval. 63, 578–608 (2006)
6. Ciardo, G., Luettgen, G., Miner, A.S.: Exploiting interleaving semantics in symbolic state-space generation. Formal Methods in System Design 31, 63–100 (2007)
7. Ciardo, G., Lüttgen, G., Siminiceanu, R.: Saturation: An efficient iteration strategy for symbolic state space generation. In: Margaria, T., Yi, W. (eds.) TACAS 2001. LNCS, vol. 2031, pp. 328–342. Springer, Heidelberg (2001)
8. Ciardo, G., Marmorstein, R., Siminiceanu, R.: Saturation unbound. In: Garavel, H., Hatcliff, J. (eds.) TACAS 2003. LNCS, vol. 2619, pp. 379–393. Springer, Heidelberg (2003)
9. Ciardo, G., Marmorstein, R., Siminiceanu, R.: The saturation algorithm for symbolic state space exploration. Software Tools for Technology Transfer 8(1), 4–25 (2006)
10. Ciardo, G., Siminiceanu, R.: Structural symbolic CTL model checking of asynchronous systems. In: Hunt Jr., W.A., Somenzi, F. (eds.) CAV 2003. LNCS, vol. 2725, pp. 40–53. Springer, Heidelberg (2003)
11. Ciardo, G., Yu, A.J.: Saturation-based symbolic reachability analysis using conjunctive and disjunctive partitioning. In: Borrione, D., Paul, W. (eds.) CHARME 2005. LNCS, vol. 3725, pp. 146–161. Springer, Heidelberg (2005)
12. Cimatti, A., Clarke, E., Giunchiglia, E., Giunchiglia, F., Pistore, M., Roveri, M., Sebastiani, R., Tacchella, A.: NuSMV Version 2: An OpenSource Tool for Symbolic Model Checking. In: Brinksma, E., Larsen, K.G. (eds.) CAV 2002. LNCS, vol. 2404, p. 359. Springer, Heidelberg (2002)
13. McMillan, K.L.: Symbolic Model Checking: An Approach to the State Explosion Problem. PhD thesis, School of Computer Science, Carnegie Mellon University, Pittsburgh, PA (May 1992), CMU-CS-92-131
14. Wan, M., Ciardo, G.: Symbolic state-space generation of asynchronous systems using extensible decision diagrams. In: Nielsen, M., Kucera, A., Miltersen, P.B., Palamidessi, C., Tuma, P., Valencia, F.D. (eds.) SOFSEM 2009. LNCS, vol. 5404, pp. 582–594. Springer, Heidelberg (2009)

LTL Model Checking for Recursive Programs

Geng-Dian Huang[1], Lin-Zan Cai[1], and Farn Wang[1,2]

[1] Dept. of Electrical Engineering, National Taiwan University
[2] Grad. Inst. of Electronic Engineering, National Taiwan University

Abstract. We propose a complete algorithm to model check LTL (Linear Temporal Logic) formulas with recursive programs. Our program models are control flow graphs extended with procedure calls. The LTL formulas may then be used to specify constraints on the global variables and the local variables in the current scope. Our algorithm is based on semi-symbolic simulation of control-flow graphs to search for counter-examples. We apply post-dominance relation to reduce the number of the exploration traces. The existence of counter-examples is reduced to Boolean satisfiability while the termination of the exploration is reduced to Boolean unsatisfiability. We report our implementation and experiment.

1 Introduction

For finite-state systems, the *LTL (Linear Temporal Logic) model checking* problem can be reduced to the problem of finding a loop, which is a counter-example for an LTL property, in a given state graph [15]. Likewise, for a recursive program, the corresponding problem can also be reduced to the problem of finding a loop in a given *control-flow graph* [7] extended with procedure calls. Such a loop corresponds to either a repetition of state sequences or a divergent recursive procedure invocation sequence. An *execution* of a recursive program can be characterized by a *state sequence*. Conceptually, a *state* is a tuple (g, Ω) where g is a valuation of global variables and Ω is a stack. A stack element consists of a location n in a control-flow graph and a valuation l of local variables. An execution forms a *loop* if (i) the valuation of global variables in the head is the same as that in the tail, (ii) the top of the stack in the head is the same as that of the tail, and (iii) the stack height of the head is the lowest in the program trace. Conditions (i) and (ii) identify a possible loop. Condition (iii) ensures that the loop is genuine, i.e., it can be repeated for infinitely many times.

Based on the dataflow algorithm in [13], we propose an algorithm to model check LTL formulas for recursive programs. We employ the *semi-symbolic simulation technique* [2], i.e., constructing a simulation tree by unfolding the control-flow graphs and record program variables symbolically in every tree node. For each tree path, a Boolean formula can be constructed to check the loop conditions. Note that we do not record the stack in tree nodes. Instead, we use the *summary* techniques to bypass procedure-call and return pairs [4]. Condition (iii) is assured by the construction of the simulation tree. To manage the complexity of formula construction, instead of constructing a whole formula for

Z. Liu and A.P. Ravn (Eds.): ATVA 2009, LNCS 5799, pp. 382–396, 2009.
© Springer-Verlag Berlin Heidelberg 2009

satisfiability checking, we present techniques to incrementally construct intermediate formulas using semi-symbolic simulation. Without recording the stack explicitly in tree nodes, each tree path has a loop diameter. We can construct another Boolean formula to check if the loop diameter is reached. Our algorithm terminates if either a counter-example is found or all tree paths reach their loop diameters.

The size of a simulation tree grows exponentially to the number of branches in a program. To reduce the size of the simulation tree, we propose to join the branches in the post-dominators. The post-dominance relation is widely used in the static analysis of programs[9]. In our experiment, the sizes of simulation trees were reduced effectively.

In section 2 reviews related work. Section 3 defines the problem of LTL model-checking with recursive programs. Section 4 explains semi-symbolic simulation [2]. Section 5 presents our LTL model-checking algorithm. Section 6 reports our experiment. Finally, section 7 concludes this work.

2   Related Work

By generalizing a dataflow algorithm [13], Ball et al. proposed a reachability analysis algorithm for recursive programs in [4]. They used BDDs (binary decision diagrams) to record *summaries* that represent pairs of program states before and after a procedure call. Based on [4], Basler et al. also proposed a reachability algorithm for recursive programs [3]. To handle recursion, they used QBF (Quantified Boolean Formulas) solvers to compute summaries. SAT solvers can replace the QBF solvers by representing the summaries in Boolean formulas which encode program traces of sufficient recursive depths and sufficient lengths [2,14]. In contrast to above work, we consider the LTL model-checking problem. Our algorithm extends the summary technique in searching for counter-examples for LTL formulas.

Esparza et al.[6] proposed an algorithm to model check LTL formulas with pushdown automata. Instead of recording summaries of procedures, their algorithm works on *head reachability graphs*. A *head* consists of a pushdown automaton state and the top symbol on the corresponding stack. In a head reachability graph, a head h connects to a head h' if there is a valid program trace from h to h'. A loop in the head reachability graph corresponds to a counter-example for the corresponding LTL formula. Esparza et al. also extended the technique to model check LTL formulas with Boolean programs [7]. Program states correspond to heads and program transition relations are encoded with BDDs in the head reachability graph. SAT-based algorithms have been shown useful for the approach [5]. In contrast, we encode the head reachability relation with a Boolean formula and reduce the loop search to Boolean satisfiability.

Huang and Wang [11] used SAT solvers to model-check the universal fragment of alternation-free μ-calculus formulas on context-free processes by encoding the local model checking algorithm in [12]. The formalization of context-free processes does not have variables. It blows up the model size to encode variables in context-free processes.

3   Problem Definition

In section 3.1, we introduce our model language, *control-flow graphs*. In section 3.2, we briefly explain *LTL (Linear Temporal Logic)* as our specification language. In LTL model checking, Büchi automatas are used to express LTL formulas [15]. In section 3.3, we define our problem in terms of control flow graphs and Büchi automatas.

3.1   Control Flow Graph with Procedure-Calls

Assume that a program P consists of a set of procedures $p_0, \ldots, p_m$, where p_0 is the main procedure. We consider variables of Boolean type. Let $\mathbb{B} = \{true, false\}$ be the domain of a Boolean variable. For simplicity, assume that all procedures have the same set of variables. Let V_G and V_L be the set of global variables and local variables. Let G and L denote the domain of global variables $\mathbb{B}^{|V_G|}$ and the domain of local variables $\mathbb{B}^{|V_L|}$ respectively. In the sequel, we use g and l to denote a valuation of V_G and of V_L respectively. Let $R = 2^{(G \times L \times G \times L)}$ be all possible transition relations. A transition relation defines the pre-condition and post-condition of a program statement. The mapping from program statements to transition relations can be found in [4]. Given a transition relation $r \in R$, we write $r(g, l, g', l')$ for $(g, l, g', l') \in r$. We model a procedure by a control-flow graph. Let $\mathcal{G}_i$ be the control-flow graph for p_i.

Definition 1. *For a procedure p_i in a program, its control-flow graph $\mathcal{G}_i$ is a directed graph $(N_i, E_i, \Delta_i, callee_i, \varsigma_i, e_i)$ where*

- *N_i is the set of nodes,*
- *$E_i \subseteq N_i \times N_i$ is the set of edges,*
- *$\Delta_i : E_i \mapsto R$ labels edges with transition relations,*
- *$callee_i \subseteq E_i \mapsto P$ labels edges with callees,*
- *$\varsigma_i, \epsilon_i \in N_i$ are the entry node and the exit node.*

Let $succ_{E_i}(n) = \{n' \mid (n, n') \in E_i\}$ denote the successors of n in E_i. E_i can be partitioned into a set of *intraprocedural* edges $E_i^{\rightarrow}$ and a set of *call-to-return* edges $E_i^{\frown}$. An intraprocedural edge e is labelled with the transition relation $\Delta_i(e)$. A call-to-return edge e represents a procedure call to procedure $callee_i(e)$. Assume that $e = (n, n')$ and $callee_i(e) = p_j$. n is a call-location and n' is a return-location. Given e, let $e^{\nearrow}$ denote the call-to-entry edge (n, ς_j) and $e^{\searrow}$ denote the exit-to-return edge (ϵ_j, n'). Assume that the passing-parameters and return values are stored by auxiliary global variables. We label $e^{\nearrow}$ with transition relation $r^{\nearrow} = \{(g, l, g, l') \mid g \in G, l \in L, l' \in L\}$ and label $e^{\searrow}$ with $r^{\searrow} = \{(g, l, g, l') \mid g \in G, l \in L, l' \in L\}$. There is no constraint on l and l' because the scope of V_L is limited to a procedure. In the sequel, we will show the valuation of V_L in the call-location n is the same as the one in the return-location n'.

Given the control-flow graphs, the program P can be represented as a control-flow graph $(N, E, \Delta, callee, s, e)$ that is the combination of the the control-flow graphs for $p_0, \ldots, p_m$ defined as follows. Let $N = \bigcup_i N_i$, $E^{\rightarrow} = \bigcup_i E_i^{\rightarrow}$, $E^{\frown} =$

$\bigcup_i E_i^\frown$, $E^\nearrow = \{e^\nearrow \mid e \in E^\frown\}$, $E^\searrow = \{e^\searrow \mid e \in E^\frown\}$, and $E = E^\rightarrow \cup E^\frown \cup E^\nearrow \cup E^\searrow$. Let $\Delta(e) = \Delta_i(e)$ for $e \in E_i^\rightarrow$ and $\Delta(e) = \{(g, l, g, l') \mid g \in G, l \in L, l' \in L\}$ for $e \in E^\nearrow \cup E^\searrow$. Let $callee(e) = callee_i(e)$ for $e \in E_i^\frown$. We may write $callee(e)$ as $callee(n, n')$ for $e = (n, n')$. A *program state* is a tuple $\langle n, g, l \rangle$ where $n \in N$ is a location, $g \in G$ is a valuation of global variables, and $l \in L$ is a valuation of local variables. We characterize the executions of the program P as *program traces*. A program trace is a sequence of program states $\langle n_1, g_1, l_1 \rangle \langle n_2, g_2, l_2 \rangle \ldots \langle n_m, g_m, l_m \rangle$ that fulfills the following constraints.

- For each consecutive pair of program states $\langle n_i, g_i, l_i \rangle$ and $\langle n_{i+1}, g_{i+1}, l_{i+1} \rangle$, $\langle n_i, g_i, l_i \rangle$ transits to $\langle n_{i+1}, g_{i+1}, l_{i+1} \rangle$ via edge $e_i = (n_i, n_{i+1})$, which is either an intraprocedural edge, a call-to-entry edge, or an exit-to-return edge.
- Each transition relation $\Delta(e_i) = r_i$ is fulfilled, i.e., $r_i(g_i, l_i, g_{i+1}, l_{i+1})$. Moreover, assume that e_i is a call-to-entry edge and ϵ_j is the corresponding exit-to return edge. The valuation of V_L in n_i is the same as the one in n_{j+1}, i.e., $l_i = l_{j+1}$, since a procedure calls only affect the valuations of global variables.
- The sequence of edges $e_1 e_2 \ldots e_{m-1}$ can be derived from the non-terminal symbol `valid` in the grammar in table 1.

Table 1. Context-free Grammar for Program Traces

valid ::= match | match $e_1^\nearrow$ valid
match ::= ε | $e_1^\rightarrow$ match | (n, ς_i) match (ϵ_i, n') match

Here $e_1^\nearrow \in E^\nearrow$ is a procedure-call transition edge. ε is a null sequence. $e_1^\rightarrow \in E^\rightarrow$ is an intraprocedural transition edge. (n, ς_i) and (ϵ_i, n') are a pair of matching procedure-call transition and procedure-return transition such that there is an $e = (n, n')$ and $callee(e) = p_i$. That is, a program trace must be context-sensitive [13]. The grammar rule for non-terminal `match` specifies that in a trace, transitions for procedure-entries and procedure-exits must match in a nested fashion. The program trace is *matched* if `match` can derive $e_1 e_2 \ldots e_{m-1}$.

The language of a program P, denoted by $\mathcal{L}(P)$, is the set of program traces.

3.2 LTL and Büchi Automata

We use LTL (Linear Temporal Logic) as our specification language for program traces. An LTL formula is constructed on top of atomic propositions for program states. Consider a program with a set of locations N and a set of Boolean variables $V_G \cup V_L$. We define the following atomic propositions for program states: $loc = n$, $v = true$, $v = false$, $true$, and $false$, where $n \in N$ and $v \in V_G \cup V_L$. $loc = n$ asserts that the location of a program state is n. v, as a proposition, asserts that the value of v is $true$. Let AP be the set of atomic propositions. A state predicate is a combination of atomic propositions with Boolean operators $\neg$, $\vee$, and $\wedge$. Let Ψ denote the set of state predicates. A program state $\langle n, g, l \rangle$ satisfies a state predicate ψ, $\langle n, g, l \rangle \models \psi$, if and only if ψ is evaluated $true$ according to $\langle n, g, l \rangle$.

Definition 2. *Suppose we are given a set AP of atomic propositions. An LTL formula φ is inductively defined with the following rule.*

$$\varphi ::= \alpha | \neg\varphi | \varphi_1 \vee \varphi_2 | \bigcirc \varphi | \varphi_1 U \varphi_2$$

$\alpha \in AP$ is an atomic proposition. "$\bigcirc\varphi$" means "φ is true on the next state". "$\varphi_1 U \varphi_2$" means "From now on, φ_1 is always true until φ_2 is true". "$\Diamond\varphi$" is the abbreviation of "$trueU\varphi$", which means "From now on, φ is eventually true". "$\Box\varphi$" is the abbreviation of "$\neg\Diamond\neg\varphi$", which means "From now on, φ is always true".

Given an LTL formula φ, we use $\mathcal{L}(\varphi)$ to denote the set of program traces satisfying φ. For LTL model checking, usually we convert LTL formulas to Büchi automata [10] with the same program traces.

Definition 3. *A Büchi automata $\mathcal{B}$ is a tuple (Q, δ, q_0, F) where*

- *Q is a finite set of states,*
- *$\delta \subseteq Q \times \Psi \times Q$ defines a finite set of transitions,*
- *q_0 is the initial state, and*
- *F is a set of final states.*

Given a $(q, \psi, q') \in \delta$ and a program state $\langle n, g, l \rangle$, we write $q \xrightarrow{\langle n,g,l \rangle} q'$ if $\langle n, g, l \rangle$ satisfies ψ. A *run* is a sequence of the form $q_1 \xrightarrow{\langle n_1,g_1,l_1 \rangle} q_2 \xrightarrow{\langle n_2,g_2,l_2 \rangle} \ldots \xrightarrow{\langle n_m,g_m,l_m \rangle} q_{m+1}$. The *word* of the run is the sequence of program states $\langle n_1, g_1, l_1 \rangle \langle n_2, g_2, l_2 \rangle \ldots \langle n_m, g_m, l_m \rangle$ of the run. Note that a word needs not be a program trace. An infinite run ρ is *accepting* if and only if it starts from q_0 and it visits a final state infinitely often. That is, ρ contains a loop which visits a final state. $\mathcal{B}$ accepts a sequence of program states w if and only if there is an accepting run whose word is w. The language of $\mathcal{B}$, denoted by $\mathcal{L}(\mathcal{B})$, is the sequences of program states accepted by $\mathcal{B}$.

3.3   LTL Model Checking Problem

A program P satisfies an LTL formula φ, denoted by $P \models \varphi$, if and only if $\mathcal{L}(P)$ is included in the sequences specified by φ. For verifying $P \models \varphi$, we negate φ and construct a Büchi automata $\mathcal{B}_{\neg\varphi}$, which accepts the sequences of program states not specified by φ. $P \models \varphi$ if and only if $\mathcal{L}(P) \cap \mathcal{L}(\mathcal{B}_{\neg\varphi}) = \emptyset$.

Given a program $P = \{p_0, \ldots, p_m\}$ and a Büchi automata $\mathcal{B} = (Q, \delta, q_0, F)$, we can simulate P and $\mathcal{B}$ concurrently to verify $\mathcal{L}(P) \cap \mathcal{L}(\mathcal{B}) = \emptyset$. A simulation state $\langle q, n, g, l \rangle$ records a state $q \in Q$ and a program state $\langle n, g, l \rangle$. A simulation state $\langle q, n, g, l \rangle$ is final if $q \in F$. Let $\mapsto$ denote the transition relation of simulation states. we have $\langle q, n, g, l \rangle \mapsto \langle q', n', g', l' \rangle$ if and only if $q \xrightarrow{\langle n,g,l \rangle} q'$ and $(g, l, g', l') \in \Delta(n, n')$. A *simulation trace* is a sequence of the form $\langle q_1, n_1, g_1, l_1 \rangle \mapsto \langle q_2, n_2, g_2, l_2 \rangle \mapsto \ldots \mapsto \langle q_m, n_m, g_m, l_m \rangle$ where $\langle n_1, g_1, l_1 \rangle$ $\langle n_2, g_2, l_2 \rangle \ldots \langle n_m, g_m, l_m \rangle$ is a program trace. The simulation trace is matched if $\langle n_1, g_1, l_1 \rangle \langle n_2, g_2, l_2 \rangle \ldots \langle n_m, g_m, l_m \rangle$ is matched. A tuple $(\langle \varsigma_i, g, l \rangle, \langle \epsilon_i, g', l' \rangle)$ is a *summary* of procedure p_i if there is a matched simulation trace from the $\langle \varsigma_i, g, l \rangle$ to $\langle \epsilon_i, g', l' \rangle$, where ς_i and ϵ_i are the entry location and exit location respectively. Assume $(n, n') \in E^{\rightarrow} \cup E^{\nearrow} \cup E^{\frown}$. A simulation state $\langle q, n, g, l \rangle$ can *reach* another simulation state $\langle q', n', g', l' \rangle$, denoted by $\langle q, n, g, l \rangle \Rightarrow \langle q', n', g', l' \rangle$, if either one of the following conditions holds.

- $(n, n') \in E^{\rightarrow} \cup E^{\nearrow}$ and $\langle q, n, g, l \rangle \mapsto \langle q', n', g', l' \rangle$.
- $(n, n') \in E^{\frown}$ and there is a matched simulation trace:
  $$\langle q, n, g, l \rangle \mapsto \langle q_1, n_1, g_1, l_1 \rangle \mapsto \ldots \mapsto \langle q_m, n_m, g_m, l_m \rangle \mapsto \langle q', n', g', l' \rangle$$
  such that $callee(n, n') = p_i$, $n_1 = \varsigma_i$, and $n_m = \epsilon_i$.
  Here, $(\langle q_1, n_1, g_1, l_1 \rangle, \langle q_m, n_m, g_m, l_m \rangle)$ is a summary of procedure p_i.

We write $\langle q, n, g, l \rangle \overset{true}{\Rightarrow} \langle q', n', g', l' \rangle$ if either $q \in F$ or $\exists 1 \le i \le m.q_i \in F$. That is, $\langle q, n, g, l \rangle$ reaches $\langle q', n', g', l' \rangle$ via a simulation trace which visits a final simulation state. Otherwise, we write $\langle q, n, g, l \rangle \overset{false}{\Rightarrow} \langle q', n', g', l' \rangle$. A *reachability path* is a sequence of the form $\langle q_1, n_1, g_1, l_1 \rangle \Rightarrow \langle q_2, n_2, g_2, l_2 \rangle \Rightarrow \ldots \Rightarrow \langle q_m, n_m, g_m, l_m \rangle$. Intuitively, the stack height of the program is monotonic increasing in a reachability path. A reachability path is matched if the stack height is not increasing, i.e., $\forall (n_i, n_{i+1}) \in E^{\rightarrow} \cup E^{\frown}$. Let $\Rightarrow^+$ denote the transitive closure, and let $\Rightarrow^*$ denote the reflexive transitive closure. If $\langle q_1, n_1, g_1, l_1 \rangle \overset{b_1}{\Rightarrow} \ldots \overset{b_{m-1}}{\Rightarrow} \langle q_m, n_m, g_m, l_m \rangle$, we have $\langle q_1, n_1, g_1, l_1 \rangle \overset{b_1 \vee \ldots \vee b_{m-1}}{\Rightarrow}{}^+ \langle q_m, n_m, g_m, l_m \rangle$. For verifying $\mathcal{L}(P) \cap \mathcal{L}(\mathcal{B}) = \emptyset$, we have the following theorem.

Theorem 1. *[7]* $\mathcal{L}(P) \cap \mathcal{L}(\mathcal{B}) \ne \emptyset$ *if and only if* $\exists g_0, l_0, \langle q, n, g, l \rangle$. $\langle q_0, \varsigma_0, g_0, l_0 \rangle \Rightarrow^* \langle q, n, g, l \rangle \overset{true}{\Rightarrow}{}^+ \langle q, n, g, l \rangle$.

Intuitively, the program trace accepted by both P and $\mathcal{B}$ shall be able to loop. The stack height at the second occurrence of $\langle q, n, g, l \rangle$ is higher or equal to that at the second occurrence of $\langle q, n, g, l \rangle$. The program trace can loop.

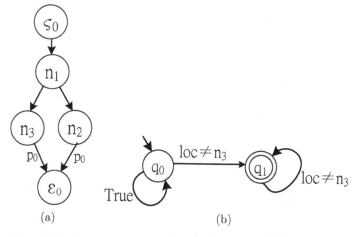

Fig. 1. (a)Control flow graph of p_0 (b) Büchi automaton $\mathcal{B}_{\Diamond \Box (loc \ne n_3)}$

Now, we show an example of $P \models \Box\Diamond(loc = n_3)$, which checks if n_3 is entered infinitely often. Assume that $P = \{p_0\}$ and we give the control flow graph of p_0 in Fig 1(a). ς_0 is the entry node, and ϵ_0 is the exit node. Location n_1 branches to location n_2 and location n_3. (n_2, ϵ_0) and (n_3, ϵ_0) are call-to-return edges, which represent procedure calls to p_0 itself. In Fig 1(b), we show a Büchi automaton $\mathcal{B}_{\Diamond\Box(loc \neq n_3))}$, where $\Diamond\Box(loc \neq n_3)) = \neg(\Box\Diamond(loc = n_3))$. By simulating P and B concurrently, we can find out a reachability path: $\langle q_0, \varsigma_0, true, true \rangle \overset{false}{\Rightarrow}$ $\langle q_1, n_1, true, true \rangle \overset{true}{\Rightarrow} \langle q_1, n_2, true, true \rangle \overset{true}{\Rightarrow} \langle q_1, \varsigma_0, true, true \rangle \overset{true}{\Rightarrow} \langle q_1, n_1, true, true \rangle$. The state $\langle q_1, n_1, true, true \rangle$ reoccurs in the reachability path so that we can infer that $\mathcal{L}(P) \cap \mathcal{L}(\mathcal{B}) \neq \emptyset$ according to the Theorem 1, and it implies $P \not\models \Box\Diamond(loc = n_3)$.

4   Semi-symbolic Simulation

Suppose a program $P = \{p_0, \ldots, p_k\}$ and a Büchi automata $\mathcal{B} = (Q, \delta, q_0, F)$. We semi-symbolic simulate P and $\mathcal{B}$ concurrently. That is, we explicitly simulate on the locations while keeping the states Q and the program variables symbolically. We use a set of Boolean variables V_Q to encode the set of states Q. That is, each state is represented by a unique valuation of V_Q. We write $[q]$ to denote the valuation for a specific state q. Let $\bar{v}$ denote a set of Boolean variables. Let $\bar{q}$, $\bar{g}$, and $\bar{l}$ be of size $|V_Q|$, $|V_G|$, and $|V_L|$ respectively. We give the definition of semi-symbolic states in definition 4.

Definition 4. *A semi-symbolic state is a tuple $\langle \bar{q}, n, \bar{g}, \bar{l} \rangle$ in which we keep a location n and sets of Boolean variables $\bar{q}$, $\bar{g}$, and $\bar{l}$.*

A semi-symbolic state $\langle \bar{q}, n, \bar{g}, \bar{l} \rangle$ can represent a set of simulation states with the same location n. An assignment π on a set of Boolean variables $\bar{v}$ is a mapping from $\bar{v}$ to $\mathbb{B}$. Let $||\bar{v}||_\pi \in \mathbb{B}^{|\bar{v}|}$ denote the valuation of $\bar{v}$ according to the assignment π. Given an assignment π of $(\bar{q} \cup \bar{g} \cup \bar{l})$, $\langle ||[\bar{q}]||_\pi, n, ||[\bar{g}]||_\pi, ||[\bar{l}]||_\pi \rangle$ is a simulation state. Let $||\langle \bar{q}, n, \bar{g}, \bar{l} \rangle||_\pi$ denote $\langle ||[\bar{q}]||_\pi, n, ||[\bar{g}]||_\pi, ||[\bar{l}]||_\pi \rangle$. Assume $\sigma = \langle \bar{q}, n, \bar{g}, \bar{l} \rangle$ and $\sigma' = \langle \bar{q}', n', \bar{g}', \bar{l}' \rangle$. Let $eq(\sigma, \sigma')$ denote a Boolean formula which is satisfied by an assignment π if and only if $||[\sigma]||_\pi = ||[\sigma']||_\pi$. Let $[F](\bar{q})$ be a Boolean formula which is satisfied by an assignment π if and only if $||[\bar{q}]||_\pi \in F$. Let $\tau(\sigma, \sigma')$ be the characteristic function for transition relation of simulation states. $\tau(\sigma, \sigma')$ is satisfied by an assignment π if and only if $||[\sigma]||_\pi \mapsto ||[\sigma']||_\pi$. The construction for these Boolean formulas is straightforward and is skipped here.

Definition 5. *A semi-symbolic state $\langle \bar{q}, n, \bar{g}, \bar{l} \rangle$ can reach another semi-symbolic state $\langle \bar{q}', n', \bar{g}', \bar{l}' \rangle$, denoted by $\langle \bar{q}, n, \bar{g}, \bar{l} \rangle \hookrightarrow \langle \bar{q}', n', \bar{g}', \bar{l}' \rangle$, if and only if $(n, n') \in E^\to \cup E^\nearrow \cup E^\frown$.*

We define the reachability relation for semi-symbolic states in definition 5. Compare with the definition for simulation states, we only check the locations since we only keep the locations explicitly in semi-symbolic states. Assuming $\sigma = \langle \bar{q}, n, \bar{g}, \bar{l} \rangle$ and $\sigma' = \langle \bar{q}', n', \bar{g}', \bar{l}' \rangle$. we define a Boolean formula $T(\sigma, b, \sigma')$ in table 4. Intuitively, $T(\sigma, b, \sigma')$ is the characteristic function for the reachability relation of simulation states. $T(\sigma, b, \sigma')$ is satisfied by an assignment π if and only if $||[\sigma]||_\pi \overset{||[b]||_\pi}{\Rightarrow} ||[\sigma']||_\pi$. That is,

- $(n, n') \in E^\rightarrow \cup E^\nearrow$ and $||[\sigma]||_\pi \mapsto ||[\sigma']||_\pi$, or
- $(n, n') \in E^\frown$, $callee(n, n') = p_i$, and there is a matched simulation trace $||[\sigma]||_\pi \mapsto \langle q_\varsigma, \varsigma_i, g_\varsigma, l_\varsigma \rangle \mapsto \ldots \mapsto \langle q_\epsilon, \epsilon_i, g_\epsilon, l_\epsilon \rangle \mapsto ||[\sigma']||_\pi$.

Moreover, $||[b]||_\pi = true$ if and only if $||[\bar{q}]||_\pi \in F$ or $\exists 1 \leq i \leq m.||[\bar{q}_i]||_\pi \in F$, and $||[b]||_\pi = false$ otherwise. For the case $(n, n') \in E^\frown$, $T(\sigma, b, \sigma')$ is defined on $\Sigma(\sigma_\varsigma, b', \sigma_\epsilon)$. Intuitively, $\Sigma(\sigma_\varsigma, b', \sigma_\epsilon)$ encodes the *summary* [2,14] of procedure p_i. By the definition, $\Sigma(\sigma_\varsigma, b', \sigma_\epsilon)$ is satisfied by an assignment π if and only if there is a matched reachability path from $||[\sigma_\varsigma]||_\pi$ to $||[\sigma_\epsilon]||_\pi$. That is, there is a matched simulation trace $\langle q_\varsigma, \varsigma_i, g_\varsigma, l_\varsigma \rangle \mapsto \ldots \mapsto \langle q_\epsilon, \epsilon_i, g_\epsilon, l_\epsilon \rangle$ where $||[\sigma_\varsigma]||_\pi = \langle q_\varsigma, \varsigma_i, g_\varsigma, l_\varsigma \rangle$ and $||[\sigma_\epsilon]||_\pi = \langle q_\epsilon, \epsilon_i, g_\epsilon, l_\epsilon \rangle$. Moreover, $||[b']||_\pi = true$ if and only if the matched simulation trace visits a final simulation state, and $||[b']||_\pi = false$ otherwise.

Table 2. Definitions of $T(\sigma, b, \sigma')$ and $\Sigma(\sigma, b, \sigma')$

$$T(\sigma, b, \sigma') \triangleq \begin{cases} \tau(\sigma, \sigma') \wedge b \Leftrightarrow [F](\bar{q}) & \text{if } (n, n') \in E^\rightarrow \cup E^\nearrow \\ \tau(\sigma, \sigma_\varsigma) \wedge \Sigma(\sigma_\varsigma, b', \sigma_\epsilon) \wedge \tau(\sigma_\epsilon, \sigma') \wedge b & \\ \Leftrightarrow ([F](\bar{q}) \vee b' \vee [F](\bar{q}_\epsilon)) & \text{if } (n, n') \in E^\frown \end{cases}$$

where $callee(n, n') = p_i$, $\sigma_\varsigma = \langle \bar{q}_\varsigma, \varsigma_i, \bar{g}_\varsigma, \bar{l}_\varsigma \rangle$, and $\sigma_\epsilon = \langle \bar{q}_\epsilon, \epsilon_i, \bar{g}_\epsilon, \bar{l}_\epsilon \rangle$.

$$\Sigma(\sigma, b, \sigma') \triangleq \begin{cases} eq(\sigma, \sigma') \wedge b \Leftrightarrow false & \text{if } n = n' \\ \bigvee_{1 \leq i \leq m} T(\sigma, b_i, \sigma_i) \wedge \Sigma(\sigma_i, b'_i, \sigma') \wedge b \Leftrightarrow (b_i \vee b'_i) & \text{if } n \neq n' \end{cases}$$

where $succ(n) = \{n_1, \ldots, n_m\}$ and $\sigma_i = \langle \bar{q}_i, n_i, \bar{g}_i, \bar{l}_i \rangle$

Definition 6. *A* semi-symbolic path *is a sequence of the form* $\sigma_1 \hookrightarrow \sigma_2 \hookrightarrow \ldots \hookrightarrow \sigma_m$.

Given a semi-symbolic path $\sigma_1 \hookrightarrow \sigma_2 \hookrightarrow \ldots \hookrightarrow \sigma_m$, we define the following Boolean formula to check the existence of loops.

$$\chi_{Loop}(\sigma_1, \sigma_2, \ldots, \sigma_m) \triangleq \bigwedge_{1 \leq i < m} T(\sigma_i, b_{\sigma_i \sigma_{i+1}}, \sigma_{i+1}) \wedge$$
$$\bigvee_{1 \leq i < j \leq m} (eq(\sigma_i, \sigma_j) \wedge \bigvee_{i \leq k < j} b_{\sigma_k \sigma_{k+1}}).$$

Intuitively, the satisfiability of $\chi_{Loop}(\sigma_1, \sigma_2, \ldots, \sigma_m)$ is corresponding to the existence of loop. $\chi_{Loop}(\sigma_1, \sigma_2, \ldots, \sigma_m)$ is satisfied by an assignment π if and only if there is a reachability path $||[\sigma_1]||_\pi \Rightarrow ||[\sigma_2]||_\pi \Rightarrow \ldots \Rightarrow ||[\sigma_m]||_\pi$ such that $\exists i, j.||[\sigma_i]||_\pi = ||[\sigma_j]||_\pi$ and $\exists k.b_{\sigma_k \sigma_{k+1}}$. We also define the following Boolean formula to check if the loop diameter is reached.

$$\chi_{Diameter}(\sigma_1, \sigma_2, \ldots, \sigma_m) \triangleq \bigwedge_{1 \leq i < m} T(\sigma_i, b_{\sigma_i \sigma_{i+1}}, \sigma_{i+1}) \wedge$$
$$\bigwedge_{1 \leq i < j \leq m} \neg eq(\sigma_i, \sigma_j).$$

The unsatisfiability of $\chi_{Diameter}(\sigma_1, \sigma_2, \ldots, \sigma_m)$ is corresponding to that the loop diameter is reached.

Construction of $T(\sigma, b, \sigma')$ *and* $\Sigma(\sigma, b, \sigma')$. We construct the Boolean formulas $T(\sigma, b, \sigma')$ and $\Sigma(\sigma, b, \sigma')$ inductively. We define a set of equations which can represent a Boolean formula. The LHS (left-hand-side) of an equation is a *term* of the form $T(\sigma, b, \sigma')$ and $\Sigma(\sigma, b, \sigma')$. **Note** that we interpret $T(\sigma, b, \sigma')$ and $\Sigma(\sigma, b, \sigma')$ as terms instead of Boolean formulas in the sequel. According to table 4, we define the LHS term by the RHS (right-hand-side) in which there may be other terms.

We illustrate the construction by example. $T(\sigma, b, \sigma') = \tau(\sigma, \sigma_\varsigma) \wedge \Sigma(\sigma_\varsigma, b', \sigma_\epsilon)$ $\wedge \tau(\sigma_\epsilon, \sigma') \wedge b \Leftrightarrow ([F](\bar{q}) \vee b' \vee [F](\bar{q}_\epsilon))$ is an equation for defining $T(\sigma, b, \sigma')$ and there is a term $\Sigma(\sigma_\varsigma, b', \sigma_\epsilon)$ in the RHS. In turn, we define an equation for $\Sigma(\sigma_\varsigma, b', \sigma_\epsilon)$. We iteratively define a set of equations Φ for $T(\sigma, b, \sigma')$. Let $Undef(\Phi)$ denote the terms which only appear in the LHS of equations. Intuitively, if a term $t \in Undef(\Phi)$, t is undefined. We can solve the set of equations by SAT solvers. The set of solutions for $T(\sigma, b, \sigma') \wedge \Phi$ over-approximates the set of solutions for the Boolean formula $T(\sigma, b, \sigma')$. In contrast, the set of solutions for $T(\sigma, b, \sigma') \wedge \Phi \wedge \bigwedge_{t \in Undef(\Phi)} \neg t$ is an under-approximation. With sufficient equations, the set of solutions for $T(\sigma, b, \sigma') \wedge \Phi$ and $T(\sigma, b, \sigma') \wedge \Phi \wedge \bigwedge_{t \in Undef(\Phi)} \neg t$ reach a fix-point, which is equivalent to the set of solutions for the Boolean formula $T(\sigma, b, \sigma')$[14].

5   Model Checking Algorithm

Suppose a program $P = \{p_0, \dots, p_k\}$ and a Büchi automata $\mathcal{B} = (Q, \delta, q_0, F)$. We construct a simulation tree to enumerate possible semi-symbolic paths. The simulation tree is constructed by unfolding the control flow graphs and by *instantiating* semi-symbolic states for the locations. An instantiation for a location n is a semi-symbolic state $\langle \bar{q}, n, \bar{g}, \bar{l} \rangle$, where $\bar{q}'$, $\bar{g}$, and $\bar{l}'$ are new sets of Boolean variables serve as a copy of V_G, V_Q, and V_L respectively. A tree node is a semi-symbolic state. A tree node $\langle \bar{q}, n, \bar{g}, \bar{l} \rangle$ has a child $\langle \bar{q}', n', \bar{g}', \bar{l}' \rangle$ if $(n, n') \in E^\rightarrow \cup E^\nearrow \cup E^\frown$. A tree node $\langle \bar{q}, n, \bar{g}, \bar{l} \rangle$ has no child if n is an exit location. A tree path in the simulation tree is a semi-symbolic path.

Example 1. In Fig 2(a), we give the control flow graph of a procedure p_0 The entry node ς_0 branches to location n_1 and location n_2. (n_1, ϵ_0) is a call-to-return edge, which represents a procedure call to p_0 itself. In Fig 2(b), we give the simulation tree constructed by unfolding the control flow graph. A node with double circles is leaf in the simulation tree.

Given a simulation tree, we define a set of equations. Let $\sigma = \langle \bar{q}, n, \bar{g}, \bar{l} \rangle$ and $\sigma' = \langle \bar{q}', n', \bar{g}', \bar{l}' \rangle$. For each tree edge (σ, σ'), we define an equation ϕ for $T(\sigma, b_{\sigma\sigma'}, \sigma')$ according to table 4. If $(n, n') \in E^\rightarrow \cup E^\nearrow$, it is straightforward to define ϕ as $T(\sigma, b_{\sigma\sigma'}, \sigma') = \tau(\sigma, \sigma') \wedge b_{\sigma\sigma'} \Leftrightarrow [F](\bar{q})$. If $(n, n') \in E^\frown$, ϕ depends on a summary of procedure $callee(n, n') = p_k$. Since $(n, n') \in E^\frown$, we have $(n, \varsigma_k) \in E^\nearrow$. Assume that σ has a child $\sigma_\varsigma = \langle \bar{q}_\epsilon, \varsigma_k, \bar{g}_\epsilon, \bar{l}_\epsilon \rangle$. We instantiate a semi-symbolic state $\sigma_\epsilon = \langle \bar{q}_\epsilon, \epsilon_k, \bar{g}_\epsilon, \bar{l}_\epsilon \rangle$ for the exit location ϵ_k. We define ϕ as $T(\sigma, b_{\sigma\sigma'}, \sigma') = \tau(\sigma, \sigma_\varsigma) \wedge \Sigma(\sigma_\varsigma, b_{\sigma_\varsigma \sigma_\epsilon}, \sigma_\epsilon) \wedge \tau(\sigma_\epsilon, \sigma') \wedge b_{\sigma\sigma'} \Leftrightarrow ([F](\bar{q}) \vee b_{\sigma_\varsigma, \sigma_\epsilon} \vee [F](\bar{q}_\epsilon))$.

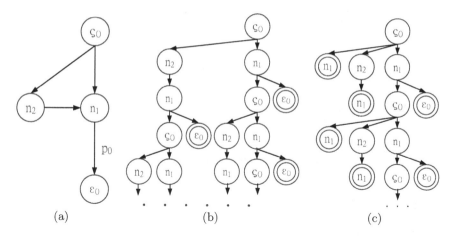

Fig. 2. (a)Control flow graph of p_0 (b)Simulation tree (c)Simulation tree applying immediately post-dominance relation

Let $\sigma_\varsigma = \langle \bar{q}_\varsigma, \varsigma_k, \bar{g}_\varsigma, \bar{l}_\varsigma \rangle$ and $\sigma_\epsilon = \langle \bar{q}_\epsilon, \epsilon_k, \bar{g}_\epsilon, \bar{l}_\epsilon \rangle$. For a summary $\Sigma(\sigma_\varsigma, b_{\sigma_\varsigma \sigma_\epsilon}, \sigma_\epsilon)$, we define a set of equations. For each tree node $\sigma = \langle \bar{q}, n, \bar{g}, \bar{l} \rangle$ reachable from σ_ς without visiting an entry location, we define an equation ϕ for $\Sigma(\sigma, b_{\sigma \sigma_\epsilon}, \sigma_\epsilon)$. Assume $n \neq \epsilon_k$ and σ has m children $\sigma_1, \ldots, \sigma_m$ where $\sigma_i = \langle \bar{q}_i, n_i, \bar{g}_i, \bar{l}_i \rangle$ and n_i is not an entry location. We define ϕ as $\Sigma(\sigma, b_{\sigma \sigma_\epsilon}, \sigma_\epsilon) = \bigvee_{1 \leq i \leq m} T(\sigma, b_{\sigma \sigma_i}, \sigma_i) \wedge \Sigma(\sigma_i, b_{\sigma_i \sigma_\epsilon}, \sigma_\epsilon) \wedge b \Leftrightarrow (b_{\sigma \sigma_i} \vee b_{\sigma_i \sigma_\epsilon})$. If $n = \epsilon_k$, σ is an instantiation for the exit location ϵ_k and the valuation of σ shall be the same as the valuation of σ_ϵ. We define ϕ as $\Sigma(\sigma, b_{\sigma \sigma_\epsilon}, \sigma_\epsilon) = eq(\sigma, \sigma_\epsilon) \wedge b_{\sigma \sigma_\epsilon} \Leftrightarrow false$.

Algorithm. We list our algorithm in table 5. We construct a simulation tree G and define a set of equations Φ on the fly. The worklist wl is used to record current leafs. In each iteration, we pop a leaf $\sigma = \langle \bar{q}, n, \bar{g}, \bar{l} \rangle$ from the worklist. We expand the simulation tree from σ and define an equation $\phi_{T(\sigma, b_{\sigma \sigma'}, \sigma')}$ for $T(\sigma, b_{\sigma \sigma'}, \sigma')$ for each new edge (σ, σ'). After the expansion, we check if $\Sigma(\sigma, b_{\sigma \sigma_\epsilon}, \sigma_\epsilon) \in Undef(\Phi)$. If so, we need define an equation $\phi_{\Sigma(\sigma, b_{\sigma \sigma_\epsilon}, \sigma_\epsilon)}$ for $\Sigma(\sigma, b_{\sigma \sigma_\epsilon}, \sigma_\epsilon)$. Then, we check all semi-symbolic paths in the simulation tree to find looping reachability path. Let $\varrho \in G$ denote that ϱ is a path from the root to a leaf in the simulation tree G. We define a Boolean formula

$$\Xi^-(G, \Phi) \triangleq \bigvee_{\varrho \in G} \chi_{Loop}(\varrho) \wedge \Phi \wedge \bigwedge_{t \in Undef(\Phi)} \neg t.$$

The satisfiability of $\Xi^-(G, \Phi)$ is corresponding to the existence of looping reachability paths. We have the following lemma.

Lemma 1. $\Xi^-(G, \Phi)$ *is satisfiable eventually if and only if* $\exists g_0, l_0, \langle q, n, g, l \rangle.$
$\langle q_0, \varsigma_0, g_0, l_0 \rangle \Rightarrow^* \langle q, n, g, l \rangle \overset{true^+}{\Rightarrow} \langle q, n, g, l \rangle.$

Table 3. Bounded Model Checking Algorithm

1: $G = \emptyset; \Phi = \emptyset; wl = \{\langle [q_0], \varsigma_0, \bar{q}, \bar{l} \rangle\}$.
2: **while** $wl \neq \emptyset$ **do**
3:    $wl = wl \setminus \sigma$, where $\sigma = \langle \bar{q}, n, \bar{g}, \bar{l} \rangle$
4:    **for** each $(n, n') \in E^{\rightarrow} \cup E^{\nearrow} \cup E^{\frown}$ **do**
5:       instantiate a semi-symbolic state $\sigma' = \langle \bar{q}', n', \bar{g}', \bar{l}' \rangle; wl = wl \cup \{\sigma'\}$
6:       $G = G \cup \{(\sigma, \sigma')\}$
7:       $\Phi = \Phi \cup \{\phi_{T(\sigma, b_{\sigma\sigma'}, \sigma')}\}$
8:    **end for**
9:    **if** $\Sigma(\sigma, b_{\sigma\sigma_\epsilon}, \sigma_\epsilon) \in Undef(\Phi)$ **then**
10:       $\Phi = \Phi \cup \{\phi_{\Sigma(\sigma, b_{\sigma\sigma_\epsilon}, \sigma_\epsilon)}\}$
11:    **end if**
12:    **if** $\Xi^-(G, \Phi)$ is satisfiable **then**
13:       print $\mathcal{L}(P) \cap \mathcal{L}(\mathcal{B}) \neq \emptyset$; exit
14:    **else if** $\Xi^+(G, \Phi)$ is unsatisfiable **then**
15:       print $\mathcal{L}(P) \cap \mathcal{L}(\mathcal{B}) = \emptyset$; exit
16:    **end if**
17: **end while**

We can stop a semi-symbolic path if it has reached its loop diameter. Otherwise, we shall continue to expand the semi-symbolic path. Our algorithm terminates if no semi-symbolic paths needs expansion. We define a Boolean formula

$$\Xi^+(G, wl) \triangleq \bigvee_{\varrho \in G} \chi_{Diameter}(\varrho) \wedge \Phi.$$

The unsatisfiability of $\Xi^+(G, \Phi)$ is corresponding to the absence of semi-symbolic paths which need expansion. In other words, our algorithm can terminate. We have the following lemma.

Lemma 2. $\Xi^+(G, wl)$ *is unsatisfiable eventually if and only if* $\nexists g_0, l_0, \langle q, n, g, l \rangle$.
$\langle q_0, \varsigma_0, g_0, l_0 \rangle \Rightarrow^* \langle q, n, g, l \rangle \overset{true^+}{\Rightarrow} \langle q, n, g, l \rangle$.

Applying Post-dominance Relation. Consider a control-flow graph $\mathcal{G} = (N, E, \Delta,$ callee, $s, e)$. A location n is *post-dominated* by a location n', denoted by $n \rightrightarrows n'$, if and only if all paths from n to e must visit n'. A location n is *immediately post-dominated* by a location n' if and only if $n \rightrightarrows n'$, and there is no location n'' such that $n \rightrightarrows n''$ and $n'' \rightrightarrows n'$. Given a location n, let $ipd(n)$ denote the location which immediately post-dominates n.

While program variables are kept symbolic, the locations are still explicitly tracked in simulation. The size of the simulation tree grows exponentially to the number of branches in a program. To reduce the size of the simulation tree, we join the branches at immediately post-dominators and continue to unfold the control flow graphs from the immediately post-dominators.

Example 2. Follow Example 1. The location ς_0 has two branches and has a immediately post-dominator n_1. In Fig 2(c), we give the simulation tree applied the immediately post-dominance relation. We stop these two branches at n_1. We add an additional edge (ς_0, n_1) (in the right-most side) and continue to unfold the control flow graphs from the n_1.

Consider a tree node $\sigma = \langle \bar{q}, n, \bar{g}, \bar{l} \rangle$ and assume that n has more than one successors. We instantiate a semi-symbolic state $\sigma_{ipd} = \langle \bar{q}_{ipd}, ipd(n), \bar{g}_{ipd}, \bar{l}_{ipd} \rangle$ for the immediately post-dominator $ipd(n)$ and add an edge $(\sigma, sigma_{ipd})$. For the edge $(\sigma, sigma_{ipd})$, we define an equation $T(\sigma, b_{\sigma\sigma_{ipd}}, \sigma_{ipd}) = \Sigma(\sigma, b_{\sigma\sigma_{ipd}}, \sigma_{ipd})$. Intuitively, $T(\sigma, b_{\sigma\sigma_{ipd}}, \sigma_{ipd})$ shall be satisfied by an assignment π if there is a matched reachability path from $|[\sigma]|_{\pi}$ to $|[\sigma_{ipd}]|_{\pi}$. It is equivalent to $\Sigma(\sigma, b_{\sigma\sigma_{ipd}}, \sigma_{ipd})$. For each node σ' in the branches, we define an equation for $\Sigma(\sigma', b_{\sigma'\sigma_{ipd}}, \sigma_{ipd})$ according to table 4. Assume that there is a function term $\Sigma(\sigma, b_{\sigma\sigma_{\epsilon}}, \sigma_{\epsilon}) \in Undef(\Phi)$. We change the equation for $\Sigma(\sigma, b_{\sigma\sigma_{\epsilon}}, \sigma_{\epsilon})$ to $\Sigma(\sigma, b_{\sigma\sigma_{\epsilon}}, \sigma_{\epsilon}) = T(\sigma, b_{\sigma\sigma_{ipd}}, \sigma_{ipd}) \wedge T(\sigma_{ipd}, b_{\sigma_{ipd}\sigma_{\epsilon}}, \sigma_{\epsilon})$ since we join the branches at $ipd(n)$.

6   Experiments

Given a program $P = \{p_0, \ldots, p_k\}$ and an LTL formula φ, we have implemented our model checking algorithm to verify $P \models \varphi$. In our implementation, we construct the Büchi automata $\mathcal{B}_{\neg\varphi}$ for the negation of φ by LTL2BA[10] and solve instances of Boolean satisfiability by Zchaff solver. We collect our data in a 1.6 GHz Intel machine with 1Gb memory.

In figure 3, we show the growth of tree size on a quicksort program [7]. We construct the simulation tree in the breadth-first order and record the number of tree nodes in each iteration. As can been seen, the growth of tree size is smooth when applying the post-dominance relation. In the $25th$ iteration, the simulation tree is constructed completely with 1682 tree nodes. Without applying the post-dominance relation, the growth of tree size is rapid and the algorithm ran out of memory in the $17th$ iteration.

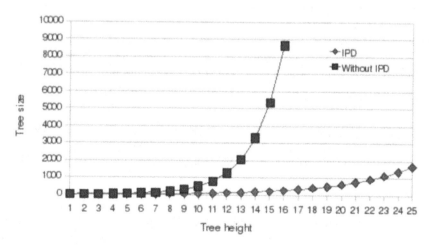

Fig. 3. Tree Size Comparison of IPD and without IPD

Table 4. Performance Comparison

#procedure/	liveness				safety			
avg. #location	ans.	moped	lmc	IPD	ans.	moped	lmc	IPD
3/1k	No	0.04	0.03	0.04	Yes	0.02	0.08	0.02
4/2k	No	0.06	0.13	0.09	No	0.12	0.02	0.11
5/4k	No	0.09	0.16	0.10	Yes	0.14	1.70	0.09
6/8k	No	0.26	0.52	0.26	Yes	0.44	6.82	0.27
7/16k	No	0.93	1.42	0.71	No	1.98	3.79	4.88
8/32k	No	14.87	6.61	2.49	No	28.32	6.88	3.04
9/64k	No	18.99	7.82	3.01	No	37.90	7.87	2.96
10/128k	No	361.47	37.46	13.24	No	O/M	42.70	17.96

moped: BDD-based model-checker. lmc: SAT-based model-checker.
O/M: out of memory

Table 5. Profiling Data

#process/ avg.	liveness				safety			
#location	lmc		IPD		lmc		IPD	
	create	solve	create	solve	create	solve	create	solve
3/1k	<0.01	<0.01	<0.01	<0.01	0.03	<0.01	<0.01	<0.01
4/2k	<0.01	<0.01	<0.01	<0.01	<0.01	<0.01	0.01	0.03
5/4k	<0.01	<0.01	<0.01	<0.01	1.22	0.24	<0.01	0.01
6/8k	<0.01	<0.01	<0.01	<0.01	4.04	2.24	<0.01	0.01
7/16k	<0.01	<0.01	<0.01	<0.01	1.89	0.31	0.04	4.01
8/32k	<0.01	<0.01	<0.01	<0.01	0.47	0.83	0.01	0.25
9/64k	<0.01	<0.01	<0.01	<0.01	0.04	<0.01	0.01	0.07
10/128k	0.32	0.04	0.01	0.02	3.09	0.31	0.75	5.18

(execution time in seconds)

Table 6. SAT Comparison

#procedure/	liveness		safety	
avg. #location	lmc	IPD	lmc	IPD
3/1k	105/349	106/270	3013/13100	251/447
4/2k	176/632	70/168	1772/8402	2529/3424
5/4k	481/2019	164/322	29407/135576	370/657
6/8k	93/297	106/270	134441/619434	1471/2036
7/16k	196/722	70/168	11564/68900	104813/68656
8/32k	316/1295	122/268	11453/55430	14313/14414
9/64k	387/1528	120/234	1544/6950	5576/9277
10/128k	10463/44562	2435/4112	84382/383924	191320/ 303415

(number of Boolean variables/number of clauses are listed)

In table 4, we compare our algorithm with a BDD-based algorithm [7] and a SAT-based algorithm [11] on randomly generated programs [11]. A location is either sequential, branching, or looping with probabilities 0.6, 0.2, and 0.2 respectively. A procedure may be called with probability 0.2 on a sequential location. We checked a liveness property and a safety property on the generated programs. The liveness property asserts that a random location of the main procedure is reachable. The safety property asserts that a random procedure is never called, i.e., ς_i is not reachable. As can be seen, our algorithm outperforms the other two for most cases. For the larger cases (8/32k, 9/64k, 10/128k), our algorithm uses less than half the time consumed by the other algorithms.

In table 5, we give the profiling data of our algorithm and the SAT-based algorithm. We measure the time for creating instances of Boolean satisfiability and the time for solving the instances[1]. Our algorithm uses less time in creating instances of Boolean satisfiability. For the cases 7/16k and 10/128k, our algorithm uses longer time in solving the instances of Boolean satisfiability. To investigate the reason, we measure the number of Boolean variables and the number of clauses in the instances of Boolean satisfiability. We show the result in table 6. As can been seen, our algorithm creates more variables and clauses for the cases 7/16k and 10/128k. It may affect the performance of the SAT solver. We believe that Further investigation is helpful to reduce the size of the instances of Boolean satisfiability.

7 Conclusions

We propose an algorithm to model check LTL formulas with recursive programs. We search counter-examples based on the semi-symbolic simulation technique. The post-dominance relation is applied to prune the search space. The experiment result suggests that the post-dominance relation is helpful. The experiment result also shows that our algorithm outperforms other algorithm in some cases. We would like to conduct more experiments to compare our algorithm with the algorithm in [11] in the future.

There are many strategies to search counter-examples, i.e., construct the simulation tree. In our preliminary implementation, we adopt breadth-first strategy. We believe that the performance can be improved with sophisticated strategies.

References

1. Burch, J.R., Clarke, E.M., McMillan, K.L., Dill, D.L., Hwang, L.J.: Symbolic Model Checking: 10^{20} States and Beyond. IEEE LICS (1990)
2. Basler, G., Kroening, D., Weissenbacher, G.: SAT-based Summarization for Boolean Programs. In: Bošnački, D., Edelkamp, S. (eds.) SPIN 2007. LNCS, vol. 4595, pp. 131–148. Springer, Heidelberg (2007)
3. Basler, G., Kroening, D., Weissenbacher, G.: A Complete Bounded Model Checking Algorithm for Pushdown Systems. In: Yorav, K. (ed.) HVC 2007. LNCS, vol. 4899, pp. 202–217. Springer, Heidelberg (2008)
4. Ball, T., Rajamani, S.: Bebop: A symbolic model checker for boolean programs. In: Havelund, K., Penix, J., Visser, W. (eds.) SPIN 2000. LNCS, vol. 1885. Springer, Heidelberg (2000)

---

[1] The rest time is used in reading inputs and building models.

5. Biere, A., Cimatti, A., Clarke, E.M., Fujita, M., Zhu, Y.: Symbolic model checking using SAT procedures instead of BDDs. In: DAC, pp. 317–320. ACM Press, New York (1999)

6. Esparza, J., Hansel, D., Rossmanith, P., Schwoon, S.: Efficient algorithms for model checking pushdown systems. In: Emerson, E.A., Sistla, A.P. (eds.) CAV 2000. LNCS, vol. 1855, pp. 232–247. Springer, Heidelberg (2000)

7. Esparza, J., Schwoon, S.: A BDD-based model checker for recursive programs. In: Berry, G., Comon, H., Finkel, A. (eds.) CAV 2001. LNCS, vol. 2102, pp. 324–336. Springer, Heidelberg (2001)

8. Ivancic, F., Yang, Z., Ganai, M., Gupta, A., Shlyakhter, I., Ashar, P.: F-Soft: Software Verification Platform. In: Etessami, K., Rajamani, S.K. (eds.) CAV 2005. LNCS, vol. 3576, pp. 301–306. Springer, Heidelberg (2005)

9. Gupta, R.: Generalized Dominators and Post-dominators. In: ACM Symp. on Principles of Programming Languages, pp. 246–257 (1992)

10. Gastin, P., Oddoux, D.: Fast LTL to Bchi Automata Translation. In: Berry, G., Comon, H., Finkel, A. (eds.) CAV 2001. LNCS, vol. 2102, pp. 53–65. Springer, Heidelberg (2001)

11. Huang, G.D., Wang, B.Y.: Complete SAT-based Model Checking for Context-Free Processes. In: Namjoshi, K.S., Yoneda, T., Higashino, T., Okamura, Y. (eds.) ATVA 2007. LNCS, vol. 4762, pp. 51–65. Springer, Heidelberg (2007)

12. Hungar, H., Steffen, B.: Local model checking for context-free processes. Nordic Journal of Computing 1(3), 364–385 (1994)

13. Reps, T., Horwitz, S., Sagiv, M.: Precise interprocedural dataflow analysis via graph reachability. In: Proc. of the ACM Symposium on Principles of Programming Languages (POPL 1995), pp. 49–61 (1995)

14. Rustan, K., Leino, M.: A SAT characterization of boolean-program correctness. In: Ball, T., Rajamani, S.K. (eds.) SPIN 2003. LNCS, vol. 2648, pp. 104–120. Springer, Heidelberg (2003)

15. Vardi, M.Y.: Automata-Theoretic Model Checking Revisited. In: Cook, B., Podelski, A. (eds.) VMCAI 2007. LNCS, vol. 4349, pp. 137–150. Springer, Heidelberg (2007)

16. Wang, B.Y.: Proving $\forall \mu$-calculus properties with SAT-based model checking. In: Wang, F. (ed.) FORTE 2005. LNCS, vol. 3731, pp. 113–127. Springer, Heidelberg (2005)

On Detecting Regular Predicates in Distributed Systems*

Hongtao Huang[1,2]

[1] State Key Laboratory of Computer Science,
Institute of Software, Chinese Academy of Sciences, Beijing 100190, China
[2] Graduate University, Chinese Academy of Sciences, Beijing 100190, China
`hht@ios.ac.cn`

Abstract. Given a distributed computation and a predicate, detection of the predicate in *Definitely* modality means checking whether in every path from the least state to the greatest state in the state space generated from the computation, there exists a state satisfying the predicate. It is well known that the state space is a lattice. The regular predicate is a class of predicates. All the states satisfying a regular predicate form a sublattice of the lattice. In this paper, we prove that detection of a regular predicate in *Definitely* modality is coNP-complete.

1   Introduction

Predicate detection in a distributed system is an important problem. It is useful in debugging and testing of the distributed system. A predicate is an interesting property that we want to check in the execution of a distributed system. Two modalities are introduced for predicate detection by Cooper and Marzullo [2]. They are denoted by *Possibly* and *Definitely*. We know that the state space of an execution of a distributed system is a distributive lattice. Given a predicate Φ, *Possibly*(Φ) means that there exists one path from the initial state to the final state in the lattice, which passes through a state satisfying Φ. *Definitely*(Φ) means that all paths from the initial state to the final state in the lattice pass through a state satisfying Φ. *Possibly*(Φ) is usually used to check the property Φ that we want to avoid, such as, the number of tokens in a system is less than a constant. While *Definitely*(Φ) is usually used to check the desired property Φ that we want to guarantee, such as, a leader is elected.

The regular predicate [4] is a special class of predicates. In the state space the consistent states satisfying the regular predicate form a sublattice of the distributive lattice of computation, which implies that the sublattice is also a distributive lattice [3]. It has an interesting property. From the original computation we can derive a computation, of which the consistent states are exactly the consistent states satisfying the regular predicate. Therefore, we can obtain

* Supported by the National Natural Science Foundation of China under Grant Nos. 60721061, 60833001 and 60603049, and the National High Technology Research and Development Program ("863"Program) of China under Grant No. 2007AA01Z112.

a succinct expression of the consistent states satisfying the regular predicate. Computation slicing [4,10] given by Garg and Mittal is the technique for obtaining the succinct expression. It also enlightens us on the forms of zones considered in this paper.

The regular predicate is also an extension of the conjunctive predicate in semantics, because it is easy to prove that every conjunctive predicate is a regular predicate. The conjunctive predicate is very useful in describing conditions in application. And detection of conjunctive predicates in both *Possibly* modality and *Definitely* modality has polynomial time algorithms [5][7][6][14].

In [11] the complexity of detection of regular predicates in *Definitely* modality is introduced as an open problem.

In [12] sufficient conditions and necessary conditions are given to detect a regular predicate in *Definitely* modality in polynomial time.

In this paper, we prove that detection of a regular predicate in *Definitely* modality is coNP-complete. For proving it, we prove that the SAT problem could be reduced into the detection of false runs in the state space in polynomial time, where a false run is a path from the least state to the greatest state which does not pass through any true state. We can see that detection of false runs is the dual problem of detection of a regular predicate in *Definitely* modality. For achieving this reduction, we first reduce the SAT problem to the problem of finding a desired path in a directed graph. Then according to the directed graph, we construct a distributed computation and a regular predicate. And we reduce the path searching problem in the directed graph to the problem of detection of false runs in the state space generated from the constructed computation.

The remainder of the paper is organized as follows: Section 2 discusses the model that we use. In section 3, we prove that detection of a regular predicate in *Definitely* modality is coNP-complete. Section 4 gives an example. Section 5 concludes the paper.

2   Model

We assume a loosely-coupled message-passing asynchronous system. A distributed system consists of n sequential processes denoted by $P_1, P_2, \ldots, P_n$. Each process in the distributed system is sequential. For each process $P_i, 1 \leq i \leq n$, the sequence of events in the process is $E_i^1 E_i^2 E_i^3 \cdots$. Let E_i denote the set of events in P_i. Let $E = E_1 \cup E_2 \cup \ldots \cup E_n$. We use Lamport's happened-before relation [8] to give an irreflexive partial order $\rightarrow$ on E. Happened-before relation is defined as the smallest relation satisfying the following conditions: for two events $e, f \in E$, (1) if e and f belong to the same process, and e occurs before f, then $e \rightarrow f$; (2) if e is an event which sends a message and f is an event which receives the message sent by e, then $e \rightarrow f$; (3) if there exists an event $g \in E$ such that $e \rightarrow g$ and $g \rightarrow f$, then $e \rightarrow f$. Based on the induced order, we model the given execution of the system as an irreflexive partial order set $\langle E, \rightarrow \rangle$. We call it a computation.

A state of a computation $\langle E, \rightarrow \rangle$ is a subset G of E such that for each event e in G, any event f occurring before e in the process that e belongs to, is in G. A state G is a consistent state, if for each event e, any event f satisfying

$f \to e$, is in G. The intuitive meaning of consistent states is that for each event in the state, all the events that should occur before it have occurred. The set of consistent states forms a distributive lattice under the relation of $\subseteq$ [9][4]. Let $L(E)$ denote the distributive lattice.

We can represent a state G by an n-dimension vector $S = (s_1, s_2, \ldots, s_n)$, where for each i, $1 \le i \le n$, if $E_i \cap G \ne \emptyset$, then $E_i^{s_i}$ is the greatest element in $E_i \cap G$; otherwise $s_i = 0$. For two states S and S' in $L(E)$, $S \le S'$ if and only if $s_i \le s'_i$, for all i, $1 \le i \le n$. $S < S'$ if and only if $S \le S'$ and $S \ne S'$. $S \sqcap S' = (min(s_1, s'_1), min(s_2, s'_2), \ldots, min(s_n, s'_n))$. $S \sqcup S' = (max(s_1, s'_1), max(s_2, s'_2), \ldots, max(s_n, s'_n))$.

A run of a computation is a total order of the events in E, which is compatible with $\to$, that is, if $e \to f$, then e comes before f in the run. A run is also a chain of states from $\perp$ to $\top$ in the lattice $L(E)$.

When detecting a predicate in a computation, each event has an associated value, and each process has an interesting variable which is used to check some properties of the execution. Given a consistent state $S = (s_1, s_2, \ldots, s_n)$, the value of the variable on P_i is the associated value of event $E_i^{s_i}$, if $s_i > 0$; otherwise, it is a given initial value.

Given a predicate Φ, two modalities are usually used in predicate detection [2]:

$Definitely(\Phi)$. It is true if for every run of the computation, there exists a consistent state satisfying Φ on this run.

$Possibly(\Phi)$. It is true if there exists a run of the computation such that a consistent state on this run satisfies Φ.

In general, detection of $Possibly(\Phi)$ is NP-complete [1] and detection of $Definitely(\Phi)$ is coNP-complete [13].

For example, in the computation of figure 1, assume the interesting variables in P_1 and P_2 are x and y respectively and the predicate we want to detect is $\Phi = x > y$. We can see that $Possibly(\Phi)$ is true, while $Definitely(\Phi)$ is false.

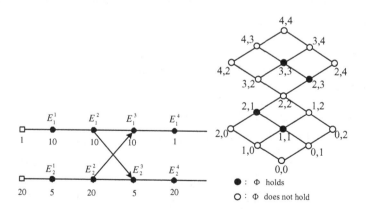

Fig. 1. A computation and its corresponding lattice

3   Detection of a Regular Predicate in *Definitely* Modality Is coNP-Complete

In this section we show that detection of a regular predicate in *Definitely* modality is coNP-complete.

Definition 1. *A predicate is regular, if given two consistent states S and T satisfying the predicate, $S \sqcup T$ and $S \sqcap T$ also satisfy the predicate.*

We can see that the consistent states satisfying a regular predicate form a sub-lattice of the distributive lattice of the computation.

For proving that detection of a regular predicate in *Definitely* Modality is coNP-complete, we give a reduction from the SAT problem to the problem of determining whether there exists a false run. A false run is a run that does not pass through any true state. It is obvious that the problem is the dual problem of detection of a regular predicate in *Definitely* modality.

Now we briefly describe the idea of the proof. A run is path from the least state to the greatest state. For associating the satisfiability of a CNF formula with a run, in step 1 we first reduce the SAT problem to a path searching problem in a directed graph. Then we have two types of paths. For associating the two types of paths, in step 2 we construct a computation, which generates a state space. Then we assign each vertex in the graph a zone of states in the state space. The constructed computation in step 2 does not have order relations. Thus all the states of the computation are consistent. In step 3, we add some order relations to the computation. It makes some states inconsistent. Using the relations we shape the state space, and put some restrictions on the runs in the state space. In step 4, we construct a regular predicate. The regular predicate defines true states and false states. Then we can consider the false runs. In the last step, we reduce the path searching problem in the directed graph to the problem of determining whether there exists a false run of the regular predicate in the state space.

3.1   Step 1

In this step, we reduce the SAT problem to a problem of finding a desired path in a directed graph.

Given a CNF formula $\Psi = (L_1^1 \vee L_1^2 \vee \ldots \vee L_1^{n_1}) \wedge \ldots \wedge (L_m^1 \vee L_m^2 \vee \ldots \vee L_m^{n_m})$, we construct a directed graph $\mathcal{G}_{SAT}$ as the following.

The graph contains an initial vertex I, a final vertex F, and m groups of vertices denoted by $\mathcal{V}_1, \ldots, \mathcal{V}_m$. $\mathcal{V}_i$ has n_i vertices, $\mathcal{V}_i^1, \mathcal{V}_i^2, \ldots, \mathcal{V}_i^{i_m}$. $\mathcal{V}_i^j$ has an assigned label L_i^j, where $1 \leq j \leq n_i$. There is an edge from the initial vertex to each vertex in $\mathcal{V}_1$. There are edges from each vertex in $\mathcal{V}_i$ to all vertices in $\mathcal{V}_{i+1}$, for all i, $1 \leq i \leq m - 1$. There is an edge from each vertex in $\mathcal{V}_m$ to the final vertex.

Lemma 1. *Ψ is satisfiable, if and only if there exists a path from the initial vertex to the final vertex in $\mathcal{G}_{SAT}$ such that in the path there do not exist two vertices with conflicting labels.*

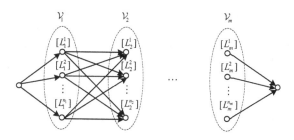

Fig. 2. The directed graph $\mathcal{G}_{SAT}$

Proof. ($\Rightarrow$): There is an evaluation satisfying Ψ. Under this evaluation, we know that for each $1 \leq i \leq m$, the set $\{L_i^1, L_i^2, \ldots, L_i^{n_i}\}$ contains at least one true literal $L_i^{\alpha_i}$.

Then $I\mathcal{V}_1^{\alpha_1}\mathcal{V}_2^{\alpha_2}\ldots\mathcal{V}_m^{\alpha_m}F$ is a desired path in $\mathcal{G}_{SAT}$.

($\Leftarrow$): Let the assigned labels in vertices in the path be true. Then Ψ is true. □

3.2 Step 2

In this step we construct a distributed computation for the directed graph $\mathcal{G}_{SAT}$. And we associate each vertex a set of states in the state space of the computation. Then in the later steps we can can reduce the problem of searching desired path in $\mathcal{G}_{SAT}$ to a problem of detection of false runs for a regular predicate.

Now we construct a computation with $2(\sum_{i=1}^{m} n_m + 2)$ processes. Each process has one event. Let $n = 2(\sum_{i=1}^{m} n_m + 2)$.

we can see that the state space has n dimensions, and contains at most 2^n states. If a state $S = (s_1, \ldots, s_n)$ is in the state space, then $s_i = 0$ or $s_i = 1$, for each $1 \leq i \leq n$.

Let the n dimensions be denoted by $\xi_1, \ldots, \xi_n$.

For associating a set of states for each vertex, we introduce a concept, zones, which can be informally seen as a hypercube in the state space.

Definition 2. *A zone* $Z[(a_1, b_1), (a_2, b_2), \ldots, (a_n, b_n)]$ *is a set of states. A state* $S = (s_1, s_2, \ldots, s_n) \in Z$ *if and only if* $a_i \leq s_i \leq b_i$ *for all* i, $1 \leq i \leq n$.

If a zone does not contain any true consistent state, we call it a false zone.

In the paper, we have two special forms of zones. They are given two denotations. Let $H[\xi_i < u, \xi_j \geq v]$ denote a zone $Z[(a_1, b_1), (a_2, b_2), \ldots, (a_n, b_n)]$ such that $a_i = 0, b_i = u - 1$, $a_j = v, b_j = |E_j|$, and $a_k = 0, b_k = |E_k|$, for all k, $1 \leq k \leq n$, $k \neq i$, $k \neq j$. Let $H[u \leq \xi_i \leq v]$ denote a zone $Z[(a_1, b_1), (a_2, b_2), \ldots, (a_n, b_n)]$ such that $a_i = u, b_i = v$, and $a_k = 0, b_k = |E_k|$, for all k, $1 \leq k \leq n, k \neq i$. If $u = v$, we can express $H[u \leq \xi_i \leq v]$ as $H[\xi_i = u]$.

Then for every vertex in $\mathcal{G}_{SAT}$ we will assign it a zone.

For each vertex, we first assign it different two numbers from 1 to n. All the numbers assigned to the vertices are required to be different. Let x be the first number, and y be the second number. If the vertex is not the initial vertex and the final vertex, the corresponding zone of the vertex is $H[\xi_x < 1, \xi_y \geq 1]$. If the vertex is the initial vertex, the corresponding zone of the vertex is $H[\xi_x < 1, \xi_y \geq 0]$. If the vertex is the final vertex, the corresponding zone of the vertex is $H[\xi_x < 2, \xi_y \geq 1]$. It is obvious that in the state space generated from the computation, $H[\xi_x < 1, \xi_y \geq 0] = H[\xi_x = 0]$ and $H[\xi_x < 2, \xi_y \geq 1] = H[\xi_y = 1]$. In this section we do this only for treating zones in a unified way.

For knowing which two numbers are assigned to a zone, we define an operation on zones, $\mathscr{X}(H) = x$ and $\mathscr{Y}(H) = y$.

Let **H** be the set of all the assigned zones for vertices.

3.3   Step 3

In the previous part we construct a computation, which has only several processes, and has no order. In this step, we add some orders into the computation, which means some states in the state space become inconsistent. Thus we shape the state space.

We know that in P_i, there is $|E_i|$ events $E_i^1, \ldots, E_i^{|E_i|}$. In the following, for convenience in each process P_i, we introduce two imaginary events E_i^0 and $E_i^{|E_i|+1}$. We assume that no event e satisfies that $e \to E_i^0$, or $E_i^{|E_i|+1} \to e$.

Given two zones $H[\xi_x < \alpha, \xi_y \geq \beta]$ and $H'[\xi_{x'} < \alpha', \xi_{y'} \geq \beta']$, where x, x', y, y' are different, we use $Disjoint(H, H')$ to denote an order relation $E_x^\alpha \to E_{y'}^{\beta'}$.

Now based the $Disjoint$ relation, we add some order relations into the computation. Given any two vertices v and v' in the directed graph, suppose that their corresponding zones are H and H' respectively. The adding rules are as the following:

(1) If v and v' belong to the same group $\mathcal{V}_k$, then we add $Disjoint(H, H')$ and $Disjoint(H', H)$ into the computation.

(2) If v and v' are not in the same group, there is path from v to v', and there is not a edge from v to v', then we add $Disjoint(H, H')$ into the computation.

(3) If v and v' are not in the same group, there is path from v to v', and v and v' have conflicting labels, then we add $Disjoint(H', H)$ into the computation.

We have added some order relations into the computation. Based on the form of $Disjoint(H, H')$, it is easy to verify that the added order relations form a partial order. Thus the computation we consider here is reasonable.

Lemma 2. *The added order relations form a partial order.*

Next we list some properties related to $Disjoint(H, H')$.

The properties considered in the remainder of the section is about consistent states. From the definition of consistent states, it is easy to get the next proposition.

Proposition 1 *A state $S = (s_1, \ldots, s_n)$ is consistent, if and only if $E_i^{s_i}.next \nrightarrow E_j^{s_j}$, for all i and j, $1 \leq i \leq n$, $1 \leq j \leq n$, $i \neq j$.*

Given a set **S** of states, we use $Con(\mathbf{S})$ to denote the consistent states in **S**.

Lemma 3 is used to determine whether a zone contains consistent states. Lemma 4 is used to find the minimal state in a zone Z, if $Con(Z) \neq \emptyset$.

Lemma 3. *None of the states in $Z[(a_1, b_1), (a_2, b_2), \ldots, (a_n, b_n)]$ is consistent, i.e. $Con(Z) = \emptyset$, if and only if there exist u and v such that $E_u^{b_u}.next \rightarrow E_v^{a_v}$.*

Proof. ($\Rightarrow$): We prove that if there do not exist such u and v, then there exists a consistent state in Z.

Let $\Theta_i = \{k | \forall j (E_i^k.next \nrightarrow E_j^{b_j})\}$. According to the precondition, we have that $\Theta_i \neq \emptyset$. Let $\theta_i = min(\Theta_i)$. Now we show that $(\theta_1, \ldots, \theta_n)$ is consistent.

Assume that it is not consistent. From proposition 1 we know that there exists $E_x^{\theta_x}$ and $E_y^{\theta_y}$ such that $E_x^{\theta_x}.next \rightarrow E_y^{\theta_y}$.

We have $\theta_y \neq b_y$ (otherwise, $E_x^{\theta_x}.next \rightarrow E_y^{b_y}$, which contradicts to $\theta_x \in \Theta_x$). Because θ_y is the minimal element in Θ_y, there exists w such that $E_y^{\theta_y - 1}.next \rightarrow E_w^{b_w}$, that is $E_y^{\theta_y} \rightarrow E_w^{b_w}$. Then $E_x^{\theta_x}.next \rightarrow E_w^{b_w}$, which contradicts to $\theta_x \in \Theta_x$. The we can conclude that $(\theta_1, \ldots, \theta_n)$ is consistent.

($\Leftarrow$): We have that $E_u^{b_u}.next \rightarrow E_v^{a_v}$. Because for any state $S = (s_1, \ldots, s_n)$ in Z, $s_u \leq b_u$ and $s_v \geq a_v$, we can conclude that $E_u^{s_u}.next \rightarrow E_v^{s_v}$. From proposition 1, S is not consistent. Thus none of the states in Z is consistent. $\square$

Lemma 4. *Suppose $Con(Z) \neq \emptyset$. $S = (s_1, s_2, \ldots, s_n)$ is the minimal consistent state in $Z[(a_1, b_1), (a_2, b_2), \ldots, (a_n, b_n)]$, if and only if $E_i^{s_i}$ is the first event in P_i satisfying that $E_i^{s_i}.next \nrightarrow E_j^{a_j}$, for all i, $1 \leq i \leq n$.*

Proof. We notice that $S = (s_1, s_2, \ldots, s_n)$ is the state $(\theta_1, \ldots, \theta_n)$ in the proof of lemma 3. Thus we can conclude that S is consistent.

Assume that there exists a consistent state $T = (t_1, t_2, \ldots, t_n)$ in Z such that $T < S$, or T can be compared with S. Then we can conclude there exists some k such that $t_k < s_k$. Because $t_k < s_k$ and $T \in Z$, $s_k \neq a_k$. Because of the precondition for S, there exists j such that $E_k^{s_k - 1}.next \rightarrow E_j^{a_j}$. Because $t_k \leq s_k - 1$ and $a_j \leq t_j$, $E_k^{t_k}.next \rightarrow E_j^{t_j}$, which contradicts to that T is consistent.

Thus S is the minimal state. $\square$

In the two previous lemmas, we see that $E_v^{a_v}$ or $E_j^{a_j}$ plays an important role. If $a_j = 0$, $E_j^{a_j} = E_j^0$. Because no event e satisfies $e \rightarrow E_j^0$, when we use lemma 3 and lemma 4, we only need to consider the $E_j^{a_j}$, where $a_j \neq 0$.

Lemma 5 shows the meaning of $Disjoint$. For two zones $H = [\xi_i < u, \xi_j \geq v]$ and $H' = [\xi_{i'} < u', \xi_{j'} \geq v']$, $Disjoint(H, H')$ or $Disjoint(H', H)$ guarantees that the two zones have not common parts.

Lemma 5. *For two zones $H = [\xi_i < u, \xi_j \geq v]$ and $H' = [\xi_{i'} < u', \xi_{j'} \geq v']$, $Con(H \cap H') = \emptyset$, if and only if $Disjoint(H, H')$ or $Disjoint(H', H)$.*

Proof. It is easy to see that $H \cap H'$ is a zone $Z[(a_1, b_1), (a_2, b_2), \ldots, (a_n, b_n)]$, where $a_i = 0, b_i = u - 1, a_{i'} = 0, b_{i'} = u' - 1, a_j = v, b_j = |E_j|, a_{j'} = v', b_{j'} = |E_{j'}|$, and $a_k = 0, b_k = |E_k|$, for all $k, k \neq i, i', j, j'$.

Among $a_1, \ldots, a_n$ only a_j and $a_{j'}$ are not 0, from lemma 3, $Con(H \cap H') = \emptyset$, if and only if $Disjoint(H, H')$ or $Disjoint(H', H)$. □

Given two consistent states $S = (s_1, s_2, \ldots, s_n)$ and $T = (t_1, t_2, \ldots, t_n)$. We use $S \triangleright T$ to denote that fact for only one dimension k, $t_k = s_k + 1$, and for all $i \neq k$, $t_i = s_i$. It means that T is the state obtained by moving one step from S.

Lemma 6 guarantees that if a run has entered into H and $Disjoint(H, H')$ holds, then when the run goes out of H, it can not directly enter into H'.

Lemma 6. *Given two zones $H = [\xi_i < u, \xi_j \geq v]$ and $H' = [\xi_{i'} < u', \xi_{j'} \geq v']$. If $Disjoint(H, H')$, then there dose not exist two consistent states S and T such that $S \in H$, $S \triangleright T$, $T \notin H$, and $T \in H'$.*

Proof. Because $S \in H$ and $T \notin H$, we can conclude that $s_i = u - 1$ and $t_i = u$. Because $Disjoint(H, H')$, $E_i^u \to E_{j'}^{v'}$. Because $T \in H'$, $v' \leq t_{j'}$. Because $S \triangleright T$, $s_{j'} = t_{j'}$. Thus we can conclude that $E_i^{s_i}.next \to E_{j'}^{s_{j'}}$, which contradicts to that S is consistent. □

Lemma 7 guarantees that if a run has entered into H and $Disjoint(H', H)$ holds, then when the run goes out of H, it can never enter into H'.

Lemma 7. *Given two zones $H = [\xi_i < u, \xi_j \geq v]$ and $H' = [\xi_{i'} < u', \xi_{j'} \geq v']$ satisfying $Disjoint(H', H)$. If a run of the computation passes through a state S in H, then the path from S to $\top$ along this run does not pass through any state in H'.*

Proof. Because a run pass through $S = (s_1, s_2, \ldots, s_n)$, S is consistent. We know that $s_{i'} \geq u'$. Otherwise because $Disjoint(H', H) = E_{i'}^{u'} \to E_j^v$, $s_{i'} < u'$ and $v \leq s_j$, we have that $E_{i'}^{s_{i'}}.next \to E_j^{s_j}$. It contradicts to that S is consistent.

If $T = (t_1, t_2, \ldots, t_n)$ is on the path from S to $\top$, then $t_i \geq s_i$ for all $1 \leq i \leq n$. Then $t_{i'} \geq s_{i'} \geq u'$, which implies that T is not in H'. □

The next lemma shows that although the added order relations make some states in the state space become inconsistent, the order relations do not make all the states in any zone become inconsistent. From the forms of added order relations and lemma 3, it easy to prove the next lemma.

Lemma 8. *Any $H \in \mathbf{H}$ contains consistent states.*

3.4   Step 4

In this step, we assign a truth value of each consistent states in the state space. And we prove that after the assignment, we obtain a regular predicate. Thus in the next step, we can reduce the problem of searching desired path in $\mathcal{G}_{SAT}$ to a problem of detection of false runs for the regular predicate.

For each consistent state S in the state space, the truth value of S is false, if and only if $S \in \bigcup_{H \in \mathbf{H}} H$. This means that we treat all zones in $\mathbf{H}$ false zones.

Then we obtain a predicate Φ. The next lemma shows that Φ is a regular predicate.

Lemma 9. Φ *is a regular predicate.*

Proof. Given two consistent states $S = (s_1, s_2, \ldots, s_n)$ and $T = (t_1, t_2, \ldots, t_n)$ satisfying the predicate. We should prove that $S \sqcap T$ and $S \sqcup T$ satisfy the predicate. Here we prove that $S \sqcap T$ satisfies the predicate. And it can be proved similarly that $S \sqcup T$ satisfies the predicate.

We prove it by contradiction. Assume that $U = S \sqcap T$ does not satisfy the predicate. We have that $u_i = min(s_i, t_i)$, for all $1 \leq i \leq n$. Because U is a false state, it must belong to a false zone H in $\mathbf{H}$.

If H has the form $H = [\xi_j = c]$, then $u_j = c$. Then $s_j = c$ or $t_j = c$. Then $S \in H$ or $T \in H$, which contradicts to that S and T satisfy the predicate.

If H has the form $H = [\xi_j < c, \xi_k \geq d]$, then $min(s_j, t_j) < c$ and $min(s_k, t_k) \geq d$. Because $min(s_k, t_k) \geq d$, we know that $s_k \geq d$ and $t_k \geq d$. Because $min(s_k, t_k) < c$, we know that $s_k < c$ or $t_k < c$. Then $S \in H$ or $T \in H$, which contradicts to that S and T satisfy the predicate. $\qquad\square$

3.5   Step 5

Based on the above construction of computation and predicate, in this step we reduce the path searching problem to detection of false runs. Thus we can show that detection of a regular predicate in *Definitely* modality is coNP-complete.

Lemma 10 shows that if a sequence of false zones satisfies the conditions stated in the lemma, then we can derive a false run. Using lemma 10 and lemma 11 we can prove lemma 12, which is the key lemma in this section.

Lemma 10. *There exists a false run, if there exists a sequence of zones $H_0 H_1 \ldots H_q$, where $H_i \in \mathbf{H}$, $1 \leq i \leq q$, satisfying the following two conditions: (1)$\bot \in H_0$, $\top \in H_q$. (2) Let $U_0 = \{\bot\}$. For each i, $1 \leq i \leq q$, let $T^{i-1} = min(\mathbf{U}_{i-1})$, and let $\mathbf{U}_i = Con(\{S | S \in (H_{i-1} \cap H_i) \wedge T^{i-1} \leq S\})$. It holds that $\mathbf{U}_i \neq \emptyset$.*

Proof. We can construct a false path using $T^0, T^1, \ldots, T^m$.

We start from $T^0 = \bot$. We know that $T^0 \in H_0$. Because $T^1 \in H_0 \cap H_1$, $T^1 \in H_0$. Because T^0 and T^1 are consistent, and $T^0 < T^1$, we have that there is a path from T^0 to T^1 in the state space. Because H_0 is a zone, it is easy to conclude that all the states in the path from T^0 to T^1 are in H_0. Thus the path from T^0 to T^1 does not pass through any true state.

Similarly, we could have those false paths from T^1 to T^2, from T^2 to T^3,..., from T^{n-1} to T^n, from T^n to $\top$. By concatenating these false paths, we obtain a false run from $\bot$ to $\top$. $\qquad\square$

Lemma 11. *Given a zone Z and a consistent state T, if $Con(\{S | S \in Z, T \leq S\}) \neq \emptyset$, then $min(Con(\{S | S \in Z, T \leq S\})) = min(Con(Z)) \sqcup T$.*

Proof. Let $U = (u_1, u_2, \ldots, u_n) = min(Con(Z))$. For all S in $Con(\{S | S \in Z, T \leq S\})$, we have that $(U \sqcup T) \sqcap S = (U \sqcap S) \sqcup (T \sqcap S) = U \sqcup T$. Thus $U \sqcup T \leq S$.

Because U and T are both consistent, we have that $U \sqcup T$ is consistent.

Then we only need to show that $U \sqcup T$ satisfies $U \sqcup T \in Z$ and $T \leq U \sqcup T$. The second condition is obvious. Now we verify the first condition. We have that $t_i \leq Z.b_i$, for all $1 \leq i \leq n$. Otherwise $Con(\{S | S \in Z, T \leq S\})$ will be empty. Let $V = (v_1, v_2, \ldots, v_n)$ be $U \sqcup T$. We can conclude that $Z.a_i \leq u_i \leq max(u_i, t_i) = v_i = max(u_i, t_i) \leq Z.b_i$. Thus $U \sqcup T \in Z$.

Thus $U \sqcup T$ is the minimal element.   □

Lemma 12. *There exists a false run, if and only if there exists a path in $\mathcal{G}_{SAT}$ which does not contain vertices with conflicting labels.*

Proof. ($\Leftarrow$): For every vertex in the path, we have a corresponding zone. Thus from the path, we have a corresponding sequence of zones $H_0 H_1 \ldots H_{m+1}$, where H_0 is the corresponding zone for the initial vertex, and H_{m+1} is the corresponding zone for the final vertex. Let $\mathbf{X}_i = \{\mathscr{X}(H_k) | i - 1 \leq k \leq m + 1\}$. According to the way of adding order relations in step 3, we have two properties about $H_0 H_1 \ldots H_{m+1}$. For all $1 \leq i \leq m + 1$, $\neg Disjoint(H_{i-1}, H_i)$ and $\neg Disjoint(H_i, H_{i-1})$. For all $1 \leq i \leq m + 1$, $\neg Disjoint(H_i, H_j)$, where $j < i$.

Now we prove that the sequence of zone satisfies the conditions stated in lemma 10, which implies that there exists a false run. We know that $\perp \in H_0$ and $\top \in H_{m+1}$. Then we show that the second condition in lemma 10 is satisfied.

By induction we prove that $\mathbf{U}_i \neq \emptyset$, where $1 \leq i \leq m + 1$. And at the same time, for $T^i = (t_1^i, \ldots, t_n^i)$ we prove that $t_j^i = 0$ for all $j \in \mathbf{X}_i$.

Induction base ($i = 1$). Because $T^0 = \perp$, $\mathbf{U}_1 = Con(\{S | S \in (H_0 \cap H_1)\})$. Because $\neg Disjoint(H_0, H_1)$ and $\neg Disjoint(H_1, H_0)$, from lemma 5, $\mathbf{U}_1 \neq \emptyset$.

Let $x = \mathscr{X}(H_0), x' = \mathscr{X}(H_1), y = \mathscr{Y}(H_0), y' = \mathscr{Y}(H_1)$. We know that $H_k \cap H_{k+1}$ is a zone $Z'[(a_1, b_1), (a_2, b_2), \ldots, (a_n, b_n)]$, where $a_x = b_x = 0, a_{x'} = b_{x'} = 0$, $a_y = b_y = 1, a_{y'} = b_{y'} = 1$, and $a_j = 0, b_j = 1$, for all $j, j \neq x, x', y, y'$. Let $T^1 = min(Z')$. Because among $a_1, \ldots, a_n$ only a_y and $a_{y'}$ are 1, from lemma 4, $t_j^1 = 1$ if and only if $E_j^{a_j}.next \rightarrow E_y^{a_y}$ or $E_j^{a_j}.next \rightarrow E_{y'}^{a_{y'}}$. Because $\neg Disjoint(H_0, H_1)$ and $\neg Disjoint(H_1, H_0)$, and for any H in $H_2 \ldots H_{m+1}$, $\neg Disjoint(H, H_0)$ and $\neg Disjoint(H, H_1)$, we can conclude that $E_j^{a_j}.next \nrightarrow E_y^{a_y}$ and $E_j^{a_j}.next \nrightarrow E_{y'}^{a_{y'}}$, if $j \in \mathbf{X}_1$. Thus $t_j^1 = 0$ for all $j \in \mathbf{X}_1$.

Induction step. Assuming that the assertion is true up to $i = k$, we prove that it holds for $i = k + 1$.

First we show that $\{S | S \in (H_k \cap H_{k+1}) \wedge T^k \leq S\} \neq \emptyset$. Let $x = \mathscr{X}(H_k), x' = \mathscr{X}(H_{k+1}), y = \mathscr{Y}(H_k), y' = \mathscr{Y}(H_{k+1})$. It is easy to conclude that $H_k \cap H_{k+1}$ is a zone $Z'[(a_1, b_1), (a_2, b_2), \ldots, (a_n, b_n)]$, where $a_x = b_x = 0, a_{x'} = b_{x'} = 0$, $a_y = b_y = 1, a_{y'} = b_{y'} = 1$, and $a_j = 0, b_j = 1$, for all $j, j \neq x, x', y, y'$. At the same time $\{S | T^k \leq S\}$ is a zone $Z''[(a_1, b_1), (a_2, b_2), \ldots, (a_n, b_n)]$, where $a_j = t_j^k$ and $b_j = 1$, for all $j, 1 \leq j \leq n$. It is easy to see that $\{S | S \in (H_k \cap H_{k+1}) \wedge T^k \leq S\} = Z' \cap Z''$. Because of the assumption to $i = k$, we know that $t_x^k = t_{x'}^k = 0$. Thus $Z' \cap Z'' \neq \emptyset$. Let a zone $Z[(a_1, b_1), (a_2, b_2), \ldots, (a_n, b_n)]$ be $Z' \cap Z''$, where

$a_x = b_x = 0, a_{x'} = b_{x'} = 0$, $a_y = b_y = 1, a_{y'} = b_{y'} = 1$, and $a_j = t_j^k, b_j = 1$, for all j, $j \neq x, x', y, y'$.

Now we prove that $\mathbf{U}_i = Con(Z) \neq \emptyset$ by contradiction. Assume that $\mathbf{U}_i = Con(Z) = \emptyset$. From the form of Z and lemma 3, $Con(Z) = \emptyset$ if and only if $\exists j (E_x^1 \to E_j^{Z.b_j})$ or $\exists j (E_{x'}^1 \to E_j^{Z.b_j})$, where $j \neq x$ and $j \neq x'$. Suppose $\exists j (E_x^1 \to E_j^{Z.b_j})$. If $j = y$, from lemma 3, H_k contains no consistent states, which leads to a contradiction. If $j = y'$, then $Disjoint(H_k, H_{k+1})$. It also leads to a contradiction. If $j \neq x, x', y, y'$, we have that $E_x^{t_x^k}.next = E_x^1 \to E_j^{Z.b_j} = E_j^{t_j^k}$, which contradicts to that T^k is consistent. We can similarly derive a contradiction for the case $\exists j (E_{x'}^1 \to E_j^{Z.b_j})$. Thus $\mathbf{U}_i = Con(Z) \neq \emptyset$.

From the properties of $H_0 \ldots H_{m+1}$, we know that $\neg Disjoint(H_k, H_{k+1})$ and $\neg Disjoint(H_{k+1}, H_k)$, and for any H in $H_{k+2} \ldots H_{m+1}$, $\neg Disjoint(H, H_k)$ and $\neg Disjoint(H, H_{k+1})$. Because of the form of $Z' = H_k \cap H_{k+1}$, similarly as the reasoning for $H_0 \cap H_1$, we can conclude that, letting $V = (v_1 \ldots v_n)$ be the minimal state of $Con(Z')$, $v_j = 0$ for all $j \in \mathbf{X_k}$. From lemma 11, $T^{k+1} = V \sqcup T$. Because $t_j^k = 0$, where $j \in \mathbf{X_k}$, we have that $t_j^{k+1} = 0$, where $j \in \mathbf{X_{k+1}}$.

Therefore, we can conclude that there exists a false run.

($\Rightarrow$): Let r be the run.

Because $\bot$ is in the zone corresponding the initial vertex I, let H_0 be this zone.

Suppose that S is the first state in the run from $\bot$, which is not in H_0. For any zone H corresponding to the vertex in $V_2 \cup \ldots \cup V_m \cup \{F\}$, according to the order relation in step 3, $Disjoint(H_0, H)$. From lemma 6, S is not in H. Then S must be in a zone, which corresponds to a vertex in V_1. Let H_1 be this zone, and ve_1 be this vertex. Because I does not have a label, there are not conflicting labels in I and ve_1. At the same time, we obtain a sequence of zones $H_0 H_1$. r passes through H_0 and H_1.

Suppose that we have obtained a sequence of vertices $I ve_1 \ldots ve_k$, where ve_i is in V_i, and the labels in these vertices are not conflicting. Let the corresponding sequence of zones be $H_0 \ldots H_k$. r passes through each zone in the sequence. Let S be the first state we encounter when the run gets out of H_k. We will show that S must be in a zone corresponding to a vertex ve_{k+1} in V_{k+1}, and the label of ve_{k+1} is not conflicting with any label in the previous vertices in the sequence.

For any zone H corresponding to a vertex in $V_{k+2} \cup \ldots \cup V_m \cup \{F\}$, we have $Disjoint(H_k, H)$. From lemma 6, S can not be in a zone corresponding to a vertex in $V_{k+2} \cup \ldots \cup V_m \cup \{F\}$. For any zone H corresponding to a vertex in $\{I\} \cup V_1 \cup \ldots \cup V_{k-2}$, $Disjoint(H, H_k)$. From lemma 7, S can not be in a zone corresponding to a vertex in $\{I\} \cup V_1 \cup \ldots \cup V_{k-2}$.

Thus S could only be in a zone corresponding to a vertex in V_{k-1} or a zone corresponding to a vertex in V_{k+1}.

If S is in a zone corresponding to a vertex in V_{k+1}, let the zone be H_{k+1} and the vertex be ve_{k+1}. From lemma 7, we have that for any H in $H_0 \ldots H_k$, $\neg Disjoint(H_k, H)$. Thus the label of ve_{k+1} is not conflicting with any label in the previous vertices in the sequence.

If S is in a zone corresponding to a vertex in $\mathcal{V}_{k-1}$, we can derive a contradiction. Based on the above reasoning, we know that if we can reach $\top$ from S along the run, the run must go through another zone H' corresponding a vertex in $\mathcal{V}_k$. From step 3, we have $Disjoint(H', H_k)$. Then from lemma 7, it is impossible.

Continue the above process until we reach a vertex ve_m in $\mathcal{V}_m$, and then reach the final vertex F. $Ive_1 \ldots ve_m F$ is the desired path in $\mathcal{G}_{SAT}$.   □

From lemma 1 and lemma 12, we can obtain the next corollary.

Corollary 1. Ψ is satisfiable, if and only if there exists a false run in the computation.

Theorem 1 is the main result of the paper.

Theorem 1. *Detection of a regular predicate in Definitely modality is coNP-complete.*

Proof. First we show that the time cost of reduction from the SAT problem to the false run searching problem is polynomial. Suppose that the number of literals in the SAT formula is l. Thus the number of vertices and the number of zones are both $l+2$. The time cost of constructing the directed graph for the SAT problem in step 1 is $O(l^2)$. The time cost of construction of the computation and assignment of zones to vertices in step 2 is $O(l)$. The time cost of adding $Disjoint$ relations in step 3 is $O(l^2)$. The time cost of construction of the predicate in step 4 is $O(l^2)$. We explain it briefly. Because $\Phi(S) \equiv \bigwedge_{H \in \mathbf{H}} S \notin H$. Then Φ can be written as the conjunction of $l+2$ formula. Given a zone $Z[(a_1, b_1), (a_2, b_2), \ldots, (a_n, b_n)]$ and a state $S = (s_1, s_2, \ldots, s_n)$, determining whether $S \in Z$ can be written as the following formula: $S \in Z \equiv \bigvee_{1 \le i \le n} (s_i < a_i \vee s_i > b_i)$. Because $n = 2l + 4$, the length of Φ is $O(l^2)$.

Thus the overall time cost is $O(l^2)$.

Next it is easy to see that the problem of determining whether there exists a false run is in NP, because from the above we know that the time complexity of determining whether a state satisfies the predicate is polynomial.

Thus determining whether there exists a false run is NP-complete. Because it it the dual problem of detection of a regular predicate in *Definitely* modality, we can conclude that detection of a regular predicate in *Definitely* modality is coNP-complete.   □

4   An Example

In this section we give an example for the five steps in the previous section. The CNF formula is $\Psi = (p \vee q \vee r) \wedge (\neg p \vee \neg q \vee \neg r) \wedge (\neg p \vee \neg q \vee r)$. The formula is satisfiable.

(Step 1) First we construct a directed graph. The graph has 11 vertices. In the graph we can find several paths satisfying the condition stated in lemma 1. The graph is drawn in figure 3 and figure 4.

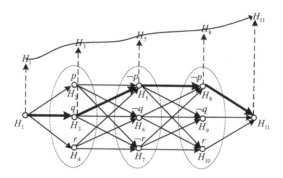

Fig. 3. The ($\Leftarrow$) part in lemma 12

(Step 2) Next we construct a computation, which has $2 \times 11 = 22$ processes. Now the state space has 22 dimensions. The 22 dimensions are denoted by $\xi_1, \ldots, \xi_{22}$. We associate each vertex a zone. H_1 is for the initial vertex. H_{11} is for the final vertex. $H_2, \ldots, H_{10}$ is for the other 9 vertices. For each zone H_i, $1 \leq i \leq 11$, the two numbers assigned to its corresponds vertex is $2 \times i - 1$ and $2 \times i$. The form of H_1 is $H[\xi_1 < 1, \xi_2 \geq 0]$. The form of H_2 is $H[\xi_3 < 1, \xi_4 \geq 1]$.

(Step 3) We add some order relations into the computation.

For example, for H_1, based on the adding rule (2), we add $Disjoint(H_1, H_5)$, $Disjoint(H_1, H_6), \ldots, Disjoint(H_1, H_{11})$ into the computation.

For H_2, based on the adding rule (1), we add $Disjoint(H_2, H_3)$, $Disjoint(H_3, H_2)$, $Disjoint(H_2, H_4)$ and $Disjoint(H_4, H_2)$ into the computation. For H_2, based on the adding rule (2), we add $Disjoint(H_2, H_8), \ldots, Disjoint(H_2, H_{11})$ into the computation. For H_2, based on the adding rule (3), we add $Disjoint(H_5, H_2)$ and $Disjoint(H_8, H_2)$ into the computation.

(Step 4) If a state is not in any zone in $H_1, \ldots, H_{11}$, then let the state be a true state. Now all the false states are in $H_1, \ldots, H_{11}$.

(Step 5) Lemma 12 is the key lemma for proving the complexity result.

Figure 3 is for the ($\Leftarrow$) part in lemma 12. There exists a path in the graph without conflicting vertices. The path is drawn in a thick line in the directed graph. From the path we obtain a sequence of zones $H_1 H_3 H_5 H_8 H_{11}$. Using lemma 10 and lemma 11 we can prove that there is a false run.

Figure 4 is for the ($\Rightarrow$) part in lemma 12.

There exists a false run. The run must start from H_1. Because we have $Disjoint(H_1, H_5), Disjoint(H_1, H_6), \ldots, Disjoint(H_1, H_{11})$, based on lemma 6 and lemma 7 we can conclude that when the run goes out of H_1 it must enter into a zone H_a in the first group, that is, H_2, H_3 and H_4. Similarly when the run goes out of H_a, it must enter into a zone H_b in the second group. The method of adding orders in step 3 and lemma 7 guarantee that the labels in the corresponding vertices of H_a and H_b do not conflict. Continue the above process. Finally we can obtain a sequence of zones $H_1 H_a H_b H_c H_{11}$ and a path of vertices in the graph which does not contain conflicting labels.

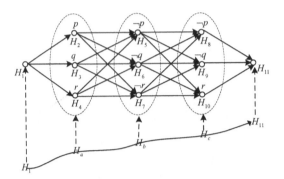

Fig. 4. The ($\Rightarrow$) part in lemma 12

5 Conclusion

In this paper, we show that detection of a regular predicate in *Definitely* modality is coNP-complete. For proving it we reduce the SAT problem to the problem of searching false runs, which is the dual problem of detection of a regular predicate in *Definitely* modality.

References

1. Chase, C., Garg, V.K.: Efficient detection of restricted classes of global predicates. In: Helary, J.-M., Raynal, M. (eds.) WDAG 1995. LNCS, vol. 972, pp. 303–317. Springer, Heidelberg (1995)
2. Cooper, R., Marzullo, K.: Consistent detection of global predicates. In: Proceedings of ACM/ONR workshop on Parallel and Distributed Debugging, pp. 163–173 (1991)
3. Davey, B.A., Priestley, H.A.: Introduction to Lattices and Order. Cambridge University Press, Cambridge (1990)
4. Garg, V.K., Mittal, N.: On slicing a distributed computation. In: Proceedings of IEEE International Conference on Distributed Computing Systems, pp. 322–329 (2001)
5. Garg, V.K., Waldecker, B.: Detection of weak unstable predicates in distributed programs. IEEE Transactions on Parallel and Distributed Systems 5(3), 299–307 (1994)
6. Garg, V.K., Waldecker, B.: Detection of strong unstable predicates in distributed programs. IEEE Transactions on Parallel and Distributed Systems 7(12), 1323–1333 (1996)
7. Hurfin, M., Mizuno, M., Raynal, M., Singhal, M.: Efficient detection of conjunctions of local predicates. IEEE Transactions on Software Engineering 24(8), 664–677 (1998)
8. Lamport, L.: Time, clocks and the ordering of events in a distributed system. Communications of the ACM 21(7), 558–564 (1978)
9. Mattern, F.: Virtual time and global states of distributed systems. In: Proceedings of the International Workshop on Parallel and Distributed Algorithms, pp. 120–131 (1989)

10. Mittal, N., Garg, V.K.: Techniques and applications of computation slicing. Distributed Computing 17(3), 251–277 (2005)
11. Sen, A., Garg, V.K.: Detecting temporal logic predicates on the happened before model. In: Proceedings of the 16th International Symposium on Parallel and Distributed Processing, pp. 76–83 (2002)
12. Sen, A., Garg, V.K.: On checking whether a predicate definitely holds. In: Petrenko, A., Ulrich, A. (eds.) FATES 2003. LNCS, vol. 2931, pp. 15–29. Springer, Heidelberg (2004)
13. Tarafdar, A., Garg, V.K.: Predicate control for active debugging of distributed programs. In: Proceedings of IEEE 9th Symposium on Parallel and Distributed Processing(SPDP), pp. 763–769 (1998)
14. Venkatesan, S., Dathan, B.: Test and debugging distributed programs using global predicates. IEEE Transactions on Software Engineering 21(2), 163–177 (1995)

Author Index